T0181897

Lecture Notes in Computer Science   13636

More information about this series at https://link.springer.com/bookseries/558

Yuen-Hsien Tseng · Marie Katsurai ·
Hoa N. Nguyen (Eds.)

From Born-Physical to Born-Virtual: Augmenting Intelligence in Digital Libraries

24th International Conference on Asian Digital Libraries, ICADL 2022
Hanoi, Vietnam, November 30 – December 2, 2022
Proceedings

 Springer

Editors
Yuen-Hsien Tseng 🆔
National Taiwan Normal University
Taipei, Taiwan

Marie Katsurai 🆔
Doshisha University
Kyoto, Japan

Hoa N. Nguyen 🆔
VNU University of Engineering
and Technology
Hanoi, Vietnam

ISSN 0302-9743   ISSN 1611-3349 (electronic)
Lecture Notes in Computer Science
ISBN 978-3-031-21755-5   ISBN 978-3-031-21756-2 (eBook)
https://doi.org/10.1007/978-3-031-21756-2

This Springer imprint is published by the registered company Springer Nature Switzerland AG
The registered company address is: Gewerbestrasse 11, 6330 Cham, Switzerland

Preface

This volume contains papers accepted at ICADL 2022: The 24th International Conference on Asia-Pacific Digital Libraries (https://icadl.net/icadl2022/). As the COVID-19 pandemic was gradually declining, the conference was organized as an onsite face-to-face conference but allowed those who could not attend to present their papers online and participate in the sessions remotely. The onsite meeting was held at Vietnam National University in Hanoi, Vietnam, from November 30 to December 2, 2022.

The ICADL conference series started in Hong Kong in 1998 and, over the years, having traveled to many countries in the Asia-Pacific region, has built a reputation as a significant digital library conference. Along with JCDL and TPDL, ICADL is held annually as one of the three top venues for connecting digital libraries, computer science, and library and information science communities. ICADL brings together researchers and practitioners in various aspects of research and practice in digital libraries. In the past few years, we have witnessed rapid advances in artificial intelligence (AI), especially in semantic search, personalized recommendation, understanding and generation of texts, images, video, and documents, together with augmented libraries, the metaverse, IoT, blockchain, and big data analytics. With these advances, many innovative applications become possible, and digital libraries could play crucial roles in AI research, applications, and practices. Thus, this year, the conference ran under the theme "From Born-Physical to Born-Virtual: Augmenting Intelligence in Digital Libraries."

In response to the conference call, 78 papers were submitted to ICADL 2022, and each paper was reviewed by at least three Program Committee (PC) members in a single-blind process. Based on the reviews and recommendations from the PC, 14 full papers, 18 short papers, and 12 posters were selected and included in the proceedings. Collectively, the submissions came from 21 countries – signifying the diversity of ICADL 2022. Based on significant contributions, the full and short papers have been classified into seven topics: Intelligent Document Analysis, Neural-based Knowledge Extraction, Knowledge Discovery for Enhancing Collaboration, Smart Search and Annotation, Cultural Data Collection and Analysis, Scholarly Data Processing, and Data Archive and Management.

The success of ICADL 2022 was the result of teamwork from many individuals. We would like to thank the PC members for their effort and time spent on reviewing submitted contributions, Son Hoang Nguyen and Shigeo Sugimoto (general chairs), and Ricardo Campos, Songphan Choemprayong, Adam Jatowt, Hao-Ren Ke, Akira Maeda, Maciej Ogrodniczuk, Muhammad Syafiq Mohd Pozi, Michael Färber, and Chutiporn Anutaria (publicity co-chairs). We are incredibly grateful to Shigeo Sugimoto for his persistent enthusiasm to guide us to be on track to hold a successful ICADL. We also thank Adam Jatowt and Emi Ishita for their leadership and support.

Finally, we would like to thank all authors, presenters, and participants of the conference. We hope that you enjoyed the conference proceedings.

December 2022

Yuen-Hsien Tseng
Marie Katsurai
Hoa N. Nguyen

Organization

General Chairs

Son Hoang Nguyen   VNU Library and Digital Knowledge Center, Vietnam
Shigeo Sugimoto   University of Tsukuba, Japan

Program Committee Chairs

Yuen-Hsien Tseng   National Taiwan Normal University, Taiwan
Marie Katsurai   Doshisha University, Japan
Hoa N. Nguyen   VNU University of Engineering and Technology, Vietnam

Publicity Co-chairs

Ricardo Campos   INESC TEC and Polytechnic Institute of Tomar, Portugal
Songphan Choemprayong   Chulalongkorn University, Thailand
Adam Jatowt   University of Innsbruck, Austria
Hao-Ren Ke   National Taiwan Normal University, Taiwan
Akira Maeda   Ritsumeikan University, Japan
Maciej Ogrodniczuk   Polish Academy of Sciences, Poland
Muhammad Syafiq Mohd Pozi   Universiti Utara Malaysia, Malaysia
Michael Färber   Karlsruhe Institute of Technology, Germany
Chutiporn Anutaria   AIT, Thailand

Program Committee

Trond Aalberg   Norwegian University of Science and Technology, Norway
Evelin Amorim   Universidade Federal do Espírito Santo, Spain
Biligsaikhan Batjargal   Ritsumeikan University, Japan
Emanuela Boros   University of La Rochelle, France
Nguyen Hai Chau   VNU, Vietnam
Chih-Ming Chen   National Chengchi University, Taiwan
Kun-Hung Cheng   National Chung Hsing University Taiwan
Songphan Choemprayong   Chulalongkorn University, Thailand
Gobinda Chowdhury   University of Strathclyde, UK

Chiawei Chu	City University of Macau, Macau, China
Mickaël Coustaty	L3i, La Rochelle Université, France
Partha Pratim Das	Indian Institute of Technology, Kharagpur, India
Antoine Doucet	University of La Rochelle, France
Yijun Duan	Kyoto University, Japan
Edward Fox	Virginia Tech, USA
Satoshi Fukuda	Chuo University, Japan
Liangcai Gao	Peking University, China
Dion Goh	Nanyang Technological University, Singapore
Emi Ishita	Kyushu University, Japan
Hiroyoshi Ito	University of Tsukuba, Japan
Adam Jatowt	University of Innsbruck, Austria
Makoto P. Kato	University of Tsukuba, Japan
Marie Katsurai	Doshisha University, Japan
Yukiko Kawai	Kyoto Sangyo University, Japan
Christopher S. G. Khoo	Nanyang Technological University, Singapore
Kangying Li	Ritsumeikan University, Japan
Shaobo Liang	Wuhan University, China
Chern Li Liew	Victoria University of Wellington, New Zealand
Chung-Ming Lo	National Chengchi University, Taiwan
Akira Maeda	Ritsumeikan University, Japan
Masaki Matsubara	University of Tsukuba, Japan
Muhammad Syafiq Mohd Pozi	Universiti Utara Malaysia, Malaysia
Jin-Cheon Na	Nanyang Technological University, Singapore
Thi-Hau Nguyen	VNU University of Engineering and Technology, Vietnam
Tri Thanh Nguyen	VNU University of Engineering and Technology, Vietnam
Viet Anh Nguyen	VNU University of Engineering and Technology, Vietnam
Hoa Nguyen Ngoc	VNU University of Engineering and Technology, Vietnam
David Nichols	University of Waikato, New Zealand
Chifumi Nishioka	National Institute of Informatics, Japan
Allard Oelen	L3S, Leibniz University Hannover, Germany
Maciej Ogrodniczuk	Institute of Computer Science, Polish Academy of Sciences, Poland
Hiroaki Ohshima	University of Hyogo, Japan
Gillian Oliver	Monash University, Australia
Christos Papatheodorou	National and Kapodistrian University of Athens, Athens, Greece
Brenda Salenave Santana	Universidade Federal do Rio Grande do Sul, Brazil

Yohei Seki	University of Tsukuba, Japan
Shigeo Sugimoto	University of Tsukuba, Japan
Kazunari Sugiyama	Kyoto University, Japan
Yasunobu Sumikawa	Takushoku University, Japan
Masao Takaku	University of Tsukuba, Japan
Yuen-Hsien Tseng	National Taiwan Normal University, Taiwan
Suppawong Tuarob	Mahidol University, Thailand
Nicholas Vanderschantz	University of Waikato, New Zealand
Diane Velasquez	University of South Australia, Australia
Shoko Wakamiya	Nara Institute of Science and Technology, Japan
Di Wang	Wuhan University, China
Yuanyuan Wang	Yamaguchi University, Japan
Chiranthi Wijesundara	University of Colombo, Sri Lanka
Dan Wu	Wuhan University, China
Yejun Wu	Louisiana State University, USA
Zhiwu Xie	Virginia Tech, USA
Maja Žumer	University of Ljubljana, Slovenia

Additional Reviewers

Ahuja, Aman	Majumdar, Srijoni
Chakravarty, Saurabh	Mohd Pozi, Muhammad Syafiq
Chattopadhyay, Nanda Gopal	Park, Sung Hee
Chekuri, Satvik	Rehman, Tohida
Das, Ananda	Roy, Subhayan
Dollack, Felix	Sanyal, Debarshi Kumar
Li, Da	Seki, Yohei

Co-hosts

Vietnam National University, Hanoi, Vietnam

Collaboration

The Asia-Pacific Chapter of iSchools

Contents

Research Activities & Digital Library

Trends in Digital Library

Intelligent Document Analysis

Fast Few Shot Self-attentive Semi-supervised Political Inclination Prediction

Souvic Chakraborty[✉], Pawan Goyal, and Animesh Mukherjee

Indian Institute of Technology, Kharagpur, West Bengal, India
chakra.souvic@gmail.com

Abstract. With the rising participation of the common mass in social media, it is increasingly common now for policymakers/journalists to create online polls on social media to understand the political leanings of people in specific locations. The caveat here is that only influential people can make such an online polling and reach out at a mass scale. Further, in such cases, the distribution of voters is not controllable and may be, in fact, biased. On the other hand, if we can interpret the publicly available data over social media to probe the political inclination of users, we will be able to have controllable insights about the survey population, keep the cost of survey low and also collect publicly available data without involving the concerned persons. Hence we introduce a self-attentive semi-supervised framework for political inclination detection to further that objective. The advantage of our model is that it neither needs huge training data nor does it need to store social network parameters. Nevertheless, it achieves an accuracy of 93.7% with no annotated data; further, with only a few annotated examples per class it achieves competitive performance. We found that the model is highly efficient even in resource-constrained settings, and insights drawn from its predictions match the manual survey outcomes when applied to diverse real-life scenarios.

1 Introduction

Political inclination refers to the political stance of an individual. Polling and surveying to understand the political leanings of people within a particular community, in a particular geopolitical region, or a specific context is a common approach. However, the manual polling mechanisms used today are hard to scale. Also, there is a significant chance of biased sampling as the samples are often too small in terms of the number of individuals surveyed and localized. On the other hand, if a survey or poll is conducted on online social platforms, it is impossible to control voters' distribution to calibrate it to resemble a random sample of opinions. Often the voters in these polls are limited to being the active audience of the pollsters sharing similar political inclination. Thus the result of the same poll can be completely different if introduced by a different pollster. Therefore, algorithmic labeling of people chosen from a controllable distribution is important, rather than asking for bias-prone active participation by influencers sharing particular political inclination or cost-inefficient manual polling.

© The Author(s), under exclusive license to Springer Nature Switzerland AG 2022
Y.-H. Tseng et al. (Eds.): ICADL 2022, LNCS 13636, pp. 3–20, 2022.
https://doi.org/10.1007/978-3-031-21756-2_1

Most of the existing approaches of political inclination detection (PID) on social networks focus on probabilistic models [8,9,13,14], which are in turn based on the texts generated by users. Researchers have also tried to exploit the network structure by making use of GCNs [24] (Graph Convolutional Networks). This method uses all second-degree features (neighbors of neighbors of the node/user to be classified in the graph) for a rich representation which makes the classification more accurate at the expense of speed. The data collection process involves collecting features of followers of followers of the user whose political inclination needs to be detected. As the collection of followers and all their tweets itself is a slow process limited by Twitter[1], the time required for the collection of the features of the second-degree neighbours increases quadratically in terms of average unique neighbors per node.

Also, the GCN-based models need to store the huge Twitter-subnetwork involving political persons and their followers. This severely violates the users' *right to erasure* as per the Article 17 of GDPR (See footnote 2) which reads as follows:

> **"The data subject shall have the right to obtain from the controller the erasure of personal data concerning him or her without undue delay and the controller shall have the obligation to erase personal data without undue delay ..."**

Further, these models are trained on a huge number of annotated examples. This makes the approaches hard to scale for newer settings and countries. In contrast, we show that certain *easy to collect features* plugged into a novel self-attentive framework can be very accurate in predicting the political inclination even if trained on a handful of annotated examples.

Our main contributions are as follows:

(1). Graph-based methods used previously raise many ethical questions [15, 17,21,23]. The users on social media platforms have the right[2]to deletion of their data from other storage systems which are dependent on social media as data source whenever their public profile on social media is deleted. Graph-based methods violate this by storing their information such as retweets, mentions, likes, and the follower-followee network. The time required to build and update such networks is huge as it will require everyday monitoring for (i) the existence of each connection and (ii) the arrival of new connections. So, the only way to use these features at inference time is to store them permanently in memory. We eliminate the need for storing such large relational graphs from past social media data of a huge number of users. We achieve this by using richer first-degree features that we collect directly at inference time along with their second degree neighbors which can be collected from the tweets of the concerned user/person to be classified directly (e.g., we collect the hashtags used by the retweeted user as it is readily available with the retweet, same for

---

[1] https://developer.twitter.com/en/docs/twitter-api/v1/rate-limits.
[2] https://gdpr-info.eu/art-17-gdpr/.

replies). Using smart augmentation of these features we beat the performance obtained by the graph-based approaches [24] at a reduced inference time.

(2). We propose a novel Fast Self-attentive Semi-supervised Political Inclination Predictor *FSSPIP* (Fig. 1). The experimental results show that even without using any gold annotation, we can achieve high accuracy of $\sim 94\%$ using weak supervision. The model is highly scalable and free from manual intervention unlike Darwish et al. (2020) [10] which needs human supervision or cluster inspection.

(3). We bring on board multiple additional datasets to show that our model can be used in many other similar settings for political inclination detection with a handful of labeled examples (or even without it). In specific, we present several case studies on media bias and political polarization using our classifier in zero-shot settings.

2   Related Work

Stefanov et al. (2020) [20] and Baly et al. (2020) [2] used Wikipedia, Twitter, YouTube, and other channels of information to detect the political leanings of the media houses. This approach is not scalable in context of persons. Conover et al. (2011) [9] had used a corpus of 1000 annotated data points to test the supervised approaches based on bag of words. Iyyer et al. (2014) [13] used advanced neural techniques like RNNs on a labeled corpus of sentences taken from speeches of democratic and republican parliamentarians. Chen et al. (2017) [8] used graph-based approaches to show the efficacy of using an opinion-aware knowledge graph. However, these techniques fail to take the richer network features into account. They also completely rely on annotated data failing to take advantage of domain knowledge of the task in hand.

Aldayel et al. (2019) [1] analyzed the features responsible for higher accuracy in stance detection setups using network features, tweet texts and text derived features. Darwish et al. (2020) [10] on the other hand used clustering based unsupervised setup to detect stance of users mainly relying on three channels of features: retweeted tweets, retweeted accounts and hashtags. Xiao et al. (2020) [24] approached the same task using manual annotation and collecting a large dataset of non-politician social media users and politicians on Twitter. They relied on variants of relational GNNs coupled with multi-task learning. However, given the need for explicit storage of information in the graph structures, even after the training phase, the graph-based algorithms often violate privacy rights of a large section of users.

Therefore, in this paper, we attempt to solve political inclination detection in a resource-constrained setup with no storage of user data after model training. We use several task-dependent augmentation techniques and unsupervised learning methods which have not been used in this context earlier thus making our model robust, easily adaptable and scalable without any human help/supervision. We only use public data available at the time of inference.

3   Model Architecture

The Base Architecture: Like previous state-of-the-art approaches [24] we too use a *GCN-like framework*. However, we, in contrast, do not store the user/feature graphs nor do we need a list of politicians in the country of the users to be classified with huge set of labelled examples. We use a long list of different *feature types* derived from *follow, mention, reply, retweet, tweets* and *likes*. We hypothesize that for a good representation of the political inclination, there are many important but easy to collect features which can be retrieved from the web directly during inference time with no need of storage. We describe these features in details below:

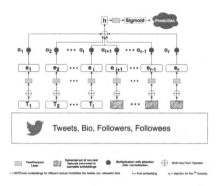

Fig. 1. The FSSPIP base architecture: The Twitter profile of a user is taken as input from which 22 different feature types are extracted and processed to predict political inclination.

Base Features

User Descriptions: We collected user descriptions of users retweeted and quoted, forming two separate documents. These user descriptions/bios often contain key information like the user's occupation, gender, religion etc.

Hashtags: Hashtags are important as similar hashtags are used to express opinions for/against a polarizing topic by users of different leanings.

Mentions: IDs mentioned in tweets are used as features.

Media Domains: It is no secret that users of different political leanings share different sets of news items that fit their ideological perspective. Considering their importance in our task, we collect domain names and domain + co-domain names from users' tweets. We use them as separate features.

Textual Content: We use pre-trained models like BERTweet [18], and Google's Universal Sentence Encoder [4] to convert the content of tweets of a user into embeddings. In our experiments, we found that BERTweet performs better (possibly because BERTweet is trained on text with vocabulary more similar to ours). Thus we report BERTweet numbers only.

Features Connected to Neighborhood:
We mentioned a total of 6 features till now. We repeat the same features for retweets and replies separately. So, the total number of features become 6+6+6=18.

In addition to all these features, we also use *friend ids, follower ids, mention ids, ids replied to,* and *ids retweeted* as features collected at test time.

So, in total we use 18+4=22 features.

Attending to Different Modalities

We use $|R| = 22$ features in our architecture. For each feature type r and user i, we obtain an embedding e_{ir} of size $d = 8$ as follows.

$$
\begin{aligned}
e_{ir} &= W_r \times BERTweet(T_{ir}), \; if \; r \in T \\
&= W_r A_{ir} H_r, \; if \; r \in T'
\end{aligned}
\tag{1}
$$

where $A_{ir} \in \{0,1\}^{1 \times Vlen_r}$ is the feature presence-absence vector for the rth feature and $H_r \in \mathbb{R}^{Vlen_r \times d}$ is the embedding matrix containing embeddings of all the features for feature type r. While pre-processing we chose only those features in the vocabulary which appeared at least in five instances of the training data to ensure having enough training instances. The length of the vocabulary for r^{th} feature type is represented as $Vlen_r$. T' and T are respectively the set of non-textual and textual feature types. For each feature type r, T_r denotes the textual content of that feature for user i, $W_r \in \mathbb{R}^{d \times d_{em}}$, where d_{em} is the embedding dimension of the output of BERTweet [18]. Now, we calculate h_i, the final embedding for the ith user as follows.

$$
h_i = \sum_r \alpha_{ir} \times \frac{e_{ir}}{|e_{ir}|}
\tag{2}
$$

FSSPIP uses a dynamic dot-product self-attention mechanism to calculate the weights for each of the feature types to finally get a weighted sum of the normalized embeddings of each feature type. We use learnable parameters $p, q, k \in [0, 1]$ to allow some flexibility in attention calculation. Learnable parameters q_r and $k_r \in R^d$ are queries and keys, respectively, for each feature type r (Here a feature type is specific social media attribute, so a collection of hashtags coming from tweets is a feature type different from the collection of hashtags coming from the retweets/replies. Please refer to the list of features mentioned at the start of the section for a broader understanding). So,

$$
\alpha_{ir} = p * \frac{e^{q_{ir} \times k_{ir}}}{\sum_r e^{q_{ir} \times k_{ir}}} + (1 - p) * |e_{ir}|
\tag{3}
$$

$$
q_{ir} = q \times e_{ir} + (1 - q) \times q_r
\tag{4}
$$

$$
k_{ir} = k \times e_{ir} + (1 - k) \times k_r
\tag{5}
$$

An illustration of this base architecture is presented in Fig. 1. It shows how input from each feature type goes through different transformation functions (BERTweet in case of textual data, trainable embeddings in case of follower ids etc.) to transform into embeddings which are then weighted by attention values calculated through three different architectural scheme as mentioned. The weighted summation of the embeddings (vector size 768) denote representation of the node/person to be classified. This embedding is further multiplied with a vector of size 768×1 and passed through a sigmoid function to obtain probability of a person being a republican in a binary classification setup. We use binary cross entropy as the loss function for supervision.

4   Augmented Semi-supervision for Superior Representation Learning

To make our architecture ready for few-shot learning, we make the model robust using regularization and multi task learning. We also use weak supervision producing high accuracy without any labelled example. Specifically, we use three different categories of techniques which are described below.

Dynamic Augmentation
Mixup: Mixup [25] is a technique that enforces linear change in output given linear change in input by training a neural network on convex combinations of pairs of examples and their annotated labels for a particular task. We adopt the method to our network data by mixing two random users for each channel (e.g. : hashtags, domains, retweetees from both users are present for the augmented user) increasing the diversity of data points and regularizing the model for unseen data points.
Sampling: Twitter users can be imagined as generative agents who generate tweets on selective issues and follow/reply/mention/interact with other users following some implicit probability distribution. So, if some of the points from the distribution are sampled out uniformly, the distribution will not change. So, we uniformly(chosen from a random uniform distribution for each feature type) sample out features from labeled examples for augmentation masking out 0–15% of the features randomly during training.
Feature Channel Dropout: While some feature types may influence the result more than others, it is important to learn to predict from the cues available if one influential feature type (e.g. *hashtags*, *followers*, *retweets* etc.) is absent. So, we randomly drop random feature types while training for better performance through adversarial training.

Weak Supervision: We hypothesize that the followers/retweeters of a particular political party often share the bias of having that particular political inclination. So, they are statistically more likely to follow the leaning of that particular political party which they are following on social media than any other. This provides some silver labels in the Twitter space for weak supervision. We crawled the Twitter handles of each political party (i.e., the official Twitter handles of *The Democratic* & *The Republican* party in case of US and *AAP*, *Congress* & *BJP* party in case of India) to collect the last 75,000 (set heuristically to contain enough examples) followers and the last 75,000 retweeters for each of these parties. We randomly selected 2,500 from each of them to get a sample representative of the timeline (as the most recent followers appear first, so collecting a big pool and resampling may help) and collected their relevant data for training. Users following both parties were removed.

Self-supervision: Self-supervision is a semi-supervised learning technique that trains the model in a new dummy task predicting part of input data using the other part of the data [18]. While in case of textual data masked language modelling and next sentence predictions [11,18] are the most frequently used pre-training technique, graph neural nets use predicting masked edges between nodes as the pre-training task. Following these methods, we pretrain our model with the task of prediction of the non-textual features which are masked in the dynamic augmentation phase during sampling the input features. We use self-supervision as pre-training method while performing few-shot learning and fine-tune later on the annotated data points. Hyperparameter details and loss function of the pretraining phase has been put in the Appendix available at https://tinyurl.com/icadlappendix).

5 Data Preparation

Dataset for the Main Task: As provided by Xiao et al. (2020) [24], we have 2,976 labeled data points (labelled *republican* or *democratic*) along with 583 politicians' data in the US setting. For a nuanced analysis, we retain the partition of the data points, used in the dataset – **PureP**[3], **P50**[4], **P20~50**[5] and **P+all**[6].

Table 1. Descriptive statistics of the labeled dataset.

	PureP	P50	P20–50	P+all
#User	579	730	946	1,125
#Retweetees	26,034	46,734	67,239	87,802
#Repliees	1,738	16,261	12,665	29,713
#Mentions	30,363	53,125	62,274	84,962

We collected the Twitter ids and labels provided by Xiao et al. (2020) [24]. We crawled the last 3,200 tweets (some tweets got deleted, some tweets were retweets, quotes, and replies), follower ids and friend ids of each labeled id in

---

[3] This dataset contains only the politicians.

[4] This dataset contains people highly interested in politics being followed or following at least 50 politicians, including the politicians themselves.

[5] This dataset contains people moderately interested in politics being followed or following anywhere between 20 to 50 politicians and the politicians themselves.

[6] This dataset contains members of **PureP**, **P20–50** along with many outliers who are following or being followed by maximum five politicians.

November, 2020 using the Twitter API[7]. We also collected the user objects (containing bios) for each id. So, after pre-processing, we have data for each feature type described in the previous section. We extracted the domain and co-domain names from the URLs shared using the tldextract[8] library. Out of 2,976 labeled users, 2,665 users were available on Twitter at the time of crawling of the tweets (November, 2020). We report our results on this dataset. A major point to be noted here is that we do not store this data once the training is over, nor do we need to collect neighborhood data at inference time making the inferece faster and memory efficient. A detailed statistics of this dataset with the count of unique features for some feature types is provided in Table 1.

Additional Datasets for Lateral Verification

We collect several other datasets to demonstrate the usefulness of FSSPIP in zero/few-shot setting. The statistics of these datasets are detailed in Table 2.

Table 2. Descriptive statistics of the collected datasets. MB: MediaBias; C: Community; MP: Multiparty; S: Statewise TPC: Topicwise; HTU: HashTagUsers (4 hashtags subset as mentioned in Fig. 3b , details in Appendix).

	MB	C	MP	S	TPC	HTU
#User	806	400	1000	2900	4000	4000
#Domains	5,629	3,829	6,651	17,285	25,679	27,287
#Hashtags	83,245	18,109	28,891	69,341	71,189	68,423
#Mentions	52,178	96,123	67,478	89,651	89,765	81,319

The Media Bias Dataset: Following Stefanov et al. (2020) [20], we use the crowdsourced labels[9] for media bias prediction. There are 806 labeled instances in the dataset with labels *left, center-left, least biased, center-right* and *right*. In order to binarize the label space (to fit in our classification model which is a binary classifier), we first discard the instances with label *least biased*; next, we merge *left, center-left* to a single label *left* and *center-right, right* to a single label *right*. We collect the friend ids, follower ids, and the last 3,200 tweets of these media houses to employ the FSSPIP classifier for prediction.

The Ethnic Community Dataset: Many post-poll surveys establish how different communities vote differently. We try to use our model to identify such divisions. We first sample recent tweets using the Twitter API (See footnote 7) mentioning names of any of the communities. Among the users tweeting, we

---

[7] https://developer.twitter.com/en/docs/twitter-api.

[8] https://pypi.org/project/tldextract/.

[9] https://mediabiasfactcheck.com/.

select only those who mention their community as one (or more) of the communities/ethnicities being probed ('black', 'white', 'hispanic/latino', 'asian'), in their bio. We put a user to a particular community if that community is mentioned in their bio.

Multi-party Leaning Dataset: In order to collect a set of users residing in a multi-party democratic system, we filter the latest 10,000 tweets (and tweeters) containing the term 'Delhi Election' using Twitter API on 17th March, 2021. We annotate random 1000 Twitter users from this list into followers of three political parties: *AAP: Aam Aadmi Party, BJP: Bhartiya Janta Party* and *Congress/INC: Indian National Congress* (AAP: 203 users, INC: 435 users, BJP: 362 users) to form the multi-party inclination dataset. We check the residency of the users and confirm it to be India through the self-declared location tag in twitter while annotating each user.

Statewise Inclination Dataset: Here, we use the Twitter API to collect tweets against a politically neutral query 'election' (all datapoints are collected before 17.05.2021). If the user has a state's name mentioned in the *Twitter's location tag*, we categorise that user to that particular state. We collected 100 users for each state in India for representative sample collection.

Hashtags User Data: In order to find out the inclination distribution behind each hashtag, we collect the tweets containing some trending hashtags (on or before 17.05.2021). We collect 1000 ($\times$ 30) tweets, excluding the retweets and replies containing each trending hashtags using the Twitter API. For a manual verification, we annotate 30 hashtags with tags Congress, BJP, and Neutral (In the date of collection, we could not find hashtags which can be attributed to be inclined towards AAP. Moreover, politically unmotivated hashtags are termed as 'neutral'). This annotation was done by a PhD student, expert in Indian Politics by reading the tweets with the hashtags.

6   Main Task: Experiments and Analysis

Baselines: We use the best performing models provided by Aldayel et al. (2019) [1] and Darwish et al. (2020) [10] (UMAP+DBSCAN with tweets containing chosen hashtags included in the Appendix). **NTF** [1] uses network/graph and textual features together in its model just like our model without attention. **UUS** [10] on the other hand uses weak supervision (a quite different method compared to ours) through dimensionality reduction and clustering, manual inspection (which also makes the algorithm less scalable) and labelling of the clusters with only three features (retweeted tweets, retweeted accounts and hashtags). We also added a modified version of the UUS algorithm for a fair comparison with our fine-tuned model as the UUS algorithm is completely unsupervised and incapable of using any supervisory signal for few-shot learning. We took the unsupervised UUS model and fine-tuned it using annotated data points, terming it **UUS+**.

We also add non-neural baselines like SVM, Logistic regression (LR) and Random Forest (RF) as we are interested to show how simple algorithms with smaller inference time tally with our methods. Here, we use the concatenation of tweets for each user as input. We used TIMME-hierarchial [24] and its other two variants as the other baselines using self-supervision on graphs with higher inference time due to second order data collection on large graph. However, we only report TIMME-hier results as it was the best-performing variant (hyperparameter stats and details on other TIMME variants in Appendix). A qualitative comparison of the baselines is added in Table 3.

Table 3. A pointwise comparison of the models used as baselines. {NNeur : Non Neural baselines}.

Models	FSSPIP	TIMME	NTF	UUS+	UUS	NNeur
Uses only neighbors?	✓		✓	✓	✓	✓
Uses textual features?	✓	✓	✓	✓	✓	✓
Uses unsupervised pretraining also while finetuning on labelled examples?	✓	✓		✓		
Performs well even without manual annotation?	✓				✓	✓
Performs well even without any human supervision ?	✓					

Results: In Table 4, we show that our best performing model *FSSPIP*[10] fairly beats other baselines for all datasets. We see that we gain most compared to other models when very few training datapoints (50) are present[11]. In the case of the non-politician datasets, i.e., **P50, P20–50** and **P+all**, the performance obtained by our model is significantly higher than other baselines, even with only 50 training data points. This may be because the non-politician datasets do not purely contain political features unlike the PureP dataset making the feature learning task less straight-forward needing finer features like domain names a user is interested in or the tweets from the retweetees.

Our model performs better than other models in terms of time required to predict for a single user. Compared to the networks using second order relational data (TIMME) we are at least $\sim$ 10x faster as shown in Table 4.

---

[10] † represents p value less than 0.05 in student's t-test while comparing FSSPIP's result with the best performing baseline.

[11] Training on the whole data, we got comparable accuracy with other state-of-the-art architectures (result in Appendix).

Table 4. Results of few-shot learning {NTF: Model proposed by [1]; UUS: Model proposed by [10]; UUS+: Model proposed by [10] fine-tuned on annotated data points; TIMME: TIMME-hier (other TIMME variants' result in Appendix); **FSSPIP: FSSPIP base architecture with the few-shot learning framework**; #T: Number of training datapoints; TTI: Time Taken for Inference per datapoint with Twitter ids as inputs. For each framework, it also includes the time taken to collect the data}.

Dataset	#T	LR	RF	SVM	NTF	UUS	UUS+	TIMME	FSSPIP
PureP	50	81.8	90.1	79.2	89.6	94.1	95.2	95.4	**97.1**[†]
	250	85.1	93.2	83.8	93.2	94.1	97.5	95.8	**98.9**[†]
	500	89.2	96.9	88.5	97.9	94.1	98.1	99.2	**99.2**
P50	50	78.2	81.7	64.2	90.9	92.2	95.5	84.6	**97.3** [†]
	250	79.2	83.8	65.4	92.3	92.2	96.8	95.1	**98.1**[†]
	500	80.4	84.1	69.3	97.8	92.2	97.5	95.2	**98.9** [†]
P20–50	50	86.1	86.6	81.2	90.2	92.5	94.9	79.1	**96.9** [†]
	250	89.6	87.3	84.8	91.8	92.5	95.8	96.9	**97.8**[†]
	500	92.1	89.9	86.1	97.7	92.5	97.1	97.1	**98.9**
P+all	50	84.2	77.1	76.2	91.5	89.1	92.8	69.5	**95.2** [†]
	250	86.5	79.5	77.9	93.9	89.1	94.5	93.8	**97.1**[†]
	500	87.6	83.2	80.8	96.7	89.1	97.4	95.2	**98.1**[†]
TTI (secs)		28.0	28.9	28.1	65.3	63.1	63.2	973.2	62.1

Table 5. Ablation study of different model variants {F1: FSSPIP-fixedattn; F2: FSSPIP-auto; FSSPIP- - -: FSSPIP base architecture; FSSPIP- -: FSSPIP without weak supervision and self supervision; FSSPIP-: FSSPIP without self supervision.}

Dataset	#T	F1	F2	FSSPIP- - -	FSSPIP- -	FSSPIP-	FSSPIP
PureP	50	90.4	91.3	91.6	92.3	94.2	97.1
	250	94.1	94.7	94.8	95.1	98.1	98.9
	500	98.9	98.7	99.0[†]	99.1	99.1	99.2
P50	50	87.2	89.4	90.9[†]	92.1	94.9	97.3
	250	92.1	91.5	92.7[†]	93.5	97.3	98.1
	500	95.6	96.8	98.4[†]	98.9	98.9	98.9
P20–50	50	87.1	87.6	90.2[†]	92.8	93.8	96.9
	250	91.6	92.4	92.8	95.2	97.2	97.8
	500	97.8	98.2	98.4	98.5	98.5	98.9
P+all	50	88.3	88.5	89.2[†]	92.5	93.0	95.2
	250	92.1	93.8	94.3[†]	95.8	96.9	97.1
	500	95.9	96.3	97.8[†]	97.8	97.9	98.1

Also, our model performs better than NTF [1] and UUS [10] by a significant margin using weak supervision[12] with better augmentation while utilizing carefully extracted network features like NTF inputs [1].

Ablation Study

Model Variants - In order to ablate our attention mechanism we employ two other varieties of attention in place of ours in FSSPIP base architecture which are as follows: We recall Eq. 2 here to understand the two new attention mechanisms: *FSSPIP-fixedattn* (F1): FSSPIP-fixedattn uses fixed learnable attention to calculate a weighted sum of embeddings of each feature type. Thus here the Eq. 2 α_r values are learnable parameters and $\alpha_{ir} = \alpha_r, \forall i$. *FSSPIP-auto* (F2): FSSPIP-auto simply sums up each of the normalized embeddings of each feature type, assuming equal attention to all the feature types while computing the final embedding vector. So, here we assume $\alpha_{ir} = 1 \ \forall i, r$.

Table 6. Important features and feature types for the predictions.

Feature type	Example features	% drop for one feature type
Hashtags	#taxreform, #maga, #medicareforall, #healthcare, #txlege, #tcot, #coleg, #gopwomen	2.7%
Domains	senate, clk, fairandsimple, house, theguardian, congress	0.9%
Followees	JimLangevin, txstdems, COHouseDem, Sam1963, MustafaTameez, pdamerica	0.3%
Retweetees	RepJoseSerrano, PuestoLoco, MustafaTameez, SenatorMenendez, ProjectLincoln, JoeBiden	0.5%
Repliees	repblumenauer, RepJoseSerrano, SenatorMenendez, Sam1963	0.3%
Mentions	kylegriffin1, MustafaTameez, WhiteHouse45, texasdemocrats, JoeBiden, Mike_Pence	0.5%

To test the few-shot learning framework we used incrementally powerful models in Table 5, where FSSPIP- - - is the base architecture without the few-shot learning framework and then each component of the framework is added sequentially to the base model (terming those intermediate models FSSPIP- -, FSSPIP-, and finally FSSPIP).

We find that the dynamic attention mechanism produces significantly[13] higher gains compared to the other two attention variants. We find that the

---

[12] We do not use any human intervention, unlike other approaches which cluster the datapoints and identify the cluster's political affiliation by manually sampling users and annotating them. This may also be subjected to randomness in the clustering process and dependent on the characteristics of the specific subsets of the social network.

[13] We ran a significance test comparing the results of other two variants with the main (dynamic) variant and found the p-value to be less than 0.05 in all the cases (compared to both F1 and F2) as marked by † in Table 5.

gains produced are higher when fewer data points are used and weak supervision has a higher impact than adding dynamic augmentation further to the weakly supervised model. This can be explained as weak supervision already trains the model with a large number of real data points which makes the model regularized enough. However, dynamic augmentation helps in regularizing the model, specially in fewshot settings to avoid over-fitting. Similarly, self-supervision also seems more useful in case of fewer training data points. Moreover, we can see that the attention variants of the model perform very close to the original model but falls short with low number of data points.

Most Important Feature Types - To determine the most important feature types, we drop each feature channel and measure the information loss by calculating the deviation in performance of the classifier (FSSPIP) trained on the combined dataset (train:test:validation datapoints = 80:10:10). The results are reported in Table 6. The highest drop is witnessed when the relevant hashtags are dropped.

Zero-Shot Gain: Inspired by the significant improvement by weak supervision as shown in Table 5, we trained our model *FSSPIP* on the weak supervision dataset *only*, which is collected without any manual annotation. We then use the whole annotated dataset for testing this model. We obtain a ***zero-shot accuracy*** of 93.7% (TIMME models are based on list of politicians of each party, and thus cannot be zero-shot. UUS, which is not easily scalable due to its clustering, purity checking by experts and soft labelling methodology, performed the best among other baselines at 91.9%). This tells that the social media followers of a political party are indeed, most of the time, followers of the party in real life also. So, training a model to classify a social media user to be a follower of one party over the other on social media also trains the model for the similar task of classifying the user to be a follower of one political party over the other in real life. We verify this conclusion again in a multi-party scenario for a diverse non-English speaking democracy like India in the next section.

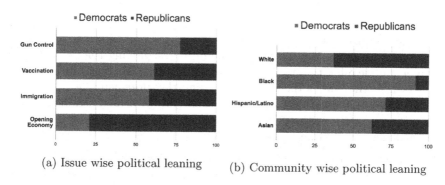

(a) Issue wise political leaning   (b) Community wise political leaning

Fig. 2. Distribution of political inclinations in the USA by topic/racial demographics.

7 Additional Task: Experiments and Analysis

We use the additionally collected datasets to show the efficacy of the zero-shot classifier. The research questions selected for this section are easy to test but important for social scientists. They had been mostly analyzed through manual surveys till now.

Media Bias Prediction: We use the trained FSSPIP classifier on the media bias dataset collected by us, taking each of the Twitter handles of the media houses as the node to be classified. We obtain an accuracy of 72.6% on the task, while we do not explicitly train for this task[14] and rely on the assumption that {democrat ≡ left} and {republic ≡ right}.

Topical Polarization - Bone(s) of Contention: In order to poll users for specific contexts and issues, we collect some hashtags (see Appendix) supporting each issue mentioned in Fig. 2a. We then use the model to classify each user and plot the % of users for each leaning in the US setting, i.e., *The Democrats & The Republicans*.

Multi-party Inclination Prediction: US political system is binary consisting of only two political parties: *The Democrats & The Republicans*. In principle, our system can work for other countries and other kinds of political systems as well. In this section, we test *zero-shot* property classification of our model on the diverse multi-party democracy like India. We take Twitter handles of three national parties in India, namely, *Aam Aadmi Party (AAP)*, *Indian National Congress (INC)* and *Bharatiya Janata Party (BJP)*. We use the weak supervision method to train our model with sampling, mixup & feature channel dropout strategy as discussed earlier. On a random sample of 1000 Twitter accounts (*AAP*: 203, *INC*: 435, *BJP*: 362), we obtain an accuracy of 81.9%. The highest confusion scores between classes (see Appendix) were between *AAP & INC*. This is fairly intuitive since both these parties are left-leaning and in opposition, while *BJP* is known to be subscribing to a right-wing leaning and is currently in power.

Statewise Leaning: In Fig. 3a, we plot the relative distribution of political leanings for each state of India (on a scale of 0–1, signifying the percentage of users in a state leaning toward *BJP*. We get the average of political leanings for each person in the state's data predicted using the aforementioned classifier). This correlates quite well (Pearson's corr coef: 0.52 with high significance and low p-value, $p < 0.01$) with the vote percentage received by *BJP* in each state in the 2019 general election.[15]

A Leopard Cannot Change Its Spots: In order to check if the political inclination changes with time, we reuse the same dataset described in the last paragraph with a temporal filtering strategy. We only use the tweets and tweet

---

[14] If we train for the task explicitly using 70:30 split for train-test data, we achieve an accuracy of 84.1%.

[15] https://eci.gov.in/.

derived features for this experiment which means the bio is always left as blank and same is done for followers/retweeters. We collect all the 3,200 tweets (limit set by the twitter API) of each user ID, directly available from Twitter. For reliable prediction, we filter the users who have tweeted at least 100 times before 2017 and at least 100 times after 2018[16] This leaves us with 2,893 users. We then predict the inclination of these Twitter users twice. Once we use the features collected from tweets before 2017 and once we use the tweets after 2018. We observe that the predictions match for 91% of the cases, which tells that political leanings are temporally (almost) invariant.

Hidden Agenda - Inclination Behind Promoted Hashtags: To find out the inclination behind each hashtag, we obtain the political leanings of the users in the collected hashtag-specific dataset using the zero-shot classifier trained on followers of Congress and BJP. We plot the percentage of users leaning toward each party for each hashtag. We correctly predicted the leaning in 25 of the 30 cases using the classifier (considering a percentage distribution of 40–60% as the neutral/apolitical zone). We plot the leanings on four different India-specific issue – *#WeAreWithYouPmModiJi*, *#BengalBurning*, *#CycloneTaukte*, *#JusticeForAsif* in Fig. 3b. While we see the disaster hashtag (#CycloneTaukte) is non-polarizing, other trending hashtags are evidently promoted by people of particular ideologies. We include the list of other hashtags in Appendix.

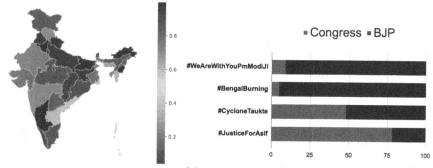

(a) Statewise distribution of average political leaning toward *BJP* in India.

(b) Distribution of political leanings of hashtag promoters

Fig. 3. Inclination distribution in India.

8   Limitations and Future Work

Our work is limited by the availability of social media data. If a country does not have enough political participation in the social media, then training a model

---

[16] We do not consider the follower-followee network as the past snapshots are not retrievable.

will not be possible. Moreover, if the profile of a person is kept private, the classifier will not be able to assign any label. We have discussed the related ethical implications of our work separately in Appendix.

Lastly, here we only evaluated our method on a dataset of users with high degree of political connection to very low degree of political connection. Collection of a dataset of users with *no political links* online but inclination toward a particular political party is a challenging task. In fact, Twitter matched voter registration data [3] also shows high partisanship evident in tweets and political connections. Research toward implicit(not explicitly tweeted/mentioned) political inclination detection (like implicit hate speech detection [5,12] or implicit aspect specific sentiment detection [6,16]) is an interesting future research direction.

9   Conclusions

We present an efficient, fast, and scalable few-shot learning framework for Twitter profiles for political inclination detection (FSSPIP). We showed that our model is explainable and learns features that humans find meaningful. Moreover, our model does not store any personal data of users unlike graph based models. It is also shown to be faster than graph-based methods. With the scalable representation learning framework, we achieve state-of-the-art accuracy, gaining significantly in unlabelled or few-shot learning setups on non-politician users. Enabling *zero-shot political inclination detection* with high fidelity, we provide a method to easily re-target this work to new countries and languages without any manual intervention/supervision unlike previous methods. We believe this will make a large-scale analysis of the political landscape throughout the globe easier and more accurate.

References

1. Aldayel, A., Magdy, W.: Your stance is exposed! analyzing possible factors for stance detection on social media. Proc. ACM Hum.-Comput. Interact. **3**(CSCW) (2019). https://doi.org/10.1145/3359307
2. Baly, R., et al.: What was written vs. who read it: News media profiling using text analysis and social media context. In: Proceedings of the 58th Annual Meeting of the Association for Computational Linguistics, pp. 3364–3374. Association for Computational Linguistics, July 2020. https://doi.org/10.18653/v1/2020.acl-main.308
3. Barberá, P.: Birds of the same feather tweet together: Bayesian ideal point estimation using twitter data. Polit. Anal. **23**(1), 76–91 (2015)
4. Cer, D., et al.: Universal sentence encoder. arXiv preprint arXiv:1803.11175 (2018)
5. Chakraborty, S., Dutta, P., Roychowdhury, S., Mukherjee, A.: CRUSH: contextually regularized and user anchored self-supervised hate speech detection. In: Findings of the Association for Computational Linguistics: NAACL 2022, pp. 1874–1886. Association for Computational Linguistics, Seattle, United States, July 2022. https://doi.org/10.18653/v1/2022.findings-naacl.144, https://aclanthology.org/2022.findings-naacl.144

6. Chakraborty, S., Goyal, P., Mukherjee, A.: Aspect-based sentiment analysis of scientific reviews. In: Proceedings of the ACM/IEEE Joint Conference on Digital Libraries in 2020, JCDL 2020, pp. 207–216. Association for Computing Machinery, New York, NY, USA (2020). https://doi.org/10.1145/3383583.3398541
7. Chakraborty, S., Goyal, P., Mukherjee, A.: (Im) balance in the representation of news? an extensive study on a decade long dataset from India. In: International Conference on Social Informatics, SocInfo (2022), arxiv.org/abs/2110.14183
8. Chen, W., Zhang, X., Wang, T., Yang, B., Li, Y.: Opinion-aware knowledge graph for political ideology detection. In: Proceedings of the Twenty-Sixth International Joint Conference on Artificial Intelligence, IJCAI-17, pp. 3647–3653 (2017). https://doi.org/10.24963/ijcai.2017/510, https://doi.org/10.24963/ijcai.2017/510
9. Conover, M.D., Goncalves, B., Ratkiewicz, J., Flammini, A., Menczer, F.: Predicting the political alignment of twitter users. In: 2011 IEEE Third International Conference on Privacy, Security, Risk and Trust and 2011 IEEE Third International Conference on Social Computing, pp. 192–199 (2011). https://doi.org/10.1109/PASSAT/SocialCom.2011.34
10. Darwish, K., Stefanov, P., Aupetit, M., Nakov, P.: Unsupervised user stance detection on twitter. Proc. Int. AAAI Conf. Web Soc. Media **14**(1), 141–152 (2020). https://ojs.aaai.org/index.php/ICWSM/article/view/7286
11. Devlin, J., Chang, M.W., Lee, K., Toutanova, K.: BERT: pre-training of deep bidirectional transformers for language understanding. In: Proceedings of the 2019 Conference of the North American Chapter of the Association for Computational Linguistics: Human Language Technologies, Vol.1 (Long and Short Papers), pp. 4171–4186. Association for Computational Linguistics, Minneapolis, Minnesota, June 2019. https://doi.org/10.18653/v1/N19-1423, https://aclanthology.org/N19-1423
12. ElSherief, M., et al.: Latent hatred: A benchmark for understanding implicit hate speech. In: Proceedings of the 2021 Conference on Empirical Methods in Natural Language Processing, pp. 345–363. Association for Computational Linguistics, Online and Punta Cana, Dominican Republic, November 2021. https://doi.org/10.18653/v1/2021.emnlp-main.29, https://aclanthology.org/2021.emnlp-main.29
13. Iyyer, M., Enns, P., Boyd-Graber, J., Resnik, P.: Political ideology detection using recursive neural networks. In: Proceedings of the 52nd Annual Meeting of the Association for Computational Linguistics (Volume 1: Long Papers), pp. 1113–1122. Association for Computational Linguistics, Baltimore, Maryland, June 2014. https://doi.org/10.3115/v1/P14-1105, https://www.aclweb.org/anthology/P14-1105
14. Kannangara, S.: Mining twitter for fine-grained political opinion polarity classification, ideology detection and sarcasm detection. In: Proceedings of the Eleventh ACM International Conference on Web Search and Data Mining, WSDM 2018, pp. 751–752. Association for Computing Machinery, New York, NY, USA (2018). https://doi.org/10.1145/3159652.3170461, https://doi.org/10.1145/3159652.3170461
15. Koops: Forgetting footprints, shunning shadows: a critical analysis of the right to be forgotten in big data practice. SCRIPTed **8**, 229 (2011)

16. Li, Z., Zou, Y., Zhang, C., Zhang, Q., Wei, Z.: Learning implicit sentiment in aspect-based sentiment analysis with supervised contrastive pre-training. In: Proceedings of the 2021 Conference on Empirical Methods in Natural Language Processing, pp. 246–256. Association for Computational Linguistics, Online and Punta Cana, Dominican Republic, November 2021. https://doi.org/10.18653/v1/2021.emnlp-main.22, https://aclanthology.org/2021.emnlp-main.22

17. Meeks, L.: Tweeted, deleted: theoretical, methodological, and ethical considerations for examining politicians' deleted tweets. Inf. Commun. Soc. **21**(1), 1–13 (2018). https://doi.org/10.1080/1369118X.2016.1257041. https://doi.org/10.1080/1369118X.2016.1257041

18. Nguyen, D.Q., Vu, T., Nguyen, A.T.: BERTweet: a pre-trained language model for English Tweets. In: Proceedings of the 2020 Conference on Empirical Methods in Natural Language Processing: System Demonstrations, pp. 9–14 (2020)

19. Sood, G., Laohaprapanon, S.: Predicting race and ethnicity from the sequence of characters in a name (2018)

20. Stefanov, P., Darwish, K., Atanasov, A., Nakov, P.: Predicting the topical stance and political leaning of media using tweets. In: Proceedings of the 58th Annual Meeting of the Association for Computational Linguistics, pp. 527–537. Association for Computational Linguistics, July 2020. https://doi.org/10.18653/v1/2020.acl-main.50, https://www.aclweb.org/anthology/2020.acl-main.50

21. Thompson, A., Stringfellow, L., Maclean, M., Nazzal, A.: Ethical considerations and challenges for using digital ethnography to research vulnerable populations. J. Bus. Res. **124**, 676–683 (2021)

22. Vahini, M., Bantupalli, J., Chakraborty, S., Mukherjee, A.: Decoding demographic un-fairness from indian names. In: International Conference on Social Informatics, SocInfo (2022), arxiv.org/abs/2209.03089

23. Williams, M.L., Burnap, P., Sloan, L.: Towards an ethical framework for publishing twitter data in social research: Taking into account users' views, online context and algorithmic estimation. Sociology **51**(6), 1149–1168 (2017). https://doi.org/10.1177/0038038517708140, https://doi.org/10.1177/0038038517708140, pMID: 29276313

24. Xiao, Z., Song, W., Xu, H., Ren, Z., Sun, Y.: Timme: Twitter ideology-detection via multi-task multi-relational embedding. In: Proceedings of the 26th ACM SIGKDD International Conference on Knowledge Discovery and Data Mining, KDD 2020, pp. 2258–2268. Association for Computing Machinery, New York, NY, USA (2020). https://doi.org/10.1145/3394486.3403275, https://doi.org/10.1145/3394486.3403275

25. Zhang, H., Cisse, M., Dauphin, Y.N., Lopez-Paz, D.: mixup: Beyond empirical risk minimization. In: International Conference on Learning Representations (2018), https://openreview.net/forum?id=r1Ddp1-Rb

Unsupervised Keyphrase Generation by Utilizing Masked Words Prediction and Pseudo-label BART Finetuning

Yingchao Ju[iD] and Mizuho Iwaihara[(✉)][iD]

Graduate School of Information, Production and Systems, Waseda University,
Kitakyushu 808-0135, Japan
jyingchao@akane.waseda.jp, iwaihara@waseda.jp

Abstract. A keyphrase is a short phrase of one or a few words that summarizes the key idea discussed in the document. Keyphrase generation is the process of predicting both present and absent keyphrases from a given document. Recent studies based on sequence-to-sequence (Seq2Seq) deep learning framework have been widely used in keyphrase generation. However, the excellent performance of these models on the keyphrase generation task is acquired at the expense of a large quantity of annotated documents. In this paper, we propose an unsupervised method called MLMPBKG, based on masked language model (MLM) and pseudo-label BART finetuning. We mask noun phrases in the article, and apply MLM to predict replaceable words. We observe that absent keyphrases can be found in these words. Based on the observation, we first propose MLMKPG, which utilizes MLM to generate keyphrase candidates and use a sentence embedding model to rank the candidate phrases. Furthermore, we use these top-ranked phrases as pseudo-labels to finetune BART for obtaining more absent keyphrases. Experimental results show that our method achieves remarkable results on both present and abstract keyphrase predictions, even surpassing supervised baselines in certain cases.

Keywords: Keyphrase generation · Unsupervised learning · Masked language model · Sentence embedding · Finetuning

1 Introduction

Keyphrases are several words or phrases that can concisely and accurately describe the subject or central concept of a document. Keyphrases are commonly used to annotate articles and essential for the categorization and fast retrieval of such items in digital libraries. Keyphrases are useful for many natural language processing and information retrieval tasks, such as text summarization [24], question answering [21], document retrieval [13] and more. Keyphrase extraction is concerned with automatically extracting a set of representative phrases which appear exactly in the target document [9]. Traditional keyphrase extraction methods have been extensively studied over the past few decades. Due to the simplicity and speed of the proposed solutions, keyphrase extraction methods had been popular in the 2000s and early 2010s.

Y.-H. Tseng et al. (Eds.): ICADL 2022, LNCS 13636, pp. 21–34, 2022.
https://doi.org/10.1007/978-3-031-21756-2_2

The main drawback of keyphrase extraction is that sometimes keyphrases are absent from the source text. Absent keyphrases are not found verbatim in the source text. Thus an extractive model will fail predicting those keyphrases. Referring to our analysis of four public research paper test datasets, a large number of keyphrases are absent from documents. Keyphrase generation is the process of predicting both extractive (present) and abstractive (absent) keyphrases from a given document. Motivated by the advances in sequence-to-sequence (Seq2Seq) applications of neural networks, the encoder-decoder paradigm was widely used in keyphrase generation task. By using the Seq2Seq framework, recent studies [5, 16] are able to generate diverse keyphrases, according to their semantic relevance to a document, no matter they are present or not. Although these methods have achieved great performance, these deep models are supervised and typically require a large quantity of document-keyphrase pairs, which requires a considerable effort to annotate documents. For example, CopyRNN [16] utilized more than 500,000 computer science domain scientific papers to train.

Recently, LOTClass [17] associates semantically related words with label names to construct category vocabulary. The model uses the masked language model (MLM) of pre-trained language model BERT [7] to predict what words can replace the label names under most contexts. This motivates us to find absent keyphrase in these replaceable words. We first do experiments that mask noun phrases in one article, then use MLM to predict replaceable words. We found that a certain number of absent keyphrases were in the phrases predicted by MLM. Figure 1 shows an example of MLM prediction. The text in the figure is selected from a document from the Inspec dataset. We replace "CT images" in the sentence with the [MASK] tag, and using MLM to predict this text will generate corresponding phrases according to the probability of the word appearing at that position. It can be seen that among the top five MLM predictions, "medical image" is one of absent keyphrases in this document.

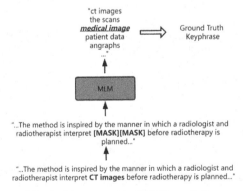

Fig. 1. The example of MLM prediction

Motivated by this observation, in this paper, we propose a novel unsupervised deep keyphrase generation method MLMPBKG, which can generate diverse keyphrases without utilizing any human annotations. Specifically, we first select present candidate noun phrases from a given text document based on POS tags. For each noun phrase in the document, we only replace each word in the phrase with a MASK tag, keeping the rest of the article unchanged. Then we use further pretrained BERT MLM to predict and return top-K tokens. For the phrases obtained in the last step, we use partial match to filter the list of predicted phrases to obtain candidate absent keyphrases.

To rank both types of keyphrases, we use sentence embedding model SimCSE [8] to generate embeddings of noun phrases (NP) and documents. These embeddings are used to calculate the cosine distance between NPs and documents. We call the above method of obtaining sorted phrases MLMKPG. We further finetune the pre-trained seq2seq model BART [18] by using top-ranked phrases as pseudo-labels to obtain more present and absent keyphrases missing from the previous steps. We call this pseudo-label finetuned BART as PL-BART. Our model combines the outputs of the MLMKPG and PL-BART model, and ranks the combined results through SimCSE, for selecting the top-k prediction as the final results. Experimental results show that our method shows remarkable results in both present and absent keyphrase generation, even surpassing the supervised baseline in several cases.

The rest of this paper is organized as follows. Section 2 covers related work. Section 3 presents the proposed models. Section 4 shows experimental evaluations based on representative benchmark datasets. Section 5 concludes this paper.

2 Related Work

Keyphrase Generation. In contrast to the extraction methods, the generative approaches aim at predicting both the present and absent keyphrases of a target document. Meng et al. [16] proposed the first generative model, known as CopyRNN, which is composed of an encoder-decoder with attention and copy mechanism. Multiple extensions of CopyRNN were also proposed in subsequent works. Chen et al. [4] proposed CorrRNN that incorporates coverage and review mechanisms. However, all these generative methods are trained to predict one keyphrase from the target document. To generate a fixed number of keyphrases, they use a beam search and select the top-k as the final predictions. In contrast, Yuan et al. [23] proposed CatSeq, which concatenate all the ground-truth keyphrases and train models to generate them as one output sequence. A et al. [1] proposed the finetuned BART-based keyphrase generation method "Key-BART" which show superior results compared with CatSeq-based models. BART [18] is a pre-trained seq2seq model combining Bidirectional and Auto-Regressive Trans-formers. BART is the combination of generalizing BERT and GPT.

All the above methods are supervised methods. Recently, Shen et al. [20] proposed an unsupervised keyphrase generation method named AutoKeyGen. The paper reports that for 56.8% of the absent keyphrases in the Inspec dataset, their partial tokens separately appear in the input document. AutoKeyGen pools the candidate present keyphrases from all documents together as a phrase bank to draw candidate absent keyphrases using partial match between the phrase bank for each document.

Masked Language Model. As a major category of pretrained language models, masked language model (MLM) [7] is trained using a denoising autoencoding objective. In a typical MLM, some tokens in a sentence are replaced by a special token [MASK]. The training objective is to predict the original tokens that are masked in the sentence. As the first large-scale pretrained masked language model, BERT chooses to mask 15% of the tokens in sentences randomly. Following BERT, various language models have been proposed with different masking schemes.

BERT randomly selects WordPiece tokens to mask. BERT-WWM [6], which use whole-word-masking in pre-training task, mask all of the tokens corresponding to a word at once. SpanBERT [12] masks tokens within a given span range, predicting the entire masked span using only the representations of the tokens at the span's boundary.

Sentence Embedding. Sentence embedding techniques represent entire sentences and their semantic information as vectors. This helps the machine in understanding the con-text, intention, and other nuances in the entire text. Doc2vec [11] represents each document by a dense vector which is trained to predict words in the document. Sent2vec [15] utilizes word n-gram features to produce sentence embeddings. Arora et al. propose SIF [19] in which sentences are represented as the weighted average of the word embeddings.

Recently, Siamese networks and contrastive learning framework have been proposed for sentence embedding models. SimCSE [8] is a simple contrastive learning framework that greatly advances the SOTA sentence embeddings. It employs unsupervised and supervised approaches. The unsupervised SimCSE takes an input sentence and predicts itself in a contrastive objective, with only standard dropout used as noise. In our work, we utilize SimCSE for calculating cosine similarities between candidate phrases and documents.

3　Methodology

3.1　Model Structure

In this paper, we propose a new unsupervised keyphrase generation method named MLMPBKG, which can generate present and absent keyphrases without any ground truth labels. Figure 2 shows the framework of MLMPBKG.

In model building stage, we first use MLMKPG to generate pseudo-labels for unlabeled documents, and use these pseudo-labels to finetune BART. The training process mainly consists of the following four steps:

1. Extracting noun phrases (NPs) from the documents according to the part-of-speech (POS) sequences as present candidate phrases. Masking the noun phrases in each document, then applying further-pretrained MLM to predict the masked phrases, to obtain semantically related phrases under most contexts.
2. MLM is applied to generate phrases obtained in Step 1, after removing duplicates and invalid phrases. Then partial match is used to filter the predictions, to obtain absent candidate phrases.
3. Ranking present and absent candidate phrases together using the similarity ranking module on embeddings.

4. Finetuning BART using the top-ranked phrases obtained in the previous steps as pseudo-labels to generate more keyphrases that may be missing from the previous steps.

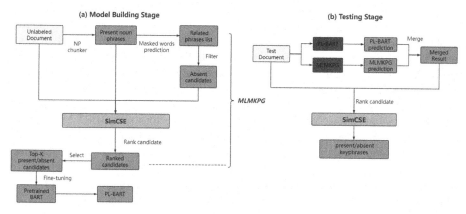

Fig. 2. Overall structure of our proposed model MLMPBKG

We call the method of obtaining top-n phrases in Steps (1)–(3) as MLMKPG, and pseudo-label finetuned BART as PL-BART.

When it comes to the inference for test documents, we combine the results of PL-BART and MLMKPG. We first merge the predictions of PL-BART and MLMKPG, then use the rank module to obtain the embedding of the document and merge predictions. We rank the phrases by cosine similarities and return the top phrases as the result.

3.2 MLM for Absent Keyphrase Generation

Masked Words Prediction. Absent keyphrases are highly related to the document and do not appear directly in the text of the document. Recently, Yu et al. [17] proposed LOTClass, which associates semantically related words using BERT with the label names to construct a category vocabulary. MLM on BERT can find replaceable words on masked tokens, where the context of the masked token is reflected. This inspires us to find absent keyphrases in these replaceable words by masking noun phrases in the document, and using MLM to predict the masked words.

We first follow the literature [2] using NP-chunker, which is a pattern wrote by regular expression, to extract noun phrases as the present candidate keyphrases. For each noun phrase in the document, one simple way is to replace each phrase with a [MASK] tag, using the MLM model which predicts one word for the single [MASK] token. However, this approach is unable to generate phrases of two or more words, which are common in ground-truth keyphrases. To generate multi-word phrases from a single masking position, for phrases of length less than 4, we replace each token in the phrase with a [MASK] token. In addition, for single token [MASK], we duplicate the single mask into double [MASK] tokens. From the single token [MASK], unigram phrases can be generated, from the double tokens [MASK] [MASK], bigram phrases can be generated, and from the triple tokens [MASK] [MASK] [MASK], trigram phrases can be generated.

As used in [7], the original MLM is only to predict for one masked token when pretraining. Instead of randomly selecting WordPiece tokens to mask, BERT-WWM [6] masks all of the tokens corresponding to a whole word at once. When predicting consecutive mask positions, BERT-WWM has a stronger ability to predict meaningful keyphrases. So in our work, we also use BERT-WWM for masked word prediction. Note that replacing a noun with four or more [MASK] tokens is possible, but we do not consider such replacements because we found that it is difficult for MLM to predict golden keyphrases in this case.

Each document with mask tokens will be given to the BERT encoder to obtain its contextualized embedding vector h. Then we feed this vector to the BERT MLM head, which can retrieve the prediction tensors at the index of the mask token. This tensor has the same size as the vocabulary, and the values are the scores attributed to each [MASK] token. The model gives higher score to tokens it deems probable in that context. We choose the top-K result on each masking noun phrases. The above process is illustrated in Fig. 3.

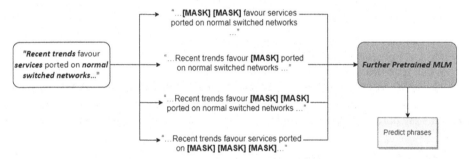

Fig. 3. Example of masked words prediction

Further Pretraining. BERT is pretrained by a general domain, which has a different data distribution from the target domain. Previous studies showed that pretraining the model towards a specific task or small corpus can provide significant benefits. Since test datasets are scientific publication datasets, in our task, we continue pretraining BERT on the unlabeled domain-specific corpus. Note that our method is applicable to any domain. Selecting domain-specific corpus for further pre-training is to perform do-main adaptation to improve the performance of in-domain tasks. Here we use only the KP20K [16] corpus for further pretraining of BERT. KP20K contains large amount of high-quality scientific metadata in the computer science domain from various online digital libraries. It contains the titles, abstracts, and keyphrases of 567830 scientific 7 articles in computer science. Here we use the training data which contain 513918 articles. The abstracts of the articles are organized into the training dataset with one sample per line. These abstracts are used for further pretraining the original BERT-WWM models with the masked language modeling task.

Partial Match Filter. The number of phrases obtained from our masked word prediction is enormous, so directly applying the ranking module to rank all the generated phrases fails to produce desirable quality phrases. We need to retain the most relevant phrases to each article using a suitable filtering method.

Recently, Shen et al. [20] reported that in many cases, tokens of an absent keyphrase can in fact be found in the source document but not in a verbatim manner. For example, in the Inspec dataset, 56.8% absent keyphrases have all their tokens separately appeared in the input document. So in our work, we filtered MLM predictions using the words in documents. Specifically, we first select adjectives, nouns and verbs in the input document as document word lists. For the phrases obtained in the masked word prediction, after removing stop words and present phrases (fully match a part of the text), we first reserve all words of length 1. For phrases longer than 2, we use partial match, such that a phrase is kept if each stemmed word of phrases separately appears in the document word lists.

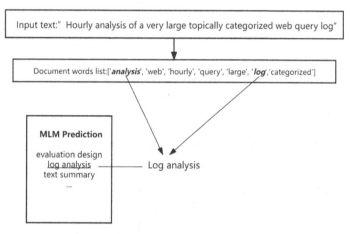

Fig. 4. The example of partial match filter

Figure 4 shows an example of the partial match filter. For the input document: "*Hourly analysis of a very large topically categorized web query log,*" after obtaining the document word list, the phrase "*log analysis*" can be kept because both log and analysis are in the document word list. By this partial match, we can filter out phrases that are less likely to be related to one article, while retaining a considerable number of candidate words.

3.3 Ranking Module

Sentence embedding models capture semantic relatedness via the distances between the corresponding vector representations within the shared vector space. Because there is a high semantic similarity between keyphrases and documents, we use the sentence embedding model to rank the candidate phrases obtained from the extraction and MLM prediction, by measuring their distance to the original document.

The unsupervised SimCSE [8] model is greatly outperforming the previous state-of-the-art models on semantic textual similarity tasks. SimCSE produces semantic relatedness between phrases through similarity measures on the corresponding vectors.

Here, we use the unsupervised SimCSE model to generate 1024-dimension vectors for both input document and its candidate phrases. The cosine similarity between NP embeddings V_{NP} and document embeddings V_d is calculated for ranking, as follows:

$$Sim(V_{NP}, V_d) = Cos(V_{NP}, V_d) = \frac{\overrightarrow{V_{NP}} \cdot \overrightarrow{V_d}}{\left|\overrightarrow{V_{NP}}\right| \cdot \left|\overrightarrow{V_d}\right|} \tag{1}$$

The phrases are sorted by their cosine similarities. We regard this similarity as how candidate keyphrases and the topic of document are semantically close.

3.4 Pseudo-label BART Finetuning

Recent study [1] has shown excellent performance on absent keyphrase prediction by fine-tuning BART. Compared with BERT, which only uses the Transformer encoder, BART achieves better performance on text generation tasks using Transformer Seq2Seq architecture. But finetuning BART require a considerable amount of annotated documents.

The paradigm of pseudo-label [14] training, which uses labeling function generating pseudo-labels on unlabeled documents to train a model, is widely used in unsupervised and semi-supervised learnings. Pseudo-labels play an important role in scenarios where the training dataset is insufficient. Since our method MLMKPG aims at directly predicting keyphrases of unlabeled texts, we use MLMKPG to annotate documents to obtain pseudo-labels to finetune BART. The specific steps to finetune BART using pseudo-labels are as follows:

1. Pair each *unlabeled* KP20K training document text with the top-5 present candidates and top-5 absent candidates using MLM-KPG.
2. Use these pairs as pseudo labels for finetuning BART. The label-smoothed cross-entropy loss is used as the loss function.

We call this pseudo-label finetuned BART as *PL-BART*. When it comes to the inference on test documents, we combine the results of PL-BART and MLMKPG. The main steps are as follows:

1. Merge Sthe predictions of the PL-BART and MLMKPG, then remove duplicate phrases.
2. Use the rank module based on SimCSE to obtain the embedding of each document and merge predictions, calculate cosine similarity and return the top-N phrases as final result.

4 Experiments

In this section, we first introduce benchmark datasets used in our work, followed by baselines, evaluation metrics, and model details. Then, we present and discuss our experimental results on present keyphrase and absent keyphrase generation.

4.1 Datasets

WE use four datasets which are commonly used for evaluating keyphrase generation. Table 1 shows statistics of documents and keyphrases in these datasets. All the models in our experiments are built on the KP20k training set which contains 513918 documents.

- **Inspec**: This dataset consists of 2000 short documents selected from scientific journal abstracts, where 500 papers are separated as the test set and their corresponding uncontrolled keyphrases for evaluation.
- **NUS**: This dataset has both author-assigned and reader-assigned keyphrases and all the 211 papers are treated as the testing data.
- **Semeval**: 288 articles are collected from the ACM Digital Library. 100 articles are used for testing.
- **Krapivin**: This dataset provides 2,304 papers with full-text and author-assigned keyphrases. We select the first 460 papers in alphabetical order as the test set.

Table 1. Statistics of documents and keyphrases in datasets. AbsDoc represent documents that have at least one absent ground-truth phrases. The same for PreDoc.

Dataset	Documents			Keyphrase		
	Number	AbsDoc	PreDoc	Number	%Present	%Absent
Inspec	500	381	497	4912	78.75	21.25
NUS	211	197	207	2283	48.01	51.99
Semeval	100	99	100	1483	44.23	55.77
Krapivin	460	424	435	2636	54.86	45.14

4.2 Baseline Models

We compare our proposed methods with three other unsupervised methods: TF-IDF, EmbedRank, and AutoKeyGen, and two supervised methods: CatSeq, and CopyRNN. Since supervised methods are trained based on golden labels, they have inherent advantages. we regard it as an upper bound of all other unsupervised methods.

- **TF-IDF** (unsupervised): TF/IDF [10] is a statistical method widely used for information retrieval. It ranks the extracted noun phrase candidates by term frequency and inverse document frequency in the given documents.
- **EmbedRank** (unsupervised): EmbedRank [2] is an unsupervised embedding-based method, which uses embedding similarity to rank present candidate keyphrases.
- **AutoKeyGen** (unsupervised): AutoKeyGen [20] is the first unsupervised keyphrase generation method. The details of this method are discussed in Sect. 2.2.

- **CatSeq** (supervised): Catseq [23] is a recent well-known keyphrase generation model, based on a recurrent generative model that generates multiple keyphrases as delimiter-separated sequences.
- **CopyRNN** (supervised): CopyRNN [16] is an encoder-decoder keyphrase generation model with attention and copy mechanism. By using the copy mechanism, the model can also predict keyphrases that contain words outside the vocabulary set.

4.3 Evaluation Metrics

Following the literature, we evaluate the model performance on generating present and absent keyphrases separately. We use R@k, F1@k, and F1@O as main evaluation metrics. Specifically, F1@5, F1@10, and F1@O are utilized for evaluating present keyphrases and R@10, R@20, R@50 and R@M for absent keyphrases. We report the macro-average scores over all documents in each test set. The formulas for calculating these metrics are as follows:

$$P@k = \frac{|\hat{y}_{:k} \cap y|}{|\hat{y}_{:k}|} \tag{2}$$

$$R@k = \frac{|\hat{y}_{:k} \cap y|}{|y|} \tag{3}$$

$$F_1@k = \frac{2*P@k*R@k}{P@k+R@k} \tag{4}$$

Here, y represents the list of ground truth keyphrases for the given source text. The symbol $\hat{y}$ represents a list of unique keyphrases ordered by the quality of the predictions. The symbol $\hat{y}_{:k}$ represents only the top-k portion of list $\hat{y}$. Since the number of ground truth keyphrases can vary drastically for different source documents, following Yuan et al.'s [23] experimental setting, we also adapt F1@O and R@M in our experiments.

– F1@O

F1@O can be viewed as a special case of F1@k when k = |Y|. In other words, we only examine the same amount of keyphrases as the number of our ground-truth keyphrases.

– R@M

M denotes the number of predicted keyphrases. In this case, $k = |\hat{y}|$ and we simply take all the predicted phrases for evaluation without truncation.

4.4 Experimental Settings

For absent candidate generation by MLM, we choose *BERT-large-WWM* models with the original masked language modeling, where further pretraining is done on the KP20k training set. The training settings are: epoch = 3, the training batch size = 4, and the masking ratio is set to 0.15.

For the masked words prediction, when the number of mask tags is more than one, we use MLM to generate top 40 phrases. When the number of mask tags is equal to one, use MLM to generate top 15 phrases, because the keyphrase of one word accounts for a relatively small proportion. Repeated and invalid phrases are removed, after stemming.

For the ranking module, we choose the unsupervised SimCSE model *unsup-simcse-roberta-large*. For domain adaptation, we use the unsupervised SimCSE training method, continuing training the unsupervised SimCSE model with raw documents of KP20K, with training batch size = 4, training epoch = 5, learning rate = $3e-5$.

For the pseudo-label finetuning of BART, we sample 350000 unlabeled documents in the KP20K training set to train "*Facebook/Bart-Large*" model, with training batch size = 4, training epoch = 6, learning rate = $3e-5$.

4.5 Experimental Results and Analysis

Present Keyphrase Evaluation. The results of present keyphrase generation are shown in Table 2. Except for the F@O metric, other metrics MLMKPG and MLMPBKG methods outperformed all the unsupervised baselines. On Inspec, our to-tally unsupervised MLMPBPG method outperformed supervised CatSeq by about ten percentage points at F@10. This indicates that the embedding-based method still has great advantages in keyphrase extraction. SimCSE can produce effective document and phrase embeddings for similarity comparison.

PL-BART showed competitive performance compared to the baseline, demonstrating the effectiveness of pseudo-label training. After combining the PL-BART results, the performance of MLMPBKG is very slightly reduced compared to MLMKPG. This indicates that during the present keyphrase prediction stage, PL-BART does not produce many of the present keyphrases that MLMKPG is missing.

Absent Keyphrase Evaluation. Table 3 presents the model comparison on absent keyphrase generation. Since all unsupervised baseline methods except AutoKeyGen are not capable of generating any absent keyphrases, we refer to them together as "Other Unsupervised Methods". Our method shows competitive results among all methods. On the Inspec and Semeval datasets, our methods MLMKPG and MLMPBKG outper-form the baseline AutoKeyGen. Except for the Kravipin dataset, MLMKPG and MLMPBKG outperform the supervised baseline CatSeq on the R@50 metric.

MLMPBKG even outperforms CatSeq by 1.4 percentage point on the inspect dataset.

Pseudo-label finetuned BART generates a number of correct absent keyphrases on different datasets. The quality of absent keyphrases generated by BART is acceptable. Correct predictions are all within the top 10. After merging with the PL-BART results, the performance of MLMPBKG on the Inspec and Kravipin datasets is greatly improved, indicating that PL-BART generates the absent keyphrases that are missing from MLMKPG.

Effect of Further Pretraining. Table 4 presents the intersection between all the MLM predictions without any filtering and the ground-truth absent keyphrases, which is the recall rate "R@M" of MLM predictions. It serves as an upper bound of the recall of the

Table 2. Present keyphrase prediction performance on four scientific publication datasets. The best unsupervised results are marked in bold. Methods marked with "*" are our methods.Supervised model results are list only for analysis. AutoKeyGen and supervised model results are from its original work.

Datasets	Inspec			SemEval			Kravipin			NUS		
	F@5	F@10	F@O	F@5	F@10	F@O	F@5	F@10	F@O	F@5	F@10	F@O
Unsupervised models												
TF-IDF	24.2	28.0	24.8	16.1	16.7	15.3	11.5	14.0	13.3	11.6	14.2	12.5
EmbedRank	32.3	38.9	**37.3**	21.6	27.7	23.7	16.3	17.4	14.1	21.7	**25.1**	21.4
AutoKeyGen	30.3	34.5	33.1	18.7	24.0	22.7	17.1	15.5	**15.8**	21.8	23.3	**23.7**
*MLMKPG	**33.7**	39.1	36.8	**26.3**	**30.5**	**28.4**	**17.9**	**18.2**	15.3	**23.7**	**25.1**	22.2
*PL-BART	30.6	31.5	29.9	21.1	22.0	21.0	14.9	15.2	13.7	18.4	18.7	16.8
*MLMPBKG	33.6	**39.2**	36.8	25.4	30.3	28.1	17.7	**18.2**	15.1	23.5	25.0	22.1
Supervised models												
CatSeq	29.0	30.0	30.7	30.2	30.6	31.0	30.7	27.4	32.4	35.9	34.9	32.4
CopyRNN	29.2	33.6	-	29.1	29.6	-	30.2	25.2	-	34.2	31.7	-

Table 3. Absent keyphrase prediction performance on four scientific publication datasets. The best unsupervised results are marked in bold. Methods marked with "*" are our methods. AutoKeyGen and supervised model results are from its original work.

Datasets	Inspec			SemEval			Kravipin			NUS		
	R@10	R@20	R@50	R@10	R@20	R@50	R@10	R@20	R@50	R@10	R@20	R@50
Unsupervised models												
Other Unsupervised methods	0	0	0	0	0	0	0	0	0	0	0	0
AutoKeyGen	2.3	2.5	-	**1.0**	1.1	-	**3.3**	**5.4**	-	**2.4**	**3.2**	-
*MLMKPG	2.4	2.5	3.4	**1.0**	**1.6**	2.6	2.3	2.5	4.7	0.8	1.7	**3.5**
*PL-BART	1.2	1.2	1.2	0.3	0.3	0.3	1.2	1.2	1.2	0.4	0.4	0.4
*MLMPBKG	**2.5**	**3.7**	**4.3**	0.8	1.5	2.6	2.1	3	**5.6**	0.8	1.5	3.2
Supervised models												
CatSeq	2.8	-	2.9	2.5	-	2.5	7.0	-	7.4	3.7	-	3.1
CopyRNN	5.1	6.8	10.1	4.9	5.7	7.5	11.6	14.2	19.5	7.8	10.0	14.4

absent keyphrases generated by MLM. Here we mainly compare three MLMs: BERT [7], BERT-WWM [6] and SpanBERT [12]. Here we use all the large models of MLM.

It can be seen from the table that original MLMs pretrained in general domain also predicted a certain number of golden keyphrases, indicating that our method can be applied in any domain. Among the listed original MLM models, BERT-WWM has the highest number of correct predictions, indicating that BERT-WWM is the most suitable MLM model for our task. After further pre-training, BERT-WWM has apparently improved the prediction performance of absent keyphrase on other three datasets except

Table 4. The recall of absent keyphrase using all the predictions of different MLMs

Datasets	Inspec	Semeval	NUS	Krapivin
	R@M	R@M	R@M	R@M
BERT	5.1	5.0	6.6	4.7
Span-BERT	5.3	6.9	6.2	6.4
BERT-WWM	**6.2**	6.5	7.8	6.7
BERT-WWM further pretrained	6.0	**8.7**	**10.6**	**10.1**

Inspec compared to the original model. This shows that further pre-training indeed enhances the performance of MLM for absent keyphrase prediction in scientific paper domain.

5   Conclusion and Future Work

In this paper, we proposed a completely unsupervised keyphrase generation method MLMPBKG which can predict high quality keyphrases. We use MLM to generate candidate words, rank them using the sentence embedding model SimCSE, and finetune the BART model using top-ranked phrases as pseudo-labels. We further combine the predictions of MLM and BART to generate the final result after sorting using SimCSE. Our experiments show that our method has competitive performance in both present and absent keyphrase predictions, even surpassing supervised baselines in some cases.

In future work, we intend to apply prompt learning to keyphrase generation. Prompt learning stimulates the potential of pre-trained language models by using templates, which greatly alleviates the problem of inconsistency between pre-training and fine-tuning, and has achieved good results in many natural language processing tasks. We plan to add a suitable template at the end of articles to train after using BART predictions.

References

1. Diya, A., Mizuho, I.: Keyphrase generation by utilizing BART finetuning and BERT-based ranking. In: DEIM Forum (2022)
2. Bennani-Smires, K., et al.: Simple unsupervised keyphrase extraction using sentence embeddings. In: Conference on Computational Natural Language Learning (2018)
3. Carbonell, J., Goldstein, J.: The use of MMR, diversity-based reranking for reordering documents and producing summaries. In: Proceedings of 21st Annual International ACM SIGIR Conference on on Research and Development in Information Retrieval, pp. 335–336 (1998)
4. Chen, J., Zhang, X., Wu, Y., Yan, Z., Li, Z.: Keyphrase generation with correlation constraints. In: Proceedings of the 2018 Conference on Empirical Methods in Natural Language Processing, pp. 4057–4066 (2018)
5. Chen, W., Gao, Y., Zhang, J., King, I., Lyu, M.R.: Title-guided encoding for Keyphrase Generation. In: Proceedings of the AAAI Conference on Artificial Intelligence, vol. 33, pp. 6268–6275 (2019)

6. Cui, Y., Che, W., Liu, T., Qin, B. and Yang, Z.: Pre-training with whole word masking for Chinese BERT. ACM Trans. Audio Speech Lang. Process. **29**, 3504–3514 (2021)
7. Devlin, J., Chang, M.W., Lee, K., Toutanova, K.: BERT: pre-training of deep bidirectional transformers for language understanding. In: Proceedings of NAACL-HLT 2019, pp. 4171–4186 (2019)
8. Gao, T., Yao, X., Chen, D.: SimCSE: simple contrastive learning of sentence embeddings. In: Proceedings of the 2021 Conference on Empirical Methods in Natural Language Processing, pp. 6894–6910 (2021)
9. Hasan, K.S., Ng, V.: Automatic keyphrase extraction: a survey of the state of the art. In: Proceedings of the 52nd Annual Meeting of the Association for Computational Linguistics, Volume 1: Long Papers, pp. 1262–1273 (2014)
10. Jones, K.S.: Index term weighting. Inf. Storage Retrieval **9**(11), 619–633 (1973)
11. Lau, J.H., Baldwin, T.: An empirical evaluation of doc2vec with practical insights into document embedding generation. In: Proceedings of the 1st Workshop on Representation Learning for NLP, pp. 78–86 (2016)
12. Joshi, M., et al: SpanBERT: improving pre-training by representing and predicting spans. Trans. Assoc. Comput. Linguist. **8**, 64–77 (2020)
13. Kim, Y., et al.: Applying graph-based keyword extraction to document retrieval. In: Proceedings of the Sixth International Joint Conference on Natural Language Processing, pp. 864–868 (2013)
14. Lee, D.H.: Pseudo-label: the simple and efficient semi-supervised learning method for deep neural networks. In: Workshop on Challenges in Representation Learning, ICML, vol. 3, No. 2, p. 896 (2013)
15. Pagliardini, M., Gupta, P., Jaggi, M.: Unsupervised learning of sentence embeddings using compositional n-gram features. In: Proceedings of NAACL-HLT, pp. 528–540 (2018)
16. Meng, R., et al: Deep Keyphrase generation. In: Proceedings of the 55th Annual Meeting of the Association for Computational Linguistics, vol. 1: Long Papers, pp. 582–592 (2017)
17. Meng, Y., et al.: Text classification using label names only: a language model self-training approach. In: Proceedings of the 2020 Conference on Empirical Methods in Natural Language Processing (EMNLP), pp. 9006–9017 (2020)
18. Lewis, M., et al.: BART: denoising sequence-to-sequence pre-training for natural language generation, translation, and comprehension. In: Proceedings of the 58th Annual Meeting of the Association for Computational Linguistics, pp. 7871–7880 (2020)
19. Arora, S., Liang, Y., Ma, T.: A simple but tough-to-beat baseline for sentence embeddings. In: ICLR (2016)
20. Shen, X., Wang, Y., Meng, R., Shang, J.: Unsupervised deep keyphrase generation. Proc. AAAI Conf. Artif. Intell. **36**(10), pp. 11303–11311 (2022)
21. Subramanian, S., et al.: Neural models for key phrase extraction and question generation. In: Proceedings of the Workshop on Machine Reading for Question Answering, pp. 78–88 (2018)
22. Wan, X., Xiao, J.: Single document keyphrase extraction using neighborhood knowledge. In: AAAI Conference on Artificial Intelligence (AAAI-08), pp. 855–860 (2008)
23. Yuan, X., et al.: One size does not fit all: generating and evaluating variable number of Keyphrases. In: Proceedings of the 58th Annual Meeting of the Association for Computational Linguistics, pp. 7961–7975 (2020)
24. Zhang, Y., et al.: Mike: keyphrase extraction by integrating multidimensional information. In: Proceedings of the 2017 ACM on Conference on Information and Knowledge Management, pp. 1349–1358 (2017)

Computer Science Named Entity Recognition in the Open Research Knowledge Graph

Jennifer D'Souza[1,2(✉)] 📔 and Sören Auer[1,2] 📔

[1] TIB Leibniz Information Centre for Science and Technology, Hannover, Germany
{jennifer.dsouza,auer}@tib.eu
[2] L3S Research Center, Leibniz University of Hannover, Hannover, Germany

Abstract. Domain-specific named entity recognition (NER) on Computer Science (CS) scholarly articles is an information extraction task that is arguably more challenging for the various annotation aims that can hamper the task and has been less studied than NER in the general domain. Given that significant progress has been made on NER, we anticipate that scholarly domain-specific NER will receive increasing attention in the years to come. Currently, progress on CS NER – the focus of this work – is hampered in part by its recency and the lack of a standardized annotation aims for scientific entities/terms. Directly addressing these issues, this work proposes a standardized task by defining a set of seven *contribution-centric scholarly entities* for CS NER viz., *research problem, solution, resource, language, tool, method,* and *dataset*.

Keywords: Named entity recognition · Information extraction

1 Introduction

Named entity recognition (NER) is an essential Natural Language Processing (NLP) function for *the lifting of entities-of-interest from unstructured text.* NER powers contemporary knowledge-graph based search engines as demonstrated in industry e.g. by Facebook [30] and Google [2]; but also the open data community with Wikidata [34]. NER has proven indispensable to machine readers of unstructured texts of common or general knowledge. Commonsense machine reading is an area where significant progress can be tracked via state-of-the-art systems such as Babelfy [29], DBpedia Spotlight [27], NELL [28], and FRED [15], to name a few. However, the same cannot be said for all domains of discourse text. Consider scholarly literature, as an exemplar, which remains relatively understudied in terms of advanced information retrieval applications that go beyond keywords toward content-based entity-centric machine readers. In the scholarly domain, obtaining fine-grained entity-centric knowledge facilitated by

Supported by TIB Leibniz Information Centre for Science and Technology, the EU H2020 ERC project ScienceGRaph (GA ID: 819536).

well-established NER systems is not yet feasible. As significant advances have been made on NER in the general domain, we believe that scholarly domain-specific NER will gain increasing attention in the years to come. This is owing to the digitalization of scholarly knowledge impetus via crowdsourcing that is growing [1, 4, 6, 8, 17, 23, 26, 35]. While expert-based crowdsourcing is effective to obtain high-quality data, it is not necessarily a scalable solution in the face of growing volumes of scientific literature [9], the processing of which would need the support of automated NLP techniques, one among which is NER. Obtaining the critical digitalized data mass via scalable methods warrant the paradigm shift toward the standardized adoption of digitalized scholarly knowledge. This data representation is advantageous for several reasons, mainly by its meaningful structured connections across entity-centric research progress, research redundancy [19] can be readily alleviated – a problem predominant in document-based silos of research records where core conceptual entities, buried within text volumes, need to be manually uncovered through human comprehension. Thus, instead of manual human comprehension of the latest and greatest scholarly knowledge within expert silos, digitalized scholarly knowledge can be routinely and centrally screened for information about past and novel discoveries.

Notably, next-generation scholarly digital library (DL) infrastructures are already emerging. The Open Research Knowledge Graph (ORKG) [3] digital research and innovation infrastructure (https://orkg.org/), argues for obtaining a semantically rich, interlinked KG representations of the "content" of the scholarly articles, specifically, focused on *research contributions*. With intelligent analytics enabled over such contributions-focused KGs, researchers can track research progress without the cognitive overhead that reading dozens of articles imposes. Via expert crowdsourcing, the information can be readily structured based on human judgements. However, the issue of needing an automated NLP system as a scalable complementary assistance technique remains; one that could even serve the purpose of making it easier for experts to structure scholarly knowledge via drag-and-drop recommendations. A typical dilemma then with leveraging automated NLP for the ORKG, specifically, w.r.t. implementing an NER module is deciding the scholarly/scientific entity extraction targets. In other words, aligned with the ORKG objective of structuring research contributions, the key challenge is: *How to select only the contribution-centric entities and what would be their types?* In this paper, we specifically tackle the scholarly *contribution-centric* NER problem for Computer Science (CS).

We define *contribution-centric* CS NER as involving the identification of a word or a phrase as an entity from CS scholarly articles, either from its title, or abstract, or full-text or a combination, which satisfies one of the following seven types, viz. *research problem, solution, resource, language, tool, method,* and *dataset*. Furthermore, since, in the context of this work, CS NER is qualified as being *contribution-centric*, only those entities that are the outcome of a particular work are candidate extraction targets. Summarily, the contributions of this paper are the following. 1) Existing CS NER language resources are examined and the problem of the lack of standardized entities therein is clarified. 2) A standardized set of entities is elicited by proposing a standardization on semantic types for extraction that satisfy the aim of being *contribution-centric* extraction targets for CS. 3) Existing resources that fulfill the aim of *contribution-centric* extraction targets are combined and, further still, additional data is annotated resulting in a large corpus which is made publicly available. 4) Finally, based on empirical evaluations from six different state-of-the-art neural architectures an automated CS NER system is created. The best model performances obtained are between 75% and 85% on the task. Our empirical analysis could serve informaticians working in the ecosphere of the contemporary digital libraries. Our system developed for the Open Research Knowledge Graph [3] is also a community release at https://tinyurl.com/orkg-cs-ner; including its underlying dataset https://github.com/jd-coderepos/contributions-ner-cs.

2   Our Corpus

To build our corpus for *contribution-centric* information extraction targets of scientific entities, we aimed: 1) to reuse existing resources for their entity annotations (see Table 1 for a survey) that already fulfill our extraction target aim (described further in Sect. 2.1); and 2) to append additional annotations to create a larger corpus for neural machine learning system development (described in Sect. 2.2).

2.1   Combining Existing Resources

This step first entailed normalizing different semantic label names with the same semantic definitions as one standard name. The mappings we used are elicited in Table 2. The table lists nine main semantic types and their semantic counterparts that were normalized. After obtaining the label names mappings as semantic type normalizations, we selected only those corpora, and specifically the semantic types within the corpora, that satisfied our CS NER *contribution-centric* entities aim. Overall, our corpus was organized as aggregations of similar aspects of the scholarly article. Thus, article titles constitute one corpus called the **Titles** corpus and article abstracts constitute a second corpus called the **Abstracts** corpus. Next we describe how some of the existing resources could be reused and combined to form the two respective corpora.

The **Titles** corpus combines annotations from two different corpora: 1) the FTD corpus [16] (row 1 in Table 1) for all three of its entities, viz. *research problem, method,* and *solution* entities. In all, 462 titles could be obtained from the FTD corpus which originally also includes exactly 462 total annotated paper titles and abstracts with one or more of the three entities' annotations. And, 2) NCG [13] (row 8 in Table 1) for its *research problem* entities. In all, 398 titles were obtained from NCG with *research problem* annotations which had a total of approximately 450 papers [13]. Thus the data from these two corpora were merged as the **Titles** corpus finally containing three entities, viz. *research problem, method,* and *solution* deemed by their original corpora respective annotation aims as *contribution-centric*, in turn fulfilling our CS NER aim.

Table 1. Comparison of Computer Science papers corpora for named entity recognition (CS NER). The corpora names in bold are the corpora merged as part of the dataset of this work. Domain Acronyms. CL - Computational Linguistics; CS - Computer Science; MS - Material Science; Phy - Physics; AI - Artificial Intelligence; STEM - Science, Technology, Engineering, Medicine; ML - Machine Learning; CV - Computer Vision. **Size** column name acronyms: P - papers; T - tokens; E - entities. A detailed version of this table is available here https://orkg.org/comparison/R150058.

Corpora	Domain	Coverage	Entity semantic types	Size		
				P	T	E
FTD [16]	CL	titles, abstracts	focus, domain, technique	426	57,182	5,382
ACL-RD TEC [33]	CL	abstracts	language resource, language resource product, measures and measurements, models, other, technology and method, tool and library	300	32,758	4,391
ScienceIE [5]	CS, MS, Phy	full text	material, process, task	500	83,753	10,994
SciERC [24]	AI	abstracts	evaluation metric, generic, material, method, task	500	60,749	8,089
NLP-TDMS [18]	CL	titles, abstracts, full text	task, dataset, metric, score	332	1,115,987	1,384
STEM-ECR [14]	10 STEM	abstracts	data, material, method, process	110	26,269	6,165
SciREX [20]	ML	titles, abstracts, full text	dataset, method, metric, task	438	248,7091	**156,931**
NCG [13]	CL, CV	titles, abstracts	research problem	405	47,127	908
ORKG-TDM [21]	AI	titles, abstracts, full text	task, dataset, metric	5,361	-	18,219
CL-Titles [12]	CL	titles	language, method, research problem, resource, solution, tool	**50,237**	284,672	87,567
PwC (this paper)	AI	titles, abstracts	research problem, method	12,271	**1,317,256**	29,273
ACL (this paper)	CL	titles	language, method, research problem, resource, dataset, solution, tool	31,044	263,143	67,270

The second corpus, i.e. the **Abstracts** corpus combines: 1) the FTD corpus paper abstracts annotated with *research problem* and *method* entities. Since no annotations for *solution* entities could be obtained in the abstracts, this type could not be included. As such, abstracts in all 462 of the FTD annotated papers were included in our corpus. Next, 2) 272 abstracts from the NCG corpus with annotations for *research problem*. And, lastly, 3) the SciERC corpus [24] (row 4 in Table 1) annotated abstracts for its *contribution-centric research problem* entity.

Table 2. Mappings of nine scientific semantic types across Computer Science papers for CS NER. The first seven italicized types are in the dataset of this work.

Types	Mappings in related work
1 *research-problem*	domain; application; task; research problem
2 *method*	technique; technology and method; method
3 *solution*	focus; solution
4 *tool*	tool and library; tool
5 *resource*	language resource; resource
6 *dataset*	language resource product; dataset
7 *language*	language
8 metric	measures and measurements; evaluation metric; metric
9 score	measures and measurements

431 of its 500 total annotated papers could be combined. Note that SciERC had annotations for additional semantic types as well, e.g., *generic, material,* and *method*. However, these annotations could not be included since they did not satisfy our *contribution-centric* entities inclusion criteria.

2.2 Our Annotated Data

ACL. This corpus of Computational Linguistics paper titles was originally released as part of the CL-Titles parser software resources [12] and was automatically annotated using the rule-based CL-Titles parser. It included all the titles in the ACL Anthology at a specific download dump timestamp (https:// aclanthology.org/anthology.bib.gz). This corpus was re-reviewed in this work for annotation quality and additional scientific semantic types that should be included. As such we noted that the semantic type *dataset* relevant particularly in the domain of Computational Linguistics was not originally included in the annotated types. We heuristically modified the annotations to include the *dataset* semantic type additionally and we further manually verified as many of the annotations as were possible in a fixed time-frame of 2 weeks. In this time, 31,041 of its 49,728 titles could be verified and amended for incorrect annotations. Thus the new verified and adapted version (which we call simply ACL) includes seven *contribution-centric* entities, viz. *language, method, research problem, resource, dataset, solution,* and *tool*. See last row in Table 1 for details.

While the corpus verification exercise was done by a single primary annotator (an NLP Postdoc), a blind IAA exercise for 50 randomly selected titles involving the primary annotator and a secondary "outsider" annotator (an NLP PhD candidate) was also conducted to gauge the replicability of the primary annotator's judgements. The results were promising. In terms of Cohen's κ, they had a strong IAA of 71.52%.

PwC. A second data source was leveraged from which additional annotations were appended to the **Titles** corpus and **Abstracts** corpus, respectively. The data was originally sourced from PapersWithCode (https://paperswithcode. com/) hence it is referred as **PwC**. Note that three of the datasets listed in Table 1, viz. NLP-TDMS [18], SciREX [20], and ORKG-TDMS [21], were indeed subsets of the PwC source. PwC is a public download dump of crowdsourced leaderboards in scholarly articles on research problems in AI annotated w.r.t. *task, dataset, metric, score*, and *method* entities. We downloaded the dump from the online source https://paperswithcode.com/about (timestamp 19–10-2021) and obtained data annotations via distance labeling of their crowdsourced annotations for only the *research problem* and *method* entities (see relevant label mappings in Table 2). Note that among their five available entities, three entities, viz. *dataset, metric, score*, were not considered since they were often not direct mentions in the text but were inferable candidates and hence did not satisfy the sequence labeling objective of this work.

Both our **Titles** and **Abstracts** corpora were appended with available PwC annotations for *research problem* and *method* entities. This was done by following two selection criteria: 1) since PwC provided over 50,000 papers, we wanted to select only a subsample of the data to avoid skewing our overall dataset annotations to just the two PwC entities (i.e., *research problem* and *method*). On the other hand, 2) we wanted to select a subsample size representative enough of PwC to capture the different nature of their crowdsourced annotations. Starting with the **Titles** corpus, the PwC titles were grouped in three categories: those with both *research problem* and *method* mentions; those with either one. From each group, roughly 2000 titles were added to dataset. Similarly, for the **Abstracts** corpus, the paper abstracts were grouped in three categories: those with both *research problem* and *method* mentions; those with either one. From each of the three groups, roughly 2000 abstracts were added.

Our final resulting corpus distributions in terms of the constituent corpora after "combining existing resources" and adding "our annotated data" was as follows. **Titles** corpus constituent subcorpora distributions: 31,041 (82%) ACL/5,885 (15%) PwC/462 (1%) FTD/398 (1%) NCG. The considered annotations were for seven *contribution-centric* entities, viz. *solution, tool, dataset, language, method, resource*, and *research problem*. And, the **Abstracts** corpus constituent subcorpora distributions were: 6756 (85%) PwC/462 (5%) FTD/272 (3%) NCG/431 (5%) SciERC.

3   Our CS NER Sequence Labeler

3.1   Experimental Setup

Model. Overall, we experimented with six different sequence labeling neural architectures. The basic building blocks to these six architectural variants, inspired from state-of-the-art neural sequence labelers in the general domain [10,22,25,32,37], were are follows: 1) a CNN, a LSTM, or a BiLSTM first layer over word representations of the data, 2) with and without a second char CNN layer, and 3) an output layer as a CRF decoder since CRFs outperformed the softmax function in sequence labeling tasks. Thus the following six

Table 3. Results with different neural architectures for CS NER over seven semantic concepts with embeddings computed on the data source (top row) and with pretained embeddings (bottom row) on the TITLES corpus (columns 2 to 4) and ABSTRACTS corpus (columns 5 to 7).

Neural architectures	Micro P	Micro R	Micro $F1$	Micro P	Micro R	Micro $F1$
Word CNN + CRF	70.28	71.24	70.76	90.55	72.51	80.53
	69.32	69.16	69.24	91.78	73.58	81.68
Word LSTM + CRF	69.24	70.08	69.65	85.45	75.54	79.62
	68.41	66.76	67.58	90.02	71.82	79.9
Word BiLSTM + CRF	71.92	73.34	72.62	88.22	76.24	81.79
	71.44	72.91	72.17	90.14	76.36	82.68
Word CNN + char CNN + CRF	71.31	72.96	72.13	78.61	71.08	74.65
	72.50	71.01	71.75	88.59	66.33	75.86
Word LSTM + char CNN + CRF	72.01	72.4	72.21	85.48	78	81.57
	71.59	69.65	70.61	87.71	76.49	81.71
Word BiLSTM + char CNN + CRF	**74.14**	**76.26**	**75.18**	**84.89**	**81.9**	**83.37**
	73.67	75.16	74.41	88.2	78.85	83.26

architectures were experimented with: i) word CNN + CRF, ii) word LSTM + CRF, iii) word BiLSTM + CRF, iv) word CNN + char CNN + CRF, v) word LSTM + char CNN + CRF, and vi) word BiLSTM + char CNN + CRF. As mentioned before, each of these architectural configurations, i.e. leveraging only word representations in the first layer or the character-based CNN as the second layer are deconstructions of state-of-the-art sequence labelers for NER in the general domain [10,22,25,32,37]. Further, the word representations for the first layer were computed one of two ways: either directly from the data, or as precomputed vectorized embedding representations.[1]

For implementing the sequence labelers, we leveraged the open-source toolkit called NCRF++ [36] (https://github.com/jiesutd/NCRFpp) that is based on PyTorch. Our experimental configuration files for model hyperparameter details including learning rate, dropout rate, number of layers, hidden size etc., are on Github https://github.com/jd-coderepos/contributions-ner-cs.

3.2   Results and Analysis

Table 3 shows the results from our six neural sequence labeling architectural configurations over our two respective corpora, viz. **Titles** and **Abstracts**, respectively, for the task of *contribution-centric* CS NER. Our best performing configuration on both datasets is *word-based BiLSTM + character CNN + CRF*. From the first three columns for **Titles** results, the highest performance is 75.18%

---

[1] We used GloVe embeddings [31].

in micro F1 over its seven entities obtained with word embeddings computed directly on the data source. And from the last three columns for **Abstracts** corpus results, we see the highest performance is 83.37% in micro F1 over its two semantic types again using word embeddings computed directly on the data source. Their performances are analyzed in detail next.

CNN versus LSTM in the first layer? From the results, we observe that word-based BiLSTMs outperform word-based CNNs which in turn outperform word-based LSTMs. Thus word-based BiLSTMs are clearly the best neural model for the first layer for *contributions-centric* CS NER. This observation is aligned with the state-of-the-art NER model configuration in the general domain as well.

Is a char CNN layer preferable in the second layer of the sequence learning neural architecture? We find that it is. Comparing the results in the last three rows with the first three rows of Table 3, shows the models discriminative ability significantly increases. This is more evident for the **Titles** corpus which had seven semantic types compared to the **Abstracts** corpus with only two. In the former case, a more robust model would be needed. The added character CNN layer satisfies this need.

Is it beneficial to leverage pre-trained embeddings? We see that it is more beneficial to compute embeddings directly on the dataset rather than using the pretrained embeddings out-of-the-box. However, present advanced embedding models based on transformers such as BERT [11] and its variants [7] also allow finetuning the pretrained embeddings on respective experimental datasets. We relegate this experiment to future work. We hypothesize that such embeddings could be leveraged with effective results in a sequence labeling setting as well. However, considering the case presented in this work, i.e. leveraging word embeddings directly computed on a large enough underlying data source versus using pretrained word embeddings, we empirically verify that the former method is better suited to the task.

4   Conclusion

This work has reported a research direction on unifying prior work on scholarly domain-specific NER, specifically for CS NER. It discussed the reuse of existing resources and the complementary addition of new annotations as a contributing publicly available language resource in the community. Furthermore, drawing on observations of state-of-the-art NER systems in the general domain where the NER task itself has garnered much research interest, six neural sequence labeling architectural variants were empirically tested for CS NER. We show that the overall CS NER task of extracting *contribution-centric* entities involving seven semantic types has performances above 75% demonstrating itself as a reliable predictor of entities in practical, real-world system usage settings. The code base is publicly released https://tinyurl.com/orkg-cs-ner, as well as service calls via a REST API https://tinyurl.com/csner-rest-api and as a Python package https://tinyurl.com/cs-ner-pypi.

References

1. SciGraph. https://www.springernature.com/de/researchers/scigraph. Accessed 2 Nov 2021
2. A reintroduction to our knowledge graph and knowledge panels. https://blog.google/products/search/about-knowledge-graph-and-knoswledge-panels/. Accessed 16 July 2020
3. Auer, S., et al.: Improving access to scientific literature with knowledge graphs. Bibliothek Forsch. Prax. **44**(3), 516–529 (2020)
4. Auer, S.: Towards an open research knowledge graph (2018). https://doi.org/10.5281/zenodo.1157185
5. Augenstein, I., Das, M., Riedel, S., Vikraman, L., McCallum, A.: SemEval 2017 task 10: ScienceIE - extracting keyphrases and relations from scientific publications. In: Proceedings of the 11th International Workshop on Semantic Evaluation (SemEval-2017), pp. 546–555. Association for Computational Linguistics, Vancouver, Canada (2017). https://doi.org/10.18653/v1/S17-2091
6. Baas, J., Schotten, M., Plume, A., Côté, G., Karimi, R.: Scopus as a curated, high-quality bibliometric data source for academic research in quantitative science studies. Quant. Sci. Stud. **1**(1), 377–386 (2020)
7. Beltagy, I., Lo, K., Cohan, A.: Scibert: a pretrained language model for scientific text. In: Proceedings of the 2019 Conference on Empirical Methods in Natural Language Processing and the 9th International Joint Conference on Natural Language Processing (EMNLP-IJCNLP), pp. 3615–3620 (2019)
8. Birkle, C., Pendlebury, D.A., Schnell, J., Adams, J.: Web of science as a data source for research on scientific and scholarly activity. Quant. Sci. Stud. **1**(1), 363–376 (2020)
9. Bornmann, L., Mutz, R.: Growth rates of modern science: a bibliometric analysis based on the number of publications and cited references. J. Am. Soc. Inf. Sci. **66**(11), 2215–2222 (2015)
10. Chiu, J.P., Nichols, E.: Named entity recognition with bidirectional LSTM-CNNs. Trans. Assoc. Comput. Linguist. **4**, 357–370 (2016)
11. Devlin, J., Chang, M.W., Lee, K., Toutanova, K.: BERT: pre-training of deep bidirectional transformers for language understanding. In: Proceedings of the 2019 Conference of the North American Chapter of the Association for Computational Linguistics: Human Language Technologies, Volume 1 (Long and Short Papers), pp. 4171–4186 (2019)
12. D'Souza, J., Auer, S.: Pattern-based acquisition of scientific entities from scholarly article titles. arXiv preprint arXiv:2109.00199 (2021)
13. D'Souza, J., Auer, S., Pedersen, T.: SemEval-2021 task 11: NLPContributionGraph - structuring scholarly NLP contributions for a research knowledge graph. In: Proceedings of the 15th International Workshop on Semantic Evaluation (SemEval-2021), pp. 364–376. Association for Computational Linguistics, Online (2021). https://doi.org/10.18653/v1/2021.semeval-1.44, https://aclanthology.org/2021.semeval-1.44
14. D'Souza, J., Hoppe, A., Brack, A., Jaradeh, M.Y., Auer, S., Ewerth, R.: The STEM-ECR dataset: grounding scientific entity references in STEM scholarly content to authoritative encyclopedic and lexicographic sources. In: Proceedings of the 12th Language Resources and Evaluation Conference, pp. 2192–2203. European Language Resources Association, Marseille, France (2020). https://aclanthology.org/2020.lrec-1.268

15. Gangemi, A., Presutti, V., Recupero, D.R., Nuzzolese, A.G., Draicchio, F., Mongiovĭ, M.: Semantic web machine reading with FRED. Semant. Web **8**(6), 873–893 (2017)

16. Gupta, S., Manning, C.: Analyzing the dynamics of research by extracting key aspects of scientific papers. In: Proceedings of 5th International Joint Conference on Natural Language Processing, pp. 1–9. Asian Federation of Natural Language Processing, Chiang Mai, Thailand (2011). https://aclanthology.org/I11-1001

17. Hendricks, G., Tkaczyk, D., Lin, J., Feeney, P.: Crossref: the sustainable source of community-owned scholarly metadata. Quant. Sci. Stud. **1**(1), 414–427 (2020)

18. Hou, Y., Jochim, C., Gleize, M., Bonin, F., Ganguly, D.: Identification of tasks, datasets, evaluation metrics, and numeric scores for scientific leaderboards construction. In: Proceedings of the 57th Annual Meeting of the Association for Computational Linguistics, pp. 5203–5213. Association for Computational Linguistics, Florence, Italy (2019). https://doi.org/10.18653/v1/P19-1513, https://aclanthology.org/P19-1513

19. Ioannidis, J.P.: The mass production of redundant, misleading, and conflicted systematic reviews and meta-analyses. Milbank Q. **94**(3), 485–514 (2016)

20. Jain, S., van Zuylen, M., Hajishirzi, H., Beltagy, I.: SciREX: a challenge dataset for document-level information extraction. In: Proceedings of the 58th Annual Meeting of the Association for Computational Linguistics, pp. 7506–7516. Association for Computational Linguistics, Online (2020). https://doi.org/10.18653/v1/2020.acl-main.670, https://aclanthology.org/2020.acl-main.670

21. Kabongo, S., D'Souza, J., Auer, S.: Automated mining of leaderboards for empirical AI research. In: Ke, H.-R., Lee, C.S., Sugiyama, K. (eds.) ICADL 2021. LNCS, vol. 13133, pp. 453–470. Springer, Cham (2021). https://doi.org/10.1007/978-3-030-91669-5_35

22. Lample, G., Ballesteros, M., Subramanian, S., Kawakami, K., Dyer, C.: Neural architectures for named entity recognition. In: Proceedings of the 2016 Conference of the North American Chapter of the Association for Computational Linguistics: Human Language Technologies, pp. 260–270 (2016)

23. Lewis, N., Wang, J., Poblet, M., Aryani, A.: Research graph: connecting researchers, research data, publications and grants using the graph technology. In: eResearch Australasia Conference (2016). https://eresearchau.files.wordpress.com/2016/03/eresau2016_paper_95.pdf

24. Luan, Y., He, L., Ostendorf, M., Hajishirzi, H.: Multi-task identification of entities, relations, and coreferencefor scientific knowledge graph construction. In: Proceedings Conference Empirical Methods Natural Language Process (EMNLP) (2018)

25. Ma, X., Hovy, E.: End-to-end sequence labeling via bi-directional LSTM-CNNs-CRF. In: Proceedings of the 54th Annual Meeting of the Association for Computational Linguistics (Volume 1: Long Papers), pp. 1064–1074 (2016)

26. Manghi, P., Manola, N., Horstmann, W., Peters, D.: An infrastructure for managing EC funded research output: the openaire project. Grey J. (TGJ) **6**(1) (2010)

27. Mendes, P.N., Jakob, M., García-Silva, A., Bizer, C.: DBpedia spotlight: shedding light on the web of documents. In: Proceedings of the 7th International Conference on Semantic Systems, pp. 1–8. ACM (2011)

28. Mitchell, T., et al.: Never-ending learning. Commun. ACM **61**(5), 103–115 (2018)

29. Moro, A., Cecconi, F., Navigli, R.: Multilingual Word Sense Disambiguation and Entity Linking for Everybody. In: ISWC, pp. 25–28. Riva del Garda, Italy (2014)

30. Noy, N., Gao, Y., Jain, A., Narayanan, A., Patterson, A., Taylor, J.: Industry-scale knowledge graphs: lessons and challenges. Queue **17**(2), 48–75 (2019)

31. Pennington, J., Socher, R., Manning, C.: GloVe: global vectors for word representation. In: Proceedings of the 2014 Conference on Empirical Methods in Natural Language Processing (EMNLP), pp. 1532–1543. Association for Computational Linguistics, Doha, Qatar (2014). https://doi.org/10.3115/v1/D14-1162, https://aclanthology.org/D14-1162

32. Peters, M., Ammar, W., Bhagavatula, C., Power, R.: Semi-supervised sequence tagging with bidirectional language models. In: Proceedings of the 55th Annual Meeting of the Association for Computational Linguistics (Volume 1: Long Papers), pp. 1756–1765 (2017)

33. QasemiZadeh, B., Schumann, A.K.: The ACL RD-TEC 2.0: a language resource for evaluating term extraction and entity recognition methods. In: Proceedings of the Tenth International Conference on Language Resources and Evaluation (LREC'16), pp. 1862–1868. European Language Resources Association (ELRA), Portorož, Slovenia (2016). https://aclanthology.org/L16-1294

34. Vrandečić, D., Krötzsch, M.: Wikidata: a free collaborative knowledgebase. Commun. ACM **57**(10), 78–85 (2014)

35. Wang, K., Shen, Z., Huang, C., Wu, C.H., Dong, Y., Kanakia, A.: Microsoft academic graph: when experts are not enough. Quant. Sci. Stud. **1**(1), 396–413 (2020)

36. Yang, J., Zhang, Y.: Ncrf++: An open-source neural sequence labeling toolkit. In: Proceedings of ACL 2018, System Demonstrations, pp. 74–79 (2018)

37. Yang, Z., Salakhutdinov, R., Cohen, W.W.: Transfer learning for sequence tagging with hierarchical recurrent networks. arXiv preprint arXiv:1703.06345 (2017)

Distantly Supervised Named Entity Recognition with Category-Oriented Confidence Calibration

Liangping Ding[1,2], Tian-Yuan Huang[1], Huan Liu[1,2], Yufei Wang[1,2], and Zhixiong Zhang[1,2(✉)]

[1] National Science Library, Chinese Academy of Sciences, Beijing 100190, China
{dingliangping,huangtianyuan,liuhuan,wangyufei,zhangzhx}@mail.las.ac.cn
[2] Department of Library Information and Archives Management, University of Chinese Academy of Sciences, Beijing 100049, China

Abstract. Named entity recognition plays an important role in extracting valuable information from digital libraries, which can help stakeholders to take full advantage of large quantities of documents to boost the development of scholarly knowledge discovery. Nevertheless, there aren't many annotated NER datasets aiming at scientific literature except medical domain, restricting to utilize abundant of advanced deep learning models. As an alternative solution, distant supervision provides a feasible way to eliminate the need of human annotations by automatically generating annotated datasets based on external resources such as knowledge base, while introducing noise inevitably. In this work, we study the noisy-labeled named entity recognition under distant supervision setting. Considering that most NER systems based on confidence estimation deal with noisy labels ignoring the fact that model has different levels of confidence towards different categories, we propose a **C**ategory-**o**riented **c**onfidence **c**alibration (**Coca**) strategy with an automatically confidence threshold calculation module. We integrate our method into a teacher-student self-training framework to improve the model performance. Our proposed approach achieves promising performance among advanced baseline models and can be easily integrated into other confidence based model frameworks (Our code is publicly available at: https://github.com/possible1402/BOND_Coca).

Keywords: Named entity recognition · Digital library · Distant supervision · Self-training · Pretrained language model

1 Introduction

There are enormous amount of scientific documents in digital libraries with large amount of unstructured information contained in nature language text, setting

The work is supported by the Project 'Research on The Semantic Evaluation System of Scientific and Technological Literature Driven by Big Data' (Grant No.21&ZD329).

Y.-H. Tseng et al. (Eds.): ICADL 2022, LNCS 13636, pp. 46–55, 2022.
https://doi.org/10.1007/978-3-031-21756-2_4

up obstacles for scholarly knowledge discovery. To facilitate the semantic enrichment, named entity recognition can be utilized to process the metadata in digital libraries, representing information in fine-grained semantics.

Named entity recognition(NER) refers to identify the real-word entity mentions and their semantic categories from text, which is a fundamental task in natural language processing and plays a vital role in a wide range of applications including information retrieval [5], knowledge base construction [2], text summarization [3] and question answering [10].

In many cases, annotated datasets for training supervised NER models are not available and it's labor-expensive and time-consuming to manually label the datasets. Distant supervision is an alternative approach which uses knowledge bases, domain ontologies and gazetteers to automatically generate annotated datasets, alleviating the need for hand-crafted datasets.

Although distant supervision [16] provides an efficient way to annotate training data, entity type labels induced by distant supervision ignore entities' local context and may have limited usage in context-sensitive applications. In addition, since knowledge bases are inherently incomplete [15], existing knowledge bases only include limited entity mentions. Thus models trained on distantly supervised datasets fail to generalize to unseen entities.

To address these challenges, it's essential to denoise the distant labels for training the robust NER system. Many existing works propose various methods such as partial annotation learning [14], self-training [9], reinforcement learning [22], positive-unlabeled learning [17], causal intervention [23] to tackle this problem.

In this work, we introduce a category-oriented confidence calibration approach accompanying with an automatically confidence threshold calculation module and apply our method to a self-training teacher-student framework to process the unreliable labels in distantly supervised NER. The inspiration of our method is that traditional NER systems usually deal with noise by setting a confidence threshold to filter out uncertain labels. While we assume that it's inconsistent of the model's certainty for distinct label types, particularly under the label imbalance scenario. It could be detrimental to the model performance if there is only one confidence threshold for all the label types, especially for highly-skewed sequence labeling tasks.

To summarize, our major contribution is two-fold:

1. We integrate category-oriented confidence calibration with teacher-student framework to tackle the problem of noisy labels in distantly supervised NER, which allows the model to adjust labels during self-training according to the confidence threshold of each label type.
2. Our proposed approach can automatically calculate the threshold of confidence estimation score for each label type instead of treating it as a hyperparameter, which can be easily adapted to different NER tasks.

2   Related Work

Distant supervision is a particular instance of weak supervision, which relies on external resources such as knowledge bases to automatically label documents with entities that are known to belong to a particular category [19,21]. NER systems achieve high performance on clean text, while their performance dramatically degrades when moved to noisy scenarios such as distant supervision [1].

Denoising is an essential step in many distantly supervised NER systems. Peng et al. formulated the task as a positive-unlabeled (PU) learning problem to adopt a weighted training loss, assigning low weights to false negative samples [17]. Shang et al. employed fuzzy CRF layer which assigned ambiguous tokens with all possible labels and maximized the overall likelihood [21]. Yang et al. designed an instance selector based on reinforcement learning to distinguish positive sentences [22].

Self-training is an effective denoising approach, which can improve model fitting and reduce the noise of pseudo labels. Our proposed method is most closely aligned with the BOND framework [12], in which a self-training algorithm is applied to guide the training of the teacher-student network. They cast confidence threshold as a hyper-parameter to tune and prevented the low-confidence labels to be involved into loss calculation. Zhang et al. integrated backdoor adjustment and causal invariance regularizer into BOND to conduct debiased method via causal interventions [23]. Liu et al. proposed a strategy to estimate confidence scores by taking advantage of the structure of entity labels [13].

3   Methodology

In this section, we introduce our teacher-student framework with category-oriented confidence calibration. Figure 1 provides a graphical overview of our model.

3.1   Task Formulation

We formally formulate the named entity recognition task as a sequence labeling task. Given a sequence of tokens $X = [x_1, ... x_i, ..., x_n]$, the aim is to predict a sequence of labels $Y = [y_1, ... y_i, ..., y_n]$ that encodes the named entities, where n is the length of sequence and y_i is the corresponding label for token x_i. Let $L_E = [1, 2, ..., C]$ represent the label set and C is the number of classes.

3.2   Model Architecture

Our model consists of four modules, termed confidence threshold calculation, category-oriented confidence calibration, teacher network, and student network, where the student network and teacher network are structurally identical.

We use pretrained language model RoBERTa to implement the teacher-student framework, which acts as the encoder and a linear classification layer is

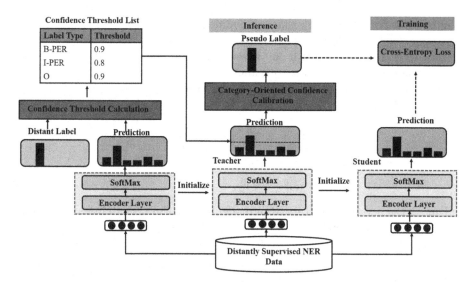

Fig. 1. The Framework of Our Model

atop it to compute the probability distribution of labels among L_E for each corresponding token x_i. Specifically, the RoBERTa layer f_θ maps the input sequence $\boldsymbol{x}$ into a sequence of hidden vectors $\boldsymbol{h} = \{h_1, ...h_i, ..., h_n\}$. After that, the classifier takes in token-wise hidden vector from the RoBERTa layer and gives the probabilities on all label types for each token x_i through $SoftMax$ function.

$$h_i = f_\theta(x_i) \tag{1}$$

$$p(x_i, \Theta) = SoftMax(Wh_i + b) \tag{2}$$

where $f_\theta(\cdot)$ produces context-sensitive representations for the input token sequence, h_i is the hidden vector of the final hidden layer corresponding to the i-th token x_i, $p(x_i, \Theta) \in \mathbb{R}^{|C|}$, and $\Theta = \{\theta, W, b\}$ denotes all the model parameters to be learned.

3.3 Self-training with Category-Oriented Confidence Calibration

Under the teacher-student framework, our model modulates the parameter update to the student network according to the posterior confidence in its label-quality estimated by a teacher network based on category-oriented confidence calibration. The whole self-training process can be mainly split into three phases.

Step 1: Confidence Threshold Calculation.

Given the distant labeled NER training set $D = \{(\boldsymbol{X}^{(m)}, \tilde{\boldsymbol{Y}}^{(m)})\}_{m=1}^M$, where $\tilde{\boldsymbol{Y}}^{(m)} = [\tilde{y}_1^{(m)}, ..., \tilde{y}_i^{(m)}, ..., \tilde{y}_n^{(m)}]$ represents a sequence of distant labels for sample

m and $\tilde{y}_i^{(m)} \in L_E$. We remark that self-training behaves poorly when encountering unreliable predicted labels namely pseudo labels, which will cause the student network to be updated towards the wrong direction. To alleviate this issue, we firstly initialize the student network and teacher network using the parameters of RoBERTa and then adapt them to acquire task dependent representation on the minibatch T_K from D whose size is K:

$$\Theta^{init} = \arg\min_{\Theta} \frac{1}{K} \sum_{m=1}^{K} l(\tilde{\boldsymbol{Y}}^{(m)}, f(\boldsymbol{X}^{(m)}; \Theta)) \tag{3}$$

$$\Theta_{tea}^0 = \Theta_{stu}^0 = \Theta^{init} \tag{4}$$

During the adaptation, RoBERTa model assigns the probabilities to all label types for the i-th token in the m-th sample, and the output probability simplex over C classes is denotes as: $\boldsymbol{P}_{\boldsymbol{x}_i}^{(m)} = [p(x_i^{(m)}, \Theta)_1, ..., p(x_i^{(m)}, \Theta)_C]$. Here $p(x_i^{(m)}, \Theta)_c$ denotes the predicted probability corresponding to the label type c. The formulas to get the pseudo label and the predicted confidence score for token x_i in m are as follows:

$$\hat{y}_i^{(m)} = \arg\max_{c} \boldsymbol{P}_{\boldsymbol{x}_i}^{(m)} \tag{5}$$

$$\hat{s}_i^{(m)} = \max \boldsymbol{P}_{\boldsymbol{x}_i}^{(m)} \tag{6}$$

To calculate confidence thresholds, we average over all confidence scores where the pseudo labels are same as the distant labels for the corresponding label type. Specifically, we firstly create an empty number sequence $\{S_j^{c,m}\}_{j=1}^{n_{c,m}}$ to gather all the predicted confidence scores corresponding to label type c for the m-th sample, in which $n_{c,m}$ represents the length of number sequence. And then for sample m in minibatch T_K, if the distant label is same as the pseudo label in the corresponding position i and the entity type is c, we add the predicted confidence score in position i to the number sequence. Finally, the confidence threshold for label type c, denoted as $\boldsymbol{V}_c$, is calculated as follows:

$$\boldsymbol{V}_c = \frac{\sum_{m=1}^{K} \sum_{j=1}^{n_{c,m}} \boldsymbol{S}_j^{c,m}}{\sum_{m=1}^{K} n_{c,m}} \tag{7}$$

Step 2: Category-Oriented Confidence Calibration.

Instead of discarding all distant labels [12], we only replace the distant labels over the confidence threshold with pseudo labels, while other distant labels remain constant. Intuitively, we consider that most distant labels are correct, and it's reasonable to do the replacement only if the model has strong confidence to believe the predicted pseudo labels.

To be precise, $p(x_i^{(m)}, \Theta)_{\tilde{y}_i^{(m)}}$ denotes the predicted probability corresponding to the distant label $\tilde{y}_i^{(m)}$ for the i-th token in the m-th sample. If the label type of the pseudo label $\hat{y}_i^{(m)}$ is c and the confidence score $\hat{s}_i^{(m)}$ is greater than or equal to $\boldsymbol{V}_c$, we assign $p(x_i^{(m)}, \Theta)_{\tilde{y}_i^{(m)}}$ to 1, and other elements in $\boldsymbol{P}_{x_i}^{(m)}$ are set to 0. After that, we update $\hat{y}_i^{(m)}$ and $\hat{s}_i^{(m)}$ according to the calibrated confidence simplex by Eq. (5) and (6). The final pseudo label for token $x_i^{(m)}$ after calibration is calculated as follows:

$$\hat{y}_i^{(m)} = \begin{cases} c & if\ \hat{s}_i^{(m)} \geq V_c \\ \hat{y}_i^{(m)} & if\ \hat{s}_i^{(m)} < V_c \\ w \end{cases} \tag{8}$$

Table 1. Experiment results (F1%) on fully supervised datasets and distantly supervised datasets

Method	Datasets				
	conll2003	twitter	webpage	wikigold	BC5CDR
Roberta-base(Fully Supervised)	90.1	52.2	72.4	86.4	–
AutoNER [21]	67.0	26.1	51.4	47.5	**84.8**
LRNT [6]	69.7	23.8	47.4	46.2	–
Noisy NER [13]	78.9	47.3	61.9	57.7	–
BOND [12]	81.5	48.0	65.7	60.1	78.7
BOND+BA+CIR [23]	81.5	**49.0**	64.7	61.5	–
BOND+Coca(Ours)	**82.7**	48.7	**68.2**	**63.0**	79.6

Step 3: Self-Training.

We integrate our approach into a teacher-student self-training framework BOND [12]. The teacher network is used to generate pseudo labels in the named entity recognition system. The student network is solving a surrogate task of approximating the output probability distribution of the entity types by the teacher network, transferring the knowledge from teacher network to student network.

The teacher network generates pseudo labels by Eq.(8) based on category-oriented confidence calibration. And then the student network is trained to fit these pseudo labels. Specifically, at the t-th iteration round, we learn the student network $\hat{\Theta}_{stu}^t$ by minimizing Eq.(3) with $\tilde{\boldsymbol{Y}}^{(m)}$ replaced by the pseudo labels counterparts $\hat{\boldsymbol{Y}}^{(m)}$, in which $\hat{\boldsymbol{Y}}^{(m)} = [\hat{y}_1^{(m)}, ..., \hat{y}_i^{(m)}, ..., \hat{y}_n^{(m)}]$. The final student model after self-training iteration is treated as the final model.

The student network is updated using stochastic gradient descent(SGD). Note that back-propagation is only through student network and the parameters of the teacher network are kept frozen during each self-training iteration. At the end of t-th iteration, we update the teacher model and student model as follows:

$$\Theta_{tea}^{t+1} = \Theta_{stu}^{t+1} = \hat{\Theta}_{stu}^t \tag{9}$$

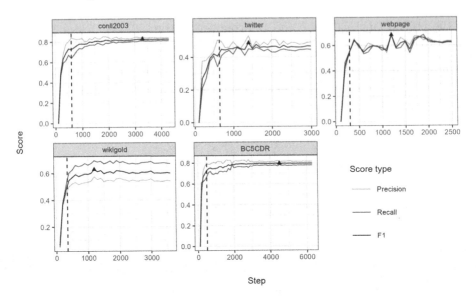

Fig. 2. Learning curves of BOND+Coca model

4   Experiments

4.1   Experimental Setup

We consider five benchmark datasets including CoNLL03 [20], Tweet [8], Wikigold [4], Webpage [18] and BC5CDR [11]. The first four datasets are processed in KB-Matching annotation setting, where the distantly supervised labels are generated following BOND [12]. And the BC5CDR dataset is processed following AutoNER [21]. We compare our model with a wide range of state-of-the-art distantly-labeled NER models including AutoNER [21], LRNT [7], BOND [12], Noisy NER [13], BOND+BA+CIR [23].

4.2   Experimental Results

Table 1 shows our primary results on fully supervised datasets and distantly supervised datasets. Experimental results demonstrate that our model is effective under distant supervision setting; it achieves promising performance on five existing named entity recognition benchmarks.

Our proposed method is mostly closely aligned with the BOND framework. We observe that integrating our category-oriented confidence calibration strategy into BOND exceeds the performance without calibration on all of the five datasets by {1.3, 0.7, 2.5, 3.0, 0.9} in terms of F1-score. The learning curves on the five datasets are summarized in Fig. 2. The position of the best F1-score is highlighted by triangle for each dataset and the starting step of self-training is labeled by dotted line. As we can see, the models achieved the best F1-scores after self-training for all datasets, which indicates that the pseudo labels used in self-training are credible.

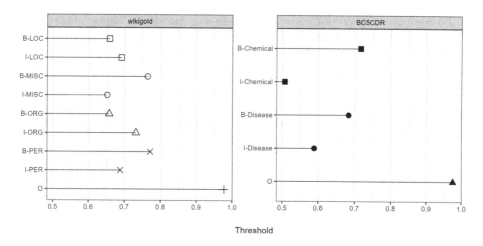

Fig. 3. Confidence thresholds on Wikigold and BC5CDR datasets

To show the effectiveness of our Coca strategy, we take wikigold and BC5CDR datasets as examples and plot the category threshold correspondingly, as shown in Fig. 3. As we can see, the thresholds varies widely across categories. The model is more confidential for category 'O' with confidence threshold almost equal to 1. While for other categories, the confidences are usually below 0.8.

In addition, We demonstrate that our proposed category-oriented confidence estimation method is beneficial not only to open-domain NER tasks, but also to specific domain such as medical domain, which can be seen from the result on BC5CDR dataset. We note that one of the reasons why our method is worse than AutoNER on BC5CDR dataset is that they use additional lexicons to boost the model performance.

5   Conclusions

In this work, we propose a category-oriented confidence calibration approach accompanying with an automatically confidence threshold calculation module to tackle the problem of noisy supervision in distantly supervised NER. We integrate our method into Roberta under a teacher-student self-training framework. Extensive experiments demonstrate the effectiveness of our method. We evaluate our model on five datasets where our method shows promising results on these datasets. We assume that our NER research can be applied to extract valuable information in the metadata, which can improve the quality of digital libraries and boost knowledge discovery.

References

1. Aguilar, G., López-Monroy, A.P., González, F.A., Solorio, T.: Modeling noisiness to recognize named entities using multitask neural networks on social media. In: Proceedings of the 2018 Conference of the North American Chapter of the Association for Computational Linguistics: Human Language Technologies, Volume 1 (Long Papers), pp. 1401–1412 (2018)
2. Al-Moslmi, T., Ocaña, M.G., Opdahl, A.L., Veres, C.: Named entity extraction for knowledge graphs: a literature overview. IEEE Access **8**, 32862–32881 (2020)
3. Aramaki, E., Miura, Y., Tonoike, M., Ohkuma, T., Mashuichi, H., Ohe, K.: TEXT2TABLE: medical text summarization system based on named entity recognition and modality identification. In: Proceedings of the BioNLP 2009 Workshop, pp. 185–192. Association for Computational Linguistics, Boulder, Colorado (2009). https://aclanthology.org/W09-1324
4. Balasuriya, D., Ringland, N., Nothman, J., Murphy, T., Curran, J.R.: Named entity recognition in wikipedia. In: Proceedings of the 2009 Workshop on The People's Web Meets NLP: Collaboratively Constructed Semantic Resources (People's Web), pp. 10–18 (2009)
5. Brandsen, A., Verberne, S., Lambers, K., Wansleeben, M.: Can bert dig it?-named entity recognition for information retrieval in the archaeology domain. J. Comput. Cult. Heritage (JOCCH) **15** (2022)
6. Cao, Y., Hu, Z., Chua, T.S., Liu, Z., Ji, H.: Low-resource name tagging learned with weakly labeled data. arXiv preprint arXiv:1908.09659 (2019)
7. Cao, Y., Hu, Z., Chua, T.s., Liu, Z., Ji, H.: Low-resource name tagging learned with weakly labeled data. In: Proceedings of the 2019 Conference on Empirical Methods in Natural Language Processing and the 9th International Joint Conference on Natural Language Processing (EMNLP-IJCNLP), pp. 261–270. Association for Computational Linguistics, Hong Kong, China (2019). https://doi.org/10.18653/v1/D19-1025, https://aclanthology.org/D19-1025
8. Godin, F., Vandersmissen, B., De Neve, W., Van de Walle, R.: Multimedia Lab@ ACL WNUT NER shared task: named entity recognition for twitter microposts using distributed word representations. In: Proceedings of the workshop on noisy user-generated text, pp. 146–153 (2015)
9. Jie, Z., Xie, P., Lu, W., Ding, R., Li, L.: Better modeling of incomplete annotations for named entity recognition. In: Proceedings of the 2019 Conference of the North American Chapter of the Association for Computational Linguistics: Human Language Technologies, Volume 1 (Long and Short Papers), pp. 729–734. Association for Computational Linguistics, Minneapolis, Minnesota (2019). https://doi.org/10.18653/v1/N19-1079, https://aclanthology.org/N19-1079
10. Lamurias, A., Couto, F.M.: Lasigebiotm at mediqa 2019: biomedical question answering using bidirectional transformers and named entity recognition. In: Proceedings of the 18th BioNLP Workshop and Shared Task, pp. 523–527 (2019)
11. Li, J., et al.: Biocreative V CDR task corpus: a resource for chemical disease relation extraction. Database **2016**, baw068 (2016)
12. Liang, C., Yu, Y., Jiang, H., Er, S., Wang, R., Zhao, T., Zhang, C.: BOND: BERT-assisted open-domain named entity recognition with distant supervision. In: Proceedings of the 26th ACM SIGKDD International Conference on Knowledge Discovery & Data Mining, pp. 1054–1064 (2020)

13. Liu, K., Fu, Y., Tan, C., Chen, M., Zhang, N., Huang, S., Gao, S.: Noisy-labeled NER with confidence estimation. In: Proceedings of the 2021 Conference of the North American Chapter of the Association for Computational Linguistics: Human Language Technologies, pp. 3437–3445. Association for Computational Linguistics, Online (2021). https://aclanthology.org/2021.naacl-main.269

14. Mayhew, S., Chaturvedi, S., Tsai, C.T., Roth, D.: Named entity recognition with partially annotated training data. In: Proceedings of the 23rd Conference on Computational Natural Language Learning (CoNLL), pp. 645–655. Association for Computational Linguistics, Hong Kong, China (2019). https://doi.org/10.18653/v1/K19-1060, https://aclanthology.org/K19-1060

15. Min, B., Grishman, R., Wan, L., Wang, C., Gondek, D.: Distant supervision for relation extraction with an incomplete knowledge base. In: Proceedings of the 2013 Conference of the North American Chapter of the Association for Computational Linguistics: Human Language Technologies, pp. 777–782 (2013)

16. Mintz, M., Bills, S., Snow, R., Jurafsky, D.: Distant supervision for relation extraction without labeled data. In: Proceedings of the Joint Conference of the 47th Annual Meeting of the ACL and the 4th International Joint Conference on Natural Language Processing of the AFNLP, pp. 1003–1011 (2009)

17. Peng, M., Xing, X., Zhang, Q., Fu, J., Huang, X.: Distantly supervised named entity recognition using positive-unlabeled learning. In: Proceedings of the 57th Annual Meeting of the Association for Computational Linguistics, pp. 2409–2419. Association for Computational Linguistics, Florence, Italy (2019). https://doi.org/10.18653/v1/P19-1231, https://aclanthology.org/P19-1231

18. Ratinov, L., Roth, D.: Design challenges and misconceptions in named entity recognition. In: Proceedings of the Thirteenth Conference on Computational Natural Language Learning (CoNLL-2009), pp. 147–155 (2009)

19. Ritter, A., Zettlemoyer, L., Mausam, M., Etzioni, O.: Modeling missing data in distant supervision for information extraction. Trans. Assoc. Comput. Linguist. 1, 367–378 (2013)

20. Sang, E.F., De Meulder, F.: Introduction to the conll-2003 shared task: language-independent named entity recognition. arXiv preprint cs/0306050 (2003)

21. Shang, J., Liu, L., Gu, X., Ren, X., Ren, T., Han, J.: Learning named entity tagger using domain-specific dictionary. In: Proceedings of the 2018 Conference on Empirical Methods in Natural Language Processing, pp. 2054–2064. Association for Computational Linguistics, Brussels, Belgium (2018). https://doi.org/10.18653/v1/D18-1230, https://aclanthology.org/D18-1230

22. Yang, Y., Chen, W., Li, Z., He, Z., Zhang, M.: Distantly supervised NER with partial annotation learning and reinforcement learning. In: Proceedings of the 27th International Conference on Computational Linguistics, pp. 2159–2169. Association for Computational Linguistics, Santa Fe, New Mexico, USA (2018), https://aclanthology.org/C18-1183

23. Zhang, W., Lin, H., Han, X., Sun, L.: De-biasing distantly supervised named entity recognition via causal intervention. In: Proceedings of the 59th Annual Meeting of the Association for Computational Linguistics and the 11th International Joint Conference on Natural Language Processing (Volume 1: Long Papers), pp. 4803–4813. Association for Computational Linguistics, Online (2021). https://doi.org/10.18653/v1/2021.acl-long.371, https://aclanthology.org/2021.acl-long.371

Neural-based Knowledge Extraction

Extractive Summarization Utilizing Keyphrases by Finetuning BERT-Based Model

Wang Xiaoye⬥ and Iwaihara Mizuho⁽⠗⁾⬥

Graduate School of InformationProduction and Systems, Waseda University,
Kitakyushu 808-0135, Japan
wangxiaoye@fuji.waseda.jp, iwaihara@waseda.jp

Abstract. Summarization is a natural language processing (NLP) task of producing a brief text, which provide a compressed text that contains the main content and key information of the source document. Both extractive summarization and keyphrase extraction are the tasks that extract shorter texts keeping salient information and main points from the source document. Compared with keyphrases, summaries composed of sentences are larger granular texts that have high probability of being related to the keyphrases of the document. On one hand, previous work lacks research on whether keyphrases are beneficial for extracting important sentences. On the other hand, with the development of deep neural network, pretrained language models, especially BERT-based models which can adapt to various natural language processing (NLP) tasks by finetuning, have attracted extensive attention. For these reasons, we propose KeyBERTSUM, in which we try to leverage keyphrases in the extractive summarization task based on a BERT encoder, guiding the model focusing on the important contents instead of the entire document. In addition, we also introduce the confidence of guiding phrases in sentence updating. Experimental evaluations of our methods on CNN/Daily Mail New York Times 50 and DUC2001 datasets have shown improvement on ROUGE scores over baselines.

Keywords: Extractive summarization · Keyphrase extraction · Pretrained language model · Attention mechanism

1 Introduction

With the explosion of information on the web, using short summaries to quickly understand the main points of an article becomes a task with enormous value. Summarization is a natural language processing (NLP) task of producing a brief text, which provides a compressed text that covers the main content and key information of the source document. According to the strategy, summarization can be divided into extractive summarization [1 –3, 9, 14, 16, 17, 23–25] and abstractive summarization [6, 7, 10]. The former extracts a short summary by extracting and combining the most representative parts of the original document, while the latter generates summaries which may contain absent words from the original document after capturing the information of the original document.

© The Author(s), under exclusive license to Springer Nature Switzerland AG 2022
Y.-H. Tseng et al. (Eds.): ICADL 2022, LNCS 13636, pp. 59–72, 2022.
https://doi.org/10.1007/978-3-031-21756-2_5

In this paper, we focus on extractive summarization, since it ensures the correctness of sentence grammar and the factuality.

A keyphrase is a noun phrase, sometimes described by one or more adjectives, which can best summarize the key topics of the original long document. Keyphrase extraction is an NLP task of automatically selecting a set of keyphrases from all candidate phrases from the document.

Both summaries and keyphrases focus on the overview contents and core ideas of the original documents, helping people to briefly understand the main idea of a long document, or capture useful information in short time. We expect that keyphrases can guide the direction of extractive summarization, highlighting the salient information. Previous work on keyphrase extraction has proven that prior summarization has ability to help extracting more accurate keyphrases [15]. On the contrary, it is possible that keyphrases is beneficial to the summarization task.

Finetuning BERT-based models for down-stream tasks have achieved state-of-the-art performance in a range of NLP tasks, due to the rich contextual knowledge derived from large-scale pre-training [5]. Therefore, we try to fine-tune the pre-trained BERT model and find reliable guiding phrases can enhance the key information in candidate sentences, so as to select sentences that can better summarize the original document.

We propose a hybrid two-step method. We select keyphrases by using a prior selector, and then use keyphrases and confidence to update sentence representations through an attention mechanism.

In summary, the approaches tried in this paper are as follows:

1. We introduce a keyphrase-guided extractive summarization model for utilizing keyphrases in selecting important sentences.
2. We apply graph attention mechanism to update sentence representations with keyphrases, and combine attentions from sentence to guiding phrases with confidence, which reflect semantic relevance between phrases and the whole document.
3. We evaluate our approach and conduct experiments on public summarization datasets, such as CNN/Daily Mail, New York Times 50 and DUC2001.

2   Related Work

2.1   Extractive Summarization

Extractive summarization retains the most important information by extracting important spans of the original text and combining them in an orderly manner. Extractive summarization is often regarded·as a span scoring and ranking task, choosing the top-ranked spans (sentences in most cases), a considering diversity to avoid redundancy.

There are a number of existing extractive summarization methods. Previous work before deep learning is mostly by unsupervised learning based on graph structures and statistical relationship. For example, TextRank [16] regards sentences as nodes and the similarity between sentences as edges to construct a graph structure, and calculates the score of each sentence through iterative convergence.

With the development of deep learning and neural network, the method of supervised learning has attracted extensive attention. Deep neural network can obtain sentence representations containing contextual semantic information, and a classification network is added to classify the sequence of sentences. RNN-based summarization models [3] played an important role in both extractive and abstractive summarization. Nallapati et al. [17] used bidirectional Gate Recurrent Unit (bi-GRU) [3] model as the encoder to capture context information from sentence-level to document-level. Cheng and Lapata [4] proposed to utilize Convolutional Neural Network (CNN) as a sentence encoder and document encoder, which allows to consider the embedding of the previous sentence encoded by the encoder to judge whether the present sentence should be selected or not. Zhou, Q., Yang, N. et al. [25] proposed an end-to-end model that jointly learns selecting and scoring based on bi-GRU model. Wang D. et al. [22] proposed a heterogeneous model for updating sentences through jointly owned words. More recently, pre-trained language models (PLMs) proved their superiority in the summarization task. By virtue of a large amount of pre-trained knowledge, PLMs obtain general features of text data, so as to produce more reliable representations. Liu Y. et al. [14] proposed a variant of BERT for extractive summarization, making full use of knowledge of BERT. Zhang X. et al. [23] proposed to pre-train a hierarchical transformer structure for summarization task.

The diversity of salient sentences in summaries also strongly influences the quality of extractive summaries. Regarding this problem, Kryściński W. et al. [9] tried to abandon the present sentence if it has n-gram overlapping with former selected sentences. Bi K. et al. [1] did researches on the difference of jointly learning saliency and redundancy in two-step learning.

Zhong M. et al. [23] created a novel paradigm shift that adopts document- level semantic similarities between the document and candidate summaries for extractive summarization task, based on a sentence transformer and contrastive learning. Their model is the first that implements extractive summarization task through document-level pretraining.

2.2 Keyphrase Extraction

Similar to extractive summarization, keyphrase extraction aims at selecting candidate phrases from the original text and selects top-ranked phrases according to their criticality. Supervised learning can define the keyphrase extraction task as a sequence labeling task, and judge whether a candidate phrase is a keyphrase through binary classification [12], but this requires sufficient labeled data to train the model. Both supervised and unsupervised learning can be viewed as candidate phrase scoring and ranking tasks. The score of a candidate phrase can be determined according to statistical, semantic or positional features.

TextRank [16] can also be used for keyword scoring, constructing graphs with key-words as nodes and co-occurrence relationships and order as edges. Wang, R. et al. [21] added pre-trained embeddings of keyphrases based on co-occurrence and considered semantic similarity.

Pre-trained language models are also widely used for keyphrase extraction. Lim Y. et al. [12] used BERT and downstream CRF to fine-tune toward keyphrase sequence labeling. Liu T. et al. [15] treated the task as a scoring and ranking task and took advantage of BERT's self-attention mechanism to calculate the importance of candidate phrases. Sharma P. et al. [18] utilized the pretrained Sentence-BERT structure to calculate the semantic similarity between candidate phrases and articles. In addition, pre-trained language models can also be used to encode contextual semantics in unsupervised learning. Liang X. et al. [11] proposed an unsupervised keyphrase scoring approach based on BERT encoding, which not only acquires keyphrase representations with rich contextual semantics, but also realizes a positional encoding.

2.3 Guided Summarization

In order to guide the model to find the salient information from long documents, summarization systems leveraging guidance information containing important contents have been proposed. C. Li et al. [10] proposed a guiding generation model for abstractive summarization, adding keyword representations into attention mechanism. Cui P. et al. [4] applied topical information to a BERT-based model by jointly integrating a topic model. Dou Z. et al. [6] applied different types of guidance signals to encoder-decoder pre-trained models, teaching the sequence-to-sequence models to pay more attentions to salient parts while generating summaries.

To the best of our knowledge, there is lack of research on how keyphrases can influence extractive summarization with deep learning, but only abstractive summarization method exists, while in our opinion, brief information carried by keyphrases can guide sentence scoring.

3   Methodology

In this section, we introduce the overall frameworks of Keyphrase Guided Summarization Model with Bidirectional Encoder Representation from Trans- formers (KeyBERT-SUM), and the specific details of KeyBERTSUM with fine- tuning methods are presented in Sects. 3.2 and 3.3, respectively.

3.1   Overall Workflow

We propose a two-stage approach. Figure 1 shows the overall structure of our model. Firstly, we apply part-of-speech tagger of each token to extract noun phrases from the source document as candidate phrases, then a keyphrase selector is used to select keyphrases which are highly relevant to important points of the document. Here we utilize pre-trained model "all-MiniLM-L6-v2" [18], applied sentence-BERT structure to score semantic similarity between candidate phrases and the document, choosing ranked top-K as guiding phrases. Then we feed the source document and keyphrase list into the encoder based on BERT, and obtain sentence embeddings that are produced with self-attention stretching over the document and the keyphrase listing. After that, the output sentence embeddings are supplied to the summarizer, from which we can continue updating sentence embeddings or directly obtain the scores of each sentence.

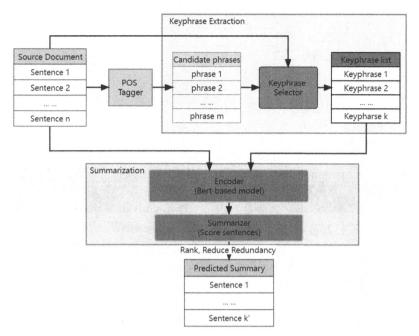

Fig. 1. Overall framework of two-step method.

Finally, the sentences are ranked according to their scores and important sentences are chosen by considering ranking and redundancy.

3.2 Keyphrase-Guided Extractive Summarization

The overall structure of the Keyphrase-guided Extractive Summarization model based on BERT (KeyBERTSUM) is shown in Fig. 2. [CLS] and [SEP] tokens, respectively, are inserted at the head and tail of each sentence, respectively, and binary interval segment embeddings are used to distinguish different sentences and phrases. The major difference is that [SEP] tokens are added between two keyphrases. Since our guiding keyphrases are extracted from the source documents, for the input sequence of guiding keyphrases to the keyphrase encoder, we retain their relative positions of the phrases in the source document, put them in the same order as their positions in the document before entering them into the encoder. In this way, we expect to identify the relative position relationships between phrases and take advantage of the positional embeddings of the BERT model. (Here only the first occurrence is considered if the phrase appears more than once).

Then, the keyphrase sequence and sentence sequence are entered separately into the two shared-weights BERT encoders, producing the phrase representations and sentence representations, respectively, and perform graph attention network in the summarizer computing inter-attentions between these representations, in which we consider the confidence of each guiding phrase produced by similarity calculation or prior keyphrase extractor is used. After encoding by the 12-layer BERT models sharing weights, the representations of *j-th* keyphrase h_k^j and documents h_d, are computed as

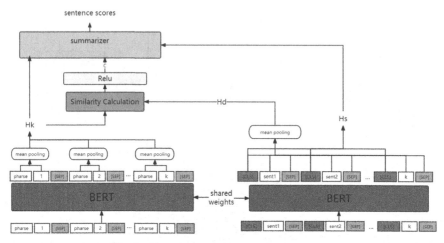

Fig. 2. The structure of KeyBERTSUM model

follows, respectively:

$$h_k^j = Meanpooling\left(h_{kj}^1, h_{kj}^2, \cdots, h_{kj}^i\right)$$
$$h_d = Meanpooling\left(h_t^1, h_t^2, \cdots, h_t^{n'}\right) \tag{1}$$

where h_{kj}^1 and h_t^1 mean the representation of first token in j-th keyphrase and document, respectively, i and n' are length of j-th keyphrase and document, respectively. Each [CLS] token aggregates the information and context of the following sentence.

Confidence Calculation. Keyphrases are defined as phrases that summarize the main topics of the document, so they are expected to be semantically similar to the entire document, which carries the main contents. It is necessary to distinguish the salience or noise of guiding phrases. By this observation, we add a similarity calculation function in our model, or directly utilize the scores from the model in the prior step. Through the BERT encoder and mean pooling, the document and keyphrases have been projected into the same vector space, and several traditional similarity and distance measures are used to calculate the confidences of the phrases. The confidence of the j-th phrase is defined as below:

$$c_j = ReLU\left(Sim\left(h_d, h_k^j\right)\right)$$

Here, we consider three similarity measures, one is cosine similarity:

$$Sim\left(h_d, h_k^j\right) = \frac{h_d \cdot h_k^j}{\|h_d\| \times \|h_k^j\|}$$

Manhattan distance is:

$$Distance\left(h_d, h_k^j\right) = \sum_{q=1}^{dim}\left|ft_{h_d}^q - ft_{h_{kj}}^q\right|$$

$$Sim\left(h_d, h_k^j\right) = \frac{1}{1 + Distance\left(h_d, h_k^j\right)}$$

where $ft_{h_d}^q$ indicates the q-th feature of h_d, The Euclidean distance is also considered:

$$Distance\left(h_d, h_k^j\right) = \sqrt{\sum_{q=1}^{dim}\left(ft_{h_d}^q - ft_{h_{kj}}^q\right)^2}$$

$$Sim\left(h_d, h_k^j\right) = \frac{1}{1 + Distance\left(h_d, h_k^j\right)}$$

We make ensure that distance values and confidence are in negative correlation.

Updating Sentence Representations. For incorporating inter-sentence relationships and phrase guidance, we propose to use self-attention mechanism and inter-attention in the summarizer to update the sentence representations in two stages, as presented in Fig. 3, called inter-sentence updating and phrase-sentence updating. To capture contextual information at sentence-level representations, we add position embeddings to the sentence representations extracted from BERT, and feed it into an additional Transformer layer, utilizing the multi-head self-attention structure.

Then we consider utilizing phrases to enrich the update of sentence representations, so as to guide the final scores of sentences. To better understand this structure, this layer can be viewed as a heterogeneous graph structure with two types of nodes. Given a set of keyphrase nodes and a set of sentence nodes, we connect edges between keyphrase nodes and sentence nodes. The keyphrase nodes are from the mean pooling regarding (1) and output of the inter-sentence updating Transformer layer, respectively.

Inspired by graph attention layer [19], we update the i-th sentence node using j-th keyphrase node through heterogeneous graph attention mechanism:

$$z_{ij} = LeakyReLU\left(W_0\left[W_s r_i^s; W_k h_j^k; W_c c_j\right]\right)$$

$$a_{ij} = \frac{exp\left(z_{ij}\right)}{\sum_{j=0}^m exp\left(z_{ij}\right)}$$

$$u_i = \|_{l=1}^L \sum_{j=0}^m tanh\left(a_{ij} W_a h_j^k\right),$$

where c_j is the confidence of j-th keyphrase; W_s, W_k and W_c are trainable weights (omit bias here). W_0 is applied to reduce the dimension of a vector into a scalar, and indicates the operation of concatenation of multi-heads features.

The vector u_i is forwarded to the dropout layer and the residual network layer, in order to prevent the degradation of the deep layer network and prevent over-fitting to a certain extent. The process formula is as follows:

$$\widetilde{r_i^s} = LN\left(r_i^s + Dropout(FFN(u_i))\right)$$

$\widetilde{r_i^s}$ is the output representation of the phrase-sentence updating layer.

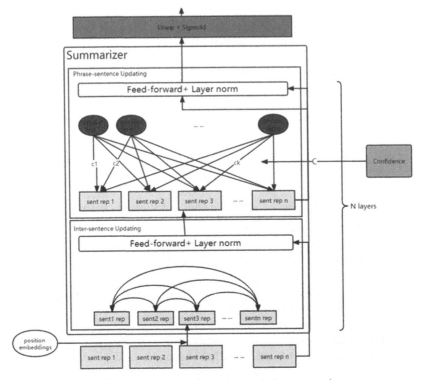

Fig. 3. Inner structure of sentence updating summarizer

We set N layers for both inter-sentence updating and phrase-sentence updating circularly, as shown in Fig. 3. Finally, a linear layer and Sigmoid layer are applied to calculate final scores using sentence representations. Since we regard extractive summarization as binary task, for finetuning the keyphrase-guided summarization model, we employ binary cross entropy loss.

4   Experiments

4.1   Datasets

CNN/Daily Mail is a combination of the CNN [16] datasets and Daily Mail [17] datasets. All the materials are news articles, and divided into training/validation/testing sets with 287,113/13,386/11,489 instances respectively. One instance of the original dataset consists of an article and associated highlights, regarded as a source document and golden summary, respectively. We use the non-anonymized version in this experiment.

New York Times Annotated corpus 50 (NYT50) contains millions of news articles published by New York Times. The metadata is collected by Newsroom and providing labels for different NLP tasks. For the summarization task, after preprocessing data following the method of Kedzie et al. [8], we acquired 44,382 (document, summary) pairs for training, 5,523 pairs for validation and 6,495 pairs for testing.

Document Understanding Conference 2001 (DUC 2001) dataset provides reference data: documents from TREC-9 and summaries produced by the National Institute of Standards and Technology for summarization tasks. X. Wan et al. [17] chose 308 articles and annotated with golden keyphrases. In our case, since the number of the articles is too small to train the model, we adopt the whole 308 instances to test the model that is finetuned on CNN/Daily Mail dataset.

4.2 Preprocessing

Oracle Summary. To generate the target labels, we firstly separate the original document D into n sentences $\{s_1, s_2, \ldots, s_n\}$ by StanfordCoreNLP server [18]. Then we select oracle sentences by comparing (ROUGE-1 + ROUGE-2) scores between concatenation of selected sentences ss_{j-1} and that of $ss_j = \left[os_1, os_2 \cdots, os_{j-1}, os_j\right]$. If $ROUGE(ss_j) > ROUGE(ss_{j-1})$, os_j will be selected as the oracle sentence. Here we select oracle sentences for 3 times.

After selection, we mark the sequence of binary labels for sentences depending on whether or not they are selected by $L_i = [l_1, l_2, \ldots, l_n]$, $l_j \in \{0, 1\}$, $1 \leq .$ We regard L_i as the target label as we mentioned above. The combination of selected sentences is called an oracle summary.

Candidate Phrases. Most Human-written keyphrases are noun phrases consisting of zero or more adjectives (e.g. electric vehicles, fuel economy standards, auto industry), so we are supposed to extract such candidate phrases from the original documents. Part-of-speech (POS) tagging from NLTK packages are utilized to tag the tokens, and RegexParser to extract candidate phrases, which makes sure that candidates are ending with noun words.

In order to filter out noisy phrases that are semantically quite far from the document, we discard candidate phrases with negative similarity and picked top-k (k = 10, 15, 20, 30) from the output of the prior keyphrase selector. Here we utilize unsupervised KeyBERT and do not consider diversity while scoring.

4.3 Configuration

We use PyTorch, and 'bert-base-uncased' version of BERT model to implement for implementation it. To finetune BERTSUM, we tried to set the batch size as 3000, 6000 (for sequence length), set $\beta_1 = 0.9, \beta_2 = 0.999$, for the Adam optimizer, and train the model for 650,000 steps with checkpoints saving every 1,000 steps. The default learning rate we tried is {2e-3, 4e-3, 6e-3}, on which we set warm up step to 10,000 steps. For hyper-parameters for the down-stream models, we set three sentence updating layers in the summarizer, with hidden size 2048 and 8 heads in the multi-head attention mechanism.

Tri-gram Blocking. The diversity of sentences in summaries ensures the reduction of information redundancy, which to some extent has effects on the quality of summaries. We follow the tri-gram blocking in [8], a method that discards sentence 3-g overlapping with the previously selected sentences along the scores iteratively.

5   Results and Analysis

In this section, we shown evaluations of our proposed KeyBERTSUM and baselines by ROUGE score. ROUGE-n (n = 1,2) measures the n-gram over- lapping degree between candidates and golden summaries, while ROUGE-L calculates 1-g overlapping degree based on the longest order matching. We show the test results on three datasets CNN/Daily Mail, New York Times 50 and DUC2001, and do controlled experiments on the CNN/Daily Mail dataset.

5.1   Experimental Results on CNN/Daily Mail

ROUGE-F1 scores (ROUGE-1, 2, L) on CNN/Daily Mail produced by our models and baselines are summarized in Table 2. In the first block, lead-3 indicates the results that

Table 1. Comparison of different extractive summarization models on CNN/Daily Mail dataset. Tri-gram blocking is applied at inference stage in this table.

	Models		ROUGE-1	ROUGE-2	ROUGE-L
	Lead-3		40.42	17.62	36.67
	Oracle		55.22	32.91	51.38
Baselines	HIBERT(Zhang et al., 2019)		42.31	19.87	38.78
	BERTSUM(Liu, 2019)		43.25	20.24	39.63
Ours	BERTSUM(Our run)		42.87	20.07	39.33
	KeyBERT +	No confidence	43.10	20.21	39.48

(continued)

Table 1. (*continued*)

Models		ROUGE-1	ROUGE-2	ROUGE-L
	Cosine Similarity	43.27	20.45	39.77
KeyBERTSUM	Manhattan Distance	43.32	20.49	39.82
	Euclidean Distance	43.24	20.44	39.74
	Scores by KeyBERT	**43.40**	**20.62**	**39.84**

simply selects the first three sentences in the document. Oracle described in Sect. 4.2.1 shows the upper bounds of extractive summarization tasks in ROUGE scores with limitation of 512 tokens (limitation of "bert-base-uncased" model). The best performance of models in our experiments are in bold. The second block shows the result reported by their corresponding papers, with pretrained language model BERT. BERTSUM is the main comparison model of our methods, since we add the new keyphrase-guided mechanism based on BERTSUM and following most settings. The results from our runs are presented in the third block.

We observe that KeyBERTSUM shows better performance than our reimplemented baselines (0.53, 0.55 and 0.51 higher on ROUGE-1, ROUGE-2 and ROUGE-L respectively). We can see that our method outperforms over the baselines in ROUGE-F1 scores, which proves that our method plays a positive role in the extractive summary task. Several confidence calculation methods are introduced in Sect. 3.2. In order to compare the results by these confidence calculations, we utilize top-20 candidate phrases from the prior selector and supply them to the KeyBERTSUM model independently. "Scores from KeyBERT" means the similarity is calculated by the prior selector pre-trained model KeyBERT.

5.2 Experimental Results on New York Times 50

The performance evaluation result on New York Times 50 is shown in Table 3. The baseline model BERTSUM (without trigram-blocking) is the results re- ported by K. Bi et al. [1], since the original paper did not report the ROUGE-F1 scores on NTY 50. The third block shows the comparison of our reimplement results on baseline models and KeyBERTSUM.

Unlike CNN/Daily Mail, the first three sentences in the NYT 50 test set are not informative enough according to the lead-3 scores. In addition, contrary to the results on the CNN/DM dataset, trigram-blocking has an apparently negative impact on the results on NYT50. We can see that both BERTSUM and KeyBERTSUM with trigram-blocking even show worse performance (decreasing by 0.66 in ROUGE-1 score).

We just utilized pre-trained KeyBERT model in Step 1 on NYT 50, and obtained higher scores (0.64 higher on ROUGE-1 without tri-gram blocking) than BERTSUM without trigram blocking. This indicates that information of guiding keyphrases has benefit on selecting sentences for both models.

Table 2. Result comparison of different models on New York Times 50 dataset. Manhattan distance and top-20 keyphrases are applied.

	Models	ROUGE-1	ROUGE-2	ROUGE-L
	Lead-3	36.65	17.65	33.37
	Oracle	56.23	37.92	49.45
Baseline	BERTSUM(Bi, 2020)	45.46	25.53	37.17
	BERTSUM(Our run)	45.90	25.98	42.21
	BERTSUM + Tri-blocking(Our run)	45.47	25.40	41.99
Ours	KeyBERTSUM	**46.54**	**26.63**	**43.10**
	KeyBERTSUM + Tri-blocking	45.88	25.92	42.25

Table 3. Comparison of different models on DUC 2001 dataset. The guiding phrases are top 8 and scores are from KeyBERT.

	Models	ROUGE-1	ROUGE-2	ROUGE-L
	Lead-3	41.35	18.83	37.50
	Oracle	50.63	33.71	47.55
	BERTSUM(Our run)	43.91	20.92	40.04
	BERTSUM + Tri-blocking(Our run)	43.45	20.45	39.56
Our runs	KeyBERTSUM	**44.67**	**21.81**	**40.84**
	KeyBERTSUM + Tri-blocking	43.85	20.93	40.05
KeyBERTSUM (Our runs)	human-written keyphrases + Tri-blocking	44.59	21.69	40.73

5.3 Experimental Results of Summarization on DUC2001

Our model achieves results better than BERTSUM baselines in our runs. (0.40 and 0.76 higher than corresponding baseline BERTSUM with and without trigram-blocking respectively on ROUGE-1).

In addition, a special feature of the DUC2001 dataset is the existence of manually-given guiding keyphrases, so we utilize human-written keyphrases and top-8 (according to the average number of human-written keyphrases) from the pre- trained model as guiding keyphrases into KeyBERTSUM for comparison. We can observe that the guiding keyphrases from pre-trained KeyBERT even outperforms in the DUC 2001 dataset than those from human-written, obtaining 0.08, 0.12 and 0.11 higher on ROUGE-1, ROUGE-2 and ROUGE-L scores respectively (without trigram-blocking). In our opinion, since the guiding keyphrases from training set of CNN/DM are selected by pre-trained KeyBERT, the model is more adaptive when tested by using keyphrases from pre-trained KeyBERT than from human-written source.

5.4 The Influence of the Top-K Keyphrases from Prior Selector

The top-K ranked keyphrases obtained from KeyBERT in Step 1 are regarded as guiding keyphrases to guide the extraction of key sentences. Because of the bi- encoder structure, we can try long sequences of keyphrases without affecting the length of the input document. Therefore, we finetune and test KeyBERTSUM by top-K ($K = 10, 15, 20, 30$) phrases on the CNN/Daily Mail dataset, based on the scores from Step 1. Table 6 shows the ROUGE-F1 score results. We observe that KeyBERTSUM achieves the best results on CNN/Daily Mail when $K = 20$, and the performance degrades with K increases or decreases. This indicates that guiding phrases with much noise or less guidance causes negative influence on the guiding effect.

Table 4. Results comparison guided by top-K keyphrases.

Top-K guiding phrases	ROUGE-1	ROUGE-2	ROUGE-L
K = 10	42.86	20.10	39.32
K = 15	43.27	20.43	39.73
K = 20	**43.40**	**20.62**	**39.84**
K = 30	43.20	20.42	39.64

6 Conclusion

In this paper, we proposed and implemented keyphrase-guided extractive summarization models for extracting important sentences using guiding keyphrases and original document. For the lack of keyphrases in traditional summarization datasets, we applied pre-trained sentence-BERT KeyBERT to extracting candidate phrases from the document and select top-K ranked phrases as guiding keyphrases. We also consider the confidence of phrases, which indicates salient parts in the document. The phrase confidence is combined with the graph attention mechanism, enhancing the features in sentence representations with information from phrases. Our experimental results show that our proposed method achieves higher ROUGE-F1 scores on three widely used datasets than BERTSUM baselines.

References

1. Bi K, Jha R, Croft W B, et al. AREDSUM: adaptive redundancy-aware itera- tive sen-tence ranking for extractive document summarization. arXiv preprint arXiv:2004.06176, 2020
2. Cheng J, Lapata M. Neural summarization by extracting sentences and words. arXiv preprint arXiv:1603.07252, 2016
3. Chung J, Gulcehre C, Cho K H, et al. Empirical evaluation of gated recurrent neural networks on sequence modeling. arXiv preprint arXiv:1412.3555, 2014

4. Cui P, Hu L, Liu Y. Enhancing extractive text summarization with topic-aware graph neural networks. arXiv preprint arXiv:2010.06253, 2020
5. Devlin J, Chang M W, Lee K, et al. Bert: Pre-training of deep bidirectional trans- formers for language understanding. arXiv preprint arXiv:1810.04805, 2018
6. Dou Z Y, Liu P, Hayashi H, et al. Gsum: A general framework for guided neural abstractive summarization. arXiv preprint arXiv:2010.08014, 2020
7. Genest P E, Lapalme G. Fully abstractive approach to guided summarization. Proceedings of the 50th Annual Meeting of the Association for Computational Lin- guistics (Volume 2: Short Papers). 2012: 354–358
8. Kedzie C, McKeown K, Daume III H. Content selection in deep learning models of summarization. arXiv preprint arXiv:1810.12343, 2018
9. Kryściński W, Keskar N S, McCann B, et al. Neural text summarization: A critical evaluation. arXiv preprint arXiv:1908.08960, 2019
10. Li C, Xu W, Li S, et al. Guiding generation for abstractive text summarization based on key information guide network//Proceedings of the 2018 Conference of the North American Chapter of the Association for Computational Linguistics: Human Language Technologies, Volume 2 (Short Papers). 2018: 55–60
11. Liang X, Wu S, Li M, et al. Unsupervised keyphrase extraction by jointly modeling local and global context[J]. arXiv preprint arXiv:2109.07293, 2021
12. Lim, Y., Seo, D., Jung, Y.: Fine-tuning BERT Models for Keyphrase Extraction in Scientific Articles[J]. Journal of advanced information technology and convergence **10**(1), 45–56 (2020)
13. Lin C Y. Rouge: A package for automatic evaluation of summaries//Text sum- marization branches out. 2004: 74–81
14. Liu Y. Fine-tune BERT for extractive summarization. arXiv preprint arXiv:1903.10318, 2019
15. Liu T, Iwaihara M. Supervised learning of keyphrase extraction utilizing prior sum- marization//International Conference on Asian Digital Libraries. Springer, Cham, 2021: 157–166
16. Mihalcea R, Tarau P. Textrank: Bringing order into text//Proceedings of the 2004 conference on empirical methods in natural language processing. 2004: 404–411
17. Nallapati R, Zhai F, Zhou B. Summarunner: A recurrent neural networkbased sequence model for extractive summarization of documents//Thirty-first AAAI conference on artificial intelligence. 2017
18. Sharma P, Li Y. Self-supervised contextual keyword and keyphrase retrieval with self-labelling (2019)
19. Veličković P, Cucurull G, Casanova A, et al. Graph attention networks. arXiv preprint arXiv: 1710.10903, 2017
20. Wan, X., Xiao, J.: Single document keyphrase extraction using neighborhood knowl- edge//AAAI. **8**, 855–860 (2008)
21. Wang, R., Liu, W., McDonald, C.: Corpus-independent generic keyphrase extraction using word embedding vectors//Software engineering research conference. **39**, 1–8 (2014)
22. Wang D, Liu P, Zheng Y, et al. Heterogeneous graph neural networks for extractive document summarization. arXiv preprint arXiv:2004.12393, 2020
23. Zhang X, Wei F, Zhou M. HIBERT: Document level pre-training of hierar- chical bidi-rectional transformers for document summarization. arXiv preprint arXiv:1905.06566, 2019
24. Zhong M, Liu P, Chen Y, et al. Extractive summarization as text matching. arXiv preprint arXiv:2004.08795, 2020
25. Zhou Q, Yang N, Wei F, et al. Neural document summarization by jointly learning to score and select sentences. arXiv preprint arXiv:1807.02305, 2018

Visualization of the Gap Between the Stances of Citizens and City Councilors on Political Issues

Ko Senoo[1]([☒]) [iD], Yohei Seki[2]([☒]) [iD], Wakako Kashino[3] [iD], and Noriko Kando[4,5] [iD]

[1] Graduate School of Comprehensive Human Sciences, University of Tsukuba,
Tsukuba, Japan
s2221652@s.tsukuba.ac.jp
[2] Faculty of Library, Information and Media Science, University of Tsukuba,
Tsukuba, Japan
yohei@slis.tsukuba.ac.jp
[3] National Institute for Japanese Language and Linguistics, Tokyo, Japan
waka@ninjal.ac.jp
[4] National Institute of Informatics, Tokyo, Japan
kando@nii.ac.jp
[5] The Graduate University for Advanced Studies, Tokyo, Japan

Abstract. In local government, clarifying the gap between the political opinions of citizens and city councilors is important for reflecting the will of the people in politics. In this study, we focus on the difference between the stances (i.e., favor or against) of citizens and city councilors on political issues, and attempt to compare the arguments of both sides. Using a dataset of texts collected from citizen tweets and city council minutes, we performed a detailed analysis of the opinions expressed, based on the fine-tuning of pretrained language models. In particular, the model predicted the labels of four attributes: stance, usefulness, regional dependency, and relevance. In our experiments, we targeted two political issues: "eliminating nursery school waiting lists" and "attracting integrated resorts (IR)." However, the clues enabling the prediction of labels for the four attributes varied depending on the target. We, therefore, introduced a target-attention mechanism, which extracted helpful information from target sentences, to improve the prediction performance. In addition, we improved the prediction of attribute labels that considered relevance-related issues, by adopting multitask learning of relevance and other attributes. Our experimental results showed that the macro F1-scores for stance and regional-dependency attributes were improved by up to 1.0% and 3.7%, respectively, when using the target-attention mechanism, and by up to 7.2% for usefulness with multitask learning. Using the trained model to analyze real opinion gaps, we found that the citizens of Osaka City were relatively more supportive of attracting IR than the citizens of Yokohama City.

Keywords: Stance prediction · Citizen opinion · City council minutes · Twitter · Bert

© The Author(s), under exclusive license to Springer Nature Switzerland AG 2022
Y.-H. Tseng et al. (Eds.): ICADL 2022, LNCS 13636, pp. 73–89, 2022.
https://doi.org/10.1007/978-3-031-21756-2_6

1 Introduction

In local government, clarifying the gap between the opinions of citizens and city councilors on political issues is important for reflecting the will of the people in politics. Many citizens express their opinions about politics via Twitter[1], and many city councils publish the minutes of their meetings on the Web. The use of such digital archives is effective in analyzing the opinions of citizens and city councilors. We define a "political issue" as an urgent issue or policy that divides opinion in local politics. We aim to predict automatically the labels (i.e., favor or against) that apply to the stance of citizens and city council members on political issues. We compare their arguments by visualizing trends in the percentages of "favor" and "agains," using a large amount of existing data with these predicted labels.

To analyze opinions on political issues in detail, it is necessary to determine not only the label attached to a stance but also whether the topics are relevant to the political issues (relevance), whether they include specific information and evidence (usefulness), and whether they are related to the place of residence (regional-dependency).

However, it is costly to create sufficiently large labeled datasets for each attribute on multiple political issues. A possible solution is to train a single model across multiple political issues to supplement the training data. Because the clues used to determine each attribute label vary according to the political issue, high-performance prediction can be difficult. Therefore, we adopted an attention mechanism [17] to extract useful information from target sentences representing political issues to help predict attribute labels. We implement this via a "target-attention" module, which weights the clues differently according to the political issue and improves the prediction performance across political issues.

In addition, not all of the input sentences to the model are relevant to the political issue. If they are not, the assigned label should be "no stance." In this way, we have attempted to improve the performance of stance prediction by considering the association between stance and relevance through multitask learning [2].

We collected the data from Twitter and from the city council minutes for two cities, Yokohama and Osaka. The political issues covered in this study and their target sentences are as follows.

1. **Children on a waiting list**: "The local government policies for children on waiting lists for nursery schools have been successful or are expected to be successful."
2. **Attracting IR**: "Integrated resorts (IR) developments, including casinos, should be attracted."

The contributions of this paper can be summarized as follows.

1. For multiple cities, we constructed a dataset of citizens' and city councilors' claims on several political issues. The dataset was labeled with four attributes: stance, usefulness, regional dependency, and relevance.

---

[1] https://twitter.com.

2. We propose the use of a new attention mechanism to predict appropriate attribute labels according to the political issue. In addition, the effectiveness of the proposed method was evaluated when applying multitask learning with respect to relevance.
3. The visualization of opinion trends revealed both gaps and commonalities in the stances of citizens and city councilors, depending on the city and the political issue.

This paper is organized as follows. Section 2 describes related work. Section 3 introduces the four attributes and the classification model proposed in this paper. In Sect. 4, we describe the dataset and the classification experiments using the proposed method. In Sect. 5, we analyze the opinions of citizens and city councilors. Section 6 summarizes the paper.

2 Related Work

2.1 Research Focusing on Citizens and City Councilors

Mohammad et al. [15] hosted SemEval-2016 Task 6, a shared task to classify tweet stances. Stefanov et al. [16] predicted Twitter users' stances on political issues and identified the political tendencies of online media and popular Twitter users. Kimura et al. [10] hosted NTCIR-14 QA Lab-PoliInfo, a shared task for evaluating prediction methods for the stances of city councilors with respect to the agenda of the Tokyo Metropolitan Assembly. Kimura et al. [9] also hosted NTCIR-15 QA Lab-PoliInfo-2, where the participants' systems predicted the stances of political parties. Although there have been many studies on the stance prediction of citizens and city councilors, there have been few studies that focus on the relationship between citizens and city councilors.

One exception is Kimura and Shibuki's study [8] that matched citizens' blogs with city council minutes. They proposed a matching method that assigns common political categories (e.g., finance, education) to citizens' blogs and city council minutes, aiming to present political information that matched the interests of citizens. This study differs from their study in that we aim to clarify the gaps between the claims of citizens and city councilors on political issues, and we also aim to investigate an effective prediction method that includes an attention mechanism and a pretrained language model.

2.2 Cross-Target Stance Prediction with Target Sentences

Augenstein et al. [1] proposed a stance prediction model that uses two BiLSTMs to encode both the target sentences (or claims) and the input sentences. This enabled them to consider information obtained from the target sentence in addition to the input sentence, and improved stance prediction even for texts without explicit reference to the target. Xu et al. [18] added an attention mechanism to the Augenstein model, to enable a focus on the parts of input sentences where the stance toward the target is described explicitly. In addition, they showed that the prediction performance of conventional stance prediction methods decreases when a single model is used across multiple targets. To address this issue, they proposed a method that considered target information, which improved the accuracy of stance prediction across a variety of targets. In this paper, we not only focus on the important words in the input sentences using the pretrained language model BERT [4] but also introduce an attention mechanism for the target sentences. Using this framework, we aim to improve the performance of stance prediction across a variety of targets.

2.3 Qualitative and Regional Attributes to Support Stance Analysis

Fact-checkability (Kimura et al. [10]) and constructiveness (Kolhatkar et al. [11]) are two issues that focus on aspects of quality other than the stance of the claim. Kimura et al. [10] classified fact-checkability in addition to stance, aiming to extract fact-checkable reasons for the stances supplied by a member of the Tokyo Metropolitan Assembly. Kolhatkar et al. [11] defined "constructiveness" as identifying constructive comments in online news articles. Constructiveness is less of an emotional response than the facilitation of discussion by providing appropriate rationales, solutions, new perspectives, and insights, as needed. In contrast to their study, we focus on citizens' tweets that contain much personal information. In this paper, we define a "usefulness" attribute that can be assigned to both tweets and city council minutes to capture the useful claims of citizens via concrete evidence and with reference to the concepts described above.

Ishida et al. [7] focused on the diversity of citizens' opinions, and automatically classified citizens' tweets from multiple viewpoints. By combining the viewpoints, they were able to specify conditions and extract opinions from among the diverse tweets of citizens. To extract citizen opinions according to their city of residence, they introduced "regional-dependency" and "relevance" viewpoints. In this paper, we also define regional-dependency and relevance attributes to enable a focus on the comments and discussions from citizens and city councilors specific to a city and to a political issue.

2.4 Multitask Learning

Multitask learning is a technique for improving the prediction performance by learning multiple tasks simultaneously in a shared model via synergistic effects among tasks. Liu et al. [14] proposed a multitask learning method for the deep learning of natural language processing and showed the effectiveness of multitask learning using BERT. Ishida et al. [7] also focused on the relationship among multiple viewpoints related to citizens' opinions and achieved high-performance predictions using a multitask learning method. In this paper, the "stance," "usefulness," and "regional-dependency" attributes have strong associations with the "relevance" attribute because they will not lead to positive labels if they are not relevant to the political issue. Therefore, we can expect to improve the prediction performance by training each attribute in association with the relevance attribute through multitask learning.

3   Proposed Method

In our proposed method, we first construct a dataset by annotating the tweets and city council minutes with the attribute labels. Next, we train the prediction models for attributes using the dataset. We then use the trained models to predict attribute labels for a large number of unknown tweets and city council minutes and visualize any gaps between them according to their city of residence.

We describe the definitions of attributes in Sect. 3.1 and explain the prediction model in Sect. 3.2.

3.1   Definition of Attributes

In this work, we trained our model using a dataset whose items were annotated with respect to the following four attributes. The labels used for the attribute annotation are given in curly brackets.

1. **Stance** {"favor," "against," "favor and against," "N/A"}: this indicates whether the opinion holder (citizen or city councilor) agrees with the target sentence (or claim) or opposes it.
2. **Relevance** {"yes," "no"}: this indicates whether the content is relevant to the target sentence (or claim). For "children on a waiting list," those sentences that refer to children waiting for elementary-school after-school care are judged as "no." In the case of "attracting IR," those sentences that refer to casino bars and online casinos, which have nothing to do with IRs, are judged as "no."
3. **Usefulness** {"yes," "no"}: this indicates whether the content is useful in facilitating a discussion of political issues. Usefulness is defined with reference to fack-checkability in Kimura et al. [10] and to constructiveness in Kolhatkar et al. [11]. "Yes" is given to those sentences that contain concrete figures or evidence, point out problems, or describe specific experiences, whereas "no" is given to those with vague evidence or slanderous comments.
4. **Regional dependency** {"yes," "no"}: this indicates whether the content covers the place of residence of the opinion holder (citizen or city councilor). If a sentence contains words that can identify the region, such as the name of a place or a facility, they are judged as "yes." Conversely, those sentences that target the world or Japan as a whole are judged as "no."

There are two types of units used for assigning attributes: sentence-level and document-level units. Sentence-level refers to a particular sentence in a tweet or in a city council minute. Document-level refers to a whole tweet in Twitter or to a whole paragraph in a speech in the city council minutes. Ishida et al. [7] considered that a single tweet may contain multiple opinions, and assigned viewpoints to each sentence. In this paper, the assignment of attribute labels is primarily at the sentence level. The regional-dependency attribute, however, is assigned only at the document level, because it is difficult to determine regional dependency at the sentence level.

3.2   Prediction Model

In this study, we predict attribute labels according to political issues by introducing a target-attention mechanism, which directs attention to important words in the target sentence (or claim). In addition, multitask learning can improve the prediction performance by jointly learning relevance together with other attributes such as stance, usefulness, and regional dependency.

An overview of the prediction model used in this paper is shown in Fig. 1. The model comprises three modules. The sentence-embedding module converts each sentence into an embedded representation using BERT and target attention. The sentence-classification module classifies the labels of the attributes for each sentence using the embedded representation. The document-classification module creates an embedded representation for a document by combining the embedded representations of each sentence and classifies the labels of the attributes for the document. Note that, in multitask learning, the target-attention, sentence-classification module, and document-classification module are prepared according to individual tasks, whereas BERT is shared by all tasks.

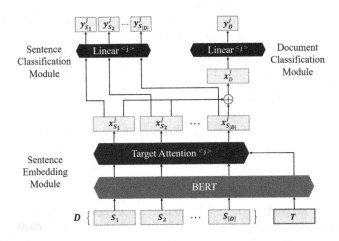

Fig. 1. Overview of the prediction model, where j is the index of the task for multitask learning.

Sentence-embedding Module. The sentence-embedding module uses BERT to create an embedded representation for a sentence and attaches information about the target sentence via target attention.

BERT. A document D that comprises one or more sentences is expressed as $D = \{S_1, ..., S_{|D|}\}$. The sentence S_i is expressed as $S_i = \{t_1, t_2, ..., t_{|S_i|}\}$, with t_n identifying each token. Given a sentence S_i as an input to BERT, the embedded representation is expressed as

$$E_{S_i} = \{e_1, e_2, ..., e_{|S_i|}\} \in \mathbb{R}^{|S_i| \times d}, \tag{1}$$

where e_n is the embedded representation of token t_n, and usually $d = 768$ for BERT. We use this $BERT_{base}$ model as the pretrained model, fine-tuned by the dataset created in this study.

Target Attention. The target sentence T is represented as $T = \{t_1, t_2, ..., t_{|T|}\}$. Given a target sentence T as an input to BERT, the embedded representation of it is expressed as

$$E_T = \{e_1, e_2, ..., e_{|T|}\} \in \mathbb{R}^{|T| \times d}.\tag{2}$$

Next, E_{S_i} and E_T are transformed in the linear layer corresponding to each task to obtain the query $Q^j_{S_i}$, key K^j, and value V^j. Note that $|S|$ is the fixed length of tokens defined for the sentence.

$$Q^j_{S_i} = W^j_Q E_{S_i} + b^j_Q \in \mathbb{R}^{|S| \times d}\tag{3}$$

$$K^j = W^j_K E_T + b^j_K \in \mathbb{R}^{|T| \times d}\tag{4}$$

$$V^j = W^j_V E_T + b^j_V \in \mathbb{R}^{|T| \times d}\tag{5}$$

where W is the weight matrix, b is the bias vector, and j is the index of the task. Note that the different tasks use different linear layers.

Then, by applying the softmax function to the inner product of $Q^j_{S_i}$ and K^j, we can compute $A^j_{S_i}$ (see Equation (6)), which represents the degree of association between each token in the sentence S_i and the target sentence T for task j. By adding the inner product of $A^j_{S_i}$ and V^j to E_{S_i}, we obtain $X^j_{S_i}$ (see Equation (7)), where each token contains information about the target sentence T. Finally, $X^j_{S_i}$ is passed through an average-pooling process that averages over each dimension of the embedded representation to obtain the output $x^j_{S_i}$ of the target-attention module (see Equation (8)).

$$A^j_{S_i} = softmax(\frac{Q^j_{S_i} K^j}{\sqrt{d}}) \in \mathbb{R}^{|S| \times |T|},\tag{6}$$

$$X^j_{S_i} = E_{S_i} + A^j_{S_i} V^j \in \mathbb{R}^{|S_i| \times d},\tag{7}$$

$$x^j_{S_i} = average(X^j_{S_i}) \in \mathbb{R}^d.\tag{8}$$

This generates the vector $x^j_{S_i}$, which contains information about important tokens in the target sentence T in addition to that for tokens in the sentence S_i.

Sentence-classification Module. The vector $x^j_{S_i}$ for the sentence S_i is input to the linear layer for sentence-level classification of task j (see Equation (9)).

$$y^j_{S_i} = softmax(W^j_S x^j_{S_i} + b^j_S) \in \mathbb{R}^c,\tag{9}$$

where $y^j_{S_i}$ is the predicted probability distribution of the attribute labels for task j, and c is the number of categories of attribute labels.

Document-classification Module. For document-level classification in task j, the vector $\boldsymbol{x}_D^j$ of a document $\boldsymbol{D}$ is calculated from the weighted sum of vectors $\boldsymbol{X}_S^j = \{\boldsymbol{x}_1^j, \boldsymbol{x}_2^j, ..., \boldsymbol{x}_{|D|}^j\}$ (see Equation (11)). By supplying $\boldsymbol{x}_D^j$ to the linear layer and the softmax function, the attribute label of the document is predicted (see Equation (12)). The weight $\boldsymbol{w}^j$ for each sentence is calculated by converting the sentence vector to a scalar quantity using the linear layer and softmax function (see Equation (10)). This enables the prediction of the attributes for each document, focusing on the important sentences contained in the document

$$\boldsymbol{w}^j = softmax(\boldsymbol{W}_w^j \boldsymbol{X}_S^j + \boldsymbol{b}_w^j) \in \mathbb{R}^{|\boldsymbol{D}|}, \tag{10}$$

$$\boldsymbol{x}_D^j = \boldsymbol{w}^j \boldsymbol{X}_S^j \in \mathbb{R}^d, \tag{11}$$

$$\boldsymbol{y}_D^j = softmax(\boldsymbol{W}_D^j \boldsymbol{x}_D^j + \boldsymbol{b}_D^j) \in \mathbb{R}^c. \tag{12}$$

4   Experiments

In Sect. 4.1, we describe the construction of the experimental dataset and the annotation. We then describe our experiments to investigate the effectiveness of target attention in Sect. 4.2 and multitask learning in Sect. 4.3.

4.1   Construction of the Experimental Dataset

As described in Sect. 1, we focused on two political issues, namely "children on a waiting list" and "attracting IR." The experimental dataset used in this study comprised eight types of texts, combining two document genres (citizen tweets and city council minutes), two cities (Yokohama and Osaka), and the above two political issues. Documents were extracted that included 1,000 to 1,500 sentences for each political issue in each city's citizen tweets and 1,000 sentences for each issue in each city's council minutes, resulting in a dataset of approximately 9,900 sentences in total. The publishing date range for the dataset was from January 1, 2016 to March 31, 2021. For the search queries, we used *"taiki-jidou"* ("Children on a waiting list" in English) and *"horyu-jidou"*[2] for "children on a waiting list," and "casino" and "IR" for "attracting IR."

Collection of Citizen Tweets. We collected tweets from 84,936 accounts for Yokohama citizens and 56,307 accounts for Osaka citizens, which were collected from Twitter based on the users' profile information, using Twitter's Streaming API. From among those tweets, we extracted tweets from Yokohama citizens and Osaka citizens that were posted during the publishing dates indicated above, giving 1,000 to 1,500 sentences for each political issue for each city. Retweets and duplicate tweets were excluded, and any URLs in the tweets were removed. The tweets were divided into sentences using the Python library function spaCy[3]. In addition to citizens, there are also accounts for city councilors, bots, and

---

[2] Children who applied for admission to nursery schools but were not included in the waiting list.

[3] https://spacy.io.

companies on Twitter. We, therefore, excluded accounts with "council," "bot," or "official" in their profiles as not representing citizen accounts.

Collection of City Council Minutes. The city council minutes for Yokohama City[4] and Osaka City[5] were collected using a Web crawler. The number of minutes matching the dates indicated above was 1,146 for Yokohama City and 809 for Osaka City. From these minutes, paragraphs containing queries about political issues were extracted, giving approximately 4,000 sentences altogether for both cities and both political issues. Paragraphs were divided into sentences based on punctuation.

Annotation of Attributes. The dataset was constructed by annotating the collected data for the attributes defined in Sect. 3. The annotation work was divided among three teams of seven annotators (the first author and six collaborators). That is, the collaborators were divided into three teams of two persons each, with the author also belonging to all teams, thereby creating teams of three annotators. The attribute label for each sentence was determined by the majority vote of the three people. First, the seven annotators annotated the common 1,000 sentences for training and updated the annotation policy based on the agreements achieved. The remaining data were then annotated by the three teams. Fleiss' κ coefficients [6] for each team are given in Table 1, representing the degree of inter-annotator agreement. The values for all attributes exceeded 0.6 (substantial agreement [13]), indicating that there were few differences in annotation between annotators.

Table 1. Fleiss' κ coefficients for each attribute

Document genre	Political issue	Attribute	κ (Team1)		κ (Team2)		κ (Team3) [a]	
			Sentence	Document	Sentence	Document	Sentence	Document
Citizen tweets	Children on a waiting list	Stance	0.617	0.674	0.614	0.662	0.632	0.690
		Relevance	0.661	0.748	0.692	0.656	0.793	0.936
		Usefulness	0.646	0.708	0.661	0.709	0.751	0.843
		Regional dependency[b]	–	0.773	–	0.686	–	0.818
	Attracting IR	Stance	0.644	0.782	0.636	0.676	0.642	0.750
		Relevance	0.693	0.919	0.763	0.827	0.786	0.920
		Usefulness	0.664	0.686	0.637	0.749	0.837	0.842
		Regional dependency[b]	–	0.745	–	0.778	–	0.816
City council minutes	Children on a waiting list	Stance	0.616	0.625	0.640	0.648	–	–
		Relevance	0.711	0.698	0.719	0.639	–	–
		Usefulness	0.649	0.662	0.716	0.702	–	–
		Regional dependency[b]	–	0.615	–	0.719	–	–
	Attracting IR	Stance	0.615	0.683	0.621	0.656	–	–
		Relevance	0.649	0.799	0.637	0.679	–	–
		Usefulness	0.638	0.649	0.718	0.711	–	–
		Regional dependency[b]	–	0.794	–	0.725	–	–

[a] In Team 3, the annotators annotated citizen tweets only.
[b] Regional dependency was annotated only at the document level, as described in Sect. 3.1.

___

[4] http://giji.city.yokohama.lg.jp/tenant/yokohama/pg/index.html.
[5] https://ssp.kaigiroku.net/tenant/cityosaka/SpTop.html.

4.2   Experiment 1: Validation of Target Attention

Objective. In this section, we examine the effectiveness of target attention in learning across the two political issues.

Method. Using the dataset described in Sect. 4.1, we trained and evaluated the prediction model for each attribute using five-fold cross validation. We used pre-trained Japanese BERT models[6] in the sentence-embedding module. The five-fold cross validation was performed using three different random seeds (1212, 1122, and 2211), and the average of a total of 15 evaluations was used to summarize the evaluation results. We evaluated the average of macro F1-scores at both the sentence level and the document level.

Note that some of the labels for the attributes involved extremely unbalanced data, and the evaluation results were very poor in the preliminary experiments. Therefore, for these labels, the sentences were downsampled by 50%. The labels involved were "N/A" for stance and "yes" for usefulness (for citizen tweets), and "N/A" for stance, "no" for regional-dependency, and "yes" for relevance (for city council minutes). In addition, because sentences labeled "favor and against" for the stance attribute represented less than 1% of the dataset, we decided not to predict the "favor and against" label in this experiment, and removed such sentences from the dataset.

As an ablation study, we also trained and evaluated a method that excluded target attention from the proposed method. In this case, the BERT outputs $E_{S_i} = \{e_1, e_2, ...e_{|S|}\}$ were given directly to the sentence and document prediction modules as inputs.

Results. The prediction performance for each attribute is given in Table 2.

Table 2. Macro F1-score (with and without target attention)

Document genre	Political issue	Target attention	Stance[*c]	Relevance	Usefulness	Regional dependency
Citizen tweets	Children on a waiting list	With	**0.408**	0.903	0.470	**0.812**
		W/O	0.406	0.903	**0.473**	0.759
	Attracting IR	With	**0.424**	0.860	0.313	**0.891**
		W/O	0.421	**0.861**	**0.316**	0.829
City council minutes	Children on a waiting list	With	**0.652**	**0.932**	0.738	**0.970**
		W/O	0.644	0.929	**0.752**	0.968
	Attracting IR	With	**0.632**	**0.924**	**0.587**	**0.967**
		W/O	0.622	0.920	0.571	0.966

[c] "*" indicates that the method with target attention is significantly better than the method without it, using paired samples t-tests. ($p < 0.05$, one-sided)

---

[6] https://github.com/cl-tohoku/bert-japanese.

Discussion. Table 2 shows that the F1-score improved by 1.0% for stance and by 3.7% on average for regional dependency when including target attention, for all four combinations of document genres and political issues. We conducted the t-tests using Pearson's r as the effect size. Note that the improvement in F1-score for stance was statistically significant. For stance, the method with target attention ($mean = 0.529$, $SD = 0.113$) was better on average than the method without it ($mean = 0.523$, $SD = 0.110$, $t(3) = 2.978$, $p = 0.029$, $r = 0.864$). Similarly, for regional dependency, the method with target attention ($mean = 0.910$, $SD = 0.065$) was better than the method without it ($mean = 0.881$, $SD = 0.090$, $t(3) = 1.813$, $p = 0.084$, $r = 0.723$). Note also that r is regarded as large for both cases according to [3]. Conversely, for the usefulness attribute, target attention did not seem to be effective because its clues tended to be independent of political issues. To visualize this effectiveness, Figs. 2 and 3 show examples of city council minutes for which the stances were correctly predicted when target attention was included.

Fig. 2. Visualization of attention (city council minutes, children on a waiting list)

Fig. 3. Visualization of attention (city council minutes, attracting IR)

In Fig. 2, the speaker criticizes the city's policy of leaving the issue of children on a waiting list to the private sector, but there is no "children on a waiting list" in the input sentence and the expression of disapproval of the political issue is ambiguous. Using target attention, however, the model paid more attention to the "children on a waiting list" in the target sentence and correctly predicted that they were "against." Fig. 3 shows the speaker's positive stance toward attracting IR, without clearly stating that it should be attracted. Nonetheless, with target attention included, we correctly predicted "favor" by paying attention to the words "casino," "IR," and "attract" in the target sentence. In addition, BERT paid attention to "understanding" and "continue" in the input sentence. This shows that words indicating a positive stance toward attracting IR were focused as clues in BERT for predicting the stance. We can, therefore, confirm that target attention is effective in improving the prediction performance for stance by extracting important information from target sentences.

4.3   Experiment 2: Validation of Multitask Learning

Objective. In this section, we investigate the effectiveness of multitask learning where the relevance attribute is used in predicting other attributes.

Method. We evaluated a multitask learning method that used the relevance attribute to predict other attributes (stance, usefulness, and regional dependency). The pretrained models, evaluation, and downsampling methods were the same as those used in Experiment 1. The results can usefully be compared with those in Experiment 1, in which each attribute was learned independently.

Results. The experimental results are shown in Table 3.

Table 3. Macro F1-score (multitask or independent)

Document genre	Political issue	Multitask learning	Stance	Usefulness	Regional dependency
Citizen tweets	Children on a waiting list	With	**0.415**	**0.478**	**0.798**
		W/O	0.408	0.473	0.759
	Attracting IR	With	**0.441**	**0.381**	**0.894**
		W/O	0.424	0.316	0.829
City council minutes	Children on a waiting list	With	**0.667**	**0.761**	**0.969**
		W/O	0.652	0.752	0.968
	Attracting IR	With	0.609	**0.606**	0.964
		W/O	**0.632**	0.571	**0.966**

Discussion. Multitask learning with relevance improved the average F1-score by 1.1%, 7.2%, and 3.2% for stance, usefulness, and regional-dependency attributes, respectively, for all four combinations of document genres and political issues. With respect to usefulness, the method with multitask learning ($mean = 0.557$, $SD = 0.143$) was better on average than the method without it ($mean = 0.528$, $SD = 0.158$, $t(3) = 2.055$, $p = 0.066$, $r = 0.765$. Note that r is again regarded as large [3]. The information learned from relevance is therefore shown to be beneficial for predicting other attributes such as stance. On the other hand, the F1-score for "relevance" itself was almost unchanged (0.1% on average) caused by multitask learning with the usefulness attribute. It is possible that information about other attributes is not necessarily beneficial for learning relevance, and that relevance would be more useful if learned independently.

To investigate the effect of relevance in predicting stance with multitask learning, Table 4 shows the distribution of stance labels according to ground-truth relevance labels in the city council minutes. That is, it shows the percentages of the predicted stance labels found by multitask learning, by independent learning, and by ground-truth labels.

Table 4. Distribution of stance and relevance in city council minutes

Political issue	Labeling method	Relevance:no				Relevance:yes				Total
		Subtotal	Percentage of stance			Subtotal	Percentage of stance			
			N/A	Favor	Against		N/A	Favor	Against	
Children on a waiting list	Multitask	671	94%	1%	5%	1184	48%	28%	24%	1855
	Independent	648	84%	4%	12%	1207	55%	23%	22%	1855
	Ground truth	582	100%	0%	0%	1273	57%	22%	21%	1855
Attracting IR	Multitask	601	94%	1%	5%	1381	61%	21%	18%	1982
	Independent	569	84%	6%	10%	1413	65%	19%	16%	1982
	Ground truth	468	100%	0%	0%	1514	65%	18%	17%	1982

Table 4 shows that for "children on a waiting list" in city council minutes, the proportion of data predicting a stance of "N/A" among the data (with relevance being "no") is 94% for multitask learning, whereas it is lower (at 84%) for independent learning. This trend is also found in the citizen tweets. Therefore, by adopting multitask learning, the stance can be predicted correctly as "N/A" for data with no relevance.

Conversely, for data with a "yes" relevance, the stance tends to be predicted as having more "favor" and "against" with multitask learning. This change has the effect of improving the recall of "favor" and "against." Among the ground truth labels, the percentage of the data with a "yes" relevance and an "N/A" stance for "children on a waiting list" and "attracting IR" are 57% and 65%, respectively. Therefore, multitasking learning was effective for "children on a waiting list," but less so for "attracting IR."

5 Visualization of the Gap in the Stance of Citizens and City Councilors

In this section, we analyze the claims of citizens and city councilors on political issues to investigate the trends and differences between them.

5.1 Method

Using prediction models trained by the proposed method, we retrieved documents with these attribute labels: "yes" in relevance, "yes" in regional dependency, and "favor" or "against" in stance. The set of documents for each city over a series of three-month periods was arranged in chronological order, with separate groups for citizens and city councilors. Within each set of documents, the number of citizens or city councilors in "favor" and "against" was counted. The stance of each person (citizen or city councilor) was defined as the majority of their stances within the interval. To obtain a sufficient quantity of data for each period, the dataset was expanded using the unannotated data in the collection, as described in Sect. 4.1.

Based on the predicted stances of citizens and city councilors for each interval, the percentages for "favor" and "against" were calculated. Line graphs were used to visualize the trends in the percentages. Focusing on the intervals for which the "favor" and "against" percentages appear skewed in the graphs, we analyzed the characteristics of the documents contained within the various periods.

5.2   Results

The results for "attracting IR" in Yokohama City and Osaka City are shown in Figs. 4 and 5, respectively. In each figure, (a) shows the percentage of each stance label for citizens in citizen tweets and (b) shows those for city councilors in city council minutes. (Because of space limitations, we omit the results for "children on a waiting list.")

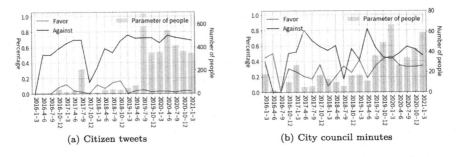

(a) Citizen tweets   (b) City council minutes

Fig. 4. Changes in stance (attracting IR, Yokohama City)

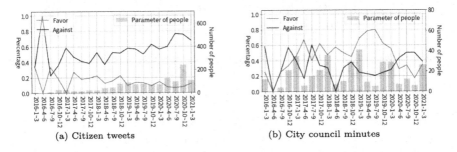

(a) Citizen tweets   (b) City council minutes

Fig. 5. Changes in stance (attracting IR, Osaka City)

5.3   Discussion

With respect to "attracting IR" in Yokohama City, Fig. 4 shows that the opposition to IR by the citizens overwhelms the support for IR, in all intervals. For city councilors, the majority are against IR in most of the intervals, although some are in favor. Overall, both citizens and city councilors in Yokohama City tended to be negative about attracting IR.

However, Fig. 5 shows that the citizens of Osaka City were more positive about attracting IR than those from Yokohama City. Although the majority are opposed to IR, there are a certain number of people who are in favor of IR at any time. For the city councilors, the majority are in favor of attracting IR in most of the intervals. In Table 5, we show the results of retrieving documents with the usefulness being "yes" in the interval from October 2019 to March 2020, when there were a large number of proponents among city councilors.

Table 5. Claims with a usefulness label of "yes" (attracting IR, Osaka City)

Citizen's tweet (favor)
Although IR has a negative aspect of casinos, it is good if Osaka can become a first-class **tourist city** like Las Vegas with the tax revenue. My store will also make money with the increase in **foreign customers**
City councilor's utterance (favor)
A budget of **7.56 billion** yen has been allocated for the next fiscal year for the design and construction of Yumeshima's infrastructure, including reclamation, roads, bridges, railroads, and water and sewage systems, in preparation for the Osaka-Kansai Expo and the formation of an **international tourism center**, including an IR

Table 5 shows a citizen tweeting that IR will stimulate the economy and make Osaka City grow as a tourist city, while pointing out that the number of foreign tourists will also increase. As for the city councilor's utterance, specific budget discussions, including figures, can be extracted as useful arguments. It also shows that they see IR as one element of the international tourism center that Osaka City aims to become. From these comments, we can conclude that both citizens and city councilors in Osaka City focus on the internationality and tourism of the IR and have high expectations for attracting IR.

By focusing on the proportion of stance labels while considering the usefulness attribute, we were able to find useful comments from both citizens and city councilors on political issues. In addition, by comparing the stances from both cities, we could show that Osaka City citizens and councilors were more positive about attracting IR than were Yokohama City citizens and councilors. Note that these results are consistent with the fact that the Yokohama mayor gave up the idea of attracting an IR in 2021 [12]. As a side note, Yokohama City's citizens were more opposed than Osaka City's to the issue of "children on a waiting list". This reflects the fact that the number of children on waiting lists is actually more of a problem in Yokohama City [5].

6   Conclusion

In this paper, we have proposed a method for comparing the stances of citizens with city councilors by identifying four attributes (stance, usefulness, regional dependency, and relevance) in tweets by citizens and in the utterances of city councilors. To improve the prediction of attribute labels, we introduced the concept of target attention, an attention mechanism that enables target sentences to be considered by the BERT-based model used. In addition, we applied multitask learning with respect to the relevance to further improve the performance. Our experimental results showed that Yokohama City citizens and councilors were less in favor of attracting IR than were Osaka City citizens and councilors (in fact, the councilors actually withdrew support for it). We also found that Yokohama City citizens were more opposed than those of Osaka City to having children on waiting lists. These results demonstrated that our method can enable us to identify differences in the stances of citizens and city councilors on social issues, depending on the city and the issue involved.

Acknowledgements. This work was partially supported by the Japanese Society for the Promotion of Science Grant-in-Aid for Challenging Exploratory Research (#22K19822), Grant-in-Aid for Scientific Research (B) (#19H04420), and by ROIS NII Open Collaborative Research 2022 (22S0103).

References

1. Augenstein, I., Rocktäschel, T., Vlachos, A., Bontcheva, K.: Stance detection with bidirectional conditional encoding. In: Proceedings of the 2016 Conference on Empirical Methods in Natural Language Processing, pp. 876–885 (2016). Association for Computational Linguistics, Austin, Texas. https://doi.org/10.18653/v1/D16-1084
2. Caruana, R.: Multitask learn. Mach. Learn. **28**(1), 41–75 (1997)
3. Cohen, J.: Power Primer. Psychol. Bull. **112**(1), 155–159 (1992). https://doi.org/10.1037/0033-2909.112.1.155
4. Devlin, J., Chang, M.W., Lee, K., Toutanova, K.: BERT: pre-training of deep bidirectional transformers for language understanding. In: Proceedings of the 2019 Conference of the North American Chapter of the Association for Computational Linguistics: Human Language Technologies, Vol. 1 (Long and Short Papers), pp. 4171–4186. Association for Computational Linguistics, Minneapolis, Minnesota (2019). https://doi.org/10.18653/v1/N19-1423
5. Digital, A.S.: Visualizing the issue of children on waiting list project. https://www.asahi.com/special/taikijido/. Accessed 20 Sept 2022
6. Fleiss, J.L.: Measuring nominal scale agreement among many raters. Psychol. Bull. **76**(5), 378 (1971)
7. Ishida, T., Seki, Y., Kashino, W., Kando, N.: Extracting citizen feedback from social media by appraisal opinion type viewpoint. J. Nat. Lang. Process. **29**(2), 416–442 (2022). https://doi.org/10.5715/jnlp.29.416
8. Kimura, Y., Shibuki, H.: Annotation of common categories for matching between minutes of municipal assemblies and inhabitants blog. In: Proceedings of the Annual Conference of JSAI. The Japanese Society for Artificial Intelligence JSAI2009(0), 3F2NFC310-3F2NFC310 (2009). https://doi.org/10.11517/pjsai.jsai2009.0_3f2nfc310
9. Kimura, Y., et al.: Overview of the NTCIR-15 QA Lab-Poliinfo-2 task. In: Proceedings of the 15th NTCIR Conference, pp. 101–112 (2020)

10. Kimura, Y., et al.: Overview of the NTCIR-14 QA lab-poliinfo task. In: Proceedings of the 14th NTCIR Conference vol. 14, pp. 121–140 (2019)
11. Kolhatkar, V., Taboada, M.: Constructive language in news comments. In: Proceedings of the First Workshop on Abusive Language Online, pp. 11–17 Association for Computational Linguistics, Vancouver, BC, Canada (2017). https://doi.org/10.18653/v1/W17-3002
12. KYODO NEWS: Yokohama withdraws bid to host casino resort due to local concerns (Sep 2021). https://english.kyodonews.net/news/2021/09/8b903ebe4a1e-yokohama-withdraws-bid-to-host-casino-resort-due-to-local-concerns.html. Accessed 13 July 2022
13. Landis, J.R., Koch, G.G.: The measurement of observer agreement for categorical data. Biometrics **33**(1), 159–174 (1977). http://www.jstor.org/stable/2529310
14. Liu, X., He, P., Chen, W., Gao, J.: Multi-task deep neural networks for natural language understanding. In: Proceedings of the 57th Annual Meeting of the Association for Computational Linguistics, pp. 4487–4496 Association for Computational Linguistics, Florence, Italy (2019). https://doi.org/10.18653/v1/P19-1441
15. Mohammad, S., Kiritchenko, S., Sobhani, P., Zhu, X., Cherry, C.: SemEval-2016 task 6: Detecting stance in tweets. In: Proceedings of the 10th International Workshop on Semantic Evaluation (SemEval-2016), pp. 31–41 Association for Computational Linguistics, San Diego, California (2016). https://doi.org/10.18653/v1/S16-1003
16. Stefanov, P., Darwish, K., Atanasov, A., Nakov, P.: Predicting the topical stance and political leaning of media using tweets. In: Proceedings of the 58th Annual Meeting of the Association for Computational Linguistics, pp. 527–537. Association for Computational Linguistics, Online (2020). https://doi.org/10.18653/v1/2020.acl-main.50
17. Vaswani, A., et al.: Attention Need (2017). https://doi.org/10.48550/ARXIV.1706.03762
18. Xu, C., Paris, C., Nepal, S., Sparks, R.: Cross-target stance classification with self-attention networks. In: Proceedings of the 56th Annual Meeting of the Association for Computational Linguistics (Volume 2: Short Papers), pp. 778–783. Association for Computational Linguistics, Melbourne, Australia (2018). https://doi.org/10.18653/v1/P18-2123

Ensembling Transformers for Cross-domain Automatic Term Extraction

Hanh Thi Hong Tran[1,2,3]([⊠])(ID), Matej Martinc[1](ID), Andraz Pelicon[1](ID),
Antoine Doucet[3](ID), and Senja Pollak[2](ID)

[1] Jožef Stefan International Postgraduate School,
Jamova Cesta 39, 1000 Ljubljana, Slovenia
`tran.hanh@ijs.si`
[2] Jožef Stefan Institute, Jamova Cesta 39, 1000 Ljubljana, Slovenia
[3] University of La Rochelle, 23 Av. Albert Einstein, La Rochelle, France

Abstract. Automatic term extraction plays an essential role in domain language understanding and several natural language processing downstream tasks. In this paper, we propose a comparative study on the predictive power of Transformers-based pretrained language models toward term extraction in a multi-language cross-domain setting. Besides evaluating the ability of monolingual models to extract single- and multi-word terms, we also experiment with ensembles of mono- and multilingual models by conducting the intersection or union on the term output sets of different language models. Our experiments have been conducted on the ACTER corpus covering four specialized domains (Corruption, Wind energy, Equitation, and Heart failure) and three languages (English, French, and Dutch), and on the RSDO5 Slovenian corpus covering four additional domains (Biomechanics, Chemistry, Veterinary, and Linguistics). The results show that the strategy of employing monolingual models outperforms the state-of-the-art approaches from the related work leveraging multilingual models, regarding all the languages except Dutch and French if the term extraction task excludes the extraction of named entity terms. Furthermore, by combining the outputs of the two best performing models, we achieve significant improvements.

Keywords: Automatic term extraction · ATE · Low resource · ACTER · RSDO5 · Monolingual · Cross-domain

1 Introduction

Automatic Term Extraction (ATE) is the task of identifying specialized terminology from the domain-specific corpora. By easing the time and effort needed to manually extract the terms, ATE is not only widely used for terminographical tasks (e.g., glossary construction [26], specialized dictionary creation [22], etc.) but it also contributes to several complex downstream tasks (e.g., machine translation [40], information retrieval [23], sentiment analysis [28], to cite a few).

© The Author(s), under exclusive license to Springer Nature Switzerland AG 2022
Y.-H. Tseng et al. (Eds.): ICADL 2022, LNCS 13636, pp. 90–100, 2022.
https://doi.org/10.1007/978-3-031-21756-2_7

With recent advances in natural language processing (NLP), a new family of deep neural approaches, namely Transformers [38], has been pushing the state-of-the-art (SOTA) in several sequence-labeling semantic tasks, e.g., named entity recognition (NER) [18,37] and machine translation [41], among others. The TermEval 2020 Shared Task on Automatic Term Extraction, organized as part of the CompuTerm workshop [31], presented one of the first opportunities to systematically study and compare various ATE systems with the advent of The Annotated Corpora for Term Extraction Research (ACTER) dataset [31,32], a novel corpora covering four domains and three languages. Regarding Slovenian, the RSDO5[1] corpus [13] was created with texts from four specialized domains. Inspired by the success of Transformers for ATE in the TermEval 2020, we propose an extensive study of their performance in a cross-domain sequence-labeling setting and evaluate different factors that influence extraction effectiveness. The experiments are conducted on two datasets: ACTER and RSDO5 corpora.

Our major contributions can be summarized as the three following points:

- An empirical evaluation of several monolingual and multilingual Transformer-based language models, including both masked (e.g., BERT and its variants) and autoregressive (e.g., XLNet) models, on the cross-domain ATE tasks;
- Filling the research gap in ATE task for Slovenian by experimenting with different models to achieve a new SOTA in the RSDO5 corpus.
- An ensembling Transformer-based model for ATE that further improves the SOTA in the field.

This paper is organised as follows: Sect. 2 presents the related work in term extraction. Next, we introduce our methodology in Sect. 3, including the dataset description, the workflow and experimental settings, as well as the evaluation metrics. The corresponding results are presented in Sect. 4. Finally, we conclude the paper and present future directions in Sect. 5.

2   Related Work

The research into monolingual ATE was first introduced during the 1990 s s [6,15] and the methods at the time included the following two-step procedure: (1) extracting a list of candidate terms; and (2) determining which of these candidate terms are correct using either supervised or unsupervised techniques. We briefly summarize different supervised ATE techniques according to their evolution below.

2.1   Approaches Based on Term Characteristics and Statistics

The first ATE approaches leveraged linguistic knowledge and distinctive linguistic aspects of terms to extract a possible candidate list. Several NLP techniques are employed to obtain the term's linguistic profile (e.g., tokenization, lemmatization, stemming, chunking, etc.). On the other hand, several studies proposed

---

[1] https://www.clarin.si/repository/xmlui/handle/11356/1470.

statistical approaches toward ATE, mostly relying on the assumption that a higher candidate term frequency in a domain-specific corpus (compared to the frequency in the general corpus) implies a higher likelihood that a candidate is an actual term. Some popular statistical measures include termhood [39], unithood [5] or C-value [10]. Many current systems still apply their variations or rely on a hybrid approach combining linguistic and statistical information [16,30].

2.2 Approaches Based on Machine Learning and Deep Learning

The recent advances in word embeddings and deep neural networks have also influenced the field of term extraction. Several embeddings have been investigated for the task at hand, e.g., non-contextual [1,43], contextual [17] word embeddings, and the combination of both [11]. The use of language models for ATE tasks is first documented in the TermEval 2020 [31] on the trilingual ACTER dataset. While the Dutch corpus winner used BiLSTM-based neural architecture with GloVe word embeddings, the English corpus winner [12] fed all possible extracted n-gram combinations into a BERT binary classifier. Several Transformer variations have also been investigated [12] (e.g., BERT, RoBERTa, CamemBERT, etc.) but no systematic comparison of their performance has been conducted. Later, the HAMLET approach [33] proposed a hybrid adaptable machine learning system that combines linguistic and statistical clues to detect terms. Recently, sequence-labeling approaches became the most popular modeling option. They were first introduced by [17] and then employed by [20] to compare several ATE methods (e.g., binary sequence classifier, sequence classifier, token classifier). Finally, cross-lingual sequence labeling proposed in [4,20,35] demonstrates the capability of multilingual models and the potential of cross-lingual learning.

2.3 Approaches for Slovenian Term Extraction

The ATE research for the less-resourced languages, especially Slovenian, is still hindered by the lack of gold standard corpora and the limited use of neural methods. Regarding the corpora, the recently compiled Slovenian KAS corpus [8] was quickly followed by the domain-specific RSDO5 corpus [14]. Regarding the methodologies, techniques evolved from purely statistical [39] to more machine learning based approaches. For example, [25] extracted the initial candidate terms using the CollTerm tool [29], a rule-based system employing a language-specific set of term patterns from the Slovenian SketchEngine module [9]. The derived candidate list was then filtered using a machine learning classifier with features representing statistical measures. Another recent approach [30] focused on the evolutionary algorithm for term extraction and alignment. Finally, [36] was one of the first to explore the deep neural approaches for Slovenian term extraction, employing XLMRoBERTa in cross- and multilingual settings.

3   Methods

We briefly describe our chosen datasets in Sect. 3.1, the general methodology in Sect. 3.2 and the chosen evaluation metrics in Sect. 3.3.

3.1   Datasets

The experiments have been conducted on two datasets: ACTER v1.5 [31] and RSDO5 v1.1 [13]. The ACTER dataset is a manually annotated collection of 12 corpora covering four domains, Corruption (corp), Dressage (equi), Wind energy (wind), and Heart failure (htfl), in three languages, English (en), French (fr), and Dutch (nl). It has two versions of gold standard annotations: one including both terms and named entities (NES), and the other containing only terms (ANN). Meanwhile, the RSDO5 corpus v1.1 [13] includes texts in Slovenian (sl), a less-resourced Slavic language with rich morphology. Compiled during the RSDO national project, the corpus contains 12 documents covering four domains, Biomechanics (bim), Chemistry (kem), Veterinary (vet), and Linguistics (ling).

3.2   Workflow

We consider ATE as a sequence-labeling task [35] with IOB labeling regime [20, 33]. The model is first trained to predict a label for each token in the input text sequence, and then applied to the unseen test data. From the token sequences labeled as terms, the final candidate term list for the test data is composed.

3.2.1   Empirical Evaluation of Pretrained Language Models

We conduct a systematic evaluation of mono- and multilingual Transformers-based models on the ATE task modeled as sequence labeling. The models were obtained from Huggingface[2] according to the number of downloads and likes criteria. The chosen models are presented in Fig. 1. Regarding the multilingual systems, we investigate the performance of mBERT [7] (*bert-base-multilingual-uncased*), mDistilBERT [34] (*distilbert-base-multilingual-cased*), InforXLM [2] (*microsoft/ infoxlm-base*), and XLMRoBERTa [3] (*xlm-roberta-base*). All the chosen multilingual models are fine-tuned in a monolingual fashion due to findings from the related work [20,35] showing that no (or only marginal) gains are obtained if the model is fine-tuned on the multilingual training data.

Regarding the monolingual models, we evaluate several English autoencoding Transformer-based models, including ALBERT [19] (*albert-base-v1* and *albert-base-v2*), BERT [7] (*bert-base-uncased*), DistilBERT [34] (*distilbert-base-uncased*), ELECTRA (*electra-small-generator*) and RoBERTa [24] (*xlm-roberta-base*), and one autoregressive model, XLNet [42] (*xlnet-base-cased*). For French, we use CamemBERT [27] (*camembert-base*) and FlauBERT [21] (*flaubert_ base_ uncased*), for Dutch, we employ BERTje (*bert-base-dutch-cased*) and RobBERT (*robBERT-base* and *robbert-v2-dutch-base*) models, and for Slovenian, we choose SloBERTa (*sloberta*), the RoBERTa-based model trained on a large Slovenian corpus.

---

[2] https://huggingface.co/models.

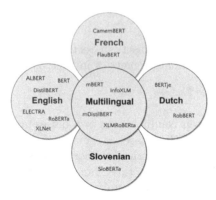

Fig. 1. Empirical evaluation of pretrained language models on the ATE task.

3.2.2   Ensemble of Transformer Models

Regarding results in Sect. 3.2.1, we propose a novel ensembling approach based on Transformer models for ATE task as we observe the general tendency for Precision to be better than Recall for all but few monolingual and multilingual models tested (see Tables 1 and 2). This leads us to believe that by combing the outputs of different models, we could achieve improvements in Recall and by extension also in the overall F1-score. We consider two strategies for combining the outputs from different models of the ensemble, namely the union and the intersection of the candidate term lists from the models of the ensemble. See the entire procedure in Fig. 2.

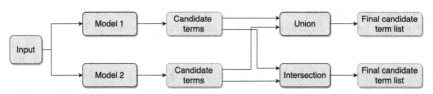

Fig. 2. The general ensembling workflow.

We hypothesize that by combining the outputs of two models, we might be able to significantly improve the Recall of the term extraction system. To validate this hypothesis, we test three combinations: Combine the outputs of the (1) best mono- and multilingual models; (2) two best monolingual models; and (3) two best multilingual models.

3.3   Evaluation Metrics

We evaluate each term extraction system by comparing the aggregated list of candidate terms extracted on the level of the whole test set with the manually annotated gold standard term list using Precision, Recall, and F1-score. These evaluation metrics have also been used in the related work [12,20,31].

4 Results

We first present the results of mono- and multilingual Transformer-based models obtained on ACTER and RSDO5 test sets compared with the SOTAs. Then, we demonstrate the impact of the ensemble post-processing step.

4.1 Monolingual Evaluation

4.1.1 ACTER Corpus

Not many approaches have been tested on the ACTER corpus v1.5 due to its novelty. Thus, we apply the approach proposed by [20] (i.e., employing XLM-RoBERTa as a token classifier), which achieved SOTA on the previous corpus version, and consider it as a baseline. The Heart failure domain is used a test set, same as in TermEval 2020.

Table 1. Results of monolingual term extraction on the ACTER dataset.

	Models	ANN			NES		
		Precision	Recall	F1-score	Precision	Recall	F1-score
Mono	albert-base-v1	52.58	47.40	49.86	54.42	54.63	54.52
	albert-base-v2	49.85	48.50	49.17	57.01	55.13	56.05
	bert-base-uncased	**59.06**	32.44	41.88	61.42	47.50	53.57
	distilbert-base-uncased	58.24	38.75	46.54	61.06	48.24	53.90
	electra-small-generator	56.46	46.80	51.18	58.17	47.31	52.18
	roberta-base	58.10	51.04	54.34	**62.28**	56.30	**59.14**
	xlnet-base-cased	56.50	**53.92**	**55.18**	58.34	**57.30**	57.82
Multi	bert-base-multilingual-uncased	55.21	35.24	43.02	**62.06**	49.44	55.04
	distilbert-base-multilingual-cased	55.14	45.45	49.83	57.10	54.20	55.61
	infoxlm-base	**57.67**	**54.64**	**56.11**	61.18	54.48	**57.64**
	xlm-roberta-base (baseline)	57.34	51.46	54.24	58.80	55.52	57.11

(a) English corpus

	Models	ANN			NES		
		Precision	Recall	F1-score	Precision	Recall	F1-score
Mono	camembert-base	**70.51**	**44.97**	**54.92**	70.74	52.23	**60.09**
	flauberta	75.91	26.17	38.92	75.28	39.01	51.39
Multi	bert-base-multilingual-uncased	67.77	37.66	48.42	69.39	**48.99**	57.43
	distilbert-base-multilingual-cased	64.45	43.45	51.91	65.20	48.78	55.81
	infoxlm-base	68.74	39.77	50.39	**71.10**	48.90	**57.95**
	xlm-roberta-base (baseline)	**68.85**	**48.61**	**56.99**	70.71	46.46	56.08

(b) French corpus

	Models	ANN			NES		
		Precision	Recall	F1-score	Precision	Recall	F1-score
Mono	bert-base-dutch-cased	65.59	**65.53**	**65.56**	67.61	**66.02**	**66.81**
	robBERT-base	69.58	36.84	48.17	71.63	55.01	62.23
	robbert-v2-dutch-base	**71.56**	36.40	48.25	**73.58**	55.72	63.42
Multi	bert-base-multilingual-uncased	**70.67**	62.49	66.33	72.34	63.71	67.75
	distilbert-base-multilingual-cased	69.80	61.28	65.26	69.45	**66.15**	67.76
	infoxlm-base	70.43	66.73	**68.53**	73.47	64.24	**68.55**
	xlm-roberta-base (baseline)	68.53	**67.94**	68.23	**73.93**	60.65	66.63

(c) Dutch corpus

In general, multilingual pretrained models outperform the monolingual ones in Recall and F1-score when applied for extraction of the ANN annotations in all three languages. If named entities are included (NES), monolingual models outperform multilingual models in two (English and French) out of three languages in the ACTER dataset. When it comes to individual models, InfoXLM outperforms other mono- and multilingual models in the F1-score on the Dutch corpus (for both ANN and NES) and on the English corpus (for ANN). If we compare the results of our study with the XLMRoBERTa baseline using the same monolingual settings from [20], our best-performing models surpass the baseline in all cases (e.g., the F1-score increases by 1.87% on ANN and 1.5% on NES in the English corpus; 4.01% on French NES; 0.3% on ANN and 1.92% on NES in the Dutch corpus) except for the French ANN annotations.

4.1.2 RSDO5 Corpus

We also compare the performance of different mono- and multilingual models on the RSDO5 corpus, Here, we evaluate the models on all domains as demonstrated in Table 2. By using two domains from the RSDO5 corpus for training, the third one for validation, and the last one for testing, all the models prove to have relatively consistent performance across different combinations. The monolingual SloBERTa model outperforms other approaches (including the XLMRoBERTa baseline from [36]) in all cases by a relatively large margin in F1-score. By employing this model and looking at the best performing train/validation combinations for each test domain, we improve the SOTA baseline in the Linguistics domain by 2.21%, in Veterinary by 2.35%, in Chemistry by 5.26%, and in Biomechanics by 2.66% regarding F1-score. Our results, thus, set a new SOTA on the Slovenian corpus.

Table 2. Results of monolingual term extraction on the RSDO5 dataset.

Training	Val	Test	xlm-roberta-base			sloberta			infoxlm-base		
			Precion	Recall	F1-score	Precion	Recall	F1-score	Precion	Recall	F1-score
bim + kem	vet	ling	69.55	64.05	66.69	73.23	70.51	71.84	68.37	71.38	69.84
bim + vet	kem	ling	66.20	72.38	69.15	73.91	73.53	73.72	67.74	71.46	69.55
kem + vet	bim	ling	69.48	73.66	71.51	**74.45**	**73.96**	**74.20**	73.71	66.90	70.14
bim + kem	ling	vet	71.06	66.72	68.82	77.56	**65.96**	**71.29**	71.04	63.69	67.16
bim + ling	kem	vet	72.66	65.59	68.94	**78.33**	65.31	71.23	66.88	68.93	67.89
ling + kem	bim	vet	69.30	68.07	68.68	76.66	64.89	70.29	72.69	63.63	67.86
bim + vet	ling	kem	68.67	55.13	61.16	72.14	65.88	68.87	67.77	60.40	63.87
bim + ling	vet	kem	70.23	59.24	64.27	70.29	**68.45**	69.36	72.00	56.58	63.37
ling + vet	bim	kem	70.14	60.27	64.83	**73.52**	66.96	**70.09**	71.22	59.49	64.83
vet + kem	ling	bim	62.25	65.20	63.69	67.97	67.36	67.66	63.60	60.59	62.06
vet + ling	kem	bim	62.35	63.99	63.16	**68.97**	66.62	**67.77**	56.66	67.53	61.62
ling + kem	vet	bim	63.51	66.80	65.11	67.15	**67.79**	67.47	60.61	64.04	62.28

Training	Val	Test	bert-base-multilingual-uncased			distilbert-base-multilingual-cased		
			Precion	Recall	F1-score	Precion	Recall	F1-score
bim + kem	vet	ling	66.77	65.86	66.31	61.82	53.38	57.29
bim + vet	kem	ling	66.80	68.01	67.40	59.14	67.20	62.91
kem + vet	bim	ling	65.97	69.62	67.75	60.94	58.16	59.52
bim + kem	ling	vet	68.18	61.56	64.70	63.76	58.70	61.13
bim + ling	kem	vet	68.58	65.46	66.98	65.83	58.15	61.75
ling + kem	bim	vet	69.12	60.61	64.59	66.01	54.02	59.42
bim + vet	ling	kem	65.35	59.73	62.41	55.73	60.52	58.03
bim + ling	vet	kem	65.53	63.22	64.35	60.15	55.83	57.91
ling + vet	bim	kem	67.32	53.96	59.90	59.53	57.70	58.60
vet + kem	ling	bim	62.63	60.85	61.73	57.84	55.84	56.82
vet + ling	kem	bim	65.25	58.30	61.58	60.62	56.36	58.41
ling + kem	vet	bim	62.69	63.61	63.15	62.04	52.44	56.84

4.2   Transformer Ensembling

We also evaluate the performance of the proposed ensembling approach described in Sect. 3.2.2. The improvements/decline in performance over the best single model on different languages of the ACTER dataset are shown in Fig. 3. The results indicate that combining the acquired term sets of the two best-performing classifiers (no matter what type of classifiers they are) using the union always results in the biggest gain.

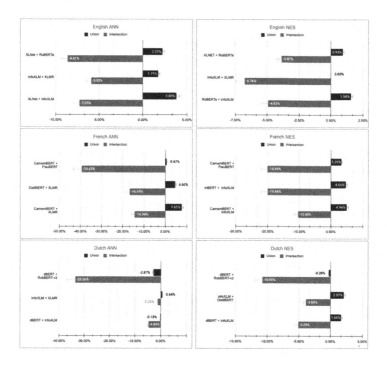

Fig. 3. F1-score improvement by combining two best classifiers in ACTER.

5   Conclusion

We proposed an empirical evaluation of different mono- and multilingual Transformers based models on the monolingual sequence-labeling cross-domain term extraction. The experiments were conducted on the trilingual ACTER dataset and the Slovenian RSDO5 dataset. Furthermore, we tested how ensembling different mono- or multilingual models affects the performance of the overall term extractor. The results demonstrate that multilingual models outperform the monolingual ones in Recall and F1-score when applied for ANN extraction. Meanwhile, monolingual models capture the information about terms better than multilingual ones when it comes to the extraction of NES annotations. We also showed that by ensembling different Transformer models we can obtain further boosts in performance for all languages. As a consequence, we established the new SOTA on the ACTER and RSDO5 datasets.

In the future, we would like to take advantage of prompt engineering by considering ATE as a language model ranking problem in a sequence-to-sequence framework, where original sentences and statement templates filled by candidate terms are regarded as the source sequence and the target.

Acknowledgements. The work was partially supported by the Slovenian Research Agency (ARRS) core research programme Knowledge Technologies (P2-0103), and the Ministry of Culture of the Republic of Slovenia through the project Development of Slovene in Digital Environment (RSDO). The first author was partly funded by Region Nouvelle Aquitaine. This work has also been supported by the TERMITRAD (2020–2019-8510010) project funded by the Nouvelle-Aquitaine Region, France.

References

1. Amjadian, E., Inkpen, D., Paribakht, T., Faez, F.: Local-global vectors to improve unigram terminology extraction. In: Proceedings of the 5th International Workshop on Computational Terminology (Computerm2016), pp. 2–11 (2016)
2. Chi, Z., et al.: InfoXLM: an information-theoretic framework for cross-lingual language model pre-training. In: Proceedings of the 2021 Conference of the North American Chapter of the Association for Computational Linguistics: Human Language Technologies, pp. 3576–3588 (2021)
3. Conneau, A., et al.: Unsupervised cross-lingual representation learning at scale. arXiv preprint arXiv:1911.02116 (2019)
4. Conneau, A., et al.: Unsupervised cross-lingual representation learning at scale. In: ACL (2020)
5. Daille, B., Gaussier, É., Langé, J.M.: Towards automatic extraction of monolingual and bilingual terminology. In: COLING 1994 Volume 1: The 15th International Conference on Computational Linguistics (1994)
6. Damerau, F.J.: Evaluating computer-generated domain-oriented vocabularies. Inf. Process. Manag. **26**(6), 791–801 (1990)
7. Devlin, J., Chang, M.W., Lee, K., Toutanova, K.: BERT: pre-training of deep bidirectional transformers for language understanding. arXiv preprint arXiv:1810.04805 (2018)
8. Erjavec, T., Fišer, D., Ljubešić, N.: The KAS corpus of slovenian academic writing. Lang. Resour. Eval. **55**(2), 551–583 (2021)
9. Fišer, D., Suchomel, V., Jakubícek, M.: Terminology extraction for academic slovene using sketch engine. In: Tenth Workshop on Recent Advances in Slavonic Natural Language Processing, RASLAN 2016, pp. 135–141 (2016)
10. Frantzi, K.T., Ananiadou, S., Tsujii, J.: The *C-value/NC-value* method of automatic recognition for multi-word terms. In: Nikolaou, C., Stephanidis, C. (eds.) ECDL 1998. LNCS, vol. 1513, pp. 585–604. Springer, Heidelberg (1998). https://doi.org/10.1007/3-540-49653-X_35
11. Gao, Y., Yuan, Yu.: Feature-less end-to-end nested term extraction. In: Tang, J., Kan, M.-Y., Zhao, D., Li, S., Zan, H. (eds.) NLPCC 2019. LNCS (LNAI), vol. 11839, pp. 607–616. Springer, Cham (2019). https://doi.org/10.1007/978-3-030-32236-6_55

12. Hazem, A., Bouhandi, M., Boudin, F., Daille, B.: TermEval 2020: TALN-LS2N system for automatic term extraction. In: Proceedings of the 6th International Workshop on Computational Terminology, pp. 95–100 (2020)
13. Jemec Tomazin, M., Trojar, M., Atelšek, S., Fajfar, T., Erjavec, T., Žagar Karer, M.: Corpus of term-annotated texts RSDO5 1.1 (2021). http://hdl.handle.net/11356/1470 slovenian language resource repository CLARIN.SI
14. Jemec Tomazin, M., Trojar, M., Žagar, M., Atelšek, S., Fajfar, T., Erjavec, T.: Corpus of term-annotated texts RSDO5 1.0 (2021)
15. Justeson, J.S., Katz, S.M.: Technical terminology: some linguistic properties and an algorithm for identification in text. Nat. Lang. Eng. **1**(1), 9–27 (1995)
16. Kessler, R., Béchet, N., Berio, G.: Extraction of terminology in the field of construction. In: 2019 First International Conference on Digital Data Processing (DDP), pp. 22–26 IEEE (2019)
17. Kucza, M., Niehues, J., Zenkel, T., Waibel, A., Stüker, S.: Term extraction via neural sequence labeling a comparative evaluation of strategies using recurrent neural networks. In: INTERSPEECH, pp. 2072–2076 (2018)
18. Lample, G., Ballesteros, M., Subramanian, S., Kawakami, K., Dyer, C.: neural architectures for named entity recognition. In: Proceedings of the 2016 Conference of the North American Chapter of the Association for Computational Linguistics: Human Language Technologies, pp. 260–270 (2016)
19. Lan, Z., Chen, M., Goodman, S., Gimpel, K., Sharma, P., Soricut, R.: ALBERT: a lite BERT for self-supervised learning of language representations. arXiv preprint arXiv:1909.11942 (2019)
20. Lang, C., Wachowiak, L., Heinisch, B., Gromann, D.: Transforming term extraction: transformer-based approaches to multilingual term extraction across domains. In: Findings of the Association for Computational Linguistics: ACL-IJCNLP 2021, pp. 3607–3620 (2021)
21. Le, H., et al.: FlauBERT: unsupervised language model pre-training for French. In: LREC (2020)
22. Serrec, A., L'Homme, M.C., Drouin, P., Kraif, O.: Automating the compilation of specialized dictionaries: use and analysis of term extraction and lexical alignment. Terminol. Int. J. Theor. Appl. Issues Special. Commun. **16**(1), 77–106 (2010)
23. Lingpeng, Y., Donghong, J., Guodong, Z., Yu, N.: Improving retrieval effectiveness by using key terms in top retrieved documents. In: Losada, D.E., Fernández-Luna, J.M. (eds.) ECIR 2005. LNCS, vol. 3408, pp. 169–184. Springer, Heidelberg (2005). https://doi.org/10.1007/978-3-540-31865-1_13
24. Liu, Y., et al.: RoBERTa: a robustly optimized BERT pretraining approach. arXiv preprint arXiv:1907.11692 (2019)
25. Ljubešić, N., Fišer, D., Erjavec, T.: KAS-term: extracting slovene terms from doctoral theses via supervised machine learning. In: Ekštein, K. (ed.) TSD 2019. LNCS (LNAI), vol. 11697, pp. 115–126. Springer, Cham (2019). https://doi.org/10.1007/978-3-030-27947-9_10
26. Maldonado, A., Lewis, D.: Self-tuning ongoing terminology extraction retrained on terminology validation decisions. In: Proceedings of The 12th International Conference on Terminology and Knowledge Engineering, pp. 91–100 (2016)
27. Martin, L., et al.: CamemBERT: a tasty French language model. arXiv preprint arXiv:1911.03894 (2019)
28. Pavlopoulos, J., Androutsopoulos, I.: Aspect term extraction for sentiment analysis: new datasets, new evaluation measures and an improved unsupervised method. In: Proceedings of the 5th Workshop on Language Analysis for Social Media (LASM), pp. 44–52 (2014)

29. Jagarlamudi, J., Daumé, H.: Extracting multilingual topics from unaligned comparable corpora. In: Gurrin, C., et al. (eds.) ECIR 2010. LNCS, vol. 5993, pp. 444–456. Springer, Heidelberg (2010). https://doi.org/10.1007/978-3-642-12275-0_39

30. Repar, A., Podpečan, V., Vavpetič, A., Lavrač, N., Pollak, S.: TermEnsembler: an ensemble learning approach to bilingual term extraction and alignment. Terminol. Int. J. Theoretical Appl. Issues Special. Commun. 25(1), 93–120 (2019)

31. Rigouts Terryn, A., Hoste, V., Drouin, P., Lefever, E.: TermEval 2020: shared task on automatic term extraction using the annotated corpora for term extraction research (acter) dataset. In: 6th International Workshop on Computational Terminology (COMPUTERM 2020), pp. 85–94 European Language Resources Association (ELRA) (2020)

32. Rigouts Terryn, A., Hoste, V., Lefever, E.: In no uncertain terms: a dataset for monolingual and multilingual automatic term extraction from comparable corpora. Lang. Resour. Eval. 54(2), 385–418 (2020)

33. Rigouts Terryn, A., Hoste, V., Lefever, E.: HAMLET: Hybrid adaptable machine learning approach to extract terminology. Terminol. (2021)

34. Sanh, V., Debut, L., Chaumond, J., Wolf, T.: DistilBERT: a distilled version of BERT: smaller, faster, cheaper and lighter. arXiv preprint arXiv:1910.01108 (2019)

35. Tran, H.T.H., Martinc, M., Doucet, A., Pollak, S.: Can cross-domain term extraction benefit from cross-lingual transfer? In: International Conference on Discovery Science, pp. 363–378. Springer (2022)

36. Tran, H.T.H., Martinc, M., Doucet, A., Pollak, S.: A transformer-based sequence-labeling approach to the slovenian cross-domain automatic term extraction. In: Submitted to Slovenian conference on Language Technologies and Digital Humanities (2022, under review)

37. Hanh, T.T.H., Doucet, A., Sidere, N., Moreno, J.G., Pollak, S.: Named entity recognition architecture combining contextual and global features. In: Ke, H.-R., Lee, C.S., Sugiyama, K. (eds.) ICADL 2021. LNCS, vol. 13133, pp. 264–276. Springer, Cham (2021). https://doi.org/10.1007/978-3-030-91669-5_21

38. Vaswani, A., et al.: Attention is all you need. arXiv preprint arXiv:1706.03762 (2017)

39. Vintar, S.: Bilingual term recognition revisited: the bag-of-equivalents term alignment approach and its evaluation. Terminol. Int. J. Theoretical Appl. Issues Specialized Commun. 16(2), 141–158 (2010)

40. Wolf, P., Bernardi, U., Federmann, C., Hunsicker, S.: From statistical term extraction to hybrid machine translation. In: Proceedings of the 15th Annual conference of the European Association for Machine Translation (2011)

41. Yang, J., et al.: Towards making the most of BERT in neural machine translation. In: Proceedings of the AAAI Conference on Artificial Intelligence, vol. 34, pp. 9378–9385 (2020)

42. Yang, Z., Dai, Z., Yang, Y., Carbonell, J., Salakhutdinov, R., Le, Q.V.: XLNet: generalized autoregressive pretraining for language understanding. arXiv preprint arXiv:1906.08237 (2019)

43. Zhang, Z., Gao, J., Ciravegna, F.: Semre-rank: improving automatic term extraction by incorporating semantic relatedness with personalised pagerank. ACM Trans. Knowl. Discov. Data (TKDD) 12(5), 1–41 (2018)

Impact Analysis of Different Effective Loss Functions by Using Deep Convolutional Neural Network for Face Recognition

Anh D. Nguyen[1], Dat T. Nguyen[1], Hai N. Dao[2(✉)], Hai H. Le[1], and Nam Q. Tran[3]

[1] VNU University of Engineering and Technology, Hanoi, Vietnam
{19021208,19020126,hailh}@vnu.edu.vn
[2] VNU Information Technology Institute, Hanoi, Vietnam
namhai249@vnu.edu.vn
[3] Dai Nam University, Hanoi, Vietnam

Abstract. Smart Library Automation System is increasingly attractive as an effective digital library system. Adapting automation in the library helps reduce the duplication of work, time-saving, and boosts work efficiency. One such significant feature is face recognition integrated. With this application, the system can use face recognition to enter and get the details of an end user. In recent years, face recognition has achieved many prodigious accomplishments based on Deep Convolutional Neural Networks (DCNN). In addition to constructing large face datasets, designing new effective DCNN architectures and loss functions are two trends to improve the performance of face recognition systems. Therefore, many studies have been published in state-of-the-art methods, making high-accuracy face recognition systems more possible than days in the past. However, it is still difficult for all research communities to train robust face recognition models because it depends heavily on their resources. This paper investigates and analyzes the effect of several effective loss functions based on softmax. Moreover, we also evaluate how hyper-parameter settings can impact the optimization process as well as the final recognition performance of the model trained by re-implementing these methods. The results of our experiments achieve state-of-the-art figures, which show the proposed method's massive potential in improving face recognition performance.

Keywords: Face recognition · DCNN · Effective loss function

1 Introduction

Face recognition (FR) has been a prominent and long-standing topic in the research community. It is widely applied in numerous areas such as social security, health, education, banking, retail, etc. FR plays a crucial role in automated library systems with a digital library. FR applications help save time and

© The Author(s), under exclusive license to Springer Nature Switzerland AG 2022
Y.-H. Tseng et al. (Eds.): ICADL 2022, LNCS 13636, pp. 101–111, 2022.
https://doi.org/10.1007/978-3-031-21756-2_8

avoid repetitive book issuing and returning work. Since Convolutional Neural Networks (CNN) have been proposed in recent years, the literature has witnessed the innovation of Deep Convolutional Neural Networks (DCNN) architectures that achieve remarkable results consecutively. There are many modern face datasets, such as MegaFace [10], MS1M [5], WebFace20M [26], ... which encompass a huge amount of identities and samples are released. It creates many chances for researchers to train effectively large and deep face recognition networks based DCNN such as [1,2,6,16] which present better performance than the human capability in FR. However, it is not enough to satisfy the expectation of the research community. Therefore, most recent researchers have focused on improving the classification loss function, which plays a crucial role in learning accurate FR models. Current popular loss functions for training DCNNs are mostly softmax-based classification loss. Since the learned features with original softmax loss cannot maximize inter-class variance and minimize the intra-class variance of embedding feature vectors, researchers try to design new effective loss functions based on it, which enhance discriminative power as well as still remain basic requirements of softmax. [15,21,23] have proposed some effective methods and gradually improved the accuracy by elaborating the objective of learning.

Challenges: The modern methods for augmenting training datasets and optimizing CNN architectures lead to significant achievements nowadays. However, most FR models that get State-of-the-Art (SOTA) accuracy have been trained on cost-strong computing hardware systems for a long time by experts. Unfortunately, the academic community is not able to access these resources. Many of them pragmatically own limited computational competence systems. In order to construct the FR system from scratch, they have to adopt medium-size datasets, customize DCNN architectures, and adjust the hyper-parameter settings for training. All of these changes can lead to unexpected results. Choosing appreciate loss functions is a easy way in order to improve performance of FR models. On the other hand, academic community makes the effort to design an effective loss function. Each loss function requires distinct constraints of data pre-processing, modifying CNN architectures,... It is necessary to select loss functions that are able to bring higher performance with respective lower implementation costs.

Contributions: From the aforementioned challenges, in this paper, we investigate state-of-the-art losses based on softmax, including CosFace, ArcFace, and MagFace to verify and understand the efficiency of these loss function for training deep neuron networks. Each function generally includes several hyperparameters, which substantially impact the final performance and is usually difficult to tune. We conducted evaluation on several face benchmarks, including LFW, CFP-FP, AgeDB-30, CALFW and CPLFW.

The remainder of this paper is organized as follows. In §2, we describe our main problem and introduce some related work in FR. §3 presents our proposal. In §4, we show our experiments, evaluate our proposed work, and provide some comparisons. Finally, §5 gives the conclusions and future work.

2 Problem Formulation and Related Work

2.1 Face Recognition

Face recognition aims to match an image of someone's face to all their representations stored in the database. Typically, most FR systems have three components, primarily face detection, feature extraction, and classification. Face detection is a preprocessing stage that detects a unique face and aligns a face in the image. Next, feature extraction, which takes input as preprocessed images, adopts a DCNN to extract deep discriminative features. It returns an embedding vector as the feature representation of a face.

The classification process contains precisely two sub-processes: *(i) face verification:* calculate the one-to-one similarity between two images to determine where those pairs belong to the identical individual, and *(ii) face identification:* seek an individual by one-to-many computing similarities between a probe and all images stored in a database to identify the specific identity of a face among a set of the facial gallery. This paper mainly focuses on feature extraction and classification in face verification tasks.

2.2 Loss Function for Deep Face Recognition

Up to now, prevailing loss functions for deep FR are mainly based on variants of softmax loss. To address a defect in the pure softmax loss, which does not run well in reducing the intra-class variation (i.e., making features of the same class compact) [19], one of the most effective approaches obtained excellent performance on FR is to add the margin into the primitive loss. We can split it into two ways:

Adding Fixed Margin into Softmax. Several efforts have been proposed to enhance the discriminative power of the softmax loss by adding a fixed penalty margin for training FR models [12,19]. Margin is added to implement the constraint: the maximum inter-class distance < the minimum inter-class distance + margin. Then, learned features can be sufficiently discriminative. These methods succeed in enforcing intra-class compactness and inter-class discrepancy to improve FR performance. At the same time, they can be implemented easily with several uncomplicated code lines in the deep learning frameworks such as Pytorch or Tensorflow.

Adding Adaptive Margin into Softmax. Although the above methods have reached the SOTA performance on a number of benchmarks, they still remain a handful of drawbacks. One of them is that low-quality images may easily impact the performance of these losses. Thus, more recently, many researchers have proposed an adaptive margin strategy to automatically tune those hyper-parameters to avoid putting too much faith in the fixed margin and generate more effective supervision during training. Some of them improve inherent fixed margin-base softmax loss functions to be more flexible [9,23]. In addition to the adaptive margin, some others also proposed adding extra factors into the function as [13] for enhancing final recognition performance. Adding adaptive margin approach attempts to adopt real data with an inconsistent inter-and intra-class variation. It might limit the discriminative power and generalizability of the FR model when using fixed marginal penalty softmax losses.

3   Analysis Approach

3.1   DCNN Architecture

Training facial recognition models can be divided into two stages: training and testing. Specifically, as illustrated in Fig. 1, face images from both training set (a) and testing set (d) are processed to handle variations before feeding into feature extraction. This process serves a purpose to alleviate the effect of the environment's condition on the performance of FR. During the training stage, a DCNN (b) is utilized to extract deep discriminative features, DCNN returns an embedding vector as a feature representation of a face. Like training stage, these embedding vectors are handled in the testing stages. However, the classification layer in the DCNN is often discarded at the testing stage. Next, during the training stage, these features will be applied to a loss function (c) which optimizes deep discriminative features. That loss function is adopted to learn the FR model accurately. After the in-depth features are extracted, face matching methods (e) come to conduct the feature classification process. While face matching methods take advantage of cosine or L2 distance, they are employed to compute similarity scores among test images in the testing stage. All our experiments are conducted based on the architecture that we demonstrated above.

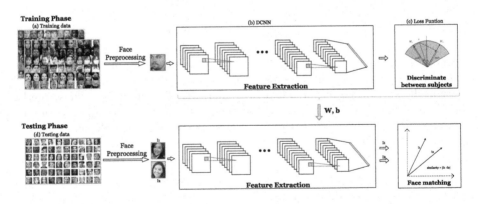

Fig. 1. Overview of training Deep Face Recognition model

Back to the problem mentioned earlier, we have to adopt the typical DCNN architecture that is ResNet50 [6] as a feature extractor and use the moderate public dataset, CASIA-WEBFACE in the training stage to be compatible with our resources. Despite being competent for these possibilities, building a facial recognition system with superior performance to humans is like [18], and there is a significant disparity between this system's accuracy and SOTA solutions. Achievements in studies of the loss function encourage us to apply these accomplishments to our situation as we search for ways to enhance our FR performance without additional hardware setup requirements. As a result, the fundamental direction we focus on in this paper is applying various loss functions to the training model in order to enhance FR performance and achieve SOTA results.

3.2 Effective Loss Function Analysis

As mentioned in 2.2, the margin-based softmax loss functions are now widely used for training FR models. Many new loss functions are published with SOTA performance for a short period. However, not all of them can easily implement or improve accuracy with our resources. Thus, we considered some functions with two criteria: (i) do not require intricately prepared samples before being fed into training; and (ii) avoid refining backbone unnecessarily and adding extra layers excessively.

Based on these criteria, we determined to use three loss functions comprise CosFace [20], ArcFace [3] and MagFace [13] for learning of DCNN model. Ideologically, to improve the discriminative competence, these loss functions implement a margin penalty on primitive softmax loss. The difference is that CosFace and ArcFace add a fixed margin while MagFace belongs to a category that adds adaptive margin into softmax.

In detail, let $\mathcal{D} = \{x_i, y_i\}_{i=1}^{N}$ where x_i denotes an input image with its corresponding label y_i and N is the number of images. In the training stage, after being fed an image, the last fully connected layer of the neuron network returns a d-dimensional embedding vector $f_i \in \mathbb{R}^d$. By defining the angle θ_j between f_i and j-th class center $w_j \in \mathbb{R}^d$ as $w_j^T f_i = \|w_j\| \|f_i\| \cos\theta_j$, CosFace, ArcFace can be formulated as follows:

$$\mathcal{L}_{CosFace} = -\log \frac{e^{s(\cos\theta_{y_i} - m)}}{e^{s(\cos\theta_{y_i} - m)} + \sum_{j \neq y_i} e^{s\cos\theta_j}} \tag{1}$$

$$\mathcal{L}_{ArcFace} = -\log \frac{e^{s\cos(\theta_{y_i} + m)}}{e^{s\cos(\theta_{y_i} + m)} + \sum_{j \neq y_i} e^{s\cos\theta_j}} \tag{2}$$

where m denotes the additive angular margin and s is the scaling parameter multiplied due to the norm of w and x in the tenet of all these loss functions. It is two key factors added into the Softmax to enhance performance. Specifically, we fix $\|w_j\| = 1$ by L_2 normalization and presume that $\|f_i\| = s$ is fixed [20]. Compared with the Softmax, margin-based variants of the Softmax loss like ArcFace and CosFace extends the decision boundary between different classes in the cosine space by a specified m and the parameter s scales up the narrow range of cosine distances, making the logits more discriminative.

In contrast, for MagFace, instead of using a specified scalar parameter as margin, it introduces two auxiliary functions related to the magnitude $a_i = \|f_i\|$

without normalization of each feature f_i, the magnitude-aware angular margin $m(a_i)$ and the regularizer $g(a_i)$ following a natural institute: High norm features are easily recognizable and large margin pushes features of high norm closer to class centers. With all previous notions, we define MagFace like:

$$\mathcal{L}_{MagFace} = -\log \frac{e^{s\cos(\theta_{y_i}+m(a_i))}}{e^{s\cos(\theta_{y_i}+m(a_i))} + \sum_{j \neq y_i} e^{s\cos\theta_j}} + \lambda_g g(a_i) \qquad (3)$$

λ_g indicates regularization losses weights. Two extra functions, $m(.)$ and $g(.)$, are convex functions that are presented in the MagFace's supplementary [13]. Due to word count constraints, we will not be able to cover everything in this paper, so we recommend reading the original paper for setting details. Based on Eqs. 1, 2 and 3, it is easy to implement three loss functions through only adjusting logits before passing it into softmax-cross entropy loss [3].

4   Evaluation

We investigate the impact analysis of several effective loss functions by performing the deep experiment of FR using DCNN models.

4.1   Dataset Preparation

For training, we choose CASIA-WEBFACE [22] containing 494,414 images of 10,575 different individuals. For evaluating the performance of DCNN-based FR, we choose several popular datasets such as LFW [7], CFP-FP [17], AgeDB-30 [14], CALFW [25] and CPLFW [24]. In there, LFW, CFP-FP, and AgeDB-30 are considered easy benchmarks and conversely, CALFW and CPLFW are higher challenges because the image quality is considered the problematic benchmark. For convenience, we fetch all datasets from the available source, InsightFace (*https://github.com/deepinsight/insightface*), in which all images are aligned to 112×112 in as the settings in ArcFace [3].

4.2   Model Training Configuration

DCNN Model Setting: All the DCNN models are trained from scratch. We implemented a widely used CNN architecture, namely ResNet50, as a backbone network. For training, we only augment training samples by random horizontal flip. Each model is trained for 32 epochs with a batch size of 128. The initial learning rate is set to 0.025 and divided by ten at 18, 28 epochs when the training loss plateaus. SGD is adopted as our optimizer with momentum is 0.9, and the weight decay parameter is set to $5e-4$. The drop ratio is fixed at 0.5 for all settings. All experiments are conducted based on Pytorch framework [8] and all the models are trained and validated for training and testing on an NVIDIA Tesla T4 (16GB) GPU.

Loss Function Hyper-parameters Setting: In ArcFace and CosFace, the margin m is choose at 0.5 and 0.35 respectively as suggested in original papers. For MagFace, there are five hyper-parameters must be selected thoroughly, as mentioned in [13]. The upper bound and lower bound of magnitude are fixed as $l_a = 10$, $u_a = 110$. Besides that, function $m(a_i)$ is described as a function defined on $[l_a, u_a]$ with $m(l_a) = l_m$, $m(u_a) = u_m$. By empirical experiment, l_m and u_m are set respectively to 0.45 and 0.8. λ_g is specified to 20 as well. The scale s has already been discussed sufficiently in several previous works [15,20], so we directly fixed its values to 64 and will not discuss its effect further.

4.3   Results

Intending to analyze the effect of the loss function in the FR DCNN model, we have built an experiment according to the method presented in Sect. 3 with the above settings. The accuracy [11] and equal error rate (ERR) metrics [4] are used to evaluate and compare our model again other SOTA. The results of specific evaluation and comparison of the accuracy of DCNN models with different loss functions and baselines are presented below:

Table 1. Accuracy metric (%) of DCNN models on five benchmarks ("*" indicates the result quoted from the original paper)

Method	LFW	CFP-FP	AgeDB-30	CALFW	CPLFW
HUMAN-Individual	97.27	–	–	82.32	81.21
HUMAN-Fusion	–	–	–	86.50	85.24
CASIA, R50, CosFace* [20]	99.33	–	–	–	–
CASIA, R50, ArcFace* [3]	99.53	95.56	95.15	–	–
MS1M-V2 , R100, MagFace* [13]	99.83	98.46	98.17	96.16	92.87
CASIA, R50, Softmax (our)	98.82	93.59	91.13	91.15	86.02
CASIA, R50, CosFace (our)	99.42	95.01	94.45	93.35	89.47
CASIA, R50, ArcFace (our)	99.43	95.12	94.88	93.88	88.98
CASIA, R50, MagFace (our)	99.43	95.11	94.55	93.82	89.27

Table 2. EER (%) of effective loss functions on all test datasets

Method	LFW	CFP-FP	AgeDB-30	CALFW	CPLFW
CosFace (our)	0.65	5.98	5.60	7.42	**12.25**
ArcFace (our)	**0.63**	6.18	**5.45**	**7.20**	12.76
MagFace (our)	0.68	**5.90**	5.68	7.23	12.70

Comparison between Effective Loss Functions and Softmax. For further understanding of the effectiveness of adding margin into softmax, we also implemented the original softmax function by the side of three proposed losses namely CosFace, ArcFace and MagFace. Results are presented in Table 1. As a baseline model, Softmax reached 98.82%, 93.59%, 91.13%, 91.15% and 86.02% accuracy on all benchmarks are LFW, CFP-FP, Age-30, CALFW and CPLFW respectively. For all other losses, they outperformed Softmax on every benchmark. Compared Softmax, CosFace archived 0.6%, 1.42%, 3.32%, 2.20%, 3.45% improvements on the respective LFW, CFP-FP, Age-30, CALFW and CPLFW. ArcFace also surpasses the baseline by 0.61%, 1.53%, 3.75%, 2.73% and 2.96% on five benchmarks respectively. As well as two previous losses, MagFace outperformed Softmax on all test datasets 0.61%, 1.52%, 3.42%, 2.67%, 3.25% consecutively. Those results clearly shown that the margin plays a key role in CosFace, ArcFace and MagFace, strengthening the discriminating power of features. Besides, our implementations for all three losses can lead to convergence without observing any difficulty similar to the advantage of Softmax.

Comparison between Effective Loss Functions. Not only compare to Softmax, we also compare among our re-implementations including CosFace, ArcFace, MagFace based EER metrics in Table 2. The result returned varied on the different benchmarks. It is interesting that CosFace showed the best result on the "hard test case", CPLFW, 12.25%, while performed more poorly on the rest of datasets. Otherwise it not surpass ArcFace and MagFace on other benchmarks. As opposed to what we had anticipated, MagFace only performed well in the CFP-FP benchmark and is good in CALFW. On the other hand, ArcFace is archived at its best in diverse age benchmarks: on AgeDB-30, it gains 5.45% EER, which is 0.15% lower than CosFace and 0.23% lower than MagFace. Similarly, on LFW and CALFW, ArcFace also archives EER values which is lower than CosFace and MagFace approximately about (0.03%–0.2%). It illuminates that ArcFace can bring the discriminative power better than CosFace and MagFace in our scenario.

Comparison with other Baselines. Besides Softmax, we also compare our re-implementations with other published results : Human-Individual and Human-Fusion as reported in Table 1. Firstly, our models easily outperformed HUMAN-Individual on CALFW and CPLFW. They achieved accuracy better than 88% on all of these benchmarks, whereas Human-Individual only achieved performance less than 83% on both. Even on the easy benchmark LFW, our models completely defeat competence of a individual about 2%. Moreover, compared to Human-Fusion which is the third baseline, our models still did outperform it by increasing about 3.0%–7.0% on CALFW and CPLFW. Those results shown us the power of our proposed models that definitely replaces human in FR tasks.

4.4 Limitations

Apart from our achievements, we also reported the limitation of our re-implementations compare to results in original papers. Although our CosFace-based DCNN model achieves even higher than the original CosFace* 0.09% for ACC, both ArcFace and MagFace re-implementations could not reach the same results as the original papers. For the ArcFace-based DCNN model, our method has 99.43% of accuracy on LFW, which is 0.1% less than the ArcFace* as well as CFP-FP and AgeDB-30. The difference in accuracy between our models and the original ones comes mainly from the difference in computing infrastructure. For instance, the ArcFace* used 4 GPU and set the batch size to 512 for training the model. Finally, with MagFace*, they used larger datasets and a deeper backbone network, so their results ultimately outperform others in Table 1.

5   Conclusion

In this paper, we have surveyed, analyzed, and identified the main challenges of CNN-based face recognition concerning specifying the loss function. To tackle these challenges independently, we re-implement and evaluate the three novel effective loss functions, including CosFace, ArcFace, and MagFace. We demonstrated the advantages of those loss functions, which perform better than their original Softmax. Our deep experiments on recent popular datasets confirm that the face recognition accuracy is clearly improved by using a suitable loss function. Our re-implementations show significant results comparing other baselines on five widely used benchmarks: LFW, CFP-FP, AgeDB-30, CALFW, and CPLFW. Hence, it asserted the discriminative power of CosFace, ArcFace, and MagFace, respectively, and the potential for deployment in the automated library system.

In future work, we will also be interested in other types of loss functions and ensemble learning methods in order to build robust face recognition applications capable of discriminating effectively in varied environments.

References

1. Baltrusaitis, T., Zadeh, A., Lim, Y.C., Morency, L.-P.: OpenFace 2.0: facial behavior analysis toolkit. In 2018 13th IEEE International Conference on Automatic Face & Gesture Recognition (FG 2018), pp. 59–66 (2018)
2. Cao, Q., Shen, L., Xie, W., Parkhi, O.M., Zisserman, A.: VGGFace2: a dataset for recognising faces across pose and age. In: 2018 13th IEEE International Conference on Automatic Face & Gesture Recognition (FG 2018), pp. 67–74 (2018)
3. Deng, J., Guo, J., Xue, N., Zafeiriou, S.: ArcFace: additive angular margin loss for deep face recognition. In: 2019 IEEE/CVF Conference on Computer Vision and Pattern Recognition (CVPR), pp. 4685–4694 (2019)
4. Du, H.P., Pham, D.H., Nguyen, H.N.: An efficient parallel method for optimizing concurrent operations on social networks. Trans. Comput. Collective Intell. 10840(XXIX), 182–199 (2018)
5. Guo, Y., Zhang, L., Hu, Y., He, X., Gao, J.: Ms-celeb-1m: a dataset and benchmark for large-scale face recognition. In: ECCV (2016)
6. He, K., Zhang, X., Ren, S., Sun, J.: Deep residual learning for image recognition. In: 2016 IEEE Conference on Computer Vision and Pattern Recognition, pp. 770–778 (2016)
7. Huang, G.B., Mattar, M., Berg, T., Learned-Miller, E.: Labeled faces in the wild: a database for studying face recognition in unconstrained environments. Technical Report 07–49, University of Massachusetts, Amherst (2007)

8. Huang, X., Du, X., Liu, H., Zang, W.: A research on face recognition open source development framework based on PyTorch. In: 2021 International Symposium on Computer Technology and Information Science (ISCTIS), pp. 346–350 (2021)

9. Jiao, J., Liu, W., Mo, Y., Jiao, J., Deng, Z., Chen, X.: Dyn-ArcFace: dynamic additive angular margin loss for deep face recognition. Multimedia Tools Appl. **80**(17), 25741–25756 (2021)

10. Kemelmacher-Shlizerman, I., Seitz, S.M., Miller, D., Brossard, E.: The megaface benchmark: 1 million faces for recognition at scale. In: 2016 IEEE Conference on Computer Vision and Pattern Recognition (CVPR), pp. 4873–4882 (2016)

11. Le, H.V., Nguyen, T.N., Nguyen, H.N., Le, L.: An efficient hybrid webshell detection method for webserver of marine transportation systems. IEEE Trans. Intell. Transp. Syst. Early Access, 1–13 (2021)

12. Liu, W., Wen, Y., Yu, Z., Yang, M.: Large-margin softmax loss for convolutional neural networks. In: Proceedings of the 33rd International Conference on International Conference on Machine Learning - Volume 48, ICML'16, pp. 507–516 (2016)

13. Meng, Q., Zhao, S., Huang, Z., Zhou, F.: MagFace: a universal representation for face recognition and quality assessment. In: 2021 IEEE/CVF Conference on Computer Vision and Pattern Recognition (CVPR), pp. 14220–14229 (2021)

14. Moschoglou, S., Papaioannou, A., Sagonas, C., Deng, J., Kotsia, I., Zafeiriou, S: AgeDB: the first manually collected, in-the-wild age database. In: 2017 IEEE Conference on Computer Vision and Pattern Recognition Workshops (CVPRW), pp. 1997–2005 (2017)

15. Ranjan, R., Castillo, C., Chellappa, R.: L2-constrained softmax loss for discriminative face verification. CoRR, abs/1703.09507 (2017)

16. Schroff, F., Kalenichenko, D., Philbin, J.: FaceNet: a unified embedding for face recognition and clustering. In: 2015 IEEE Conference on Computer Vision and Pattern Recognition (CVPR), pp. 815–823 (2015)

17. Sengupta, S., Chen, J.-C., Castillo, C., Patel, V.M., Chellappa, R., Jacobs, D.W.: Frontal to profile face verification in the wild. In: 2016 IEEE Winter Conference on Applications of Computer Vision (WACV), pp. 1–9 (2016)

18. Tao, K., He, Y., Chen, C.: Design of face recognition system based on convolutional neural network. In: 2019 Chinese Automation Congress (CAC), pp. 5403–5406 (2019)

19. Wang, F., Cheng, J., Liu, W., Liu, H.: Additive margin softmax for face verification. IEEE Signal Process. Lett. **25**(7), 926–930 (2018)

20. Wang, H., et al.: CosFace: large margin cosine loss for deep face recognition. In: 2018 IEEE/CVF Conference on Computer Vision and Pattern Recognition, pp. 5265–5274 (2018)

21. Wen, Y., Zhang, K., Li, Z., Qiao, Yu.: A discriminative feature learning approach for deep face recognition. In: Leibe, B., Matas, J., Sebe, N., Welling, M. (eds.) ECCV 2016. LNCS, vol. 9911, pp. 499–515. Springer, Cham (2016). https://doi.org/10.1007/978-3-319-46478-7_31

22. Yi, D., Lei, Z., Liao, S., Li, S.Z.: Learning face representation from scratch (2014)

23. Zhang, X., Zhao, R., Qiao, Y., Wang, X., Li, H.: AdaCos: adaptively scaling cosine logits for effectively learning deep face representations. In: 2019 IEEE/CVF Conference on Computer Vision and Pattern Recognition (CVPR), pp. 10815–10824 (2019)

24. Zheng, T., Deng, W.: Cross-pose LFW: a database for studying cross-pose face recognition in unconstrained environments. Technical Report 18–01, Beijing University of Posts and Telecommunications (2018)

25. Zheng, T., Deng, W., Hu, J.: Cross-age LFW: a database for studying cross-age face recognition in unconstrained environments. CoRR, abs/1708.08197 (2017)
26. Zhu, Z., et al.: Webface260m: a benchmark unveiling the power of million-scale deep face recognition. In: 2021 IEEE/CVF Conference on Computer Vision and Pattern Recognition (CVPR), pp. 10487–10497 (2021)

Knowledge Discovery for Enhancing Collaboration

Singlish Checker: A Tool for Understanding and Analysing an English Creole Language

Lee-Hsun Hsieh🆔, Nam-Chew Chua, Agus Trisnajaya Kwee, Pei-Chi Lo,
Yang-Yin Lee, and Ee-Peng Lim(✉)🆔

Living Analytics Research Centre, Singapore Management University,
Singapore, Singapore
eplim@smu.edu.sg

Abstract. As English is a widely used language in many countries of different cultures, variants of English also known as English creoles have also been created. Singlish is one such English creole used by people in Singapore. Nevertheless, unlike English, Singlish is not taught in schools nor encouraged to be used in formal communications. Hence, it remains to be a low resource language with a lack of up-to-date Singlish word dictionary and computational tools to analyse the language. In this paper, we therefore propose **Singlish Checker**, a tool that is able to help detecting Singlish text, Singlish words and phrases. To develop this tool, we first construct a large set of Singlish words and phrases by identifying different sources of Singlish words and their definitions and integrating them. We later propose a Singlish classifier model based on a BERT model fine-tuned with a large number of classified Singlish sentences. Our experiment show that the BERT-based classifier can achieved very high F1 performance, outperforming the baseline.

Keywords: Singlish · Singlish classification · Singlish dictionary

1 Introduction

Motivation. As English is a widely used language in many countries of different cultures, variants of English also known as English creoles have also been created. Singlish is one such English creole used by people in Singapore, a country of slightly more than 5.5 millions. Singlish has been influenced by other major non-English languages used in the country and they include, in decreasing order of popularity, Chinese (and its dialects such as Hokkien, Teochew, and Cantonese), Malay, and Tamil.

Consider the sentence example: "The weather is so hot, I buay tahan." The word phrase "buay tahan" is Singlish and it combines a Hokkien (a southern Chinese dialect) word "buay" and another Malay word "tahan" carrying the meanings of "cannot" and "tolerate" respectively. The above sentence therefore says that a person cannot tolerate the hot weather. Without a good vocabulary of Singlish words or phrases, one will have difficulty understand the sentence. To

© The Author(s), under exclusive license to Springer Nature Switzerland AG 2022
Y.-H. Tseng et al. (Eds.): ICADL 2022, LNCS 13636, pp. 115–124, 2022.
https://doi.org/10.1007/978-3-031-21756-2_9

make understanding Singlish harder, an existing English word could acquire a new meaning when it appears in Singlish text. For example, the word "uncle" in Singlish often refers to some unrelated older man such as an old taxi male driver ("taxi uncle" in Singlish) and policeman ("police uncle" in Singlish). Singlish sentences may also have grammatical structures different from that of English.

Unlike English, Singlish is not taught in schools nor encouraged to be used in formal communications. Nevertheless, Singlish is still highly popular in informal conversations and online communications as the language has become an integral part of the Singapore identity. Due to its informal nature and a lack of formal research, Singlish is a low resource language with a lack of up-to-date Singlish word dictionary and computational tools to analyse the language. Several individuals have in the past tried to construct dictionaries of Singlish words and phrases. These dictionaries are however not integrated with one another and are not well utilized in any tools for analysing Singlish content.

Objective. In this paper, we therefore propose Singlish Checker, a tool that is able to help detecting Singlish text, Singlish words and phrases. Our long term goal is to develop a set of NLP tools for helping non-Singlish users understand the language and researchers analyse Singlish content for studying the language trends and the underlying content topics and sentiments. To develop the Singlish Checker tool, we first aim to construct a large pool of Singlish words and phrases by identifying and integrating different sources of Singlish words and their definitions. We also want to build a classifier to determine Singlish content. This classifier will be very useful to the construction of a large corpus of Singlish text for future research purposes.

Contributions. In the following, we summarize our research contributions:

- We have found six disparate sources of Singlish words/phrases and their definitions and integrated them into a combined list. This combined list covers more than 1600 distinct Singlish words/phrases, which to our best knowledge is the largest so far.
- We propose a Singlish classification model based on a BERT mode fine-tuned with many likely Singlish sentences. Our experiment show that the classification model can achieved F1 performance of more than 0.9.
- We have developed a working Singlish Checker system which has a web-based demo interface to showcase the classification and Singlish word extraction functions.

Outline of Paper. We organize the rest of the paper as follows. Section 2 covers the relevant previous research. Section 3 outlines the construction of Singlish dictionary. We then propose our Singlish classification model and conduct experiment evaluation of the model in Sect. 4. The Singlish checker system is then presented in Sect. 5. Section 6 concludes the paper.

2   Related Works

Linguistic studies on Singlish. While Singlish is largely used in the informal settings, linguists have shown great interests in the analysis of this creole language, finding the origins of Singlish words, and linking them with the user culture. For example, Wong studied the use of "one", an English particle, in Singlish sentences and postulated that the frequent use of "one" can be attributed to Singlish users wanting to speak more definitively than the Anglo English speakers [14]. Gupta studied how Singlish is used in different settings on the web and suggested the use of Singlish is related to establishing the Singapore identity [6]. In [2], the use of Singlish particles such as "ah", "lah", "leh", etc., in Singlish users' social networks was analysed. The work concluded that some particles are more frequently used in personal topics than in non-personal topics. The use of particles is also influenced by the user's ethnicity.

NLP Works on Singlish. As a creole language, there are limited NLP tools for analysing Singlish. Wang et al. was the first to construct Singlish dependency treebank using the Universal Dependencies scheme. They further proposed a neural stacking model-based Singlish parser integrated with English syntactic knowledge [13]. In a subsequent work, they further extended the treebank, and introduced a neural multi-task model-based parser which outperforms the previously proposed stacking model [12]. Both [12,13] develop their parser models based on manually labelled Singlish sentences, and they do not address the recognition of Singlish words. To aid future Singlish NLP sudies, Chow and Bond constructed computational grammar for Singlish, which was built upon standard English Head-driven Phrase Structure Grammar (HPSG) [3]. They included newly defined lexical types and rules to cover Singlish use-of-words. This work also does not address the recognition of Singlish words.

One popular task in NLP is sentiment polarity identification. Early works in Singlish sentiment polarity identification focused on constructing sentic dictionaries. For instance, Lo et al. employed a semi-supervised approach to derive Singlish sentic patterns [9]. Experiment results suggested that considering both English and Singlish sentic patterns lead to better sentiment prediction accuracy compared to English-only models. Ho et al. focused on concept-level sentiment knowledge base and proposed SenticNet, which consisted of semantics and sentics associated with Singlish words and phrases [7]. In a more recent study, Leow and Lo developed deep neural networks (DNNs) models for Singlish polarity detection [8]. They found that proper pre-processing is the key to high prediction accuracy. In addition, RNN was reported to outperform CNN in Singlish polarity classification task. In the above works, the Singlish sentences and words were manually determined.

Finally, there are also previous works that investigated the analysis of Singapore user generated content. Silva et al. predicted Singapore users' personal value by analysing their social network content with Singapore-Linguistic Inquiry and Word Count (S-LIWC) [11]. S-LIWC is a text analytic toolkit which counts the use of words and captures writers' psychometric properties specifically developed for Singlish content. [4] explored the linguistic factors that affect the popularity of Reddit posts in r/Singapore, where both Singlish (basilect) and standard English (acrolect) co-exist. Results showed that popular posts drawn on basilect-induced features as they connected better to the local audience.

3   Singlish Dictionary Construction

As we need a comprehensive and up-to-date set of Singlish words and phrases to determine known Singlish words and phrases in a sentence, we first search for existing online sources of Singlish words and phrases. With some efforts, we found the following six sources:

- Coxford Singlish Dictionary (**Coxford**): This dictionary is located at http://colingoh.com /project/the-coxford-singlish-dictionary/ and it covers 809 Singlish words and phrases. The dictionary has no longer been maintained nor updated since 2001.
- Eat Drink Men and Women forum (**EDMW**): This is a forum at Hardwarezone.com.sg and the first post in this forum defines about 277 Singapore acronyms and Singlish words commonly used by the forum users. The forum can be found at https://forums.hardwarezone.com.sg/eat-drink-man-woman-16/acronyms-lingo-peculiar-edmw-1738415.html. We manually determine the Singlish words to be included in our research.
- SinglishWiki Singapore Internet Lingo (**SinglishWiki**): This list of 103 Singlish words can be found at https://singternet.fandom.com/wiki/Singapore_ Internet_Lingo_Wiki. It was last updated in June 2011.
- Singaporelang (**Singaporelang**): This list of 113 Singlish words was compiled by Zinkie Aw in 2015. It is no longer available online.
- Singlish Vocabulary Wikipedia pages (**Wiki_Singlish**): This list of 285 Singlish words appeared at https://en.wikipedia.org/wiki/Singlish_vocabulary
- Singlishdictionary.com (**SinglishDict**): This list was compiled by Jack Tsen-Ta Lee and it covers 1,193 Singlish words and phrases (as at May 2016). This list can be found at http://www.mysmu.edu/faculty/jacklee/.

For data sources that involve webpages, we first develop separate crawlers to collect the Singlish words/phrases along with their definitions. Finally, we merge the words/phrases together, removing the duplicates (as they appears in more than one source), and removing the well known organization and location entities commonly mentioned in Singapore's content. We finally obtain the integrated set of 1628 distinct Singlish words and phrases known as **Merged_SinglishDict**.

4   Singlish Classification

4.1   BERT-Based Singlish Classification Model

We adopt a classification model that uses a specially trained BERT model known as SinglishBERT as shown in Fig. 1. As SinglishBERT is a transformer-encoder trained with large amount of Singlish text, it is able to generate contextualized word embeddings for each word and special token of the input sentence. We shall elaborate the training of SinglishBERT in Sect. 4.2. The classification model takes the input sentence of n word tokens $w_1, w_2, \cdots, w_n$, adds the special tokens [CLS] and [SEP] to be beginning and end of sequence, respectively, before passing the token sequence to the SinglishBERT. The output embeddings of the [CLS] token generated by SinglishBERT is used as the representation of the sentence and fed to a feed forward neural network before the output is passed to a sigmoid cross entropy loss function for optimization so as to generate a prediction of Singlish label with a score between 0 and 1.

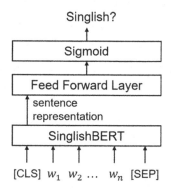

Fig. 1. Singlish Classification Model

4.2   SinglishBERT: A BERT-Based Classifier

SinglishBERT is an important module in our classification model responsible for generating contextualized token embeddings for every word and special token. Each token embedding is a vector representation that allows the token to be compared with other token. When two tokens from different sentences share the same sense or meaning, SinglishBERT is expected to return their embeddings to be close to each other in the representation space.

As the name suggests, SinglishBERT is a version of BERT which has been trained with large amount of English text to generate token embeddings [5]. Nevertheless, SinglishBERT is not developed by directly fine-tuning BERT. Instead, we fine-tune another BERT variant called SingBERT, which has been fine-tuned with a text corpus collected from subreddits r/singapore and r/malaysia (due to the similar way of speaking English in Singapore and Malaysia), and online forums popular among Singapore users [1]. As this corpus may still carry substantial amount of English text, we construct another text corpus to further fine-tune SingBERT to become SinglishBERT.

This new large text corpus consisting of 673,205 classified public Singlish tweet sentences generated by more than 150,000 Singapore users in 2020. These sentences are selected based on the following selection criteria:

– They have been assigned "en" language suggesting that the language used is likely to be English (or some English variants);
– Each sentence contains at least 5 and at most 30 words as an overly short or long sentence may be spam;

– Less than $\frac{1}{4}$ of the letters or characters in the sentence are in uppercase or non-English as we want to rule out spam and advertisement content;
– Less than a quarter of the words in the sentence are Malay words with the help of an online Malay dictionary; and
– Every sentence has a confidence score higher 0.999 assigned by our baseline classifier which will be introduced in the experiment section (see Sect. 4.3). We have intentionally selected a very confidence score threshold to ensure that the selected sentences are likely to be classified Singlish correctly by the baseline classifier.

With the above Singlish corpus, we fine-tune SingBERT to obtain Singlish-BERT.

4.3   Experiments

In this section, we conduct experiments to evaluate the accuracy of our BERT-based Singlish classifier and compare it with some baseline classifier.

Baseline Singlish Classifier. To compared against the above BERT-based classifier, we introduce a strong baseline Singlish classification model as shown in Fig. 2. The baseline classifier utilizes three distilled-GPT2 models: Distil-GPT2(Singlish), DistilGPT2(English) and DistilGPT2(Malay). DistilGPT2 is a lightweight version of Generative Pre-trained Transformer 2 (GPT-2) [10]. It is not only a decoder that can generate a sentence, but also a language model that returns a perplexity defined as the exponentiated average negative log-likelihood of the input sentence. A small perplexity suggests that the distilled-GPT2 is likely to be able to generate the input sentence. DistilGPT2(Singlish) is a distilled-GPT2 pre-trained with English corpus consisting of about 100,000 standard English sentences generated by Singapore users. We also pre-train distilled-GPT2 with Singlish and Malay corpuses to obtain DistilGPT2(Singlish) and DistilGPT2(Malay) respectively. Our Singlish and Malay corpuses consists of 10,000 and 120,000 Singlish and Malay sentences respectively. When the same input sentence is fed to the three DistilGPT2 models, we obtain three perplexity scores corresponding to the three models. We concatenate these three scores into a feature set and pass to an SVM classifier with a Radial Basis Function (RBF) kernel.

Labeled Datasets. While the different classifiers are built upon different pre-trained models which use different pre-training datasets, we construct a common labeled datasets for training and testing the classification models. We first gather a set of 9060 manually labeled Singlish sentences from Reddit and Twitter as positive sentences. These sentences are authored by Singapore users who are active in subreddits covering Singapore matters or have indicated Singapore location in their Twitter profiles. The negative sentences consists of 20,000 manually labeled English sentences and another 20,000 manually labeled Malay sentences which are authored by Singapore users on Twitter. Malay sentences are chosen largely because Malay language is commonly used in Singapore and the language adopts the same alphabet as English.

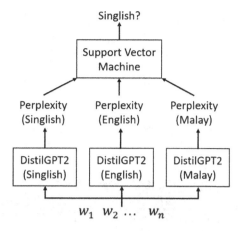

Fig. 2. Baseline Singlish Classifier

Accuracy Metrics. To report the model accuracy, we use the 5-fold cross validation approach dividing the labeled dataset into 5 disjoint subsets or folds of the same size such that each subset has the same proportions of positive (or Singlish) and negative (or English/Malay) sentences. We then use one of the folds for testing and remaining four folds for training the model. This evaluation is repeated for every fold used for testing. The final accuracy of prediction results over the five folds is obtained by averaging the fold-specific accuracy results. In our experiment, we define Singlish to be our target class and adopt the performance metrics: Precision, Recall and F1. Let S be a set of sentences. For a sentence $s \in S$, we use $g(s)$ and $p(s)$ denote the ground truth and predicted labels of the sentence s respectively. Precision (Pr), recall (Re) and $F1$ are defined as follows:

$$Pr = \frac{|\{s \in S | g(s) = p(s) = \text{``Singlish''}\}|}{|\{s \in S | p(s) = \text{``Singlish''}\}|}$$

$$Re = \frac{|\{s \in S | g(s) = p(s) = \text{``Singlish''}\}|}{|\{s \in S | g(s) = \text{``Singlish''}\}|}$$

$$F1 = \frac{2 \cdot Pr \cdot Re}{Pr + Re}$$

Results. Table 1 shows the accuracy results of our proposed BERT-based classifer and the baseline classifier. While the baseline classifier yields fairly good performance with an F1 of 0.842, BERT-based classifier still outperforms it by a substantial margin. This could be attributed to larger set of features (768 of them) provided by the BERT-based classifier compared with the three-only features used by the baseline classifier. The precision and recall results of BERT-based classifier are surprisingly very high contributing to the F1 of 0.944. This accuracy level also suggests that the model is ready to be deployed in real world applications.

Table 1. Classification results

	Precision	Recall	F1
Baseline Classifier	0.897	0.793	0.842
BERT-based Classifier	0.957	0.932	0.944

5   Singlish Checker: System Features and User Interface

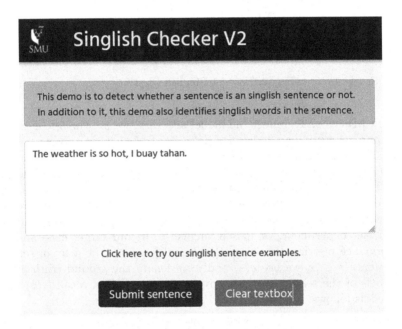

Fig. 3. Singlish Checker UI: Input sentence

In this section, we describe the web-based Singlish Checker application that utilizes both the MergedSinglistDict and Singlish classification model. Functionally, this application takes a sentence as input and returns the a score between 0 and 1. When the score is closer to 1 when the sentence is predicted to be Singlish, and 0 otherwise. Figure 3 depicts the user interface of Singlish Checker which contains a text box for one or more input sentence. In this figure, we show the sentence "The weather is so hot, I buay tahan.". When the input consists of multiple sentences, the Singlish Checker will return the average of sentence scores instead. To illustrate the use of Singlish Checker, the user interface includes several example sentences for the user to select. Once the input sentence(s) is entered, the user should click on the "Submit sentence" button.

Figure 4 depicts the results after the user submit the input sentence. The results include a sentence score, and the list of Singlish words or phrases detected

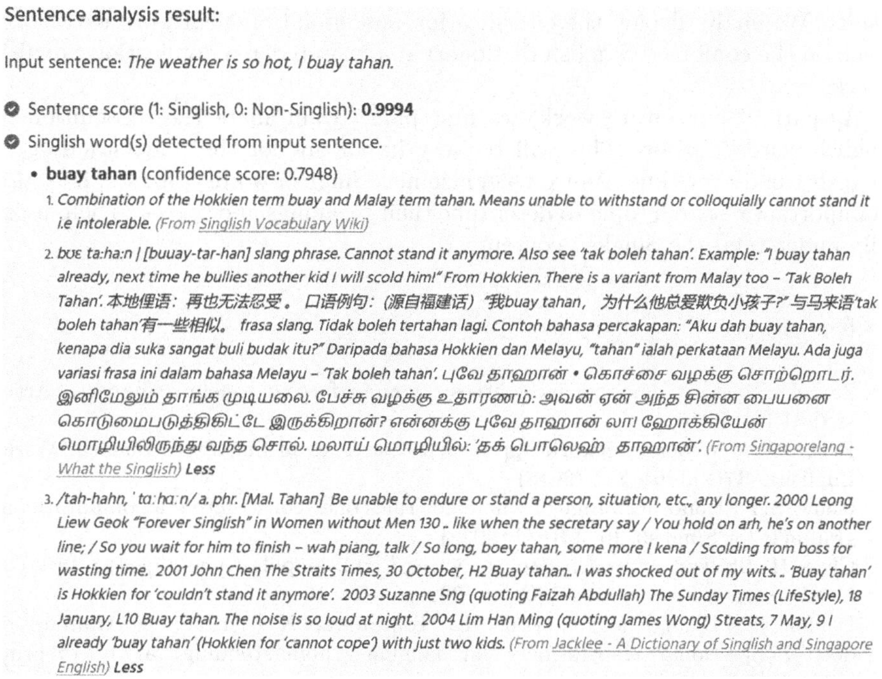

Sentence analysis result:

Input sentence: *The weather is so hot, I buay tahan.*

✅ Sentence score (1: Singlish, 0: Non-Singlish): **0.9994**

✅ Singlish word(s) detected from input sentence.

- **buay tahan** (confidence score: 0.7948)

  1. *Combination of the Hokkien term buay and Malay term tahan. Means unable to withstand or colloquially cannot stand it i.e intolerable. (From Singlish Vocabulary Wiki)*

  2. *bʊɛ ta:ha:n / [buuay-tar-han] slang phrase. Cannot stand it anymore. Also see 'tak boleh tahan'. Example: "I buay tahan already, next time he bullies another kid I will scold him!" From Hokkien. There is a variant from Malay too – Tak Boleh Tahan'. 本地俚语：再也无法忍受。 口语例句：(源自福建话) "我buay tahan， 为什么他总爱欺负小孩子?" 与马来语'tak boleh tahan'有一些相似。 frasa slang. Tidak boleh tertahan lagi. Contoh bahasa percakapan: "Aku dah buay tahan, kenapa dia suka sangat buli budak itu?" Daripada bahasa Hokkien dan Melayu, "tahan" ialah perkataan Melayu. Ada juga variasi frasa ini dalam bahasa Melayu – Tak boleh tahan'. புவே தாஹரான் • கொச்சை வழக்கு சொற்றொடர். இனிமேலும் தாங்க முடியலை. பேச்சு வழக்கு உதாரணம்: அவன் ஏன் அந்த சின்ன பையனை கொடுமைபடுத்திகிட்டே இருக்கிறான்? என்னக்கு புவே தாஹரான் லா! ஹொராக்கியேன் மொழியிலிருந்து வந்த சொல். மலாய் மொழியில்: 'தக் பொலெஹ் தாஹரான'. (From Singaporelang - What the Singlish) Less*

  3. */tah-hahn, ˈta:ha:n/ a. phr. [Mal. Tahan] Be unable to endure or stand a person, situation, etc., any longer. 2000 Leong Liew Geok "Forever Singlish" in Women without Men 130 .. like when the secretary say / You hold on arh, he's on another line; / So you wait for him to finish – wah piang, talk / So long, boey tahan, some more I kena / Scolding from boss for wasting time. 2001 John Chen The Straits Times, 30 October, H2 Buay tahan.. I was shocked out of my wits. .. 'Buay tahan' is Hokkien for 'couldn't stand it anymore'. 2003 Suzanne Sng (quoting Faizah Abdullah) The Sunday Times (LifeStyle), 18 January, L10 Buay tahan. The noise is so loud at night. 2004 Lim Han Ming (quoting James Wong) Streats, 7 May, 9 I already 'buay tahan' (Hokkien for 'cannot cope') with just two kids. (From Jacklee - A Dictionary of Singlish and Singapore English) Less*

Fig. 4. Singlish Checker UI: Sentence Results

in the sentence by checking against MergedSinglishDict. In this example, the sentence score of 0.9994 returned by our classification model suggests that the sentence is Singlish. For each Singlish word or phrase, Singlish Checker also returns its confidence score, its corresponding definition(s), or meaning(s). The confidence score is assigned by a Singlish word phrase recognition module. Due to space constraint, we shall not elaborate this module in this paper. In the figure, the word phrase "buay tahan" has been detected with a confidence score of 0.7948. There are three definitions found for this word phrase and they come from Wiki_Singlish, Singaporelang and SinglishDict respectively. Note that these definitions have not yet been integrated and shall be a topic for future research.

6 Conclusion

This paper introduces Singlish as a English creole language widely used in Singapore. To help analysing this low-resource language, our research integrates several data sources of Singlish words and their definitions. This combined set of Singlish words to our knowledge serves as the largest Singlish dictionary. To detect Singlish sentences or to select them for downstream research or analysis, we propose a BERT-based classification model utilizing SinglishBERT a BERT variant pre-trained or fine-tuned with a large Singlish corpus. Through our experiments, we show that our proposed classification model can achieve very accurate results. We finally deploy the classification model and Singlish word extraction based on the combined Singlish dictionary in our web demo application Singlish Checker.

As part of our future work, we first plan to automate the recognition of Singlish words/phrases. This will be very important for the understanding of Singlish trend over time. As we recognize new Singlish words/phrases, it is also an important research topic to determine their meanings and senses to help users fully understand the Singlish content.

References

1. Zanelim/singbert. hugging face. https://huggingface.co/zanelim/singbert,. Accessed 31 Dec 2010
2. Botha, W.: A social network approach to particles in Singapore English. World Englishes **37**(2), 261–281 (2018)
3. Chow, S.Y., Bond, F.: Singlish where got rules one? constructing a computational grammar for Singlish. In: LREC (2022)
4. Chua, H.: Stylistic approaches to predicting Reddit popularity in diglossia. In: ACL (2021). https://doi.org/10.18653/v1/2021.acl-srw.10
5. Devlin, J., Chang, M.W., Lee, K., Toutanova, K.: BERT: pre-training of deep bidirectional transformers for language understanding. arXiv preprint arXiv:1810.04805 (2018)
6. Gupta, A.F.: Singlish on the web. In: Varieties of English in South East Asia and Beyond, pp. 19–37. University of Malaya Press (2006)
7. Ho, D., Hamzah, D., Poria, S., Cambria, E.: Singlish SenticNet: a concept-based sentiment resource for Singapore English. In: 2018 IEEE Symposium Series on Computational Intelligence (SSCI), pp. 1285–1291 (2018)
8. Leow, Y.S., Lo, S.L.: Singlish polarity study using deep learning. In: First International Workshop on Social Media Analytics for Smart Cities (SMASC) (2017)
9. Lo, S.L., Cambria, E., Chiong, R., Cornforth, D.: A multilingual semi-supervised approach in deriving Singlish sentic patterns for polarity detection. Knowl.-Based Syst. **105**, 236–247 (2016). https://doi.org/10.1016/j.knosys.2016.04.024
10. Sanh, V., Debut, L., Chaumond, J., Wolf, T.: Distilbert, a distilled version of BERT: smaller, faster, cheaper and lighter. In: NeurIPS EMC2 Workshop (2019)
11. Silva, A., Lo, P.C., Lim, E.P.: On predicting personal values of social media users using community-specific language features and personal value correlation. In: ICWSM, pp. 680–690 (2021)
12. Wang, H., Yang, J., Zhang, Y.: From genesis to creole language: transfer learning for Singlish universal dependencies parsing and POS tagging. ACM Trans. Asian Low-Resour. Lang. Inf. Process. **19**(1), 1–29 (2019)
13. Wang, H., Zhang, Y., Chan, G.L., Yang, J., Chieu, H.L.: Universal Dependencies parsing for colloquial Singaporean English. In: ACL (2017). https://doi.org/10.18653/v1/P17-1159
14. Wong, J.: "Why you so Singlish one?" a semantic and cultural interpretation of the Singapore English particle one. Lang. Soc. **34**(2), 239–275 (2005)

"S × UKILAM" Collaboration to Connect Local Digital Resources and School Education: Workshop and Archiving to Construct Network of "People" and "Data"

Masao Oi[1,2](✉) ⓘ, Boyoung Kim[1] ⓘ, and Hidenori Watanave[1] ⓘ

[1] The University of Tokyo, Tokyo, Japan
oi-masao519@g.ecc.u-tokyo.ac.jp
[2] TRC-ADEAC, Tokyo, Japan

Abstract. The purpose of this study is to construct a network of people and data to connect diverse local digital resources and school education. Accordingly, we propose the S × UKILAM (School × University, Kominkan, Industry, Library, Archives, and Museum) collaboration, in which school teachers and institutions that hold and publish resources cooperate to create learning materials. As part of the project, three national workshops were held involving participants from 83% of prefectures and 197 institutions. The questionnaire suggested the effectiveness of the workshops and also identified the problems encountered in utilizing the resources. The 62 diverse learning materials co-created based on the workshops were made available as a secondary-use archive, creating a database in a format that can be machine-readably linked to various learning contents and resources.

Keywords: Digital archive · Local resources as learning materials · Educational metadata, MLA · S × UKILAM · IIIF · LOD · Digital humanities · Japan search

1 Introduction

In 2015, UNESCO emphasized the educational functions of museums and recommended collaboration with schools [1]. Subsequently, the "Education for Sustainable Development 2030 [2]" adopted by the United Nations also indicated learning tangible and intangible cultural heritage [3].

In addition, the Courses of Study, which are considered the basis of Japan's education program, were revised between 2017 to 2019. These guidelines aim to foster an respect for local cultural heritage in cooperation with institutions such as libraries and museums and conduct inquiry-based learning that utilizes various resources based on "questions" [4]. It was also indicated that learning to access digital materials using ICT should be included in the curriculum. Furthermore, in the context of the "GIGA (Global and Innovation Gateway for All) school concept" and online learning, which assumed significance in the wake of the COVID-19 pandemic, there has been a growing demand for using diverse resources as digital materials for learning.

© The Author(s), under exclusive license to Springer Nature Switzerland AG 2022
Y.-H. Tseng et al. (Eds.): ICADL 2022, LNCS 13636, pp. 125–134, 2022.
https://doi.org/10.1007/978-3-031-21756-2_10

Accordingly, it is imperative to facilitate the use of digital data of diverse resources from different regions in school education.

2 Relevant Research and Issues

2.1 Local Resources and School Education

The use of local resources can help students associate national history and contemporary issues with their daily lives and perceive them as familiar [5–8]. Meanwhile, local resources are difficult to utilize in their original form in school education. The resources used in primary and secondary education should be contextualized in line with the objectives of the unit and should be read and understood by the learners themselves.

Therefore, teachers are required to convert them into learning materials based on their developmental stage [9]. Accordingly, the importance of visiting Museums, Libraries, and Archives (MLA) facilities to collect materials has also been suggested [10].

However, these methods are subject to constraints of time and distance. Many teachers face time constraints to prepare for classes due to work overload [11], so they may not have the time to visit MLA facilities. There may also be situations where there are no facilities nearby or where sufficient resources are not held in local facilities.

In this backdrop, a survey asking teachers about the barriers they experience in teaching the subject indicated a "lack of appropriate learning materials," with many expressing anxiety about collecting and utilizing "local resources" [12]. Although the need to use local resources has been demonstrated, the linkage between daily learning and diverse local resources has not been sufficiently examined [13].

2.2 Digital Archive and School Education

One of the methods to solve time and distance issues when using local resources as learning materials is the utilization of digital archives built by MLAs in various regions. However, although some practical examples are reported [14, 15], their educational utilization has been limited, which can be attributed to the following issues.

Absence of Learning Design Linking Resources and School Education. First, a systematic method of linking digital resources to learning in school education has not been established [16]. The resources stocked in digital archives are not categorized based on the educational field, such as the units in which they can be utilized. Therefore, many teachers and learners are not aware of the existence. Therefore, there is a need to con-sider methods for connecting digital archive resources with the school's curriculum [17].

Unclear and Strict Guidelines Regarding Secondary Use of Resources. Second, there are issues surrounding the rights of digital archive resources. In Japan, there are many cases where the rights and conditions of use of resources in digital archives are unclear or restrictive [18]. This situation is a barrier to the utilization of the materials.

Accessibility to Diverse Resources. Third, with the acceleration of information technology, digital resources are widely available online, making it difficult to recognize what resources are available where, and access the required resources. Using "Japan Search", a integrated platform that enables cross-search of various metadata [19], can be a good solution. However, it is still labor-intensive to search for learning materials from a vast amount of information and consider how to utilize them in the classroom.

2.3 Comparison of Digital Archives Utilization

Europe and the USA operate integrated digital archives and content linking of educational use to these resources. For example, Europeana has aggregated metadata of digital content from EU countries and established dedicated pages to support thematic views and educational use [20]. The Digital Public Library of America has also developed educational activities based on the establishment of "Primary Source Sets," which compiles and publishes resources, learning materials and teaching guides [21]. With regard to this project, ABBOTT et al. (2015) argue that curation of resources specific to educational purposes, outreach activities, and collaboration with institutions of education are important for the effective use of digital heritages [22].

Meanwhile, although local authorities in Japan have been releasing learning guidance plans or operating websites for sharing learning materials with limited membership [23], these contents are mainly text-based, and no scheme has been established to link a variety of primary sources with school education. In addition, an open-access environment has not been developed in which learning materials and their material resources can be freely used for secondary purposes in schools. In order to promote the use of digital resources, in addition to cooperation with various institutions, accessibility should be improved by relying on the highly interoperable IIIF (International Image Interoperability Framework) [24]. It is also necessary to consider schemes for sharing meaningful cases of using the resources [25].

3 Methods

3.1 Overview

The purpose of this study is "to construct a network of people and data to connect diverse local digital resources and school education."

We propose the following methods to achieve the elements extracted from the issues of previous research: "linking diverse local resources and school education" and "sharing in a format that enables secondary use." The overall diagram of this study, including the proposed methods, is shown (see Fig. 1).

1 Organize workshops in which school teachers and institutions that hold and publish resources such as MLAs, can collaboratively create learning materials from diverse resources.
2 Prepare a learning materials archive based on the products created in the workshops.

a. To enable easy sharing and utilization of the workshop results in primary and secondary education, metadata based on the perspectives of the educational field ("educational metadata") are added.
b. To enable free secondary use, educational materials and educational metadata are comprehensively displayed and published using the IIIF.
c. Develop LOD (Linked Open Data) as a basis for educational metadata to facilitate the retrieval of resources and learning materials to other digital contents.

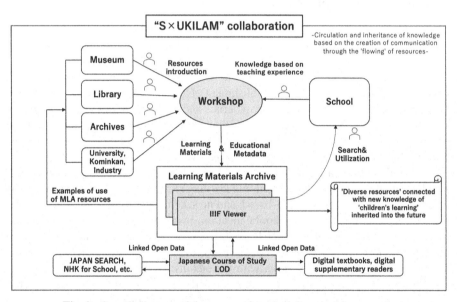

Fig. 1. Overall diagram of the proposed methodology in this research.

3.2 Organizing Workshops

In order to connect diverse local digital resources and school education, it is imperative to construct a network of "people." Accordingly, we organized workshops where school teachers and personnel from institutions that hold and publish resources collaboratively create educational materials.

To facilitate participation from remote locations, the workshop is held online (zoom). In addition, to encourage active discussion, breakout functions are used during the core time for discussion and development of learning materials, in which school teachers and personnel from institutions that hold and publish resources are categorized into mixed teams for minor group work. As a collaborative workspace, Google drive is utilized and a shared folder for each group of participants to support the collaborative work. After conducting the group-based discussions and learning material development work, all participants share their results. The workshop flow is shown below.

- Part I: Explanation about the workshop: 30 min.
- Part II: Discussions and work on the creation of learning materials: 110 min.
- Part III: Presentation of discussions and learning materials created: 40 min.

3.3 Preparing the "Learning Materials Archive"

For collaboration between diverse resources and school education based on digital archive, it is essential to construct a network of "data." Therefore, we develop a learning material archive that stores the materials produced in the workshops in a form available for secondary use. Furthermore, "educational metadata" which is critical for connecting diverse resources and school education in terms of "data," are assigned to the learning materials. Some of the elements that are assigned to the material are:

- Target of learning (grade, subject, area, unit, etc.)
- Time information and Location information (period, latitude and longitude etc.)
- Key words (President Roosevelt, WWII, etc.)
- Meta-learning information (learning scenarios, learning guide codes)

The aforementioned "educational metadata" is stored with the material metadata in the internationally interoperable IIIF viewer's manifest file, thereby improving accessibility and providing a better understanding of the material. In addition, as the specifications of IIIF are based on the premise of open data sharing, the license indication is mandatory, and downloading is possible.

The interface design of the archive enables users to search for educational materials by sorting them according to the elements of the assigned "educational metadata." The econdary use criteria for the learning materials are basically CC BY 4.0 [26], which is recommended. For resources with copyright or secondary use restrictions, the basic policy is to grant a license of EDUCATIONAL USE PERMITTED [27], provided the criteria will ultimately be decided through discussion in the workshops.

Among the "educational metadata" described in the previous section, the Code of Study Guidelines is expected to become a particularly important factor in the future. The Code of Study Guidelines is open data released by MEXT (Ministry of Education, Culture, Sports, Science and Technology) in 2020 [28]. By considering a LOD model using this as a hub, it is believed that it will be possible to connect digital archive materials, including digital textbooks and digital supplementary readers in the future.

We have developed and published the "Japanese Course of Study LOD" as a data set using RDF (Resource Description Framework) and SPARQL when the URI is attached to the guidelines and codes and made publicly available [29]. The LOD data is published in structured RDF format under the same license as the original code tables [30].

4 Results and Discussion

4.1 Organizing the Workshop

We held three workshops between July 2021 and March 2022, with entries from 39 (83%) prefectures and 197 institutions from Hokkaido to Okinawa, thereby creating an opportunity for professionals with diverse affiliations and attributes to converge at one place. The attributes of the participants' institutional affiliations are listed below.

Elementary, junior high and high school, school librarians (49 schools), educational committees and local government officials (22 institutions), university students and researchers (34 institutions), libraries, museums, archives and art galleries personnel (62 institutions), companies and NPOs personnel (30 institutions).

The workshop discussions were based on the common goal of making diverse resources into learning materials, and communication sparked by daily concerns, issues, and questions about the utilization of resources from different attributes.

In this research, a questionnaire survey of the participants was conducted. The results are shown below. Note that the data presented in this paper are based on the results of the questionnaire from the first to the third workshops, which were cumulated (N = 159).

Regarding the evaluation of the workshop in relation to purpose and motivation, 97.4% of respondents (n = 156) noted that the workshop was either extremely helpful or helpful. The perspectives expressed by participants on the "purpose and motivation for joining the workshop" are shown in (Fig. 2, Fig. 3). Regarding the question "What issues from the workshop topics do you feel are especially important?" (n = 155, *multiple answers possible), the results are shown in (Fig. 4).

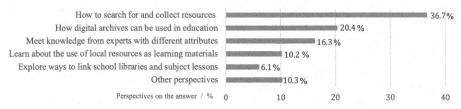

Fig. 2. Purpose and motivation for joining the workshop; School personnel (n = 49)

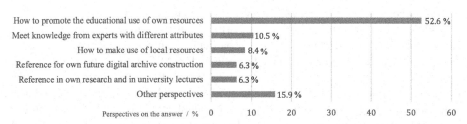

Fig. 3. Purpose and motivation for joining the workshop; Personnel from MLAs, research institutions, companies and NPOs (n = 95)

The results showed that many participants believed that creating opportunities for collaboration and networking between school and MLAs et al. was particularly important, thereby confirming the significance of creating opportunities for communication.

The results also showed that many participants believed that understanding the conditions for secondary use of resources was also important, which can be attributed to the fact that the concerns and issues from different perspectives, which are usually difficult to interact with, were shared through the workshop. It is worth noting that interest

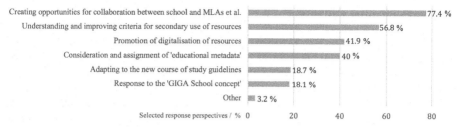

Fig. 4. "What issues from the workshop topics do you feel are especially important?" (n = 155, *multiple answers possible)

was also shown in consideration and assignment of educational metadata as a point of discussion for connecting education and digital archive resources in the future.

Others suggested that the track record of utilization of digital archive resources is necessary as evidence for budget requests. This indicates the importance of creating opportunities to make school personnel aware of the existence of MLA resources from the perspective of digitalization of the archive and its sustainability, to gain knowledge of what is needed to promote their use in schools through dialogue, and to develop and accumulate classroom practice using the materials produced. Consequently, we believe that it is important to create dialogue and communication between school and MLA personnel, in order to connect diverse local digital resources and school education.

4.2   Preparing the "Learning Materials Archive"

The "Learning Materials Archive" included a compilation of learning materials that were the deliverables of the workshop and was made available in September 2021. The archive has since been expanded with each workshop, and as of July 2022, 62 learning materials have been released with "educational metadata" and licenses to enable secondary use [31].

Although the content of learning materials tends to be more social studies and history-related due to the resource characteristics of the institutions participated, it is characteristic that learning materials were produced from various perspectives, such as inquiry learning, Japanese, art, disaster prevention, geology, biology, ESD (Education for Sustainable Development), etc. Furthermore, learning materials produced from cross-curricular perspectives, such as social studies × Japanese, social studies × health and physical education, which are unique due to discussions between participants with diverse attributes, resulting in creation that is not bound by preconceived notions.

As indicated by the characteristics of the learning materials that were awarded good practices in the Europeana Education Competition [32], upcoming learning materials need to go beyond subject boundaries and contribute to the development of competencies related to equality, diversity and sustainability. Our "Learning Material Archive" could serve as a foundation to support new learning designs that break away from the traditional teaching frameworks and perspectives of the Japanese education system.

4.3 Developmental Expansion of the S × UKILAM Collaboration

This section provides examples of development that emerged from participation in the workshops. As a first stage of development, Hamamatsu and Minato city held workshops. They focused more on local resources and local school teachers and MLAs gathered to discuss how to develop learning materials that utilize local resources.

Furthermore, based on this local workshop, the next stage of development was initiated in both municipalities in a different way. In Hamamatsu, the study of the use of local digital resources as learning materials was carried out as an "official duty" throughout the year, namely as a formal task within work hours. In Minato, a plan is underway to gather examples of the use of local digital resources and to award prizes for exceptional learning materials and practices. Despite their different approaches, it is hoped that these developments will make the use of local digital archive resources routine for more teachers and learners in schools, rather than just for a few teachers.

5 Conclusion

In this paper, we discussed the practice of the S × UKILAM collaboration, as a methodology for constructing a network of people and data to connect diverse local resources and school education.

This practice has created a community of diverse experts collaboratively developing local resources into learning materials. Furthermore, released diverse learning materials as an archive for secondary use. The results of the questionnaire revealed the importance of dialogue with experts of different attributes. Additionally, there are developing community-based activities, such as local authorities emerging as official duty to make local digital resources into learning materials.

In conclusion, our proposal method of the S × UKILAM collaboration has enabled the construction of a network of people and data to connect diverse local resources and school education. We will continue to consider the possibility of connecting diverse resources and school education in a more effective and serendipitous way through community interactions by holding regular workshops.

However, there is a problem to the assignment of educational metadata, which requires a certain knowledge and experience in education. Therefore, it is necessary to consider the creation of a framework to facilitate the assignment of "educational metadata" even without specialist educational knowledge. In the future, we are going to solve these problems and develop the LOD of the archive of educational materials. Through these practices, we will create methods for flowing the various resources stocked in each region to as many learners as possible and inheriting new knowledge that emerges from these resources to the future.

Referencess

1. UNESCO.: Recommendation concerning the Protection and Promotion of Museums and Collections, their Diversity and their Role in Society. (2015). https://www.j-muse.or.jp/02p rogram/pdf/UNESCO_RECOMMENDATION_ENG.pdf. Accessed 15 July 2022

2. United Nations.: Education for sustainable development in the framework of the 2030 Agenda for Sustainable Development. (2017). https://digitallibrary.un.org/record/1318978, Accessed 15 July 2022

3. Ministry of Education.: Policy on UNESCO activities for 2020–2021 (Report). (2019). https://www.mext.go.jp/unesco/001/2019/1422386.htm. Accessed 15 July 2022

4. Ministry of Education.: Revised Courses of Study. (2017, 2018, 2019). https://www.mext.go.jp/a_menu/shotou/new-cs/1384661.htm. Accessed 15 July 2022

5. Atsushi, N..: A study on the schoolchildren's concept of historical time in their "community". The New Geogr. **34**(3), 31–44 (1986)

6. 安井,俊夫.:国際化社会における人間形成と地域;共感と子どもの主体形成. 社会科教育研究, **1986**(54), 72–76 (1986)

7. Masami, U.: Strategies for the Teaching of local social history in secondary schools; in the case of Minnesota social history project. J. Soc. Stud. **1995**(72), 16–26 (1995)

8. Yasushi, A.: Incorporating Local History into the teaching materials for geography and history; an examination of regions and nation in the HIstory of Hokkaidou by the case of Otobe-Shinagawa farm. J. Soc. Stud. **2000**(84), 1–10 (2000)

9. 藤野, 敦.: 新学習指導要領における公文書館等との連携について. 国立公文書館アーカイブズ, **72**(2019). https://www.archives.go.jp/publication/archives/no072/8866. Accessed 15 July 2022

10. Hiroshi, N.: The significance of archives of social studies education. J. Soc. Stud. **2004**(91), 34–40 (2004)

11. HATOプロジェクト.: 教員の仕事と意識に関する調査. 愛知教育大学. 6–13 (2016). https://www.aichi-edu.ac.jp/center/hato/mt_files/p4_teacher_image_2_160512.pdf. Accessed 15 July 2022

12. Syoji, O.: The hindrance in teaching social studies and the wishes for the improvement in university education; based upon survey of teachers with experiences of one and five years. J. Soc. Stud. **1985**(53), 48–58 (1985)

13. Naotoshi, M.: Study trend on cooperation school and community in the journal of social studies. J. Soc. Stud. **2007**(102), 1–12 (2007)

14. 中村, 賢.: 文書館資料などを活用した指導教材作成について; 学校向けアーカイブズガイドの作成を中心に. 福井県文書館紀要. **2017**(14), 33–46 (2017)

15. Michihiro, M.: Concept of distributed digital commons for area-based learning; The Shinshu digital commons: "Our Shinshu" model. J. Japan Soc. Digit. Arch. **2**(2), 107–110 (2018)

16. Kazuki, K.: A proposal for using digital archives in the school education. J. Jpn. Soc. Digit. Arch. **3**(2), 211–212 (2019)

17. Yurio, K.: Practical research of using local digital visual archives in education: possibilities and problems. J. Jpn. Soc. Digit. Arch. **2**(2), 83–86 (2018)

18. Soichi, T.: Presenting digital archive to the public: rights statements. J. Jpn. Soc. Digit. Arch. **1**(Pre), 76–79 (2017)

19. Masao, O., Hidenori, W.: Curation class design for elementary, middle and high schools utilizing Japan search: significance and potential of educational use of digital archives. J. Jpn. Soc. Digit. Arch. **4**(4), 352–359 (2020)

20. Europeana Classroom Homepage. https://www.europeana.eu/en/europeana-classroom. Accessed 15 July 2022

21. DPLA Primary Source Sets Homepage. https://dp.la/primary-source-sets. Accessed 15 July 2022

22. Franky, A., Dan C.: Using Large Digital Collections in Education; Meeting the Needs of Teachers and Students. Digital Public Library of America, pp. 1–28 (2015)

23. 高大連携歴史教育研究会.: 教材共有サイト Homepage. https://kodai-kyozai.org/, Accessed 15 July 2022

24. Kiyonori, N.: An ecosystem of scholarly digital resources and potential of IIIF. J. Jpn. Soc. Digit. Arch. **1**(Pre), 84–85 (2017)
25. Kenji, T.: Some efforts to make development of a digital archive system – ADEAC. . Jpn. Soc. Digit. Arch. **2**(4), 324–329 (2018)
26. Creative commons Homepage. https://creativecommons.org/licenses/by/4.0/deed.ja, Accessed 15 July 2022
27. RIGHTS STATEMENTS Homepage, https://rightsstatements.org/page/InC-EDU/1.0/?language=en. Accessed 15 July 2022
28. Ministry of Education.: Educational Data Standards, Code Table of the Code of Study Guidelines (Whole Edition) (2020). https://www.mext.go.jp/a_menu/other/data_00002.htm. Accessed 15 July 2022
29. Masao, T., Masao, O., Satoshi, E., Yuka, E., Yumiko, A., Takayuki, A.: Japanese course of study LOD. https://jp-cos.github.io/en/about.html. Accessed 15 July 2022
30. Satoshi, E., et al.: Study of utilization for learning with linked open data created from courses of study. In: Research Report of JET Conferences, vol. 1, pp. 135–142 (2022)
31. Masao, Oi.: S×UKILAM collaboration; Learning Materials Archive utilizing diverse resources. https://trc-adeac.trc.co.jp/Html/Home/9900000010/topg/SxUKILAM/index.html?_fsi=GABUIi3Q. Accessed 15 July 2022
32. The Europeana Education Competition 2021. Teaching with EUROPEANA Homepage. https://teachwitheuropeana.eun.org/updates/europeana-education-competition-2021-winners/. Accessed 15 July 2022

Active Learning for Efficient Partial Improvement of Learning to Rank

Koki Shibata$^{(\boxtimes)}$ and Makoto P. Kato

University of Tsukuba, Tsukuba, Japan
s2221646@s.tsukuba.ac.jp, mpkato@slis.tsukuba.ac.jp

Abstract. In this study, we propose a framework that allows partial improvement of ranking algorithms based on feedback from search engine administrators, where partial improvement refers to changing the rank of a particular document for a particular type of query. The proposed framework consists of two models: a query identification model to identify which query rankings should be updated, and a ranking model to generate the ranking that the administrator expects. By repeatedly performing steps (1) to (3), these models are trained based on feedback from search engine administrators: (1) A search engine administrator selects a query for which rankings should be improved; (2) the search engine administrator gives feedback on the documents in the ranking returned in response to the selected query; and (3) the models are trained with the feedback given by the administrator. In this framework, it is critical to elicit effective feedback from administrators to achieve partial improvement effectively. Thus, we propose an active learning method for recommending queries that are likely to be selected by the administrator and lead to informative feedback for producing expected rankings. We conducted simulation-based experiments with three learning-to-rank datasets to verify the effectiveness of the proposed active learning method. The experimental results showed that the proposed active learning method enabled efficient partial improvement of rankings.

Keywords: Active learning · Learning to rank · Search engine

1 Introduction

In the learning-to-rank paradigm, many query-document features are extracted and combined to rank documents, and ranking models are trained with users' feedback (e.g., clicks on search results).

While users' feedback enables search engines to reflect users' preferences in the rankings, there is a concern that a biased view of users might reinforce various biases, such as racial bias, gender bias, etc., in the learning-to-rank paradigm.

Search engine administrators (e.g., search quality team members in a company) must change the search algorithms when problems are found in the ranking. However, it is not easy to manually modify a complex learning-to-rank model as anticipated. Updating the whole ranking algorithm could solve a problem in

© The Author(s), under exclusive license to Springer Nature Switzerland AG 2022
Y.-H. Tseng et al. (Eds.): ICADL 2022, LNCS 13636, pp. 135–143, 2022.
https://doi.org/10.1007/978-3-031-21756-2_11

search results for multiple queries, while there is a risk of causing unexpected ranking changes for some queries.

Therefore, we propose a framework that allows partial improvement of ranking algorithms based on feedback from search engine administrators, where partial improvement refers to changing the rank of a particular document for a particular type of query.

The most similar research topic is *relevance feedback*. However, our proposal is clearly distinguished from relevance feedback, since our framework aims to improve *the ranking algorithm for a particular set of queries* rather than search results for a single query. Detailed discussion is given in Sect. 2.1.

It is critical to elicit effective feedback from administrators to achieve partial improvement in this framework effectively. Thus, we propose an active learning method for suggesting queries that are likely to be selected by the administrator and lead to informative feedback for producing expected rankings.

We used three learning-to-rank datasets, namely, OpenLiveQ [10] and LETOR's MQ2007 and MQ2008 [12] to verify the effectiveness of the proposed active learning method. Building artificial query groups and ranking changes on these datasets, we conducted simulation-based experiments. The experimental results showed that the proposed active learning method enabled efficient partial improvement of rankings.

The main contributions of the paper are summarized as follows: (1) We proposed a framework of partial improvement of rankings based on feedback from search engine administrators; (2) We proposed a new active learning method for the proposed framework; and (3) We conducted experiments and demonstrated the effectiveness of the proposed active learning method.

2   Related Works

2.1   Ranking Improvement Based on User Feedback

This subsection describes existing works for improving rankings based on user feedback. These works can be broadly divided into the following two categories: those based on implicit feedback and those based on explicit feedback.

A method using implicit feedback [1,6,8,13,14] estimates the relevance of the document from the user's behavior, and the ranking algorithm ranks documents based on the estimated relevance. In this method, distinction exists in the problem settings. In our setting, a ranking algorithm has already been trained with user's implicit feedback, but it has to behave differently for certain queries.

A method using explicit feedback [16–18] is the method that trains the ranking algorithm using the relevance of documents obtained directly from the user. An example of explicit feedback is user's relevance feedback. The user gives either relevant or irrelevant to the displayed document in relevance feedback.

However, in the method using relevance feedback, the feedback from the user is binary: relevant/irrelevant. Therefore, it is difficult to specify the rank of the documents to be changed. In addition, these methods focus only on improving ranking for queries for which feedback is given, and do not consider the impact on other search results. In our task, it is required that the ranking should be improved not only for queries used for feedback, but also for those that have not received feedback if they are in the scope of the improvement.

2.2 Active Learning for Learning to Rank

This subsection discussed existing research on active learning in ranking learning. There is many researches on active learning in ranking learning [2–4, 7]

These researches assumed to make efficient for the learning of only one model. However, in the proposed framework, two different models are used: a query identification model (classification model) and an improved ranking model (ranking function). As we need to find a query that can simultaneously train these two models, it is difficult to apply existing active learning methods to our framework simply.

3   Methodology

In this section, we first describe the problem setting. Then, the details of the framework and the proposed active learning method are described.

3.1   Problem Setting

Given a query set Q and a document set D, we define ranking model r as $r : Q \times D \to \mathbb{R}$. Given query $q \in Q$ and documents D, ranking model r gives a score for each query-document pair and generates a list of documents ranked in the descending order of the score, i.e., $r(q, d_i) < r(q, d_j) \Rightarrow d_i \prec d_j$, where $r(q, d_i)$ indicates the score of document $d_i \in D$ for query q, and $\prec$ represents a total order on D indicating which document is ranked higher.

Suppose that r_0 denotes an *original ranking model*. Typically, this model is the one that has already been trained with a large numbers of clicks and deployed in service. A search engine administrator finds that rankings should be improved for a particular set of queries, denoted by $S \subseteq Q$. S/he also has *improved ranking model* (IRM) $r^\star$ in her/his mind. Partial improvement of the ranking is the problem of updating the search engine so that it applies the IRM $r^\star$ for a query in S; otherwise, it applies the existing ranking model r_0.

3.2   Framework

To solve the problem defined in the previous subsection, one of the simple ways is to estimate S, a set of queries for which rankings should be updated, and $r^\star$, a ranking model that reflects the intent of a search engine administrator. We propose a framework for addressing the problem of the partial improvement of rankings focusing on this specific setting. As we briefly explained, this framework consists of two models. One is the query identification model (QIM) m, a binary

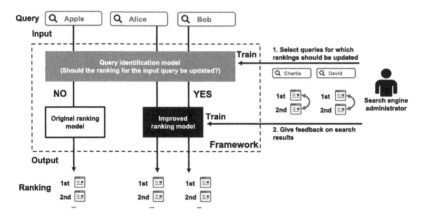

Fig. 1. Overview of the proposed framework.

classifier for identifying S, a set of queries for which rankings should be updated. Specifically, m takes a query as input and is expected to return 1 if it is in S; otherwise 0. The other is the improved ranking model (IRM)[1] r. These two models are trained with feedback from a search engine administrator.

Figure 1 shows our proposed framework. In our proposed framework, steps (1) to (3) below are repeated to train these models:

1. The administrator selects the queries for which rankings should be improved;
2. The administrator gives feedback on search results returned in response to the selected queries; and
3. The models are trained with the given feedback.

In step(1), $q \in Q$ are selected from the entire set of queries Q for which feedback is given in the next step. This step can be completed solely by an administrator or conducted with the support of the system. In step(2), the QIM m was trained with the true labels, while the IRM r was trained with true pairwise preferences of the rankings for the query. In step(3), two models are trained with these feedback.

Repeating the query selection, feedback, and model train n times, we finally obtained the QIM and IRM trained with n feedback. With these trained models, the framework produces a ranked list by r_{n+1} for queries identified by m_{n+1} which are trained n times with administrator feedback, and uses the original ranking model r_0 for the other queries.

3.3   Active Learning for Efficient Partial Improvement of Rankings

Since there is a limitation on the amount of feedback an administrator can provide, it is critical to enable the administrator to provide informative feedback by

---

[1] As r is an estimate of $r^\star$, this should be called *estimated improved ranking model*. For simplicity, r is called *improved ranking model* when there is no ambiguity.

selecting appropriate queries. Therefore, we propose an active learning method that suggests a set of queries by which informative feedback is likely to be given, and support the query selection of a search engine administrator for efficient partial improvement of rankings. This corresponds to the improvement of training step(1) in Sect. 3.2.

In the proposed active learning method, queries are prioritized by a scoring function consisting of two factors. One is the likelihood of being in the scope of the feedback. While some negative (i.e., out of the scope) queries are useful to train the QIM, negative queries do not increase the amount of the feedback for search results. The other factor is the estimated informativeness of feedback on search results. Feedback on search results is considered informative if it contains new information about the ranking that an administrator expects. Thus, it is important to prioritize queries that can produce rankings strongly disagreeing with the estimated IRM.

Based on the discussion above, the scoring function is defined as follows:

$$\text{score}(q) = \alpha P(y = 1|q) + (1 - \alpha)\text{diff}(r_0, r|q) \tag{1}$$

where α is a hyperparameter and $P(y = 1|q)$ is the probability of q being in the scope of the feedback (i.e., S). $\text{diff}(r_0, r|q)$ indicates the ranking difference between r_0 and r for search results returned in response to the query q. Note that r is an estimated IRM (i.e., r_i at i-th iteration).

The ranking difference $\text{diff}(r_0, r|q)$ can be measured by a ranking coefficient between the two ranking models. We define the ranking difference by the negative value of $\text{coef}(r_0, r|q)$:

$$\text{diff}(r_0, r|q) = \text{sigmoid}(1 - \text{coef}(r_0, r|q))$$

where $\text{coef}(r_0, r|q)$ is the Spearman's rank correlation coefficient between for the ranking of r_0 and the ranking of r for q and we amplify a value distant from zero by using the sigmoid function.

4   Experiments

We conducted simulation-based experiments to show the effectiveness of our framework and proposed active learning method. Since there is no publicly available dataset, we first give a brief overview of the dataset development. We then introduce the experimental settings and present the experimental results.

Datasets. The simulation was based on three learning-to-rank datasets, namely, OpenLiveQ [10] and LETOR's MQ2007 and MQ2008 [12]. OpenLiveQ is a dataset for Japanese question retrieval, while MQ2007 and MQ2008 are popular datasets for learning to rank.

To build S, we identified DBpedia [9,11] entities from each query, assigned their categories, and grouped queries by the estimated categories. We manually examined each query group and selected 25 sufficiently large query groups for each dataset. To build r_0, we trained a ranking model using the training data of each dataset. To simulate $r^\star$, we first selected *prototype documents* which is s/he wants to rank higher or lower for each of query groups. A prototype document was randomly selected from the top ten documents returned by r_0 for a randomly selected query. The IRM $r^\star$ was simulated by the application of either of the following updates to a ranking for each query in S: (**Down**) We first selected the five closest documents to the prototype document, from the top 100 documents returned for a query. The document similarity was measured by the cosine of query-document feature vectors. The selected documents were placed as the bottom five documents in the whole ranking. (**Up**) For each query included in S, the five closest documents to the prototype document were placed as the top five documents in the whole ranking.

Since those updates are highly dependent on the base document, we randomly selected ten prototype documents for each of 25 query groups. Therefore, we obtained a total of 250 settings with different IRMs. Note that in OpenLiveQ, we conducted only the down operation to update rankings.

Procedure. First, we initialized a QIM and an IRM based on four queries in S and a query not in S. These queries were selected randomly. The QIM m_1 was trained with the true labels for those five queries, while the IRM r_1 was trained with true pairwise rankings preferences for the four queries. This initialization was conducted in exactly the same way for all the comparative methods.

After obtaining m_1 and r_1, we simulated as follows. At each iteration, an active learning method was used to select five queries at a time. We then got a label for each query, and obtained pairwise preferences of the rankings for a query in the scope of feedback. At the end of iteration, QIM and IRM were trained with the given feedback. We repeated this procedure 15 times ($n = 15$).

4.1 Experimental Settings

Implementation Details. A linear SVM was used as the QIM m, though an arbitrary binary classifier could be used. We used one of the simplest pairwise learning-to-rank algorithm, RankNet [5,15], as the original ranking model r_0 and estimated improved ranking model (IRM) r. Feature vectors of queries were the word frequency vectors of documents which is relevant. Hyperparameters were determined with validation data.

Evaluation Metrics. One of the straightforward evaluation metrics for our experiments is a rank correlation coefficient between rankings by the IRM and its estimate. However, we consider that the averaged correlation coefficient is often insensitive to the partial improvement. This is because rankings of most of the queries do not change, and those of only a subset of queries (say, 0.01% of queries) are expected to be improved in our scenario.

The problem of existing evaluation metrics motivated us to propose a unique evaluation metric called *pairwise difference*. This measure quantifies how many document pairs whose order in a ranking should be swapped are actually

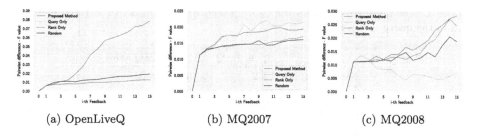

(a) OpenLiveQ   (b) MQ2007   (c) MQ2008

Fig. 2. Pairwise difference F-value for active learning method after i-th feedback.

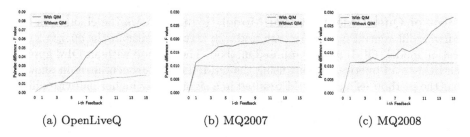

(a) OpenLiveQ   (b) MQ2007   (c) MQ2008

Fig. 3. Pairwise difference F-value for each feedback comparing methods with/without QIM (Query Identification Model).

swapped by partial improvement. For a query group S, let $P_{r^\star}$ be a set of document pairs on which the original ranking model r_0 and IRM $r^\star$ disagree:

$$P_{r^\star} = \{(d_i, d_j) \mid q \in S \land (d_i, d_j) \in D_q \land (r_0(q, d_i) - r_0(q, d_j))\,(r^\star(q, d_i) - r^\star(q, d_j)) < 0\}$$

If d_i is ranked higher than d_j by r_0, $r_0(q, d_i) - r_0(q, d_j)$ is positive. If $r^\star$ disagrees with the pairwise preference of r_0 or ranks d_j higher tahn d_i, $r^\star(q, d_i) - r^\star(q, d_j)$ is negative. In this case, $(r_0(q, d_i) - r_0(q, d_j))\,(r^\star(q, d_i) - r^\star(q, d_j))$ is negative, as we expect.

4.2   Experiment Results

Comparison of Active Learning Methods. Figure 2 shows the mean pairwise difference F-value after i-th feedback for each active learning method. The vertical axis indicates the mean F-value of the pairwise difference, while the horizontal axis indicates the round of feedback. The proposed method performed significantly better than the other methods in the OpenliveQ dataset. In MQ2007, while Query Only was slightly better than the proposed method, both of the methods performed equally well. In contrast, Rank Only performed well among the comparative methods in MQ2008. The proposed method using both criteria worked almost the best in all the datasets. The experimental results suggest that both criteria are necessary to elicit effective feedback from search engine administrators. Since the performance of partial improvement changes significantly depending on the choice of query, it can be considered that the query selection is very important in our proposed framework.

Table 1. The number of queries that were presented by each active learning method and in the query group S.

	OpenLiveQ	MQ2007	MQ2008
Proposed method	**14.2**	9.43	6.85
Query only	4.92	**9.91**	**7.33**
Rank only	5.50	6.57	6.77
Random	5.90	6.03	7.00

Effect of Query Identification Model. Figure 3 shows the changes in the pairwise difference F-values for each feedback with and without the query identification model (QIM) in the proposed method. The method without QIM applies the IRM to all queries without using the QIM. The experimental result showed that the method using the QIM resulted in a significantly higher pairwise difference F-values, suggesting that the QIM is vital to selectively apply an improved ranking algorithm to search engine results.

Effect of Number of Suggested Queries in Scope of Feedback. Table 1 shows the average number of queries that were presented by each active learning method and given feedback by the search engine administrator (or those belong to S). Overall, there is a trend that, if more queries were given feedback (or the QIM was successfully trained for identifying queries for which ranking should be improved), the pairwise difference F-value is likely high. Whereas, Query Only shows a slight different trend in MQ2008, in which F-value is not as high as the proposed method and Rank Only in spite of the success of the QIM. These results suggest that a QIM needs to identify queries in S for acquiring more feedback to rankings, while it can be only a necessary condition. For example, more feedback can be useless if such feedback has already been predicted by an estimated IRM and is not informative at all.

5   Conclusions

In this study, we proposed a framework that enables the partial improvement of ranking algorithms based on feedback from search engine administrators. It was critical to elicit effective feedback from administrators to achieve efficient partial improvement in this framework. Thus, we proposed an active learning method for suggesting queries that is likely to be selected by the administrator and lead to informative feedback for producing expected rankings. We conducted simulation-based experiments to verify the effectiveness of the proposed active learning method. The experimental results showed that the proposed active learning method accelerated the partial improvement in rankings.

References

1. Agichtein, E., Brill, E., Dumais, S.: Improving web search ranking by incorporating user behavior information. In: Proceedings of the 29th Annual International ACM SIGIR Conference on Research and Development in Information Retrieval, pp. 19–26 (2006)
2. Aibo, T., Matthew, L.: Active learning to maximize accuracy vs. effort in interactive information retrieval. In: SIGIR '11, pp. 24–28 (2011)
3. Bilgic, M., Bennett, P.N.: Active query selection for learning rankers. In: Proceedings of the 35th International ACM SIGIR Conference on Research and Development in Information Retrieval, pp. 1033–1034 (2012)
4. Bo, L., Chapelle, O., Ya, Z., Yi, C., Zheng, Z., Tseng, B.: Active learning for ranking through expected loss optimization. In: SIGIR 2010, pp. 19–23 (2010)
5. Burges, C., et al.: Learning to rank using gradient descent. In: Proceedings of the 22nd International Conference on Machine Learning, pp. 89–96 (2005)
6. Filip, R., Thorsten, J.: Query chains: learning to rank from implicit feedback. In: KDD 2005, pp. 239–248 (2005)
7. H.S. Seung, M.Opper, H.Sompolinsky: Query by committee. In: COLT, pp. 287–294 (1992)
8. Joachims, T., Swaminathan, A., Schnabel, T.: Unbiased learning-to-rank with biased feedback. In: Proceedings of the Tenth ACM International Conference on Web Search and Data Mining, pp. 781–789 (2017)
9. Kato, F., Takeda, H., Koide, S., Ohmukai, I.: Building dbpedia japanese and linked data cloud in japanese. In: 2013 Linked Data in Practice Workshop (LDPW2013), pp. 1–11 (2014)
10. Kato, M.P., Takehiro, Y., Tomohiro, M., Akiomi, N., Sumio, F.: Overview of the ntcir-13 openliveq task. In: Proceedings of the NTCIR 2013 Conference (2017)
11. Lehmann, J., et al.: Dbpedia-a large-scale, multilingual knowledge base extracted from Wikipedia. Semantic web **6**(2), 167–195 (2015)
12. Qin, T., Liu, T.Y.: Introducing letor 4.0 datasets. arXiv preprint arXiv:1306.2597 (2013)
13. Thorsten, J.: Optimizing search engines using clickthrough data. In: KDD 2002, pp. 133–142 (2002)
14. Xinyi, D., et al.: U-rank: Utility-oriented learning to rankwith implicitfeedback. In: CIKM 2020, pp. 2373–2380 (2020)
15. Yu, H.T.: Pt-ranking: a benchmarking platform for neural learning-to-rank (2020)
16. Yuanhua, L., Zhai, C.: Adaptive relevance feedback in information retrieval. In: CIKM 2009, pp. 255–264 (2009)
17. Zhai, C., Lafferty, J.: Model-based feedback in the language modeling approach to information retrieval. In: Proceedings of the tenth international Conference on Information and Knowledge Management, pp. 403–410 (2001)
18. Zuobing, X., Ram, A.: A bayesian logistic regression model for activerelevance feedback. In: SIGIR 2008, pp. 20–24 (2008)

Differences Between Research Projects in Computer Science Funded by Japanese and American Agencies

Emi Ishita[1](✉) and Tetsuya Nakatoh[2]

[1] Kyushu University, Fukuoka 819-0395, Japan
ishita.emi.982@m.kyushu-u.ac.jp
[2] Nakamura Gakuen University, Fukuoka 814-0198, Japan

Abstract. Understanding the relationship between funding agencies' expectations and researchers' activities in funded research projects will contribute to improved policy-making by funding agencies and better research activity by researchers. Thus, the purpose of this study is to investigate how research project size, international collaboration, and publication in international journals of articles resulting from funded research projects in Japan have progressed over the last decade. We focused on publications resulting from research projects funded by the major grants agencies in Japan and the USA using bibliographic data for computer science papers published from 2011 to 2020. Based on the numbers of authors of published journal articles and conference papers, the results showed that the size of projects funded by the National Science Foundation has been growing. In terms of international collaboration, both countries have increasingly collaborated with China, and researchers involved in research projects funded by the Japan Society for the Promotion of Science have increasingly published in English-language journals with less diverse audiences.

Keywords: Bibliometrics · Structure of funded research projects · Funding agencies

1 Introduction

Researchers' activities and research topics are often based on their own interests and preferences, although researchers may also be influenced by social expectations, the expectations of institutions or funding agencies, and current research trends. One of those trends is international collaborations, which have developed in numerous disciplines and countries over recent years. González-Alcaide, et al. [1] examined international collaborations of research papers in a specific field from 1980 to 2016 [1]. Of the total number of papers published in the periods 1980–1989 and 2010–2016, 19.1% and 32.5%, respectively, involved international collaborations. McManus et al. [2] analyzed international collaborations by Brazilian scientists and found that the number of papers published with foreign partners increased between 2004 and 2019. In Japan, the Japan Society for the Promotion of Science (JSPS) administers grant programs such as the "Fund for the Promotion of Joint International Research" and "Enhancement of International Dissemination of Information" [3], the title of which indicate that funding agencies encourage researchers to engage in international collaborations. Another trend is growth in research project size. This can be explained by the emergence of Big Science, which is characterized by "large-scale instruments and facilities, supported by funding from government or international agencies, in which research is conducted by teams or groups of scientists and technicians" [4]. For example, the Japan Science and Technology Agency (JST) has called for research proposals for its JST-Mirai Program (Large-scale Type) [5]. In Japan, researchers have been used to presenting their contributions to and building their communities in Japanese academic associations, and thus Japanese academia has become well-developed. However, as noted above, funding agencies are increasingly expecting researchers in Japan to conduct large-scale research and engage in international collaborations, although these expectations are rarely made explicit.

In this study, we investigated how researchers working on funded research projects reacted to these expectations by focusing on the size, internationalization, and presence of research project funding based on published literature. We examined the number of authors in relation to project size, the combination of authors' countries regarding internationalization, and popular journals regarding the presence of funding contributions. There are numerous ways to measure their reactions, but publications are one of the main avenues. We also examined changes over a decade using publications from the last 10 years. Understanding these researchers' activities will help research funding agencies to develop future funding policies, while also enabling researchers to develop research proposals that lead to better outcomes.

Our main focus is funded research projects in Japan, but we also examined funded research projects in the USA for comparison. The JSPS [6] was selected as the main research funding agency in Japan, while the National Science Foundation (NSF) [7] was selected as the main funding agency in the USA. We examined funded computer science research projects from 2011 to 2020 because the research groups in this field were in a dynamic state of change. Japanese researchers in computer science are expected to publish in international journals and at international conferences, which facilitated this analysis. The data used in this study were obtained from the Scopus database. If researchers' projects are funded by grant agencies, they are strongly advised to include information regarding this funding in their acknowledgments. Therefore, the Scopus database enabled us to obtain a list of publications funded by grant agencies.

2 Related Works

Bibliometric studies have previously been used to investigate research trends in various fields and to understand the structure of research activities. For example, Guiling et al. [8] investigated global research trends in organizational citizenship behavior over the last two decades by analyzing the top authors, journals, institutions, and countries in the field using the Scopus database. Wang et al. [9] performed a comprehensive bibliometric analysis of uncertain group decision-making over the last four decades by analyzing factors such as publication types, the most prolific countries/regions, highly authoritative publications, the development of publications, citations, and cooperating publications, the most prolific institutions, the countries/regions involved in institutional collaborative networks, and keyword timelines. In this study, we analyzed publications that resulted from funded research projects. Faisal et al. [10] analyzed 225 government-funded research projects on science education in Indonesia from 2014 to 2018 and identified the key topics, research context, content, and outcomes. In this study, we focused on the number of authors, the combinations of authors' home countries, and journal popularity over the last decade.

3 Data Collection

The bibliographic data used were obtained from the Scopus database using query searches. We focused on computer science publications from 2011 to 2020 using the search option "SUBJAREA(comp)" to specify the field of computer science and the search options "(DOCTYPE,"ar")" and "(DOCTYPE,"cp")" to identify journal articles and papers from conference proceedings, respectively. The search option "(FUND-SPONSOR, "National Science Foundation")" was used to identify projects funded by the NSF in the USA and the search option "(FUND-SPONSOR, "Japan Society for the Promotion of Science")" was used to identify projects funded by the JSPS in Japan. Table 1 shows the number of search results for each funding agency, publication year, and literature type. Scopus is constantly adding bibliographic data, including for previous publication years, and thus the results shown in Table 1 are those that were obtained in June 2021, when we conducted the search. Because Scopus only permitted a maximum of 2,000 bibliographic items including the abstract and other detailed information to be downloaded, when the number of search results exceeded this number, the 2,000 most highly cited papers were selected for analysis.

During data processing, we found that some studies were shown as being funded by the NSF, even though they were actually funded by the National Natural Science Foundation of China (NSFC). Therefore, we manually checked the grant name, grant number, and acknowledgment statement in papers published by authors belonging to Chinese institutions and papers with NSF or NSFC displayed in the fund-sponsor field. For example, NSF fund numbers consist of seven digits, the first two of which represent the funding year, as well as a three-letter prefix in some cases, such as CNS-1018108, while NSFC fund numbers consist of eight digits, for example, 61071061. We used this information to identify NSF-funded studies. In cases where it was unclear whether the funding was provided by the NSF or the NSFC, we looked up the grant numbers in the NSF's award database [11]. In cases where authors stated that they had received an NSF CAREER award but no award number was cited, we considered the project to be a funded project even though we were unable to ascertain when the author had received funding. Following these manual checks, we deleted any papers that did not appear to be funded by the NSF. In addition, when examining journals and conference papers, we found that some papers, for example, in Lecture Notes in Computer Science, were incorrectly indexed as journal articles, and some journal articles were incorrectly indexed as conference proceedings. We excluded IEEE/ACM/IEICE Transactions and publication titles including the word "journal" from the conference paper lists, and Lecture Notes in Computer Science from the article lists. The final numbers of papers used are shown in Table 1.

Table 1. Numbers of journal articles and conference papers used for analysis.

| Year | NSF | | | | | JSPS | | | |
| | Jour | | Conf | | | Jour | | Conf | |
	Result	Used	Result	Used		Result	Used	Result	Used
2011	3,264	1,975	1,053	927		723	722	774	735
2012	3,574	1,960	1,365	1,182		1,049	1,048	979	905
2013	3,756	1,950	4,942	1,924		1,198	1,197	1,501	1,445
2014	3,459	1,957	1,323	1,223		1,273	1,220	1,228	1,138
2015	3,091	1,961	2,711	1,922		1,380	1,370	1,309	1,262
2016	4,362	1,958	7,335	1,891		1,531	1,520	1,850	1,752
2017	4,898	1,964	8,654	1,886		1,803	1,800	2,777	1,911
2018	6,086	1,925	9,656	1,911		2,179	1,998	3,477	1,915
2019	6,096	1,932	11,704	1,945		1,939	1,939	3,776	1,976
2020	6,865	1,953	9,354	1,966		2,068	2,000	2,671	1,965

4   Results

4.1   Numbers of Papers

It can be seen from Table 1 that the numbers of journal articles and conference papers resulting from NSF- and JSPS-funded research projects grew substantially over the decade from 2011 to 2020. The number of journal articles resulting from NSF-funded projects more than doubled, while the number of conference papers was nearly nine times greater. The number of journal articles resulting from JSPS-funded projects nearly tripled, while the number of conference papers was five times greater by 2019 before declining in 2020. Thus, the growth in the number of articles resulting from JSPS-funded

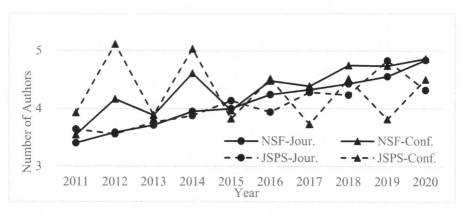

Fig. 1. Numbers of authors of publications.

research projects was less than that of articles resulting from NSF-funded research projects. As another factor, the Scopus has tried to include many publications in its database.

4.2 Numbers of Authors

Figure 1 shows the numbers of authors of published papers resulting from funded research projects. The number of authors of journal articles resulting from NSF-funded research projects (slope $= 0.15$, $p < 0.001$, $R^2 = 0.99$ by regression analysis), conference papers resulting from NSF-funded research projects (slope $= 0.12$, $p = 0.002$, $R^2 = 0.72$), and journal articles resulting from JSPS-funded research projects (slope $= 0.11$, $p < 0.001$, $R^2 = 0.78$) all increased over the decade, while the numbers of authors of conference papers resulting from JSPS-funded research projects varied considerably from year to year (slope $= -0.02$, $p = 0.70$, $R^2 = 0.02$). The number of authors of NSF-funded articles increased more than that of JSPS-funded articles, indicating that the size of NSF-funded research projects increased over the decade.

4.3 Authors' Countries

Figures 2 and 3 show the country combinations of collaborating authors of JSPS- and NSF-funded journal articles, respectively. The country names have been abbreviated using ISO 3166-1 country codes. We included all countries included in the affiliation fields from the bibliographic data, and only counted each combination once. For example, if three researchers belonged to a US institution and two researchers belonged to Chinese institutions, the combination of countries was recorded as "US & CN." It can be seen from Fig. 2 that the biggest research group consisted of authors from Japan (i.e., no international collaboration), followed by collaborative groups of authors from Japan and China. The ratio of combination of countries from only Japan was within 66.1% and 71.7%, and it has not been detected any statistically significant increase or decrease ($R^2 = 0.45$). The proportion of collaborations between Japan and China increased from 4.3% in 2011 to 7.1% in 2020 ($R^2 = 0.9044$). China was becoming a stronger partner in later years. It can be seen from Fig. 3 that in 2011, 64.9% of USA research groups were based solely in the USA, but this had decreased to 55.8% by 2020 ($R^2 = 0.93$). Conversely, the proportion of research groups based in the USA and China grew from 6.6% to 13.6% during the decade ($R^2 = 0.91$). The ratio of combination of author's countries in research groups consisting only of researchers belonging to Japanese institutions in JSPS-funded projects was higher than that in NSF-funded projects. In NSF-funded projects, the ratio of authors comprising only the USA was relatively lower, and that ratio was decreasing year by year. NSF-funded projects are more internationalized. In addition, it can be seen that both Japan and the USA are increasingly collaborating with China.

In the preliminary analysis, we also examined the combinations of authors' countries in NSF- and JSPS-funded conference papers, and the results were similar to those for journal articles.

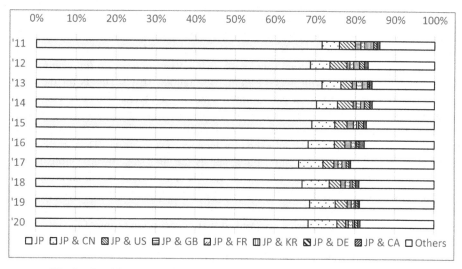

Fig. 2. Combinations of authors' countries for JSPS-funded journal articles.

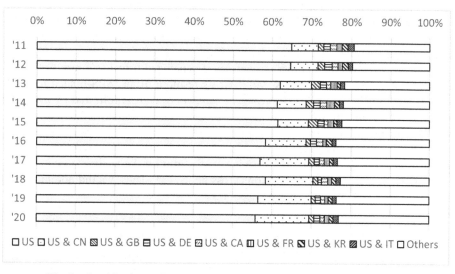

Fig. 3. Combinations of authors' countries for NSF-funded journal articles.

4.4 Journal Popularity

We counted the number of articles published in each journal in each year, and then for the three top-ranked journals in any year, we counted the number of articles in other years. Tables 2 and 3 show the numbers of journal articles resulting from JSPS- and NSF-funded research projects. The solid orange borders indicate the top-ranked journal in terms of the number of articles, the dashed green borders indicate the second-ranked journal, and the dotted blue borders indicate the third-ranked journal.

In terms of journals publishing JSPS-funded articles, *IEICE Transactions on Fundamentals of Electronics, Communications and Computer Sciences* published the most articles in the first five years, while *International Journal of Molecular Sciences* published the most articles in the final four years. *IEICE Transactions on Information and Systems* maintained its fourth-placed ranking throughout. IEICE stands for the Institute of Electronics, Information and Communication Engineers, which is a Japanese academic association that publishes journals and transactions in English, as well as in Japanese. Several Japanese groups have begun to publish papers in English, but they tend to choose international journals published by Japanese associations. Thus, researchers might choose a Japanese association publisher as the first step toward publishing in international journals. *International Journal of Molecular Sciences*, which is an international open access journal, was also the top-ranked journal in some years, and some researchers prefer to publish in open access journals. It can be seen from Table 3 that *Journal of Computational Physics* was ranked first or second in terms of the number of articles published from 2013 to 2017, *Journal of Chemical Theory and Computation* was ranked first or second from 2017 to 2020, and five of the eight most popular journals were published by the IEEE. No journal maintained its top ranking throughout the decade. The rankings of journals publishing NSF-funded articles were even more inconsistent, with no journal maintaining a high ranking throughout the decade. This indicates that NSF-funded projects are more varied. *IEEE Access* was the only journal ranked in both groups. Journal articles resulting from NSF-funded research projects appeared in a more diverse range of publications than those resulting from JSPS-funded research projects.

We also examined the number of conference papers published as a result of JSPS- and NSF-funded research projects. Most papers resulting from JSPS-funded research projects were published in *Lecture Notes in Computer Science*, followed by *Proceedings of SPIE*, which publish the proceedings of various international conferences. Papers were also published in *Procedia Computer Science*, the *ACM International Conference Proceeding Series*, *Leibniz International Proceedings in Informatics*, and *CEUR Workshop Proceedings*. The Scopus database is not as useful for the analysis of conference proceedings because of the aggregation across publishers. Thus, we did not undertake any further analysis of conference proceedings.

Table 2. Most Popular Journals for JSPS-funded Articles.

	2011	2012	2013	2014	2015	2016	2017	2018	2019	2020
IEICE Trans. Fundamentals	35	44	53	55	73	52	56	35	65	51
IEICE Trans. Inf. & Syst.	22	31	36	37	61	65	72	59	71	79
Int. J. Mol. Sci.	5	25	39	26	49	60	102	148	180	212
IEICE Trans. Commun.	27	34	25	19	32	26	24	33	43	23
IEEE Access	NA	NA	NA	3	10	13	41	60	120	123
Applied Sciences	NA	NA	NA	NA	2	8	22	65	64	92
Total	722	1048	1197	1220	1370	1520	1800	1998	1939	2000

Table 3. Most popular journals for NSF-funded articles.

	2011	2012	2013	2014	2015	2016	2017	2018	2019	2020
IEEE Trans. Inf. Theory	124	86	59	41	40	40	47	22	28	35
IEEE Trans. Signal Process.	85	65	38	43	40	48	56	42	41	18
J. Comput. Phys.	77	46	66	99	92	76	65	50	38	53
PLoS Comput. Biol.	49	65	72	72	97	72	41	33	28	26
J. Chem. Theory Comput.	13	32	61	75	65	69	66	63	61	65
IEEE Trans Smart Grid	11	26	17	19	24	25	29	61	43	53
IEEE Internet Things J.	NA	NA	NA	2	1	7	34	31	62	46
IEEE Access	NA	NA	1	4	7	20	43	37	58	44
Total	1975	1960	1950	1957	1961	1958	1964	1925	1932	1953

5   Conclusion

We analyzed the number of authors, combinations of collaborating authors' countries, and popular journals in relation to the publication of journal articles and conference papers resulting from funded research projects. The results showed that the numbers of authors jointly publishing journal articles resulting from JSPS-funded research is increasing, but this is not the case for conference papers. Thus, this requires further analysis. Regarding the combinations of collaborating authors' countries, we found that authors participating in JSPS-funded research projects are increasingly collaborating with China, and are increasingly tending to publish in a diverse range of English-language journals published by Japanese associations. From these results, Japanese-funded research projects are reacting to the part of fund agency expectations.

In this study, we used Scopus bibliographic data, and conducted data cleaning as described in Sect. 3. These data might still contain errors, however, we intend to make these data available to the public to the extent that this does not breach the Scopus guidelines.

The results of this study raise several questions regarding the funding of research projects that are worthy of further investigation. For example, the influence of gender on research projects and publications [12] would be interesting to examine if such data are available, and it would also be worth investigating the differences between various types of research funding. We are also interested in exploring the research topics that various funding agencies are focused on, regardless of whether they express their interest implicitly or explicitly. The analysis of research topics between both funded research projects over the decade would be a next step. We plan to conduct topic analysis in an effort to identify the major research topics in Japan and the USA. Previous studies have conducted topic analyses using topic modeling [13–15]. Our aim is to apply the latent Dirichlet allocation model to titles and abstracts of publications to enable a more in-depth analysis.

Acknowledgments. This work is supported by the Japan Society for the Promotion of Science (JSPS) KAKENHI Grant Number JP18K11990.

References

1. González-Alcaide, G., Salinas, A., Ramos, J.M.: Scientometrics analysis of research activity and collaboration patterns in Chagas cardiomyopathy. PLoS Negl. Trop. Dis. **12**(66), e0006602 (2018). https://doi.org/10.1371/journal.pntd.0006602
2. McManus, C., Baeta Neves, A.A., Maranhão, A.Q., Souza Filho, A.G., Santana, J.M.: International collaboration in Brazilian science: financing and impact. Scientometrics **125**(3), 2745–2772 (2020). https://doi.org/10.1007/s11192-020-03728-7
3. Japan Society for the Promotion of Science. Grants-in-Aid for Scientific Research (KAKENHI), https://www.jsps.go.jp/english/e-grants/grants01.html. Accessed 5 June 5 2022
4. Britannica, Big Science, https://www.britannica.com/science/Big-Science-science. Accessed 8 June 2022
5. Japan Science and Technology Agency (JST), JST-Mirai Program Large-scale Type. https://www.jst.go.jp/mirai/en/program/large-scale-type/index.html. Accessed 5 June 5 2022
6. Japan Society for the Promotion of Science. Homepage. https://www.jsps.go.jp/english/index.html. Accessed 16 Mar 2022
7. National Science Foundation. Homepage. https://www.nsf.gov/. Accessed 16 Mar 2022
8. Guiling, Y., Panatik, S.A., Sukor, M.S.M., Rusbadrol, N., Cunlin, L.: Bibliometric analysis of global research on organizational citizenship behavior from 2000 to 2019. SAGE Open **12**(1), 1–16 (2022). https://doi.org/10.1177/21582440221079898
9. Wang, X., Xu, Z., Su, S.-F., Zhou, W.: A comprehensive bibliometric analysis of uncertain group decision making from 1980 to 2019. Inf. Sci. **547**, 328–353 (2021). https://doi.org/10.1016/j.ins.2020.08.036
10. Faisal, F., Gi, G.M., Martin, S.N.: Analysis of government-funded research in Indonesia from 2014–2018: implications for research trends in science education. Indonesian J. Sci. Educ. **9**(2), 146–158 (2020). https://doi.org/10.15294/jpii.v9i2.23174
11. National Science Foundation. Award Simple Search. https://www.nsf.gov/awardsearch/. Accessed 16 Mar 2022
12. Mihaljević-Brandt, H., Santamaría, L., Tullney, M.: The effect of gender in the publication patterns in mathematics. PLoS ONE **11**(10), e0165367 (2016). https://doi.org/10.1371/journal.pone.0165367
13. Han, X.: Evolution of research topics in LIS between 1996 and 2019: an analysis based on latent Dirichlet allocation topic model. Scientometrics **125**(3), 2561–2595 (2020). https://doi.org/10.1007/s11192-020-03721-0
14. Miyata, Y., Ishita, E., Yang, F., Yamamoto, M., Iwase, A., Kurata, K.: Knowledge structure transition in library and information science: topic modeling and visualization. Scientometrics **125**(1), 665–687 (2020). https://doi.org/10.1007/s11192-020-03657-5
15. Wieczorek, O., Unger, S., Riebling, J., Erhard, L., Koß, C., Heiberger, R.: Mapping the field of psychology: trends in research topics 1995–2015. Scientometrics **126**(12), 9699–9731 (2021). https://doi.org/10.1007/s11192-021-04069-9

Smart Search and Annotation

Bibrecord-Based Literature Management with Interactive Latent Space Learning

Shingo Watanabe[✉][iD], Hiroyoshi Ito[iD], Masaki Matsubara[iD],
and Atsuyuki Morishima[iD]

University of Tsukuba, Tsukuba, Japan
watanabe.shingo.ss@alumni.tsukuba.ac.jp,
{ito,masaki,mori}@slis.tsukuba.ac.jp

Abstract. Every researcher must conduct a literature review, and the document management needs of researchers working on various research topics vary. However, there are two significant challenges today. First, traditional methods like the tree hierarchy of document folders and tag-based management are no longer effective with the enormous volume of publications. Second, although their bib information is available to everyone, many papers can be accessed only through paid services. This study attempts to develop an interactive tool for personal literature management solely based on their bibliographic records. To make such a tool possible, we developed a principled "human-in-the-loop latent space learning" method that estimates the management criteria of each researcher based on his or her feedback to calculate the positions of documents in a two-dimensional space on the screen. Since a set of bibliographic records forms a graph, our model is naturally designed as a graph-based encoder-decoder model that connects the graph and the space. The experiments with ten researchers from humanities, science, and engineering domains show that the proposed framework gives much superior results to a typical graph convolutional encoder-decoder model.

Keywords: Graph neural network · Human-in-the-loop system · Document management

1 Introduction

Every researcher must conduct a literature review, and there is a personalized need for researchers working on various research topics in their document management. They must organize publications according to their criteria to find relevant research and understand their field trends.

However, there are two significant challenges faced in personalized literature management. First, researchers must manage much research. Fire [4] found that recently, more than seven million new scholarly studies have been published yearly. Therefore, the traditional approaches, like the tree hierarchy of document folders and tag-based management, are no longer effective. There is a need for automated literature management techniques.

Y.-H. Tseng et al. (Eds.): ICADL 2022, LNCS 13636, pp. 155–171, 2022.
https://doi.org/10.1007/978-3-031-21756-2_13

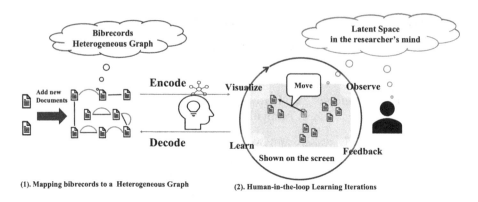

Fig. 1. Overview of the framework. (1) A graph of bib records is constructed for the arrived documents; documents are connected if they mention the same terms, are written by the same author, etc. (2) Next, we have a human-in-the-loop learning iteration for learning the latent space in the user's mind. Then, the learner *predicts* the positions of newly arrived papers in the space.

Second, accessing the paper's content was challenging. Although their bib information is available to everyone, many papers can be accessed through paid service only. According to Nicolson et al. [13], 65% out of the 100 most cited papers were paywalled. This is a major barrier for researchers to accessing pertinent papers for their research. Therefore, methods for automatic literature management that use the literature contents [22, 30, 38] have limited applicability.

With this background, this study attempts to develop an interactive tool for personal literature management based on bibliographic records *without the need to access the contents of papers*. The tool asks the researcher to put icons corresponding to papers in the two-dimensional space on the screen with their own criteria, and then *predicts the positions of newly arrived papers that the user would put in*. Figure 1 illustrates how it works. First, since the relationships among bibliographic records are naturally modeled as a graph, the set of bib records is represented as a heterogeneous graph of bib records whose nodes correspond to papers, authors, conference names, years, etc. (Fig. 1(1)). The graph connects papers that share the same authors, the same years, and so on. Then, the machine learner, which implements our human-in-the-loop latent space learning method (Sect. 4), computes and visualizes the positions in a *two-dimensional space on the screen* that corresponds to the space for papers that exists in the researcher's mind (Fig. 1(2)). Next, the researcher gives feedback on the suggested positions by *moving papers in incorrect positions in her criteria to the correct position*. In the feedback phase, the researchers are given details about the literature, including the title, authors, publication place, and year. Then, the learner takes the feedback and updates the criteria in the space so that it can correctly predict positions of newly arrived papers. The *interactive* nature not only captures the current latent space of papers in each researcher's mind, but also allows the system to follow the researcher's criteria that are evolving over time [1].

Then, our problem can be thought of as a *latent space learning* with a graph convolutional encoder-decoder model [17]; here, the encoder and decoder map paper nodes in the graph to points in the latent space and vice versa, and the objective function is cross-entropy loss for generating adjacency matrices for document clusters in the space. However, existing models do not support our *human-in-the-loop* nature, i.e., do not allow the user to give interactive feedback to the latent space. Therefore, we developed a principled "human-in-the-loop latent space learning" method that estimates the management criteria of each researcher based on his or her feedback on the estimated positions of documents in a two-dimensional space on the screen. Our challenge is how to make the model capture the characteristics of the latent space for literature management.

Challenges and Contributions. (1) We show a *principled* framework for interactive latent space learning for literature management. It is based on a common graph convolutional encoder-decoder model, in which the criteria for individual literature management are represented by the weights of a set of *meta-paths* (i.e., sequences of attributes at the schema of bib-records data), which are a popular means to capture the semantics of heterogeneous graph [22,31]. Our model is unique in that it is based on the following two assumptions. First, the user's criteria in the latent space are consistent *only locally*. This is inspired by the results in psychology such as [34]. Thus, our first research question **(RQ1)** is whether each researcher has criteria at different sub-spaces in the latent space or not. Second, two papers are connected through paths on the graph if they are close to each other in the latent space. Therefore, unlike other popular graph convolutional encoder-decoder models, our decoder is based on the Euclidean distance of latent vectors. Thus, our second question **(RQ2)** is whether our decoder is effective or not.

(2) We show experimental results where the subjects are ten academic researchers from *science, engineering, and the humanities domains*. The results answer the two research questions positively and show that the approach is much superior to a typical graph convolutional model, and the resulting quality is practically good in that it can put the new paper in the position close to the correct one although it does not necessarily exact one. This implies that our tool can help researchers manage relevant publications with their own criteria.

Limitations. This research does not intend to find the best feature set and the best performance of learning the latent space with bibliographic data potentially available on public. The experimental result only shows to what degree we can learn the latent space, given a minimum set of information from bib records.

2 Related Work

Literature Management Tools. Tools to assist researchers in organizing related papers are widely used, and studies have been conducted on such tools. Francese [5] conducted a survey at the University of Turin to determine how students and researchers manage their bibliographies. The results of the survey showed that EndNote was the most popular bibliography management software for researchers to manage their electronic literature online, used by 49% of respondents, followed by BibTex (11%) and Mendeley (9%). In general, such tools can automatically classify the documents with *objective criteria* such as years and authors, and need explicit inputs from users (such as tags given to each paper) to manage them with the users' criteria for document management. In contrast, our system automatically estimates the *user's* document management criteria and can map new documents onto the space so that the user can easily grasp how they are related to other papers.

Document Classification, Clustering, Recommendation. Various methods have been proposed, such as hierarchical Bayesian clustering [12], metric learning [23,36], but almost all the approach use natural language processing methods [10,29]. Unlike our method, most existing methods classify, cluster, and recommend documents by analyzing abstracts and content of papers assuming that they can access the *document contents*, which limits the applicability in the current digital library situation.

We found that there are studies on personalized paper recommendation methods that do not need the document contents [15,20,22,35,37]. The paper recommendation is orthogonal to the latent space learning problem in that the former does not identify any criteria on how researchers manage the papers, and our method does not address the problem of identifying papers to recommend. Combining the two approaches to help researchers is an interesting future work.

Active Learning. Active learning has also been the subject of various studies like distance-based active learning [2,24,39]. Recently, numerous studies on interactive recommendation systems based on machine learning models and human interaction have been conducted [14], and some studies have used an active learning approach to determine user interests [26]. Our feedback system on the placement of documents in the latent space serves as an oracle for latent-space learning while allowing the criteria of organizing documents to *evolve* with the interactive interface.

Latent Space Learning. Latent space learning has been used for learning data features and comprehending data patterns and/or structural similarities in various contexts. For example, PTE [32] is a semi-supervised latent-space learning technique for textual data. Additionally, doc2vec [19] creates representations for each document using latent space learning.

For graphs, network embedding techniques considering latent semantics have drawn considerable attention [6,9,11,27,28]. Some of the techniques such as Deepwalk [25] and Node2vec [7] rely on random walks to produce a distributed representation of nodes; LINE [33] consider and embed nodes that indirectly have edges attached to one another; The Kipf and Welling GCN [17] method learns the latent vectors of nodes while considering the network structure. Additionally, to fit autoencoders [16] to network data, the GCN was used in graph autoencoders (GAE) and variational graph autoencoders (VGAE) [18]. Both methods involve a two-layer graph convolutional network and reconstruct the adjacency matrix using an encoder-decoder algorithm. Our model is unique in that it deals with local consistency of criteria in the latent space and adopts the distance-based decoder tailored for literature management.

Table 1. Notations used in this paper

Symbol	Description
$\mathcal{D}$	A set of documents $\{d_1, \cdots, d_{|\mathcal{D}|}\}$
$\mathcal{P}$	A set of meta-path $\{p_1, \cdots, p_{|\mathcal{P}|}\}$
$\mathcal{V}$	A set of nodes
$\mathcal{E}$	A set of edges
$G(\mathcal{D}, \mathcal{E})$	Undirected graph
$\mathcal{A}$	A set of object types of nodes
$\mathcal{R}$	A set of relation types of edges
L	Embedding dimension
$\mathcal{W}_p$	The weight of a meta-path p
$\mathbf{A}^p \in \mathbb{R}^{\mathcal{D} \times \mathcal{D}}$	Adjacency matrix of a meta-path p
$\mathcal{C}_k \subseteq \mathcal{D}$	k-th cluster consists of a set of documents
$\vec{\mu}_k \in \mathbb{R}^L$	A centroid of k-th cluster
$\tilde{\mathbf{A}} \in \mathbb{R}^{\mathcal{D} \times \mathcal{D}}$	Adjacency matrix weighted with W
$\tilde{\mathbf{A}}_{d_i, d_j}$	The (i, j) element of $\tilde{\mathbf{A}}$
$\mathbf{X} \in \mathbb{R}^{\mathcal{D} \times \mathcal{D}}$	Features
$\vec{z}_{d_i} \in \mathbb{R}^L$	Latent vector of d_i
$\mathbf{Z} \in \mathbb{R}^{\mathcal{D} \times L}$	Matrix of $\vec{z}$
$\hat{\mathcal{Z}}$	A set feedback by a user $\{(\vec{z}_{d_i}, \hat{\vec{z}}_{d_i}), \cdots, (\vec{z}_{d_j}, \hat{\vec{z}}_{d_j})\}$
θ	Decoder network parameters
ψ	Encoder network parameters
$\mathcal{Q}$	A set of unknown documents $\{q_1, \cdots, q_{|\mathcal{Q}|}\}$

3   Definitions and the Problem

We discuss our problem with the notations in Table 1. First, we define important concepts we use in the discussion, and then define our problem.

Heterogeneous Information Network. Real-world systems, such as bibliographic information networks, are structured into HINs [3,31]. A heterogeneous information network (HIN) is a special type of network structure that has multiple types of nodes and edges.

Definition 1 (Heterogeneous Information Network). *An HIN is defined as a directed graph $G(\mathcal{V}, \mathcal{E})$ with an object-type mapping function $\tau : \mathcal{V} \rightarrow \mathcal{A}$ and* relation-type mapping function $\phi : \mathcal{E} \rightarrow \mathcal{R}$, where $mathcalV$ and $\mathcal{E}$ represent set of the nodes and edges, and $\mathcal{A}$ and $\mathcal{R}$ are the set of the object types and the relation types, respectively. In general, $|\mathcal{A}| + |\mathcal{R}| > 2$. For example, in a bibliographic information network, there are object types, such as paper (P), author (A), term (T), year (Y), and relation types: e.g., published a paper (A-P), a paper is published in a venue (P-V). By constructing a schema of paths called a _meta-path_ from these types of objects and relations, we can explain the rich semantics from the HIN.

Meta-Path. Intuitively, a _meta-path_ is a sequence of object-types that can have an instance in the graph. For example, A-P and P-A-P are meta-paths. Meta-paths are commonly used to capture rich semantics of [22,31].

Definition 2 (Meta-Path). The meta-path P is defined as $\mathcal{A}_1 \xrightarrow{R_1} \mathcal{A}_2 \xrightarrow{R_2}$ $\cdots \xrightarrow{R_l} \mathcal{A}_{l+1}$ and defines a composite relation $\mathcal{R} = \mathcal{R}_1 \circ \mathcal{R}_2 \circ \cdots \mathcal{R}_l$ between types $\mathcal{A}_1$ and $\mathcal{A}_{l+1}$ where $\circ$ denotes the composition operator of the relations. Because this study is interested in the relationships between papers, we consider a meta-path in which both the starting and ending points of the meta-path are papers (P). For example, the meta-path "Paper (P)– Author (A)– Paper (P)" indicates the relationship between papers written by the same author.

Problem. We assume that a set of documents represents an HIN, and each document has features. In this study, we assume the attribute is an index of the document, which is represented as a matrix $\mathbf{X} \in \mathbb{R}^{|\mathcal{D}| \times |\mathcal{D}|}$. We construct adjacency matrices $\{\mathbf{A}^p \in \mathbb{R}^{|\mathcal{D}| \times |\mathcal{D}|}\}_{p \in \mathcal{P}}$, each of which represents the relationships between documents in a meta-path p. Additionally, the user interaction processes are provided to estimate the user's document management criterion. This interaction is denoted as a set of tuples $(\vec{z}, \hat{\vec{z}}) \in \hat{\mathcal{Z}}$, where $\vec{z}_{d_i}$ represents the initial point of the d_i's latent vector and $\hat{\vec{z}}_{d_i}$ represents the point of the vector after the interaction. Our research is defined formally as follows: given a set of adjacency matrices $\{\mathbf{A}^p\}_{p \in \mathcal{P}}$, the feature of documents X, and a set of interactions $\hat{\mathcal{Z}}$, we find $Z_{\mathcal{Q}}$, which is a set of latent vectors of a set of unknown documents $\mathcal{Q}$.

4   Proposed Learning Method

To make the model captures the problem of identifying the positions of documents of the latent space in the user's mind, our method was designed based on the two assumption. First, there is some locality of the criteria of managing documents in the space in mind — when the researcher moves papers to the place near some of the other papers, there is a consistent criterion in the neighborhood, but the consistency is not guaranteed in other places. Second, two papers will be connected through many paths some way on the graph if they are close

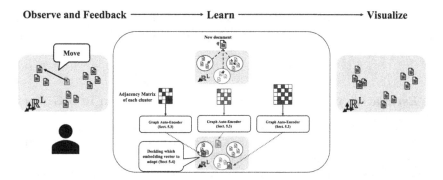

Fig. 2. One iteration of Observe-Feedback-Learn-Visualize. Given the visualized latent space of papers, the user gives the feedback by moving papers in incorrect positions to the correct ones, then the learning process updates the space based on the feedback.

to each other in the latent space. Therefore, unlike other popular graph convolutional network-based encoder-decoder models, our model's decoder is based on the Euclidean distance of latent vectors.

The learning phase of our proposed framework comprises four steps:

1. Clustering the latent vectors
2. Estimating document management criterion in each cluster
3. Learning the latent vectors of documents based on Graph Auto-Encoders
4. Choosing a cluster where a new document is located and acquiring the latent vector for the new document

This step is included in our iteration of our human-in-the-loop framework; each time a user provides feedback, we apply this step to update the clusters and fine-tune the models. Figure 2 illustrates the learning phase in one "move-learn-display" iteration in our framework in Fig. 1.

4.1 Clustering the Latent Vectors

The first step of our proposed method is to cluster the latent space in which the user provides feedback. K-means clustering method was used [8]. Clustering by K-means results in an adjacency matrix and center of mass for each cluster. The K-means optimization problem is as follows:

$$\{\mathbf{r}_{d_i}\}_{d_i \in \mathcal{D}}, \{\vec{\mu}_k\}_{k \in [n_c]} = \underset{\{\mathbf{r}_{d_i}\}, \{\vec{\mu}_k\}}{\arg\min} J, \tag{1}$$

where $\mathbf{r}_{d_i} = (r_{d_i,1}, \cdots, r_{d_i,k})^\top$ represents the cluster assignment vector of the document d_i. Each element $r_{d_i,j}$ is one if document d_i belongs to cluster j and zero otherwise. $\vec{\mu}_k \in \mathbb{R}^L$ is the centroid vector of cluster k. Objective function J is defined as follows:

$$J = \sum_{d_i \in \mathcal{D}} \sum_{k \in [n_c]} r_{d_i,k} \|\vec{z}_{d_i} - \vec{\mu}_k\|_2^2, \tag{2}$$

where $\vec{z}_{d_i}$ is a latent vector for a document d_i. After solving the K-means clustering, we obtain the k-th cluster

$$\mathcal{C}_k = \{d_i \in \mathcal{D} \mid r_{d_i,k} = 1\}. \tag{3}$$

4.2   Estimation of Document Management Criterion in a Given Cluster

This section describes how to estimate a user's document management criterion from the space they have generated. We used meta-paths as a management criterion for documents and weighed the meta-paths from the user's space. Here, we assume that the management criterion is unique for each cluster the user creates. The fundamental concept of determining the weight of the meta-path is that when two documents in a cluster are related to a meta-path, the user manages the cluster considering the meta-path. From this insight, we calculate the weight of meta-path p for k-th cluster from the adjacency matrix as follows:

$$w_k^p = \left| \left\{ d_i \in \mathcal{C}_k \mid \exists d_j \in \mathcal{C}_k : \mathbf{A}_{d_i,d_j}^p = 1 \right\} \right|. \tag{4}$$

Once the weights of the meta-paths within a cluster k have been determined, the adjacency matrices are weighted accordingly. The weighted adjacency matrix for the k-th cluster is defined as follows

$$\tilde{\mathbf{A}}_k = \sum_{p \in \mathcal{P}} w_k^p \mathbf{A}_{\mathcal{C}_k}^p, \tag{5}$$

where $\mathbf{A}_{\mathcal{C}_k}^p$ is an adjacency matrix for a meta-path p of which elements are only for a cluster $\mathcal{C}_k$.

4.3   Learning the Latent Vector of Documents Based on Graph Auto-Encoders

In this section, we explain how our model learns the latent vector of documents. From an overview, we use the weighted adjacency matrix $\tilde{\mathbf{A}}_k$ to obtain a latent vector in the latent space for each document. To this end, we construct a graph convolutional network(GCN)-based encoder-decoder model with supervision from the user's interactions. In our system, we create the models for each cluster the user created.

Encoder: Our encoder is GCN [17] with two layers. Particularly, the latent vectors of the documents in cluster $\mathcal{C}_k$ were calculated using the following equation:

$$\mathbf{Z}_k = GCN_{\phi_k}(\mathbf{X}_k, \tilde{\mathbf{A}}_k), \tag{6}$$

where $\mathbf{X}_k$ is the feature matrix only for a cluster $\mathcal{C}_k$. GCN is defined as

$$GCN_{\phi_k}(\mathbf{X}_k, \tilde{\mathbf{A}}_k) = \hat{\mathbf{A}}_k ReLU(\hat{\mathbf{A}}_k \mathbf{X}_k \mathbf{W}_k^{(0)}) \mathbf{W}_k^{(1)} \tag{7}$$

with the GCN parameter set for k-th cluster $\phi_k = \left\{ \mathbf{W}_k^{(0)}, \mathbf{W}_k^{(1)} \right\}$ where $\mathbf{W}_k^{(0)} \in \mathbb{R}^{|\mathcal{D}| \times k_1}$ is the weight of first layer and $\mathbf{W}_k^{(1)} \in \mathbb{R}^{k_1 \times L}$ is the weight of the second layer. $\hat{\mathbf{A}}$ is defined as

$$\hat{\mathbf{A}}_k = \mathbf{D}^{-\frac{1}{2}} \tilde{\mathbf{A}}_k \mathbf{D}^{-\frac{1}{2}}. \tag{8}$$

The decoder reconstructs the adjacency matrix $\tilde{\mathbf{A}}_k$ by computing the probability $p_\theta(\tilde{\mathbf{A}}_k | \mathbf{Z}_\mathcal{D})$ of edge generation based on the latent vector of each document where

$$p_{\theta_k}(\tilde{\mathbf{A}}_k | \mathbf{Z}_k) = \prod_{d_i \in \mathcal{C}_k} \prod_{d_j \in \mathcal{C}_k} p_{\theta_k}(\tilde{\mathbf{A}}_{k_{d_i,d_j}} | \vec{z}_{d_i}, \vec{z}_{d_j}). \tag{9}$$

The decoder in the generative model was configured using the Euclidean distance of the latent vectors. This is intended to increase the probability of generating edges between documents that are placed closer together because the user provides feedback to the system based on the distance between documents. The decoder expressed as follows:

$$p_{\theta_k}(\tilde{\mathbf{A}}_{k_{d_i,d_j}} | \vec{z_{d_i}}, \vec{z_{d_j}}) = \sigma \left(\frac{a_k}{\|\vec{z_{d_i}} - \vec{z_{d_j}}\|_2^2} + b_k \right), \tag{10}$$

where $\sigma(\cdot)$ denotes a sigmoid function and $\theta_k = \{a_k, b_k\}$ denotes a set of parameters used in the decoder.

Objective Function: The objective function consists of cross-entropy loss for generating the adjacency matrix and supervision from the interaction by the user. Parameters $\boldsymbol{\phi} = \{\phi_k\}_{k \in [n_c]}$, and $\boldsymbol{\theta} = \{\theta_k\}_{k \in [n_c]}$ are learned to maximize them.

The cross-entropy used to generate the adjacency matrix is defined as follows:

$$\mathcal{L}_{GAE} = \sum_{k \in [n_c]} \log p_{\theta_k}(\tilde{\mathbf{A}}_k | GCN_{\phi_k}(\mathbf{X}_k, \tilde{\mathbf{A}}_k))) \tag{11}$$

$$= \sum_{k \in [n_c]} \sum_{d_i \in \mathcal{C}_k} \sum_{d_j \in \mathcal{C}_k} \tilde{\mathbf{A}}_{k_{d_i,d_j}} \log p_{\theta_k} \left(\tilde{\mathbf{A}}_{k_{d_i,d_j}} | \vec{z_{d_i}}, \vec{z_{d_j}} \right) \tag{12}$$

Moreover, we define a loss function that measures the difference between the user's feedback and the learned latent vectors to minimize disagreement. We measure this disagreement using the conditional probability that, given user feedback, the generation probability of the latent vector. The objective function is defined as follows:

$$\mathcal{L}_{feedback} = \sum_{k \in [n_c]} \log p \left(GCN_{\phi_k}(\mathbf{X}_k, \tilde{\mathbf{A}}_k) | \hat{\mathcal{Z}} \right) \tag{13}$$

$$= \sum_{k \in [n_c]} \sum_{(\vec{z_{d_i}}, \vec{z_{\hat{d_i}}}) \in \hat{\mathcal{Z}}} \delta(d_i \in \mathcal{C}_k) \log \mathcal{N}(\vec{z_{d_i}}^k | \vec{z_{\hat{d_i}}}, \sigma^2 \mathbf{I}) \tag{14}$$

$$= -\sum_{k \in [n_c]} \sum_{(\vec{z_{d_i}}, \vec{z_{\hat{d_i}}}) \in \hat{\mathcal{Z}}} \delta(d_i \in \mathcal{C}_k) \left\| \vec{z_{d_i}}^k - \vec{z_{\hat{d_i}}} \right\|_2^2 + const., \tag{15}$$

where $\mathcal{N}(\vec{x} \mid \vec{\mu}, \mathbf{\Sigma})$ denotes the multivariate normal distribution, $\delta(\cdot)$ denotes an indicator function, and $\vec{z_{d_i}}^k$ represents a latent vector which is generated by k-th encoder. The overall optimization problem is defined as follows:

$$\phi, \boldsymbol{\theta} = \underset{\phi, \boldsymbol{\theta}}{\arg\max} \, \mathcal{L}_{GAE} + \alpha \mathcal{L}_{feedback}, \tag{16}$$

where α denotes a hyper-parameter.

4.4 Choosing a Cluster Where a New Document Locates and Acquiring the Latent Vector for the New Document

This section explains the method used to determine the latent vectors of the new document. Because the input adjacency matrix for the encoder differs for each cluster, we must determine the most appropriate cluster and the corresponding latent vector for the new document. The fundamental principle for determining the most appropriate cluster is when the latent vector of a new document belongs to a cluster, the similarity between the documents in that cluster will be higher than that in the other clusters, that is, the cluster's centroid will have the closest similarity. Based on this principle, we determine the latent vector of the new document q as follows

$$\vec{z_q} = \underset{\vec{z_q} \in \{\vec{z_q}^k\}_{k \in [n_c]}}{\arg\min} \frac{1}{|\mathcal{C}_k|} \sum_{\vec{z_d} \in \mathcal{C}_k} \|\vec{z_q}^k - \vec{z_d}\| \tag{17}$$

$$= \underset{\vec{z_q} \in \{\vec{z_q}^k\}_{k \in [n_c]}}{\arg\min} \|\vec{z_q}^k - \vec{\mu_k}\|, \tag{18}$$

where $\vec{z_q}^k \in \mathbb{R}^L$ represents the latent vector generated from the encoder using the k-th cluster's adjacency matrix $\tilde{\mathbf{A}}_k$.

5 Experiment

We conducted an experiment to answer our two research questions and how effective the method was. For RQ1, we compared our method with its variation that assumes the consistency of the criteria across the latent space. For RQ2, we compared our framework with a popular encoder-decoder-model for graphs as a baseline, which uses the inner-product-based decoder. In this section, **ISLE** (Interactive latent Space Learning) denotes our method.

5.1 Settings

Participants. We recruited ten researchers (a library domain researcher, two data engineering domains, three HCI domains and four ML domain researchers).

Data Collection. First, we asked each of the participants to send us the Bib-TeX records of any 50 papers related to his or her research. Second, we asked them to use our tool, in the way that the tool shows the bib records in random order and the user puts each into the two-dimensional space. As a result, we obtained the history of how they behaved in the 50 iterations, i.e., how they moved their papers to put all of the 50 papers in their spaces incrementally. The user saw the title, author, conference, and year of publication of each paper in the phase.

Evaluation. For each subsequence of iterations 1 to $10i$ of collected data for each participant, we compared the predicted position for $(10i + 1)$th paper and its correct positions in the collected data. In the experiments, we set hyperparameters as $L = 2$, $\alpha = 100$, $n_c = 6$, and $k_1 = 4$.

Metrics. We used Recall@k and nDCG@k [21] where k=6. Recall@k is expressed using the following equation

$$Recall@k = \frac{|\mathcal{U} \cap \mathcal{P}_k|}{|\mathcal{U}|}, \tag{19}$$

where $\mathcal{U}$ denotes the set of the closest (with the Euclidean distance) k documents in the latent space to the test data placed by the user, and $\mathcal{P}_k$ is the set of the closest k latent vectors to the position of the test data predicted by the model. nDCG@k [21] is obtained by dividing the value of DCG@k by the most ideal value of DCG@k, that is, if all model predictions are correct. We use the inverse of the distance from the correct position as a relevance value.

5.2 Baselines and Variations

(1) VGAE. VGAE is a popular encoder-decoder-model for graphs [18]. VGAE in our experiment is a variant of ISLE in which the decoder is replaced by the decoder used in ordinary VGAE. In other words, the decoder expressed by the equation (10) in Sect. 5 is replaced with the inner product of each latent representation, which is expressed as follows:

$$p_\theta(\mathbf{A}_{d_i,d_j} | \vec{z_{d_i}}, \vec{z_{d_j}}) = \sigma(\vec{z_{d_i}} \cdot \vec{z_{d_j}}), \tag{20}$$

where σ represents the sigmoid function.

(2) ISLE and VAGE Without Clustering. We used **VGAE** and **ISLE** that omits step 1 (clustering) (Sect. 4.1), to address RQ1.

(3) ISLE with Different Sets of Meta-paths. The meta-paths used are listed in Table 2. We compared the following five cases for **ISLE**, while we used all meta-paths for **VGAE**. (a) **ALL**: An adjacency matrix is composed of PAP, PTP, PYP, and PVP meta-paths. (b) **PAP Only**: An adjacency matrix is composed only of PAP. (c) **PTP Only**: An adjacency matrix is composed only of PTP. (d) **PYP Only**: An adjacency matrix is composed only of PYP. (e) **PVP Only**: An adjacency matrix is composed only of PVP.

5.3   Results

Figures 3a–4b show the result. The solid line in each figure represents the mean, and the shaded area represents the 95% confidence interval. The red lines in each figure indicate the results of our proposed method when the adjacency matrix given as input consists of **ALL**, as described in Sect. 5.2. The blue lines in Fig. 3 indicate the results of **VGAE** when the adjacency matrix given as the input consists of **ALL**, as described in Sect. 5.2. The yellow and olive lines in the Fig. 3 show the result of estimating document management criteria without using clusters in the proposed method. The green, peach, purple, and gray lines in Fig. 4 depict the limited types of meta-paths given as inputs in the proposed method. The figures demonstrate ISLE outperformed all methods and that the accuracy improves as the number of feedback increases.

Table 2. Meaning of each meta-path

Meta-path	Meaning
PAP	Papers which the same author wrote
PTP	Papers that mention the same word in the title
PYP	Papers published in the same year
PVP	Papers presented at the same conference

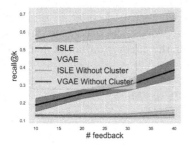

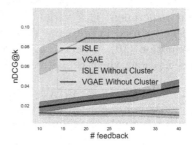

(a) Value of recall@k for the proposed method and VGAE

(b) Value of nDCG@k for the proposed method and VGAE

Fig. 3. The horizontal axis represents the number of times feedback is received from the user. The results of ISLE outperformed other methods.

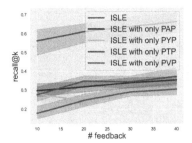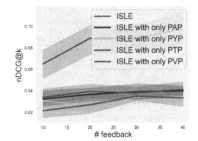

(a) Value of recall@k for the proposed method and when the type of meta-path is limited

(b) Value of nDCG@k for the proposed method and when the type of meta-path is limited

Fig. 4. The horizontal axis represents the number of times feedback is received from the user. The results of ISLE using multiple meta-paths were more accurate.

Note that in our context, recall@k indicates how the predicted position is close to the correct one, while nDCG@k indicates how it keeps the order of distances. Unlike ordinary information retrieval context, Recall@k is more critical for our problem because the order of distances can dramatically change even if the position is slightly moved.

Figure 4a compares the results with different sets of meta-paths. The result shows that ISLE performs the best when we use all of the four meta-paths. As we noted in the limitation part, finding the best feature set is not our research question. However, this implies that researchers are aware of multiple criteria when managing papers and the proposed method can flexibly express these criteria by using multiple meta-paths.

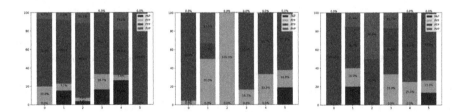

Fig. 5. The normalized distribution of meta-path weights in each cluster

6 Discussion

The Locality of Criteria in the latent space (RQ1). The results shown in Figs. 3a and b clearly indicate that methods with a clustering phase are superior to those without clustering. This shows that the clusters of each researcher have a different set of weights of meta-paths, which means that researchers use different criteria in sub-spaces in their latent space. Figure 5 shows the normalized

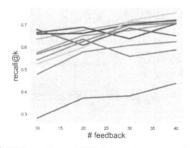 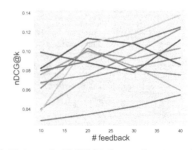

(a) Value of recall@k by each researcher   (b) Value of nDCG@k by each researcher

Fig. 6. Comparison of accuracy by each researcher

distribution of meta-path weights in each cluster of three of the ten subjects. In their distributions, although PTP accounts for a large proportion, the weights are often considerably different to each cluster even for the same researcher.

Effectiveness of the Euclidean Distance-Based Decoder (RQ2). The idea behind our second assumption is that the user provides feedback in the latent space based on the Euclidean distance rather than the angle between documents (which is the principle for VGAE's decoder). So ISLE's decoder would be more accurate, which calculates the generation probability of edges based on the Euclidean distance between documents. The results shown in Fig. 3a and 3b clearly support this assumption.

Individual Difference. We collected data from ten researchers, and Fig. 6 shows how each researcher's feedback affected the accuracy of the data. Similar colors represent researchers in similar research domains. Figures 6a and 6b show that the accuracy generally improves as the number of feedback cycles increases. Our findings are the management criteria of each researcher can be captured with meta-paths, although there are individual differences. The following are possible reasons for the decrease in accuracy during the experiment: (1) The criteria changed during the experiment and the cluster was reconstructed. (2) The English paper is mixed with papers in another language.

7   Conclusion and Future Work

In this study, we proposed a method that estimates a user's document management criterion based on human-in-the-loop latent-space learning.

The experimental results showed that the proposed method accurately places unknown documents at the user's desired position compared with the baseline method. Additionally, experiments with multiple and limited number of meta-paths showed that proposed method (ISLE) is more accurate when multiple meta-paths are used, indicating that ISLE is effective even when users manage documents according to various criteria. In the future, we intend to (1) consider a method that enables to learn efficiently with a small amount of feedback (2) develop a document management system based on ISLE that can be used in the real-world (3) consider using longer meta-paths. The realization of these three goals will provide not only a better method for human-in-the-loop latent-space learning but will also provide support for researchers in literature management.

Acknowledgement. This work was partially supported by Kumagai Gumi Co., Ltd., JSPS KAKENHI Grant Number 22H00508, 22K17944 and 21H03552. This work was approved by the IRB of University of Tsukuba. We are grateful to Masao Takaku for his valuable comments.

References

1. Bates, M.J.: The design of browsing and berrypicking techniques for the online search interface. Online Rev. **13**(5), 407–424 (1989)
2. Deng, Y., Yuan, Y., Fu, H., Qu, A.: Query-augmented active metric learning. J. Am. Stat. Assoc. 1–14 (2022)
3. Dong, Y., Chawla, N.V., Swami, A.: metapath2vec: scalable representation learning for heterogeneous networks. In: Proceedings of the 23rd ACM SIGKDD International Conference on Knowledge Discovery and Data Mining, pp. 135–144 (2017)
4. Fire, M., Guestrin, C.: Over-optimization of academic publishing metrics: observing Goodhart's law in action. GigaScience **8**(6), giz053 (2019)
5. Francese, E.: Usage of reference management software at the university of Torino. Usage Ref. Manage. Softw. Univ. Torino **4**, 145–174 (2013)
6. Fu, X., Zhang, J., Meng, Z., King, I.: MAGNN: metapath aggregated graph neural network for heterogeneous graph embedding. In: Proceedings of The Web Conference 2020, pp. 2331–2341 (2020)
7. Grover, A., Leskovec, J.: node2vec: scalable feature learning for networks. In: Proceedings of the 22nd ACM SIGKDD International Conference on Knowledge Discovery and Data Mining, pp. 855–864 (2016)
8. Hartigan, J.A., Wong, M.A.: Algorithm as 136: a k-means clustering algorithm. J. Roy. Stat. Soc. Ser. C (Applied Statistics) **28**(1), 100–108 (1979)
9. Hsu, Y.L., Tsai, Y.C., Li, C.T.: FinGAT: financial graph attention networks for recommending top-k profitable stocks. IEEE Transactions on Knowledge and Data Engineering (2021)
10. Hu, X., Yoo, I.: A comprehensive comparison study of document clustering for a biomedical digital library medline. In: Proceedings of the 6th ACM/IEEE-CS Joint Conference on Digital Libraries (JCDL2006), pp. 220–229. IEEE (2006)
11. Huang, X., Qian, S., Fang, Q., Sang, J., Xu, C.: Meta-path augmented sequential recommendation with contextual co-attention network. ACM Trans. Multimedia Comput. Commun. Appl. (TOMM) **16**(2), 1–24 (2020)
12. Iwayama, M., Tokunaga, T.: Hierarchical Bayesian clustering for automatic text classification. In: Proceedings of the 14th International Joint Conference on Artificial Intelligence, vol. 2, pp. 1322–1327 (1995)
13. Josh, N., Pepe, A.: 65 out of the 100 most cited papers are paywalled. https://www.authorea.com/users/8850/articles/125400-65-out-of-the-100-most-cited-papers-arepaywalled (2019). Accessed 30 June 2022

14. Jugovac, M., Jannach, D.: Interacting with recommenders-overview and research directions. ACM Trans. Interact. Intell. Syst. (TiiS) **7**(3), 1–46 (2017)
15. Kang, Y., Hou, A., Zhao, Z., Gan, D.: A hybrid approach for paper recommendation. IEICE Trans. Inf. Syst. **104**(8), 1222–1231 (2021)
16. Kingma, D.P., Welling, M.: Auto-encoding variational bayes. arXiv preprint arXiv:1312.6114 (2013)
17. Kipf, T.N., Welling, M.: Semi-supervised classification with graph convolutional networks. arXiv preprint arXiv:1609.02907 (2016)
18. Kipf, T.N., Welling, M.: Variational graph auto-encoders. arXiv preprint arXiv:1611.07308 (2016)
19. Le, Q., Mikolov, T.: Distributed representations of sentences and documents. In: International Conference on Machine Learning, pp. 1188–1196. PMLR (2014)
20. Lee, J., Lee, K., Kim, J.G.: Personalized academic research paper recommendation system. arXiv preprint arXiv:1304.5457 (2013)
21. Liang, D., Krishnan, R.G., Hoffman, M.D., Jebara, T.: Variational autoencoders for collaborative filtering. In: Proceedings of the 2018 World Wide Web Conference, pp. 689–698 (2018)
22. Ma, X., Wang, R.: Personalized scientific paper recommendation based on heterogeneous graph representation. IEEE Access **7**, 79887–79894 (2019)
23. Mikawa, K., Goto, M.: Regularized distance metric learning for document classification and its application. J. Jpn. Ind. Manage. Assoc. **66**(2E), 190–203 (2015)
24. Nadagouda, N., Xu, A., Davenport, M.A.: Active metric learning and classification using similarity queries. arXiv preprint arXiv:2202.01953 (2022)
25. Perozzi, B., Al-Rfou, R., Skiena, S.: Deepwalk: online learning of social representations. In: Proceedings of the 20th ACM SIGKDD International Conference on Knowledge Discovery and Data Mining, pp. 701–710 (2014)
26. Elahi, M.: Adaptive active learning in recommender systems. In: Konstan, J.A., Conejo, R., Marzo, J.L., Oliver, N. (eds.) UMAP 2011. LNCS, vol. 6787, pp. 414–417. Springer, Heidelberg (2011). https://doi.org/10.1007/978-3-642-22362-4_40
27. Salehi, A., Davulcu, H.: Graph attention auto-encoders. arXiv preprint arXiv:1905.10715 (2019)
28. Salha-Galvan, G., Hennequin, R., Chapus, B., Tran, V.A., Vazirgiannis, M.: Cold start similar artists ranking with gravity-inspired graph autoencoders. In: Fifteenth ACM Conference on Recommender Systems, pp. 443–452 (2021)
29. Scharpf, P., Schubotz, M., Youssef, A., Hamborg, F., Meuschke, N., Gipp, B.: Classification and clustering of arxiv documents, sections, and abstracts, comparing encodings of natural and mathematical language. In: Proceedings of the ACM/IEEE Joint Conference on Digital Libraries in 2020, pp. 137–146 (2020)
30. Sherkat, E., Nourashrafeddin, S., Milios, E.E., Minghim, R.: Interactive document clustering revisited: a visual analytics approach. In: 23rd International Conference on Intelligent User Interfaces, pp. 281–292 (2018)
31. Sun, Y., Han, J.: Meta-path-based search and mining in heterogeneous information networks. Tsinghua Sci. Technol. **18**(4), 329–338 (2013)
32. Tang, J., Qu, M., Mei, Q.: PTE: predictive text embedding through large-scale heterogeneous text networks. In: Proceedings of the 21st ACM SIGKDD International Conference on Knowledge Discovery and Data Mining, pp. 1165–1174 (2015)
33. Tang, J., Qu, M., Wang, M., Zhang, M., Yan, J., Mei, Q.: Line: large-scale information network embedding. In: Proceedings of the 24th International Conference on World Wide Web, pp. 1067–1077 (2015)
34. Vlaev, I.: Local choices: rationality and the contextuality of decision-making. Brain Sci. **8**(1), 8 (2018)

35. Waheed, W., Imran, M., Raza, B., Malik, A.K., Khattak, H.A.: A hybrid approach toward research paper recommendation using centrality measures and author ranking. IEEE Access **7**, 33145–33158 (2019)
36. Wang, J., Wu, S., Vu, H.Q., Li, G.: Text document clustering with metric learning. In: Proceedings of the 33rd International ACM SIGIR Conference on Research and Development in Information Retrieval, pp. 783–784 (2010)
37. Wang, W., Tang, T., Xia, F., Gong, Z., Chen, Z., Liu, H.: Collaborative filtering with network representation learning for citation recommendation. IEEE Trans. Big Data **8**(5), 1233–1246 (2020)
38. Wei, C.P., Chiang, R.H., Wu, C.C.: Accommodating individual preferences in the categorization of documents: a personalized clustering approach. J. Manag. Inf. Syst. **23**(2), 173–201 (2006)
39. Yang, L., Jin, R., Sukthankar, R.: Bayesian active distance metric learning. arXiv preprint arXiv:1206.5283 (2012)

Can a Machine Reading Comprehension Model Improve Ad-hoc Document Retrieval?

Kota Usuha[1(✉)], Makoto P. Kato[1], and Sumio Fujita[2]

[1] University of Tsukuba, Tsukuba, Japan
k-ush@klis.tsukuba.ac.jp, mpkato@acm.org
[2] Yahoo Japan Corporation, Tokyo, Japan
sufujita@yahoo-corp.jp

Abstract. We propose a method to solve ad-hoc document retrieval tasks using a reading comprehension model. To solve the ad-hoc retrieval task, the proposed method generates a question for the given query, and a reading comprehension model is employed to determine whether the target document contains a corresponding answer to the generated question, thereby estimating the relevance of the document. Experimental results show that a simple application did not improve the performance in ad-hoc retrieval tasks. Through extensive analysis of the experimental results, however, we found that the proposed method was effective for improving the performance when it was applied to queries containing proper nouns.

Keywords: Information retrieval · Question answering · Reading comprehension

1 Introduction

The ad-hoc retrieval task, which is the central task in information retrieval, involves ranking documents based on their estimated relevance for a given query. On the other hand, the *machine reading comprehension* task attempts to extract an answer to a given question from a given text.

The ad-hoc retrieval and machine reading comprehension algorithms, which we refer to as the *retriever* and *reader*, respectively, have been developed rapidly due to recent advances in neural network models and large-scale datasets, e.g., MS MARCO [1] and SQuAD [18]. State-of-the-arts in those tasks are based on a neural language model pre-trained using a large text corpus, e.g., bidirectional encoder representations from transformers (BERT) [7]. In open-domain question answering tasks, which include the ad-hoc passage retrieval and machine reading comprehension tasks, pre-trained models fine-turned on the same question answering dataset are used as the retriever and reader [6,11,16,22]. Thus, the distinction between ad-hoc retrieval and machine reading comprehension becomes less clear due to the universal models that can be used for various NLP tasks.

Y.-H. Tseng et al. (Eds.): ICADL 2022, LNCS 13636, pp. 172–181, 2022.
https://doi.org/10.1007/978-3-031-21756-2_14

However, despite the many similarities between these two tasks, the applicability of employing a model fine-tuned for one task to the other task has not been investigated extensively. If a fine-tuned reader model could be employed in ad-hoc retrieval tasks, task efficiency could be improved in various ways:

Zero Training Time. The training time for a retriever model can be eliminated, because we no longer have to fine-tune a model for the ad-hoc retrieval tasks.

Zero Resource. The preparation of datasets to train retriever models is not required, which is beneficial to developing multi-lingual retrievers. Various multi-lingual resources are available for reading comprehension tasks [3, 10]; however, only synthetic multi-lingual datasets are available for ad-hoc retrieval [2].

High Research Efficiency. The performance improvement of reading comprehension tasks can be introduced to ad-hoc retrieval tasks, which may lead to more efficient development of ad-hoc retrieval algorithms.

Thus, in this paper, we propose a method to directly apply a fine-tuned reader model to ad-hoc retrieval tasks. The proposed method, which we refer to as the **Ad**-hoc **I**nformation **R**etrieval model based on machine **Read**ing comprehension (AIRRead), transforms a keyword query into the latent questions hidden behind the query. Then, a reader estimates the relevance of each document by determining whether a corresponding answer is contained in a given document. Our experimental results demonstrated that selective application of AIRRead improved the ad-hoc retrieval performance compared to the standard baselines.

2   Related Work

BERT-based ad-hoc retrieval can be divided into two main categories. The first is where BERT is employed to embed documents and queries separately in order to obtain embedded representations. Then, the cosine similarity between the embedded representations of the query and the document is used as the relevance score [8, 24]. In the second category, BERT is employed to encode documents and queries jointly. We expect BERT to output a relevance score of the input document for the given query [14, 23].

The machine reading comprehension is used in the question answering task, which involves extracting an answer to a given question from a passage. Otsuka et al. proposed a method that transforms input questions to questions with more detailed content prior to inputting them into a reading comprehension model [15]. In question answering tasks, reading comprehension is responsible for extracting answers; however, in an open-domain question answering task, it is necessary to efficiently search for passages to input to the reading comprehension model. Nishida et al. proposed a method that incorporates multi-task learning in an open-domain reading comprehension task, where the same model is employed to retrieve the passages and extract the answers [13].

Similarly, in AIRRead, we employ a reading comprehension model and input documents and queries to BERT jointly. However, the task we tackle is an ad-hoc retrieval task and we directly apply a machine reading model to ad-hoc retrieval tasks. In addition, AIRRead employs a trained model for the machine reading task; thus, additional model training is not required.

3   Methodology

Here, we describe the methodology used to generate a question from a query, and how relevance estimation is performed using a trained reading comprehension model (or *reader*).

3.1   Problem Setting

Let D be a document collection. We estimate the relevance score s_i of documents $d_i \in D$ for the given q_r, and rank documents in descending order of the relevance score. To estimate the relevance score, we do not train a relevance estimation model, but employ a trained reader. Thus, a training process is not required for the relevance estimation.

3.2   Framework

Here, given a query, we first retrieve an initial ranked list of documents D' from the document set D with a search model that can be retrieved rapidly via indexing, e.g., BM25. Query q_r is transformed to a question q_s by the question generation model g, which is used as input to the reader, and the relevance score is estimated for each document in D' by the reader f. A question-document pair is an input to the reader to obtain the relevance score. Formally, the relevance score s_i of the i-th document d_i in D' is estimated as follows:

$$q_s = g(q_r),$$

$$s_i = f(q_s, d_i).$$

When translating a query into a question, the information needs must be shared between query and question to capture the original information needs. If the information needs of the query are ambiguous or underspecified, multiple questions may be necessary to represent hidden information needs. In such cases, the relevance of a document is estimated based on multiple questions, and the relevance scores for each question are aggregated into a single score. A document can be highly relevant if it covers major questions behind a query. Thus, when multiple questions are generated from a query, the maximum value is used as the relevance score as follows:

$$Q_s = g(q_r),$$

$$s_i = \max_{q \in Q_s} f(q, d_i),$$

where Q_s is the set of questions generated by $g(q_r)$.

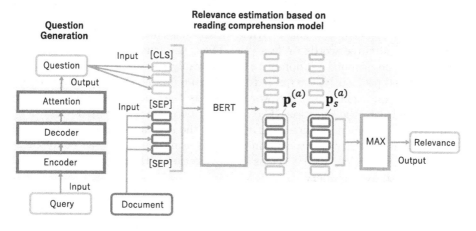

Fig. 1. Flow of the proposed method

Algorithm 1. Generating a query from a question

---

tokens ← Tokenize(question)
length ← get uniformly distributed random number from 1 to 3
length ← max(length, GetLength(question))
query ← {}
for 1 … length **do**
   token ← $\underset{token \in tokens}{\arg\max}$ idf(token)
   query ← query ∪ {token}
end for

return query

3.3   AIRRead

In this section, we describe the proposed method, AIRRead, in detail. Figure 1 shows the flow of the proposed method.

3.4   Question Generation

To generate questions from queries, several methods have been proposed [4,9,20]. In AIRRead, We treat the process of generating a question from a query as a text-to-text translation process [9]; thus, we employed a machine translation model to generate the query into a question. We constructed a dataset in which queries and questions are paired by generating queries from questions to train a machine translation model.

Algorithm 1 describes the procedure used to generate a query from a question. For Generally, queries are shorter than questions, and approximately 76% of queries include three words or less [21]. Thus, the length of the query to be generated is determined randomly to be uniformly distributed in the range of 1–3. As stated previously, the query to be generated must share the information needs of the question; thus, the words used as the query are extracted from words included in the question. The words to be extracted are determined by their inverse document frequency (IDF) under the assumption that a word with a lower occurrence frequency contains more information. Then, as many times as the query length, one of the tokens in the question with the highest IDF value is extracted to form a query.

3.5   Relevance Estimation Based on Reading Comprehension

Here, we describe the method used in AIRRead to estimate relevance in ad-hoc document retrieval using a trained reading comprehension model (or *reader*).

Typically, a reader is employed for the question answering task, which takes a passage and a question, and then extracts the answer to the question from the given passage [5]. Here, the answer is presented as a span in the passage. Thus, a reader outputs two probabilities for each token. i.e., one is the probability that the answer span begins with that token, and the other is the probability that the answer span ends with that token.

We employ BERT as the reader, where a sequence of questions and passages is input, and the probability of the beginning and end of the answer span for each input token is output. When inputting a question q_s and passage a, we add [SEP] between the question and the passage and at the end of the input sequence, and we add [CLS] at the beginning of the input sequence. In this case, the output is two probability distributions over each token in the input sequence. As we are especially interested in whether an answer exists in the given passage, let $\mathbf{p}_s^{(a)}$ be the probability that the passage token is the beginning of the answer span, and $\mathbf{p}_e^{(a)}$ be the probability that the passage token is the end of the answer span. More specifically, the answer beginning probability $\mathbf{p}_s^{(a)}$ is defined as $\mathbf{p}_s^{(a)} = (p_{s,1}^{(a)}, p_{s,2}^{(a)}, \ldots, p_{s,|a|}^{(a)})$ where $|a|$ is the length of the passage a. The answer end probability $\mathbf{p}_e^{(a)}$ is defined similarly.

A passage is considered relevant if it contains at least an answer to a generated question. Thus, the relevance score of the passage a in the document d_i, denoted by $s_{i,a}$, is defined as the maximum beginning probability of passage tokens:

$$s_{i,a} = \max_{1 \leq j \leq |a|} p_{s,j}^{(a)}$$

We fine-tune BERT on SQuAD 2.0 [17], which is a dataset for reading comprehension tasks. Unlike SQuAD 1.0, SQuAD 2.0 includes questions cannot be answered from the passage. If a question is determined to be unanswerable, BERT is trained such that the position of the [CLS] token at the beginning of the input sequence becomes the answer interval. As a result, when the reader

Table 1. Statistics of the constructed query-question dataset.

Data size	Average query length	Average question length
727,858	1.99	6.38

finds a passage not able to answer a question, we expect the reader to output low probabilities for all the passage tokens and, accordingly, a low relevance score for the given passage.

4 Experiments

In this section, we describe the experimental settings and results.

4.1 Datasets

To train a model that can translate a query to a question, we constructed a dataset of query-question pairs using the questions in the MS MARCO dataset. For the constructed dataset, the construction process is as described in Sect. 3.4, and the statistics are given in Table 1.

To evaluate AIRRead, we employed the English NTCIR WWW-2 [12] and WWW-3 [19] test collections, which are standard test collections for ad-hoc document retrieval tasks.

4.2 Experimental Settings

The following methods were used as baselines in our experiments: *BM25 (WWW)*, which is provided as a baseline in NTCIR WWW-2 and WWW-3; *BM25 (Ours)*, which is BM25 used in our experiment (slightly different from BM25 (WWW) due to some configuration differences); and *Birch* [23], which achieved the best performance in the NTCIR-15 WWW-3 English subtask. Birch is a BERT-based ad-hoc retrieval model that estimates the document relevance by aggregating sentence-level evidence. We used three standard evaluation metrics for retrieval tasks, i.e., nDCG@10, Q@10, and nERR@10.

For the question generation model, we used an encoder-decoder with an attention mechanism trained on the constructed query-question dataset (Sect. 4.1). While we generated multiple questions and performed relevance estimation, we found that this did not contribute to performance improvement. Thus, we opt to use a single question for each query.

4.3 Initial Results

Table 2 shows the experimental results obtained by the baselines and AIRRead. As can be seen, on the WWW-3 test collection, AIRRead outperformed BM25

Table 2. Experimental results of the baselines and AIRRead.

Method	WWW-3			WWW-2		
	nDCG	Q	nERR	nDCG	Q	nERR
BM25 (WWW)	0.575	0.585	0.676	0.326	**0.304**	0.478
BM25 (Ours)	0.628	0.639	0.744	0.317	0.291	0.459
Birch	**0.694**	**0.712**	**0.796**	**0.334**	0.300	**0.486**
AIRRead	0.627	0.636	0.735	0.303	0.281	0.424

(WWW) in terms of all considered metrics but did not outperform Birch. However, when we look at the results for BM25 (Ours), we see that BM25 (Ours) outperformed AIRRead for all metrics. These results suggest that a simple application of the reader cannot improve the performance of ad-hoc retrieval baselines. We then hypothesized that AIRRead is effective for a special type of queries, and devised a selective application of AIRRead based on extensive analysis of the experimental results.

4.4   Selective Application of AIRRead

From the document rankings obtained by BM25 (Ours), for each query, we examined how much reranking by the reader improved the rankings. We define the improvement rate of reranking by the reader as follows.

$$\text{Improvement rate} = \frac{\text{nDCG}_{RC}}{\text{nDCG}_{BM25}}$$

where nDCG_{RC} is the nDCG of the document rankings obtained by AIRRead, and nDCG_{BM25} is the nDCG of the document rankings obtained by BM25 (Ours). When nDCG_{BM25} is 0, nDCG_{RC} is also 0; thus, the improvement rate is set to 0. An improvement rate greater than 1 indicates that AIRRead improved the ranking of BM25 in terms of nDCG.

For the WWW-3 queries, we sorted the rankings obtained by AIRRead (Manual)[1] in descending order of improvement rate and examined the percentage of parts of speech in the top-20 and bottom-20 queries. Table 3 shows the results of sorting in descending order by the percentage of parts-of-speech in the overall, top-20, and bottom-20 queries, as well as the difference between the percentage of each part-of-speech in the top-20 and bottom-20 queries. As can be seen, the difference between the top-20 and bottom-20 in terms of the improvement rate for proper nouns was the largest; thus, we consider that reranking via AIR-Read is effective for queries containing proper nouns. For nouns, the difference between the top-20 and bottom-20 was the smallest; however, considering that the ratio of nouns to all queries is as high as 0.459, more research is required to conclude that the AIRRead method's reranking process has a negative effect on performance improvement for queries containing nouns.

---

[1] Here, we used *Manual* configuration to isolate the effect of the question generation.

Table 3. Percentage of POS in the top-20 queries when queries were sorted in descending order of improvement rate. The difference is the percentage of parts of speech in the top-20 queries minus the percentage of parts of speech in the bottom-20 queries. Only the top three and bottom three of POS are shown.

POS	All	Top-20	Bottom-20	Top-20 − Bottom-20
Proper noun	0.238	0.486	0.245	**+0.241**
Adverb	0.022	0.057	0.019	+0.038
Other	0.006	0.029	0.000	+0.029
Determiner	0.022	0.000	0.019	−0.019
Adposition	0.050	0.029	0.075	−0.046
Noun	0.459	0.257	0.472	−0.215

Table 4. Experimental results of selective application of AIRRead.

Method	WWW-3			WWW-2		
	nDCG	Q	nERR	nDCG	Q	nERR
AIRRead	0.627	0.636	0.735	0.303	0.281	0.424
Selective	0.627	0.635	0.745	**0.320**	**0.295**	**0.474**
Manual and Selective	**0.629**	**0.639**	**0.749**	0.319	**0.295**	0.472
WhatIs and Selective	0.627	0.635	0.737	0.319	**0.295**	0.469

Since AIRRead was particularly effective for queries containing proper nouns, we devised *Selective* approach, which only applies AIRRead to queries that contain at least a proper noun. For the other queries, the documents list ranked by BM25 was output without reranking. Table 4 compared Selective methods with following different question generation strategies. *WhatIs*, which generated questions by simply adding "What is" to the beginning of the given query. *Manual*, which manually transformed the queries given in the English subtask of NTCIR15 WWW-3 and WWW-2 into questions. The transformation was performed by the authors, who read the description field describing the information needs of the query. From Table 4, we found that AIRRead (Selective) outperformed AIRRead for all evaluation metrics, except for Q of the WWW-3 test collection. While the selective application alone was effective for the WWW-2 test collection, high-quality questions (Manual) were necessary to achieve decent performance improvements for the WWW-3 test collection. Comparing the best performances achieved by the selective approaches with the baselines in Table 2, we can observe some improvements over the BM25 baselines in the WWW-3 test collection. These results indicate that the reading comprehension model contributed to the performance improvement via selective reranking.

5   Conclusion

In this paper, we have proposed a method to address the problem of generating questions from queries and handle ad-hoc document retrieval tasks using trained machine reading comprehension models. We found that, compared to the BM25 method, the trained reading comprehension model worked well in terms of document reranking for queries containing proper nouns. In future, we would like further investigate the tendency of effective queries.

References

1. Bajaj, P., et al.: MS MARCO: a human generated machine reading comprehension dataset (2018). https://arxiv.org/abs/1611.09268
2. Bonifacio, L.H., Campiotti, I., Jeronymo, V., Lotufo, R., Nogueira, R.: MMARCO: a multilingual version of the MS MARCO passage ranking dataset. arXiv preprint arXiv:2108.13897 (2021)
3. Clark, J.H., Choi, E., Collins, M., Garrette, D., Kwiatkowski, T., Nikolaev, V., Palomaki, J.: TYDI QA: a benchmark for information-seeking question answering in typologically diverse languages. Trans. Assoc. Comput. Linguist. **8**, 454–470 (2020)
4. Dror, G., Maarek, Y., Mejer, A., Szpektor, I.: From query to question in one click: suggesting synthetic questions to searchers. In: Proceedings of the 22nd International Conference on World Wide Web, pp. 391–402 WWW 2013, Association for Computing Machinery, New York, NY, USA (2013). https://doi.org/10.1145/2488388.2488423
5. Hermann, K.M., et al.: Teaching machines to read and comprehend. In: Proceedings of the 28th International Conference on Neural Information Processing Systems, vol. 1, pp. 1693–1701. NIPS2015, MIT Press, Cambridge, MA, USA (2015)
6. Karpukhin, V., et al.: Dense passage retrieval for open-domain question answering. In: Proceedings of the 2020 Conference on Empirical Methods in Natural Language Processing (EMNLP), pp. 6769–6781 (2020)
7. Kenton, J.D.M.W.C., Toutanova, L.K.: BERT: pre-training of deep bidirectional transformers for language understanding. In: Proceedings of NAACL-HLT, pp. 4171–4186 (2019)
8. Khattab, O., Zaharia, M.: ColBERT: efficient and effective passage search via contextualized late interaction over BERT. In: Proceedings of the 43rd International ACM SIGIR Conference on Research and Development in Information Retrieval, pp. 39–48 (2020)
9. Kumar, A., Dandapat, S., Chordia, S.: Translating web search queries into natural language questions. In: Proceedings of the Eleventh International Conference on Language Resources and Evaluation (LREC 2018). European Language Resources Association (ELRA), Miyazaki, Japan (2018). https://aclanthology.org/L18-1151
10. Longpre, S., Lu, Y., Daiber, J.: MKQA: A linguistically diverse benchmark for multilingual open domain question answering. arXiv preprint arXiv:2007.15207 (2020)
11. Luan, Y., Eisenstein, J., Toutanova, K., Collins, M.: Sparse, dense, and attentional representations for text retrieval. Trans. Assoc. Comput. Linguist. **9**, 329–345 (2021)

12. Mao, J., Sakai, T., Luo, C., Xiao, P., Liu, Y., Dou, Z.: Overview of the NTCIR-14 we want web task. In: NTCIR-14 Conference (2019)
13. Nishida, K., Saito, I., Otsuka, A., Asano, H., Tomita, J.: Retrieve-and-read: multi-task learning of information retrieval and reading comprehension. ACM (2018). https://doi.org/10.1145/3269206.3271702
14. Nogueira, R., Yang, W., Cho, K., Lin, J.: Multi-stage document ranking with BERT (2019). https://arxiv.org/abs/1910.14424
15. Otsuka, A., Nishida, K., Saito, I., Asano, H., Tomita, J., Satoh, T.: Reading comprehension based question answering technique by focusing on identifying question intention. vol. 34, pp. 1–12 (2019).https://doi.org/10.1527/tjsai.A-J14
16. Qu, Y., et al.: Rocketqa: An optimized training approach to dense passage retrieval for open-domain question answering. In: Proceedings of the 2021 Conference of the North American Chapter of the Association for Computational Linguistics: Human Language Technologies, pp. 5835–5847 (2021)
17. Rajpurkar, P., Jia, R., Liang, P.: Know what you don't know: unanswerable questions for SQuAD. In: Proceedings of the 56th Annual Meeting of the Association for Computational Linguistics (Volume 2: Short Papers), pp. 784–789 Association for Computational Linguistics, Melbourne, Australia (2018). https://doi.org/10.18653/v1/P18-2124
18. Rajpurkar, P., Zhang, J., Lopyrev, K., Liang, P.: SQuAD: 100,000+ questions for machine comprehension of text. In: Proceedings of the 2016 Conference on Empirical Methods in Natural Language Processing, pp. 2383–2392 Association for Computational Linguistics, Austin, Texas (2016). https://doi.org/10.18653/v1/D16-1264
19. Sakai, T., et al.: Overview of the NTCIR-15 we want web with centre (WWW-3) task. In: NTCIR-15 Conference (2020)
20. Shiqi, Z., Haifeng, W., Chao, L., Ting, L., Yi, G.: Automatically generating questions from queries for community-based question answering. In: Proceedings of 5th International Joint Conference on Natural Language Processing, pp. 929–937. Asian Federation of Natural Language Processing, Chiang Mai, Thailand (2011)
21. Spink, A., Wolfram, D., Jansen, M.B.J., Saracevic, T.: Searching the web: the public and their queries. vol. 52, pp. 226–234
22. Xiong, L., et al.: Approximate nearest neighbor negative contrastive learning for dense text retrieval. In: International Conference on Learning Representations (2020)
23. Yilmaz, Z.A., Yang, W., Zhang, H., Lin, J.: Cross-domain modeling of sentence-level evidence for document retrieval. In: Proceedings of the 2019 Conference on Empirical Methods in Natural Language Processing and the 9th International Joint Conference on Natural Language Processing (EMNLP-IJCNLP), pp. 3490–3496. Association for Computational Linguistics (2019)
24. Zhan, J., Mao, J., Liu, Y., Zhang, M., Ma, S.: RepBERT: contextualized text embeddings for first-stage retrieval (2020). https://arxiv.org/abs/2006.15498

Experimenting with Unsupervised Multilingual Event Detection in Historical Newspapers

Emanuela Boros[1]([⊠])[iD], Luis Adrián Cabrera-Diego[1,2][iD],
and Antoine Doucet[1][iD]

[1] University of La Rochelle, L3i, F-17000 La Rochelle, France
{emanuela.boros,antoine.doucet}@univ-lr.fr
[2] Jus Mundi, F-75008 Paris, France
a.cabrera@jusmundi.com

Abstract. To prevent historical knowledge's fading, research in event detection could facilitate access to digitized collections. In this paper, we propose a method for annotating multilingual historical documents for event detection in an unsupervised manner by leveraging entities and semantic notions of event types. We automatically annotate the documents by relying on dependency parse trees and automatic semantic mapping to event-based frames, with a focus on the multilingual transfer between frames and candidate events. The documents are afterward verified by native speakers, Digital Humanities researchers. We also report on experimental results of event detection in historical newspapers with a state-of-the-art model. We demonstrate that our approach allows for easy language adaptation by presenting two study cases with knowledge extracted from German newspapers from 1911 to 1933 regarding events surrounding International Women's Day and from French newspapers between 1900 and 1944 related to the abolition of guillotine executions in France. Our preliminary findings show that this type of approach could alleviate the need for manual annotation by also providing a practical course of action toward unsupervised event detection from multilingual digitized and historical documents.

Keywords: Event detection · Named entity recognition · Historical documents · Historical newspapers

1 Introduction

The digitization of newspapers has greatly improved accessibility and clearly changed the nature of historical research, by enabling easier data access and analysis at scale through multilingual semantic data enrichment [6,7,10,42]. Through better document analysis results and semantic enrichment e.g., named entity recognition (NER), relation extraction (RE), event extraction (EE), the quality of the newspaper data offered by the libraries to its users is substantially improved [12–15]. Preserving the historical memory of entities and events

Y.-H. Tseng et al. (Eds.): ICADL 2022, LNCS 13636, pp. 182–193, 2022.
https://doi.org/10.1007/978-3-031-21756-2_15

from historical documents and making them accessible to a larger audience, not only limited to humanities scholars and experts, could lead to better organization of our historical knowledge [2,38,44]. Following this statement, this process can be viewed as an area where the detection of events in historical documents can contribute to the construction of more nuanced knowledge bases that could enable further data exploration and help to shape the humanities and historians' research [38]. Extracting event information from text documents into a structured knowledge base or ontology enables several technologies. For example, text summarization might benefit from the selection of one or more events to yield the best summary with the least extraneous information [18,30]. Question answering can take advantage of the detected events and they will be able to answer queries about types of events (wars, disease outbreaks, political movements, climate catastrophes, terrorist attacks, etc.) [29,43].

Therefore, for enabling the development and evaluation of event detection in historical documents, benchmarking plays an important role. However, most of the current datasets in event detection (i.e., MUC [19], ACE 2005 [48]) are not suitable for several reasons, including the high cost of manual annotation of historical texts and the difficulty in defining an event [45]. Besides, different studies have explored how different natural language processing (NLP) tasks, such as named entity recognition (NER) [3,20,34,41] and entity linking (EL) [35,46], can be impacted by the digitization process. However, to the best of our knowledge, there are no previous works regarding this type of analysis for the event detection task, mostly because there is no data.

Thus, in this paper, we develop a method to automatically discover a set of distinct, salient events from historical newspapers. This is done by leveraging the semantic similarity of contextual representations for detecting event triggers in an unsupervised manner that can be easily adaptable to other languages. The detected events can be used then to speed up the manual annotation or validation of historical corpora.

2   Event Detection in Modern and Historical Datasets

Event Detection in Modern Datasets. Prior work in event detection can be divided in: pattern-based systems [39,40,50], machine learning systems based on engineered features (i.e. feature-based) [8,21,24,27], and neural-based approaches [9,17,36,37]. There also has been a lot of interest in approaching this task with external resource-based models which are either feature-based [28,31] or neural-based [32] combined with resources such as FrameNet [1] which is a linguistic corpus that defines complete semantic frames and frame-to-frame relations, or event data generation as in [22,49,51]. The approach proposed in [31] used a probabilistic soft logic (PSL) based approach and a neural network by also leveraging FrameNet to alleviate the data sparseness problem of event detection based on the observation that frames in FrameNet are analogous to events. The authors of [33] also consider that arguments provide significant clues to this task, and adopt a supervised attention mechanism to exploit argument information explicitly for event detection, while also using events from FrameNet, as extra training data. The model described in [28] also leverages FrameNet by tackling the challenge of the annotation cost and data scarcity by considering that ACE 2005 dataset defines limited and specific event schemes based on FrameNet by expressing event information with frame and building a hierarchy of event schemas that are more fine-grained and have much wider coverage than ACE.

Event Detection in Historical Datasets. When it comes to historical and digitized documents, models rely more on external resources, such as FrameNet and WordNet [16], than on event detection approaches used in the state of the art for modern datasets. FrameNet, for instance, has been highly investigated for event detection in historical and digitized, mostly due to the lack of annotated data. A project proposed in 2004 [25] involved the enhancement of materials drawn from the *Franklin D. Roosevelt Library and Digital Archives* and enabled data exploitation for providing a deeper search and access methods for historians of World War II. The documents were scanned, hand-validated, and enriched with various entities such as person names, dates, locations, and job titles. The work focused on the identification of communicative events in the Memorandum of conversation and implied the extraction of verbs associated with any of the FrameNet "Communication" frames and this communicative event utilized a scheme that assigned the role of communicator to a tagged person or pronoun preceding the verb. Another historical event detection module was proposed to be used for museum collections [10], allowing users to search for exhibits related to particular historical events or actors within time periods and geographic areas, extracted from Dutch historical archives. The authors focused on event detection from manually tagged textual data about the Srebrenica Massacre (July 1995). They specified event triplets and Wordnet concepts denoting event actions, participants, and locations or time markers and identified the historical events through recognition of historical actions. A novel FrameNet-based method was also proposed for performing a computational analysis of Italian war bulletins in World War I and II [7] that had never been digitized before. The bulletins were annotated with different types of information, such as named entities, events, participants, time, and georeferenced locations. Instances of major event types (e.g., bombing, sinking, battles) were established before applying the FrameNet mapping [25].

3   Data Collection

For the data collection and our experiments, we utilized the NewsEye collection[1] that consists of a large selection of European newspapers (1850–1950) in several languages that have been digitized and made available online. The difficulty of detecting events in the NewsEye dataset does not only refer to the automatic text recognition (ATR) or digitization errors, but also to the lack of annotated data in a multilingual setting.

Thus, we decided to annotate two subsets of documents in two low-resource languages, German and French, and to experiment with a state-of-the-art event

---

[1] https://www.newseye.eu/.

detection system in a domain and language adaptation scenario. The documents were collected using the NewsEye platform [26], and annotated by the Digital Humanities groups (native speakers) from the NewsEye consortium, University of Innsbruck (UIBK-ICH), Austria, and the Paul Valéry University Montpellier 3, France. The subjects of the datasets were selected by the annotators, depending on their line of research and interests.

4   Unsupervised Data Annotation

Following the recommendation of Sprugnoli, [45], in this work, we defined an event to be consistent with ACE 2005 [48] and chose the event types and subtypes according to their annotation guidelines[2]. We then automatically assigned a frame category to each event type by consulting the English FrameNet database. FrameNet, as indicated in Sect. 2, is a linguistic corpus containing considerable information about lexical and predicate-argument semantics in the form of frames. A frame, in FrameNet, is defined as a triplet composed of a name, like *Execution*, a set of Frame Elements (FEs), and a list of Lexical Units (LUs).[3] An LU is a word or phrase that evokes the corresponding frame, such as *executioner* and *guillotine*. FEs indicate a set of semantic roles associated with the frame, such as *reason, instrument* or *place*. Most frames contain a set of exemplars with annotated LUs and FEs.

For linking ACE 2005 event subtypes to FrameNet frames, we start by processing the corpus by extracting all the verbs of the corpus and grouping them using WordNet [16] synsets. Then, the grouped verbs are matched to FrameNet lexical units (LU). Finally, we associate different ACE 2005 event subtypes[4] to FrameNet by matching frames names to the event subtype names as in [28]. In summary, ACE 2005 event subtypes, are linked indirectly to FrameNet lexical units (LU), which in turn can be seen as event triggers.

For the creation of candidate event mentions, we generate dependency parse trees for each sentence in the dataset[5]. Next, we focus on the extraction of noun-phrases (NPs) that can be pronouns, proper nouns, or nouns, potentially bound with other tokens that act as modifiers, e.g., adjectives or other nouns, that are generally subjects (*nsubj*) or objects (*obj*) (complements of prepositions). Finally, we obtain a triplet composed of the tree *root*, which is generally the verb of the sentence, and its dependents, the *nsubj* and the *obj*. A candidate event mention is, thus, represented by a triplet, where the *root* is commonly a verb, which can possibly be mapped to a lexical unit (LU), similarly as we did for the event trigger candidates. In Fig. 1, we present the dependency parse tree of a sentence in French.

---

[2] https://www.ldc.upenn.edu/sites/www.ldc.upenn.edu/files/english-events-guidelines-v5.4.3.pdf.

[3] An example of the *Execution* frame can be viewed at Framenet2 website.

[4] We chose movements, conflictual events, and membership in organizations.

[5] We used spaCy 3.1+ [23] with the model xx_ent_wiki_sm https://spacy.io/models/xx.

Fig. 1. Example of the correspondence between syntactic arguments of the verbs and participants of the event denoted by the verb (Translation: *From the same place where I had seen Danton disappear, I saw Robespierre disappear.*)

For example, in Fig. 1, there are two triplets both with "disparaître" (to disappear) as root. Specifically, the first triplet is composed of *j'* as subject (*subj*) and "Danton" as object (*obj*). The second triplet has for subject (*subj*) *j'* and for object (*obj*) "Robespierre". In both triplets, "Danton" and "Robespierre", besides being objects, they are entities of type person.

For linking candidate event mentions to ACE 2005 event subtypes, we make use of multilingual BERT [11]. To be precise, we use BERT to obtain the contextual representation x of each token in every sentence in the corpus having at least one candidate event mention; $X = [x_0, x_1 \ldots x_n]$ where n is the sentence length. Then, from X, we isolate the contextual representation x_i of the token i that represents the candidate root event mention. For example, the first "disparaître" from Fig. 1.

At the same time, we use as well BERT to obtain the contextual representation of the ACE 2005 event subtype by processing FrameNet lexical units (LU) associated, in step 1 as event triggers, for each explored event subtype. Specifically, for a specific event subtype, we concatenated all its event triggers, i.e. lexical units, to generate a pseudo-sentence that is processed by BERT. Then BERT outputs a contextual embedding of the pseudo-sentence, which represents the event subtype.[6]

Finally, in order to consider a candidate event mention, we compare, through cosine similarity, the contextual embedding of an ACE 2005 subtype, with the one of the root of the event mention candidate. If the obtained cosine similarity is greater than 0.7, then the mention candidate is considered to belong to the analyzed ACE 2005 subtype.

For example, for the *Attack* event type in French, we compared the extracted *roots* with the following set of lexical units that was retrieved from FrameNet: *attack, assault, strike, ambush, assail, raid, bomb, bombing, raid, infiltrate, hit, fire, small, take up arms, fire, airstrike, bombardment, counter-attack, counter-offensive.* After analyzing the results, we observed that two separate sets of event triggers were extracted: (1) known events: *foudroyer* (strike down), *armer* (take up arms), *attaquer* (attack), *frapper* (strike); (2) unseen events: *arracher* (snatch), *déchiqueter* (tear off), *étouffer* (suffocate), *empoigner* (grab), *trancher* (shred).

---

[6] We are aware that BERT was trained for representing true sentences rather than pseudo-sentences. However, we consider that BERT might generate an embedding that represents the context in which all the event triggers are frequently used.

5   Evaluation

As indicated in Sect. 2, there is no annotated data for historical event detection, and its creation can be expensive. Thus, to evaluate the unsupervised annotation (Sect. 4), we rely on an indirect assessment based on a fine-tuned language model.

Specifically, we train an event detection system by fine-tuning multilingual BERT [11] on English ACE 2005 following the work of Boros et al. [5]. The goal is that through zero-shot[7], the event detection system will be able to detect a subset of events in the historical corpus (Sect. 3), which would intersect with those found by the unsupervised method (Sect. 4). Ideally, the spans of tokens found by the fine-tuned model should match the spans set by the unsupervised annotation, and thus, we will be able to determine precision, recall, and F-score.

As well, following the work of Boros et al. [5], we explore for our evaluation, the fine-tuning of multilingual BERT on English ACE 2005 along with entity markers. The use of *entity markers* consists in augmenting the input data with a series of special tokens that include the entity type. For example, the sentence from Fig. 1 becomes *From the same place where I had seen [PER$_{start}$] Danton [PER$_{end}$] disappear, I saw [PER$_{start}$] Robespierre [PER$_{end}$] disappear*. To do this, we train beforehand a NER system based on a hierarchical architecture that includes a stack of Transformer layers [47] on top of a BERT encoder (BERT-n× *Transformer-CRF*). This architecture, described in [4], has proved to be robust against OCR errors. The performance of the NER system on this collection is, in terms of F-score 48.32 for German, and 72.71 for French. Once the NER system has been created, we annotate the historical corpus and add the entity markers to the input of the event detection system.

6   Results and Discussion

We present the results obtained through two study cases defined by researchers from the NewsEye project and then, we discuss these results.

International Women's Day. For this study case, we selected a subset of 207 German articles that mentioned the keyword "Women's Day" ("Frauentag") and "International Women's Day" ("Internationaler Frauentag") published between 1911 and 1933 in order to analyze the events organized on or around the International Women's Day. For this subset, we selected events regarding *gatherings* or *movements*. These are revealed by the *Conflict* event type with the *Demonstrate* and *Attack* subtypes and the *Contact* with *Meet* event subtype.

To understand the meaning of the event types in a deeper analysis, we detail several types in the following paragraphs. *Demonstrate* and *Attack* are subtypes of the *Conflict* event type. An *Attack* event is defined as a violent physical act causing harm or damage. For example, in *Um diesen ersehnten Zustand herbeizuführen, entsenden wir unseren Schwestern in der ganzen Welt unsere Grüße und rufen sie auf, beim internationalen Frauentag mit uns gemeinsam gegen die*

---

[7] As we use multilingual BERT, even when the training is English, the model should be able to predict events in other languages in a zero-shot manner.

Fortdauer des Krieges zu demonstrieren.[8], the triggers are: for *Demonstrate*, demonstrieren, and for *Attack*, Krieges. Thus, there are, in this case, two mentions of different types of events.

Table 1. Evaluation of NewsEye German event detection.

Type	Subtype	P	R	F1
BERT-multilingual-cased				
Conflict	Attack	33.33	4.55	8.00
Conflict	Demonstrate	50.00	9.09	15.38
Contact	Meet	50.00	15.38	23.53
		44.44	9.65	15.63
BERT-multilingual-cased+*Entity Type Markers*				
Conflict	Attack	27.27	42.86	33.33
Conflict	Demonstrate	47.06	66.67	55.17
Contact	Meet	83.33	38.46	52.63
		52.55	49.33	**47.04**

We can observe from Table 1 that in the results for the model that does not utilize entity markers, the performance drops significantly, while their presence increases the scores values.

Death Penalty Abolition. In the 1900s, in France, there were regular debates regarding the abolition of the death penalty. For this study case, we selected a subset of 207 French articles that mentioned "guillotine" (same in French) and "death penalty" ("peine de mort") published between 1900 and 1944. from the following newspapers: *Le Matin, L'œuvre* and *Le Gaulois*. We selected events regarding *life*, through the *Die* event subtype, conflictual events (*Conflict* with the *Attack* subtype), and criminal *Justice* events with *Execute* subtype. Due to the digitization and article separation processes, some articles contained an insignificant amount of tokens, thus, we removed those with less than ten tokens[9].

The results, summarized in Table 2, reveal the capacity of our approach for extracting events while establishing a strong baseline. However, we notice that the scores are rather imbalanced, favoring precision, which could indicate a close similarity between the chosen event types.

Discussion. It must be stated that the low F-scores (Tables 1 and 2) for certain event subtypes are not unexpected. In the first place, we compare two approaches in an indirect way, one using an unsupervised method, and another using a supervised method but trained on different types of documents and language. As well,

---

[8] Translation: *In order to bring about this desired state, we send our greetings to our sisters all over the world and call on them to demonstrate together with us against the continuation of the war on International Women's Day.*

[9] This threshold was chosen experimentally after we verified the dismissed articles.

Table 2. Evaluation of NewsEye French event detection.

Type	Subtype	P	R	F1
BERT-multilingual-cased				
Conflict	Attack	13.31	18.22	15.41
Life	Die	42.30	19.60	26.83
Justice	Execute	40.00	10.00	16.00
		31.87	15.94	19.40
BERT-multilingual-cased+*Entity Type Markers*				
Conflict	Attack	20.10	18.21	19.21
Life	Die	30.82	21.41	25.30
Justice	Execute	100.0	15.00	26.08
		50.30	18.20	**23.53**

the results of the NER system are not perfect, especially for German, which could affect their performance. Nonetheless, the results presented in Tables 1 and 2, show that there is an intersection between the unsupervised annotations and those predicted by the fine-tuned models. Thus, this can signal that the unsupervised approach presented here could be useful for pre-annotating historical documents before being seen by a human. This could accelerate the creation of actual corpora annotated with events and, in the future, automatize the detection of events through machine learning. However, it is clear that the unsupervised method has some limitations. We need to evaluate how well the semantics could have affected the matching of verbs and lexical units in FrameNet, if these mistakes are, for example, the reasons why certain events were not detected in French, as the low recall shows in Table 2.

7   Conclusions

In this paper, we proposed an unsupervised event detection method for detecting events in historical newspapers by relying on available resources. We also obtained promising preliminary results in event detection from multilingual articles surrounding International Women's Day in German, and the death penalty abolition, in French. We plan in making the dataset publicly available for enabling further research, while envisioning subsequent work regarding an enhanced list of event types and studies concerning the adaptability to other languages.

Acknowledgments. This work has been supported by the European Union's Horizon 2020 research and innovation program under grants 770299 (NewsEye) and 825153 (Embeddia). Also, it has been supported by the ANNA (2019-1R40226) and TER-MITRAD (2020–2019-8510010) projects funded by the Nouvelle-Aquitaine Region, France.

References

1. Baker, C.F., Fillmore, C.J., Lowe, J.B.: The Berkeley frameNet project. In: 36th Annual Meeting of the Association for Computational Linguistics and 17th International Conference on Computational Linguistics, vol. 1, pp. 86–90 (1998)
2. Bedi, H., Patil, S., Hingmire, S., Palshikar, G.: Event timeline generation from history textbooks. In: Proceedings of the 4th Workshop on Natural Language Processing Techniques for Educational Applications (NLPTEA 2017), pp. 69–77 (2017)
3. Boros, E., et al.: Alleviating digitization errors in named entity recognition for historical documents. In: Proceedings of the 24th Conference on Computational Natural Language Learning, pp. 431–441. Association for Computational Linguistics (2020). https://doi.org/10.18653/v1/2020.conll-1.35
4. Boros, E., et al.: Robust named entity recognition and linking on historical multilingual documents. In: Cappellato, L., Eickhoff, C., Ferro, N., Névéol, A. (eds.) CLEF 2020 Working Notes. Working Notes of CLEF 2020 - Conference and Labs of the Evaluation Forum. CEUR-WS (2020)
5. Boros, E., Moreno, J.G., Doucet, A.: Event detection with entity markers. In: Hiemstra, D., Moens, M.-F., Mothe, J., Perego, R., Potthast, M., Sebastiani, F. (eds.) ECIR 2021. LNCS, vol. 12657, pp. 233–240. Springer, Cham (2021). https://doi.org/10.1007/978-3-030-72240-1_20
6. Boschee, E., Natarajan, P., Weischedel, R.: Automatic extraction of events from open source text for predictive forecasting. In: Subrahmanian, V. (ed.) Handbook of Computational Approaches to Counterterrorism, pp. 51–67. Springer, New York (2013). https://doi.org/10.1007/978-1-4614-5311-6_3
7. Boschetti, F., et al.: Computational analysis of historical documents: an application to Italian war bulletins in World War I and II. In: Workshop on Language resources and technologies for processing and linking historical documents and archives (LRT4HDA 2014), pp. 70–75. ELRA (2014)
8. Bronstein, O., Dagan, I., Li, Q., Ji, H., Frank, A.: Seed-based event trigger labeling: how far can event descriptions get us? In: ACL, vol. 2, pp. 372–376 (2015)
9. Chen, Y., Xu, L., Liu, K., Zeng, D., Zhao, J.: Event extraction via dynamic multipooling convolutional neural networks. In: Proceedings of the 53rd Annual Meeting of the Association for Computational Linguistics and the 7th International Joint Conference on Natural Language Processing, vol. 1, pp. 167–176 (2015)
10. Cybulska, A., Vossen, P.: Historical event extraction from text. In: Proceedings of the 5th ACL-HLT Workshop on Language Technology for Cultural Heritage, Social Sciences, and Humanities, pp. 39–43 (2011)
11. Devlin, J., Chang, M.W., Lee, K., Toutanova, K.: BERT: pre-training of deep bidirectional transformers for language understanding. arXiv preprint arXiv:1810.04805 (2018)
12. Ehrmann, M., Romanello, M., Bircher, S., Clematide, S.: Introducing the CLEF 2020 HIPE shared task: named entity recognition and linking on historical newspapers. In: Jose, J.M., et al. (eds.) ECIR 2020. LNCS, vol. 12036, pp. 524–532. Springer, Cham (2020). https://doi.org/10.1007/978-3-030-45442-5_68
13. Ehrmann, M., Romanello, M., Doucet, A., Clematide, S.: Introducing the HIPE 2022 shared task: named entity recognition and linking in multilingual historical documents. In: Hagen, M., et al. (eds.) ECIR 2022. LNCS, vol. 13186, pp. 347–354. Springer, Cham (2022). https://doi.org/10.1007/978-3-030-99739-7_44

14. Ehrmann, M., Romanello, M., Flückiger, A., Clematide, S.: Overview of CLEF HIPE 2020: named entity recognition and linking on historical newspapers. In: Arampatzis, A., et al. (eds.) CLEF 2020. LNCS, vol. 12260, pp. 288–310. Springer, Cham (2020). https://doi.org/10.1007/978-3-030-58219-7_21
15. Ehrmann, M., Romanello, M., Najem-Meyer, S., Doucet, A., Clematide, S.: Overview of HIPE-2022: named entity recognition and linking in multilingual historical documents. In: Barrón-Cedeño, A., et al. (eds.) Experimental IR Meets Multilinguality, Multimodality, and Interaction. CLEF 2022. LNCS , vol. 13390. Springer, Cham (2022). https://doi.org/10.1007/978-3-031-13643-6_26
16. Fellbaum, C.: Wordnet. In: Poli, R., Healy, M., Kameas, A. (eds) Theory and Applications of Ontology: Computer Applications, pp. 231–243. Springer, Dordrecht (2010). https://doi.org/10.1007/978-90-481-8847-5_10
17. Feng, X., Huang, L., Tang, D., Ji, H., Qin, B., Liu, T.: A language-independent neural network for event detection. In: Proceedings of the 54th Annual Meeting of the Association for Computational Linguistics (vol. 2: Short Papers), vol. 2, pp. 66–71 (2016)
18. Filatova, E., Hatzivassiloglou, V.: Event-based extractive summarization (2004)
19. Grishman, R., Sundheim, B.: Message understanding conference-6: a brief history. In: COLING 1996, pp. 466–471 (1996)
20. Hamdi, A., Jean-Caurant, A., Sidere, N., Coustaty, M., Doucet, A.: An analysis of the performance of named entity recognition over OCRed documents. In: 2019 ACM/IEEE Joint Conference on Digital Libraries (JCDL), pp. 333–334. IEEE, Illinois, USA (2019)
21. Hong, Y., Zhang, J., Ma, B., Yao, J., Zhou, G., Zhu, Q.: Using cross-entity inference to improve event extraction. In: Proceedings of the 49th Annual Meeting of the Association for Computational Linguistics: Human Language Technologies-vol. 1, pp. 1127–1136. Association for Computational Linguistics (2011)
22. Hong, Y., Zhou, W., Zhang, J., Zhou, G., Zhu, Q.: Self-regulation: employing a generative adversarial network to improve event detection. In: Proceedings of the 56th Annual Meeting of the Association for Computational Linguistics (vol. 1: Long Papers), pp. 515–526 (2018)
23. Honnibal, M., Montani, I., Van Landeghem, S., Boyd, A.: spaCy: industrial-strength natural language processing in python (2020). https://doi.org/10.5281/zenodo.1212303
24. Huang, R., Riloff, E.: Peeling back the layers: detecting event role fillers in secondary contexts. In: ACL 2011, pp. 1137–1147 (2011)
25. Ide, N., Woolner, D.: Exploiting semantic web technologies for intelligent access to historical documents. In: Proceedings of the Fourth International Conference on Language Resources and Evaluation (LREC'04). European Language Resources Association (ELRA), Lisbon, Portugal (2004). https://www.lrec-conf.org/proceedings/lrec2004/pdf/248.pdf
26. Jean-Caurant, A., Doucet, A.: Accessing and investigating large collections of historical newspapers with the NewsEye platform. In: Proceedings of the ACM/IEEE Joint Conference on Digital Libraries in 2020, pp. 531–532 (2020)
27. Li, Q., Ji, H., Huang, L.: Joint event extraction via structured prediction with global features. In: Proceedings of the 51st Annual Meeting of the Association for Computational Linguistics (vol. 1: Long Papers), pp. 73–82. Association for Computational Linguistics, Sofia, Bulgaria (2013). https://www.aclweb.org/anthology/P13-1008
28. Li, W., Cheng, D., He, L., Wang, Y., Jin, X.: Joint event extraction based on hierarchical event schemas from FrameNet. IEEE Access **7**, 25001–25015 (2019)

29. Liu, J., Chen, Y., Liu, K., Bi, W., Liu, X.: Event extraction as machine reading comprehension. In: Proceedings of the 2020 Conference on Empirical Methods in Natural Language Processing (EMNLP), pp. 1641–1651 (2020)
30. Liu, M., Li, W., Wu, M., Lu, Q.: Extractive summarization based on event term clustering. In: Proceedings of the 45th Annual Meeting of the Association for Computational Linguistics Companion Volume Proceedings of the Demo and Poster Sessions, pp. 185–188 (2007)
31. Liu, S., et al.: Leveraging FrameNet to improve automatic event detection (2016)
32. Liu, S., Chen, Y., Liu, K., Zhao, J.: Exploiting argument information to improve event detection via supervised attention mechanisms. In: 55th Annual Meeting of the Association for Computational Linguistics (ACL 2017), pp. 1789–1798. Vancouver, Canada (2017)
33. Liu, S., et al.: Exploiting argument information to improve event detection via supervised attention mechanisms (2017)
34. Miller, D., Boisen, S., Schwartz, R., Stone, R., Weischedel, R.: Named entity extraction from noisy input: speech and OCR. In: Proceedings of the sixth conference on Applied natural language processing, pp. 316–324. Association for Computational Linguistics, Seattle, Washington, USA (2000)
35. Mutuvi, S., Doucet, A., Odeo, M., Jatowt, A.: Evaluating the impact of ocr errors on topic modeling. In: Dobreva, M., Hinze, A., Žumer, M. (eds.) ICADL 2018. LNCS, vol. 11279, pp. 3–14. Springer, Cham (2018). https://doi.org/10.1007/978-3-030-04257-8_1
36. Nguyen, T.H., Cho, K., Grishman, R.: Joint event extraction via recurrent neural networks. In: Proceedings of the 2016 Conference of the North American Chapter of the Association for Computational Linguistics: Human Language Technologies, pp. 300–309 (2016)
37. Nguyen, T.H., Grishman, R.: Event detection and domain adaptation with convolutional neural networks. In: Proceedings of the 53rd Annual Meeting of the Association for Computational Linguistics and the 7th International Joint Conference on Natural Language Processing (vol. 2: Short Papers), pp. 365–371. Association for Computational Linguistics, Beijing, China (2015). https://doi.org/10.3115/v1/P15-2060
38. Oberbichler, S., et al.: Integrated interdisciplinary workflows for research on historical newspapers: perspectives from humanities scholars, computer scientists, and librarians. J. Assoc. Inf. Sci. Technol. **73**(2), 225–239 (2021)
39. Riloff, E.: Automatically generating extraction patterns from untagged text. In: AAAI1996, pp. 1044–1049 (1996)
40. Riloff, E.: An empirical study of automated dictionary construction for information extraction in three domains. Artif. Intell. **85**(1), 101–134 (1996)
41. Rodriquez, K.J., Bryant, M., Blanke, T., Luszczynska, M.: Comparison of named entity recognition tools for raw OCR text. In: Jancsary, J. (ed.) 11th Conference on Natural Language Processing, KONVENS 2012, Empirical Methods in Natural Language Processing, 19–21 Sept 2012. Scientific series of the ÖGAI, vol. 5, pp. 410–414. ÖGAI, Wien, Österreich, Vienna, Austria (2012). https://www.oegai.at/konvens2012/proceedings/60_rodriquez12w/
42. Rovera, M., Nanni, F., Ponzetto, S.P.: Event-Based access to historical Italian war memoirs. J. Comput. Cult. Heritage **14**(1), 1-23 (2021). https://doi.org/10.1145/3406210

43. Saurí, R., Knippen, R., Verhagen, M., Pustejovsky, J.: Evita: a robust event recognizer for QA systems. In: Proceedings of Human Language Technology Conference and Conference on Empirical Methods in Natural Language Processing, pp. 700–707. Association for Computational Linguistics, Vancouver, British Columbia, Canada (2005). https://aclanthology.org/H05-1088
44. Shaw, R.B.: Events and periods as concepts for organizing historical knowledge. University of California, Berkeley (2010)
45. Sprugnoli, R.: Event Detection and Classification for the Digital Humanities, Ph. D. thesis, University of Trento (2018)
46. van Strien, D., Beelen, K., Ardanuy, M.C., Hosseini, K., McGillivray, B., Colavizza, G.: Assessing the impact of OCR quality on downstream NLP tasks. In: ICAART 2020 - Proceedings of the 12th International Conference on Agents and Artificial Intelligence vol. 1, pp. 484–496 (2020)
47. Vaswani, A., et al.: Attention is all you need. In: Advances in Neural Information Processing Systems, pp. 5998–6008 (2017)
48. Walker, C., Stephanie, S., Julie, M., Kazuaki, M.: ACE 2005 multilingual training corpus. Linguistic Data Consortium, Technical report (2005)
49. Yang, S., Feng, D., Qiao, L., Kan, Z., Li, D.: Exploring pre-trained language models for event extraction and generation. In: Proceedings of the 57th Annual Meeting of the Association for Computational Linguistics, pp. 5284–5294 (2019)
50. Yangarber, R., Grishman, R., Tapanainen, P., Huttunen, S.: Automatic acquisition of domain knowledge for information extraction. In: 18th International Conference on Computational Linguistics (COLING 2000), pp. 940–946 (2000)
51. Zhang, T., Ji, H., Sil, A.: Joint entity and event extraction with generative adversarial imitation learning. Data Intell. **1**(2), 99–120 (2019)

Towards a Polish Question Answering Dataset (PoQuAD)

Ryszard Tuora[(✉)], Natalia Zawadzka-Paluektau, Cezary Klamra,
Aleksandra Zwierzchowska, and Łukasz Kobyliński

Institute of Computer Science, Polish Academy of Sciences, Jana Kazimierza 5,
01–248 Warszawa, Poland
{r.tuora,natalia.zawadzka-paluektau,c.klamra,a.zwierzchowska,
lkobylinski}@ipipan.waw.pl

Abstract. This paper presents the efforts towards creating **PoQuAD**, a dataset for training automatic question answering models in Polish. It justifies why having native data is vital for training accurate Question Answering systems. PoQuAD broadly follows the methodology of SQuAD 2.0 (including impossible questions), but detracts from it in a few aspects. The first of these concerns reducing annotation density in order to broaden the range of topics included. The second is the inclusion of a generative answer layer to better suit the needs of a morphologically rich language. PoQuAD is a work in progress and so far consists of over 29000 question-answer pairs with contexts extracted from Polish Wikipedia. The planned size of the dataset is over 50 thousand such entries. The paper describes the annotation process and the guidelines which were given to annotators in order to ensure quality of the data. The collected data is subjected to analysis in order to shed some light on its linguistic properties and on the difficulty of the task.

Keywords: Natural language processing · Question answering · Machine reading comprehension

1 Introduction

Automatic question answering (**QA**) is a burgeoning field within natural language processing (**NLP**). A robust QA system can be used to gather information from a digital library in a much more natural way than standard information-retrieval (**IR**) methods, i.e. by asking questions, as opposed to forming search queries. As in other domains of NLP, the best contemporary QA methods rely on utilizing general-purpose language models, which are then fine-tuned on question answering datasets. The models are usually embedded in a retrieve-and-read pipeline in which a document is first recovered using conventional IR techniques, and then the fine-tuned reading-comprehension model extracts an answer from the document. The latter task is data-heavy, and for this reason, high-quality data is crucial in achieving good performance of the entire system.

Y.-H. Tseng et al. (Eds.): ICADL 2022, LNCS 13636, pp. 194–203, 2022.
https://doi.org/10.1007/978-3-031-21756-2_16

This paper presents the ongoing efforts in creating **PoQuAD** — Polish Question Answering Dataset, a resource designed for training machine-learning QA models in Polish. First, the related datasets and experiments are discussed, then the annotation procedure is explained in detail, and lastly some analysis of the collected data is presented.

2   Previous Work

The paradigm dataset for the retrieve-and-read approach is SQuAD [18], which contains over 100 thousand question-answer pairs annotated by crowdsources to be answered based on articles collected from the English Wikipedia. This dataset has subsequently been extended to form SQuAD 2.0 [17] by adding so-called *impossible questions*, i.e. questions which are relevant to the text, but nevertheless cannot be answered based on the information within it.

When working with languages other than English, a range of approaches can be proposed. We distinguish:

1. Zero-shot transfer based on multilingual models
2. Training monolingual models on translated datasets
3. Training monolingual models on native datasets

It is generally the case that 3 is superior to 1 and 2. For French the best **F1** results for each paradigm are 86.1%, 87.5%, and 91.8%, respectively [8]. In the case of German, when models of similar size are compared, the **F1** scores for each category are 68.6%, 78.8%, and 88.1%, respectively [14]. These results suggest that providing native data is important in achieving high accuracy even when the native datasets are substantially smaller, as is the case for both of these studies (60k for French, and 14k for German). The general SQuAD formula was therefore used for preparing native datasets for other languages, such as Russian [9], Korean [10], Persian [1], Vietnamese [15], and Chinese [5].

A case which deserves a more detailed discussion is that of Czech because of its linguistic proximity to Polish. The first Czech dataset for QA, named SQAD [12], was created in 2014 (and therefore the naming similarity to SQuAD is purely coincidental). It has been iteratively enriched in [19,22], and it has a different approach to annotation, more suited to Slavic languages. Additionally, [11] represents the efforts to use machine-translated data for training QA models. In that study, the best model trained on translated data fares worse on Czech (79.2%) than the same architecture on the original data (86.2%), which suggests that translation does lead to a substantial data degradation. [11] also raises an important point, namely the fact that SQuAD's overrepresentation of named entities may artificially inflate the results, as these are usually represented more uniformly across different languages. For a more general task, these cross-lingual strategies might fare even worse than ones which use native data.

With respect to Polish data, [16] is the sole native resource, but the questions are not paired with the relevant paragraphs, and therefore it cannot be used for extractive QA as is. [2] offers a machine-translation of the SQuAD 2.0 dataset, but the reported top score of 61.9%, when evaluated on the translated dev-set, is not satisfactory. The translated data is of lower quality because of 1. translation errors, and 2. additional difficulties in aligning answer spans between the translated documents. Additionally, the data in SQuAD are biased towards the anglophone culture, with questions about American pop stars, cities in the US, or intricacies of the political systems of the anglosphere being much more frequent than what would be of interest to the average Polish reader. The previous work is therefore insufficient with respect to providing satisfactory question answering capabilities for Polish, and a resource filling that gap would be an important addition to Polish NLP. **PoQuAD** is planned as a means of bridging this gap.

3   Data Gathering

3.1   Textual Data

Textual data was obtained from Polish Wikipedia by scraping articles falling into one of three categories which are recognized by the Wikipedia community: 1. Featured Articles, 2. Good Articles, or 3. Most popular articles.

These criteria were imposed in order to ensure the quality of textual data and also relevance to the interests of an average Polish reader. Articles were then divided into a summary (usually everything before the first header) and the rest of the article. The remaining paragraphs were narrowed down by imposing the criterion of length (over 500 characters). Subsequently, textRank algorithm was used to rank the centrality of these paragraphs, and only the top scoring paragraph of each article was selected for annotation.

This is a substantial difference from the original SQuAD approach, where entire articles were annotated. The original method is perhaps more cost efficient as it does not require annotators first familiarizing themselves with the article, and usually makes it impossible for a paragraph to be incomprehensible for the annotator. On the other hand, this method focuses on the more interesting paragraphs (as per textRank), and covers a broader range of topics. However, because even with the summary available, a paragraph can be incomprehensible without the fuller context, we allow annotators to entirely skip paragraphs if they are unable to ask questions about them. Including such a possibility can also nudge them against forcing trivial questions.

3.2   Annotation Process

Four in-house annotators were given instructions about the desiderata for the data, which were mostly similar to those from SQuAD, i.e. emphasized lexical differences between the question and context, and encouraged asking interesting, hard questions. The proportion between possible and impossible questions was to be kept roughly around 4:1. All the annotations were done *via* LabelStud.io [20], with a custom interface built for the task. After collection, the annotations were validated by both automatic methods and manual supervision by a linguist. The automatic validation relied on using a custom Polish spaCy model[1], and it aimed to identify: 1. technical errors, e.g. missing labels or questions, 2. misspellings in question or generative answer text, 3. questions with high lexical similarity to the corresponding text fragment, and 4. overrepresentation of a particular type of questions or answers, e.g. yes-no questions or dates. Validation results served to identify systematic problems, before proceeding onto manual curation, which included marking incorrect annotations for a random sample of each tranche (200 paragraphs) as falling into one of error types, e.g. WRONG EXTRACTIVE ANSWER SPAN, or MULTIPLE PLAUSIBLE ANSWERS. The annotators were then asked to correct their annotation based on the results of both phases of validation, and only the tranches which passed both phases were admitted into the dataset.

3.3   Differences with Respect to SQuAD

As stipulated, there were some deviations from the original SQuAD formula of the task. The most important ones are as follows:

Ambiguous Questions. Because a satisfactory question answering system should be able to answer ambiguous questions in context (e.g. in a series of questions about the same topic, or based off the metadata about the user, e.g. which page they are currently on), some degree of ambiguity in the data would be essential for training. For this reason, annotators are not discouraged to ask such ambiguous questions as long as it is clear, for an average reader, how the ambiguities should be resolved based on the paragraph. For example:

Czy Jerzy Płażewski wydał negatywną opinię o filmie Wajdy?
[Did Jerzy Płażewski review Wajda's film negatively?]

It is only in the context of the paragraph, which is wholly devoted to the film "Popiół i Diament", that it becomes clear what film is the subject of the question. This is an acceptable level of ambiguity. On the other hand:

Jak on ocenił to dzieło?
[How did he rate this piece?]

is too ambiguous and therefore would not be accepted into the dataset, as it would introduce noise into the training process.

Generative Question Answering. In English QA, a fragment extracted from text can usually be used as an answer without any alterations. This does not apply to the morphologically rich Polish. A word or an entire phrase can appear in the text in an inflected form. Returning it as is can be ungrammatical and confusing, as shown in Fig. 1. In such cases a generative method is needed.

---

[1] https://github.com/ipipan/spacy-pl-trf.

Context: [...] *Ministerstwo Skarbu Pastwa wystpio do Centralnego Biura Antykorupcyjnego z prob o podjcie dziaa sprawdzajcych proces pozyskiwania rodków przez Stpnia na potrzeby finansowania komercyjnej produkcji filmowej z udziaem Anny Szarek, czyli yciowej partnerki Prezesa GPW* Ludwika Sobolewskiego. [...]
Question: *Z kim w zwizku bya Anna Szarek?*
[With whom was Anna Szarek in a relationship?]
Extractive Answer: *Ludwika Sobolewskiego* [GEN case]
Generative Answer: *z Ludwikiem Sobolewskim* [INSTR with a preposition added]

Fig. 1. Differences between both annotation layers

For this reason, similarly to [19], we add a second layer of annotation, which is done by hand, and includes answers in a "normalized" form. The cue for the annotator is to convert the extracted fragment into a form which would be most natural and grammatical to use while answering the question during, for example, a conversation. This operation usually involves making necessary inflections, but can also require adding words (e.g. prepositions), subtracting words (e.g. interjections), or expanding abbreviations. Additionally this layer can be used to store answers to yes-no questions; in this case, the extracted answer is usually a sentence which clearly supports "yes" or "no" (which rarely occur explicitly in the contexts) as a generative answer. In these more nuanced cases, the skills demanded by the generative task are not limited to purely linguistic matters, but also to being able to determine which elements are superfluous, what might an abbreviation corefer with, and whether a given fragment supports or contradicts a supposition.

4   Data Analysis

A random sample of 100 question and answer pairs has been analyzed manually (largely following the methodology of [18]). The answers to each question have been grouped into the following categories: common noun phrase, person, other proper nouns, adjective phrase, verb phrase, date, and other numeric answers, as well as yes/no for polar questions. As can be observed in Table 1, noun phrases account for more than half of all the answers in the sample (similar results have been reported by [8,18]). Among them, proper nouns not referring to people prevail, followed by common noun phrases, and references to people. Numerical answers are three times less frequent than noun phrases. Among them, other numbers are slightly more common than dates. The least frequently selected answers are those forming adjectival and verb phrases. Finally, with respect to the polar questions, it can be observed that the annotators had a preference for questions that could be answered affirmatively.

Table 1. Answer type by frequency (in a sample of 100)

Answer type	Freq.	Example
Other proper nouns	28	**Q:** *Jakiego zespołu album jest uważany za najważniejszy w historii MTV Unplugged* [Which band's album is thought to be the most important album in the history of MTV Unplugged]?, **A:** *Alice in Chains*
Common noun phrase	19	**Q:** *Jakie są cechy charakterystyczne klimatu oceanicznego* [What are the characteristics of the oceanic climate]?, **A:** *Wysokie opady* [High precipitation]
Person	10	**Q:** *Jaki naukowiec, między innymi, prowadził badania nad RNA* [Which scientist, among others, did studies on RNA]?, **A:** *Kreiter*
Other numeric	10	**Q:** *Jak wysoko zbudowano miasto Pompeje* [How high was Pompeii located]?, **A:** *40 m n.p.m.* [40 m above sea level]
Date	8	**Q:** *Kiedy trwał konflikt zbrojny pomiędzy Rosją a Japonią* [When were Russia and Japan in conflict]?, **A:** *W 1905 r.* [In 1905]
Adjective phrase	7	**Q:** *Jakie zdolności posiadał przyszły mąż Krystyny z dynastii Wazów* [What talents did the future husband of Christina of the House of Vasa possess]?, **A:** *Wojskowe* [Military]
Verb phrase	7	**Q:** *Jakie są cele "Iustitii"* [What are Iustitia's goals]?, **A:** *Umacnianie niezależności sądów i niezawisłości sędziów* [Strengthening the autonomy of courts and the independence of judges]
Yes/No	8/3	**Q:** *Czy chciano wybudować port lotniczy* [Did they want to build an airport]? **A:** *Tak* [Yes]

Additionally, the relationship between the question and the answer for each of the pairs from the same sample was analyzed (see Table 2) in order to shed light on the type of reasoning required to arrive from one to the other. This has shown that lexical and, to a slightly lesser extent, syntactic variation, were the two most frequently adopted procedures in the formation of questions. The following is an example of both lexical and syntactic variation (it also illustrates the fact that some question and answer pairs fall into more than one category):

W jakim miejscu Dee Dee miała **spotkać** *chłopaka swojej córki?*
[Where was Dee Dee supposed to **meet** her daughter's boyfriend?]

Context:

Wedle jej planu miał **wpaść na** *nią, gdy ona z Dee Dee były w kinie w kostiumach.*
[According to her plan, he was supposed to **bump into** her when she and Dee Dee were at the cinema in costumes.]

With respect to lexical choices, the original *wpaść na* [bump into] is replaced in the question by the more neutral *spotkać* [meet]. As regards the syntactic variation, the question swaps the original text's subject and object and requires the original complex sentence to be restructured into a simple one:

(He was supposed to bump into her when she and Dee Dee were at the cinema in costumes → He was supposed to bump into her at the cinema)

The question and answer pair analysed above also provides an example of another type of reasoning – multiple sentence reasoning as knowledge that *her* refers to Dee Dee and that *her daughter's boyfriend* is the elided subject of the original sentence needs to be accessed from the preceding sentence:

Rok później Gypsy zaaranżowała spotkanie matki z Godejohnem oraz zapłaciła mu, gdy ten przybył do Springfield.

[A year later, Gypsy arranged a meeting between her mother and Godejohn and paid him when he arrived in Springfield.]

Table 2. Reasoning required to answer questions

Type of reasoning	Frequency
Lexical variation	47
Syntactic variation	43
World knowledge	11
No reasoning	11
Multiple sentence reasoning	8
Ambiguous	7

Other, less populous categories include WORLD KNOWLEDGE where the lexical gap to be bridged is less about linguistic knowledge, and more based in knowledge about the world, NO REASONING where the answer is explicitly stipulated as such in the text, and AMBIGUOUS which includes questions where it is not entirely clear whether the annotated answer is the correct one.

4.1 Evaluation

The 29k collected questions were divided into train, dev and test sets in a 8:1:1 proportion. 3 paradigms of training are considered: training an extractive model on PoQuAD, training an extractive model on translated SQuAD-PL [2], and training a generative model on PoQuAD. In all paradigms, the test set of PoQuAD was used for evaluation. Two metrics are employed: **EM** which requires gold and system answers to be identical, and a macro average of token-wise **F1** coverage between these. Results on answerable and impossible questions are also considered separately, as **HasAns** and **NoAns** respectively.

Generally, native models are significantly superior to multilingual models, and models trained on native data outperform ones trained on the translated dataset. It may be argued that the latter fact stems from the detours from the original SQuAD formula, nevertheless the translated dataset is much larger than PoQuAD, which should at least partialy counteract this factor. All this amounts to a strong argument in favour of working with native data. For extractive QA, the best performer is **HerBERT-large**, with 76.36% **Total F1**, whereas in the generative paradigm, **plT5 large** scores the highest. The extractive results are around 12 p.p. lower than those reported for datasets of similar size (e.g. **F1** of 88.1% in [14], or 87.02% in [15]). The likely cause of this is that these datasets do not include impossible questions, which, as [17] shows, substantially raise the difficulty level of the task. Although not directly comparable, the generative paradigm, as expected, leads to lower results. What is surprising is the particularly weak performance on impossible questions, which might be due to the inherent bias for producing text, as opposed to returning empty sequences. A full evaluation of both of these hypotheses would require obtaining human performance metrics.

Table 3. Evaluation results on PoQuAD

QA paradigm	Train set	Model	HasAns		NoAns	Total	
			EM	F1	EM	EM	F1
Extractive	PoQuAD	mBERT [7]	52.14	67.26	53.74	52.42	64.90
		XLM-R base [4]	55.93	70.77	48.03	54.55	66.80
		XLM-R large [4]	59.76	75.38	56.89	59.26	72.15
		HerBERT base [13]	59.26	73.64	56.50	58.78	70.65
		HerBERT large [13]	**63.59**	**78.90**	**64.37**	**63.72**	**76.36**
	SQuAD-PL	XLM-R base	36.45	54.25	47.44	38.37	53.06
		HerBERT base	42.99	63.80	42.13	42.84	60.01
		HerBERT large	48.27	70.85	41.34	47.06	65.70
Generative	PoQuAD	mT5 base [21]	51.85	66.34	14.96	45.41	57.37
		BART [6]	48.77	64.32	28.74	45.28	58.11
		PlT5 base [3]	55.89	69.71	17.32	49.16	60.57
		PlT5 large [3]	**67.08**	**80.27**	**36.22**	**61.70**	**72.58**

5   Conclusions

This paper presents a work in progress concerning the creation of a native resource for QA in Polish — PoQuAD. The motivation for the project, annotation methods, aims, and preliminary results were discussed. It is proposed and argued that this work will be an important step in enriching Polish QA and NLP in general. The dataset is available[2] in the SQuAD JSON format, with some additional keys storing the extra annotation layers. As of September 2022, PoQuAD consists of 29k questions, but in the following months, the threshold of 50k is to be reached. The final dataset, besides increased number of examples, would benefit from additional annotation for estimating human performance and robust error analysis, with respect to question types and their quantitative properties.

---

[2] The repository at https://github.com/ipipan/poquad will be continually updated with new data. It is licensed on **GNU GPL 3.0** license.

Acknowledgements. This work was supported by the European Regional Development Fund as a part of the 2014–2020 Smart Growth Operational Programme: (1) Intelligent travel search system based on natural language understanding algorithms, project no. POIR.01.01.01–00-0798/19; (2) CLARIN — Common Language Resources and Technology Infrastructure, project no. POIR.04.02.00-00C002/19.

References

1. Ayoubi, S., Davoodeh, M.Y.: PersianQA: a dataset for Persian question answering. https://github.com/SajjjadAyobi/PersianQA (2021)
2. Borzymowski, H.: Polish QA model (2020), model trained on HuggingFace. https://huggingface.co/henryk/bert-base-multilingual-cased-finetuned-polish-squad2
3. Chrabrowa, A., et al.: Evaluation of transfer learning for polish with a text-to-text model. arXiv preprint arXiv:2205.08808 (2022)
4. Conneau, A., et al.: Unsupervised cross-lingual representation learning at scale. CoRR (2019). https://arxiv.org/abs/1911.02116
5. Cui, Y., et al.: A span-extraction dataset for Chinese machine reading comprehension. In: Proceedings of the 2019 Conference on Empirical Methods in Natural Language Processing and the 9th International Joint Conference on Natural Language Processing (EMNLP-IJCNLP), pp. 5883–5889 Association for Computational Linguistics, Hong Kong, China (2019). https://doi.org/10.18653/v1/D19-1600
6. Dadas, S.: Polish BART. https://github.com/sdadas/polish-nlp-resources#bart
7. Devlin, J., Chang, M., Lee, K., Toutanova, K.: BERT: pre-training of deep bidirectional transformers for language understanding. CoRR (2018). https://arxiv.org/abs/1810.04805
8. d'Hoffschmidt, M., Belblidia, W., Brendlé, T., Heinrich, Q., Vidal, M.: FQuAD: French question answering dataset (2020). https://arxiv.org/abs/2002.06071
9. Efimov, P., Chertok, A., Boytsov, L., Braslavski, P.: SberQuAD – Russian reading comprehension dataset: description and analysis. In: Arampatzis, A., et al. (eds.) CLEF 2020. LNCS, vol. 12260, pp. 3–15. Springer, Cham (2020). https://doi.org/10.1007/978-3-030-58219-7_1
10. Lim, S., Kim, M., Lee, J.: Korquad1.0: korean QA dataset for machine reading comprehension (2019). https://arxiv.org/abs/1909.07005
11. Macková, K., Straka, M.: Reading comprehension in Czech via machine translation and cross-lingual transfer (2020). https://arxiv.org/abs/2007.01667
12. Medved, M., Horak, A.: SQAD: Simple question answering database. In: RASLAN (2014)
13. Mroczkowski, R., Rybak, P., Wróblewska, A., Gawlik, I.: HerBERT: efficiently pretrained transformer-based language model for polish. In: Proceedings of the 8th Workshop on Balto-Slavic Natural Language Processing, pp. 1–10. Association for Computational Linguistics, Kiyv, Ukraine (2021). https://www.aclweb.org/anthology/2021.bsnlp-1.1
14. Möller, T., Risch, J., Pietsch, M.: GermanQuAD and GermanDPR: improving non-english question answering and passage retrieval (2021). https://arxiv.org/abs/2104.12741

15. Nguyen, K., Nguyen, V., Nguyen, A., Nguyen, N.: A Vietnamese dataset for evaluating machine reading comprehension. In: Proceedings of the 28th International Conference on Computational Linguistics. pp. 2595–2605. International Committee on Computational Linguistics, Barcelona, Spain (2020). https://doi.org/10.18653/v1/2020.coling-main.233

16. Ogrodniczuk, M., Przybyła, P.: PolEval 2021 task 4: question answering challenge (2021)

17. Rajpurkar, P., Jia, R., Liang, P.: Know what you don't know: Unanswerable questions for squad (2018). https://doi.org/10.48550/ARXIV.1806.03822

18. Rajpurkar, P., Zhang, J., Lopyrev, K., Liang, P.: Squad: 100,000+ questions for machine comprehension of text. In: Proceedings of the 2016 Conference on Empirical Methods in Natural Language Processing. pp. 2383–2392. Association for Computational Linguistics, Austin, Texas (2016). https://doi.org/10.18653/v1/D16-1264

19. Sabol, R., Medved' M., Horák, A.: Czech question answering with extended sqad v3.0 benchmark dataset. In: Horák, A., Rychlý, P., Rambousek, A. (eds.) Proceedings of the Thirteenth Workshop on Recent Advances in Slavonic Natural Languages Processing, RASLAN 2019, pp. 99–108. Tribun EU, Brno (2019)

20. Tkachenko, M., Malyuk, M., Holmanyuk, A., Liubimov, N.: Label studio: data labeling software (2020–2022). https://github.com/heartexlabs/label-studio

21. Xue, L., et al.: mT5: a massively multilingual pre-trained text-to-text transformer. CoRR (2020). https://arxiv.org/abs/2010.11934

22. Šulganová, T., Marek, M., Horák, A.: Enlargement of the Czech question-answering dataset to SQAD v2.0. In: Proceedings of the Eleventh Workshop on Recent Advances in Slavonic Natural Language Processing, RASLAN, pp. 79–84. Brno (2017)

Cultural Data Collection and Analysis

Accessing Digital Cultural Heritage Information: Users vs Institutional Perspectives of Metadata and Searching

Ryan Colin Gibson, Sudatta Chowdhury, and Gobinda Chowdhury(✉)

Department of Computer and Information Sciences, University of Strathclyde, Glasgow, UK
{ryan.gibson,sudatta.chowdhury,gobinda.chowdhury}@strath.ac.uk

Abstract. A controlled experiment with ten participants, involving two tasks and a selected set of digital cultural heritage content, explored (a) how does the metadata assigned by cultural heritage organisations meet or differ from the search needs of users? and (b) how can the search strategies of users inform the search pathways employed by cultural heritage organisations? Findings reveal that collection management standards like *Spectrum* encourage a variety of different characteristics to be considered when developing metadata, yet much of the content is left to the interpretations of curators e.g. description or physical description. Rather, user- and context-specific guidelines could be beneficial in ensuring the aspects considered most important by consumers are indexed, thereby producing more relevant search results. A user-centred approach to designing cultural heritage websites would also help to improve an individual's experience when searching for information. However, a process is needed for institutions to form a concrete understanding of who their target users are before developing features and designs to suit their specific needs and interests.

Keywords: Cultural heritage information · Information access · Users · Metadata · Spectrum

1 Introduction

Users of cultural heritage can be diverse, and may include members of the general public, cultural heritage professionals, academics, historians, and industry workers, amongst others. Such audiences have different backgrounds and experiences, meaning cultural heritage objects can have multiple interpretations based on varied user types, as well as their cultural context and information needs [1]. Identifying user interests in different parts of an online collection, and investigating the related search behaviour, can help to improve system support in Interactive Information Retrieval where users are engaged in purposeful and directed searching.

Users of cultural heritage information can have specific characteristics that need to be considered in order to design the most effective digital information systems that will facilitate interactive and contextual access to information [2–5]. The findings of user behaviour studies can also change what an organisation is doing [6]. A further challenge

© The Author(s), under exclusive license to Springer Nature Switzerland AG 2022
Y.-H. Tseng et al. (Eds.): ICADL 2022, LNCS 13636, pp. 207–221, 2022.
https://doi.org/10.1007/978-3-031-21756-2_17

to understanding user experience and information needs online comes from the variable quality of digital objects and collections themselves. Most of the time the metadata associated with cultural objects, such as images, is either sparse or inconsistent, and this makes keyword-based exploratory search difficult and therefore slows down the research or engagement process [7]. User modelling can describe the interaction process between users and cultural heritage applications and products [8]; however, despite a myriad of research reported over the past two decades or so, there is a lack of a richer and deeper understanding of digital users [9].

Research reported in this paper is part of a larger project, funded by the Arts & Humanities Research Council (AHRC) in the UK that aimed to investigate how people accessed cultural heritage information during the COVID-19 pandemic. The main project examined user search behaviour and patterns via the log analysis of access data collected from two national institutions in Scotland, viz. National Museums Scotland (NMS) and National Galleries of Scotland (NGS). Details of the log analysis, findings and conclusions, are available online.[1] This paper complements the report by providing additional discourse on two controlled experiments that were conducted with two groups of users, and selected sets of digital content from NMS and NGS, to explore whether there are any differences in the way collection items are indexed by the institutions and searched for by the users. More specifically, the research aimed to understand what barriers exist across the search pathways and interfaces of cultural heritage institutions – like NGS and NMS – and what improvements can be made to enhance user experience. This consisted of a user study to identify the characteristics of collection items deemed most important when searching, in addition to the search strategies employed across the sites. As such, we were able to compare current metadata standards with end user search queries, whilst also identifying user experience enhancers/barriers across the interfaces of NGS and NMS. Two primary research questions shaped the design of the user studies:

1. How does the metadata assigned by cultural heritage organisations meet or differ from the search needs of users?
2. How can the search strategies of users inform the search pathways employed by cultural heritage organisations?

The rest of the paper presents the methodology and protocols used in this research, along with key findings and discussions around how various user-defined metadata can be accommodated within the existing framework of the collection management standard, called Spectrum[2], used throughout the cultural heritage sector in the UK.

2 Methodology

2.1 Study Participants

In total, 10 people completed the virtual study, via Zoom, between the months of January and March 2022. Table 1 includes the demographics of these participants, where a

---

[1] https://doi.org/10.5281/zenodo.6602364.

[2] https://collectionstrust.org.uk/spectrum.

deliberate decision was made to recruit both experienced and first-time users of the NGS and NMS sites to understand whether there were any differences in the search behaviour between these two groups. Inexperienced users who had some knowledge of search were recruited from higher education institutions across Scotland, whilst more experienced users were contacted directly from the mailing lists of NMS. All participants had access to an information sheet during the recruitment process and provided informed consent before contributing to the study.

2.2 Protocol

The user study was split into two separate tasks, which were completed virtually via the Zoom video conferencing system to adhere to social distancing measures imposed during the COVID-19 pandemic in UK. Both tasks were performed on Mural[3] with task one consisting of an item categorization process, where participants assigned search phrases to items from NGS and NMS before grouping them together to form 'collections', similar to [10]. The second task involved a scenario-based search observation process, where participants performed live searches across the NGS and NMS websites to fulfil their information needs, similar to [11].

Table 1. Profiles of study participants

ID	Gender	Age	Education	Profession	Regular user	English as a first language
1	M	25–34	Bachelors	PhD Student	No	Y
2	M	25–34	Masters	PhD Student, Teaching Assistant	No	Y
3	F	25–34	Masters	PhD Student	No	N
4	F	25–34	Masters	PhD Student, Teaching Assistant	No	N
5	M	25–34	Masters	PhD Student	No	Y
6	F	25–34	Masters	Post-graduate Student	NMS	N
7	F	45–54	PhD	Teaching Fellow	NMS	Y
8	F	18–24	Bachelors	Post-graduate Student	NMS, NGS	Y
9	F	25–34	Bachelors	Post-graduate Student	NMS, NGS	Y
10	M	35–44	Bachelors	Post-graduate Student	NMS	N

For task one, NGS and NMS selected one regularly accessed item and one less popular item from five of their collection departments. This was to ensure that consideration

---

[3] https://www.mural.co/.

was also placed on harder to find items, which may have less impactful meta-data. Digital flashcards were then developed for each of these items, which included the available metadata and an associated image; see Appendix A[4] for some examples. These flashcards were pooled into a Mural worksheet (Fig. 1 for an example of a completed sheet), with the participant selecting the first item and assigning tags that would assist in its retrieval. They were then asked to describe their reasons for the tags they assigned, before placing the flashcard in an appropriate space in the worksheet, which may have included grouping similar items together to form 'collections.' This process was repeated until the resource pool was empty, at which point the participant was given the opportunity to make amendments to the tags and/or groupings. Such a procedure enabled the participants to consider, outside of the infrastructures of NGS and NMS, the characteristics of collection items that are most important to them when searching. A comparison between these characteristics and the data management standards employed by NGS and NMS were made.

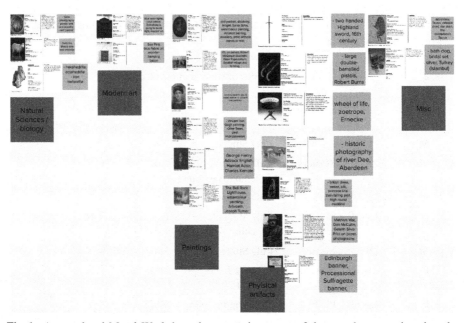

Fig. 1. A completed Mural Worksheet demonstrating some of the search tags assigned to the collection items.

It was also important to consider the search strategies of users when fulfilling their information needs within the real digital infrastructures of NGS and NMS, including the search terms employed. Therefore, task two involved a search observation process, with each participant being required to locate various items across each site. Based on

---

[4] https://docs.google.com/document/d/1hQPm75YXN_PhfEEUBpOCv6tV3CsoDGCvoqhajz ma7xk/edit?usp=sharing.

Borlund's evaluation framework [12] for interactive retrieval systems, four simulated search scenarios were created by NGS and NMS focusing on the following goals:

1. Researching a well-defined topical information need
2. Researching topics via data elements only e.g. titles and locations
3. Researching an ill-defined topical information need
4. Researching a known item via data elements

The specific search scenarios can be found in Appendix B[5] and were designed to ensure all features across both sites were accessed. Participants completed one search task at a time and were permitted to utilise as many features and access as many pages as they deemed necessary to satisfy the information need. Whilst locating search items, each participant was encouraged to 'think aloud' [13]: to talk through the rationale behind their actions as they were carried out. Help was not provided by the investigator unless explicitly requested, and no time limit was placed on the search tasks. On completion, a discussion took place about the features the participant liked on each site and the potential improvements that could be implemented.

3 Analysis

Both tasks were recorded and transcribed verbatim with participant consent for further analysis. The first task was primarily subjected to a deductive content analysis, using the *Spectrum* data management standard as the driving structural framework, since *Spectrum* is employed by both NGS and NMS. Content analysis is a term used to describe a number of text analysis strategies:

> "It is a systematic coding and categorising approach used for exploring large amounts of textual information unobtrusively to determine trends and patterns of words used, their frequency, their relationships, and the structures and discourses of communication…The purpose of content analysis is to describe the characteristics of the document's content by examining who says what, to whom, and with what effect." [14]

With its added focus on the use of particular words, content analysis was an ideal method to determine the characteristics users find most interesting when searching for cultural heritage items and whether these align with *Spectrum*. An in-depth description of the steps involved in content analysis is described by Erlingsson and Brysiewicz [15]. During task two, participants employed a range of search strategies and therefore encountered a variety of barriers. Consequently, an inductive framework analysis [16] was considered to be the most appropriate method since it facilitates the natural comparison of participants' views, which led to more concrete recommendations on how to improve the search pathways across NGS and NMS.

---

[5] https://docs.google.com/document/d/1hQPm75YXN_PhfEEUBpOCv6tV3CsoDGCvoqhajz ma7xk/edit?usp=sharing.

In addition, quantitative measures (such as time to completion, success rates, number of pages accessed etc.) were recorded for task two. Nevertheless, there were several factors that skewed the results for certain participants, including: poor internet connectivity that made if difficult to converse via Zoom; and a more limited proficiency of the English language. Since the n-size of the study was relatively small, we decided to omit these results and focus exclusively on the richer qualitative data.

3.1 Results: Metadata Tagging

Overall, the majority of the search tags created by the ten participants could be retrofitted to meet the cataloguing fields proposed by *Spectrum*. Nevertheless, this process often consisted of assigning tags to wider encasing fields, such as description or physical description, where curators have some freedom in determining the characteristics that should be included. As such, there is a risk that potentially important information could be overlooked due to the structures of expertise and knowledge frameworks, or the lack of it, that inform the institutions' indexing practices [20]. For example, in Ian Hamilton Finlay's 'Sea Pink' (see Appendix A[6]), most of the less familiar participants focused on the colours pink and teal when assigning search tags due to their lack of knowledge about the object, yet such descriptors are not included in the metadata. NMS in particular offer no specific search functionalities related to colour, which participant eight suggests would be helpful to distinguish between similar items from the same era: *"I think something that might also be helpful to include within the websites is if you can kind of also add colours as ways to sort objects, especially within fashions and textiles. If there's a lot of similar objects within the same era, then being able to identify them by colour might be helpful."*
Some of the tags proposed by the participants could not be modelled under the existing Spectrum standards, with the majority of these aligning with the ability to link loosely coupled objects together. For example, in reflecting contemporary concerns with inclusion and equality, many of the participants honed-in on characteristics that related to disability (such as Mrs E.M. Wright being painted by an artist with no hands) and women's rights (e.g. the suffragette banner) and therefore suggested that such topics could be grouped together under the same collection. This included highlighting female subjects or artists from older time periods, due to their previous exclusion from the field of art and culture. Currently, such information could be captured in *Spectrum's* description field, yet this would not be sufficient to link inherently different items together, meaning an additional field would be necessary.
Similarly, some of the participants assigned search tags based on the presence of an animal or person, regardless of whether they were well known: participant four: *"There's also people in this painting [Great Expectations] so I'll put it here [next to portraits] and I'll just put like a theme like people in general or something";* participant one: *"People do look for art that relates to animals in particular."* Creating new fields that enable users to search for people or animals in general (e.g. linking the zoetrope with more obvious items such as Dolly the sheep) could help facilitate future research into

---

[6] https://docs.google.com/document/d/1hQPm75YXN_PhfEEUBpOCv6tV3CsoDGCvoqhajz
ma7xk/edit?usp=sharing.

areas such as class or the role of animals in human culture. Sub-categories may also be developed to support more specific research, as highlighted by participant two: *"This is going to be such an awkward one to do but it's like famous or renowned. Yeah, it's like famous faces. And I'm going to put in Stevenson, you can put in Dolly the Sheep, uh, where's Van Gogh gone. I'm going to put him there and connect him to Burns."*

Participants also consistently assigned tags that group items from a particular domain. Some of these tags cited well indexed areas such as anatomy, Scottish history, space and war; nevertheless, many were poorly captured by NGS and NMS, including animation, activism, taxidermy etc. Spectrum's Object Category / Classification field can permit the retrieval of items from a particular subject, yet once again the nature of these subjects relies on the views of curators, which can differ from end users.

Finally, there was a difference observed in the manner in which participants from outside of Scotland tagged specific items compared to the available metadata. Those individuals with English as an additional language particularly relied upon *Spectrum's* Object name category when tagging items, which encapsulates more basic descriptions. Nevertheless, there were instances of local or culturally specific terms being embedded in this category, for example 'claymore' in the highland sword, which had no meaning to these participants, who instead opted for simpler terms such as 'sword': participant six: *"Because I don't know what [a] claymore [is], so I will just type sword."* This highlights the importance of providing synonyms to support search from a range of users. Non-native participants where English was their first language also had similar experiences. In addition, less knowledgeable participants tended not to tag more scientific terms and opted for terms that were used on a more general basis: participant eight: *"I don't think most people know a hexahedrite or things like that in their daily vocabulary. But meteorite would be something that more people of any age can sort of search for and maybe if you are a younger audience, you might just search rocks."*

3.2 Spectrum Fields

This section provides a discussion some of the interesting tags assigned by the participants and how they relate to *Spectrum* fields. Note that *Spectrum* has a far wider catalogue and not all fields were referenced by the participants.

Dimensions: Participants consistently referred to the size of tangible items (i.e. physical, 3-D objects) when providing tags. This did not solely involve specific dimensions, particularly with the less experienced participants where other more general descriptors were applied such as 'miniature'. On the other hand, the more knowledgeable participants requested further information on the size of certain items, such as the claymore, which highlights the variability of the metadata being assigned to collection objects: participant seven: *"Has it got the dimensions? No it doesn't, um, because some of these were symbolic, you know, they were so big that they weren't actually weapons but they're classed as weapons."*

Location: The location tag in *Spectrum* calls for full location audit information, including current display locations. Some of the frequent visitors of NGS and NMS were interested in the exact rooms items were held, yet others cared more about whether they were on display to support their decision for an in person visit: participant one: *"You want to group together things that were on display...but also if it wasn't on display they [users] wouldn't waste their time going to the museum to go see it if it wasn't there because obviously, you know, during the pandemic everyone's working from home. Some people may have moved away from the city and a lot of people who visit museums aren't actually from the city...they might not want to visit or come to travel that far if that wasn't there. And a lot of international people go to the museum."*

Materials: Materials were one of the most commonly tagged aspects for both experienced and inexperienced users, particularly when an unusual or defining substance was utilised by an artist: participant four: *"If I want like a more specific [tag] I would look at material, so here, like, it's really different to have a wood material [for paintings]."* In addition, the participants would often fall back on the physical characteristic of items if they lacked knowledge on an artefact, participant eight: *"I don't think people would necessarily remember it's a bridal set or anything like that, I think a keyword to be in here would be silver."*

Production Dating: The *Spectrum* Production Dating field urges indexers to provide a specific date an item was made or a broader range if one is not available. This was evident in the participants' own tags, where four different classes of date were mentioned: the exact date; the century; an era such as Victorian; and modern vs old art. Different indexing strategies could link vastly diverse items together, particularly via the latter method as highlighted by participant two: *"I would have guessed that [mummy portrait] would have been like, you know, maybe pre Victorian times but if that's where that's from then it's ancient, that's pretty amazing. So yes, to go with modern history there's also your ancient history. Anything that's over 1000 years would go into ancient history. Or like anything over 800 years. Yeah, I'd say 800 years cause then you get into like the middle ages, your dark ages and middle ages."*

Production Place: *Spectrum* also places significance on the area an item is associated with, which may include multiple locations such as the place it was designed and the place it was manufactured. Both sets of participants also felt such information was important, and suggested emphasising Scottish and non-Scottish objects for tourists who may want to prioritise local artefacts: participant nine *"When I go to [anon] and they like present some Scottish local artists and some creation in a particular space. So I think some of the audience will be interested in Scottish artists. So I might put these kind of key words in it."*

School /Style /Culture and Title: IN terms of the style of an object and its title, many of the participants who had little experience in certain sub-domains of art and culture were hesitant to tag such fields unless they contained common knowledge such as Dolly the Sheep. Nevertheless, they recognised that users with more experience would deem these characteristics to be important, as also found in [20], where expert users were searched for more characteristics than novice: participant eight *"I mean I'm not an artist, I'm not, but is he classified as an impressionist or something? But I guess if people are looking for Van Gogh though they know about him."* Participant ten *"I don't know a lot about guns so I wouldn't know that [flintlock]. But I bet if someone knew something about guns and they were searching for it I'm sure they would know that term."*

Personalisation: Following on from the 'School / Style / Culture and Title' section, participants recognised that search terms are personal and are influenced by an individual's preferences and experiences: participant ten: *"Yeah so it was easier because I have a background knowledge on Dolly I know what search terms would probably work for that one, whereas the other ones I don't have any background knowledge on those"*; participant two: *"It's not something that I'd be particularly interested in looking at, I mean it's a very pretty dress but again it needs to be something a lot more outlandish. You know, some sort of famous person...but if it's just a pretty dress, it doesn't appeal to me as much as a lot more smaller, physical objects."*

In terms of the tagging process, the variability of the metadata available had an effect on the depth of the search terms assigned to an item. Some participants had great difficulty tagging items that had little description; whereas others were absorbed by more complex items and found themselves applying less relevant tags; participant five: *"Because there's no information on it, it makes it hard to classify it and give it worth. I'd imagine walking past that and being like you'd want to know why it's there and then when there's no information on it you're like there's nothing there to tell me why it's here and that someone made it"*; participant one: *"I could list everything in that photo, waves, sea, boat, lighthouse but you know then I'm just listing everything in it rather than trying to generalise a theme...I don't want thousands of themes. How do I encompass most of them?"* There was also some evidence of participants breaking wider encompassing tags into smaller sub-tags.

Physical vs Digital Space: When attempting to group items, participant eight consistently referred to the physical spaces of museums and how collections are formed: *"Thinking about the actual physical space of where these objects would be and I think that is really important for a lot of people when it comes to sorting things especially if you've been to the physical spaces, they're like oh this was probably in this room whereas this was in this room."* This was surprising since literature (e.g. Burke et al., [17]) focuses on taking advantage of the different experiences offered by digital spaces and moving away from simply mirroring the layout of physical museums and galleries.

3.3 Results: Search Tasks

In addition to evaluating the search tags employed by NGS and NMS, it is also important to consider the overall user experience of individuals searching for information across the sites. Whilst completing the search tasks, the participants discussed aspects relating to the way they search, the search features (pathways) available, and the structure of the items returned.

Search Procedures: Continuing on from the first task, the search terms employed by participants were generally basic, consisting of a few descriptive phrases such as 'brooch, love.' Most, centred on terms that could be captured by *Spectrum's* Object Name field, with colour, style, and materials also being used to narrow searches that returned a wide range of results. Barriers related to search terms primarily consisted of a lack of support for synonyms, misspellings, and grammatical constructs such as pluralisation: participant two: *"It would be dreadful if you type in something and it turns out you've missed your spelling slightly. Instead of archaeology I put archaeologists and got nothing."*

Two main search strategies were utilised by the participants depending on the topic being explored and their familiarity with the websites. First, if a topic was particularly broad, or the participant was new to the NGS or NMS websites, then they would prefer to use the site-wide search box: participant four: *"I feel like the advanced search is too narrow for this, like I don't know where to put the Covid-19, like should this go into the collection or description, so I'm just gonna go with the normal search, Covid-19."* There was also evidence of participants falling back to the site-wide search bar if other features such as advanced search produced no relevant results: participant seven: *"So when in doubt usually my last step, I think, is just going to the actual search bar up here and searching like art and culture."* Second, participants who were familiar with the websites tended to use more of the available search features, often beginning with advanced search when the object had a particularly distinguishable feature.

In general, participants tolerated between four and six pages of items being returned. If the results became too obscure, then they would narrow the search by adding further terms to the advanced search bar: participant five: *"We're getting a bit obscure, well there's a brooch but if I started to see like it was getting a bit abstract, like that plaid I'd be like, oh right, I may be going too far."*

Search Features: The motivations behind utilising each of the available search features across NGS and NMS, as well as the advantages and barriers to using these features are presented below.

Advanced Search Bars: AS discussed earlier, the participants tended to use advanced search features when they were familiar with the websites and had a particular characteristic in mind that they wanted to search for, especially when narrowing results. Figure 2 highlights the differences in the advanced search features of NGS and NMS.

Users of NMS felt that the advanced search bar was missing crucial characteristics such as colour, whilst they were also unsure on what information to include in the categories that were provided. For example, all were hesitant to input a collection when searching for items as there was no easy way to find a list of collections made available by the museum: participant five *"Knowing what the collections are called helps. But then again, I feel like that should just be something I can find out very easily rather than having to look for one example then work my way back up the chain."* In addition, the results were overly restrictive, in that inputting a wrong word or misspelling in one category would simply break the search.

The participants preferred the ability to select pre-determined search categories - like those offered by NGS - since this supports users who are less familiar with their item to find what they are looking for: participant one: *"I like that they both had an advanced search option. I like the fact that this one has the search option, where it kind of gives you things - if I wanted to search Van Gogh, you can see the artist and his artworks. It will give you, like, very specific things that might have been the actual search term to use."* Nevertheless, they felt that the free-text search bar was difficult to locate within the 'More' menu item and should instead be embedded in the main Artworks page. Improvements to NMS' advanced search feature focused on guiding the user on what terms to use either via an autocomplete feature or similar drop-down menus to NGS: participant two *"I think something that pops up with recommendations of tags that do exist...I think that would help."*

Artists Search NGS: The participants who utilised the 'Artists' search feature from NGS appreciated the additional information that may be obtained - such as a link to the artists Wikipedia entry and biography - and felt that the pages were well structured overall. Yet, there were some instances where they attempted to find an unlisted artist using this feature and subsequently requested a more complete catalogue.

Collections at NGS Site: The 'Collections' feature from NGS was misused by the participants who were unfamiliar with the site, as they felt that the page would offer a way to search for collection items (like the advanced search bar found in 'Artworks'), as opposed to describing collections that are available in the gallery. This may suggest that a re-think of the headings may be necessary to support new users in accessing the features they are looking for but also encourage them to utilise a wider range of functionalities.

Glossary at NGS Site: Surprisingly, NGS' glossary was underutilised by the participants, especially those who were less familiar with art and culture. Nevertheless, when shown the feature, most suggested it could be extremely useful to identify potential search terms, with participant four advocating for a link to be embedded within the site-wide and advanced search features: *"It's difficult to find it. I feel like it should be near the search bar and then, like, under the search bar it should be written like 'don't know what terms to search, look at our glossary' or something like that."*

Site-wide Search Bars: AS discussed previously, the site-wide search bars were mostly utilised by new users or when participants were researching more open or new topics such as Covid-19. In addition, the experienced users of NMS used this feature in circumstances where an article would be more insightful than a collection page: participant six: *"The phrasing of that question, which was art is addressing the topic of climate change, that doesn't make me think I'm looking for artwork for climate change because there's probably lots of that but more maybe articles."* On the other hand, less experienced users expected a combination of articles and collection pages to be returned by the NMS site-wide search bar, which was not the case. In terms of the NGS bar, the participants appreciated the suggested terms drop-down menu that appears when typing but found it distracting when a suggestion permanently fills the search box once you have hovered over it.

Stories and Resources NMS: This feature was mainly used by participants who were familiar with the NMS site. They suggested that 'Stories and resources' offered an alternative way of gaining additional information on items via articles that are grouped together by themes and subjects: participant seven: *"This is quite an interesting way to go because this includes lots more than just the actual artefacts, so I think the themes are quite good. I have found you've got to know to go there, and I think that that could be clearer. Romans' life in the frontier, Romans, the Roman army. These are really, really good, these sorts of articles. I think that's actually gonna tell me a bit more."* Improvements to the feature centred on the ability to restrict search results via subject,

Fig. 2. NGS and NMS advanced search bars.

theme, and type as opposed to just one of those categories: participant eight *"I think if there was a way to sort of more narrow down, like if you could choose both the theme and subject because as you can see you can't choose both. So having, like, explorer by type or subject or theme or a mixture of all of them I think would be a lot more helpful."*

Item Descriptions: Three barriers relating to the descriptions of items were observed across both sites. First, participants found the collection search results to be difficult to navigate when the items were presented with the same, basic tags: participant five *"It's frustrating how they're all called brooch. If they even had brooch brackets, something, a year, a period, a style anything because otherwise what you've got is brooch, brooch, brooch...even like a preview of what it could be [would be helpful]."* Some of the participants were also hesitant to conclude that their search tasks had been completed due to the omission of important metadata such as a date: participant three *"I would be really missing a year. At the least, I like an approximate year because if it says Roman site at Newstead I don't know whether there might be, like, an actual Roman site still now at Newstead and it's been found like a week ago so it's dated like 2021. I know I'm overthinking this but it's clear for this object, but it might not be clear for other objects that are not so well known in history."* Finally, the lack of associated images hindered participants during the tasks where they had to use a picture of an object as a reference.

4   Conclusion

The population for the study was small, yet the results enabled a conclusion to be formed that the knowledge of stakeholder needs and preferences can help drive user-centred improvements to the digital infrastructures of cultural heritage institutions. All of the participants were highly educated and were either pursuing or had obtained a postgraduate degree. Professional and highly educated people form the majority of users of cultural heritage [18], and hence our selected user group may reflect the bulk of users visiting the NGS and NMS sites. Nevertheless, future studies should also consider individuals who may be representative of one-time users looking for information, for instance in relation to in-person visits.

Overall, this research provides some insights into the online search behaviour of NMS and NGS users that can inform future policies around digital presence and provisions for these institutions, and the sector as a whole. Existing collection management standards like *Spectrum*[7] are not user-centred and often the metadata implemented by collection institutions to index objects are not designed for the diverse needs and contexts of users. This calls for more research – with diverse groups of both users and non-users, and selected collections/objects, to capture multiple perspectives of items. Such a process has the potential to ensure metadata is more user-centred and the search interface employed takes into consideration the needs of people with different backgrounds, motivations, ethnicities, and varied experience in cultural heritage. Research literature shows promising prospects for the use of AI (artificial intelligence) and ML (machine learning) to support more timely and wide-reaching metadata tagging [19]. However, this would require items to have a standard of existing data that neither NMS nor NGS currently have across their collections, which could be true for most cultural heritage institutions. Future investigations into this approach should start off small, focusing on collection items that have no licensing issues, good data standards, and which speak to diverse sets of users and their search motivations, before upscaling across entire collections.

---

[7] https://collectionstrust.org.uk/spectrum/.

Results from the first experiment highlight that indexing cultural heritage objects for a range of target users is an extremely difficult and time-consuming task, even with curators being guided by data management standards such as *Spectrum*. These standards encourage a variety of different characteristics to be considered when developing metadata, yet much of the content is left to the interpretations of curators e.g. description or physical description. Rather, user- and context-specific guidelines could be beneficial in ensuring the aspects considered most important by consumers are indexed, whilst AI and ML techniques can expand on the resulting descriptions, thereby producing more relevant search results based on user profiles and access patterns.

Results from the second experiment indicate that a user-centred approach to designing cultural heritage websites would help to improve an individual's experience when searching for information. Such a process requires institutions to form a concrete understanding of who their target users are before developing features and designs to suit their specific needs and interests. To elaborate, those participants who had less experience with art and culture, including the NGS and NMS sites, experienced different barriers than those who did, and used a narrower range of search features - primarily the site-wide and advanced search.

Acknowledgement. Research reported in this paper forms part of a larger project funded by the Arts & Humanities Research Council (AHRC) in UK (Ref: AH/V015443/1). We would like to express our sincere thanks to AHRC and all the partners of this project, especially Dr. Jen Ross (University of Edinburgh), Chanté St Clair Inglis (National Museums of Scotland) and Christopher Ganley (National Galleries of Scotland).

References

1. Hooper-Greenhill, E.: Museums and the Interpretation of Visual Culture. Routledge, Abingdon (2000)
2. Ruthven, I., Chowdhury, G.: Cultural Heritage Information: Access and Management. Facet Publishing, London (2015)
3. Chowdhury, G.: Cultural heritage information services: sustainability issues. In: Ruthven, I., Chowdhury, G. (eds.) Cultural Heritage Information: Access and Management, pp. 221–245. Facet Publishing, London (2015)
4. Chowdhury, S.: Cultural heritage information: users and usability. In: Ruthven, I., Chowdhury, G. (eds.) Cultural Heritage Information: Access and Management, pp. 135–151. Facet Publishing, London (2015)
5. Han, H.J., Wolfram, D.: An exploration of search session patterns in an image-based digital library. J. Inf. Sci. **42**, 477–491 (2016)
6. Farrell, S.: Search-log analysis: the most overlooked opportunity in web UX research, (2017). https://www.nngroup.com/articles/search-log-analysis/. Accessed 16 July 2022
7. Eramian, M., Walia, E., Power, C., Cairns, P., Lewis, A.: Image-based search and retrieval for biface artefacts using features capturing archaeologically significant characteristics. Mach. Vis. Appl. **28**(1–2), 201–218 (2016). https://doi.org/10.1007/s00138-016-0819-x
8. Konstantakis, M., Aliprantis, J., Teneketzis, A., Caridakis, G.: Understanding user experience aspects in cultural heritage interaction. In: PCI 2018: Proceedings of the 22nd Pan-Hellenic Conference on Informatics, November 2018, pp 267–271 (2018). https://doi-org.proxy.lib.strath.ac.uk/10.1145/3291533.3291580. Accessed 16 July 2022

9. Bailey-Ross, C.: Online user research literature review: UK gallery, library, archive and museum (GLAM) digital collections Commissioned report. Towards a national collection (2021).https://doi.org/10.5281/zenodo.5779826. Accessed 16 July 2022
10. Rainbow, R., Morrison, A. and Morgan, M.: 'Providing accessible online collections. In: Proceedings of Museums and the Web 2012 (2012). https://www.museumsandtheweb.com/mw2012/papers/providing_accessible_online_collections.html. Accessed 27 Sep 2022
11. Skov, M., Ingwersen, P.: Museum web search behavior of special interest visitors. Libr. Inf. Sci. Res. **36**, 91–98 (2014)
12. Borlund. P.: Experimental components for the evaluation of interactive information retrieval systems. J. Document. **56**, 71–90 (2000)
13. Nielsen, J., Clemmensen, T., Yssing, C.: Getting access to what goes on in people's heads? - Reflections on the think-aloud technique. In: NordiCHI 2002 (2002)
14. Vaismoradi, M., Turunen, H., Bonda, T.: Content analysis and thematic analysis: Implications for conducting a qualitative descriptive study. Nurs. Health Sci. **14**, 398–405 (2013)
15. Erlingsson, C., Brysiewicz, P.: A hands-on guide to doing content analysis. African J. Emerg. Med. **7**(3), 93–99 (2017)
16. Gale, N.K., Heath, G., Cameron, E., Rashid, S., Redwood, S.: Using the framework method for the analysis of qualitative data in multi-disciplinary health research. BMC Med. Res. Methodol. **13**, 117 (2013)
17. Burke, V., Jørgensen, D., Jørgensen, F.A.: Museums at home: digital initiatives in response to COVID-19. Norsk museumstidsskrift **6**(2), 117–123 (2020)
18. Walsh, D., Clough, P., Foster, J.: User categories for digital cultural heritage. In Proceedings of 1st International Workshop on Accessing Cultural Heritage at Scale (ACHS 2016). http://ceur-ws.org/Vol-1611/paper6.pdf. Accessed 20 July 2022
19. Bordoni, L., Mele, F., Sorgente, A.: Artificial Intelligence for Cultural Heritage. Cambridge Scholars Publishing, Cambridge (2016). https://www.cambridgescholars.com/resources/pdfs/978-1-4438-9085-4-sample.pdf. Accessed 22 July 2022
20. Koolen, M., Kamps, J., de Keijzer, V.: Information retrieval in cultural heritage. Interdisc. Sci. Rev. **34**(2–3), 268–284 (2009). https://doi.org/10.1179/174327909X441153

A Comparison of Information Retrieval Pre-processing Algorithms Applied to African Historical Data

Soham Singh and Hussein Suleman[(✉)] [iD]

University of Cape Town, Cape Town, South Africa
sngsoh004@myuct.ac.za, hussein@cs.uct.ac.za
http://dl.cs.uct.ac.za/

Abstract. African historical data presents unique challenges to search algorithms because much of the data was produced by colonial authorities or archivists far from the source of the data. Contemporary datasets include descriptions of museum artefacts in European museums and books written by colonial administrators, both of which encode African history. These are both arguably biased collections and the information retrieval algorithms used to search through such data collections may not provide modern researchers with relevant results. The goal of this study was therefore to investigate the degree to which common text and image pre-processing algorithms affect the quality of search results when users search through a current African historical data collection. Nine common algorithms were compared in terms of recall, precision and NDCG. The results indicate that text pre-processing performs better when stemming and stopping are used but thesaurus use may depend on the thesaurus chosen. Results from the image pre-processing experiment indicate that shape detectors generally work better than colour detectors.

Keywords: Bias · Retrieval · Heritage data

1 Introduction

African historical and heritage collections are composed of many objects collected during colonial and pre- colonial times. These objects are today found in museums and libraries around the world, with metadata produced by curators in what are often the museums of colonising countries (e.g., UK). Further, many historical accounts were documented by colonial authorities, and are today studied as among the primary sources of information on African history. The Five Hundred Year Archive [17] is a project to convene this dispersed information but also allow for re-contextualisation and decolonisation of the narrative.

Decolonisation encompasses initiatives that must be undertaken at a variety of levels, including at the epistemic level [9]. Given that retrieval systems (also known as search engines) in digital archives can be considered as epistemically significant [15] and that a museum is an epistemic space [11], it is reasonable to consider that the process of decolonising heritage retrieval systems, from a

© The Author(s), under exclusive license to Springer Nature Switzerland AG 2022
Y.-H. Tseng et al. (Eds.): ICADL 2022, LNCS 13636, pp. 222–230, 2022.
https://doi.org/10.1007/978-3-031-21756-2_18

humanitarian perspective, is strongly coupled with the mitigation of the biases that stem from the pre-colonial annotations. The current approach of immutable information retrieval for such systems will not satisfy the requirements of a decolonised system and the belief of "neutrality of technology" has overshadowed the inherent problematic social values embedded in modern day search engines [13]. Thus, in this work, an experiment was conducted to determine how different core retrieval algorithms for text and images perform when applied to African historical data with known biases.

With regards to text retrieval pre-processing algorithms, we specifically explore the effects of stemming, stopword removal and synonym query expansion [2]. The effects of stemming were explored due to the inconsistency in the language used between the curators of the artefacts in the heritage data and the modern researchers using heritage data retrieval systems. There is also a mixture of low-resource languages that do not contain a standard-zed vocabulary in the data. While the queries used in this study were all in English, many of the documents contained annotations, or the names of places and people, borrowed from African languages such as isiZulu. Given the language-based nature of stemming, this could result in isiZulu words being stemmed and incorrectly matched with the stems of the English query phrases. Stopword removal could potentially improve retrieval effectiveness by promoting retrieval based on the matching of rarer, shorter words that add more meaning to documents and queries. Lastly, for text retrieval, this research explores whether the use of thesauri can address the potential issue of differences in language as a result of modern researchers being in a different era, belonging to a different culture, or speaking language differently, to the curators of the artefacts.

For image retrieval pre-processing algorithms, we specifically wanted to investigate the differences between shape-based pre-processing algorithms, image-based pre-processing algorithms, and pre-processing algorithms based on both colour and shape, to determine if these elements are influential in the retrieval effectiveness of this African heritage data. The image dataset was found to contain many images that were comprised mainly of brown colours and Earthy tones. Many of the artefacts had also experienced degradation, meaning their shapes were no longer wholly intact.

This paper is organized as follows. Section 2 elaborates on the literature available for decolonization and algorithms for data pre-processing. Sections 3 and 4 outline the research methodology and results, followed by the conclusions for the study in Sect. 5.

2   Literature Review

Decolonisation and African Heritage Data. In 2015, student-led protests throughout Universities in South Africa for the #RhodesMustFall movement brought recognition and promoted discourse regarding the inequalities that were systematically built into tertiary education institutions [9]. Decolonisation is the process of unlearning unjust practices and ideals and dismantling institutions with the intention of facilitating other perspectives of knowledge [9]. Through decolonising, society can recognize that historically marginalized groups are agents of their own experiences and pasts [6,12,14] and can provide the foundation to redeem African theory across diverse disciplines and domains [9]. Four dimensions of decolonisation have been identified as important to the initiative, these being: structural, epistemic, personal, and relational [9]. Of these, what should be of interest to information sciences and technology is the epistemic dimension. Given that museums are epistemic spaces [11], it is reasonable to suggest that digital retrieval systems containing the very heritage data present in museums are also in need of undergoing the process of decolonisation. Research conducted on the Google search engine's retrieval integrity for the query term: "black girls" was noted for undertaking decolonising work by questioning the nature of Web searches and results in relation to social justice [14] and questioned the inability for users to be able to "see Google's algorithm" to understand the associations made by the search engine [13]. A core concept of decolonisation - interrogation - strongly encourages questioning what qualifies as "expert" and why certain knowledge is presented or omitted [9].

2.1   Information Retrieval Pre-processing Algorithms

Text Retrieval. Most text retrieval systems use a collection of pre-processing algorithms to improve on the quality of retrieval (either recall, precision, or both). Stemming, stopping and use of a thesaurus (synonyms) [2] are standard techniques to increase recall, precision, and recall, respectively. Stemming is the reduction of a word to its root form (e.g., driving -> drive). Stopping is the removal of common words (e.g., the). Thesauri are used for the expansion of queries using their synonyms (e.g., car -> car auto motor).

Image Retrieval. Image retrieval algorithms extract features from images that can be used in order to determine a degree of similarity. Common algorithms include: Edge Histogram (EH), Pyramid Histogram of Oriented Gradients (PH), Auto Colour Correlogram (AC), Colour and Edge Directivity Descriptor (CE), Colour Layout (CL) and Joint Composite Descriptor (JC). Edge Histogram [18] optimises matching performance by initially using global and semi-local edge histograms, then determines similarity by combining global, semi-global, and local histograms. This is then compared against the MPEG-7 descriptor of the local histogram. Pyramid Histogram of Oriented Gradients [3] determines spatial layout information by tiling the image, across multiple resolutions, into various regions. Local shape information is also determined by iterating over regions and acquiring the distribution of edge orientations used for similarity calculations. Auto Colour Correlation computes the probability of finding a pixel of a particular colour in a specified distance from a pixel of another colour [7]. Colour and Edge Directivity use fuzzy rules and texture filters for subregions of an image, eventually combined into a histogram [5]. Colour Layout computes a spatial distribution of colour [8]. Finally, the Joint Composite Descriptor combines colours and texture descriptors [4].

3   Experimental Design

In this section, we present an experiment that aimed to provide an offline evaluation of pre-processing algorithms for text and image retrieval to determine if algorithmic variation has the potential to have a significant difference on retrieval effectiveness.

3.1   The Five Hundred Year Archive Dataset (FHYA)

The dataset of the FHYA contains multimodal digitized artefacts from South Africa from the period of 1750 to the late 19th century and includes data that was created during the colonial era, as well as data that is being curated in postcolonial times [17]. Some artefacts were curated outside of the Southern Africa region while others were curated within the country during the Apartheid period. This variation in curation circumstances results in the different perspectives of each curator reflecting in the data.

The FHYA dataset provided for use in this study consists of artefacts that have a JPEG image (in some instances multiple images) and related XML metadata. The metadata consisted of descriptive information of the artefacts such as the name of the parent series/collection, the title of the artefact, a material designation (e.g.: textual record, object, sound recording etc.), a unique identifier, and a list of events with associated dates (e.g.: curation, custody, collection, making etc.). The subset of the FHYA used for this study consisted of 1345 text documents and 5708 images - this was the complete collection at the time of the study.

3.2   System Design and Implementation

It was decided that the multimodal information retrieval system would be built using Apache Solr [1] and LIRE, an open-source, Java plug-in to facilitate image retrieval and search within Solr [10]. To support algorithmic variation, multiple indexes (or cores) were created in the Solr retrieval system, each with their own respective pre- and post-processing algorithmic procedures defined in their configuration schemas. All cores were then indexed with the same subset of the FHYA dataset that was provided for use in this study.

Text Retrieval. For text retrieval, the retrieval system supported stemming, stopping and synonyms. Combinations of these algorithms were also added to the retrieval system. This included the following combinations (the names of the pre-processing algorithms that are used for the rest of this paper are in brackets following each description): Stemming and Stopping (stemmingAndStopping), Stopping and Synonyms (stoppingAndSynonyms), Synonyms and Stemming (synonymsAndStemming), Stemming, Stopping and Synonyms (allConfig) and a pre- processing algorithm using none of the techniques (noConfig) that was added to be used as a baseline for comparison. Queries were compared against all textual content in the documents (i.e. not just the short titles but also descriptions and other fields).

Image Retrieval. Image retrieval was supported by integrating LireSolr, an implementation of the LIRE library that makes use of deep learning processes to extract features from images, with the Solr text retrieval system [10]. 6 of the available image-retrieval algorithms in LIRE were included in the system: Edge Histogram [18], Pyramid Histogram of Oriented Gradients [3], Auto Colour Correlogram [7], Colour and Edge Directivity Descriptor [5], Colour Layout [8] and Joint Composite Descriptor [4]. These pre-processing algorithms were selected to specifically investigate the differences between shape-based pre-processing algorithms, image-based pre- processing algorithms, and pre-processing algorithms based on both colour and shape.

3.3 Sample Queries

This experiment required sample queries, as well as relevance judgements for their results, to evaluate retrieval effectiveness.

Text Queries. The Google Trends tool was used to obtain a list of candidate information needs and associated text-based queries. This was done by submitting topics, such as "History of Africa", into the tool and storing the related queries for the topic, as well as parsing any related topics and their respective related queries. This ultimately resulted in a list of 54 candidate information needs that were verified as being relevant to the domain of precolonial African heritage by the Archive & Public Culture Research Initiative at the University of Cape Town. The associated queries were submitted to the text retrieval system described in Sect. 3.2, and any query where less than 10 results was retrieved was removed from being a candidate for use in the experiment. From this process, a final list of 70 sample text-based queries was obtained.

Image Queries. Sample image queries were obtained by finding an online digital library containing African heritage image data. The Smithsonian National Museum of African Art (NMAfA) [16] was identified as being a suitable candidate, given it contains traditional African art and artefacts, as well as having suitable accessibility. The NMAfA allows for image files to be used for educational use under "fair use", thus permission was not required to be obtained from NMAfA. 133 candidate images related to "Pre-colonial South African heritage" were obtained, from which 70 were randomly sampled for consistency with the number of sample text queries used in the experiment.

3.4 Experiment Procedure

The process for conducting the experiment was as follows: 70 text-based and 70 image-based queries (obtained from the process outlined in 3.3) were submitted to the retrieval system across all text and image retrieval pre-processing algorithms. Afterwards, the unique results from each pre- processing algorithm for a given query were recorded and a superset of results for each query was compiled (resulting in 140 total supersets). Supersets were compiled in CSV format such that the file name was the respective query, and each of the retrieved documents was listed. Alongside the link to each of the retrieved documents were 3 columns for relevance of the document to be graded. 10 participants were then allocated 14 supersets each (7 image supersets and 7 text supersets) and were asked to grade the relevance of results in the superset to its respective query by adding an "X" in the column that best represented the relevance of the document.

3.5 Participants

The requirements for participants were that they were aged 18 or older and had access to a computer with an Internet connection and browser. For the filtering of sample image queries, 3 participants were sampled using the convenience sampling method. The participants were 2 males and 1 female, all between the ages of 23 and 30. 10 participants were recruited for the formal experiment using the convenience sampling method. Participants were 70% male and 30% female, with all participants aged between 23 and 35 years of age.

4   Results

The results of nonparametric, asymptotic Friedman tests revealed that there was a statistically significant difference in the recall of the different image algorithms, $\chi^2(5) = 29.708$, p < .001. Significant differences were also found for precision and NDCG@10 (all p < .001). This would suggest that algorithmic variation for heritage image data retrieval can significantly improve retrieval effectiveness for image retrieval across many metrics. This led to further detailed inspection of the differences between algorithms. Figure 1 illustrates the differences between image algorithms with respect to their average precision and recall at different ranking positions (n = 1 to n = 10), indicating that AC, EH and PH outperformed other algorithms for these two metrics across all 10 ranking positions. Table 1, which contains mean values for image algorithms across all recorded metrics, also shows that these three algorithms had the best ranking performance given their relatively high NDCG@10 values. The presence of EH and PH in the top 3 performing algorithms would suggest that shape-based image pre-processing algorithms potentially perform better for this heritage data retrieval compared to colour-based pre-processing algorithms (which is further supported by the worst-performing algorithm being CL).

While significant differences were recorded between image pre-processing algorithms, this was not the case for the text pre-processing algorithms. For text retrieval pre-processing algorithms, significant differences were only observed for precision ($\chi^2(7) = 47.801$, p < .001). It can be seen from Table 2 that the addition of stemming to the baseline algorithm (noConfig) leads to an improvement in recall and precision performance. This would suggest that stemming processing on heritage text data can potentially lead to the improvement of text retrieval effectiveness, despite the variety of language usage in the data, although there are no significant differences. This is also potentially supported by the fact that every pre-processing algorithm that contained stemming processing had better mean recall performance compared to the baseline, and all except synonymsAndStemming and allConfig had better precision and NDCG performance compared to the baseline (see Table 2). Conversely, the addition of thesaurus processing appears to worsen retrieval effectiveness when compared to the baseline. This requires further inspection as to whether it is an issue with the thesaurus used for this research (i.e. the WordNet thesaurus) or thesaurus processing in general. Lastly, stopword removal appears to have no significant impact on retrieval effectiveness of this heritage text data. This could be a result of the lack of stopwords in the queries used for the evaluation (about 11%).

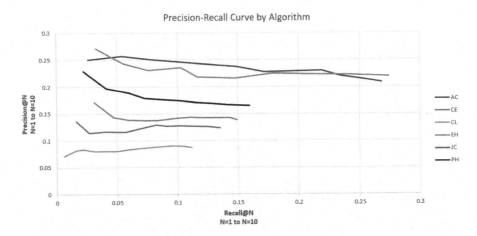

Fig. 1. Precision-Recall curve by image algorithms

Table 1. Mean and standard deviation for retrieval metrics for image algorithms (*= statistically significant differences)

Algorithm	Recall*		Precision*		NDCG@10*	
	Mean	SD	Mean	SD	Mean	SD
AC	0.268	0.272	0.211	0.219	0.330	0.289
CE	0.150	0.185	0.145	0.183	0.216	0.246
CL	0.112	0.170	0.093	0.129	0.129	0.186
EH	0.274	0.261	0.221	0.219	0.337	0.299
JC	0.135	0.174	0.129	0.164	0.188	0.222
PH	0.159	0.166	0.165	0.207	0.234	0.252

Table 2. Mean and standard deviation for retrieval metrics for text algorithms (*= statistically significant differences)

Algorithm	Recall		Precision*		NDCG@10	
	Mean	SD	Mean	SD	Mean	SD
AllConfig	0.619	0.347	0.338	0.337	0.574	0.359
NoConfig	0.558	0.384	0.389	0.335	0.591	0.379
Stemming	0.684	0.338	0.416	0.335	0.667	0.343
StemmingAndStopping	0.649	0.343	0.442	0.348	0.657	0.349
Stopping	0.539	0.382	0.421	0.347	0.585	0.380
StoppingAndSynonyms	0.505	0.375	0.319	0.326	0.504	0.368
Synonyms	0.521	0.376	0.314	0.316	0.524	0.368
SynonymsAndStemming	0.621	0.336	0.341	0.340	0.577	0.351

5   Conclusions

African historical datasets are critical for modern researchers, but they are often cautious about the data having been produced by colonial authorities and museums in remote parts of the world. This study was motivated by that hesitation to accept search algorithms applied to sensitive and contested datasets. The results indicate that stemming and stopping improve relevance, as they are typically expected to. The use of a thesaurus was not as successful and suggests that widely accepted thesauri may not work for historical data in a specific context. Future work could investigate the production of specialized thesauri. Image pre-processing results indicate that shape detection works significantly better with images of historical artefacts than colour detection. Thus, the selection of algorithms and their parameters are specific and sensitive to the nature of the dataset, and this must be considered or mitigated for when designing search systems for historical datasets.

Acknowledgements. This research was partially funded by the National Research Foundation of South Africa (Grant numbers: 105862, 119121 and 129253) and University of Cape Town. The authors acknowledge that opinions, findings and conclusions or recommendations expressed in this publication are that of the authors, and that the NRF accepts no liability whatsoever in this regard.

We would like to acknowledge the Archive & Public Culture research initiative at the University of Cape Town for allowing this research to use the Five Hundred Year Archive data collection for the purposes of this study.

References

1. Apache: Solr. https://lucene.apache.org/solr/
2. Baeza-Yates, R., Ribeiro-Neto, B., et al.: Modern Information Retrieval, vol. 463. ACM Press, New York (1999)

3. Bosch, A., Zisserman, A., Munoz, X.: Representing shape with a spatial pyramid Kernel. In: Proceedings of the 6th ACM International Conference on Image and Video Retrieval, pp. 401–408. CIVR 2007. Association for Computing Machinery, New York, NY, USA (2007). https://doi.org/10.1145/1282280.1282340

4. Chatzichristofis, S., Boutalis, Y., Lux, M.: Selection of the proper compact composite descriptor for improving content based image retrieval. In: Proceedings of the 6th IASTED International Conference, vol. 134643, p. 064 (2009)

5. Chatzichristofis, S.A., Boutalis, Y.S.: CEDD: color and edge directivity descriptor: a compact descriptor for image indexing and retrieval. In: International Conference on Computer Vision Systems, pp. 312–322. Springer (2008). https://doi.org/10.1007/978-3-540-79547-6_30

6. Fanon, F., Sartre, J.P., Farrington, C.: The Wretched of the Earth. Grove Press, New York (1963)

7. Huang, J., Kumar, S., Mitra, M., Zhu, W.J., Zabih, R.: Image indexing using color correlograms. In: Proceedings of IEEE Computer Society Conference on Computer Vision and Pattern Recognition, pp. 762–768 (1997). https://doi.org/10.1109/CVPR.1997.609412

8. Kasutani, E., Yamada, A.: The mpeg-7 color layout descriptor: a compact image feature description for high-speed image/video segment retrieval. In: Proceedings 2001 International Conference on Image Processing (Cat. No.01CH37205), vol. 1, pp. 674–677 (2001). https://doi.org/10.1109/ICIP.2001.959135

9. Kessi, S., Marks, Z., Ramugondo, E.: Decolonizing African studies (2020)

10. Lux, M., Riegler, M., Halvorsen, P., MacStravic, G.: LireSolr: a visual information retrieval server. In: Proceedings of the 2017 ACM on International Conference on Multimedia Retrieval, pp. 466–469. ICMR 2017. Association for Computing Machinery, New York, NY, USA (2017). https://doi.org/10.1145/3078971.3079014

11. Mbembe, A.: Decolonizing knowledge and the question of the archive (2015)

12. Memmi, A.: The Colonizer and the Colonized. Routledge (2013). https://dx.doi.org/10.4324/9781315065670

13. Noble, S.U.: Google search: Hyper-visibility as a means of rendering black women and girls invisible. InVisible Culture (2013)

14. Parker, K.R.: Introduction: decolonizing the university: a battle for the African mind. CLA J. 60(2), 164–171 (2016)

15. Simpson, T.W.: Evaluating google as an epistemic tool. Philosophical Engineering: Toward a Philosophy of the Web, pp. 97–115 (2013)

16. Smithsonian Institute: National museum of African art. https://africa.si.edu/collections/collections

17. The Five Hundred Year Archive: About. https://fhya.org/about

18. Won, C.S., Park, D.K., Park, S.J.: Efficient use of mpeg-7 edge histogram descriptor. ETRI J. 24(1), 23–30 (2002). https://dx.doi.org/10.4218/etrij.02.0102.0103

Opening Access to Digital Collections: The State of Cultural Materials in Indonesian Higher Education Institutions

Widiatmoko Adi Putranto[1]([⊠]) (iD), Regina Dwi Shalsa Mayzana[2] (iD), and Emi Ishita[1] (iD)

[1] Department of Library Science, Kyushu University, Fukuoka, Japan
`putranto.widiatmoko.761@s.kyushu-u.ac.jp`
[2] Archives and Records Management Study Program, Universitas Gadjah Mada, Yogyakarta, Indonesia

Abstract. This paper discusses the issue of opening access to digitized cultural heritage materials by examining the current state of their digital collections at the Indonesian higher education (HE) institutions in terms of their accessibility to the users. The accessibility is based on the online presence of the university libraries and the ability of the websites to provide sufficient information about the cultural heritage collections from the perspectives of the users. Eight Indonesian HE institutions with cultural heritage collections were identified. However, they have not been able to provide sufficient or explicit information on the cultural heritage collections online, including information on what collections are available, the basic descriptions of the items, and what users can do with the material. Therefore, raising awareness among Indonesian HE institutions, particularly the libraries, on the importance of opening access to cultural heritage collections is required.

Keywords: Higher education · Libraries · Cultural heritage materials · Open access

1 Introduction

UNESCO labels Indonesia as a "superpower country" for its wealth of cultural resources manifested in different forms [1]. Libraries, archives, or museums (LAMs) that belong to Indonesian higher education (HE) institutions manage not only scholarly research in the commercial databases and institutional repositories, but also part of those numerous cultural heritage materials collections. These cultural heritage materials are not necessarily related to the HE institutions; however, they often reflect and record the local or native culture of the region where the institution is located. Some may be in the form of rare books or manuscripts, while others may be in the form of historical photographs or artifacts. Similar to scholarly research in the digital environment, these cultural heritage materials collections can be sources of valuable information [2].

In addition to being taken over by either public or private LAMs, some cultural heritage materials are acquired by or donated to the HE institutions by other cultural institutions or communities. For example, the Central Library of Universitas Gadjah Mada, Indonesia, holds and digitizes some materials from the private collections of Indonesia's first vice-president, Mohammad Hatta[1]. Conversely, the Kyushu University library in Japan is currently working on an ongoing project to open its rare book collections to the public[2]. In Australia, both libraries of the University of Melbourne[3] and the University of South Australia[4] offer digitized cultural materials from photographs to architectural drawings with different levels of accessibility. Most of these collections are put under the rare, historical, or special collections category because of their distinctive uniqueness, historical value, and limited numbers.

Nowadays, digital or digitized materials are the preferred or main resources, without feeling the need to consult physical materials [3]. Opening access to cultural heritage materials or at least making them available online is argued to be the next step after opening access to academic papers. However, this study recognizes that there may be cases where making digital collections open is not an option because of copyright restrictions, conservation concerns, donor demands, infrastructural gaps, or maybe culturally sensitive issues. Nevertheless, there is a potential to explore the greater benefits of opening access to this type of collection.

Despite the growing discussions of opening access to digital resources in HE institutions, little research has been conducted on the state of digital cultural heritage materials in Indonesia, particularly related to online accessibility. This study aims to examine (1) the number of HE institutions using the official university website and the university library website, (2) the number of university library websites providing sufficient information regarding the digital cultural heritage collections, and (3) the accessibility of the online materials and to what extent they provide open access to these collections to the public.

2   Literature Reviews

Opening access to scientific research papers in the HE institutional repositories has been significantly explored [3–9]; however, the accessibility of other cultural heritage materials as special collections in HE institutions is still rarely discussed. A study by Netshakhuma [10] examines the lack of policy, including accessibility issues, in preserving cultural heritage materials kept by South African universities. Dowding [11] provides an example of how a university library can technically challenge the removal of the restrictions and initiate opening access to digital heritage collections. The urge to disseminate various women's cultural heritage in Nigerian university libraries by making them available in virtual forms to improve awareness is explored by Anasi et al. [12]. Although it is still a relatively new research area, accessibility to the digital collections of cultural heritage materials is a common interest in diverse institutional contexts, and the concerns are expanding from policy to preservation.

---

[1] https://lib.ugm.ac.id/.

[2] https://www.lib.kyushu-u.ac.jp/.

[3] https://library.unimelb.edu.au/.

[4] https://www.library.unisa.edu.au/.

In Indonesia, Asaniyah [13] discusses different definitions of rare collections and their preservation methods in principle. Winastwan [14] explains the technical aspects of the digitization of rare collections at the Bung Karno (Indonesia's first president) Library, whereas Yasa [15] explores Ganesha University's management of Gedong Kirtya Museum, which houses the collections from the Dutch colonial era.

3   Method

3.1   The Outline of the Survey

We identify the issue of opening access to cultural heritage materials that belong in the special collections of the library in HE institutions by examining their availability and accessibility. We examined the library websites based on 1) the existence of the website(s), 2) the provision of information regarding the digital cultural heritage collections on the websites, and 3) the accessibility of the collections.

3.2   Sample

According to the HE statistical yearbook 2020 [16], there are 3,473 institutions that offer higher education in Indonesia, consisting of 122 public institutions (2.7%), 3,044 private institutions (66.3%), 1,240 academies (27.0%), and 187 government-affiliated institutes (4.1%). In this study, we examined 122 public institutions, which consist of 63 universities, 12 institutes, 4 academies, and 43 polytechnics.

3.3   Data Collection

There were three survey items for the websites of the libraries, as shown above. We employed different coding methods for each survey item. For the first item, both Annotators A and B examined the existence of 122 HE institution library websites to double-check. In some cases, several websites a) could not be accessed in either one of the researcher's countries of stay or b) were doubled for one institution without any clarification. The first one was considered non-existent, and the latter one was described as existent.

For survey item 2, two annotators conducted coding. Before the coding, we measured Cohen's Kappa intercoder agreement [17] to obtain reliable results. First, Annotator A, who was the principal annotator, conducted a training session for Annotator B. After the training session, two rounds of annotation were performed with 20 institutions for Round 1 and 40 institutions for Round 2. Both annotators conducted coding independently. We calculated Cohen's Kappa intercoder agreement based on their coding results. We obtained 0.74 in Round 1 and 0.62 in Round 2, and these scores were in substantial agreement. Thereafter, each annotator independently coded the rest of the websites.

Further analysis was conducted for survey item 3) by adopting OpenGLAM's state of accessibility categories, as shown in Table 1 [18].

Table 1. State of accessibility

Closed	Declared	Explicitly provides information that they own the collections of cultural materials without specific itemization or further details
	Member-Only	Declares that the institution owns collections but are available for only members, and a sign-in is required
	Listed	Collections are made partly available online or itemized and further specified into one or more lists
Available online		Provides full online access to the content and metadata; however, it is either or combination of (a) non-downloadable, (b) downloadable, (c) restricted in use (e.g., for research purpose only), and (d) no clear licenses
Open		Releases full online access to the collections and encourages reuse for free

If an institution gets a score of 1 in the second item, it is almost certain that it will reach as minimum as the "declared" stage. Subsequently, Annotator A discussed with Annotator B to analyze each website identified to hold cultural heritage collections and adjudicated the result of the analysis of each item. Once the institutions had been identified, the annotators conducted further analysis on the content of the websites to determine the quality of the provided information on the collections, based on several indicators, including but not limited to content and description, categorization, metadata, or license. These are important elements to ensure the discoverability, accessibility, usability, and validity of information for the users.

4   Results

4.1   The Existence of the Library Websites

Table 2 shows the number of existing library websites and institution websites. Nearly all public HE institutions in Indonesia have a library website, and only 15 of the total 122 institutions (12.3%) had no library website. Six websites were considered non-existent because of obsolete/error URLs.

Additionally, we identified eight institutions, consisting of seven universities and one institute, of the 107 public HE institutions that provide information or explicitly state that they house cultural heritage collections. This number is considered low.

Table 2. The existence of library websites and institution websites in Indonesian HE institutions

Web	Indicators	#HE		#HE with CH Information	
		Available	Unavailable	Available	Unavailable
Library	Universities	63 (100%)	0	7 (5.7%)	56 (45.9%)
	Institutes	10 (83.3%)	2 (16.7%)	1 (0.9%)	11 (9%)
	Academies	1 (25%)	3 (75%)	0	4 (3.3%)
	Polytechnics	33 (76.7%)	10 (23.3%)	0	43(35.2%)
Total		107 (87.7%)	15 (12.3%)	8 (6.6%)	114 (93.4%)
Institution	Universities	63 (100%)	0	-	-
	Institutes	12 (100%)	0		
	Academies	4 (100%)	0		
	Polytechnics	43 (100%)	0		
Total		122 (100%)	0		

Table 3. Cultural heritage material collections on the HE institution library websites.
HE = institutions websites; OL = openness level; L = listed; D = declared.

HE	OL	Type of cultural heritage collections
A	L	Historical Islamic manuscripts in Arabic and Malay, folklore
B	L	Several historical administrative and academic documents
C	L	Private collections that belong to the first vice-president of Indonesia
D	L	An extensive list of collections of 2,471 historical manuscripts and 1,807 classic books related to Javanese history and folklore
E	D	Cultural collections of Osing, Tengger, and Madura tribes
F	D	Collections of books older than 1980
G	D	Digital and Special Collections (Java Collection and Grant)
H	D	Rare collections about Papuan history in the Dutch language

4.2   The Provision of Information on the Cultural Heritage Collections

As seen in Table 2, out of 107 library websites, there are only eight institutions that, at minimum, explicitly provide information regarding the holdings of cultural heritage material collections. The openness level of each institution varied between half "declared" and half "listed"; however, all were still classified in the "closed" category.

From 4 institutions that list their collections, it was observed that most of the collections were paper-based media, such as manuscripts, books, or documents in 2D formats. Ultimately, many of the collections of these libraries with cultural heritage materials were not available online. There was no description of the cultural heritage collections on the websites of institutions A and B, except for a menu on the website connected to a search catalog. Institutions E, F, G, and H did not itemize or list their collections online.

To categorize and name collections, rare collections are the most common term used. At Institution A, the metadata for online items were available and considerably informative; however, the other items were scarce. Conversely, limited metadata were available for the rare-book collections at Institution B, and no metadata was available on the library websites of Institution C. On the website of Institution D, the institution owner was written as part of the metadata; however, almost no other information was available. The findings showed that, presently, no libraries provide a clear license or explicit information regarding copyrights on the website, making it hard for the users to understand, except they visit the library.

5 Discussion

5.1 Accessibility of Cultural Heritage Collections in HE Institutions

Cultural heritage materials in rare or special collections are significant because they distinguish one library collection from another [19]. Opening access to these collections by putting them on the library website will make them discoverable and accessible and promote the library to attract new users, as well as allow space for interaction [20]. One of the first steps to improve accessibility for opening access is to establish an online platform, i.e., websites, for providing sufficient information on the collections. The American Library Association [21] defines accessibility as "an ethic and set of design approaches that attempt to ensure that the fullest use of any resource is open to the greatest number of people." IFLA [22] adds that "all people…should have access to information through ICTs and the skills needed to participate fully in society." In the current internet culture, accessibility is crucial not only to ensure the relevance of the institution and its compliance with the standard, but also to allow users to discover, learn, and share information and for the cultural heritage material collections to reach their fullest and maximum potential as information resources.

This study finds that the number of Indonesian HE institution libraries opening access to their digital cultural heritage materials by making them online is arguably low, with only 8 out of 122 (see Table 1 and Table 2) HE institutions explicitly stating that they provide such collections. Only 4 institutions provide more than just statements in the form of listed, itemized collections. In some cases, the collections menu refers users to the catalog directly with no suggestions. Resultantly, users may be confused if they are not sure what to search for. Furthermore, as institutions that provide information, it is a challenge to identify basic information, such as how to access the collections and what they are about, on these library websites. It is unfortunate that they have the same traits with poor information on the collections, with limited explicit description, limited accessible online content, and a lack of metadata.

Another identical characteristic among these library websites is that they do not provide or mention any license, use policy, or copyright information. For instance, Institution A enables the download feature for their publicly available online collections. This is interesting because users may be able to obtain a digital copy of the collections; however, there is no explicit information about what they are legally allowed to do with the copy. In HE institution libraries, such as Leiden University in the Netherlands[5] or Kyoto University in Japan[6], the heritage collections accessible online are provided with comprehensive and descriptive copyright information, use policy, or license. This is important not only to ensure legal compliance but also to encourageusers about what they can and cannot do with the collections to maximize the potential of the resources.

Thus, libraries need to formulate a strong policy regarding copyright status. According to Indonesian Constitution No 28 [23], digitizing cultural heritage materials are mostly allowed for non-commercial purposes or any purposes that do not harm the economic rights of the original creator. According to Gunawan [24], the State of Indonesia owns the copyright of orphan works; however, as a form of respect, it is recommended to seek permission from the heir of the original creator to digitize public-domain heritage materials. It is hard to find a statement or interpretation about whether cultural institutions can apply new copyright for a digital surrogate of heritage materials. Open-access movement encourages institutions to not apply new copyright for a work of digitized cultural heritage materials that was originally out of copyright to ensure that users can get maximum benefits from the materials.

5.2 Opening Access by Making Collections Online

Making digital cultural heritage material collections online with sufficient information does not only mean that university libraries adapt and transform their service to the choice of access of the users. Instead, it opens up relatively wide possibilities while offering essential challenges.

Manaf [25] discusses how the digital materials in the open digital repository of a memory institution may increase accessibility, the rediscovery of resources, preservation, and the promotion of information on the national cultural heritage collections. Wiedemann et al. [26] stress that open access is significantly urgent on the global level at German memory institutions, as digital materials are considered to have the same value as the original physical objects.

As the collections become more visible, making collections online broadens the likelihood of collaborations across institutions. Currently, the libraries of several HE institutions in the Netherlands, such as Leiden University, or Oxford University's Bodleian Library, UK, also manage Indonesian cultural heritage materials. Drooglever et al. [27] show how archives related to colonial Indonesia are dispersed among diverse countries from the Netherlands, UK, Australia, to Belgium. Hence, Ricardo Punzalan's [28] proposal of virtual reunification to recombine dispersed materials between multiple heritage institutions can arguably be considered. Additionally, Mi and Pollock [29] examine how the University of South Florida conducts multidisciplinary collaborations in developing the metadata schema of their collections of cultural heritage materials for increased access and exposure. The beauty of the online networks of academic scholars and institutions is that there is a great opportunity for collaboration to connect, combine, or integrate these dispersed heritage resources. Further, users can map and locate the collections. Finally, if the collections are available to the public, this will allow an

---

[5] https://www.bibliotheek.universiteitleiden.nl/.

[6] https://rmda.kulib.kyoto-u.ac.jp/en.

even broader scope of users to reconnect or reimagine the collections to produce new knowledge or works.

However, making collections open and accessible online does not come without risks. McCormick [30] describes the policy challenges of ensuring long-term access to both digital and physical cultural heritage materials housed at the University of Toronto, Canada. Hamilton and Saunderson [31] summarize several types of risks of an open approach, including the loss of income, control, visits, position, and aura. Nevertheless, in the end, they argue that "it is crucial that the institution does not assume restriction or restrict material as a default." Similarly, in the report of the European Public Sector Information Platform on Open Data in Cultural Heritage Institutions [32], although there are concerns about the cost-intensive aspects, such as time and money, as well as technical knowledge, they conclude that the project "goes beyond mere economic value and addresses the value for society and future generations."

6   Conclusion

This study shows that only a few academic libraries in Indonesian HE institutions provide sufficient and explicit information about their collections of cultural heritage materials. The online accessibility of cultural heritage materials is still low and most of the materials available online are closed. Therefore, this current state prevents them to be accessible, discoverable, and optimized as potential knowledge resources by a relatively wide audience, thereby hindering the process of making libraries, as cultural institutions, to be more inclusive. Further, libraries should provide transparency by explicitly making this information accessible to the users, including what users can and cannot do because of the legal framework of the collections.

Acknowledgments. This work is supported by the Japan Society for the Promotion of Science (JSPS) KAKENHI Grant Number JP18K18508.

References

1. Antara. UNESCO Sebut Indonesia Negara super power bidang budaya. Antara News. https://m.antaranews.com/berita/663307/unesco-sebut-indonesia-negara-super-power-bid ang-budaya. Accessed 2 Aug 2022
2. Darbey, N., Hayden, H.: Special Collections for Beginners: A Case Study of Special Collections at Waterford Institute of Technology Library Service. New Library World (2008)
3. McCarthy, D., Wallace, A.: Survey of GLAM open access policy and practice. Copyright Cortex. 18 (2018). 'Museums around the World in the Face of COVID-19'. http://bit.ly/Ope nGLAMsurvey
4. Priyanto, I.F.: Readiness of Indonesian academic libraries for open access and open access repositories implementation: a study on Indonesian open access repositories registered in OpenDOAR. Ph.D. Dissertation, University of Texas, Austin (2015). https://digital.library. unt.edu/ark:/67531/metadc804888/
5. Allamki, Z.: The readiness of open access policy implementation: a case study within a Kuwaiti higher education institute. Unpublished doctoral dissertation, University of Salford, UK (2013). http://usir.salford.ac.uk/29413/1/Zuwainah_Thesis_Final_2013.pdf

6. Lewis, D.: The inevitability of open access. Coll. Res. Libr. **73**(5), 493–506 (2012)
7. Schmidt, B., Shearer, K.: Licensing revisited: Open access clauses in practice. LIBER Q. **22**(3), 176–189 (2012)
8. Rufai, R., Gul, S., Shah, T.A.: Open access journals in library and information science: the story so far. TRIM **7**(2), 218–228 (2011)
9. Antelman, K.: Do open-access articles have a greater research impact? Coll. Res. Libr. **65**(5), 372–382 (2004)
10. Netshakhuma, S.: Preservation of cultural heritage materials at the University of Witwatersrand. Collections (Walnut Creek, Calif.) **17**(4), 411–429 (2021). https://doi.org/10.1177/155 0190620987838
11. Dowding, H.: The role of the national university in developing nations' digital cultural heritage projects: a perspective from Kazakhstan. OCLC Syst. Serv. **30**(1), 52–61 (2014). https://doi. org/10.1108/OCLC-06-2013-0016
12. Anasi, S.N., Ibegwam, A., Oyediran-Tidings, S.O.: Preservation and dissemination of women's cultural heritage in Nigerian university libraries. Lib. Rev. (2013). https://www. emerald.com/insight/content/10.1108/LR-11-2012-0126/full/html
13. Asaniyah, N.: Pelestarian Informasi Koleksi Langka. Buletin Perpustakaan: Direktorat Perpustakaan Universitas Islam Indonesia. No. 57 (2017)
14. Winastwan, R. E.: Mekanisme Digitalisasi Terhadap Koleksi Langka di UPT Perpustakaan Proklamator Bung Karno Blitar. Jurnal El-Pustaka **1**(2) (2020). http://ejournal.radenintan.ac. id/index.php/elpustaka/article/view/7287/4277
15. Yasa, I.: Museum Gedong Kirtya Sebagai Sumber Pembelajaran Sejarah Lokal Di Jurusan Pendidikan Sejarah, Fakultas Ilmu Sosial, Universitas Pendidikan Ganesha-Singaraja. Doctoral dissertation, Sebelas Maret University, Kota Surakarta (2011)
16. Secretariat Directorate General of Higher Education, Ministry of Education and Culture, Indonesia. (2020). Higher Education Statistical Year Book 2020 [Higher Education Online Database]
17. Wildan, M.: Kabupaten Jember. https://kebudayaan.kemdikbud.go.id/ditwdb/kabupaten-jem ber/. Accessed 11 Aug 2022
18. Wallace, A.: Introduction. OpenGLAM (2020). https://doi.org/10.21428/74d826b1.be9df175
19. Michel, P.: Digitizing special collections: to boldly go where we've been before. Library Hi Tech. (2005). https://www.emerald.com/insight/content/doi/10.1108/07378830510621793/ full/html
20. Lyons, B.: Louis round Wilson special collections library. J. Am. Folk. **124**(493), 244–246 (2011). https://www.proquest.com/docview/927983580?parentSessionId=hR6zSLfywPGF wvt0BGmfO4mBk8o2yEgCQ4BcZjrP640%3D&pq-origsite=summon&accountid=13771
21. American Library Association. Introduction: Why Accessibility? (2012). https://journals.ala. org/index.php/ltr/article/view/4688/5577. Accessed 11 Aug 2022
22. Zuyev, A.E.: Principles on Public Access in Libraries. Bibliotekovedenie. Russian J. Lib. Sci. **65**(6), 679–681. The International Federation of Library Associations and Institutions and Electronic Information for Libraries (2016). https://cdn.ifla.org/wp-content/uploads/files/ass ets/hq/topics/info-society/documents/handout-principles-on-public-access-in-libraries.pdf
23. Indonesian Constitution. Number 28. (2014). Copyright. [Online]
24. Gunawan, A.: Dreamsea Webinar 06: Hak Cipta dan Digitalisasi Manuskrip Nusantara [Online webinar] (2021). https://youtu.be/QR_26cusdbs
25. Abd Manaf, Z.: Establishing the national digital cultural heritage repository in Malaysia. Lib. Rev. (Glasgow) **57**(7), 537–548 (2008). https://doi.org/10.1108/00242530810894059
26. Wiedemann, J., Schmitt, S., Patzschke, E.: Responding to open access: how German museums use digital content. Mus. Soc. **17**(2), 193–209 (2019)

27. Drooglever, P.J., Schouten, M.J., Lohanda, M.: Guide to the Archives on Relations Between the Netherlands and Indonesia 1945–1963 (vol. 1) (1999). Institute of Netherlands History, The Hague. http://resources.huygens.knaw.nl/indonesischebetrekkingen1945-1969/Ned erlands-indonesischeBetrekkingen1945-1950/Archiefgids/archiefgids.pdf
28. Punzalan, R.L.: Virtual reunification: bits and pieces gathered together to represent the whole. Doctoral dissertation, University of Michigan, Ann Arbor, Michigan (2013). https://rpunza lan.com/wp/wp-content/uploads/2011/07/Punzalan-Dissertation.pdf
29. Mi, X., Pollock, B.M.: Metadata schema to facilitate linked data for 3D digital models of cultural heritage collections: a University of South Florida Libraries case study. Catal. Classif. Q. **56**(2–3), 273–286 (2018). https://www.tandfonline.com/doi/abs/10.1080/01639374.2017. 1388894
30. McCormick, P.: Preserving Canada's cultural heritage: University of Toronto libraries. Feliciter (Ottawa) **54**(4), 178–181 (2008)
31. Hamilton, G., Saunderson, F.: Open Licensing for Cultural Heritage. Facet Publishing, London (2017)
32. Dietrich, D., Pekel, J.: European public sector information platform topic report: OpenData in Cultural Heritage Institutions. European PSI Platform, No. 2012/04, April 2012

Using Archivematica and Omeka S for Long-Term Preservation and Access of Digitized Archive Materials

Boyoung Kim[1,2]([⊠]) [iD], Satoru Nakamura[1] [iD], and Hidenori Watanave[1] [iD]

[1] The University of Tokyo, Tokyo, Japan
`kim-boyoung688@g.ecc.u-tokyo.ac.jp, nakamura@hi.u-tokyo.ac.jp,`
`hwtnv@iii.u-tokyo.ac.jp`
[2] Shibusawa Eiichi Memorial Foundation, Tokyo, Japan
`kim@shibusawa.or.jp`

Abstract. This study proposes a workflow using Archivematica, an application for long-term preservation of digital archives, and Omeka S for system accesses, for the long-term preservation of digitized archival materials and their access based on the Open Archival Information System (OAIS) Reference Model. The workflow requires three steps. First, metadata for ensuring authenticity is analyzed based on the OAIS information model. Second, information packages for preservation and accessing are generated using Archivematica. Third, an original tool is developed for metadata interoperability between Archivematica and Omeka S. Consequently, a consistent preservation and access workflow for digitized materials is successfully established.

Keywords: Long-term preservation · Authenticity · Archivematica · Omeka S · Digital archive

1 Introduction

Recently, the digitization of archival materials has been actively promoted in Japan. In particular, Japan Search [1], which launched services in 2020 and is linked to 175 databases in Japan containing over 25 million metadata elements as of June 2022 [2], has become an established tool for searching and browsing digitized content in various fields. However, note that the responsibility for ensuring the authenticity and long-term preservation of archival materials to be digitized belongs to each holding institution. However, few institutions have a proper workflow for their long-term preservation.

To solve this situation, this study proposes a long-term preservation of digitized archives and their reliable access by improving a workflow based on the Open Archival Information System (OAIS) Reference Model [3] using Archivematica [4] and Omeka S [5].

2 Research Subject and Issues

In this study, we use the "Shimbun no Nihon" collection (Japan of Newspaper, 1929–1931) held by the Multimedia and Socio-information Studies Archive of the University of Tokyo [6]. This material is publicly available on Digital Cultural Heritage (DCH) [7], which is a platform created by Omeka S [8].

Fig. 1. Digitized "Shimbun no Nihon" (The University of Tokyo, Multimedia and Socio-information Studies Archive/ Graduate School of Interdisciplinary Information Studies Inter-faculty Initiative in Information Studies Library)

The original "Shimbun no Nihon" was preserved in a bound form (385×270 mm) and each page was photographed and digitized (see Fig. 1). The data were preserved as sets of images (JPEG) and catalogs (CSV)—one before importing into Omeka S and the other after importing into and exporting from Omeka S (see Fig. 2). However, the measures for the long-term preservation are currently under consideration.

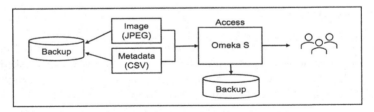

Fig. 2. Current workflow

3 Method

3.1 OAIS Information Model

Applying specific standards such as the OAIS Reference Model is ideal when considering the long-term preservation of "Shimbun no Nihon." The OAIS Reference Model is an international standard (ISO 14731:2012) that defines a high-level conceptual model for a digital repository.

However, constructing a fully OAIS-compliant repository is not within the scope of this study. This study aims to demonstrate the handling of digital objects and metadata of digitized archival materials for a long time. Therefore, we focus on the information model of the OAIS Reference Model, which defines the Submission Information Package (SIP), Archival Information Package (AIP), and Dissemination Information Package (DIP).

3.2 Workflow Using Archivematica

To create and preserve information packages that ensure their authenticity, metadata management is essential. Manually handling all metadata is difficult; thus, various applications should be used in an appropriate manner in the workflow.

We suggest a workflow using Archivematica (see Fig. 3) to conduct efficient metadata imports and exports. Archivematica is open-source software used to support long-term preservation. Its strengths include: the ability to manage data according to the OAIS Reference Model; perform critical preservation tasks, such as normalization, characterization, format identification; and packages the SIPs, AIPs, and DIPs.

However, the workflow has two issues. First, we must clarify the metadata for authenticity before transferring the data (A). Second, we require tools to import DIPs into Omeka S from Archivematica (B).

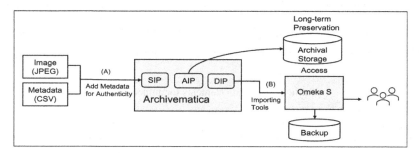

Fig. 3. Improved workflow using Archivematica

4   Ensuring Authenticity

4.1   Definition of Authenticity

To clarify the metadata of digital material before transferring them into Archivematica, we must consider authenticity. To maintain the authenticity of digitized archival materials, reliability, integrity, and availability must be ensured [9]:

1. Reliability: Establishing a curatorial process for a trustworthy object and maintaining its original context. That is, it requires transparent and fully documented preservation strategies, and the provision of metadata necessary to describe the content, context, and provenance of the object.

2. Integrity: Protecting the data from unauthorized or accidental alterations; this is ensured through bitstream preservation and the provision of metadata to describe all actions taken in the preservation process.
3. Availability: Allowing authorized users to access and understand information across time and technological environments. To this end, logical preservation features and sufficient metadata must be provided to enable users to locate, retrieve, and interpret records.

Metadata play an important role in ensuring authenticity. Metadata for digital preservation is of two types. Description metadata include the information for discovery, interpretation, rights, provenance, context, structure, etc. Technical metadata include the technical properties of data, preservation management process, packaging, and transmission information. In general, the former can be manually captured; the latter can be captured automatically, such as with Archivematica as in this study.

4.2 Analyzing Metadata

Table 1 shows an analysis of the three elements of authenticity discussed in Sect. 4.1 and compliance with the OAIS information model. Among the digitized materials in "Shimbun no Nihon," image data managed by Omeka S are assigned a checksum and unique ID, which serve to identify the data and prevent modifications. Both are necessary for providing access. However, this is only for data currently being released to the public and is not intended for long-term preservation, as it does not guarantee the integrity of the data. Therefore, we analyzed the metadata currently assigned and determined that some information was missing for authenticity, as presented in Table 1.

Table 1. Metadata elements for authenticity

Authenticity elements	Related metadata	Necessary information	OAIS information model	Currently assigned
Reliability	Metadata for content, context, and provenance	Contents	Content Data Object	Yes
		Unique identification	Reference	Yes
		Terms of preservation and use	Access Rights	Insufficient
		Creator information	Context	Yes

(*continued*)

Table 1. (*continued*)

Authenticity elements	Related metadata	Necessary information	OAIS information model	Currently assigned
		Administrative/Biographical history		Insufficient
		Archival history	Provenance	Yes
		Doner information	Descriptive Information	Insufficient
		Arrangement information		No
		Hierarchical information		No
Integrity	Metadata for the bitstream preservation and processing performed	Checksum	Fixity	No
		Migration information	Provenance	No
		Record of all processes and changes		No
Usability	Metadata to enable use, retrieval, representation, and interpretation	Descriptive information about the object to be preserved	Descriptive Information	Yes
		Information on S/W and H/W for representation	Representation Information	No
		AIP packaging information	Packaging Information	No

5 Constructing Workflow

5.1 Creating AIPs and DIPs with Archivematica

To ensure the authenticity of digitized materials, missing metadata were added based on the analysis presented in Table 1. The metadata.csv file with descriptive metadata and four image files as digital objects were then transferred to Archivematica to create a SIP. Figures 4 and 5 show the AIP for long-term preservation and DIP for dissemination created by feeding the SIP to Archivematica.

As suggested by the workflow in Fig. 3, AIPs are transferred into an archival storage for long-term preservation. DIPs are transferred into Omeka S, which is the access system for "Shinbun no Nihon." However, we do not preserve SIPs because Archivematica uses them inside of the system to generate AIPs.

```
ex02-1-TIFF-007c28cc-4671-4d5d-be2a-facace4c7b84
├── bag-info.txt
├── bagit.txt
├── manifest-sha256.txt
├── tagmanifest-sha256.txt
└── data
    ├── METS.007c28cc-4671-4d5d-be2a-facace4c7b84.xml
    ├── README.html
    ├── logs
    │   ├── FileUUIDs.log
    │   ├── fileFormatIdentification.log
    │   ├── filenameChanges.log
    │   └── transfers
    │       └── ex02-1-TIFF-f3a140bf-5761-4a30-8039-0cf9f1fee3e7
    │           └── logs
    │               ├── FileUUIDs.log
    │               ├── bulk-60500ba0-2d60-4fd4-af2e-db7686f528bbj
    │               ├── bulk-65292df4-d068-4770-bd97-9fc824bb2118
    │               ├── bulk-aed38fc7-84b4-4193-85d5-8956daa368b4
    │               ├── bulk-e7074752-b600-482a-a9bb-4520a238ece8
    │               ├── fileFormatIdentification.log
    │               └── filenameChanges.log
    ├── objects
    │   ├── N
    │   └── SN
    │       ├── SN1_19291001
    │       │   ├── shimbunnonihon1_0004-f6afda8e-68f1-4e68-b067-7dc308668eb0.tif
    │       │   ├── shimbunnonihon1_0004.jpg
    │       │   ├── shimbunnonihon1_0005-68a7fbb7-5e71-4c77-ab2b-3bf15b4f511b.tif
    │       │   └── shimbunnonihon1_0005.jpg
    │       └── SN1_19291002
    │           ├── shimbunnonihon1_0012-1f3a2391-90fe-4990-bfa7-bb3503db8505.tif
    │           ├── shimbunnonihon1_0012.jpg
    │           ├── shimbunnonihon1_0013-8eb35202-9394-4fa3-afc1-fea1a08066ae.tif
    │           └── shimbunnonihon1_0013.jpg
    ├── metadata
    │   ├── OCRfiles
    │   │   ├── shimbunnonihon1_0004-aed38fc7-84b4-4193-85d5-8956daa368b4.txt
    │   │   ├── shimbunnonihon1_0005-65292df4-d068-4770-bd97-9fc824bb2118.txt
    │   │   ├── shimbunnonihon1_0012-e7074752-b600-482a-a9bb-4520a238ece8.txt
    │   │   └── shimbunnonihon1_0013-60500ba0-2d60-4fd4-af2e-db7686f528bb.txt
    │   └── transfers
    │       └── ex02-1-TIFF-f3a140bf-5761-4a30-8039-0cf9f1fee3e7
    │           ├── directory_tree.txt
    │           └── metadata.csv
    ├── submissionDocumentation
    │   └── transfer-ex02-1-TIFF-f3a140bf-5761-4a30-8039-0cf9f1fee3e7
    │       └── METS.xml
    └── thumbnails
        ├── 60500ba0-2d60-4fd4-af2e-db7686f528bb.jpg
        ├── 65292df4-d068-4770-bd97-9fc824bb2118.jpg
        ├── aed38fc7-84b4-4193-85d5-8956daa368b4.jpg
        └── e7074752-b600-482a-a9bb-4520a238ece8.jpg
```

Fig. 4. AIP directory tree

```
ex02-1-TIFF-007c28cc-4671-4d5d-be2a-facace4c7b84
├── METS.007c28cc-4671-4d5d-be2a-facace4c7b84.xml
├── OCRfiles
│   ├── shimbunnonihon1_0004-aed38fc7-84b4-4193-85d5-8956daa368b4.txt
│   ├── shimbunnonihon1_0005-65292df4-d068-4770-bd97-9fc824bb2118.txt
│   ├── shimbunnonihon1_0012-e7074752-b600-482a-a9bb-4520a238ece8.txt
│   └── shimbunnonihon1_0013-60500ba0-2d60-4fd4-af2e-db7686f528bb.txt
├── objects
│   ├── 60500ba0-2d60-4fd4-af2e-db7686f528bb-shimbunnonihon1_0013.jpg
│   ├── 65292df4-d068-4770-bd97-9fc824bb2118-shimbunnonihon1_0005.jpg
│   ├── aed38fc7-84b4-4193-85d5-8956daa368b4-shimbunnonihon1_0004.jpg
│   └── e7074752-b600-482a-a9bb-4520a238ece8-shimbunnonihon1_0012.jpg
├── processingMCP.xml
└── thumbnails
    ├── 60500ba0-2d60-4fd4-af2e-db7686f528bb.jpg
    ├── 65292df4-d068-4770-bd97-9fc824bb2118.jpg
    ├── aed38fc7-84b4-4193-85d5-8956daa368b4.jpg
    └── e7074752-b600-482a-a9bb-4520a238ece8.jpg
```

Fig. 5. DIP directory tree

5.2 Importing DIPs into Omeka S

When utilizing DIPs, Archivematica makes Access to Memory (AtoM) [10] the default access system. It also provides integrated workflows with ArchivesSpace, CONTENTdm, and Binder [11]. However, Archivematica does not provide an official workflow for Omeka S. Therefore, we constructed a new system for importing Archivematica DIPs to Omeka S [12].

In particular, we developed a program using Python to input Archivematica DIPs and output the files in formats that can be imported into Omeka S by analyzing the Metadata Encoding and Transmission Standard (METS) files in DIPs. The program was linked to Omeka S by retrieving descriptive metadata, hierarchy information, and paths to the media from the METS file. In Fig. 6, "Media" indicates that the DIP object files (see Fig. 5) are registered. When importing to Omeka S, we used the "Create" operation of Omeka S's REST API [13].

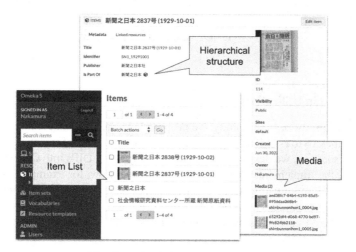

Fig. 6. Uploaded results to Omeka S

6 Considerations

6.1 Achievements

We established a consistent preservation and access workflow for digitized materials using Archivematica and Omeka S and made three main improvements to the process as follows:

a. Enhanced the metadata to support authenticity;
b. Clarified long-term preservation targets by creating AIPs; and
c. Realized the imports of DIPs into Omeka S.

Furthermore, this improvement enables the preservation of information in compliance with the Preservation Metadata Implementation Strategies (PREMIS) and METS (see Fig. 7).

```
▼<mets:mets xmlns:mets="http://www.loc.gov/METS/" xmlns:xsi="http://www.w3.org/2001/XMLSchema-instance"
  xmlns:xlink="http://www.w3.org/1999/xlink" xsi:schemaLocation="http://www.loc.gov/METS/
  http://www.loc.gov/standards/mets/version1121/mets.xsd">
    <mets:metsHdr CREATEDATE="2022-06-23T08:40:13"/>
  ▼<mets:dmdSec ID="dmdSec_1">
    ▼<mets:mdWrap MDTYPE="PREMIS:OBJECT">
      ▼<mets:xmlData>
        ▼<premis:object xmlns:premis="http://www.loc.gov/premis/v3" xsi:type="premis:intellectualEntity"
          xsi:schemaLocation="http://www.loc.gov/premis/v3 http://www.loc.gov/standards/premis/v3/premis.xsd" version="3.0">
          ▼<premis:objectIdentifier>
            <premis:objectIdentifierType>UUID</premis:objectIdentifierType>
            <premis:objectIdentifierValue>007c2cc-4671-4d5d-be2a-facace4c7b84</premis:objectIdentifierValue>
          </premis:objectIdentifier>
          <premis:originalName>ex02-1-TIFF-007c2cc-4671-4d5d-be2a-facace4c7b84</premis:originalName>
        </premis:object>
      </mets:xmlData>
    </mets:mdWrap>
  </mets:dmdSec>
```

Fig. 7. Example of PREMIS metadata in METS

6.2   Challenges in Utilization

Workflow Automation. In this study, we proposed a workflow that combines Archivematica and Omeka S to establish long-term preservation and access for authentic digitized materials. In addition, we developed a system for importing DIPs into Omeka S.

However, the implementation of the proposed workflow, for example, the manual copying of DIPs output using Archivematica, can be labor expensive. To optimize the workflow, the entire process must be automated from Ingest to Access. In the future, we intend to use the API provided by Archivematica and consider automated processing to improve workflow efficiency.

Managing Descriptive Metadata. Because Archivematica is not an application for managing description metadata, it must be used with other systems that can access and manage entire descriptive metadata[14]. For example, AtoM conforms to the General International Standard Archival Description (ISAD(G)), which describes materials from overview (fonds or series) to detail (item) levels; therefore, representing groups of materials in a hierarchical manner is essential. In addition, AtoM has a full range of description elements for contextual information. These descriptive metadata play an important role in maintaining the authenticity of materials. That is, combining Archivematica and AtoM enables the management of the preservation information suitable for archival materials.

On the other hand, Omeka S is primarily focused on managing materials at the item level and is suitable for viewing individual materials. Therefore, in this study, we decided to include some descriptive metadata such as history, organization, and hierarchical information in the AIP. Future studies should further consider how to add and maintain such metadata.

Managing Archival Storge. As a temporary measure, the AIP of "Nihon no Shimbun" is stored in a distributed manner using offline PCs, HDDs, and online storage such as Google Drive. However, the OAIS Reference Model defines some functions for archival storage, such as managing the storage hierarchy, refreshing the media, error checking, disaster recovery, and providing access. Although this issue is not within the scope of this study, it is a critical issue to be solved in the future.

7 Conclusion

In this study, we proposed a method for long-term preservation with a workflow corresponding to the OAIS information model. Using Archivematica and Omeka S, we proposed an improved workflow and achieved the following three results: 1) provided metadata that supports authenticity, 2) clarified long-term preservation targets by creating AIPs, and 3) realized the importation of DIPs into Omeka S by developing a unique tool.

The long-term preservation of digitized materials involves high costs and requires technical capabilities. For example, compliance with the OAIS Reference Model is desirable when building a reliable repository, and Archivematica's support for this is highly significant. However, several issues must be addressed—the cost and maintenance during implementation and interoperability with systems such as Omeka S that are already installed and in use. We hope that the tools developed and released in this study will help in considering the use of Archivematica in archival institutions that use Omeka S, as well as in the long-term preservation of digitized materials.

References

1. Japan Search Homepage. https://jpsearch.go.jp/. Accessed 21 Sep 2022
2. Japan Search Current data. https://jpsearch.go.jp/stats. Accessed 25 July 2022
3. Consultative Committee for Space Data Systems–CSSDS: Reference Model for an Open Archival Information System (OAIS). Magenta Book. Issue 2. June 2012 CCSDS 651.0-M-2. https://public.ccsds.org/Pubs/650x0m2.pdf. Accessed 21 Sep 2022
4. Archivematica Homepage. https://www.archivematica.org/en/. Accessed 21 Sep 2022
5. Omeka, S.: Homepage. https://omeka.org/s/. Accessed 21 Sep 2022
6. Multi-media and Socio-Information Studies Archive, Interfaculty Initiative in Information Studies/Graduate School of Interdisciplinary Information Studies, https://www.center.iii.u-tokyo.ac.jp/. Accessed 21 Sep 2022
7. Digital Cultural Heritage Homepage. https://dch.iii.u-tokyo.ac.jp/s/dch/page/home. Accessed 21 Sep 2022
8. 高嶋, 朋子: 東京大学情報学環社会情報研究資料センターニュース **28**, 3–5 (2018). http://hdl.handle.net/2261/0002000860
9. Adrian, B.: Practical Digital Preservation: A How-to Guide for Organizations of Any Size. Facet Publishing, London (2013)
10. Access to Memory (AtoM) Homepage. https://accesstomemory.org/en/. Accessed 21 Sep 2022
11. Archivematica Access. https://www.archivematica.org/en/docs/archivematica-1.13/user-manual/access/access/. Accessed 21 Sep 2022

12. Customized tool. https://github.com/nakamura196/archivematica-omekas. Accessed 21 Sep 2022
13. Omeka, S.: Developer Documentaion Create. https://omeka.org/s/docs/developer/api/rest_api/#create. Accessed 21 Sep 2022
14. Archivematica FAQ No.12: You can ingest metadata as a CSV file or through the dash-board while processing. However, Archivematica is not an archival description system. In-depth contextual and content description can be done through an access system like AtoM. https://www.archivematica.org/en/docs/archivematica-1.13/getting-started/troubleshooting/faq/#faq. Accessed 21 Sep 2022

Scholarly Data Processing

KGMM - A Maturity Model for Scholarly Knowledge Graphs Based on Intertwined Human-Machine Collaboration

Hassan Hussein[1]([✉])(ID), Allard Oelen[1](ID), Oliver Karras[1](ID), and Sören Auer[1,2](ID)

[1] TIB Leibniz Information Centre for Science and Technology, Hannover, Germany
{hassan.hussein,allard.oelen,oliver.karras,soeren.auer}@tib.eu
[2] L3S Research Center, Leibniz University of Hannover, Hannover, Germany

Abstract. Knowledge Graphs (KG) have gained increasing importance in science, business and society in the last years. However, most knowledge graphs were either extracted or compiled from existing sources. There are only relatively few examples where knowledge graphs were genuinely created by an intertwined human-machine collaboration. Also, since the quality of data and knowledge graphs is of paramount importance, a number of data quality assessment models have been proposed. However, they do not take the specific aspects of intertwined human-machine curated knowledge graphs into account. In this work, we propose a graded maturity model for scholarly knowledge graphs (KGMM), which specifically focuses on aspects related to the joint, evolutionary curation of knowledge graphs for digital libraries. Our model comprises 5 maturity stages with 20 quality measures. We demonstrate the implementation of our model in a large scale scholarly knowledge graph curation effort.

Keywords: Knowledge graph · Linked Open Data (LOD) · Maturity model · Human-machine collaboration

1 Introduction

Knowledge graphs have gained increasing importance in science, business, and society in the last years [42]. However, most knowledge graphs were either extracted or compiled from existing sources. There are few knowledge graphs that were created by an intertwined human-machine collaboration, e.g., Wikidata [43], Google's knowledge graph [41], or the Open Research Knowledge Graph [23].

A number of data quality assessment models have been proposed, since the quality of data and knowledge graphs is of paramount importance [4,36,48]. A shortcoming of these existing assessment models is that they do not take the specific aspects of intertwined human-machine curated knowledge graphs into account. Intertwining human and machine collaboration can work in various ways [32]. For example, on the one hand, machine intelligence can assist humans in the curation of scholarly knowledge graphs, e.g., by suggesting properties and

Y.-H. Tseng et al. (Eds.): ICADL 2022, LNCS 13636, pp. 253–269, 2022.
https://doi.org/10.1007/978-3-031-21756-2_21

values to be filled in a curation form. On the other hand, human intelligence can be used to validate the results of machine intelligence, e.g., by voting about the correctness of automatically extracted information pieces. In such scenarios, it is important to assist a community of curators in assessing and *gradually* improving the quality of the scholarly knowledge graph.

Furthermore, there are some quality problems arise when creating KGs from digital libraries. Kroll et al. [26] ask, "Why is automatically building knowledge graphs so difficult?" They think that the content selected by digital libraries may be too varied for rule-based methods to produce high-quality knowledge graphs. Yadagiri, and Ramesh [47] pointed out that organizations' privacy concerns were a significant barrier to linked data technologies adaption in digital libraries. Gonzales [14] mentioned that copyright restrictions and legalities are the primary barriers for libraries to publishing data on the web. As, the libraries must acquire licenses for numerous periodicals, databases, and other online resources. Charles et al. [7] and Cole et al. [8] remarked that a significant problem for Linked Open Data (LOD) on the web is multilingual and data heterogeneity. Sergio et al. [34] mentioned the challenge of enhancing the user experience when the KG is automatically created from a digital library. The "general validity of facts" is mentioned by Kroll et al. [25], as they think that the current knowledge graphs on the web wildly vary from those utilized in scientific digital libraries. Even though entity-centric data in reputable LOD sources on the web may or may not be authentic, it is nevertheless likely to be genuine. Cole et al. [8] add that, practical LOD uses in a library setting are still few, immature, and mostly untested.

In this work, we propose a graded knowledge graph maturity model (KGMM), which specifically focuses on aspects related to the joint, evolutionary curation of knowledge graphs. Our research approach leads to the following research question: *How can a maturity model for a scholarly knowledge graph look like?* In that regard, we hypothesize that if the KG developers use our model, then the data will be available for the consumers in the most mature, complete, representable, stable, and linkable shape.

Our model comprises 5 maturity stages with 20 quality measures. In addition, the measures are prioritized in three categories in each level to further support the applicability of the model. The model is inspired by the FAIR data principles [46], the Linked Open Data star scheme by Berners-Lee[1], the Linked Data Quality Framework [48] but tailors and augments these frameworks specifically for scholarly knowledge graphs intertwining human-machine collaboration. Especially for realizing and implementing the FAIR principles aiming at making data Findable, Accessible, Interoperable and Reusable, we need clear guidance for the developers of knowledge graph applications as well as curators following a principled knowledge graph quality model.

We demonstrate the implementation of our model in a large scale scholarly knowledge graph curation effort with more than 500 collaborators. We show how the model is implemented and can be used to incrementally assess and

---

[1] https://www.w3.org/DesignIssues/LinkedData.html.

improve specific parts of the scholarly knowledge graph. Curators are given clear guidelines on how the maturity of a certain part of the scholarly knowledge graph can be improved to reach the next maturity stage.

The article is structured as follows: We review related work in Sect. 2. The research method is explained in Sect. 3. Our proposed maturity model is introduced in Sect. 4. In Sect. 5, we present a use case based on the previously introduced model. Finally, we discuss and conclude our work in Sect. 6.

2 Related Work

According to Proenca [37], a maturity model is a methodology used to effectively assess elements of objects, such as processes or organizations, in various domains. Based on this assessment, maturity models enable to evaluate the current maturity level of a respective object in order to contribute to its continuous improvement by providing guidance on how to reach the next maturity level. In a literature review [19], we found eleven maturity models from six different domains, such as Software (Engineering), Information Management, and Business Information, that have an average of five maturity levels (minimum: 4, median: 5, maximum: 6) and cover an average of six attributes (minimum: 3, median: 6, maximum: 30). Table 1 shows an excerpt of this comparison. One of the most well-known maturity models is the Capability Maturity Model (CMM) by Paule et al. [35]. CMM enables software development organizations to enhance their consistency and capability to deliver high-quality software within budget and on time. In this work, we follow the same line of thought but focus on maturity in general for all sorts of knowledge graphs. Similar to CMM, our proposed KGMM enables the assessment of the quality of a knowledge graph in order to determine its current maturity level and thus provide guidance on how to achieve its next level.

A knowledge graph is a special kind of database that manages data in a graph structure. Therefore, the quality of knowledge graphs is closely related to the quality of its data. For any information system, data quality is crucial, as data is the cornerstone of the system [10]. Wang and Diane [45] define data quality as data that is "fit-for-use" for a certain application or use case so that it fulfills its users' needs. This consideration of data quality is in line with ISO 19113 (2002) that describes data quality as the "totality of characteristics of a product that bear on its ability to satisfy stated and implied needs". Consequently, high data quality ensures that a system or product provides benefits for its users by satisfying their needs. In contrast, low data quality has several negative implications for the users, such as decreased customer satisfaction, increased operating costs, ineffective decision-making processes, and poor performance [36]. Therefore, any issues in the quality of data harms its use and thus restricts the value of the system or product from the users' point of view [48].

For this reason, Berners-Lee introduced the star rating system and the Linked Data Principles as instruments for a "good linked data". This work was the starting point for the development of several approaches that examine and support the quality of knowledge graphs. One of the most well-known and currently prominent approaches is the FAIR principles by Wilkinson et al. [46] to boost machines' ability to automatically find and use data (i.e., machine-actionability). Zaveri et al. [48] analyzed 30 of these existing approaches, resulting in 23 data quality measures, which they summarized in the Linked Data Quality Framework. This work is one of the most recent and comprehensive frameworks on data quality. We built our KGMM model adopting the work of Berners-Lee, Wilkinson et al. [46], and Zaveri et al. [48], as their work is widely adopted in the data management domain and provides comprehensive guidelines for data quality assurance.

A shortcoming of these works is that they do not consider specific aspects of intertwined human-machine collaboration. However, Zogaj and Bretschneider [49] explain that successful information system projects often also include crowdsourcing. In this context, Wang et al. [44] further stated that expert crowd members produce extremely accurate knowledge graphs. However, crowdsourcing is often not sustainable due to the limited human resources available. Therefore, crowdsourcing is usually used to refine knowledge graphs for three reasons. First, automatic methods struggle to achieve both high accuracy and broad coverage. Second, the network's documents have a long tail effect, implying that a large amount of knowledge is poorly dispersed. Finally, automatic processing technology is prone to flaws such as excessive noise levels and problems ensuring knowledge accuracy [6]. We consider these reasons and their effects on the data quality by reflecting these human-machine dimensions in KGMM.

3   Research Method

For developing and realizing the KGMM we followed a design science approach including the following five-step methodology:

1. Reviewing different existing data quality and maturity models [19].
2. Eliciting requirements for a KG maturity model from the large-scale knowledge graph application Open Research Knowledge Graph (ORKG) aiming at intertwining human and machine collaboration.
3. Studying the different quality dimensions in the previous works.
4. Develop the KGMM by prioritizing and weighting various quality dimensions and measures based on the reviewed literature.
5. Extension of the ORKG application by implementing features catering for the various KGMM measures and their evaluation.

4   Knowledge Graph Maturity Model

In this study, we are proposing a tool to assess the KG maturity by measuring the data quality at each level. In the KGMM maturity model, we define and

Table 1. Overview of selected maturity models in various domains.

Module name	Levels/ Attributes	Domain	Maturity definition	Practicality
Capability Model Integration (CMMI)[1]	5/ 22	Software	✓	Specific improvement activities
Model-driven Development (MDD) Maturity Model [39]	5/ 3	Product Lifecycle	-	General recommendations
Assessing Business-IT [27] Alignment Maturity	5/ 5	Business Information Technology	-	General recommendations
Gartner Enterprise Information Management Maturity Model [31]	6/ 4	Information Management	-	General recommendations
A Capability Maturity Model for Research Data Mgmt. [38]	5/ 6	Research Data Management	-	General recommendations

[1] https://resources.sei.cmu.edu/library/asset-view.cfm?assetid=9661

prioritize quality measures for each level to boost the data quality and elevate the KG maturity. We adapted the three priority levels from the FAIR Data Maturity Model Working Group [15] and apply them to prioritize the quality measures for each level. The three priorities are defined as follows:

- **Essential:** denotes a quality metric that is crucial for approaching a maturity level, or, on the contrary, that maturity would be practically impossible to reach if the priority was not fulfilled.
- **Important:** addresses a quality metric that may or may not be vital in some situations. Achieving it, if at all possible, would significantly boost maturity.
- **Useful:** is a type of measure that concentrates on a nice-to-have quality metric that is not required.

We also use the pass-or-fail approach from the same publication, the FAIR Data Maturity Model Working Group [15], to identify whether the quality measures for KG are meeting a given maturity level requirement or not. First of all, we associate each quality metric with a priority (Essential, Important, or Useful). In any event, if a specific quality metric is "essential", then the KG must fulfill this quality metric (pass) to advance to the next maturity level. Furthermore, at least 50% of the quality measures that are "important" at a given maturity level should "pass". Otherwise, the maturity level will be "fail". In conclusion, to make the KG pass a certain level, the KG should fulfill all the "essential" quality measures and at least 50% of the "important" quality measures.

In Table 2 we list the seven data quality dimensions in the rows and the five maturity levels in the columns. The 20 quality measures themselves are displayed in the table cells.

Table 2. *Overview on the KGMM maturity model.* The five maturity levels are listed in the columns and the quality dimensions in the rows. We also indicate priority levels and relevance for human-machine curation. For more concrete examples of the quality problems and the relevance for human-machine curation, please check our detailed table available on Zenodo. [20]

Quality dimensions	Level 1: Published	Level 2: Completeness	Level 3: Representation	Level 4: Stability	Level 5: Linkability
Accuracy	Syntactic accuracy**[H,M]	Timeliness***[H] Correctness***[H,M] Semantic accuracy**[H,M]			
Completeness		Trustworthiness[H] *** Instance completeness**[H,M] Property completeness**[H,M] Population completeness**[M]			Linkability*[H,M]
Findability				Identifier stability**[M]	
Accessibility	Responsiveness***[H,M] Easiness**[H]			Queryability**[H,M]	Dereferencability *[M]
Interoperability		Provenance***[H]	Data representation*[H]	Trackability***[H,M]	
Reusability	License***[H,M]		Reusability***[M]		
Succinctness			Conciseness***[H,M]		

*** Essential, ** Important, * Useful
Indicates the relevance to human curation.
Indicates the relevance to machine-actionability.

4.1   Level 1: Published

At this level, the KG should be published on the web (in any format) with an open license fulfilling the following requirements:

- **Responsiveness (Essential):** It is marked as "essential" because the KG is not useful for the end user if the KG is not accessible in a reasonable time. Nah [30] recommends that the loading time should be below two seconds. The exploration and curation Web interface for the KG should be accessible in a responsive manner with small page loading times.
- **Licences (Essential):** The KG should be licensed under an open licence in order to make the data available for everyone. The licensing information should integrated into the KG interface in a machine-readable manner. The Creative Commons organization created an ontology to provide a machine-actionable representation of license information [1].
- **Syntactic Accuracy (Important):**
  The syntactic accuracy according to Hogan et al. [17], is the degree to which the data are accurate in terms of the grammatical rules set for the domain and/or data model. The syntactic accuracy is marked as "important" because even without complete syntactic accuracy the KG might still be usable for both human and machine. Syntactic accuracy can be ensured by restricting the user interface (e.g., by form-based interactions) to only allow the entering of syntactically accurate representations.
- **Easiness (Important):** We mean by easiness, an intuitive way to navigate, explore and curate a KG. Also, Garett et al. [12] find the easiness (easy navigation) as one of the unique (important) design factors that affect user engagement. Easiness also according to Hogan et al. [18] means, the simplicity with which a user can interpret data without confusion, which includes at least the availability of human-readable labels and descriptions that allow them to grasp what is being presented.
  We mark this measure as "important" because it is a key factor for sustaining user engagement with a KG.
  While the other measures in this layer can be largely automatically validated, checking for easiness requires more qualitative assessment means such as user studies, Web analytic, surveys or interviews.

4.2   Level 2: Completeness

Wang and Diane [45] define completeness as the degree to which data has enough breadth, depth, and scope for the task at hand. Furthermore, according to Hogan et al. [17], data completeness is the extent to which a data set provides all the needed data. Issa et al. [21] conducted a review that revealed nine of the most frequently used techniques (automatically or semi-automatically) for assessing dataset completeness. We adopt semi-automatic techniques to let humans (crowd-members) and machines work jointly to complete KG data. In Sect. 5, we discuss in more detail how we implemented a mechanism that allows intertwined human-machine collaboration. Based on the previous listed work, we consider complete and current data as a key aspect of KGs. Therefore, we define the following quality measures relates to completeness:

- **Correctness (Essential):** Hogan et al. [17] use the term "validity" to refer to correctness. This is accomplished by imposing restrictions to prevent validity infringements within the KG. According to Batini and Scannapieco [3], corrections are essential when the KG data comes from sources that are subject to error (e.g., caused by manual data entry) or from sources whose dependability is unknown. We consider correctness as "essential" because incorrect KG data leads to misleading forecasts for the data consumers. If the data is inaccurate, resources, time, and money are wasted.
- **Timeliness (Essential):** According to Pipino et al., [36] timeliness refers to how current the data is regarding the use case or objective. Fürber and Hepp [11] think that we can compare two timestamps to discover possible data obsoleteness if at least timestamps describing the last update of data are available in the source and destination data sources. We consider timeliness as "essential" because outdated knowledge can lead to inaccurate analyses, which in turn leads to wrong decisions. Additionally, outdated knowledge can be considered incorrect, which relates to the previously described metric.
- **Provenance (Essential):** Provenance data is widely acknowledged as essential for facilitating the reuse, management, and reproducibility of published data [40]. According to Golbeck and Mannes [13], when it comes to filtering and aggregation, tracking the provenance of Semantic Web metadata is essential, especially when the trustworthiness of the data is in question. As previously mentioned, we leverage a crowdsourced approach for KG data creation and curation. To ensure data validity, provenance tracking is a crucial aspect to keep track of the history, and to be able to link data to the original source. Therefore, we consider provenance as "essential".
- **Trustworthiness (Essential):** According to Zaveri et al. [48], trustworthiness is the degree to which the data is considered correct, verifiable, actual, and believable. The data trustworthiness, according to Jacobi et al. [22], is either: trustworthiness of the source, relative content trust (i.e., depending on the domain knowledge of the source, claims are either trustworthy or not), and a combination of factors. We have marked trustworthiness as "essential" because when a KG cannot be trusted, the data consumer cannot make a well-informed decision.
- **Semantic Accuracy (Important):** Hidalgo-Delgado et al. [16] define semantic accuracy as the level to which data values accurately represent real-world phenomena, as impacted by inaccurate extraction outputs, an imperfect number of claims, destruction, and other considerations.
- **Instance Completeness (Important):** According to Micic et al. [29], an instance is complete if a dataset includes all of the real-world objects required for a given task.
- **Property Completeness (Important):** According to Batini and Scannapieco [3], the property completeness is an estimate of the incomplete extent for any property in a KG. Hogan et al. [17] define property completeness as the measure of missing values for a given property in a KG.

- **Population Completeness (Important):** According to Batini and Scannapieco [3], population completeness compares missing values to a reference population. Pipino et al. [36]. define population completeness as the ratio of the number of represented objects to the total number of real-world objects known to population completeness.

Completeness assessment particularly benefits from intertwined human-machine collaboration, because deficiencies of automated or manual completeness assessment methods can be mitigated by the complementary strategy.

4.3 Level 3: Representation

At this level, the KG should fulfill the following requirements:

- **Reusability (Essential):** Wilkinson et al. [46] state that for data to be reusable, it should be:
  - its meta (data) is thoroughly specified with a variety of precise and important properties.
  - its (meta) data are published with a clear and accessible utilization agreement.
  - its (meta) data are coupled with comprehensive provenance.
  - its (meta) data conform to community-relevant domain guidelines.
  Moreover, Hogan et al. [17] state that reusability is the ability of a dataset to be coupled with other datasets. We have marked reusability as "essential" because it is one of the main FAIR principles. In addition, reusability emphasizes machine-actionability so that the data consumers can use the KG without any or little human intervention.
- **Conciseness (Essential):** According to Pablo et al. [28], a KG is concise when there are no non-essential schema and data elements in the given KG. Hidalgo Delgado et al. [16] differentiate between:
  - **Intentional conciseness (schema level):** meaning the absence of redundant schema components (properties, classes, shapes, etc.) in the KG.
  - **Extensional conciseness (data level):** meaning the absence of duplicated entities and relations in the KG.
  Batini et al. [2] refer to conciseness as "uniqueness." They define it as the degree to which data is devoid of duplicates in areas of breadth, depth, and scope. [11] considers OWL helpful to avoid data redundancy on the semantic web. OWL can be used to flag synonymous identifiers with *owl:sameAs*. Batini and Scannapieco [3] see that when more than one state of the information system matches a state of the real-world system, data values are consistent. We mark conciseness as "essential" because the more prominent the KG's conciseness, the more readable and understandable the KG is.
- **Data representation (Useful):** Batini and Scannapieco [3] assert that the KG should present the data in a suitable language and unit, with explicit data definitions. They differentiate between different levels of data representation:

- **Concise representation:** the KG presents data concisely without being encumbered.
- **Representational consistency:** Data is always displayed in the same format and is compatible with the older data.

4.4 Level 4: Stability

The KG should be available using open W3C standards[1] (e.g., RDF or SPARQL). In particular, the following requirements should be fulfilled:

- **Trackability (Essential):** [5,9,50] agree that keeping track of where the data originates from is of paramount importance when working with KGs. So it is "essential" to verify the data sources in KGs to have a better reputation for accuracy, truthfulness, and fairness in the KG.
- **Identifier stability (Important):** The WC3[2] recommends using URIs as a distinctive identifier for real-world objects. In addition, Hogan et al. [17] state that when the KG should be augmented with external data sources, it is necessary to use globally unique IDs to avoid name conflicts and use external identity connections to distinguish a node from an external source. They provide examples of stable identifiers like Digital Object Identifiers (DOIs) for papers, ORCID IDs for authors, International Standard Book Numbers (ISBNs) for books, Alpha-2 codes for counties, and other persistent identifier (PID) schemes.
- **Queryability (Important):** The KG should furnish a SPARQL, GraphQL and/or API endpoint to make it straightforward for the data consumers to retrieve data from the KG. According to Hidalgo Delgado et al., [16] queryability necessitates data availability via SPARQL endpoints and RDF dumps. SPARQL endpoints likewise streamline federated search across several data sources, enhancing and enriching data accessibility.

4.5 Level 5: Linkability

At this level, the KG should achieve the following prerequisites:

- **Dereferencability (Useful):** Hidalgo-Delgado et al. [16] state that we can dereference resources based on URIs. We can correspondingly address the URIs using HTTP calls to return appropriate and authentic data. The resource dereferencing is complete if the HTTP call yields an RDF document and the HTTP status code is 200.
- **Linkability (Useful):** According to Hogan et al., [17], linkability is the degree to which data set instances are connected. This measure is again a good example, where human-machine collaboration is beneficial. Automated linking techniques can be applied by machines using human input for training, validation and coherence assessment.

---

[1] https://www.w3.org/standards/semanticweb/query.

[2] https://www.w3.org/TR/cooluris/.

5   Application of KGMM to a Large-Scale Use Case

The Open Research Knowledge Graph (ORKG) [23] represents a perfect testbed for implementation and experimentation with the KGMM. The ORKG comprises machine extracted and human curated semantic descriptions of research contributions from more than 10.000 scientific articles in 500 scientific fields [24].

A key element of the ORKG are tabular research contribution comparisons give an overview on the state-of-the-art for a certain research problem [33]. We implemented the KGMM for the ORKG in particular also for evaluating the maturity of comparisons. In this section, we first clarify how the ORKG satisfies the KGMM's requirements and then illustrate in detail how we implemented the KGMM for ORKG comparisons.

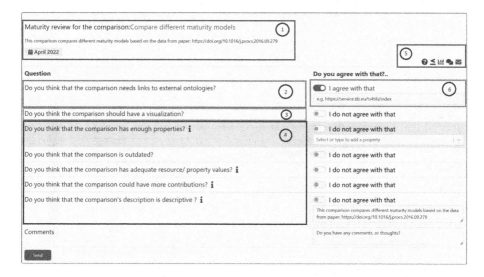

Fig. 1. *Comparison peer review form for feedback from crowd members.* Box one (orange) contains the comparison's metadata. Box two (purple) contains a question asking the reviewers about the linkability (KGMM level 5). The question in box three (lime) asks the reviewers about the data representation (KGMM level 3). Questions in box four (blue) ask the reviewers about the KG completeness (KGMM level 2). The icons in box five (brown) enable the user to find all the needed reports or send the review to another expert. Box six (yellow) let the reviewers add links to external ontologies, if they can recommend any. (Color figure online)

5.1   ORKG Maturity Levels

The ORKG comparison has five maturity levels, identical to the KGMM model. We have illustrated a detailed table that demonstrates how the ORKG implemented the various KGMM maturity levels, quality dimensions, metrics, and measures available on Zenodo. [20]

5.2   Application of KGMM to ORKG Comparisons

One crucial type of content in the ORKG are comparisons of research contributions addressing a specific research question. We now discuss how the KGMM was specifically applied to this type of content.

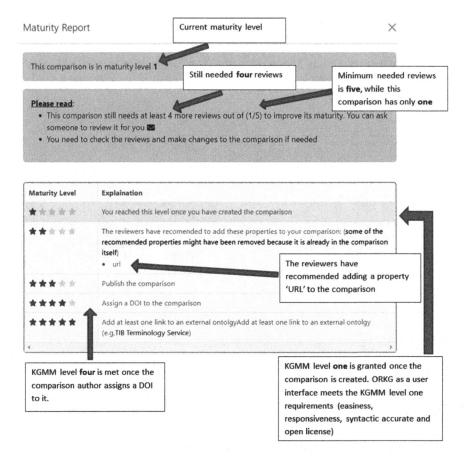

Fig. 2. *Full report about the current maturity level, and the number of added reviews.* The report aims at answering the following questions: (1) What is the current maturity level? (2) What are the properties, that the reviewers have recommended? (3) How many reviews in total are needed for a comparison? (4) How many reviewers have reviewed the comparison so far?

The Reviews. Once a comparison is published in the ORKG, peer community members (other than the original author) can add reviews for this comparison. The comparison author can invite others to review the comparison by sending an email with the review URL. The comparison review is publicly accessible for all users resembling an open review process. To ensure data quality and provenance tracking, only registered users can add reviews.

We followed the design approach proposed by Cao et al. [6] regarding to crowdsourcing task design. Implicit crowdsourcing tasks excel better in terms of cost and outcomes. The implicit crowdsourcing task implies that the crowd members are unaware of the existence of the task since it is part of the genuine user interaction with the application. Additionally, they suggest designing binary choice (true or false) questions for more acceptable results. As shown in Fig. 1, our implemented review is a relatively straightforward, implicit agree/disagree task, where the reviewers inform us of their thought on the constructed comparison.

Determination of the Minimum Review Number by the Community. We do not know how many reviews would be adequate to review a given comparison. A reasonable solution here is to allow the community to determine that by themselves. We enable the crowd members to decide what the minimum of required reviews should be for a comparison in their field.

The Maturity Report. The report illustrates the maturity level of a particular comparison. Moreover, the report answers the question "Why is a particular comparison at a certain maturity level?" The report helps the comparison author to comprehend what should be done to advance the maturity level by providing concrete steps. Also, the report is publicly available to the community, so others can help to improve the maturity of the comparison (cf. Fig. 2).

The Feedback Report. The report reveals how the reviewers evaluate a given comparison. It is an aggregative, publicly available report of the reviewer's feedback for a given comparison. The report draws the comparison author's attention to what the reviewers think about his comparison. On the other hand, the report also assists the community in drawing an image of the others' thoughts.

6   Conclusions and Future Work

This work is a first of a larger research and development agenda. We want to lift knowledge graphs to a novel level, by more 1) systematically intertwining human and machine intelligence and 2) developing means for managing more complex information assets in KGs then mere entity descriptions. For both of these aspects, a maturity model for gradually improving the representations in the KG is of utmost importance. With KGMM we presented a first version of a graded maturity model for knowledge graph applications aiming to intertwine human-machine collaboration. The proposed model consists of 5 maturity levels, comprising 20 quality measures. It has a strong foundation in existing quality assessment frameworks, including the FAIR data guidelines, LOD stars, and a set of additional work related to linked data quality. The maturity model is complemented with dimensions specifically related to human-machine curated knowledge graphs.

We plan also to do either a qualitative or empirical evaluation. In that sense, we have to wait for one to one and a half years until we have adequate peer-reviews for the KGMM by our users. Afterward, we can have an extended version of the paper as a journal paper describing a detailed evaluation of the KGMM.

Supplemental Material Statement: Source code for Sect. 5 is available on Github.[3]

References

1. Abelson, H., Adida, B., Linksvayer, M., Yergler, N.: CC REL: the creative commons rights expression language, vol. 2, pp. 149–188. Open Book Publishers, 1 edn. (2012). https://www.jstor.org/stable/j.ctt5vjsx3.16
2. Batini, C., Cappiello, C., Francalanci, C., Maurino, A.: Methodologies for data quality assessment and improvement. ACM Comput. Surv. **41**(3), 16:1–16:52 (2009). https://doi.org/10.1145/1541880.1541883
3. Batini, C., Scannapieco, M.: Data Quality: Concepts, Methodologies and Techniques (Data-Centric Systems and Applications). Springer-Verlag, Berlin, Heidelberg (2006). https://doi.org/10.1007/3-540-33173-5
4. Bizer, C., Cyganiak, R.: Quality-driven information filtering using the WIQA policy framework. Web Semant. **7**(1), 1–10 (2009). https://doi.org/10.1016/j.websem.2008.02.005
5. Bonatti, P.A., Hogan, A., Polleres, A., Sauro, L.: Robust and scalable linked data reasoning incorporating provenance and trust annotations. J. Web Semant. **9**(2), 165–201 (2011) https://doi.org/10.1016/j.websem.2011.06.003, https://www.sciencedirect.com/science/article/pii/S1570826811000394
6. Cao, M., Zhang, J., Xu, S., Ying, Z.: Knowledge graphs meet crowdsourcing: a brief survey. In: Qi, L., Khosravi, M.R., Xu, X., Zhang, Y., Menon, V.G. (eds.) Cloud Computing, vol. 363, pp. 3–17. Springer International Publishing (2021), https://link.springer.com/10.1007/978-3-030-69992-5_1, series Title: Lecture Notes of the Institute for Computer Sciences, Social Informatics and Telecommunications Engineering
7. Charles, V., Freire, N., Isaac, A.: Links, languages and semantics: linked data approaches in the European library and Europeana. IFLA, Lyon (2014)
8. Cole, T., Han, M., Weathers, W., Joyner, E.: Library marc records into linked open data: challenges and opportunities. J. Librar. Metadata **13**(2–3), 163–196 (2013). https://doi.org/10.1080/19386389.2013.826074
9. Dividino, R., Sizov, S., Staab, S., Schueler, B.: Querying for provenance, trust, uncertainty and other meta knowledge in RDF. J. Web Semant. **7**(3), 204–219 (2009) https://doi.org/10.1016/j.websem.2009.07.004, https://www.sciencedirect.com/science/article/pii/S1570826809000237
10. English, L.P.: Improving Data Warehouse and Business Information Quality. John Wiley, and Sons, Inc. (1999)
11. Fürber, C., Hepp, M.: Swiqa - a semantic web information quality assessment framework. In: ECIS (2011)
12. Garett, R., Chiu, J., Zhang, L., Young, S.D.: A literature review: website design and user engagement, July 2016. https://www.ncbi.nlm.nih.gov/pmc/articles/PMC4974011/

---

[3] https://gitlab.com/TIBHannover/orkg/orkg-frontend/-/merge_requests/883.

13. Golbeck, J., Mannes, A.: Using trust and provenance for content filtering on the semantic web. In: MTW (2006)
14. Gonzales, B.M.: Linking libraries to the web: linked data and the future of the bibliographic record. Inf. Technol. Librar. **33**, 10–22 (2014)
15. Group, F.D.M.M.W.: FAIR Data Maturity Model. Specification and Guidelines, June 2020. https://doi.org/10.15497/rda00050
16. Hidalgo-Delgado, Y., López, Y.A., Rodríguez, J.P.F., Mederos, A.L.: Quality assessment of library linked data: a case study. In: Villazón-Terrazas, B., Ortiz-Rodríguez, F., Tiwari, S., Goyal, A., Jabbar, M. (eds.) Knowledge Graphs and Semantic Web, vol. 1459, pp. 93–108. Springer International Publishing (2021). https://link.springer.com/10.1007/978-3-030-91305-2_8, series Title: Communications in Computer and Information Science
17. Hogan, A., et al.: Knowledge graphs. ACM Comput. Surveys **54**(4), 1–37 (2022). https://doi.org/10.1145/3447772. arxiv:2003.02320
18. Hogan, A., Umbrich, J., Harth, A., Cyganiak, R., Polleres, A., Decker, S.: An empirical survey of linked data conformance. J. Web Semant. **14**, 14–44 (2012). https://doi.org/10.1016/j.websem.2012.02.001, https://www.sciencedirect.com/science/article/pii/S1570826812000352
19. Hussein, H., Oelen, A., Karras, O., Auer, S.: A comparison of different maturity models (2022). https://doi.org/10.48366/R186111, https://www.orkg.org/orkg/comparison/R186111/
20. Hussein, H., Oelen, A., Karras, O., Auer, S.: Knowledge graph maturity model, June 2022. https://doi.org/10.5281/zenodo.6732786
21. Issa, S., Adekunle, O., Hamdi, F., Cherfi, S.S.S., Dumontier, M., Zaveri, A.: Knowledge graph completeness: a systematic literature review. IEEE Access **9**, 31322–31339 (2021) https://doi.org/10.1109/ACCESS.2021.3056622, https://ieeexplore.ieee.org/document/9344615/
22. Jacobi, I., Kagal, L., Khandelwal, A.: Rule-based trust assessment on the semantic web. In: Bassiliades, N., Governatori, G., Paschke, A. (eds.) Rule-Based Reasoning, Programming, and Applications, vol. 6826, pp. 227–241. Springer, Berlin Heidelberg (2011). https://link.springer.com/10.1007/978-3-642-22546-8_18, series Title: Lecture Notes in Computer Science
23. Jaradeh, M.Y., Auer, S., Prinz, M., Kovtun, V., Kismihók, G., Stocker, M.: Open research knowledge graph: towards machine actionability in scholarly communication. arXiv preprint arXiv:1901.10816, p. 42 (2019)
24. Karras, O., Groen, E.C., Khan, J.A., Auer, S.: Researcher or crowd member? Why not both! the open research knowledge graph for applying and communicating crowdRE research. In: IEEE 29th International Requirements Engineering Conference Workshops (REW). IEEE (2021)
25. Kroll, H., Kalo, J.C., Nagel, D., Mennicke, S., Balke, W.T.: Context-compatible information fusion for scientific knowledge graphs. In: Digital Libraries for Open Knowledge: 24th International Conference on Theory and Practice of Digital Libraries, TPDL 2020, Lyon, France, 25–27 August 2020, Proceedings, pp. 33–47. Springer-Verlag, Berlin, Heidelberg (2020). https://doi.org/10.1007/978-3-030-54956-5_3
26. Kroll, H., Pirklbauer, J., Balke, W.T.: A toolbox for the nearly-unsupervised construction of digital library knowledge graphs. In: 2021 ACM/IEEE Joint Conference on Digital Libraries (JCDL), pp. 21–30 (2021). https://doi.org/10.1109/JCDL52503.2021.00014

27. Luftman, J.N.: Assessing business-IT alignment maturity. AIS Journals (2022). https://www.researchgate.net/publication/228681894_Assessing_Business-IT_Alignment_Maturity

28. Mendes, P.N., Mühleisen, H., Bizer, C.: Sieve: linked data quality assessment and fusion. In: EDBT-ICDT 2012 (2012)

29. Micic, N., Neagu, D., Campean, F., Zadeh, E.H.: Towards a data quality framework for heterogeneous data. In: 2017 IEEE International Conference on Internet of Things (iThings) and IEEE Green Computing and Communications (GreenCom) and IEEE Cyber, Physical and Social Computing (CPSCom) and IEEE Smart Data (SmartData), pp. 155–162 (2017)

30. Nah, F.F.H.: A study on tolerable waiting time: how long are web users willing to wait? Behav. Inf. Technol. **23**(3), 153–163 (2004). https://doi.org/10.1080/01449290410001669914

31. Newman, D., Logan, D.: Gartner introduces the EIM maturity model. In: Gartner Introduces the EIM Maturity Model (2008)

32. Oelen, A., Jaradeh, M.Y., Stocker, M., Auer, S.: Organizing scholarly knowledge leveraging crowdsourcing, expert curation and automated techniques. Linking Knowledge: Linked Open Data for Knowledge Organization, pp. 182–99 (2021)

33. Oelen, A., Jaradeh, M.Y., Stocker, M., Auer, S.: Generate FAIR literature surveys with scholarly knowledge graphs. In: Proceedings of the ACM/IEEE Joint Conference on Digital Libraries in 2020, pp. 97–106. Association for Computing Machinery (2020). https://doi.org/10.1145/3383583.3398520

34. Oramas, S., Sordo, M., Serra, X.: Automatic creation of knowledge graphs from digital musical document libraries. Fontes Artis Musicae (2014)

35. Paulk, M., Curtis, B., Chrissis, M., Weber, C.: Capability maturity model, version 1.1. IEEE Softw. **10**(4), 18–27 (1993). https://doi.org/10.1109/52.219617

36. Pipino, L.L., Lee, Y.W., Wang, R.Y.: Data quality assessment. Commun. ACM **45**(4), 211–218 (2002). https://doi.org/10.1145/505248.506010

37. Proenca, D.: Methods and techniques for maturity assessment. In: 2016 11th Iberian Conference on Information Systems and Technologies (CISTI), pp. 1–4. IEEE (2016). https://doi.org/10.1109/CISTI.2016.7521483, https://ieeexplore.ieee.org/document/7521483/

38. Qin, J., Crowston, K., Kirkland, A.: A capability maturity model for research data management. asis and t (2014). https://surface.syr.edu/istpub/184

39. Rios, E., Bozheva, T., Bediaga, A., Guilloreau, N.: MDD maturity model: a roadmap for introducing model-driven development. In: Rensink, A., Warmer, J. (eds.) Model Driven Architecture - Foundations and Applications, pp. 78–89. Springer. Lecture Notes in Computer Science (2006). https://doi.org/10.1007/11787044_7

40. Simmhan, Y.L., Plale, B., Gannon, D.: A survey of data provenance in e-science. SIGMOD Record **34**, 31–36 (2005). https://citeseerx.ist.psu.edu/viewdoc/summary?doi=10.1.1.130.6325

41. Singhal, A.: Introducing the knowledge graph: things, not strings. Official Google Blog **5**, 16 (2012)

42. Stocker, M., et al.: SKG4EOSC-scholarly knowledge graphs for EOSC: establishing a backbone of knowledge graphs for fair scholarly information in EOSC. Res. Ideas Outcomes **8** (2022)

43. Vrandečić, D., Krötzsch, M.: Wikidata: a free collaborative knowledgebase. Commun. ACM **57**(10), 78–85 (2014)

44. Wang, B., Luo, J., Zhu, S.: Research on domain ontology automation construction based on Chinese texts. In: Proceedings of the 2019 8th International Conference on Software and Computer Applications, pp. 425–430. ICSCA 2019. Association for Computing Machinery (2019). https://doi.org/10.1145/3316615.3316685

45. Wang, R.Y., Strong., D.M.: Beyond accuracy: what data quality means to data consumers. J. Manage. Inf. Syst. **12**(4), 5–33 (1996)

46. Wilkinson, M.D., et al.: The FAIR guiding principles for scientific data management and stewardship. Scient. Data **3**, 1–9 (2016). https://doi.org/10.1038/sdata.2016.18

47. Yadagiri, N., Ramesh, P.: Semantic web and the libraries: an overview. Int. J. Library Sci. **7**(1), 80–94 (2013)

48. Zaveri, A., Rula, A., Maurino, A., Pietrobon, R., Lehmann, J., Auer, S.: Quality assessment for linked data: a survey. Semant. Web **7**(1), 63–93 (2016)

49. Zogaj, S., Bretschneider, U.: Analyzing governance mechanisms for crowdsourcing information systems: a multiple case analysis. In: ECIS, pp. 9–11 (2014)

50. Zou, L., Chen, L., Özsu, M.T.: K-automorphism: a general framework for privacy preserving network publication. Proc. VLDB Endow. **2**(1), 946–957 (2009). https://doi.org/10.14778/1687627.1687734

Technostress on Academic Librarians Working in Digital Scholarship During the Pandemic in Indonesia

Nurrochmah Febrianti Nadyasari[1], Rahmi[1(✉)] [iD], and Hideo Joho[2]

[1] Department of Library and Information Science, Faculty of Humanities, Universitas Indonesia, Kampus Baru UI, Depok, West Java 16424, Indonesia
{nurrochmahfebrianti,rahmi.ami}@ui.ac.id
[2] Department Faculty of Library, Information and Media Science, University of Tsukuba, Tsukuba, Japan
hideo@slis.tsukuba.ac.jp

Abstract. Technostress can arise when individuals use information and communications technology (ICT) in their work, and academic librarians who work in digital scholarship are especially susceptible. Librarians use ICT to provide information to the academic community; one of their roles is to disseminate research results from researchers, lecturers and students. The importance of digital scholarship has increased, mainly due to a shift towards digital teaching, learning and research in academic institutions and a transition from face-to-face to virtual meetings. This study aims to measure the technostress level across six variables and investigates the significant differences in the technostress levels of academic librarians during the pandemic based on demographic data. This study uses a quantitative approach; its research subjects are 92 academic librarians in Indonesia, from whom data was collected through questionnaires. The results reveal that academic librarians tended to experience low technostress during the pandemic. This research is helpful as a reference for future studies on technostress and for reviewing policies related to digital scholarship that may be implemented in academic libraries.

Keywords: Technostress · Digital scholarship · Academic librarian · Academic library

1 Introduction

The performance of academic librarians in Indonesia was high in 2021, particularly in digital resource technology [27]. However, Davis and Newstrom [14] in Iskamto [20] explain that if stress increases, performance will tend to decrease; employees' behavior changes, and it becomes difficult to do their work. This changed behavior contributes to job performance. One factor that creates stress in workplaces using technology is known as technostress.

Craig Brod introduced the term "technostress" in 1980 because of the emergence of automation in the workplace. The term then evolved to include the problems associated

Y.-H. Tseng et al. (Eds.): ICADL 2022, LNCS 13636, pp. 270–289, 2022.
https://doi.org/10.1007/978-3-031-21756-2_22

with employees using information and communications technology (ICT) [41]. Technostress can occur when individuals use ICT in their work; the subjects of this study, academic librarians, are especially susceptible to technostress. Librarians use ICT to provide information to the academic community, particularly for digital scholarship. Digital scholarship involves actively using digital media in academic activities, including referencing information obtained from digital media and used in research or college assignments [48].

Tarafdar et al. [56] reveal 5 (five) components that create technostress in employees: techno-invasion, techno-overload, techno-uncertainty, techno-insecurity and techno-complexity. Research by Ahmad and Amin [2] states that academic librarians in Malaysia experienced techno-uncertainty, techno-overload and techno-complexity. In addition, the triggering factors for technostress can differ significantly based on gender, education level and unemployment [24]. In Indonesia, Mustika et al. [31] found that technostress creators can increase stress during a pandemic if the pandemic interferes with individuals' work, and technology cannot provide effective help in their jobs.

Digital scholarship is important because of the shift in teaching, learning and research in academic institutions from face-to-face to a combination of face-to-face and digital. This shift means that one or more individuals, such as academic librarians, are required to actively disseminate information using technology. The scope of digital scholarship includes digitization, the preservation of archives and special digital collections, and the creation and enhancement of metadata and computing, including text mining analysis, programming and web development [30]. The emergence of digital scholarship has created a new role for academic librarians as collaborators with researchers, lecturers and students [22]. Andayani [3] stated that librarians play an important role as partners in research in universities by providing research consulting services, teaching research skills, and publishing and disseminating research results.

Several studies have used a quantitative approach to examine technostress in Indonesia. Examples include the fields of information technology (IT) by Ferziani et al. [17] and psychology by Mustika et al. [31]. However, there is currently no research on the concept of digital scholarship, and no known study of technostress in the field of library and information science uses a quantitative approach. Murgu's research [30] shows that organizational conditions contribute to the technostress levels of digital scholarship librarians at Association of Research Libraries (ARL) institutions.

This study will answer the following questions: 1) What is the technostress level of 92 academic librarians in Indonesia working in digital scholarship during the Covid19 pandemic? 2) Is there a significant difference among the technostress levels of higher-education librarians based on differences in demographic data?

This study aims to measure the technostress level during the pandemic across six variables and investigate the significant differences between the technostress levels of academic librarians grouped by demographic data.

2 Literature Review

2.1 Technostress

Salazar-Concha et al. [41] state, "Technostress is defined as stress experienced by people due to information and communication systems and technologies." Arnetz and Wiholm [5] in la Torre et al. [24] offer another opinion, suggesting that "Technostress is a psychophysiological state characterized by high levels of stress-sensitive hormones, as well as cognitive symptoms, such as poor concentration, irritability and impaired memory." Suryanto and Sasi [54] add, "Technostress is a condition of discomfort caused by the inability of individuals to adapt to technological changes and/or a condition of individual dependence on technology that results in physical and psychological discomfort." Thus, it can be concluded that technostress is stress caused by ICT that harms a person.

Research by Kwanya et al. [23] found the following major causes of technostress experienced by academic librarians in eastern and southern Africa: (1) the number of users accessing multiple access points to multiple technology systems, (2) systems impeding performance, (3) eye strain, (4) the need to manage several user profiles, (5) using outdated systems, (6) the pressure to stay up-to-date and work efficiently with new technologies, (7) the pressure to adapt quickly and adopt new trends, (8) the desire to stay ahead of the market, (9) the feeling of failure if unable to get expected results from the technology, (10) inadequate technology infrastructure, (11) the need to learn many things, (12) lack of support; (13) spam, (14) tight deadlines for a high volume of work, (15) insufficient technological skills, (16) heavy workload, (17) inadequate technology standards, and (18) unreliable technology.

Atanasoff and Venable [6] in Murgu [30] categorize 3 (three) perspectives that are generally used to approach the issue of technostress: transactional, biological and occupational. The transactional perspective was analyzed by Tarafdar et al. [56], who defined the following components of technostress in the work environment:

1. Techno-invasion describes the impact of invasive ICT, which means that users can potentially be contacted at any time. Employees feel the need to be constantly "connected," and the boundaries between personal life and work are blurred.
2. Techno-overload describes a situation where ICT users are forced to work faster and longer.
3. Techno-uncertainty describes user unrest and uncertainty about changes and improvements in ICT that force users to constantly learn and re-educate themselves.
4. Techno-insecurity is a perceived threat of job loss to potential candidates who are more ICT-savvy.
5. Techno-complexity is when users feel that their skills are insufficient to understand the complexities of ICT and, therefore, must spend time and effort learning and understanding various aspects of ICT.

The biological perspective focuses on the physiological implications of increased technology use in the workplace, such as increased blood pressure and other health markers. Lastly, theories related to occupational health are used to consider job demand, lack of technological resources and lack of human resources, which may contribute to the perception of increased technostress. This perspective suggests mitigation measures that human resources departments can use to reduce the number and severity of stressors experienced by employees.

la Torre et al. [24] stated that women often experience more technostress than men, mainly triggered by techno-overload, techno-invasion, techno-complexity and role overload. Other results show that non-workers experience more techno-overload and techno-uncertainty than workers. Individuals educated to the degree level feel particularly pressured by techno-invasion and experience the effect of using technology on productivity. From the study results described, it can be concluded that the triggers for technostress differ significantly by gender, level of education and unemployment.

Ahmad and Amin [2] show that academic librarians' overall level of technostress in Malaysia is moderate. Academic librarians in Malaysia experience technostress due to techno-uncertainty, techno-overload and techno-complexity. New findings from Imam et al. [19] show that the largest causes of technostress among academic librarians in southwest Nigeria are environmental incidents, poor working conditions and poor lighting, while social factors are job fragmentation and changing hierarchies. The symptoms of technostress in these librarians include eye strain, backache, dizziness, chest pain, loss of patience, high levels of anxiety when separated from their computer, feeling frustrated at work and during routine work, and feeling too comfortable with computers.

In Indonesia, research on technostress in IT has been carried out by Ferziani et al. [17], who found that the types of technostress experienced by IT consulting company employees include communication society technostress and boundary technostress. Mustika et al. [31] found that technostress creators can increase stress if the pandemic interferes with individuals' work, and ICT cannot help them work effectively; to a certain extent, however, technostress creators can also increase employee innovation in completing work. As for library science, Sulistyo-Basuki et al. [53] in Samosir and Syahfitri [42] have emphasized that librarian technostress can arise because of an imbalance between the penetration of IT into various library in-house activities and the availability of training programs to improve the ability to manage IT. However, no study of technostress in libraries in Indonesia has used a quantitative approach, so it is difficult to determine the level of technostress among librarians.

2.2 Digital Scholarship

The exact definition and meaning of digital scholarship are still under debate. Mulligan [29] in Li et al. [26] stated that "Digital scholarship is a very broad general term, which includes data curation and management, digital publishing and visualization, database support, software development and interface design." Rumsey [39], in "Digital Scholarship Support in ARL Member Libraries: An Overview" [15], describes digital scholarship as "the use of digital evidence and methods, digital authoring, digital publishing, digital curation and preservation, and digital use and reuse of scholarship." Stefany et al. [51] and Setyaningsih et al. [48] explain that "Digital scholarship is an element that includes the active participation of digital media users in academic activities to make information from digital media as a data reference, for example, in research practice or completing college assignments." In summary, digital scholarship is the use of digital tools by libraries to organize information in various formats and provide it as reference data to academic fields.

Ayers [7] mentions that digital scholarship most often describes discipline-based scholarship produced with digital tools and presented in a digital form, although it can also refer to copyrights, open access and scholarship analysis in the online world. More specifically, the scope of digital scholarship can include digitization, the preservation of archives and special digital collections, the creation and enhancement of metadata, and computing, such as data mining analysis, programming and web development [30]. In addition, King [22] emphasized that the skills and competencies of librarians needed in the field of digital scholarship include collaborating/partnering in project management in the digital humanities field, having content and collection expertise, understanding metadata enrichment and user access, knowing how to use an XML editor (Oxygen/TEI), mastering language processing tools (such as parts-of-speech taggers), performing lexicography, recognizing named entity recognition tools, performing data analysis and modeling, knowing statistical analysis, and having knowledge of programming tools (Python, JavaScript). The current digital scholarship reveals that librarians are expected to be able to follow and apply advanced technology for the advancement of knowledge in the academic world.

According to Cox [13], digital scholarship relies on collections of information and data, along with tools, infrastructure and people. Libraries have embraced this opportunity to redefine their role, representing a fundamental change toward digital content publishing and active participation in research projects [13]. The following are activities that provide excellent opportunities for librarians, as summarized by Cox [13]:

1. Digitization and digital preservation, often in archives and special collections;
2. Creation and enhancement of metadata for linked data, exchange and reuse;
3. Assignment of identifiers to promote discovery;
4. Hosting digital collections in library repositories;
5. Publishing edited faculty journals;
6. Dissemination of open access research results and learning materials;
7. Research data management;
8. Curation of original (not converted) digital collections;
9. Advice on copyright, digital rights management and standards implementation;
10. Participation in text mining, data analysis and geographic information systems (GIS) projects; and
11. Provision of space, equipment and digital scholarship training.

Abrigo and Labangon [1] conducted a quantitative-approach study to research digital scholarship services at 50 of Asia's top universities (as identified in the Times Higher Education [THE] Asia University Rankings 2020). The results indicate that the dynamics of the universities' digital scholarship environments are very mature, with an emphasis on Big Data, collaboration and partnerships in research, and a powerful interdisciplinary drive towards research and innovation. Furthermore, research from Ocran and Afful-Arthur [34] shows that the role of librarians at the Sam Jonah Library, University of Cape Coast, involves digital scholarship seminars and training, digital technology support services, digital research, humanities data services, scientific communication and digital publishing, as well as the provision of physical space and research tools. Meanwhile, the challenges include inadequate facilities to increase digital scholarship, inadequate access to reading materials, inadequate platforms or tools for librarians and insufficient training for librarians.

Until now, there has been no conceptual study of digital scholarship in Indonesia, but there is research related to the role of librarians in digital scholarship. Andayani [3] argues that academic librarians can play an important role as partners in research at universities by providing research consulting services, teaching research skills, and publishing and disseminating research results. Nurkamilah and Nashihuddin [33] found that the efforts made by librarians at Sebelas Maret University Surakarta in building librarian–research collaborations were as follows:

1. Improving the writing and research culture for librarians;
2. Reviewing regulations regarding the role of libraries and librarians in academic research activities;
3. Increasing the role of librarians in academic research activities;
4. Improving the research competence of librarians; and
5. Synergizing university research maps with library services.

3 Methods

A quantitative approach is used as the research method in this study. The quantitative approach was chosen because it provides statistical results and can build, support or refute previous theories by testing hypotheses [25]. The subject of this research is academic librarians in Indonesia. The simple random sampling technique was used, which provides equal opportunities for each element in the research population to be selected [25]. This sampling technique aims to generalize the research results [44] and is suitable for a homogeneous population [38].

Data collection was performed using a questionnaire because it can save time and costs and has the broad scope necessary to reach respondents who live in remote areas [36]. The questionnaires were administered online through the SurveyMonkey platform. Questionnaires were also distributed via personal emails to librarians through the Indonesian Higher Education Library Forum (FPPTI) from March 4 to March 25, 2022. Data analysis used SPSS as a statistical data processing tool.

The research instrument took aspects from Murgu [30] and Tarafdar et al. [56]. The questions address 6 (six) technostress variables: techno-overload, techno-complexity, techno-invasion, techno-insecurity, techno-uncertainty and role overload, and also examine demographic data (gender, age, study program, last education, work experience and position). According to Tarafdar et al. [56] in Murgu [30], role overload refers to the feeling that the individual's role requirements exceed their capacity in terms of difficulty or amount of work. Each item in the research instrument is assessed based on the librarian's work over the last 6 (six) months. The value of this research instrument uses a Likert-type scale of 1–4 (1 = strongly disagree, 2 = disagree, 3 = agree and 4 = strongly agree).

The paired samples t-test was used to investigate the significant differences between technostress variables grouped by demographic data. The test was used to determine significant differences by comparing the two mean values of variables of related individuals, objects or units [50]. The output of the paired sample t-test is in the form of paired sample correlations (to determine the strength of the relationship between the two variables) and paired samples tests (to investigate whether there is a significant difference between the two variables). A p-value of less than 0.05 indicates a significant difference, while a p-value greater than 0.05 indicates no significant difference between the two variables.

In April 2022, 143 respondents filled out the questionnaires emailed to them. The remaining 92 respondents filled out the online survey, and their combined responses ultimately comprised the research sample. The reliability test of the technostress variables was carried out using Cronbach's alpha with an overall result of 0.86, derived from techno-overload (0.90), techno-complexity (0.53), techno-insecurity (0.56), techno-uncertainty (0.62) and role overload (0.78). The techno-invasion variable was not included because it had only one question item and could not be tested. Nevertheless, the result is a reliable technostress question item because values of 0.45–0.98 are acceptable [55].

4   Research Results

4.1   Descriptive Analysis

In Table 1, the techno-uncertainty variable has the highest value (M = 2.84), while the techno-insecurity variable has the lowest value (M = 1.89). The average value of technostress is 2.23, and the standard deviation (SD) is 0.696. In addition, the overall interpretation of the technostress level can be seen through the technostress scale category in Table 2. These results indicate that the technostress level of higher-education librarians in the field of digital scholarship in Indonesia is low, but it tends to be higher for techno-uncertainty, techno-complexity and techno-overload.

Table 1. Correlation results between technostress variables

Variable	N	Item	Mean	SD	1	2	3	4	5	6
Techno-overload	92	5	2.53	0.977	1.00					
Techno-invasion	92	1	2.12	0.899	0.639**	1.00				
Techno-complexity	92	5	2.78	0.571	0.367**	0.415**	1.00			
Techno-insecurity	92	4	1.89	0.687	0.284**	0.306**	0.388**	1.00		
Techno-uncertainty	92	4	2.84	0.598	0.188	0.139	0.185	0.117	1.00	
Role Overload	92	5	2.25	0.657	0.407**	0.451**	0.381**	0.524**	0.021	1.00

**Significant correlation at the $p \leq 0.01$ level

.   Statistical correlation tests were used to determine the relationship between each technostress variable. First, there is a significant relationship between techno-overload and techno-invasion, techno-complexity, techno-insecurity and role overload. Second, techno-invasion has a significant relationship with techno-complexity, techno-insecurity and role overload. Third, techno-complexity has a significant relationship with techno-overload, techno-insecurity and role overload. Techno-insecurity has a significant relationship with role overload. Finally, role overload has a significant relationship with all technostress variables except techno-uncertainty. Techno-uncertainty does not significantly correlate with any of these variables.

Table 2. Categories of the technostress scale

Scale	Category
1.00–1.75	Very low
1.76–2.51	Low
2.52–3.27	High
3.28–4.00	Very high

Figure 1 shows the respondents' answers to questions related to techno-overload. The fourth techno-overload item has the highest average value (M = 2.82), indicating that the respondents experienced techno-overload when forced to adapt to new technology. Meanwhile, the third techno-overload item has the lowest average score (M = 2.35), reflecting the respondents' ability to work with tight schedules. Overall, the techno-overload experienced by the respondents was relatively high (M = 2.53).

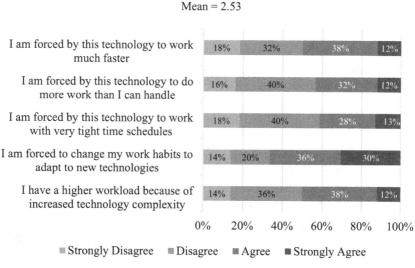

Fig. 1. Calculation results of the techno-overload variable

Figure 2 illustrates the respondents' answers on techno-invasion (average M = 2.12). The low average is a response to the statement that respondents feel their personal lives are being invaded by technology related to digital scholarship. This indicates that they did not feel that digital scholarship technology was invading their personal lives.

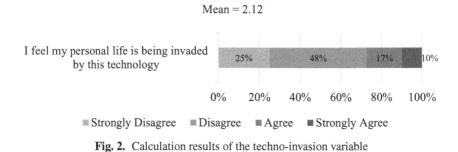

Fig. 2. Calculation results of the techno-invasion variable

Figure 3 illustrates the respondents' answers on techno-complexity. The first techno-complexity item, whether the technology used by the respondents could handle their work satisfactorily (M = 3.23), received the highest average score. The second techno-complexity item, whether respondents took a long time to understand and use new technology, has a low average value (M = 2.15). Overall, the respondents experienced high techno-complexity (M = 2.78).

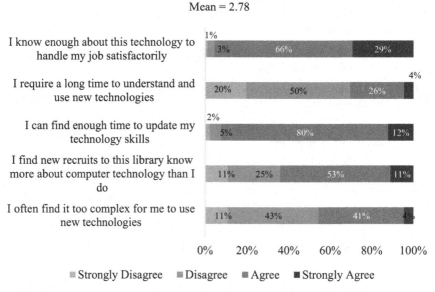

Fig. 3. Calculation results of the techno-complexity variable

Below illustrates the respondents' answers concerning techno-insecurity. The second techno-insecurity item had the highest average score (M = 3.29), whereas the fourth techno-insecurity item had the lowest average score (M = 1.61). Respondents all admitted that they had a sense of insecurity, so they had to update their skills continuously. Nevertheless, overall techno-insecurity experienced by respondents tended to be low (M = 1.89) (Fig. 4).

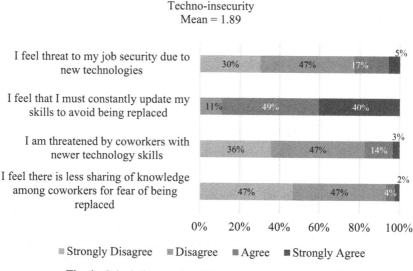

Fig. 4. Calculation results of the techno-insecurity variable

Figure 5 illustrates the respondents' answers on techno-uncertainty. The highest average score (M = 3.16) was for the respondents' response to the statement that the technology used in their libraries always had new developments. The lowest average score (M = 2.57) was for the statement that the library they occupied did not often change hardware. The processed results show a relatively high techno-uncertainty component (M = 2.83).

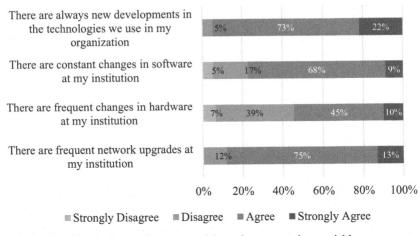

Fig. 5. Calculation results of the techno-uncertainty variable

Figure 6 presents the respondents' answers on role overload. The fifth role overload item, where respondents agreed that they felt they could not meet everyone's expectations at a given time, had the highest average score (M = 2.70). The fourth role overload item has the lowest average value (M = 1.84), which means that most respondents have time for themselves. Over all items, the role overload component is rated as low (M = 2.25).

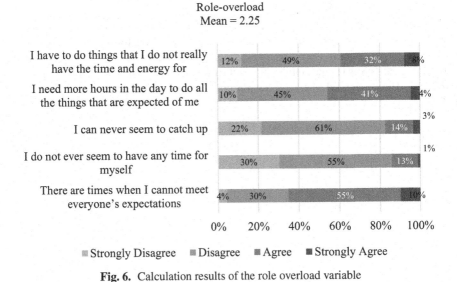

Fig. 6. Calculation results of the role overload variable

4.2 Demographic Analysis

The respondents' demographic data are shown in Table 3. Of the 92 respondents, 52 were men (56.5%), and the rest were women (43.5%). Most respondents were 40–65 years old (65.2%) and had a work experience of 16 years or more (57.6%). The study program taken by most of the respondents was library science (65.2%), and most respondents occupied the job position of "librarian" (48.9%).

Table 3. Demographic data of technostress respondents ($N = 92$)

Variable	Category	N	%
Gender	Male	52	56.5
	Female	40	43.5
Age	20–39 years	32	34.8
	40–65 years	60	65.2
Last education	High school/equivalent	1	1.1
	Diploma 2	3	3.3
	Diploma 3	7	7.6
	Diploma 4 or undergraduate degree	46	50
	Master's degree	32	34.8
	Doctoral degree	3	3.3
Work experience	1–5 years	9	9.8
	6–10 years	17	18.5
	11–15 years	13	14.1
	16 and over	53	57.6
Study Program in Last Education	Library and information science	60	65.2
	Non-library and information science	32	34.8
Position	Head of library	8	8.7
	Librarian	45	48.9
	Library technician	13	14.1
	Experts in the field of libraries	26	28.3

Table 4 presents the relationships between the demographic factors and technostress variables using paired samples t-tests. Significant differences were detected in both techno-overload and techno-complexity with gender, work experience, last education, study program and position, but there is no significant difference with age. Furthermore, there are significant differences between the techno-invasion, techno-insecurity and technostress variables and gender, age, work experience, last education and study program. However, there is no significant difference between job position and techno-invasion, techno-insecurity and technostress. Techno-uncertainty and role overload have the same results, meaning that there are significant differences within the overall demographic data.

Table 4. Paired samples t-tests between demographic factors and technostress

	Techno-overload	Techno-invasion	Techno-complexity	Techno-insecurity	Techno-uncertainty	Role Overload	Technostress
Gender	9.403**	6.842**	18.014**	4.963**	16.547**	9.191**	9.000**
Age	−1.008 $p = 0.316$	−4.851**	1.715 $p = 0.090$	−8.652**	2.497*	−4.669**	−4.758**
Last education	−21.191**	−25.867**	−22.296**	−29.305**	−20.500**	−26.474**	−27.728**
Study program	10.536**	7.054**	18.830**	6.176**	18.049**	10.473**	9.940**
Work experience	−4.349**	−7.249**	−3.417, $p = 0.001$*	−10.330**	−3.231, $p = 0.002$*	−7.400**	−7.736**
Position	3.786**	1.00, $p = 0.320$	6.176**	−0.527, $p = 0.599$	6.620**	2.093, $p = 0.002$*	1.865, $p = 0.065$

* $p < 0.05$, ** $p < 0.000$

5 Discussion

5.1 Main Findings

This study found that academic librarians experienced low technostress during the pandemic because they could use digital scholarship technology well. Most respondents are in the 40–65-year-old age group. Techno-overload and techno-uncertainty scored highly because of the increased use of digital tools. This is in line with the research of Karr-Wisniewski and Lu [21] and Schmitt et al. [46], which focused on a change in work routines or expectations of working longer and faster. Technological complexity is a challenge when carrying out tasks because unexpected requests for new skills and tight deadlines can cause health problems [28, 45].

However, the first, second and third techno-complexity items were edited into positive questions to prevent respondents from inadvertently providing a wrong answer [11]. This positive question contradicts the concept of techno-complexity from Tarafdar et al. [56], so there is a possibility that the overall calculation was affected. The researcher tried to calculate the level of technostress without the techno-complexity variable, which showed low scores (M = 2.22, SD = 0.677). Meanwhile, the calculation involving the techno-complexity variable, which consisted of three items, also showed that the level of technostress was low (M = 2.22, SD = 0.724). Thus, the results of the two arithmetical experiments show that the change in the wording of the questions did not change the outcome of the experiment.

The results of this study have similarities and differences with research conducted by Murgu [30]. In those results [30], the technostress level of librarians is not high, with an average score of 2.19. Furthermore, the research variable with the highest average score was role overload, whereas the techno-insecurity variable received the lowest average score. Meanwhile, in the current study, the techno-uncertainty variable had the highest average score, and techno-insecurity had the lowest average score. The other similarities are as follows: 1) Librarians must change their work habits to adapt to new technologies; 2) They must update their technology skills so that they are not replaced; 3) There are new technological developments; 4) Librarians are not able to meet everyone's expectations in a given time.

There were 86 respondents in Murgu's study [30] from ARL institutions, and the demographic data consisted of full-time equivalency, team and age. A total of 44 respondents (51%) worked full time at 1–75%, while the rest (42) worked at 75–100%. A total of 59 respondents (69%) worked in teams with an average of 5 (five) members, and the rest worked independently. Most respondents were 26–45 years old (78%), and the remainder were 46–60 years old. Significant difference testing was conducted using the independent sample t-test, and the results showed no significant difference between technostress based on full-time equivalency, team and age.

This study's findings were different from those of Murgu's [30] research in several ways. There were 92 respondents, and the demographic data consisted of gender, age, final education, work experience, study program and position. The research sample covers all of Indonesia because the study intends to discover the number of academic librarians in Indonesia who work in digital scholarship. Most of the respondents in this study were 40–65 years old (65.2%), and others were 20–39 years old (34.8%). The results of the paired samples t-test in this study revealed that there were significant differences and relationships between technostress and demographic data, with the exception of job position.

5.2 Implications of Technostress in Digital Scholarship

Changing work habits to adapt to new technology is the main trigger for librarians to experience technostress. Gillespie et al. [18] in Ahmad and Amin [2] say that introducing new technologies can increase workloads and stress among academic staff. In addition, individuals already using ICT proficiently can adapt and be proactive more quickly, but this does not apply to those who do not have good digital literacy [31]. Therefore, a librarian who does not have strong digital literacy skills will be challenged to adapt to new technology and change work habits.

Change becomes a scourge to organizations when it generates uncertainty that can threaten the continuity of working life, and concerns arise about the ability to continue working [40, 43, 47]. Similarly, job insecurity motivates librarians to update their library skills continuously so that they can retain their jobs and not be replaced. Job insecurity is defined as a condition experienced by a person because of changes in the environment (external factors) and the character, personality or mentality of the person who experiences these conditions (internal factors) [47]. Two triggering factors are unprecedented technological changes [32] and increased competitiveness within a company [8].

The development and deployment of new technology that librarians need to use also causes higher technostress. Andre [4] in Ahmad and Amin [2] revealed that the slightest change could be disruptive as technology continues to change. According to Cooper and Straw [12] in Wartono and Mochtar [57], introducing new technology at work requires employees to adapt. Continuous introductions of new technology will put pressure on employee schedules, leading to overwork. In addition, automated equipment gives employees fewer roles in production, which leads to work stress, according to Suci [52]. Both excessive and light workloads due to the development of new technologies are equally stressful.

Feelings of not being able to meet people's expectations are found in employees who are required to fulfill their roles at their workplaces. This feeling is one of the signs of impostor syndrome, which occurs when success is achieved not as a result of one's abilities but instead due to favorable circumstances or excessive effort [35]. Bravata et al. [10] found that employees who do not accept recognition when they are successful or who often question their professional abilities are at high risk of developing impostor syndrome. Pannhausen et al. [35] stated that someone with a high level of impostor syndrome believes that other people have high expectations of them, feels pressured to be perfect, and feels criticized when presenting their results. Both studies suggest that impostor syndrome makes a person feel their ability is insufficient to carry out their duties and roles at work.

A group of 40–65-year-old respondents in this study contradicts the stereotype that older workers find it challenging to adapt because they are less creative, less interested in developing technology and less suitable for teamwork [9]. Older workers are freer and have more flexible time to complete their work when faced with limited time in which to solve problems [49]. Bartkowiak et al. [9] found that the older workers with more work experience coped well with stress and experienced less stress. Many librarians in Indonesia are older, with long work experience. Because of the moratorium on hiring, there has been no employee recruitment for 5 (five) years in Indonesian academic libraries [37].

5.3 Limitations

The technostress instrument used is based on an adaptation of Murgu's [30] research, which was translated into Indonesian to suit environmental conditions. The translation enabled the academic librarians to understand each question clearly. Until now, the total number of academic librarians in Indonesia has not been known for certain, so this study uses simple random sampling. This study considers academic librarians to be professionals because FPPTI members work at private and public universities. As a result, the study does not include the origin and the region of the academic institution, so it cannot locate the type of educational institution in the demographic data.

The scale in the research instrument is from 1 to 4 because Indonesians are prone to central tendency bias, namely, the tendency to choose a scale value that is closer to the midpoint and avoid the ends of the scale [16]. The data collection period was only a month that coincided with the pandemic; a longer collection period may yield different results. Librarians were not interviewed directly, so the study was unable to investigate the primary triggers of technostress as deeply as interviews might have revealed.

6   Conclusion and Suggestions for Future Research

The results reveal that academic librarians in Indonesia experienced low technostress during the Covid-19 pandemic. However, librarians have difficulties in adapting to new technological developments and feel unable to meet the expectations and needs of others. therefore, librarians change work habits and add technology skills so that they are not replaced when changes occur in the organization for which they work. These findings are similar to those of Murgu [30] at the ARL institutions and Ahmad and Amin [2] in Malaysia, in that they all agree that the level of Academic Librarians' Technostress is not high.

These findings are expected to act as a reference for future technostress studies and for policies related to digital scholarship that may be implemented in academic libraries especially in Indonesia. This research can also offer a resource for library science and information related to psychology, IT and library management. Future research should also include the type of work based on career length to distinguish between the levels of technostress among librarians. Research in other fields, such as health sciences or other fields of science, can explore the concept of digital scholarship in the Indonesian language, which has not yet been examined.

Acknowledgements. The authors thank the anonymous reviewers for their constructive comments to improve the article. This work was supported in part by the PUTI Q2 contract NKB-1201/UN2.RST/HKP.05.00/2022. Any opinions, findings, and conclusions described here are the authors' and do not necessarily reflect those of the sponsors.

References

1. Abrigo, C., Labangon, D.L.G.: The library as a digital scholarship hub: opportunities for leveraging learning support. Qual. Quant. Methods Libr. **10**(4), 585–608 (2022). http://78.46. 229.148/ojs/index.php/qqml/article/view/742
2. Ahmad, U.N.U., Amin, S.M.: The dimensions of technostress among academic librarians. Procedia. Soc. Behav. Sci. **65**, 266–271 (2012). https://doi.org/10.1016/j.sbspro.2012.11.121
3. Andayani, U.: Pustakawan akademik sebagai mitra riset di perguruan tinggi. Al Maktabah **15**(1), 29–40 (2016). https://doi.org/10.15408/almaktabah.v15i1.4712
4. Andre, R.: Organizational Behavior: An Introduction to Your Life in Organizations. Pearson Education Inc, Upper Saddle River, New Jersey (2008)
5. Arnetz, B.B., Wiholm, C.: Technological stress: psychophysiological symptoms in modern offices. J. Psychosom. Res. **43**(1), 35–42 (1997). https://doi.org/10.1016/S0022-3999(97)000 83-4
6. Atanasoff, L., Venable, M.A.: Technostress: implications for adults in the workforce. Career Dev. Q. **65**(4), 326–338 (2017). https://doi.org/10.1002/cdq.12111
7. Ayers, E.D.: Does digital scholarship have a future? EDUCAUSE Review. https://er.educause. edu/articles/2013/8/does-digital-scholarship-have-a-future/. Accessed 10 Mar 2022
8. Balz, A., Schuller, K.: Always looking for something better? The impact of job insecurity on turnover intentions: do employables and irreplaceables react differently? Econ. Ind. Democr. **42**(1), 142–159 (2018). https://doi.org/10.1177/0143831X18757058
9. Bartkowiak, G., Krugiełka, A., Kostrzewa-Demczuk, P., Dachowski, R., Gałek-Bracha, K.: Experiencing stress among different professional groups in the context of their age. Int. J. Environ. Res. Publ. Health. **19**(2), 1–7 (2022). https://doi.org/10.3390/ijerph19020622
10. Bravata, D.M., et al.: Prevalence, predictors, and treatment of impostor syndrome: a systematic review. J. Gen. Intern. Med. **35**(4), 1252–1275 (2019). https://doi.org/10.1007/s11606-019-05364-1
11. Bryman, A.: Social Research Methods, 4th edn. Oxford University Press, New York, NY (2012)
12. Cooper, C., Strow, A.: Stres Manajemen yang Sukses Dalam Sepekan. Mega Poin, Jakarta (2000)
13. Cox, J.: Communicating new library roles to enable digital scholarship: a review article. New Rev. Acad. Librariansh. **22**(2–3), 132–147 (2016). https://doi.org/10.1080/13614533.2016. 1181665
14. Davis, K., Newstrom, J.W.: Perilaku Dalam Organisasi. 7th edn. Erlangga, Jakarta (2008)
15. Digital Scholarship Support in ARL Member Libraries: An Overview. https://www.arl.org/ digital-scholarship-support-in-arl-member-libraries-an-overview/. Accessed 11 Mar 2022
16. Douven, I.: A Bayesian perspective on Likert scales and central tendency. Psychon. Bull. Rev. **25**(3), 1203–1211 (2018). https://doi.org/10.3758/S13423-017-1344-2/FIGURES/3
17. Ferziani, A., Rajagukguk, R.O., Analya, P.: Types of technostress on employees of IT consulting company. In: 2018 International Conference on Orange Technologies (ICOT), pp. 1–5. IEEE (2018). https://doi.org/10.1109/ICOT.2018.8705838
18. Gillespie, N.A., Walsh, M., Winefield, A.H., Dua, J., Stough, C.: Occupational stress in universities: staff perceptions of the causes, consequences and moderators of stress. Work Stress. **15**(1), 53–72 (2001). https://doi.org/10.1080/02678370117944
19. Imam, A., Ilori, M.E., Shittu, R.A., Oluwafemi, V.S., Adeyemi, O.R.: Techno-stress incidence of occupational stress on job productivity of academic librarians in three selected federal universities in southwest Nigeria. Libr. Philos. Pract. 1–12 (2022). Retrieved from https://www.proquest.com/scholarly-journals/techno-stress-incidence-occ upational-on-job/docview/2632217568/se-2

20. Iskamto, D.: Stress and its impact on employee performance. Int. J. Soc. Manage. Stud. **2**(3), 142–148 (2021). https://doi.org/10.5555/IJOSMAS.V2I3.42

21. Karr-Wisniewski, P., Lu, Y.: When more is too much: operationalizing technology overload and exploring its impact on knowledge worker productivity. Comput. Hum. Behav. **26**(5), 1061–1072 (2010). https://doi.org/10.1016/j.chb.2010.03.008

22. King, M.: Digital scholarship librarian: what skills and competences are needed to be a collaborative librarian. Int. Inf. Libr. Review **50**(1), 40–46 (2018). https://doi.org/10.1080/10572317.2017.1422898

23. Kwanya, T., Stilwell, C., Underwood, P.: Technostress and technolust: coping mechanisms among academic librarians in eastern and southern Africa. In: Proceedings of the International Conference on ICT Management for Global Competitiveness and Economic Growth in Emerging Economies, pp. 302–313. ICTM, Wroclaw (2012). https://citeseerx.ist.psu.edu/viewdoc/download?doi=10.1.1.690.8438&rep=rep1&type=pdf#page=306

24. la Torre, G., de Leonardis, V., Chiappetta, M.: Technostress: how does it affect the productivity and life of an individual? Results of an observational study. Public Health **189**, 60–65 (2020). https://doi.org/10.1016/J.PUHE.2020.09.013

25. Leavy, P.: Research Design: Quantitative, Qualitative, Mixed Methods, Arts-Based, and Community-Based Participatory Research Approaches. The Guildford Press, New York (2017)

26. Li, B., Song, Y., Lu, X., Zhou, L.: Making the digital turn: identifying the user requirements of digital scholarship services in university libraries. J. Acad. Librariansh. **46**(2), 1–11 (2020). https://doi.org/10.1016/j.acalib.2020.102135

27. Masrek, M.N., Yuwinanto, H.P., Atmi, R.T., Soesantari, T., Mutia, F.: Cultural intelligence and job performance of academic librarians in Indonesia. J. Acad. Librariansh. **47**(5), 102394 (2021). https://doi.org/10.1016/J.ACALIB.2021.102394

28. Morris, M.G., Venkatesh, V.: Enterprise resource planning systems implementation and organizational change: impacts on job characteristics and job satisfaction. MIS Q. **34**(1), 143–161 (2010)

29. Mulligan, R.: SPEC Kit 350: supporting digital scholarship (May 2016). Association of Research Libraries (2016).https://doi.org/10.29242/spec.350

30. Murgu, C.: A modern disease of adaptation…?: Technostress and academic librarians working in digital scholarship at ARL institutions. J. Acad. Librariansh. **47**(5), 1–14 (2021). https://doi.org/10.1016/J.ACALIB.2021.102400

31. Mustika, M.D., Handoko, A.M., Mamoen, H.A., Siahaan, D.U., Yasyfin, A.: Your gadgets, stress, and performance: the influence of technostress on individual satisfaction and performance. Psychol. Res. Urban Soc. **4**(2), 18–28 (2021). https://doi.org/10.7454/proust.v4i2.113

32. Nam, T.: Technology usage, expected job sustainability, and perceived job insecurity. Technol. Forecast. Soc. Chang. **138**, 155–165 (2019). https://doi.org/10.1016/j.techfore.2018.08.017

33. Nurkamilah, S., Nashihuddin, W.: Upaya Perpustakaan dalam Membangun Kolaborasi Riset Pustakawan di Universitas Sebelas Maret Surakarta. Tik Ilmeu: Jurnal Ilmu Perpustakaan Dan Informasi **5**(1), 1–16 (2021). https://doi.org/10.29240/tik.v5i1.2279

34. Ocran, T.K., Afful-Arthur, P.: The role of digital scholarship in academic libraries, the case of University of Cape Coast: opportunities and challenges Libr. Hi Tech. (2021).https://doi.org/10.1108/LHT-09-2020-0238

35. Pannhausen, S., Klug, K., Rohrmann, S.: Never good enough: the relation between the impostor phenomenon and multidimensional perfectionism. Curr. Psychol. **41**(2), 888–901 (2020). https://doi.org/10.1007/s12144-020-00613-7

36. Questionnaire method of data collection. https://microbenotes.com/questionnaire-method-of-data-collection/. Accessed 12 Mar 2022

37. Rachmawati, R., Royani, Y.: Pengaruh Psikologis selama WFH Terhadap Produktivitas Kerja Pustakawan di Lingkungan PDDI-LIPI. VISI PUSTAKA: Buletin Jaringan Informasi Antar Perpustakaan **23**(1), 23–32 (2021). https://doi.org/10.37014/visipustaka.v23i1.1044

38. Rinaldi, A., Novalia, Syazali, M.: Statistika Inferensial untuk Ilmu Sosial dan Pendidikan. IPB Press, Bogor (2021)

39. Rumsey, A.S.: Scholarly Communication Institute 9 (New-Model Scholarly Communication: Road Map for Change). (2011). http://uvasci.org/institutes-2003-2011/SCI-9-Road-Map-for-Change.pdf

40. Salasa, S., Murni, T.W., Emaliyawati, E.: Pemberdayaan pada Kelompok Remaja melalui Pendekatan Contingency Planning dalam Meningkatkan Kesiapsiagaan terhadap Ancaman Kematian Akibat Bencana. Jurnal Pendidikan Keperawatan Indonesia **3**(2), 154 (2011). https://doi.org/10.17509/jpki.v3i2.9421

41. Salazar-Concha, C., Ficapal-Cusí, P., Boada-Grau, J., Camacho, L.J.: Analyzing the evolution of technostress: a science mapping approach. Heliyon. **7**(4),1–9 (2021). doi:https://doi.org/10.1016/j.heliyon.2021.e06726

42. Samosir, Z.Z., Syahfitri, I.: Faktor Penyebab Stres Kerja Pustakawan pada Perpustakaan Universitas Sumatera Utara. Pustaha: Jurnal Studi Perpustakaan Dan Informasi **4**(2), 60–69 (2008). http://203.189.121.7/~puslit2_ejournal/ejournal/index.php/pus/article/view/17236

43. Santosa, T.E.C.: Analisis Hubungan Antara Kontrak Psikologi Baru, Pengalaman Kerja, Kepuasan Kerja, dan Kreativitas Pekerja : Studi Empiris pada Pekerja di Industri Perbankan. Jurnal Kajian Bisnis **13**(1), 74–93 (2005)

44. Sari, R.: Pengantar Penelitian Kuantitatif. Deepublish, Yogyakarta (2017)

45. Satpathy, S., Patel, G., Kumar, K.: Identifying and ranking techno-stressors among IT employees due to work from home arrangement during Covid-19 pandemic. Decision **48**(4), 391–402 (2021). https://doi.org/10.1007/s40622-021-00295-5

46. Schmitt, J.B., Breuer, J., Wulf, T.: From cognitive overload to digital detox: psychological implications of telework during the COVID-19 pandemic. Comput. Hum. Behav. **124**, 106899 (2021). https://doi.org/10.1016/J.CHB.2021.106899

47. Setiawan, R., Hadianto, B.: Job Insecurity dalam Organisasi. Jurnal Manajemen Maranatha **7**(2), 69–79 (2008). https://doi.org/10.28932/JMM.V7I2.206

48. Setyaningsih, R., Abdullah, A., Prihantoro, E., Hustinawaty, H.: Model Penguatan Literasi Digital Melalui Pemanfaatan E-learning. Jurnal ASPIKOM **3**(6), 1200–1214 (2019). https://doi.org/10.24329/aspikom.v3i6.333

49. Shultz, K.S., Wang, M., Crimmins, E.M., Fisher, G.G.: Age differences in the demand–control model of work stress: an examination of data from 15 European countries. J. Appl. Gerontol. **29**(1), 21–47 (2009). https://doi.org/10.1177/0733464809334286

50. SPSS Tutorials : Paired Samples t Test. https://libguides.library.kent.edu/SPSS/PairedSamplestTest. Accessed 13 Apr 2022

51. Stefany, S., Nurbani, Badarrudin: Literasi Digital dan Pembukaan Diri: Studi Korelasi Penggunaan Media Sosial Pada Pelajar Remaja di Kota Medan. Sosioglobal: Jurnal Pemikiran Dan Penelitian Sosiologi. **2**(1), 10–31 (2017). https://doi.org/10.24198/jsg.v2i1.15268

52. Suci, I.S.M.: Analisis Hubungan Faktor Individu dan Beban Kerja Mental dengan Stres Kerja. Indonesian J. Occup. Saf. Health **7**(2), 220 (2018). https://doi.org/10.20473/ijosh.v7i2.2018.220-229

53. Sulistyo-Basuki, Lawanda, I.I., Hariyadi, U.B.R., Laksmi.: Perpustakaan dan Informasi dalam Konteks Budaya. Departemen Ilmu Perpustakaan dan Informasi - Fakultas Ilmu Budaya - Universitas Indonesia, Depok (2006)

54. Suryanto, S., Sasi, T.R.: Technostress: Pengertian, Penyebab dan Koping Pustakawan. Pustabiblia: J. Libr. Inf. Sci. **1**(2), 209–221 (2006). https://doi.org/10.18326/pustabiblia.v1i2.209-222

55. Taber, K.S.: The use of Cronbach's Alpha when developing and reporting research instruments in science education. Res. Sci. Educ. **48**(6), 1273–1296 (2016). https://doi.org/10.1007/s11 165-016-9602-2

56. Tarafdar, M., Tu, Q., Ragu-Nathan, B.S., Ragu-Nathan, T.S.: The impact of technostress on role stress and productivity. J. Manag. Inf. Syst. **24**(1), 301–328 (2007). https://doi.org/10. 2753/MIS0742-1222240109

57. Wartono, T., Mochtar, S.: Stres dan Kinerja di Lingkungan Kerja yang Semakin Kompetitif. KREATIF : Jurnal Ilmiah Prodi Manajemen Universitas Pamulang. **2**(2), 153–171 (2007). https://doi.org/10.32493/jk.v2i2.y2014.p%25p

MORTY: Structured Summarization for Targeted Information Extraction from Scholarly Articles

Mohamad Yaser Jaradeh[1]([✉]) [iD], Markus Stocker[2] [iD], and Sören Auer[2] [iD]

[1] L3S Research Center, Leibniz University, Hannover, Germany
`jaradeh@l3s.de`
[2] Leibniz Information Centre for Science and Technology, Hanover, Germany
`{markus.stocker,auer}@tib.eu`

Abstract. Information extraction from scholarly articles is a challenging task due to the sizable document length and implicit information hidden in text, figures, and citations. Scholarly information extraction has various applications in exploration, archival, and curation services for digital libraries and knowledge management systems. We present MORTY, an information extraction technique that creates structured summaries of text from scholarly articles. Our approach condenses the article's full-text to property-value pairs as a segmented text snippet called structured summary. We also present a sizable scholarly dataset combining structured summaries retrieved from a scholarly knowledge graph and corresponding publicly available scientific articles, which we openly publish as a resource for the research community. Our results show that structured summarization is a suitable approach for targeted information extraction that complements other commonly used methods such as question answering and named entity recognition.

Keywords: Information extraction · Scholarly knowledge · Summarization · Natural language processing · Literature review completion

1 Introduction

By their very nature, scholarly articles tend to be dense with information and knowledge [20]. The task of information extraction (IE) has been widely researched by the community in a variety of contexts [3,13,22], including the scholarly domain [19,35]. However, information extraction from scholarly articles continues to suffer from low accuracy. Reasons include ambiguity of scholarly text, information representation in scholarly articles, and lack of training datasets [29].

Other than retrospective information extraction, initiatives such as the ORKG [9], Hi-Knowledge [11], and Coda [31] collect structured scholarly information by engaging researchers in the knowledge curation process. In ORKG,

© The Author(s), under exclusive license to Springer Nature Switzerland AG 2022
Y.-H. Tseng et al. (Eds.): ICADL 2022, LNCS 13636, pp. 290–300, 2022.
https://doi.org/10.1007/978-3-031-21756-2_23

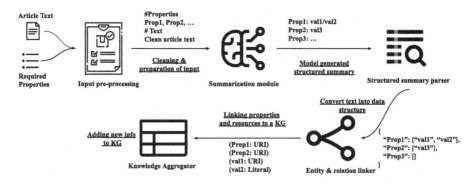

Fig. 1. Bird's eye view on the complete workflow of employing structured summarization in the context of information extraction from scholarly documents and articles (MORTY).

information is collected by experts that extract and structure the essential information from articles. However, experts might not use the exact wording from the original article or might put forward a novel segment of text that did not exist before in the original text.

Information extraction techniques [28] could play a supporting role through automated extraction, suggestions to experts or autonomously adding extracted information to a a data source (e.g. database or knowledge graph). However, blindly extracting information (i.e. factual extractions) is not suitable for scholarly data due to the large amount of information condensed into little text. Blind extraction refers to Open Information Extraction [8] that relies on propositions and facts as well as common entities and relations between them. For scholarly articles, a more targeted approach is required, whereby a system is able to extract a set of predefined properties and their corresponding values while ignoring others.

We propose MORTY, a method that leverages summarization tasks conducted by deep-learning language models to create structured summaries that can be parsed into extracted information, stored in a knowledge graph. We present, evaluate, and discuss MORTY. Furthermore, we highlight the research problems, possible solutions, limitations of the approach, and review open questions and future prospects.

The core contributions of this article are: First, a dataset of paper full texts with a list of property-value pairs of human-expert annotated information. Second, an approach for information extraction from scholarly articles using structured summarization.[1]

---

[1] Code & data (with stats): https://github.com/YaserJaradeh/MORTY.

2   Related Work

Information Extraction. Several information extraction methods have been proposed by the community, each with their own advantages and disadvantages. Ji et al. [12] proposed an end-to-end system that uses a multi-task model to perform sentence classification and information extraction on legal documents. TRIE [42] uses end-to-end system to jointly perform document reading and information extraction on everyday documents such as invoices, tickets, and resumes. Chua and Duffy [4] proposes a method for finding the suitable grammar set for the parsing and the extraction of information. Specifically for scholarly context, various systems has been created to extract and retrieve information from publications and scholarly articles. exBERT [10] uses triple classification to perform knowledge graph completion. Dasigi et al. [6] proposed a method to retrieve information from papers to answer natural language questions. FNG-IE [32] is an improved graph-based approach for the extraction of keywords from scholarly big-data. Furthermore, Liu et al. [15] presents the TableSeer system that is capable of metadata extraction from tables of scholarly nature.

Language Models. With regards to automated text summarization, various language models relying on attention mechanisms [34] displayed state-of-the-art results superseding human performance. BERT [7] (scholarly counterpart SciB-ERT [1]) are some of the most commonly used transformer models capable to automatically summarize text. Similarly, RoBERTa [16] is an optimized approach to represent language and is capable of producing summarizations of text. BART [14] is a sequence-to-sequence model trained as a denoising autoencoder, which improves on the pre-training phase. Zhang et al. [41] presents the PEGA-SUS model trained for abstractive summary generation of text. These and other models are usually built to handle "short" input sequences, e.g. 512-1K tokens. Other attempts address the issue of processing longer inputs. BigBird [40] and Longformer [2] present models that are capable of handling a much larger input, e.g. 4K-16K tokens. Other generational models aren't created specifically for one task; instead, they are capable of performing multiple tasks depending on the input text. For instance, GPT2 [23] supports unconditional text generation. Raffel et al. [24] describe T5, a model that can perform summarization, translation, and question answering based on keywords in the input text. Some of these language models have been either pre-trained on scholarly data such as PubMed[2] and arXiv [5] datasets, or have been fine-tuned on such data for empirical evaluation in their original publication. Our contribution in this article leverages the capabilities of automatic summarization for the objective of information extraction form scholarly documents.

---

[2] https://www.nlm.nih.gov/databases/download/pubmed_medline.html.

3   MORTY

Scholarly text is ambiguous and information dense. We illustrate the problem by taking a look at the abstract of this article. If we want to extract a single piece of information (i.e. a property) such as the "research problem" addressed by the article, it is necessary to comprehend the text and look even behind the textual representation. In this example, the research problem is "information extraction from scholarly articles". The method of looking up certain properties such as "research problem" in the text, proves insufficient because the phrase may not exist as is or is spelled differently. This can be extend by looking up synonyms for the property or by finding verbs that represent the same intent (e.g., addresses, tackles, etc.). Other times, regardless of how the property is represented, the value itself is implicit or not represented as expected, which requires more abstractive answers than extractive ones [33].

We argue that these cases barely scratch the surface of the problem. Certain properties could require values placed throughout the text, combined together, and even morphed into dissimilar wording. Others, cannot be found in the text, but are included in figures, tables, or even in citations [26,37]. Furthermore, some properties could be of annotation-nature, i.e. the property and the value are not in the original text, but tacit knowledge of an expert annotating an article.

MORTY leverages the capabilities of deep learning language models to comprehend the semantics of scholarly text and perform targeted information extraction via text summarization. Scholarly articles typically follow a certain structure. IMRaD [30] refers to Introduction, Methods, Results, Discussion. The concept has been applied to abstracts for a high-level overview of the four essential aspects of the work. Structured abstracts [18] follows the IMRaD principles by including the same points in the abstract. This motivated us to incorporate structure into automatic textual summaries, which can be easily parsed for the sake of information extraction (a.k.a. structured summary).

Figure 1 depicts a high-level view of the MORTY approach to information extraction on scholarly articles comprising several workflow phases. It starts with pre-processing of the article text (i.e., the conversion from traditional PDF into text as well as cleaning and removing some needless segments of the text). A summarization model is then capable of rendering a large text snippet into a much shorter structured summarization that contains pairs of properties and their corresponding values. Later stages take care of parsing the produced summary via finding pre-defined syntactical patterns in the produced text. Then interlinking extracted values to knowledge graph entities via exact lookup functionalities. Lastly the newly extracted and aligned data gets added it to a destination knowledge graph. The fundamental component of the approach is the summarization module due to the fact that all other components of MORTY are self-consistent. This article tackles the following research question (**RQ**): *How can we leverage structured summaries for the task of scholarly information extraction?*

4   Evaluation

Since the main component of MORTY is the structured summary generation, **we focus our evaluation on that component solely**. Other components of the approach are deterministic in behavior and can be disregarded for the sake of this evaluation. We created a dataset using the ORKG infrastructure, and empirically evaluated the feasibility of the summarization task with various models and approaches based on this dataset.

4.1   Dataset Collection

We require a source for human-curated annotations of scholarly articles. ORKG is a knowledge graph that contains this sort of information. Hence, we leverage the ORKG to create a dataset of scholarly articles' texts with a set of property-value pairs. First, we took a snapshot of the ORKG data[3] and we filtered on papers that are open access or have pre-prints on arXiv. This ensures restriction-free access to the PDF files of articles. Second, we parse the PDF files using GROBID [17] into text. Furthermore, we employ a heuristic to clean the text. The heuristic involves the following steps: i) Remove a set of pre-defined sections (such as abstract, related work, background, acknowledgments, and references); ii) Remove all URLs from the text, as well as all Unicode characters; iii) Remove tables, figures, footnotes, and citation texts. Lastly, we collect all annotations from the ORKG excluding some properties that contain values of URIs and other structural properties[4]. Afterwards that data was collected in a format that the summarization model is trained on and can process. We split the data in 80–10-10 training-validation-testing split in favor of the testing set.

4.2   Baselines

Throughout the evaluation, multiple baselines were investigated (see Table 1). Various language models were used that are capable and pre-trained on summarization tasks. The maximum input size for each model varies depending on its architecture. In our created dataset, the average entry contained around 5K tokens, with a maximum around 9K and a minimum around 1.5K. Some of the models we used (e.g. Pegasus) are capable of abstractive summarization, i.e. can create summaries with words that don't exist in the original input text. This is important when annotated properties and values are not present in the text, but are formulated differently.

Furthermore, the feasibility of the task is evaluated using two other categories of NLP tasks. Extractive question answering (similarly to [39]) language models are leveraged to try to extract values for certain questions. The questions are formulated as follows: "what is the {property-label}?". This type of baselines is

---

[3] Data snapshot was taken on 02.02.2022.
[4] Properties that are used solely for information organization and have no semantic value.

Table 1. Overview of models used in the evaluation, categorized per task. With the number of parameters, the max input size they can handle, and what dataset they are fine-tuned on beforehand to our training.

Model	# of Params	Input Size	Finetuned on
Summarization			
ProphetNet-large [38]	391 M	2 K	CNN
BART-large [14]	460 M	4 K	CNN
GPT2-large [23]	774 M	2 K	–
Pegasus-large [41]	568 M	2 K	Pubmed
BigBird-large [40]	576 M	4 K	Pubmed
T5-large [24]	770 M	4 K	–
Longformer-large [2]	459 M	8 K	Pubmed
Question Answering			
BERT-large [7]	335 M	1 K	SQuAD2
Longformer-large [2]	459 M	8 K	SQuAD2
Named Entity Recognition			
BERT-large [7]	335 M	1 K	CoNLL
RoBERTa-large [16]	355 M	2 K	CoNLL

inherently flawed because some of the properties and values from the datasets are not as is in the input text. Another method for evaluation is to perform named entity recognition by recognizing the individual values as entities of interest and then classifying them into one of the classes (properties).

4.3   Evaluation Results and Discussion

The evaluation took place on a machine with 2 GPUs RTX A6000 each with a 48GB vRAM. Training scripts where adapted from the fine-tuning scripts of each of model's code repositories with the help of the Transformers [36] library. The training used a batch size = 2 and epochs = 20 with early stopping enabled.

First, we evaluate the performance of various language models for structured summarization. Table 2 shows the results of the Rouge F1 metric (following [41]) for all considered language models. Second, we evaluate the feasibility of the task using techniques other than summarization, namely extractive question answering and using named entity recognition. Though the tasks of summarizations, named entitiy recognition, and question answering are not directly comparable; we include this analysis to show the validity of summarization as a candidate for targeted IE tasks compared to other approaches. Table 3 describes the performance of the two different approaches using two models for each case. Each model has different maximum input size and for the QA task the models were previously tuned on the SQuAD2 [25] and the CoNLL [27] datasets for the NER task. For the QA metrics, the reported number are computed @1, meaning only candidate results at the first place.

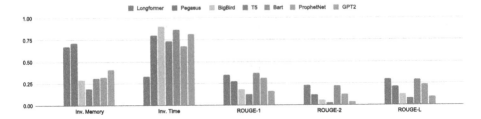

Fig. 2. Summarization metrics overview of used models including the inverse time needed for training, and inverse memory consumption. Time and memory values are normalized and inversed. Higher values are better.

Table 2. Rouge F1 scores for 1-gram, 2-grams, and longest-gram variations of the summarization models. Top best results are indicated in bold, second best in italic.

Table 3. Precision, recall, f1-score results of other baseline models on the question answering (QA) and named entity recognition (NER) tasks.

	Rouge-1	Rouge-2	Rouge-L
ProphetNet	31.1	12.5	23.7
BART	**36.7**	*22.0*	*29.4*
GPT2	16.1	3.6	9.3
Pegasus	27.1	11.7	21.2
BigBird	17.9	5.9	12.5
T5	12.2	2.8	7.9
Longformer	*34.7*	**22.4**	**29.6**

	Precision	Recall	F1-score
Question Answering			
BERT	20.8	18.1	19.1
Longformer	23.7	22.8	23.2
Named Entity Recognition			
BERT	17.2	17.0	17.0
RoBERTa	19.7	19.5	19.6

The results show that the task is viable using summarization and that structured summaries are able to extract the required information out of the scholarly articles. When considering the normal summarization task, i.e. summarizing text into a coherent shorter text snippet, the top model [21] at the time of writing this article are performing with 51.05, 23.26, 46.47 for Rouge 1–2-L respectively[5]. This kind of summarization is far easier than structured summarization since the aim is merely coherent text creation, not structured summary of text fragments. Examining Tables 1 and 2, we note that input size affects the performance of the model. The summarization model requires the processing of the complete input article text to extract values from it, and if the model can not handle the full article then it will suffer in performance metrics. We note that, BART and Longformer summarization models performed best across all metrics.

ProphetNet and Pegaus performed well compared to other models, but they were not able to beat Longformer in part due to limited maximum input size. GPT2 model suffered due to its nature as a generative model. It was not able to generate the structured summary rather generating more coherent text. Surprisingly, although big models with a 4K max input size BigBird and T5 did not perform comparatively to top models in the list.

---

[5] https://paperswithcode.com/sota/text-summarization-on-pubmed-1.

Table 4. Examples: Expected vs. model predicted values.

Property	Expected	MORTY prediction
Preprocessing steps	Topic segmentation Anaphora resolution Pronoun resolution	Anaphora resolution
Data size	139 meetings	20 meetings
Summarization type	Abstractive	Abstractive
Evaluation metrics	ROUGE-2 ROUGE-SU4	F1
Study location	Singapore	The City of Singapore

Figure 2 depicts an overview of the Rouge metrics of the summarization models as well as time and space requirement of each. Though Longformer is the best performing model on average, it requires more time to train compared to BART. On the other hand, BART requires almost twice the memory compared to Longformer.

In order to empirically judge if the summarization method is suitable for the task of information extraction, we evaluate the approach against two categories of tasks: Question Answering (QA) and Named Entity Recognition (NER). Table 3 shows the precision, recall, and f1-score metrics for two models in each category. Due to the nature of the training data and the task itself, these two categories are inherently flawed because they are extractive and not abstractive, meaning that they aim at finding values from within the text, rather than compute with novel values. Thus, these tasks are only able to retrieve parts of the values that are in the text and the rest are unattainable to them. This explains why different models in both tasks preform poorly.

Table 4 shows some examples of five properties from three different articles with the expected values and the predicted values by the summarization model (here Longformer). We observe that the model is able to extract partial values or similar values but with different wordings, as well as exact values, and completely different values. For instance, "Data size" is an annotation property, were the expected value is not in the text, rather it is a summation of other values. "Preprocessing steps" property aggregate values from multiple places in the text. The remarks made in this section answers our research question.

5   Conclusion and Future Directions

The objective of this work was to leverage structured summarization for the task of IE from scholarly articles. We evaluated various models on the summarization task, as well as compared against models performing question answering and named entity recognition. The results show that summarization is a viable and feasible approach for the IE task on scholarly articles. Based on our observations, we suggest the following open points in this domain: i) Enable longer input sizes for large language models and evaluate them. ii) Experiment with various structured summary formats and study their effect. iii) Incorporate active learning with user feedback collected from a user interface within a scholarly infrastructure. iv) Perform a user evaluation to study the efficacy of the IE task on scholarly data for users.

References

1. Beltagy, I., Lo, K., Cohan, A.: SciBERT: a pretrained language model for scientific text. In: Proceedings of the 2019 Conference on Empirical Methods in Natural Language Processing and the 9th International Joint Conference on Natural Language Processing (EMNLP-IJCNLP), pp. 3615–3620. Association for Computational Linguistics, Hong Kong, China (2019). https://doi.org/10.18653/v1/D19-1371

2. Beltagy, I., Peters, M.E., Cohan, A.: Longformer: the long-document transformer. arXiv preprint arXiv:2004.05150 (2020)

3. Chang, C.H., Kayed, M., Girgis, M.R., Shaalan, K.F.: A survey of web information extraction systems. IEEE Trans. Knowl. Data Eng. **18**(10), 1411–1428 (2006)

4. Chua, F.C., Duffy, N.P.: DeepCPCFG: deep learning and context free grammars for end-to-end information extraction. In: Lladós, J., Lopresti, D., Uchida, S. (eds.) Document Analysis and Recognition - ICDAR 2021, pp. 838–853. Springer International Publishing, Cham (2021)

5. Clement, C.B., Bierbaum, M., O'Keeffe, K.P., Alemi, A.A.: On the use of arxiv as a dataset (2019)

6. Dasigi, P., Lo, K., Beltagy, I., Cohan, A., Smith, N.A., Gardner, M.: A dataset of information-seeking questions and answers anchored in research papers. In: Proceedings of the 2021 Conference of the North American Chapter of the Association for Computational Linguistics: Human Language Technologies, pp. 4599–4610. Association for Computational Linguistics (2021). https://doi.org/10.18653/v1/2021.naacl-main.365

7. Devlin, J., Chang, M.W., Lee, K., Toutanova, K.: BERT: pre-training of deep bidirectional transformers for language understanding. arXiv preprint arXiv:1810.04805 (2018)

8. Etzioni, O., Banko, M., Soderland, S., Weld, D.S.: Open information extraction from the web. Commun. ACM **51**(12), 68–74 (2008)

9. Jaradeh, M.Y., et al.: Open research knowledge graph: next generation infrastructure for semantic scholarly knowledge. In: Proceedings of the 10th International Conference on Knowledge Capture, pp. 243–246 (2019)

10. Jaradeh, M.Y., Singh, K., Stocker, M., Auer, S.: Triple classification for scholarly knowledge graph completion. In: Proceedings of the 11th on Knowledge Capture Conference, pp. 225–232. K-CAP 2021, Association for Computing Machinery, New York, NY, USA (2021). https://doi.org/10.1145/3460210.3493582

11. Jeschke, J., et al.: Hi-knowledge, version 2.0. https://hi-knowledge.org/ (2020). Accessed 23 May 2022

12. Ji, D., Tao, P., Fei, H., Ren, Y.: An end-to-end joint model for evidence information extraction from court record document. Inf. Process. Manage. **57**(6), 102305 (2020). https://doi.org/10.1016/j.ipm.2020.102305

13. Pinheiro, V., Pequeno, T., Furtado, V., Nogueira, D.: Information extraction from text based on semantic inferentialism. In: Andreasen, T., Yager, R.R., Bulskov, H., Christiansen, H., Larsen, H.L. (eds.) FQAS 2009. LNCS (LNAI), vol. 5822, pp. 333–344. Springer, Heidelberg (2009). https://doi.org/10.1007/978-3-642-04957-6_29

14. Lewis, M., et al.: BART: denoising sequence-to-sequence pre-training for natural language generation, translation, and comprehension. arXiv preprint arXiv:1910.13461 (2019)

15. Liu, Y., Bai, K., Mitra, P., Giles, C.L.: TableSeer: automatic table metadata extraction and searching in digital libraries. In: Proceedings of the 7th ACM/IEEE-CS Joint Conference on Digital Libraries, pp. 91–100 JCDL 2007, Association for Computing Machinery, New York, NY, USA (2007). https://doi.org/10.1145/1255175.1255193

16. Liu, Y., et al.: RoBERTa: a robustly optimized BERT pretraining approach. arXiv preprint arXiv:1907.11692 (2019)

17. Lopez, P.: GROBID: combining automatic bibliographic data recognition and term extraction for scholarship publications. In: Agosti, M., Borbinha, J., Kapidakis, S., Papatheodorou, C., Tsakonas, G. (eds.) ECDL 2009. LNCS, vol. 5714, pp. 473–474. Springer, Heidelberg (2009). https://doi.org/10.1007/978-3-642-04346-8_62

18. Nakayama, T., Hirai, N., Yamazaki, S., Naito, M.: Adoption of structured abstracts by general medical journals and format for a structured abstract. J. Med. Libr. Assoc. 93(2), 237–242 (2005)

19. Nasar, Z., Jaffry, S.W., Malik, M.K.: Information extraction from scientific articles: a survey. Scientometrics 117(3), 1931–1990 (2018). https://doi.org/10.1007/s11192-018-2921-5

20. Palmatier, R.W., Houston, M.B., Hulland, J.: Review articles: purpose, process, and structure. J. Acad. Mark. Sci. 46(1), 1–5 (2018)

21. Pang, B., Nijkamp, E., Kryściński, W., Savarese, S., Zhou, Y., Xiong, C.: Long document summarization with top-down and bottom-up inference. arXiv preprint arXiv:2203.07586 (2022)

22. Piskorski, J., Yangarber, R.: Information extraction: past, present and future. In: Poibeau, T., Saggion, H., Piskorski, J., Yangarber, R. (eds) Multi-source, Multilingual Information Extraction and Summarization. Theory and Applications of Natural Language Processing. Springer, Heidelberg(2013). https://doi.org/10.1007/978-3-642-28569-1_2

23. Radford, A., et al.: Language models are unsupervised multitask learners. OpenAI blog 1(8), 9 (2019)

24. Raffel, C., et al.: Exploring the limits of transfer learning with a unified text-to-text transformer. arXiv preprint arXiv:1910.10683 (2019)

25. Rajpurkar, P., Jia, R., Liang, P.: Know what you don't know: unanswerable questions for squad. arXiv preprint arXiv:1806.03822 (2018)

26. Ray Choudhury, S., Mitra, P., Giles, C.L.: Automatic extraction of figures from scholarly documents. In: Proceedings of the 2015 ACM Symposium on Document Engineering, pp. 47–50 (2015)

27. Sang, E.F., De Meulder, F.: Introduction to the CoNLL-2003 shared task: language-independent named entity recognition. arXiv preprint arXiv:cs/0306050 (2003)

28. Sarawagi, S.: Information extraction. Now Publishers Inc (2008)

29. Singh, M., et al.: OCR++: a robust framework for information extraction from scholarly articles. CoRR arXiv preprint arXiv:abs/1609.06423 (2016)

30. Sollaci, L.B., Pereira, M.G.: The introduction, methods, results, and discussion (imrad) structure: a fifty-year survey. J. Med. Libr. Assoc. **92**(3), 364–367 (2004). https://pubmed.ncbi.nlm.nih.gov/15243643

31. Spadaro, G., Tiddi, I., Columbus, S., Jin, S., Teije, A.t., Balliet, D.: The cooperation databank: machine-readable science accelerates research synthesis (2020). https://doi.org/10.31234/osf.io/rveh3

32. Tahir, N., et al.: FNG-IE: an improved graph-based method for keyword extraction from scholarly big-data. PeerJ Comput. Sci. **7**, e389 (2021)

33. Tas, O., Kiyani, F.: A survey automatic text summarization. PressAcademia Procedia **5**(1), 205–213 (2007)

34. Vaswani, A., et al.: Attention is all you need. CoRR arXiv preprint arXiv:abs/1706.03762 (2017)

35. Williams, K., Wu, J., Wu, Z., Giles, C.L.: Information extraction for scholarly digital libraries. In: Proceedings of the 16th ACM/IEEE-CS on Joint Conference on Digital Libraries, pp. 287–288 (2016)

36. Wolf, T., et al.: Transformers: state-of-the-art natural language processing. In: Proceedings of the 2020 Conference on Empirical Methods in Natural Language Processing: System Demonstrations, pp. 38–45. Association for Computational Linguistics (2020). www.aclweb.org/anthology/2020.emnlp-demos.6

37. Xia, F., Wang, W., Bekele, T.M., Liu, H.: Big scholarly data: a survey. IEEE Trans. Big Data **3**(1), 18–35 (2017). https://doi.org/10.1109/TBDATA.2016.2641460

38. Yan, Y., et al.: ProphetNet: predicting future N-Gram for sequence-to-sequence pre-training. arXiv preprint arXiv:2001.04063 (2020)

39. Yao, X., Van Durme, B.: Information extraction over structured data: question answering with freebase. In: Proceedings of the 52nd Annual Meeting of the Association for Computational Linguistics (vol. 1: Long Papers), pp. 956–966 (2014)

40. Zaheer, M., et al.: Big bird: transformers for longer sequences. Adv. Neural. Inf. Process. Syst. **33**, 17283–17297 (2020)

41. Zhang, J., Zhao, Y., Saleh, M., Liu, P.: Pegasus: pre-training with extracted gap-sentences for abstractive summarization. In: International Conference on Machine Learning, pp. 11328–11339. PMLR (2020)

42. Zhang, P., et al.: TRIE: end-to-end text reading and information extraction for document understanding, pp. 1413–1422. Association for Computing Machinery, New York, NY, USA (2020). https://doi.org/10.1145/3394171.3413900

Scholarly Knowledge Extraction
from Published Software Packages

Muhammad Haris[1]([✉]) [iD], Markus Stocker[1,2] [iD], and Sören Auer[1,2] [iD]

[1] L3S Research Center, Leibniz University Hannover, 30167 Hannover, Germany
haris@l3s.de, {markus.stocker,auer}@tib.eu
[2] TIB—Leibniz Information Centre for Science and Technology, Hannover, Germany

Abstract. A plethora of scientific software packages are published in
repositories, e.g., Zenodo and figshare. These software packages are
crucial for the reproducibility of published research. As an additional
route to scholarly knowledge graph construction, we propose an approach for automated extraction of machine actionable (structured) scholarly knowledge from published software packages by static analysis of
their (meta)data and contents (in particular scripts in languages such
as Python). The approach can be summarized as follows. First, we
extract metadata information (software description, programming languages, related references) from software packages by leveraging the Software Metadata Extraction Framework (SOMEF) and the GitHub API.
Second, we analyze the extracted metadata to find the research articles
associated with the corresponding software repository. Third, for software contained in published packages, we create and analyze the Abstract
Syntax Tree (AST) representation to extract information about the procedures performed on data. Fourth, we search the extracted information
in the full text of related articles to constrain the extracted information
to scholarly knowledge, i.e. information published in the scholarly literature. Finally, we publish the extracted machine actionable scholarly
knowledge in the Open Research Knowledge Graph (ORKG).

Keywords: Analyzing software packages · Open research knowledge
graph · Code analysis · Abstract syntax tree · Scholarly
communication · Machine actionability

1 Introduction

A variety of general and domain-specific knowledge graphs have been proposed
to represent (scholarly) knowledge in a structured manner [7, 26]. General purpose knowledge graphs include DBpedia[1] [18], Wikidata[2] [25], YAGO [23],
etc., whereas domain-specific infrastructures include approaches in Cultural

---

[1] https://www.dbpedia.org.
[2] https://www.wikidata.org/wiki/Wikidata:Main_Page.

Y.-H. Tseng et al. (Eds.): ICADL 2022, LNCS 13636, pp. 301–310, 2022.
https://doi.org/10.1007/978-3-031-21756-2_24

Heritage [13], KnowLife in Life Sciences [9], Hi-Knowledge in Invasion Biology[3] [8,10], COVID-19 Air Quality Data Collection[4], Papers With Code in Machine Learning[5], Cooperation Databank in Social Sciences[6] [21], among others. In addition, knowledge graph technologies have also been employed to describe software packages in a structured manner [2,16].

Extending the state-of-the-art, we propose an approach for scholarly knowledge extraction from published software packages by static analysis of package contents, i.e., (meta-)data and software (in particular, Python scripts), and represent the extracted knowledge in a knowledge graph. The main purpose of this knowledge graph is to capture information about the materials and methods used in scholarly work described in research articles.

We address the following research question: Can structured scholarly knowledge be automatically extracted from published software packages? Our approach consists of the following steps:

1. *Mining software packages* deposited in Zenodo[7] using its REST API[8] and analyzing the API response to extract the linked metadata information, i.e., associated scholarly articles. We complement the approach by leveraging the Software Metadata Extraction Framework (SOMEF) to parse the README files and extract other related metadata information (i.e., software name, description, used programming languages).
2. *Perform static code analysis* to extract information about the procedures performed on data. We utilize Abstract Syntax Tree (AST) representations to statically analyze program code and identify operations performed on data.
3. *Identify scholarly knowledge* by performing keyword-based search of extracted information in article full text. Thus, among all the information extracted from software packages we identify that which is scholarly knowledge.
4. *Construct a knowledge graph* of scholarly knowledge extracted from software packages. For this purpose, we leverage the Open Research Knowledge Graph (ORKG)[9] [14], a production research infrastructure that supports producing and publishing machine actionable scholarly knowledge.

2   Related Work

Several approaches have been suggested to retrieve metadata from software repositories. Mao et al. [19] proposed the Software Metadata Extraction Framework (SOMEF) to extract metadata from software packages published on GitHub. Specifically, the framework employs machine learning-based methods

---

[3] https://hi-knowledge.org.
[4] https://covid-aqs.fz-juelich.de.
[5] https://paperswithcode.org.
[6] https://cooperationdatabank.org.
[7] https://zenodo.org.
[8] https://developers.zenodo.org.
[9] https://www.orkg.org/orkg/.

to extract repository name, software description, citations, reference URLs, etc. from README files and to represent the metadata in structured formats (JSON-LD, JSON and RDF). SOMEF was later extended to extract additional metadata and auxiliary files (e.g., Notebooks, Dockerfiles) from software packages [16]. Moreover, the extended work also supports creating a knowledge graph of parsed metadata, thus improving search of software deposited in repositories. Abdelaziz et al. [1] proposed CodeBreaker, a knowledge graph with information about 1.3 million Python scripts published on GitHub. The graph was embedded in an IDE to recommend code functions while writing software. Similarly, Graph-Gen4Code [2] is a knowledge graph with information about software included in GitHub repositories. It was generated by analyzing the functionalities of Python scripts and linking them with the natural language artefacts (documentation and forum discussions on StackOverflow and StackExchange). The knowledge graph contains 2 billion triples. Several other machine learning-based approaches for searching [11] software scripts and summarization [3,12] have been proposed. The Pydriller [22] and GitPython[10] frameworks were proposed to mine information from GitHub repositories, including source code, commits, branch differences, etc. Similarly, ModelMine [20] mines and analyzes models included in repositories. Vagavolu et al. [24] presented an approach that leverages Code2vec [17] and includes semantic graphs with Abstract Syntax Tree (AST) for performing different software engineering tasks. [4] presented an AST based-approach for code representation and considered code data flow mechanisms to suggest code improvements.

3   Methodology

In this section, we present our methodology for automatically extracting *scholarly* knowledge from software packages and building a knowledge graph from the extracted meta(data). Figure 1 provides an overview of the key components.

3.1   Mining Software Packages

We mine software packages from the Zenodo repository by leveraging its REST API. The metadata of each package is analyzed to retrieve its DOI and metadata about related versions and associated scholarly articles. The versions of software packages are retrieved by interpreting `relation: isVersionOf` metadata, whereas the DOI of the linked article, if available, is fetched using the `relation: cites` or `relation: isSupplementTo` metadata. We also leverage the Software Metadata Extraction Framework (SOMEF) and GitHub API to extract additional metadata from software packages, in particular software name, description, used programming languages, GitHub URL. Since not all software packages include the `cites` or `isSupplementTo` relations in metadata, we utilize SOMEF to parse the README files of software packages as an additional approach to extract the DOI of the related scholarly article.

---

[10] https://github.com/gitpython-developers/GitPython.

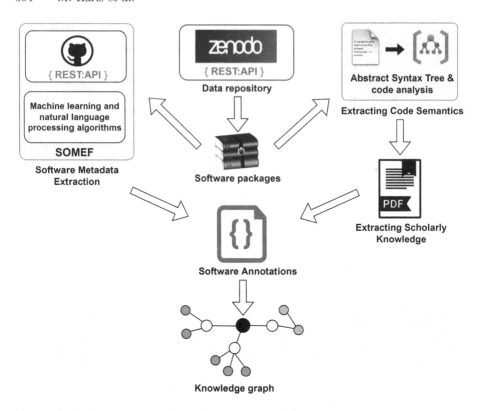

Fig. 1. Pipeline for constructing a knowledge graph of scholarly knowledge extracted from software packages: 1) Mining software packages from the Zenodo repository using its REST API; 2) Extracting software metadata by analyzing the Zenodo API results as well as the GitHub API, using SOMEF; 3) Performing static code analysis using AST representations of software to extract code semantics, in particular operations on data; 4) Performing keywords-based search in article full texts to identify scholarly knowledge; 5) Knowledge graph construction with scholarly knowledge extracted from software packages.

Static Code Analysis. We utilize Abstract Syntax Tree (AST) representations for static analysis of Python scripts included in software packages. AST provides structured representations of scripts, omitting unnecessary syntactic details (e.g., semicolons, commas, and comments). Our goal is to extract information about the data used in scripts and the procedures performed on that data. Our developed Python-based module sequentially reads the scripts contained in software packages and generates the AST. The implemented procedures and variables are tokenized and represented as nodes in the tree, which facilitates the analysis of the code flow. Thus, by traversing the tree we extracts the information about the data used in the scripts, the procedures performed on the data and, if available, the output data.

```
1   test_data = pd.read_csv("Sample.csv")
2   reference = pd.        ("Reference.csv")
3   train = reference.drop("MF_name",1)
4   test_data = test_data.drop("gene",1)
5
6   score_adj = []
7   for o in range(len(test_data.columns)):
8       test = test_data.loc[:,test_data.columns[o]]
9       im_name = train.columns
10      svr = LinearSVR(random_state=0)
11      model = svr.fit(train, test)
12      score = model.coef_
13      score[np.where(score<0)] = 0
14      score_adj.append((score/sum(score)))
15  score_adj = pd.DataFrame(score_adj)
16  score_adj.to_csv("score.csv")
```

Input datasets (lines 1–2)

Output dataset (line 16)

Fig. 2. Static code analysis: Exemplary Python script (shortened) included in a software package. The script lines highlighted with same color show different procedural changes that a particular variable has undergone. (Color figure online)

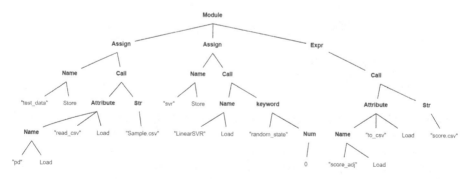

Fig. 3. Abstract Syntax Tree (AST) of the script shown in Fig. 2. For simplicity, the AST is shown only for Lines 1, 10 and 16.

Figure 2 shows the Python script included in the software package[11]. The script shows an example in which `Sample.csv` and `Reference.csv` used as input data, then the operation `LinearSVR` is performed on the data, and finally the resulting data `score.csv` is generated.

Figure 3 shows the AST of the Python script (Fig. 2) created using a suitable Python library[12]. For simplicity, we show the AST of lines 1, 10, and 16. In the tree structure, the name of the node represents the functionality of each line of the script. For example, line 1 performs a task that reads data and `assigns` it to a variable. Therefore, the relevant node in the tree is labelled `Assign`. We retrieve all leaf nodes since they represent variables, their values, and procedures. Analyzing these script semantics, we can then find the flow of data between procedures. We investigate the flow of variables that contain the input data, i.e., examining which operations used a particular variable as a parameter.

3.2   Identifying Scholarly Knowledge

Not all information extracted from software packages and AST-analyzed program code is scholarly knowledge. Information is scholarly knowledge if it is included in a scholarly article. Hence, we filter the information extracted from software packages for information referred to in the article citing the software package. For this, we employ keyword-based search. Specifically, we search for the terms extracted in AST-analyzed program code in the related article full text. Assuming that the DOI of the related article has been identified, we fetch the PDF version of the article by utilizing the Unpaywall REST API[13]. We make use of the Unpaywall API because, contrary to DOI metadata, it provides the URL to the PDF version of scholarly articles. In our example (Fig. 2), the extracted terms (`Sample`, `Reference`, `read_csv`, `LinearSVR`, `svr.fit`, and `to_csv`) are searched in the PDF and we find `Sample`, `Reference` and `LinearSVR` are cited in the scholarly article. We thus assume that the extracted information is scholarly knowledge.

3.3   Knowledge Graph Construction

We now construct the knowledge graph with the scholarly knowledge obtained in the analysis of software packages. For this, we leverage the Open Research Knowledge Graph (ORKG) [14]. The ORKG aims to represent scholarly articles in a machine actionable and structured form. Abstractly speaking, the ORKG represents research contributions describing key results, the materials and methods used to obtain the results, and the addressed research problem.

The scholarly information extracted from software packages in organized in triples and ingesting into ORKG using its REST API. Figure 4 shows the

---

[11] https://zenodo.org/record/5874955.

[12] https://docs.python.org/3/library/ast.html.

[13] https://api.unpaywall.org/v2/10.1186/s12920-019-0613-5?email=unpaywall_01@example.com.

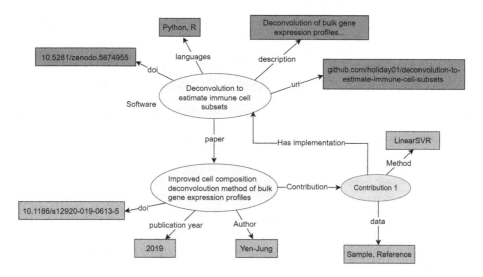

Fig. 4. Knowledge graph depicting the scholarly knowledge extracted from a software package related to an article, describing key aspects (e.g., method used) of a research contribution of the work described in the article.

resulting knowledge graph for a paper and its research contribution[14]. The figure also shows the metadata of corresponding software package[15].

4   Results and Discussion

At the time of writing, there are more than 80,000 software packages available on Zenodo. To expedite the execution process, we discard packages larger than 400 MB. We thus consider 52,236 software packages. We further process only those software packages that are also available on GitHub, that is 40,239 packages. We analyze the metadata of the software packages and the respective README files and find a total of 6221 research articles, of which 642 articles are associated with the related software packages in metadata through the `cites` or `isSupplementTo` relations. The remaining 5579 articles are extracted by analyzing the README files of the software packages using SOMEF. We only analyze software packages that include Python scripts and have linked scholarly articles, that is 2172 packages. Table 1 summarizes the statistics.

Out of 6221 articles, 4328 are described in ORKG because for the remaining articles the DOIs in README files are not parsed correctly. The articles added to ORKG include ORKG research contribution descriptions linking the software package and including information about computational methods and data used in research extracted by analyzing the software packages.

---

[14] https://orkg.org/paper/R209873.
[15] https://orkg.org/content-type/Software/R209880.

Table 1. Statistics about the (scholarly) information extracted from software packages.

Entity	Total
Software package	52236
Paper	Explicit links in metadata: 642; SOMEF-based link extraction: 5579 (Total: 6221)
GitHub URL	40,239
Python-based software packages, linked with articles	2172
Analyzed Python scripts	67,936

Software Semantics and Named Entity Recognition (NER) Models. There exist numerous approaches for the extraction of scholarly knowledge from articles using machine learning and natural language processing, including scientific named entity recognition [6, 15] and sentence classification [5]. These approaches process the entire text to extract the essential entities in scholarly articles, which is costly in terms of data collection and training. Moreover, the approaches require large training data to achieve acceptable performance. We argue that extracting scholarly knowledge from software packages as proposed here is a significant step towards automated and cheap construction of scholarly knowledge graphs. Instead of extracting scholarly entities from full texts using machine learning models, the scholarly knowledge is extracted from related software packages with more structured data.

Future Directions. In future work, we aim to develop a pipeline that will automatically execute the software packages that contain scholarly knowledge. Such an approach can be integrated into software repositories (zenodo, figshare) to automatically execute the published software and determine whether the (extracted) scholarly knowledge is reproducible.

5   Conclusions

Our work is an important step towards automated and scalable mining of scholarly knowledge from published software packages and creating the knowledge graph using the extracted data. The resulting knowledge graph holds the links between articles and software packages, as well as and most interestingly descriptions of the computational methods and materials used in research work presented in articles. Evaluated on zenodo, our approach can be extended to other repositories, e.g., figshare, as well as software in languages other than Python, e.g., R, Java, Javascript, and C++—potentially further increasing the number of articles and related scholarly knowledge added to ORKG.

Acknowledgment. This work was co-funded by the European Research Council for the project ScienceGRAPH (Grant agreement ID: 819536) and TIB–Leibniz Information Centre for Science and Technology.

References

1. Abdelaziz, I., Srinivas, K., Dolby, J., McCusker, J.P.: A demonstration of code-breaker: a machine interpretable knowledge graph for code. In: SEMWEB (2020)
2. Abdelaziz, I., Dolby, J., McCusker, J., Srinivas, K.: A toolkit for generating code knowledge graphs. In: Proceedings of the 11th on Knowledge Capture Conference, pp. 137–144. K-CAP 2021. Association for Computing Machinery, New York, NY, USA (2021). https://doi.org/10.1145/3460210.3493578
3. Ahmad, W., Chakraborty, S., Ray, B., Chang, K.W.: A transformer-based approach for source code summarization. In: Proceedings of the 58th Annual Meeting of the Association for Computational Linguistics, pp. 4998–5007. Association for Computational Linguistics, July 2020. https://doi.org/10.18653/v1/2020.acl-main.449
4. Allamanis, M., Brockschmidt, M., Khademi, M.: Learning to represent programs with graphs. arXiv preprint arXiv:1711.00740 (2017)
5. Brack, A., Hoppe, A., Buschermöhle, P., Ewerth, R.: Cross-domain multi-task learning for sequential sentence classification in research papers. In: Proceedings of the 22nd ACM/IEEE Joint Conference on Digital Libraries. JCDL 2022. Association for Computing Machinery, New York, NY, USA (2022). https://doi.org/10.1145/3529372.3530922
6. Brack, A., Müller, D.U., Hoppe, A., Ewerth, R.: Coreference resolution in research papers from multiple domains. In: Hiemstra, D., Moens, M.F., Mothe, J., Perego, R., Potthast, M., Sebastiani, F. (eds.) Advances in Information Retrieval, pp. 79–97. Springer International Publishing, Cham (2021). https://doi.org/10.1007/978-3-030-72113-8_6
7. Chao, K., Tao, L., Li, M., Guoyu, J., Yuchao, W., Yu, Z.: Construction and application research of knowledge graph in spacecraft launch. J. Physi. Conf. Ser. **1754**, 012180 (2021). https://doi.org/10.1088/1742-6596/1754/1/012180
8. Enders, M., et al.: A conceptual map of invasion biology: integrating hypotheses into a consensus network. Global Ecol. Biogeograph. **29**(6), 978–991 (2020)
9. Ernst, P., Meng, C., Siu, A., Weikum, G.: KnowLife: a knowledge graph for health and life sciences, pp. 1254–1257, March 2014. https://doi.org/10.1109/ICDE.2014.6816754
10. Heger, T., et al.: Conceptual frameworks and methods for advancing invasion ecology. Ambio **42**(5), 527–540 (2013)
11. Husain, H., Wu, H.H., Gazit, T., Allamanis, M., Brockschmidt, M.: Codesearchnet challenge: evaluating the state of semantic code search, June 2020. https://www.microsoft.com/en-us/research/publication/codesearchnet-challenge-evaluating-the-state-of-semantic-code-search/
12. Iyer, S., Konstas, I., Cheung, A., Zettlemoyer, L.: Summarizing source code using a neural attention model. In: Proceedings of the 54th Annual Meeting of the Association for Computational Linguistics (Volume 1: Long Papers), pp. 2073–2083. Association for Computational Linguistics, August 2016. https://doi.org/10.18653/v1/P16-1195

13. Jain, N.: Domain-specific knowledge graph construction for semantic analysis. In: Harth, A., et al. (eds.) ESWC 2020. LNCS, vol. 12124, pp. 250–260. Springer, Cham (2020). https://doi.org/10.1007/978-3-030-62327-2_40
14. Jaradeh, M.Y., et al.: Open research knowledge graph: next generation infrastructure for semantic scholarly knowledge. In: Proceedings of the 10th International Conference on Knowledge Capture, p. 243–246. K-CAP 2019. Association for Computing Machinery, New York, NY, USA (2019). https://doi.org/10.1145/3360901.3364435
15. Jiang, M., D'Souza, J., Auer, S., Downie, J.S.: Improving scholarly knowledge representation: Evaluating BERT-based models for scientific relation classification. In: Ishita, E., Pang, N.L.S., Zhou, L. (eds.) Digital Libraries at Times of Massive Societal Transition, pp. 3–19. Springer International Publishing, Cham (2020). https://doi.org/10.1007/978-3-030-64452-9_1
16. Kelley, A., Garijo, D.: A framework for creating knowledge graphs of scientific software metadata. Quant. Sci. Stud. 2(4), 1423–1446 (12 2021). https://doi.org/10.1162/qss_a_00167
17. Le, Q., Mikolov, T.: Distributed representations of sentences and documents. In: International Conference on Machine Learning, pp. 1188–1196. PMLR (2014)
18. Lehmann, J., et al.: Dbpedia - a large-scale, multilingual knowledge base extracted from Wikipedia. Semant. Web J. 6 (2014). https://doi.org/10.3233/SW-140134
19. Mao, A., Garijo, D., Fakhraei, S.: SoMEF: a framework for capturing scientific software metadata from its documentation. In: 2019 IEEE International Conference on Big Data (Big Data), pp. 3032–3037 (2019). https://doi.org/10.1109/BigData47090.2019.9006447
20. Reza, S.M., Badreddin, O., Rahad, K.: ModelMine: a tool to facilitate mining models from open source repositories. Association for Computing Machinery, New York, NY, USA (2020). https://doi.org/10.1145/3417990.3422006
21. Spadaro, G., Tiddi, I., Columbus, S., Jin, S., Teije, A.T., Team, C., Balliet, D.: The cooperation databank: machine-readable science accelerates research synthesis. Perspect. Psychol. Sci. 17456916211053319 (2020)
22. Spadini, D., Aniche, M., Bacchelli, A.: PyDriller: Python framework for mining software repositories, pp. 908–911. ESEC/FSE 2018. Association for Computing Machinery, New York, NY, USA (2018). https://doi.org/10.1145/3236024.3264598
23. Suchanek, F., Kasneci, G., Weikum, G.: YAGO: a core of semantic knowledge, pp. 697–706, January 2007. https://doi.org/10.1145/1242572.1242667
24. Vagavolu, D., Swarna, K.C., Chimalakonda, S.: A mocktail of source code representations. In: 2021 36th IEEE/ACM International Conference on Automated Software Engineering (ASE), pp. 1296–1300 (2021). https://doi.org/10.1109/ASE51524.2021.9678551
25. Vrandečić, D., Krötzsch, M.: Wikidata: A free collaborative knowledgebase. Commun. ACM 57(10), 78–85 (2014). https://doi.org/10.1145/2629489
26. Zhao, Z., Han, S.K., So, I.M.: Architecture of knowledge graph construction techniques (2018)

Data Archive and Management

Aggregator Reuse and Extension for Richer Web Archive Interaction

Mat Kelly[(✉)][iD]

Drexel University, Philadelphia, PA 19104, USA
mkelly@drexel.edu
https://matkelly.com

Abstract. Memento aggregators enable users to query multiple web archives for captures of a URI in time through a single HTTP endpoint. While this one-to-many access point is useful for researchers and end-users, aggregators are in a position to provide additional functionality to end-users beyond black box style aggregation. This paper identifies the state-of-the-art of Memento aggregation, abstracts its processes, highlights shortcomings, and offers systematic enhancements.

1 Introduction

Web archives act as a historical record of the web. The Internet Archive (IA) possesses the largest number of web archive holdings. These holdings are accessible through a set of interfaces to the Wayback Machine. Beyond IA, other web archives exhibit focused collection efforts, often providing unique captures within IA's temporal and spatial (i.e., URL [7]) voids [17]. A common usage pattern in accessing IA's captures is to request the archive's web site at archive.org, submit a URL of interest by providing it in a text input field, then selecting a date and time from the set of available captures for that URL in the past. This pattern may differ between web archives' respective web interfaces. Memento [27] provides the standards-based interoperable means, dynamics, syntax, and semantics for representing identifiers for archival captures (mementos) from a set of web archives. Each archive that supports the Memento Framework provides an HTTP endpoint for retrieving mementos from their respective archival holdings. Users can send a request for all captures of a URL to a variety of supporting archives through a single endpoint by an accessible tool that performs the logic of querying and combining results from multiple sources—a Memento aggregator.

Memento aggregators typically have reference to a set of endpoints to web archives that implement the Memento Framework. An aggregator may express this through a URI "template" like Fig. 1 or as a URI with an implicit append operation of a URI-R [27]. Upon receiving a request from a client with a parameterized URL (e.g., the URI-R applied to the template URI), an aggregator relays the argument received in this request as parameters for subsequent requests to each archive. When the aggregator receives a sufficient response,[1] as dictated

---

[1] This criteria is implementation-specific and may be associated with a temporal threshold, memento count, etc.

© The Author(s), under exclusive license to Springer Nature Switzerland AG 2022
Y.-H. Tseng et al. (Eds.): ICADL 2022, LNCS 13636, pp. 313–328, 2022.
https://doi.org/10.1007/978-3-031-21756-2_25

```
t₀: {scheme & hostname}/{resource type}/{format}/{URI-R}
t₁: https://myarchive.org/timemap/link/http://example.com
m₀: {scheme & hostname}/{datetime}/{URI-R}
m₁: http://archive.md/20210619183508/https://icadl.net/icadl2021/
m₂: https://archive.ph/eoQRZ
```

Fig. 1. An aggregator must be configured to supply parameters to an HTTP endpoint (like t_1), often exhibited in the form of a "templated URI" (t_0) for a URI-T as shown here. The suffixed red portion represents a URI-R http://example.com as used in practice. This URI templating is replicated (m_0) with URI-Ms (e.g., m_1), though a web archive need not identify its captures in this non-opaque manner (m_2 and m_1 identify the same memento). (Color figure online)

by the logic of the aggregator in-practice, the aggregator combines the results through a procedure that aligns with Memento syntax, often inclusive of temporal sorting.[2] The aggregator returns this "aggregated" response to the client. This description somewhat encompasses the conventional role of the aggregator. Its place as a means for users to interface with multiple web archives through a single request has the potential to be further utilized, exploited, and be more generally useful.

This paper examines the hierarchical (yet decoupled) relationship between a Memento aggregator and Memento-compliant web archives. While an aggregator and a set of archives often exhibit a static one-to-many relationship (respectively), there exists both more fundamental and more potentially complex hierarchies that may be exhibited using existing infrastructure. These exhibitions may be strategically and efficiently enhanced through consideration of this potential additional capability for the sake of enhancing the role of the aggregator in use cases for web archives. We build on existing work in defining a framework for aggregating public and private web archives [16]. Our focus will be on identifying (Sect. 6) and mitigating (Sect. 7) some outstanding issues both introduced by the framework as well as those that exist in current practice of interfacing with web archives using Memento aggregation.

2   Background

The Memento Framework [27] introduces the ability to perform temporal negotiation on the web by relating the current and past representations of a web page. Past representations are identified by "URI-Ms" and the original representation by a "URI-R", per Memento. Memento also introduces a resource to associate URI-Ms and URI-Rs through a structured listing called a TimeMap, identified by a "URI-T". A web archive may return a TimeMap representing its holdings, inclusive of URI-Ms, a URI-R, URI-Ts, and a URI-G for a "TimeGate". A TimeGate allows a client, through HTTP request headers, to specify a datetime basis for a likewise included URI-R. This paper relates to the information

---

[2] It is important to note here that TimeMaps do not need to be temporally sorted to be Memento compliant.

(a)   (b)

Fig. 2. The "Time Travel" service provides a graphical, web-based endpoint to interface with LANL's Memento aggregator. After submitting a URI and date range in the interface (Fig. 2a), the results are displayed (Fig. 2b), showing the extent of the captures from a variety of pre-configured, server-defined web archives.

retrieval and relational aspects of Memento TimeMaps and not specifically to the temporal negotiation of Memento, the latter being a feature of TimeGates. We focus on the association of past and present URIs and not the ability to resolve the closest datetime, both of which Memento provides.

The concept of aggregation goes beyond the Memento specification by leveraging a similar structure to TimeMaps but allowing the URIs contained within the aggregated TimeMap to identify resources at multiple archives instead of a single archive. The Research Library at Los Alamos National Laboratory (LANL) deployed the original Memento aggregator [8,11], currently accessible through a web interface via the Time Travel service at https://timetravel. mementoweb.org/. This web service (Fig. 2a) provides an HTML form field for a user to specify the URI-R and a datetime then uses temporal negotiation to query a set of archives and return links to the results (Fig. 2b).

A central point of access also implies a central point of failure—if the aggregator goes down, no further aggregation may be performed, and users must again resort to querying individual web archives. In response, Alam and Nelson created MemGator [1], a portable, open-source, cross-platform, user-deployable Memento aggregator. This tool enables individuals to no longer solely rely on a single web-accessible aggregator but also configure, use, and potentially deploy their own. Also, unlike Time Travel, a user has the ability to control *which* web archives are queried for mementos. This newfound ability provided the accessibility of the aggregation capability to be further explored by researchers.

Memento is an extension to the Hypertext Transfer Protocol (HTTP). HTTP is a stateless, client-server based protocol on which the web is built. In the context of Memento, a client provides an HTTP request for a TimeMap of a URI in the past, often by appending a URI-R to a templated endpoint (Fig. 1). Both the identifiers for a TimeMap and a memento are returned with corresponding Link [20] HTTP response headers giving additional context to the representation. A user (e.g., person) will typically act as a client through a user-agent (e.g., web browser, cURL[3]) and may send an HTTP request to a Memento aggregator with the expectation of receiving an HTTP response. The aggregator, in-turn, acts as a client to the web archives, relaying the request for the URI-R in the past and expects HTTP responses. This use case of a Memento aggregator playing the role of a server and a client is abridged in Sect. 7.4.

3   Related Work

Most research involving Memento aggregation relates to usage of the aggregator rather than enhancement of the aggregation process. In the same way that prior to MemGator, researchers would state "we requested URIs from the Time Travel Service", this statement was transformed to "we used MemGator to request URIs", indicative that it was useful for researchers to utilize their own aggregator instance [4,14,21]. A facet of this use case is the ability for researchers to customize the set of web archives to be used as the basis for querying, which is performed prior to running MemGator by modifying a configuration file.[4] This paper examines the aggregation process beyond accessing an aggregator and does so at a more abstract level than the ability to customize the archival sources.

3.1   Using Aggregators Beyond End-User Aggregation

As MemGator is free and open-source software (cf. Time Travel), many research endeavors on evolving the aggregation process have centered around enhancing its development beyond the limited endpoint-based Time Travel ecosystem. While the set of archives to be aggregated is static, both in accessing the Time Travel service as well as a deployed MemGator instance, other standards-based mechanisms like HTTP Prefer [26] provide a means of allowing a client to specify the set of archives aggregated to an "enhanced" aggregator—in this case, an extended version of MemGator [13]. This approach [13] entailed encoding the set of archives that normally reside in a server-side configuration file to be customizable at *query* time. The specification of custom archival sources utilizes the "Prefer" HTTP request header with a value being the self-describing, base-64 encoded JSON representing the aggregator's configuration of endpoints. A prototypical extension of MemGator referenced by the authors required the aggregator to read the HTTP request header and respond accordingly at runtime to request captures only from the archives specified by the client.

---

[3] https://curl.se/.

[4] An aside: researchers that need to control the process do so either through manipulation of their internal software (LANL experimenting with Time Travel [8]) or those outside of LANL utilizing MemGator.

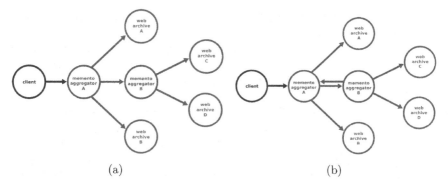

(a)   (b)

Fig. 3. An aggregator is configured to query HTTP endpoints (Fig. 3a), which are typically from web archives, but could equally be configured to be to other aggregators causing an "aggregator chaining" effect (Sect. 4.3). Aggregators are agnostic of whether their requester is a client, script, or aggregator itself (Fig. 3b) and thus may send a request that ultimately resolves to a requester causing an infinite loop.

3.2   Abstractions from Other Domains

The process of HTTP requests as recursively applied through an aggregator subsequently querying additional sources resembles a graph structure, typically reduced to a tree in the conventional case (Sect. 4.2). As this work reiterates the potential for an aggregator querying an aggregator [16], the scenario arises of graph-style cycles (Fig. 3) that must be mitigated. Additionally, we may encounter redundancies in this "chaining" process (Fig. 5) where aggregators down the request chain are configured to query identical, previously queried archives with the same parameters. The similarity of this problem resembles a singly linked list wherein a child does not know the capacity of its parent and is in adherence of HTTP being stateless. Here, an origin node is aware of that to which it links but a node is likely not aware of the linkages from its parent, to which the node itself is one.

3.3   Aggregation Optimization

The process of aggregation can be complex [19], both in programmatic logic to accomplish it as well as largely so in the temporal, spatial, and computational requirements. In conventional practice (Sect. 4.2), upon receiving a request, an aggregator will then send a request to each web archive, as defined by the endpoints in the aggregator's configuration. The process of sending these requests can typically be performed asynchronously [1], as the response time from a particular archive may be affected by a variety of factors including its infrastructure capabilities, the quantity of its holdings, the temporal spread of its holdings, etc.

Different web archives inherently possess a different set of archival holdings.[5] For example, an archive may only collect web pages within a limited set of ccTLDs [22] like .ac.uk and .gov.uk for academic and government websites in the United Kingdom (respectively). Repeated requests for TimeMaps from web archives that consistently have no mementos for a structured type of URI produce inefficiencies that are exacerbated when aggregated and affect the aggregation process. AlSum et al. [5] generated profiles to identify the distribution of URIs across archives and the effect on recall by both including and excluding IA from the aggregated results. MementoMap [3] provided an approach to remedy this issue with the cooperation of a web archive. By an archive supplying indexes of its holdings, a "map" can be created to abstractly represent (using wildcards) the extent of the holdings for specific URI patterns. This may be abstracted to the level of TLD (e.g., the extent of the holdings within the .uk TLD) down to the specificity of the quantity of holdings within a specific path of the URI. MementoMaps also provide a format to represent this extent both on the level of URI-R and URI-M. Through the cooperation of one such scoped archive, the Portuguese Web Archive, Alam et al. [3] were able to demonstrate the increase in efficiency of selectively sending requests to a subset of archives informed by their respective holdings. This work leveraged MemGator. Aturban et al. [6], through a longitudinal study on the web archives themselves, identified the disappearance of the base URI of an archive, further highlighting the need for an aggregator to be updated to ensure resolution as archives change their hostnames.

In related work, Bornand et al. [8] consulted logs from the aggregator created by the Time Travel service (the authors are from LANL) to create classifiers to effectively route queries rather than relying on a web archive to provide a profile. They analyzed over 1.2 million URI-Rs from the aggregator's cache (with over 239,000 URI-Ms) to identify a point-of-compromise for optimizing the requests sent to an archive based on the true and false positive rate as informed by prior requests.

Part of this work entails enabling the user to have more extensive interaction with web archives using Memento. This is frequently enabled through the use of browser extensions [15,25] and dedicated applications [12,18,28]. Mink[6] is an extension for the Chrome web browser that allows a user to extend the context of the web page they are currently viewing to be used as the basis of a request to a Memento aggregator. Some preliminary efforts have been performed to provide further user control over archival selection from the web browser using the extension, but have not been formalized nor deployed in the primary extension. Doing so entails either the approach of requiring an enhanced aggregator that receives a request to adapt their set of archives queried at runtime based on the user's request (a server-side approach) or for Mink to filter the results on the client after the aggregator returns the results. In the latter, client-side approach,

---

[5] We distinguish "archival holdings" from mementos in that the latter implies compliance with the Memento Framework.

[6] https://github.com/machawk1/mink.

the logic of aggregation becomes the responsibility of the extension when an aggregator does not comply with sending requests to archives outside of its base configuration.

4   Base Querying Models

Per Sect. 3, Memento aggregators are often configured to be used as a web service; in the case of MemGator, specifying a list of archives, timeouts, etc.; and "used" by querying the aggregator's HTTP endpoints with the URI as a parameter. In this Section we define aggregator "querying models" for further discussion.

4.1   Proxy-Style Querying (S_0)

An aggregator may be configured to query a single web archive. This is typically not exhibited because of redundancy (i.e., the user would normally just send the request to the archive directly), but serves as a base case for the querying models for further discussion. Here, the "aggregator" acts as a simple relay or proxy between the client and the web archive. This might potentially be useful for specifying a configuration to the aggregator beyond what can be expressed with a request to URI,[7] e.g., timeouts for a response.

4.2   Conventional Querying (S_1)

Typical aggregator usage entails a client sending a request to an aggregator that then queries multiple web archives, aggregates the responses, and returns this response to the client (Fig. 4). The internal logic of the aggregator is not necessarily as relevant in defining this model but is critical for an aggregator's operation. For example, an aggregator may pipeline the requests for more efficient querying. An aggregator also might require archives to respond within a time threshold and "short-circuit" the response to disregard archives that do not respond in time. The abbreviated set of results could then be aggregated based on the subset archives that have responded up to that point in time. Some of these aspects are discussed further in Sect. 7.

4.3   Aggregator Chaining (S_2)

A Memento aggregator may successfully query any endpoint that is Memento compliant. The response from an aggregator is itself also typically Memento compliant. This begets the possibility that what is typically considered a "web archive" configured as an endpoint to query by an aggregator may be an aggregator itself, i.e., an aggregator querying an aggregator (Fig. 3a). One reason this is not typically exhibited is because the set of archives that are queried are (in

---

[7] Tools like cURL can also specify timeouts as command-line flags, but this moves the responsibility to the client.

```
1  $ curl https://memgator.example/timemap/link/https://icadl.net/
2
3  <https://icadl.net>; rel="original",
4  <https://memgator.example/timemap/link/https://icadl.net>; rel="self";
5  type="application/link-format",
6  <https://web.archive.org/web/20180503103914/http://icadl.net/>; rel="first memento";
7  datetime="Thu, 03 May 2018 10:39:14 GMT",
8  <https://web.archive.org/web/20200815050320/https://icadl.net/>; rel="memento";
9  datetime="Sat, 15 Aug 2020 05:03:20 GMT",
10 <https://web.archive.org/web/20200826164340/https://icadl.net/>; rel="memento";
11 datetime="Wed, 26 Aug 2020 16:43:40 GMT",
12 <https://web.archive.org/web/20201101023226/https://icadl.net/>; rel="memento";
13 datetime="Sun, 01 Nov 2020 02:32:26 GMT",
14 <http://web.archive.org/web/20220602205625/https://icadl.net/>; rel="last memento";
15 datetime="Thu, 02 Jun 2022 20:56:25 GMT",
16 <https://memgator.example/timemap/link/https://icadl.net>; rel="timemap";
17 type="application/link-format",
18 <https://memgator.example/timemap/json/https://icadl.net>; rel="timemap";
19 type="application/json",
20 <https://memgator.example/timemap/cdxj/https://icadl.net>; rel="timemap";
21 type="application/cdxj+ors",
22 <https://memgator.example/timegate/https://icadl.net>; rel="timegate"
```

Fig. 4. A typical use case for a Memento aggregator is for a user to specify a URL and receive a TimeMap representing a list of identifiers (URI-Ms) in the past—S_1. Shown here is a Link [20] formatted aggregated TimeMap from MemGator containing a URI-R (line 3 in orange), URI-Ts (lines 4, 16–21 in green), URI-Ms (lines 6–15 in purple) and a URI-G (line 22 in blue). (Color figure online)

practice) manually validated before being put in-place in the configuration. In the case of the Time Travel service, there is no indication that an aggregator is queried by the basis aggregator handling the initial response. For MemGator, however, the set of endpoints is user-configurable, and thus this valid scenario may arise and has implications. The merits of "aggregator chaining" were discussed in the seminal work introducing the concept [16], but did not go into detail or highlight some problems that may occur. We reiterate and address these in Sect. 6.

As above, an aggregator may plausibly query a second aggregator. More fundamentally, and problematically, an aggregator can specify itself in its own definition of sources to query. This can be mitigated by the aforementioned manual validation, but the more scalable and programmatic approach might be accomplished through short-circuiting conditional logic in the querying function, i.e., preventing an aggregation web service from sending a request to itself and causing an infinite loop (Fig. 3b). Doing so in the self-referencing case is straight-forward but through the indirection introduced through aggregator, an "aggregator-in-the-middle" prevents this logic from being enforced, as a request from a secondary aggregator would be handled as if from any other client. We discuss this problem further in Sect. 7.2.

5   Core Features

In this paper we define approaches to extend the capability of the aggregator abstraction without regard to implementation. This brief but important Section defines the empirical assumptions and expectations currently exhibited by an aggregator. These premises of an aggregator set forth the foundational base cases of expectations of an implementation. We build on these assumptions in Sect. 7.

Expectation 1. An aggregator must treat web requests received as clients and the requests it sends to archival sources as agnostic of the dynamics of the receiver.

Expectation 2. An aggregator must treat clients' requests equally, regardless of whether a requestor is a user-agent, a script, or an aggregator itself.

Expectation 3. An aggregator is unaware of whether its own configuration incurs any sources queries of its parent.

Expectation 4. An aggregator must treat clients as stateless and return results from its queries sources.

6   Existing Problematic Scenarios

What might be deemed as "mis-"configuration of a Memento aggregator may only be exhibited and discoverable upon execution of a request for aggregation. Typical approaches for including a web archive as an aggregation source are (1) the popularity of the archive itself to merit inclusion, (2) manual discovery by those responsible for configuring the aggregator, or (3) efforts toward publicity on the part of the archive itself to make those responsible for the archive's existence and Memento compliance. There is no established process for an archive to declare the availability of its holdings in an effort to be included in a publicly accessible aggregator [23,24]. Web archives with restricted holdings may be unsuitable to aggregate for reason of privacy of the holdings [16] or the requirement to limit accessibility beyond the conventional public scope. For example, the UK Web Archive requires a client to be physically on-site to access some of its holdings, otherwise returning an HTTP 451 (Unavailable For Legal Reason) [9] status code.

Aggregators like the Time Travel service also supply TimeGate functionality, allowing for temporal negotiation (per Sect. 2), which is outside of this paper's scope. As temporal negotiation requires an index for efficient selection (required for scale cf. query time indexing), an aggregator would need to retain the extent of the captures on a URI-R basis from their set of sources. As this is dynamic due to the availability of various archives' web services, the non-static nature of the set of mementos in an archive, etc., a heuristic-based approach or some form of caching [8] might suffice for "good enough" temporal negotiation. For optimal precision of the representation of sources' holdings, runtime querying of said sources' respective indexes produces a more representative result. Thus, the abstraction of a TimeGate service being co-located with an aggregator would still succumb to the effects described in this Section. The remainder of this Section describes three effects that can plague current aggregation instances: aggregation cycles (Sect. 6.1), self-reference (Sect. 6.2), and source redundancy (Sect. 6.3).

6.1 When a Tree Becomes a Graph

As an extension of S_2 in Sect. 4.3, an aggregator (A) requesting captures from a second aggregator (B) may cause a cycle if the latter aggregator is configured to query aggregator A. This can be mitigated using a few approaches, one of which we describe in Sect. 7.2. Figure 3b illustrates an abstract scenario where this might occur with user-configurable Memento aggregators.

6.2 Self-reference

A simpler example of the abstraction where an aggregator, through the request chain, is requested to respond to a request that it initiated is exhibited in an aggregator's own endpoints being within its configuration. A web service might be naive of the URI to which it is accessible, blindly sending responses after consuming and processing the parameters in the requests received. Likewise, the solution described in Sect. 7.2 would prevent this from occurring.

6.3 Duplication of Sources

The combination of aggregators being user-configurable and the potential for aggregators to query aggregators may result in duplication of results. For example, in Fig. 5, aggregator A queries web archive A, web archive B, and aggregator B. Aggregator B queries web archive A, web archive C, and web archive D. It could be useful for the clients of aggregator A to obtain the results from aggregator B, for instance, aggregator B may be privy to access restrictive web archives C and D. However, the results returned from aggregator B from web archive A will likely be redundant of those requested from aggregator A. Thus, the results may need to be deduplicated. This characteristic may also exist outside of aggregation. For instance, aggregators currently configured to request mementos from archive.org and archive-it.org (both hosted by Internet Archive) will often receive URI-Ms from each archive with precisely the same 14-digit time stamp represented in the URI-M. While it is possible that two services have unique captures (based on the tools used), this requires dereferencing the URI-Ms, which is out of the scope of this paper that focuses on TimeMaps.

7 Newfound Capabilities

In this paper we emphasize the contribution of the untapped functional potential of a Memento aggregator beyond simple aggregation. Section 5 outlined the

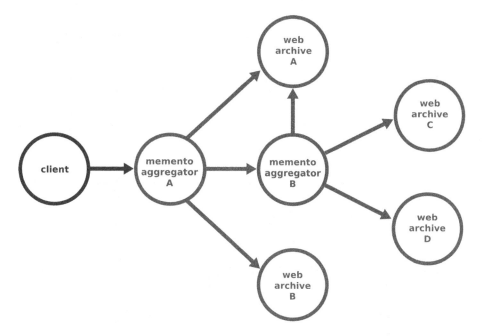

Fig. 5. An aggregator (A) configured to request captures from a set of sources $\{S\}$ inclusive of a second aggregator (B) can result with B redundantly querying one of A's sources, i.e., $|S_A \cap S_B| \geq 1$.

fundamental expectations of an aggregator that are exhibited and must be maintained as core functions. While the logic itself of strategically querying the set of archives with which an aggregator is configured has been explored in other works using profiles or machine-learning (Sect. 3.3), these do not consider the breadth of potential improvements like enabling the client to have further control of the aggregation beyond URI (e.g., using HTTP Prefer [13]), efficiency in returning partial results through HTTP endpoints, and mitigation of a non-curated set of archival sources.

7.1   User-Defined Set of Archives

HTTP provides a standardized means [13] for enabling the end-user (one querying an aggregator through HTTP) to specify the archival sources for aggregation – the HTTP Prefer request header [26]. The value for this header may include an encoded, modified version of the JSON data that is typically used to configure MemGator and contain custom values and transporting through the header. The expectation of an enhanced aggregator is that it will be required to decode this JSON and at its discretion, use that as the basis for the set of archives to query. Some nuances to this approach that have not been explored are (for example) whether the configuration can and should be applied to all users, the rules that should restrict which clients should be authorized to affect this change in the

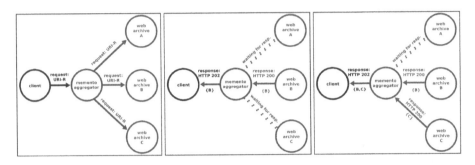

Fig. 6. Rather than an aggregator waiting for the slowest archival source to respond, the response can be progressively built based on the data received thus far. This response may be served to a client as a preliminary response as indicated by HTTP 202.

aggregator's operation, and how to further express the semantics to the extent to which the preference was applied (beyond supplying the Preference-Applied response header).

7.2   Cycle Detection

In Sect. 6.1, we introduced the potential for a cycle to occur when Memento aggregators are user-configurable and oblivious to the sources subsequently queried by aggregators further in the request chain. Approaches at mitigating cycles admittedly require the notion of HTTP being stateless to be violated. For instance, including a nonce or unique value to the request and propagating that to the sources queried (whether a web archive or aggregator), and likewise reading this value would allow the process to be short-circuited and provide a requestor some indication that the requestee was a requestor earlier in the hierarchical chain.

7.3   Preliminary Results Streaming

HTTP provides an often unused but standardized mechanism for a server to convey that a request is still processing (HTTP 202 status code) and that a client should wait and check back later [10], often at some indicated amount of time. In the context of Memento aggregation, web archives or other archival sources (e.g., other aggregators per Sect. 4.3), a set of sources from which resources are requested likely returns results in respectively varying amounts of time. This can create a bottleneck while the aggregation service waits for the slowest endpoint to respond but can be optimized by progressively building the result (Fig. 6). MemGator, for instance, merges TimeMaps as they arrive from the requesting aggregator and provide timeouts that can be specified by the user (i.e., the "user" that is executing the MemGator binary – not one making the HTTP request).

An important precondition for optimizing aggregators' processing through streaming is the recognition that Memento does not guarantee nor enforce internal temporal order of the identifiers in TimeMaps. When progressively merging TimeMaps from a partial set of sources requested, the merging process can be performed asynchronously relative to responses being received or more simply, not at all. For an aggregator to wait until all web archives have responded (which may never occur in the case of transient errors at an archive) is temporally inefficient. However, an incomplete (i.e., containing results only from a subset of archives), partially sorted, or unsorted aggregated TimeMap being returned to an end-user while an aggregator continues to wait can help to inform the end-user of the degree of success thus far. This may be potentially useful in cases where the results of the archives referenced in the aggregated TimeMap are explicit (e.g., through included metadata) instead of needing to be inferred (e.g., zero URI-Ms from an archive *might* mean no captures). This latter point can be helpful to end-users in making an informed decision to prematurely close the request if the results from an archive, as expressed in the partially aggregated TimeMap, are not to their expectations.

While the ability to return a TimeMap containing results from a subset of archives from which TimeMaps were requested may be useful and more efficient, the temporal burden for an aggregator to sort results is relatively less expensive, as it can be performed asynchronously and progressively. Despite this, partial, unsorted, concatenated TimeMaps returned using either a mechanism of streaming or through the HTTP 202 mechanism allows results, even if intermediate, to be immediately used rather than waiting on a likely unrevealed (to the end-user) set of conditions that are used prior to the response being returned.

7.4   Rescoping the Aggregator for Client-side Execution

In Sect. 2, we alluded to the propagation model, which may itself become recursive, of a client querying an aggregator that then similarly becomes the client through propagation of parameters. With Memento, a user-agent conventionally represents a client, transforming the request to the appropriate format (e.g., HTTP headers) as expected by a server (e.g., an aggregator).

From the client's perspective, the set of archives that an aggregator queried is not typically revealed. For example, if a client sends a request to an aggregator for `icadl.net` and receives back a TimeMap containing URI-Ms (Fig. 4), the set of archives represented by the URI-Ms *might* be representative of the entirety of the set, but that fact is not explicitly conveyed. It is likely and common, because of archival scoping and based on the URI-R provided, that archives within the set queried possessed no mementos for the URI-R and thus are not represented. It is wasteful and temporally inefficient to send requests to archives that possess no captures for a URI-R [16]. A priori knowledge as established by profiling archives of their holdings [2] or more specifically MementoMap [3], helps to mitigate this problem. These advancements allow the set of archives to be strategically defined so requests for URI-Rs that are unlikely to be in an archives' respective holdings are not requested. However, MementoMap requires archival cooperation and is not foolproof if the index of the captures [8] is not updated to be representative of newly collected captures. It is also heuristic-based, so has false positive built in, i.e., likelihoods may result in no URI-Ms being returned in the TimeMap from an archive that was queried, despite their profile stating that they have captures.

8 Discussion and Future Work

Implicit to this work is the continuous effort to enable the end-user, for which aggregators are typically deployed, to be able to be more specific about that which they would like aggregated. As described in Sect. 3.3, allowing for this degree of interaction with a web service will likely have ramifications to efficiency, for example, caching mechanism may not be beneficial if archival sources vary with each request. For the Time Travel service, this might be moot, as the set of archives queried is controlled server-side. For open-source aggregators, however, which have the potential for extended capability, this process can be further optimized and explored.

There is also the notion of functional cohesion, that is, a service should ideally do one job and do it well. This cohesion is already violated in practice with the addition of TimeGate functionality being co-located with TimeMap querying (i.e., aggregation) endpoints. We hope to see further work done in investigating use cases for both the end-user querying aggregators, researchers deploying their own aggregators, and the functions and processes inherent to the aggregation procedure to enhance the capability to make the aggregation concept generally more usable.

9 Conclusion

This paper focused on the aspect of Memento aggregation. We identified the state-of-the-art in pure server-side aggregators (Time Travel) and user-deployable aggregators (MemGator). Through an aggregator being user-configurable and -deployable, which has proven useful to researchers, other potential issues may arise based solely on the current functionality of an aggregator. We proposed further functional extensions to the internal aggregation process.

From the perspective of a web service where a client sends an HTTP request to an endpoint, the aspects of this work may not much matter. However, the capacity of aggregators in the status quo still contains untapped potential capability beyond that the typical use case (S_1). By enumerating these potential concerns with a user-controlled Memento aggregator, the ultimate goal of enabling a client to have more expression and preference in the process of aggregating web archives will hopefully be improved.

Acknowledgement. For initial discussions on aggregator chaining and potential pitfalls, we would like to thank Chuck Cartledge, Sawood Alam, Michael Nelson, and Michele Weigle.

References

1. Alam, S., Nelson, M.L.: MemGator - a portable concurrent memento aggregator. In: Proceedings of the ACM/IEEE Joint Conference on Digital Libraries (JCDL), pp. 243–244 (2016). https://doi.org/10.1145/2910896.2925452
2. Alam, S., Nelson, M.L., Van de Sompel, H., Balakireva, L.L., Shankar, H., Rosenthal, D.S.H.: Web archive profiling through CDX summarization. Int. J. Digit. Libr. **17**(3), 223–238 (2016). https://doi.org/10.1007/s00799-016-0184-4
3. Alam, S., Weigle, M.C., Nelson, M.L., Melo, F., Bicho, D., Gomes, D.: MementoMap framework for flexible and adaptive web archive profiling. In: Proceedings of the ACM/IEEE Joint Conference on Digital Libraries (JCDL), pp. 172–181 (2019). https://doi.org/10.1109/JCDL.2019.00033
4. Alkwai, L., Nelson, M.L., Weigle, M.C.: Comparing the archival rate of Arabic, English, Danish, and Korean language web pages. ACM Trans. Inf. Syst. (TOIS) **36**(1), 1–34 (2017). https://doi.org/10.1145/3041656
5. AlSum, A., Weigle, M.C., Nelson, M.L., Van de Sompel, H.: Profiling web archive coverage for top-level domain and content language. Int. J. Digit. Libr. (3), 149–166 (2014). https://doi.org/10.1007/s00799-014-0118-y
6. Aturban, M., Nelson, M.L., Weigle, M.C.: Where did the web archive go? In: Proceedings of the Theory and Practice of Digital Libraries Conference (TPDL), pp. 73–84, September 2021. https://doi.org/10.1007/978-3-030-86324-1_9
7. Berners-Lee, T., Fielding, R.T., Masinter, L.: Uniform Resource Identifier (URI): generic syntax. IETF RFC 3986, January 2005
8. Bornand, N.J., Balakireva, L., Van de Sompel, H.: Routing memento requests using binary classifiers. In: Proceedings of the ACM/IEEE Joint Conference on Digital Libraries (JCDL), pp. 63–72 (2016). https://doi.org/10.1145/2910896.2910899
9. Bray, T.: An HTTP status code to report legal obstacles. IETF RFC 7725, February 2016
10. Fielding, R.T., Reschke, J.F.: Hypertext Transfer Protocol (HTTP/1.1): semantics and content. IETF RFC 7231, June 2014
11. Jones, S.M., Klein, M., Van de Sompel, H., Nelson, M.L., Weigle, M.C.: Interoperability for accessing versions of web resources with the memento protocol. In: The Past Web, pp. 101–126. Springer, Cham (2021). https://doi.org/10.1007/978-3-030-63291-5_9
12. Jordan, W., Kelly, M., Brunelle, J.F., Vobrak, L., Weigle, M.C., Nelson, M.L.: Mobile Mink: merging mobile and desktop archived webs. In: Proceedings of the ACM/IEEE Joint Conference on Digital Libraries (JCDL), pp. 243–244 (2015). https://doi.org/10.1145/2756406.2756956
13. Kelly, M., Alam, S., Nelson, M.L., Weigle, M.C.: Client-assisted memento aggregation using the prefer header. Presented at the ACM/IEEE JCDL 2018 workshop on web archiving and digital libraries (WADL) (2018)
14. Kelly, M., Alkwai, L.M., Alam, S., Nelson, M.L., Weigle, M.C., Van de Sompel, H.: Impact of URI canonicalization on memento count. In: Proceedings of the ACM/IEEE Joint Conference on Digital Libraries (JCDL), pp. 303–304 (2017). https://doi.org/10.1109/JCDL.2017.7991601
15. Kelly, M., Nelson, M.L., Weigle, M.C.: Mink: Integrating the live and archived web viewing experience using web browsers and memento. In: Proceedings of the ACM/IEEE Joint Conference on Digital Libraries (JCDL), pp. 469–470 (2014). https://doi.org/10.1109/JCDL.2014.6970229

16. Kelly, M., Nelson, M.L., Weigle, M.C.: A framework for aggregating private and public web archives. In: Proceedings of the ACM/IEEE Joint Conference on Digital Libraries (JCDL), pp. 273–282 (2018). https://doi.org/10.1145/3197026.3197045

17. Lobbé, Q.: Where the dead blogs are - a disaggregated exploration of web archives to reveal extinct online collectives. In: International Conference on Asian Digital Libraries (ICADL), pp. 112–123 (2018). https://doi.org/10.1007/978-3-030-04257-8_10

18. Nelson, M.L.: Right-click to the past - memento for chrome, October 2013. https://ws-dl.blogspot.com/2013/10/2013-10-14-right-click-to-past-memento.html. Accessed 1 Nov 2020

19. Nelson, M.L., Van de Sompel, H.: Adding the dimension of time to HTTP. In: Fagerberg, J., Mowery, D.C., Nelson, R.R. (eds.) The SAGE Handbook of Web History, chap. 14, pp. 189–214. SAGE Publications Ltd, 55 City Road (2019)

20. Nottingham, M.: Web linking. IETF RFC 8288, October 2017

21. Nwala, A.C., Weigle, M.C., Nelson, M.L., Ziegler, A.B., Aizman, A.: Local memory project: providing tools to build collections of stories for local events from local sources. In: Proceedings of the ACM/IEEE Joint Conference on Digital Libraries (JCDL), pp. 219–228 (2017). https://doi.org/10.1109/JCDL.2017.7991576

22. Postel, J.: Domain name system structure and delegation. IETF RFC 1591, March 1994

23. Rosenthal, D.S.H.: The importance of discovery in memento, December 2010. https://blog.dshr.org/2010/12/importance-of-discovery-in-memento.html. Accessed 30 Nov 2020

24. Rosenthal, D.S.H.: Memento & the marketplace for archiving, January 2011. https://blog.dshr.org/2011/01/memento-marketplace-for-archiving.html. Accessed 30 Nov 2020

25. Sanderson, R., Shankar, H., Ainsworth, S., McCown, F., Adams, S.: Implementing time travel for the web. Code4Lib J. (13) (2011). https://journal.code4lib.org/articles/4979

26. Snell, J.M.: Prefer header for HTTP. IETF RFC 7240, June 2014

27. Van de Sompel, H., Nelson, M., Sanderson, R.: HTTP framework for time-based access to resource states - memento. IETF RFC 7089, December 2013

28. Tweedy, H., McCown, F., Nelson, M.L.: A memento web browser for iOS. In: Proceedings of the ACM/IEEE Joint Conference on Digital Libraries (JCDL), pp. 371–372 (2013). https://doi.org/10.1145/2467696.2467764

Caching HTTP 404 Responses Eliminates Unnecessary Archival Replay Requests

Kritika Garg[1]([✉])[iD], Himarsha R. Jayanetti[1][iD], Sawood Alam[2][iD],
Michele C. Weigle[1][iD], and Michael L. Nelson[1][iD]

[1] Old Dominion University, Norfolk, VA 23529, USA
{kgarg001,hjaya002}@odu.edu, {mweigle,mln}@cs.odu.edu
[2] Wayback Machine, Internet Archive, San Francisco, CA 94118, USA
sawood@archive.org

Abstract. Upon replay, JavaScript on archived web pages can generate recurring HTTP requests that lead to unnecessary traffic to the web archive. In one example, an archived page averaged more than 1000 requests per minute. These requests are not visible to the user, so if a user leaves such an archived page open in a browser tab, they would be unaware that their browser is continuing to generate traffic to the web archive. We found that web pages that require regular updates (e.g., radio playlists, updates for sports scores, image carousels) are more likely to make such recurring requests. If the resources requested by the web page are not archived, some web archives may attempt to patch the archive by requesting the resources from the live web. If the requested resources are not available on the live web, the resources cannot be archived, and the responses remain HTTP 404. Some archived pages continue to poll the server as frequently as they did on the live web, while some pages poll the server even more frequently if their requests return HTTP 404 responses, creating a high amount of unnecessary traffic. On a large scale, such web pages are effectively a denial of service attack on the web archive. Significant computational, network, and storage resources are required for web archives to archive and then successfully replay pages as they were on the live web, and these resources should not be spent on unnecessary HTTP traffic. Our proposed solution is to optimize archival replay using Cache-Control HTTP response headers. We implemented this approach in a test environment and cached HTTP 404 responses that prevented the browser's requests from reaching the web archive server.

Keywords: Web archiving · Archival replay · Web traffic · Memento · HTTP Cache-Control

1 Introduction

Web archives allow users to replay and browse archived web pages, or mementos, as they were on the live web. However, playback of the archived web pages may not be complete if the embedded resources are missing from the archive [7]. We

Y.-H. Tseng et al. (Eds.): ICADL 2022, LNCS 13636, pp. 329–344, 2022.
https://doi.org/10.1007/978-3-031-21756-2_26

discovered that upon replay some archived web pages make recurring requests for missing embedded resources, creating unnecessary and wasteful traffic for the web archive. These recurring requests could only be seen by observing the network activity of the archived web page. To users browsing the web archive, these web pages would appear like any other regular mementos replaying in their browser. They would not see the web traffic generated by these recurring requests. Thus, if a user leaves such an archived page replaying in a browser tab for a long time, they would be unaware that their browser is generating a huge amount of unnecessary traffic to the web archive. Our previous work [16] on analyzing the access logs of Arquivo.pt [12] revealed a similar user session. This long-running user session ran for almost four days and issued over 4.3M recurring requests to the web archive for the embedded images of a single memento of `radiocomercial.iol.pt`. We discuss this memento further in Sect. 3.2.

This discovery inspired us to investigate the kinds of web pages that would generate recurring requests to web archives similar to `radiocomercial.iol.pt`. By examining the network traffic on numerous archived web pages, we found that web pages that require regular updates (e.g., sports scores updates, stock market updates, news updates, chat applications, new tweets) and poll the server periodically for the updates may generate the recurring requests. For example, a popular and well-archived domain like `twitter.com` also exhibits this behavior when it polls for new tweets and the latest trends. The example of `twitter.com` is different from `radiocomercial.iol.pt` as it makes fewer recurring requests per minute. However, the cumulative load of many people globally replaying the mementos of `twitter.com` would result in a significant amount of wasted bandwidth for the web archive. We also saw that web pages with image carousels, banners, widgets, etc. are also more likely to cause the recurring requests.

We studied the behavior of such web pages in different web archives. Some web archives may patch the memento by requesting missing embedded resources from the live web. The patch/write requests would be successful only if the requested resources are accessible on the live web. However, if the requested resources are not accessible on the live web, the resources cannot be archived, and the patch/write requests would result in HTTP 404 responses. In this case, patching the memento from the live web would create unnecessary writes and reads. We describe a memento displaying this behavior in Sect. 3.3.

We found that some mementos would send requests to the server as often as they did on the live web, while others would poll the server even more rapidly if their requests returned HTTP 404 responses, resulting in excessive load on the web archive. On a large scale, web pages like these could effectively be denial of service attacks, squandering network resources, overloading web archive servers, and possibly depriving other users access to the archive. Web archiving and archival replay are resource-intensive processes, and these resources should not be spent on unnecessary HTTP traffic. That is why it is important to be aware of such issues and optimize the replay system accordingly for an effective playback. Eliminating this wasteful HTTP traffic to the web archives will also have a positive, although small, environmental impact. In this paper, we have describe various sources that could cause unnecessary HTTP traffic for the web archives. In Sect. 3, we have provide examples of the mementos that generate unnecessary recurring requests. In Sect. 4, we demonstrate a minimal reproducible example web page containing a carousel that generates recurring requests for the missing embedded resources. In Sect. 5, we implement a solution for eliminating the unnecessary requests by using the Cache-Control HTTP response header to cache HTTP 404 responses.

2   Background and Related Work

Web archiving involves recording HTTP traffic from web servers and then replaying them in a different context. A memento, or URI-M, is a snapshot of a URI-R (URI of an original resource) captured at a specific Memento-Datetime (the date-time a particular URI-M was archived). These terms are defined in the Memento Protocol [25].

The objective of successful archival replay is that when replaying an archived web page, the page should be viewable and behave exactly as it did at the time of archiving. To render a web page the way it looked in the past, the base HTML page and all the related embedded resources, such as images, stylesheets, JavaScript, fonts, and other media, should be archived around the same time as the base page. However, not every embedded resource of the page that is attempted to be archived is captured by web archives. As a result, some of the embedded resources on archived pages are missing. Brunelle et al. [7] have measured the impact of missing resources in web archives. The missing embedded resources may introduce anomalies during archival replay. For example, in our study, we saw that various mementos repeatedly made requests to missing resources during the replay, causing unnecessary or wasteful traffic for the web archive. In our previous work [9], we documented the difficulties in replaying mementos of Twitter's new user interface due to missing embedded JSON files. Missing resources could also lead to temporal discrepancies during replay. In the Internet Archive's Wayback Machine, the Memento-Datetime of the base HTML page and the Memento-Datetime of the corresponding embedded resources may or may not be temporally aligned, which could result in a temporal violation during the replay [1,2].

These anomalies can cause security vulnerabilities in web archives. As an example, these unnecessary recurring requests on a wide scale may overwhelm a web archives with excessive web traffic, leading to the denial of archival services. Additional research into security of high-fidelity web archives [20,26] has revealed a number of security risks to web rehosting services. Lerner et al. [21] detected several vulnerabilities and security attacks specific to the Internet Archive's Wayback Machine. The security issues raised above show the importance of optimizing and upgrading the archival replay systems. Goel et al. [11] proposed a design to reduce storage needs by discarding JavaScript code with functionality that will not work or would remain unexecuted during replay. Our work focuses on the effects of JavaScript code that executes during replay and triggers recurring

HTTP requests. Our proposed solution does not cause an overhaul of the system, because we are adding the header to the server layer without changing the application. We can eliminate the wasteful network traffic caused by the executing JavaScript code by returning a Cache-Control HTTP header.

3   Things We Found in the Archive

We examined several mementos that cause recurring requests upon replay. We noticed this behavior in mementos with missing resources for the banners, widgets, carousels, playlists, and web pages that request regular updates (e.g., updates for sports scores). In this section, we provide examples of four such mementos.

3.1   Banner Example

Figure 1 shows a memento of http://esdica.pt/ captured on 2013-11-06T21:59:54 in Arquivo.pt and its network activity in Chrome DevTools [13]. The memento is of the homepage of a high school website that contains a large banner trying to display a series of images in the form of a slideshow. The banner slideshow is generated by a jQuery Advanced Slider component that cycles through a list of images in an endless loop.[1] The network tab of Chrome DevTools shows that the HTTP GET requests for the embedded images received HTTP 404 Not Found responses from the web archive. This means that the requested mementos of the embedded images are not available in the web archive. We noticed that this memento is making recurring HTTP GET requests to Arquivo.pt for the missing images.[2] This banner is shared across many pages at `esdica.pt`, which means all the archived pages would generate similar loads.

3.2   Carousel Example

Figure 2 shows a memento of http://www.radiocomercial.iol.pt/ captured on 2009-06-28T04:40:51 in Arquivo.pt. Upon replay, it makes recurring HTTP GET requests for the embedded images[3] to the web archive server. This memento of the Rádio Commercial website contains a carousel with a slideshow cycling through a series of images of musicians. The carousel is built with Cascading Style Sheets (CSS) and JavaScript.[4] The JavaScript contains a loader function that iterates through a series of 12 images in form of

---

[1] https://arquivo.pt/wayback/20131105212033js_/http://esdica.pt/js/slider/jquery.advancedSlider.min.js.

[2] https://arquivo.pt/wayback/20131105211447/http://esdica.pt/imagens/banners/img03b.jpg.

[3] https://arquivo.pt/wayback/20090628044051im_/http://www.radiocomercial.iol.pt/styles/slideshow/loader-0.png.

[4] https://arquivo.pt/wayback/20090628052553js_/http://www.radiocomercial.iol.pt/jscript/slideshow/slideshow.js.

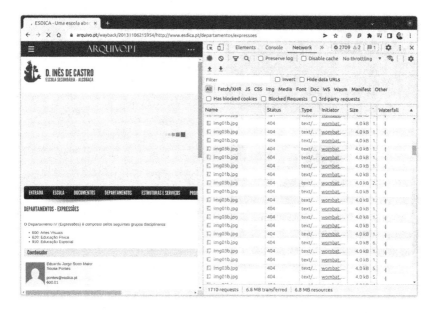

Fig. 1. Memento of a school website with a banner making recurrent requests for missing embedded images to Arquivo.pt https://arquivo.pt/wayback/20131105211447/http://esdica.pt/

`/styles/slideshow/loader-#.png`, where # is replaced by numbers from 0 to 11, and loads them for the slideshow. If an image is not available, then the next time through the slideshow, another GET request would be made for the image. The Network tab in Fig. 2 shows that the HTTP GET requests for the images received HTTP 404 Not Found responses from the web archive. Therefore, the JavaScript keeps sending requests for the embedded images, as it is unable to load them for the slideshow. This results in unnecessary traffic to the web archive server. We observed that replaying this memento causes 122,204 requests in 10 min (1098.36 requests per minute on average) to the web archive.

3.3 Playlist Example

Figure 3 shows another memento of http://www.radiocomercial.iol.pt/ captured on 2010-08-22T13:36:54 in the Internet Archive's Wayback Machine, a year after the memento described in Sect. 3.2. Between the two captures, the Rádio Commercial website completely changed its user interface. However, the behavior of generating recurring HTTP GET requests persisted. This allowed us to observe how different web archives handle such mementos.

Fig. 2. Memento of a radio station web page with a carousel making recurrent requests for missing embedded images to Arquivo.pt https://arquivo.pt/wayback/20090628044051/http://www.radiocomercial.iol.pt/

The memento contains a playlist of songs and cover images for the songs. We identified that the memento captured by the Internet Archive (IA) was missing many embedded resources such as CSS, JavaScript, images, etc. The memento was not rendered correctly due to missing CSS. We inspected the network activity in Chrome DevTools and noticed that the memento was also making the same recurring GET requests and receiving HTTP 404 responses for the images in the playlist (Fig. 3).

IA tries to patch mementos by requesting the missing embedded resources from the live web to archive them during the replay. This is done with their Save Page Now (SPN) service [14], which issues a request in the form `https://web.archive.org/save/_embed/{URL}` (Fig. 4, left). The request to patch the missing resource received an HTTP 404 response, indicating that the image does not exist on the live web (Fig. 4, right). This resulted in multiple recurring requests for the same resource, recurring read requests for the memento, and recurring SPN requests (via `save/_embed/`) for the memento to the IA web server. We observed that, on average, 30 s after the first request, the new SPN requests receive HTTP 429 Too Many Requests responses from IA in an effort to throttle the excessive number of SPN requests made to its server.

3.4   Latest Feed Example

Figure 5 shows the memento of https://www.livesport.com/en/ captured on 2021-09-01T09:27:55 in the Internet Archive's Wayback Machine. The memento is of a sports website that provides live score updates for different sports. When the memento is loaded, the web page tries to fetch the memento of the scores API feed. The XMLHttpRequest (XHR) request returned an HTTP 404 response since the feed is not archived. The web archive cannot archive the feeds because it requires authorization. The memento keeps requesting the feed resulting in recurring unsuccessful requests. For example, the memento in Fig. 5 is making recurring requests for two feeds.[5,6]

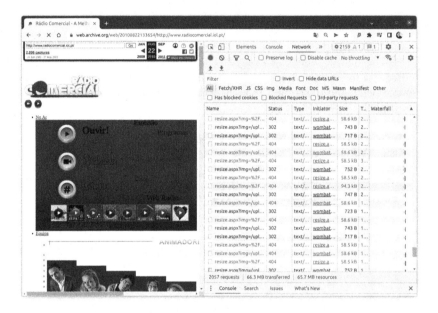

Fig. 3. Memento of a radio webpage with a playlist making recurrent requests for missing embedded images to the Internet Archive web server https://web.archive.org/web/20100822133654/http://www.radiocomercial.iol.pt/

---

[5] https://web.archive.org/web/20210901092756/https://d.livesport.com/en/x/feed/u_0_1.

[6] https://web.archive.org/web/20210901092756/https://d.livesport.com/en/x/feed/sys_1.

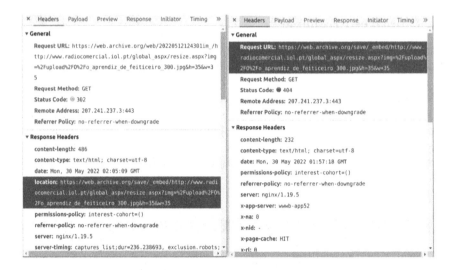

Fig. 4. Request for the missing resource is redirected to IA's SPN service to archive the resource (left), and the request to archive the missing resource returned HTTP 404 response (right)

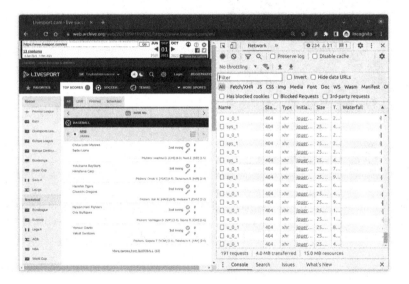

Fig. 5. Memento making recurrent XHR requests to fetch the live score API feeds https://web.archive.org/web/20210901092755/https://www.livesport.com/en/

4   Abstract Model: Minimal Reproducible Example

In our examples, web pages that require regular feed updates or contain carousels, banners, widgets, etc. are more likely to make these recurring requests, causing a surge in web traffic. We implemented a minimal reproducible example (MRE) web page[7] with a carousel to assess this behavior in a simpler environment.

Our implementation is similar to the radio commercial example we described in Sect. 3.2. We used jQuery [23], a feature-rich JavaScript library, to create a dynamic carousel. We created a carousel that displays three images every second and generates an HTTP GET request for each image. We hosted this carousel demo using GitHub Pages [10] and then tested it in the Chrome browser to observe its behavior. We made two variations of this demo. In the first variation, the requested image resources are available, and in the second variation, the requested image resources are not available. When the images are available, the browser caches the images received from the first request and then serves the consecutive image requests from the disk cache. When the images are not available, the carousel requests the images continuously from the server. Since the requested images are not available, the browser receives HTTP 404 Not Found responses. We noticed that in this scenario the browser does not cache the HTTP 404 response to the first image request (Fig. 6). This means continuous requests are made to the web server for unavailable resources.

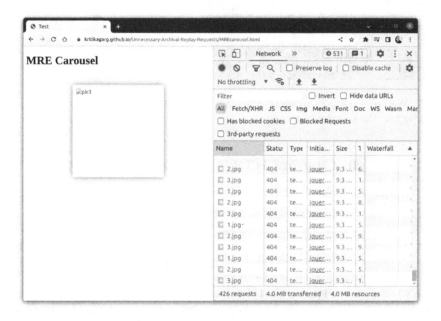

Fig. 6. MRE carousel making recurring requests for missing embedded resources (request in Chrome DevTools) https://kritikagarg.github.io/Unnecessary-Archival-Replay-Requests/MREcarousel.html

---

[7] https://kritikagarg.github.io/Unnecessary-Archival-Replay-Requests/MREcarousel.html.

We archived this demo page to test its behavior in a web archive environment. We generated a HAR (HTTP Archive) file which tracks all the detailed logging of web browser's HTTP transactions with the demo page. We used the har2warc Python package [18] to convert this HAR file into a WARC (Web Archive) format. We replayed the WARC file locally using pywb, a web archive replay system that allows users to replay archived web content in their browser [17]. Figure 7 shows the archived demo page continuously sending requests to the pywb server for the missing images. The terminal in Fig. 7 shows the web server logs for the requested images.

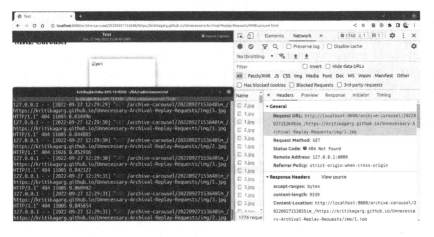

Fig. 7. Web server logs of pywb (the black terminal screen) showing recurring requests made by the MRE carousel memento

5 Approach: Caching HTTP 404 Responses

After studying the behavior of our demo carousel, we understood that we could avoid recurring requests without being obtrusive to the web archives by caching HTTP 404 responses. We set up Nginx [22] as a reverse proxy server to control the network traffic between a client and the archive server. This allowed us to intercept responses headed for the server and enable Cache-Control for them. Cache-Control is an HTTP header consisting of a set of directives that define when/how a response should be cached and the response's maximum age before expiring. We configured our Nginx proxy server to add the Cache-Control HTTP header to all outgoing responses (Fig. 8), which means responses other than HTTP 404 would also be cached. Web archives generally have a cache mechanism to cache successful responses. However, HTTP 404 error responses are not cached because if the missing resource later becomes available, it could be served immediately to the client. Replaying mementos with missing resources can trigger wasteful network requests to the archive. Our simplified and practical method of caching HTTP 404 responses might cause a brief delay in the time between archiving and serving the missing resource. However, it will help web archives reduce the unnecessary overload on their system caused by these mementos without disrupting the application.

We ran pywb with the uWSGI server application [24] on port 8081 and ran the Nginx proxy server on port 80. We replayed the demo carousel on localhost:80 to test its behavior with the Cache-Control HTTP response header in place. In this case, we have set the Cache-Control response header to public. The public response directive indicates that the response can be stored in a shared cache that exists between the origin server and clients. We have also set the max-age directive to indicate the length of time a response is considered fresh, in this case, 600 s (10 min).[8] We observed the effect of the change in the web server logs after setting the Cache-Control response header (Fig. 9). The web server logs did not display any recurring requests because the HTTP 404 responses were cached.

```
/etc/nginx/sites-available$ cat custom_server.conf
server {
  listen 80;
  location /static {alias /home/kritika/RA/radiocommercial/
    static;}

  location / {
    uwsgi\_pass localhost:8081;
    include uwsgi_params;
    uwsgi_param UWSGI_SCHEME $scheme;

    proxy_pass_request_headers   on;
  add_header Cache-Control "public, max-age=600" always;
  }
}
```

Fig. 8. Nginx configuration file to set the Cache-Control HTTP header

6   Evaluating Rate of Recurring Requests

To evaluate the rate of the recurring requests, we first looked at the memento of radiocomercial.iol.pt described in Sect. 3.2. We evaluated the number of requests made by the memento before and after introducing the Cache-Control HTTP header. We replayed the memento and recorded the HTTP session using Chrome DevTools. We downloaded this session as a HAR file and analyzed it using haralyzer [8]. We obtained the number of requests the memento made to the server every second and plotted the cumulative number of requests over

---

[8] The max-age value could be adjusted to reflect an archive's accession frequency, the existence of patching/Save Page Now functionality, and other archive-specific preferences.

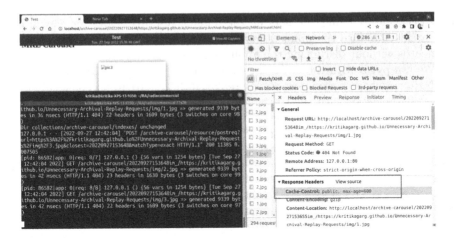

Fig. 9. Web server logs (the black terminal screen) showing no recurring requests after setting the HTTP Cache-Control response header (request in Chrome DevTools)

time as shown in Fig. 10a. The x-axis represents the time in seconds, and the y-axis represents the cumulative sum of the number of requests. The slope of the line indicates how many new requests are issued every second. The red line demonstrates the wasteful recurring requests. The red line becomes linear after the first 13 s. We measured that the memento made 1098.36 requests every minute on average to the web archive. The memento made 203 requests in the first 13 s for the essential resources required to replay the memento and the rest are the wasteful requests made for the missing resources. The blue line demonstrates the scenario if the Cache-Control HTTP header were in place. Since we do not control the web archive, we cannot control which headers are returned. After the primary 203 requests for the required resources, there would be no further new requests with the responses being cached. This anticipated behavior is shown in the figure with the blue line becoming flat.

Figure 10b shows the number of requests made by the memento of MRE described in Sect. 4. In this case, because we control the server, we implemented the HTTP Cache-Control header on responses. We obtained the number of requests our MRE memento made to the server before and after introducing the Cache-Control HTTP header. We found that our example memento's growth matches the projected behavior in Fig. 10a. We measured that our MRE memento made 174 requests every minute on average to the server. The red line is linear after the first 3 s (or first seven requests) due to recurring requests. The blue line shows how this linear growth changed into a flat straight line after caching, which demonstrates that we successfully eliminated the unnecessary recurring requests.

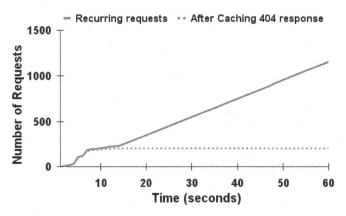

(a) The cumulative number of requests made per second by `radiocomercial.iol.pt` memento and the anticipated number of requests after introducing the Cache-Control HTTP response header

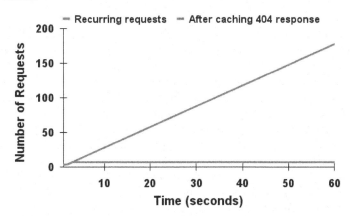

(b) The cumulative number of requests made per second by MRE memento before and after introducing the Cache-Control HTTP response header

Fig. 10. The cumulative number of requests made per second before and after introducing the Cache-Control HTTP response header. (Color figure online)

7 Future Work

For future work, we propose to look at other examples of frequent requests, such as where the URL changes with an increment variable or a timestamp in the query parameter. For example, appending random query strings to each requested resource would make each request unique. Most web archives do not have a generalizable method to recognize and ignore these query strings, which leads to HTTP 404 responses for the requests for the mementos of these URI-Rs.

One potential solution could be for archival replay systems to have more strategic canonicalization [3,6,15] in place to eliminate such requests. For example, pywb performs fuzzy matching[9] on the query strings, where it ignores the query parameters and content is loaded from the URL under the Content-Location header. This problem cannot be mitigated by caching because although the server may recognize these multiple URLs to be for the same resource, the client would see them as different URLs. So any caching header applied on one request will not be applied to another from the client's perspective. We propose future work to explore the possibility of adding intelligence in client-side replay libraries like reconstructive [4,5] and wombat.js [19]. These client-side libraries could watch the requests and limit them if they detect any patterns of repetition or similarity in the URLs or the responses they are receiving from the archive. They could serve a prior response of one of the requests to the client using service workers so the request will not go to the web archive server.

8   Conclusions

Replaying an archived web page should not cause hundreds or thousands of recurring requests per minute to web archives. In this paper, we described various forms in which web archival replay can generate wasteful requests using example web pages archived by Arquivo.pt and the Internet Archive. We provided examples of web pages with banners, carousels, playlists, and web pages that request regular updates (e.g., updates for sports scores, stock prices, new tweets). We identified that JavaScript triggers recurring HTTP GET requests for the same URL of the missing embedded resources upon replaying the memento. Web archives that try to patch these missing embedded resources from the live web may cause even more unnecessary traffic to the web archive. On a large scale, excessive web traffic could lead to the denial of archival services. We presented that web archives can mitigate unnecessary requests by sending a Cache-Control header on the HTTP 404 responses. We demonstrated this simplified and effective method on a minimal reproducible example memento that initially made 174 requests per minute. After introducing a Cache-Control response header, the memento only made seven requests, eliminating the unnecessary recurring requests.

Acknowledgement. We are grateful to Daniel Gomes and Fernando Melo of Arquivo.pt for sharing access log data from the Arquivo.pt web archive with us.

References

1. Ainsworth, S.G., Nelson, M.L., Van de Sompel, H.: A framework for evaluation of composite memento temporal coherence. Technical Report. arXiv:1402.0928, Old Dominion University (2014)

---

[9] https://github.com/webrecorder/pywb/blob/main/pywb/warcserver/index/fuzzymatcher.py.

2. Ainsworth, S.G., Nelson, M.L., Van de Sompel, H.: Only one out of five archived web pages existed as presented. In: Proceedings of the 26th ACM Conference on Hypertext & Social Media, pp. 257–266 (2015)

3. Alam, S.: MementoMap: a web archive profiling framework for efficient memento routing. Ph.D. thesis, Old Dominion University, December 2020. https:// doi.org/10.25777/5vnk-s536, https://digitalcommons.odu.edu/computerscience_ etds/129/

4. Alam, S., Berlin, J.A.: Reconstructive: A ServiceWorker for Client-Side Reconstruction of Composite Mementos. https://oduwsdl.github.io/Reconstructive/ (2017)

5. Alam, S., Kelly, M., Weigle, M.C., Nelson, M.L.: Client-side reconstruction of composite mementos using ServiceWorker. In: Proceedings of the 17th ACM/IEEE-CS Joint Conference on Digital Libraries, JCDL 2017, pp. 237–240 (2017). https:// doi.org/10.1109/JCDL.2017.7991579

6. Alam, S., Weigle, M.C., Nelson, M.L., Melo, F., Bicho, D., Gomes, D.: MementoMap framework for flexible and adaptive web archive profiling. In: Proceedings of the 19th ACM/IEEE-CS Joint Conference on Digital Libraries, JCDL 2019, pp. 172–181. IEEE, June 2019. https://doi.org/10.1109/JCDL.2019.00033

7. Brunelle, J.F., Kelly, M., SalahEldeen, H., Weigle, M.C., Nelson, M.L.: Not all mementos are created equal: measuring the impact of missing resources. In: IEEE/ACM Joint Conference on Digital Libraries, pp. 321–330 (2014). https:// doi.org/10.1109/JCDL.2014.6970187

8. Crown, J.: Haralyzer. https://pypi.org/project/haralyzer/ (2015)

9. Garg, K., Jayanetti, H.R., Alam, S., Weigle, M.C., Nelson, M.L.: Replaying archived twitter: when your bird is broken, will it bring you down? In: 2021 ACM/IEEE Joint Conference on Digital Libraries (JCDL), Los Alamitos, CA, USA, pp. 160–169. IEEE Computer Society, September 2021. https://doi.org/10. 1109/JCDL52503.2021.00028

10. GitHub: GitHub Pages. https://pages.github.com/ (2008)

11. Goel, A., Zhu, J., Netravali, R., Madhyastha, H.V.: Jawa: web archival in the era of JavaScript. In: Proceedings of the 16th USENIX Symposium on Operating Systems Design and Implementation (OSDI 22), Carlsbad, CA, pp. 805–820. USENIX Association, July 2022. https://www.usenix.org/conference/osdi22/presentation/ goel

12. Gomes, D., Costa, M., Cruz, D., Miranda, J., Fontes, S.: Creating a billion-scale searchable web archive. In: Proceedings of the Temporal Web Analytics Workshop, TempWeb 2013, pp. 1059–1066 (2013). https://doi.org/10.1145/2487788.2488118

13. Google: Chrome DevTools. https://developer.chrome.com/docs/devtools/ (2008)

14. Graham, M.: The wayback machine's save page now is new and improved. https:// blog.archive.org/2019/10/23/the-wayback-machines-save-page-now-is-new-and- improved/ (2019)

15. Internet Archive: Sort-friendly URI Reordering Transform (SURT) python package. https://github.com/internetarchive/surt (2017)

16. Jayanetti, H.R., Garg, K., Alam, S., Nelson, M.L., Weigle, M.C.: Robots still outnumber humans in web archives, but less than before. In: Proceedings of the 26th International Conference on Theory and Practice of Digital Libraries (TPDL) (2022). https://doi.org/10.1007/978-3-031-16802-4_19

17. Kreymer, I.: pywb. https://pypi.org/project/pywb/ (2014)

18. Kreymer, I.: har2warc. https://pypi.org/project/har2warc/ (2018)

19. Kreymer, I., Berlin, J.: Wombat.js client-side rewriting library. https://github. com/webrecorder/wombat (2018)

20. Kreymer, I., Cushman, J.: Thinking like a hacker: security considerations for high-fidelity web archives. https://labs.rhizome.org/presentations/security.html (2019)
21. Lerner, A., Kohno, T., Roesner, F.: Rewriting history: changing the archived web from the present. In: Proceedings of the 2017 ACM SIGSAC Conference on Computer and Communications Security, CCS 2017, pp. 1741–1755 (2017). https://doi.org/10.1145/3133956.3134042
22. Sysoev, I.: Nginx. https://www.nginx.com/ (2004)
23. The jQuery Team: Jquery. https://github.com/jquery/jquery (2006)
24. Unbit: uWSGI. https://github.com/unbit/uwsgi (2016)
25. Van de Sompel, H., Nelson, M.L., Sanderson, R.: HTTP framework for time-based access to resource states - Memento, Internet RFC 7089. https://tools.ietf.org/html/rfc7089 (2013)
26. Watanabe, T., Shioji, E., Akiyama, M., Mori, T.: Melting pot of origins: compromising the intermediary web services that rehost websites. In: Proceedings of Network and Distributed System Security (2020). https://doi.org/10.14722/ndss.2020.24140

Documenting Architectural Styles Using CIDOC CRM

Michail Agathos[1], Eleftherios Kalogeros[1], Manolis Gergatsoulis[1(✉)],
and Georgios Papaioannou[2]

[1] Laboratory on Digital Libraries and Electronic Publishing, Department of
Archives, Library Science and Museology, Ionian University, Ioannou Theotoki 72,
49100 Corfu, Greece
{agathos,kalogero,manolis}@ionio.gr
[2] Museology Research Laboratory, Department of Archives, Library Science and
Museology, Ionian University, Ioannou Theotoki 72, 49100 Corfu, Greece
gpapaioa@ionio.gr

Abstract. Documenting cultural heritage information is of major
importance and significance nowadays in the emerging world of digital
libraries, computing and information studies across the globe. Architecture and architectural styles fall within this big effort, as architecture is
strictly connected with human societies and heritage. The CIDOC CRM
is a well-established and continuously emerging reference model aiming
to represent cultural heritage information. This paper connects the dots
and offers for the first time a model for documenting architectural styles
via CIDOC CRM and its extensions. In this paper, we discuss the notion
of architectural style and the previous work on documenting architecture.
Via classes and properties of CIDOC CRM and its extensions, we model
the historical context of architectural styles/periods, we represent specific
elements that characterize architectural styles using Gothic Architecture
as an example, and we document various and complex spatial and temporal relationships and influences among architectural styles and periods,
such sub-styles of given architectural styles, regional variations among
architectural styles, and architectural influences from one architectural
style to another.

Keywords: Architectural style · CIDOC CRM · Ontologies · Cultural
heritage documentation

1 Introduction

The CIDOC CRM ontology and its extensions comprise a modern documentation tool to model heritage, art, and history-related concepts, including modeling
work, perceptions and notions associated to architecture. Architecture has been
practiced in countless styles and types worldwide. Buildings of specific architectural styles and traditions (e.g. Roman, neo-classical, Victorian, modern, etc.)
define areas, shape spaces, affect human actions and behaviors, and characterize

© The Author(s), under exclusive license to Springer Nature Switzerland AG 2022
Y.-H. Tseng et al. (Eds.): ICADL 2022, LNCS 13636, pp. 345–359, 2022.
https://doi.org/10.1007/978-3-031-21756-2_27

civilizations. Architectural styles are both static and dynamic, as they can be solid and striking for a period, but they also evolve through time by influencing one another. CIDOC CRM [4] and its extensions (e.g. CRMba [28]) contribute to their digital documentation. Can CIDOC CRM and CIDOC CRM based models sufficiently represent architectural styles? To what extent are they able to offer a framework to support the documentation of architectural styles and therefore their interpretation? We approach these questions by working towards an automated CRM-based system for modeling architectural styles.

This paper offers a section (Sect. 2) on what is architectural style, followed by a section (Sect. 3) on related work in terms of documenting architecture and architectural styles. We then, in Sect. 4, present our proposed model. In particular, in Subsect. 4.1 we show how we can model the historical context of an architectural period, in Subsect. 4.2 we present our proposal for the representation of architectural style elements, in Subsect. 4.3 we demonstrate how we can model the relation between architectural styles and periods, in Subsect. 4.4 we show how we can relate specific buildings (or parts of buildings) to the architectural styles affecting their construction, while in Subsect. 4.5 we present an example of the use of the models presented in previous subsections. Finally, Sect. 5 concludes the paper and presents our plans for future work.

2   What Is Architectural Style?

Architecture has been defined in numerous ways: it is "the crystallization of ideas. It has been defined many ways-as shelter in the form of art, a blossoming in stone and a flowering of geometry (Ralph Waldo Emerson), frozen music (Goethe), human triumph over gravitation and the will to power (Nietzsche), the will of an epoch translated into space (architect Ludwig Mies van der Rohe), the magnificent play of forms in light (architect Le Corbusier), a cultural instrument (architect Louis I. Kahn), and even inhabited sculpture (sculptor Constantin Brancusi)" [29]. Numerous architectural styles define architecture all over the world, e.g. the Greek and Roman architectural style, the Gothic, the Baroque, the neoclassical, the Victorian, the modern, the post-modern, etc. An architectural style is much more than a set of characteristics for walls and ceilings produced for sheltering humans and human activities. Beauty, aesthetics, functionality, sustainability, adaptation to the geography, the environment and the weather, building materials, location, structure design, political views, ideologies, religions, approaches to how people (should/must/deserve/choose to) live are notions that have affected architectural styles in different times and places. An architectural style is "a definite type of architecture, distinguished by special characteristics of structure and ornament", one reads in the Oxford English Dictionary. We like the definition in Archisoup, a resource portal for architects and students of architecture[1]: "an architectural style is a collection of external influences that shape the materiality, method of construction, and form of a building, helping it to be identified and characterized in both historical and design terms". This emphasis on the visual allows an architectural style to incorporate different functions [26]. On the structural side, the architectural style of a building is evident by specific visual building elements and features, which lead to building acting both as architectural instances and as architectural classification systems [36]. An example is the Gothic architectural style which is characterized by pointed arches, rib vaults, rose windows and ornate façades [31]. Moreover, architectural styles in their historical span have adopted features and attributes that reflect and illustrate cultural circumstances and social aspects.

In the literature there are numerous comparative studies, guides, volumes and manuals analyzing architectural styles in depth [19,29]. Unfortunately, there is less on holistic ontological approaches for architectural styles. This work aims to help towards this. Architectural features and attributes (we mentioned some of them above) can serve as denominators to theoretically represent an architectural style, addressing it as an entity that possesses certain properties that can be measured [12]. On the other hand, there are complicated interrelationships between different architectural styles and approaches (e.g. interpretations and re-interpretations, style revivals, special territorialities), and little analysis on entities and properties for architectural styles [19,26,35].

3   Related Work

The CIDOC Conceptual Reference Model (CIDOC CRM) is a formal ontology for modelling cultural heritage heterogeneous information towards integration, mediating, interoperability, and information interchange. Over the last 15 years, CIDOC CRM-related research and work have been conducted to integrate cultural heritage information. Examples include archaeological data integration via the ARIADNE project [22], the ARIADNEplus project [1] and other projects, which resulted to the CIDOC CRM extensions like CRMarchaeo [3], and CRMba [2], as well as to models on documenting excavation context sheets and archaeological buildings [7–10,13,16–18,25,33].

[30] presents a CIDOC CRM based data model representing monuments and concepts of the architectural style of European Megalithism. However, to the best of our knowledge, there is no general conceptual model covering a wide range of architectural styles and periods based on CIDOC CRM.

CIDOC CRM is considered most appropriate for modeling interrelations and mappings between different heterogeneous sources [15]. Examples include EAD mappings to CIDOC CRM [11], VRA mappings in [14] and Dublin Core mappings in [20].

In terms of documenting architecture, the Architecture Metadata Object Schema (ARMOS) [6] has been proposed. ARMOS acts as an application profile and uses elements from other metadata schemas, especially from the CDWA

---

[1] https://www.archisoup.com/architectural-styles.

(Categories of Description of Works of Arts). In the DBpedia's dataset (the RDF knowledge database of Wikipedia) information about historical buildings is organized under the ontology class dbo:HistoricBuilding. In this ontology, Architectural Style is considered a property of the class dbo:ArchitecturalStructure, the superclass of dbo:Building class, without further possibilities for semantic organization. The need for better semantic organization of DBpedia's historic buildings instances is studied in [5].

The accurate classification of architectural styles is significant towards studying architecture, cultural heritage, human history, societies and civilizations [34]. It is also a very challenging endeavor, given the rich and complex inter-class relationships between different architectural styles [37]. In their work, [21] proposed an algorithm which automates the determination of building style through classification of architectural styles from façade images. In another study, [37] proposed a feature extraction module based on preprocessed images with Deformable Part-based Models (DPM). With similar goals, [23] focused on the effectiveness of using the data mining techniques to determine the architectural style(s) of buildings and proposed an algorithm to automate the detection process based on images of several buildings. To this end, they also utilized artificial intelligence technology and clustering techniques [24]. Recently, studies used models based on convolutional neural network (CNN) and achieved highly competitive results due to the capabilities of feature expression. More specifically, [36] adopted a convolutional neural network model for classifying house styles in the United States of America. They also explore the possibility of using state-of-the-art image recognition algorithms in house style recognition. To improve the accuracy of architectural style classification, [34] proposed an architectural style classification method based on CNN and channel-spatial attention. Finally, recent research in deep learning and computer vision has highlighted the great potential in analyzing urban environments from images. [32] proposed a deep learning-based framework for understanding architectural styles and age epochs by deciphering building façades based on street-level imagery.

[30] presents a CIDOC CRM based data model representing monuments and concepts of the architectural style of European Megalithism.

4   Data Model

4.1   The Historical Context of an Architectural Period

Periods and styles flow together. Architectural movement grow from ideas and construction techniques influenced by historical periods and the specific landscapes and cultural needs, reflecting the philosophy, intellectual currents, hopes and aspirations of given places and times. Architectural styles are not the result of mere accident or caprice, but of intellectual, moral, social, religious, and even political conditions [19].

Figure 1 depicts the data model based on CIDOC CRM classes used to document the historical context of an architectural style, including its period of creation, its origin, its denomination and its creators.

In order to present the two-fold role of an architectural style we represent the historical period in which a specific style was developed, flourished and formed using the E4 Period class. A specific style, with its characteristic features that occur in time even after the end of a given historical period, is the cultural and artistic production that is classified with the fixed value Architectural Style in the E55 Type class. It is represented using the class E29 Design or Procedure. We have highlighted these three classes in Fig. 1.

The participants in the creation of a style could be either individual actors (e.g. an architect) presented in the data model via the E21 Person class and/or a group of people (belonging to a civilization, religious doctrine, political movement etc). They are presented via the E74 Group class. The class E55 Type connected with the E74 Group class exemplifies the identity of this group.

Using the Gothic Architecture Style as an example, our data model approach has as follows: The *Gothic period* (E4 Period) spanned a long period of history - *between the mid-12th century and the 16th century* (E52 Time-Span). *Gothic Architectural Style* (E29 Design or Procedure) originated in the *Île-de-France and Picardy regions of northern France* (E53 Place). The *creation of this style* (E65 Creation) is attributed to *Abbot Suger (1081-1151 CE)* (E21 Person), one of the earliest patrons of Gothic Architectural Style who built the Basilica Church of Saint-Denis in France, a Gothic Cathedral that acts as a prime example of Gothic Architectural Style. In its life span, Gothic architectural style found its own name as *International Gothic* (E41 Appellation), (*Getty AAT* (E32 Authority Document), record: *300020786* (E42 Identifier)).

4.2   Architectural Style Elements

Architectural styles are characterized by certain architectural elements which distinguish them from other styles of architecture [31] and make a building or other structure notable and historically identifiable. Among these, decoration, materials, techniques, and plans belong to elements that play a vital role in the recognition and identification of a particular style.

Figure 2 depicts the data model based on CIDOC CRM classes used to document the architectural elements of an architectural style. These include materials that are related to a particular style, floor and other plans showing structural arrangements, design details and points of support [19].

The above elements are represented using the E29 Design or Procedure class, classified by the E55 Type class, taking each time the appropriate value (decoration, techniques, plans). Building materials of an architectural style are represented by the E57 Material class. The above two classes are highlighted in Fig. 2.

Continuing with the Gothic Architectural Style as an example, our data model approach has as follows: *Gothic Architectural Style* (E29 Design or Procedure) is typically associated with achievements in the use of *stone* (E57 Material) and *glass* (E57 Material). In the case of *Gothic Architectural Style* (E29 Design or Procedure), *techniques* (E55 Type) such as the *pointed* (E29 Design or Procedure) or *ogival arch* (E29 Design or Procedure), the large *stained glass* windows (E29

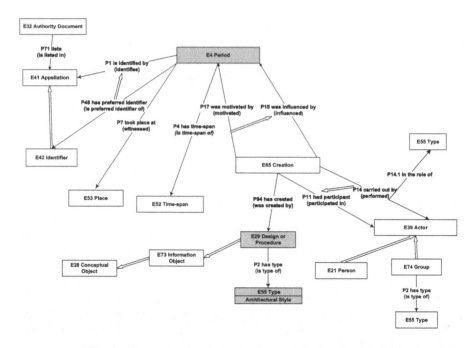

Fig. 1. The historical context of an architectural period.

Design or Procedure), the *rib vaults* (E29 Design or Procedure) and the *flying buttresses* (E29 Design or Procedure), are fundamental for its definition. Decoration elements (E29 Design or Procedure) such as *Gothic Sculpture* (E55 Type), are also important and notable features for Gothic Architectural Style (E29 Design or Procedure). The *plan* (E55 Type) of Gothic cathedrals and churches was usually based on the *Latin cross (or "cruciform") plan* (E29 Design or Procedure), taken from the ancient Roman Basilica and from the later Romanesque churches [27].

4.3   Relations Between Architectural Styles and Periods

The history of Architectural has revealed that there are complex and complicated relationships between different chronological periods and the architectural styles within them. Similar to almost all aspects and manifestations of life within human societies, sharp edges among architectural styles do not exist. Within the theory and the history of architecture, we often come across subdivisions of styles with the prefixes early, middle, late, neo, proto etc. [26]. A data model depicting these architectural sub-period related relations based on CIDOC CRM is in Fig. 3. In Fig. 3 we have highlighted in red the properties connecting the main period of an architectural style (left side of Fig. 3) with a sub-period of it (right side of Fig. 3). It is the property P9 consists of (forms part of) that connects the main period with its sub-period (E4 Period). The property P17 was motivated by (motivates) connects the creations of the main and the sub- periods, while the

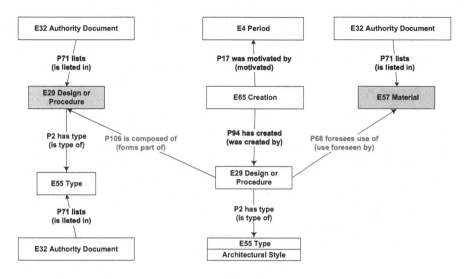

Fig. 2. Representing architectural style elements.

property P69 has association with (is associated with) indicates that the design(s) or procedure(s) of both periods (i.e. the main and the sub-) are related. Note that P69.1 has type defines this association via the E55 type class, which comes with an instance clarifying the sub-period.

An architectural style may also be influenced by other styles from different chronological periods. It is very common for architectural periods to appear consecutively, influencing one another [19]. Figure 4 offers a CIDOC CRM -based data model depicting this, with the properties connecting the two periods (the influencing and the influenced) highlighted in red. It is the property P183 ends before the start of (starts after the end of) and/or the property P182 ends before or with the start of (starts after or with the end of) that connects one period with the other (E4 Period). The property P15 was influenced by (influenced) connects the creations of the two periods, while the property P69 has association with (is associated with) indicates that the design(s) or procedure(s) of both periods are related. Note that P69.1 has type defines this association via the E55 type class, which comes with an instance clarifying the predecessor/successor.

Within an architectural style, there are also spatial interrelationships such as special territorialities and/or revivals. An architectural style may not be limited to one place or region; it can spread from its place of origin to other areas where it may continue to develop in different ways. Moreover, we observe revivals and re-interpretations of an architectural style at a given space and time. Each time the original style revives, we deal with the creation of a new type of style, as the design or procedure may present minor and/or major changes and modifications. A CIDOC CRM -based data model for this is depicted in Fig. 5 and its red-highlighted properties. The properties P17 was motivated by (motivated) and P15 was influenced by (influenced) connect the E65 creation classes of both interrelated

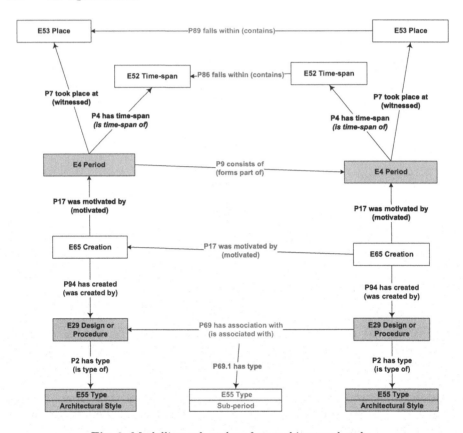

Fig. 3. Modelling sub-styles of an architectural style.

periods (E4 Period), while the property P69 has association with (is associated with) indicates that the design(s) or procedure(s) of both periods are also related. Note that P69.1 has type defines this association via the E55 type class, which comes with an instance clarifying the regional variation.

Continuing with the Gothic Architectural Style as an example, in Fig. 3, for *Gothic period* (E4 Period) different sub-typologies are identified: *Early to High Gothic and Early English* (E4 Period) from *c.1130* to *c.1240* (E52 Time-Span), *Rayonnant and Decorated Style* (E4 Period) from *c.1240* to *c.1350* (E52 Time-Span), *Late Gothic: flamboyant and perpendicular* (E4 Period) from *c.1350* to *c.1500* (E52 Time-Span).

In Fig. 4, the *Gothic Period* (E4 Period) *evolved* (E55 Type) from the *Romanesque architecture* (E4 Period) by adopting and adapting Romanesque elements (E29 Design or Procedure) to produce a *new style* (E65 Creation) that featured exaggerated arches, increased vaulting, and enlarged windows which was then succeeded by *Renaissance architecture* (E4 Period). One of the most

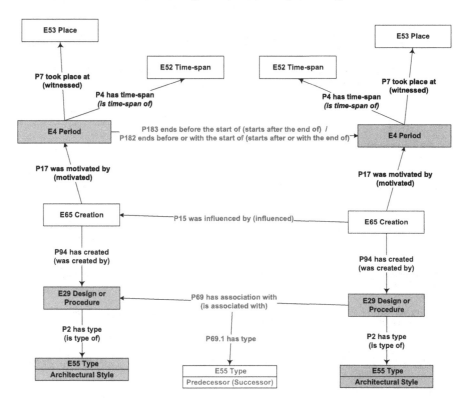

Fig. 4. A data model for the influences between Architectural Periods due to their temporal correlations based on CIDOC CRM.

fundamental elements of the Gothic Architectural Style, the pointed arch, was likely borrowed from the *Islamic architecture*[2] (E4 Period).

Finally, in Fig. 5, the *Gothic Architectural Style* (E29 Design or Procedure) was not just limited to *France* (E53 Place). This type of ornate architecture spread across *Europe* (E53 Place), finding a foothold in *Italy* (E53 Place), *Germany* (E53 Place), *Spain* (E53 Place), and *England* (E53 Place). Though each country gave the style its *own twist* (E65 Creation), international Gothic still retains the basic elements found in *France* (E53 Place). A good example of a style's revival is the *Gothic Revival*[3] (E29 Design or Procedure) (also referred to as *Victorian Gothic, neo-Gothic, or Gothick* (E41 Appellation)). It is an architectural movement that began in the *late 1740s* (E52 Time-Span) in *England* (E53 Place) and *influenced* (E55 Type) on the *medieval Gothic Architecture* (E29 Design or Procedure). This new style intended to complement or even supersede the neoclassical styles that prevailed at the time.

---

[2] https://www.khanacademy.org/.
[3] https://en.wikipedia.org/wiki/Gothic_Revival_architecture.

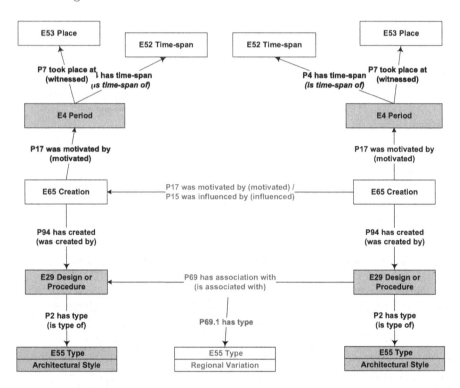

Fig. 5. A data model for spatial Architectural Periods relations based on CIDOC CRM.

4.4   Relating Buildings to Architectural Styles

Buildings can categorized and related with one or more architectural styles. Specific buildings or parts of them may act as prime examples of the application of a particular style. Buildings may have architectural elements that are easily notable and historically identifiable that belong to a specific architectural style. As many historic buildings have been altered through time, different styles of different periods may be evident to one or more building parts. A data model to relate an architectural style with its related buildings or building parts based on CIDOC CRM is depicted in Fig. 6. In this model the classes B1 Build Work and B2 Morphological Building Section from the CRMba [2] extension are used. B1 Build Work class is used to represent instances of buildings that their construction (represented by E12 Production class) refers to a particular architectural style, while B2 Morphological Building Section is used to represent instances of parts of buildings that their construction relates to a particular architectural style.

Continuing with the Gothic Period as an example, the *Basilica of Saint-Denis* (B1 Build Work), a large medieval abbey church, currently the cathedral of the commune of Saint-Denis in Vienna, is widely considered the first structure to

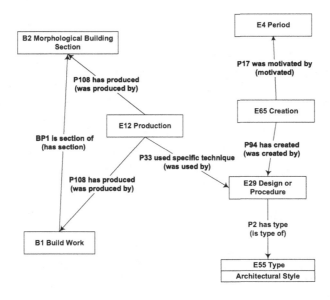

Fig. 6. Relating buildings to their architectural style.

employ all the elements of Gothic architecture[4] (E29 Design or Procedure), thus a prime example of the Gothic period (E4 Period). On the other hand, *St. Stephen's Cathedral* (B1 Build Work) in Vienna is a combination of *Romanesque* and *Gothic styles* (E29 Design or Procedure). The exterior (B2 Morphological Building Section) of St. Stephen's Cathedral in Vienna (B1 Build Work) is an amalgamation of *Romanesque* and *Gothic Architectural Styles* (E29 Design or Procedure) while its *Towers* (B2 Morphological Building Section) on the west front of the cathedral are inspired by *Romanesque Style* (E29 Design or Procedure).

4.5   An Example of the Use of Our Model

In Fig. 7 we present an example of the use of our proposed model. We represent the *Gothic Architectural Style* (E29 Design or Procedure) of the *Gothic Period* (E4 Period). The *Gothic Period* (E4 Period) motivated the creation of the *Gothic Architectural Style* (P17 motivated, E65 Creation). This creation by *Abbot Suger* (P14 carried out by, E21 Person) created the *Gothic Architectural Style* (P94 has created, E29 Design or Procedure). Characteristics of the *Gothic Period* (E4 Period) are: its time-span between the *mid-12th and the 16th century* (P4 has time-span, E52 Time-span), its place in the areas of the *Ile-de-France and Picardy regions of northern France* (P7 tool place at, E53 Place), its appellation *"International Gothic"* and its identifier *"300020786"* (P1 is identified by, E41 Appellation, P47 has preferred identifier, E42 Identifier). Elements of *Gothic Architectural Style* are represented with the classes E57 Material (connected with

---
[4] https://en.wikipedia.org/wiki/Basilica_of_Saint-Denis.

the property P68 foresees use of), E12 Production (connected with the property P33 used specific technique), E29 Design or Procedure (connected with the property P106 is composed of), and E55 Type (connected with the property P2 has type). In the proposed model we recommend the use of AAT vocabulary (P71i is listed in, E32 Authority Document) in certain classes, namely E57 Material, E41 Appellation, and E42 Identifier. To refer to a specific building, we used a class from the CRMba (bottom right part of Fig. 7): the process of the production of Construction of the Basilica Church of Saint-Denis (E12 Production) led to the Basilica Church of Saint-Denis (P108 has produced, B1 Built Work).

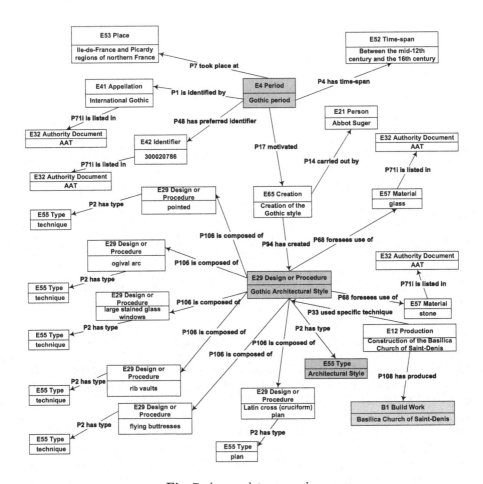

Fig. 7. A complete example.

5   Conclusions and Future Work

By using CIDOC CRM and its extensions, this paper has modelled the way that architectural styles and periods interact, forming human-built historic environments, parts of the world's cultural heritage. This piece of ongoing research adds to the documentation and management of cultural heritage information, contributing to the discussion on shared interests and endeavors among digital humanities, computing, and information studies. We have focused on representing the historical context of an architectural style/period and on documenting the main elements of architectural styles. We also addressed and modelled the various and complex spatial and temporal relationships and influences among architectural styles and periods, including sub-styles of an architectural style, regional variations among architectural styles, and architectural influences from one style to another. The architectural style of Gothic Architecture served as an example. As part of our future work, we aim to study specific architectural style cases, including vernacular architectural styles. We also intend to produce a data value vocabulary for the types of relationships in architectural styles by further addressing the relevant semantics.

References

1. ARIADNEplus - a data infrastructure serving the archaeological community worldwide. https://ariadne-infrastructure.eu/. Accessed 9 July 2021
2. Definition of the CRMba: An extension of CIDOC CRM to support buildings archaeology documentation. Version 1.4. Technical report, December 2016
3. Definition of the CRMarchaeo: an extension of CIDOC CRM to support the archaeological excavation process. Version 1.4.8. Technical report, February 2019
4. Definition of the CIDOC Conceptual Reference Model (Vol. A). Version 7.1.1. Technical report, April 2021
5. Agathos, M., Kalogeros, E., Kapidakis, S.: A case study of summarizing and normalizing the properties of DBpedia building instances. In: Fuhr, N., Kovács, L., Risse, T., Nejdl, W. (eds.) TPDL 2016. LNCS, vol. 9819, pp. 398–404. Springer, Cham (2016). https://doi.org/10.1007/978-3-319-43997-6_33
6. Agathos, M., Kapidakis, S.: A meta - model agreement for architectural heritage. In: Garoufallou, E., Greenberg, J. (eds.) MTSR 2013. CCIS, vol. 390, pp. 384–395. Springer, Cham (2013). https://doi.org/10.1007/978-3-319-03437-9_37
7. Binding, C.: Implementing archaeological time periods using CIDOC CRM and SKOS. In: Aroyo, L., et al. (eds.) ESWC 2010. LNCS, vol. 6088, pp. 273–287. Springer, Heidelberg (2010). https://doi.org/10.1007/978-3-642-13486-9_19
8. Binding, C., May, K., Souza, R., Tudhope, D., Vlachidis, A.: Semantic technologies for archaeology resources: results from the STAR project. In: Contreras, F., Farjas, M., Melero, F.J. (eds.) Proceedings 38th Annual Conference on Computer Applications and Quantitative Methods in Archaeology, BAR International Series 2494, pp. 555–561. BAR Publishing (2013)
9. Binding, C., May, K., Tudhope, D.: Semantic interoperability in archaeological datasets: data mapping and extraction via the CIDOC CRM. In: Christensen-Dalsgaard, B., Castelli, D., Ammitzbøll Jurik, B., Lippincott, J. (eds.) ECDL 2008. LNCS, vol. 5173, pp. 280–290. Springer, Heidelberg (2008). https://doi.org/10.1007/978-3-540-87599-4_30

10. Binding, C., Tudhope, D., Vlachidis, A.: A study of semantic integration across archaeological data and reports in different languages. J. Inf. Sci. **45**(3), 364–386 (2019)
11. Bountouri, L., Gergatsoulis, M.: The semantic mapping of archival metadata to the CIDOC CRM ontology. J. Arch. Organ. **9**(3–4), 174–207 (2011)
12. Chan, C.-S.: Can style be measured? Des. Stud. **21**(3), 277–291 (2000)
13. Deicke, A.J.E.: CIDOC CRM-based modeling of archaeological catalogue data. In: William De Luca, E., Bianchini, P. (eds.) Proceedings of the First Workshop on Digital Humanities and Digital Curation co-located with the 10th Conference on Metadata and Semantics Research (MTSR 2016), volume 1764 of CEUR Workshop Proceedings, Goettingen, Germany. CEUR-WS.org (2016)
14. Gaitanou, P., Gergatsoulis, M.: Defining a semantic mapping of VRA core 4.0 to the CIDOC conceptual reference model. Int. J. Metadata Semant. Ontol. **7**(2), 140–156 (2012)
15. Gergatsoulis, M., Bountouri, L., Gaitanou, P., Papatheodorou, C.: Query transformation in a CIDOC CRM based cultural metadata integration environment. In: Lalmas, M., Jose, J., Rauber, A., Sebastiani, F., Frommholz, I. (eds.) ECDL 2010. LNCS, vol. 6273, pp. 38–45. Springer, Heidelberg (2010). https://doi.org/10.1007/978-3-642-15464-5_6
16. Gergatsoulis, M., Papaioannou, G., Kalogeros, E., Carter, R.: Representing archeological excavations using the CIDOC CRM based conceptual models. In: Garoufallou, E., Ovalle-Perandones, M.-A. (eds.) MTSR 2020. CCIS, vol. 1355, pp. 355–366. Springer, Cham (2021). https://doi.org/10.1007/978-3-030-71903-6_33
17. Gergatsoulis, M., Papaioannou, G., Kalogeros, E., Mpismpikopoulos, I., Tsiouprou, K., Carter, R.: Modelling archaeological buildings using CIDOC-CRM and its extensions: the case of Fuwairit, Qatar. In: Ke, H.-R., Lee, C.S., Sugiyama, K. (eds.) ICADL 2021. LNCS, vol. 13133, pp. 357–372. Springer, Cham (2021). https://doi.org/10.1007/978-3-030-91669-5_28
18. Giagkoudi, E., Tsiafakis, D., Papatheodorou, C.: Describing and revealing the semantics of excavation notebooks. In: Proceedings of the CIDOC 2018 Annual Conference, 19 September–5 October, Heraklion, Crete, Greece (2018)
19. Hamlin, A.D.F.: A Text-Book of the History of Architecture, 7th edn., revised. Project Gutenberg (2008)
20. Kakali, C., et al.: Integrating Dublin core metadata for cultural heritage collections using ontologies. In: Proceedings of the 2007 International Conference on Dublin Core and Metadata Applications, DC 2007, Singapore, 27–31 August 2007, pp. 128–139 (2007)
21. Mathias, M., Martinovic, A., Weissenberg, J., Haegler, S., Gool, L.V.: Automatic architectural style recognition. Int. Arch. Photogram. Remote Sens. Spat. Inf. Sci. XXXVIII-5/W16, 171–176 (2011)
22. Meghini, C., et al.: ARIADNE: a research infrastructure for archaeology. ACM J. Comput. and Cult. Herit. **10**(3), 18:1–18:27 (2017)
23. Mercioni, M.A., Holban, S.: The recognition of the architectural style using data mining techniques. In: 2018 IEEE 12th International Symposium on Applied Computational Intelligence and Informatics (SACI), pp. 331–338 (2018)
24. Mercioni, M.A., Holban, S.: A study on hierarchical clustering and the distance metrics for identifying architectural styles. In: 2019 International Conference on ENERGY and ENVIRONMENT (CIEM), pp. 49–53 (2019)
25. Niccolucci, F.: Documenting archaeological science with CIDOC CRM. Int. J. Digit. Libr. **18**(3), 223–231 (2017)

26. Poppeliers, J.C., Chambers, S.A.: What Style Is It?: A Guide to American Architecture. Wiley (2003)
27. Renault, C.: Les Styles de l'architecture et du mobilier. Éditions Jean-Paul Gisserot (2000)
28. Ronzino, P., Niccolucci, F., Felicetti, A., Doerr, M.: CRMba a CRM extension for the documentation of standing buildings. Int. J. Digit. Libr. **17**(1), 71–78 (2016)
29. Roth, L.M.: Understanding Architecture: Its Elements, History, and Meaning. Routledge (2018)
30. Santos, I., Vieira, R., Trojahn, C., Rocha, L., Cuenca, E.C.: Megalithism representation in CIDOC-CRM. In: Chiusano, S., et al. (eds.) New Trends in Database and Information Systems - ADBIS 2022 Short Papers, Doctoral Consortium and Workshops: DOING, K-GALS, MADEISD, MegaData, SWODCH, Turin, Italy, 5–8 September 2022, Proceedings, volume 1652 of Communications in Computer and Information Science, pp. 550–558. Springer, Cham (2022). https://doi.org/10.1007/978-3-031-15743-1_50
31. Shalunts, G., Haxhimusa, Y., Sablatnig, R.: Classification of gothic and baroque architectural elements. In: 2012 19th International Conference on Systems, Signals and Image Processing (IWSSIP), pp. 316–319 (2012)
32. Sun, M., Zhang, F., Duarte, F., Ratti, C.: Understanding architecture age and style through deep learning. Cities **128** (2022)
33. Vlachidis, A., Binding, C., May, K., Tudhope, D.: Automatic metadata generation in an archaeological digital library: semantic annotation of grey literature. In: Przepiórkowski, A., et al. (eds.) Computational Linguistics - Applications, volume 458 of Studies in Computational Intelligence, pp. 187–202. Springer, Cham (2013). https://doi.org/10.1007/978-3-642-34399-5_10
34. Wang, B., Zhang, S., Zhang, J., Cai, Z.: Architectural style classification based on CNN and channel-spatial attention. Signal, Image and Video Processing (2022)
35. Xu, Z., Tao, D., Zhang, Y., Wu, J., Tsoi, A.C.: Architectural style classification using multinomial latent logistic regression. In: Fleet, D., Pajdla, T., Schiele, B., Tuytelaars, T. (eds.) ECCV 2014. LNCS, vol. 8689, pp. 600–615. Springer, Cham (2014). https://doi.org/10.1007/978-3-319-10590-1_39
36. Yi, Y.K., Zhang, Y., Myung, J.: House style recognition using deep convolutional neural network. Autom. Constr. **118**, 103307 (2020)
37. Zhao, P., Miao, Q., Song, J., Qi, Y., Liu, R., Ge, D.: Architectural style classification based on feature extraction module. IEEE Access **6**, 52598–52606 (2018)

Exploiting Views for Collaborative Research Data Management of Structured Data

David Broneske[1]([✉]) [iD], Ian Wolff[2] [iD], Veit Köppen[3] [iD], and Martin Schäler[4] [iD]

[1] DZHW, Hannover, Germany
`broneske@dzhw.eu`
[2] University of Magdeburg, Magdeburg, Germany
`ian.wolff@ovgu.de`
[3] Zentral- und Landesbibliothek Berlin, Berlin, Germany
`veit.koeppen@zlb.de`
[4] Salzburg University, Salzburg, Austria
`martin.schaeler@sbg.ac.at`

Abstract. Data-driven analysis plays a vital role in research projects, and sharing data with collaborators inside or outside a project is supposed to be daily scientific work. There are various tools for research data management, which offer features like storing data, meta-data indexing, and provide options to share data. However, currently, none of them offers capabilities for sharing data in different levels of detail without excessive data duplication. Naturally, sharing data by duplication is a tedious process, as preparing data for sharing typically involves changing temporal resolution (i.e., aggregation) or anonymization, e.g., to ensure privacy. In this paper, instead of re-inventing the wheel, we ask whether the concept of views, a well-established concept in relational databases, fulfills the above requirement. Conducting a case study for a project employing sharing of learning analytics data, we propose a framework that allows for fine-granular configuration of shared content based on the concept of views. In the case study, we a) analyze a data reuse scenario based on the FAIR principles, b) suggest a concept for using views for data sharing, and c) demonstrate its feasibility with a proof-of-concept.

Keywords: Research data management · Data sharing · Provenance

1 Introduction

In the last decade, there was a substantial rise in the importance of research data management. This shift does not only come from scientists, but is more and more enforced by scientific organizations and funding organizations [2]. For instance, funding programs require specifically for a data management plan. Especially in bigger projects featuring a consortium of partners, it is essential to define what data are gathered and how can they be shared. Here, sharing refers to partners within the consortium as well as to other external researchers, even beyond project lifetime. This is especially challenging, if data of human participants are collected. Thus, internally, researchers are allowed to see more participant details

Y.-H. Tseng et al. (Eds.): ICADL 2022, LNCS 13636, pp. 360–376, 2022.
https://doi.org/10.1007/978-3-031-21756-2_28

than external researchers. In such a scenario, sharing represents a significant challenge, i.e., how to *suit the data needs* for different stakeholders (internal or external partners) on the same data basis in a *flexible* and *non-redundant* way.

Current research data management repositories (e.g., DSpace, EPrints, Fedora, or Invenio) already allow for research data storage and indexing. Currently, none of them offers any capabilities to prepare data for different levels of detail that are required in collaborative research projects as described above. Hence, a straight-forward workaround for a collaborative research data management is creating one dataset per stakeholder. Naturally, this is a tedious and resource-intensive approach as all redundant copies have to be kept consistent, e.g., when correcting minor errors or updating data. Moreover, preparing data for public access often involves significant modifications due to changing the temporal resolution (i.e., aggregation), pseudonymization, grouping data of individuals to ensure k-anonymity [30], or introducing a well-defined amount of noise to ensure differential privacy [8]. Therefore, *provenance* of the newly created data is essential to be able to reproduce datasets and, thus, allow for easy validation of scientific results extracted from them. Finally, a requirement or proof is sometimes necessary for data anonymization concepts. As a result, we require an alternative approach to limit data duplication. The approach shall furthermore provide means to allow for fine-tuned data representation and keeping track of data provenance, which may also be the proof for proper anonymization.

In this paper, we address the problem of research data sharing among different stakeholders on our use case in the learning analytics area. However, instead of re-inventing the wheel, we ask whether we can rely on a well-established concept, which can be easily integrated into existing data management repositories. As a result, we propose a framework for fine-granular configuration of shared content, based on the concept of views. In summary, our contributions:

- We analyze a reuse scenario of research data in our collaborative research project and define a set of requirements and limitations.
- Based on the requirements, we propose a framework that allows to flexibly share structured research data.
- We exemplarily show, as a proof of concept, how to implement our structured research data management on the use case of a collaborative learning analytics project with three collaboration levels and derive open challenges.

2   Collaborative Reuse Scenarios in Learning Analytics

In this section, we describe the problem statement of collaborative sharing of research data at different levels. To this end, we introduce our use case of learning analytics, as well as the data collected therein. Then, we discuss objectives and challenges of sharing the collected data. Finally, we discuss the envisioned re-use scenario in detail, describing what our proposed framework has to support.

2.1   Learning Analytics Use Case

In learning analytics, one collects and analyzes data about learners and their contexts, aiming at understanding and optimizing the learning process [32].

Table 1. Learning analytics data collected at both universities

	OVGU	TU BAF
Initial skill assessment and student characterization	Questionnaire data in SQLValidator	Questionnaire data in LiaScript
Student activities	Moodle log (CSV)	N/A
Student collaboration	Log-data in SQLValidator	GitHub commits, issues
Student exercise performance	Moodle log (CSV)	Code submitted via GitHub
Student learning behavior	Error data from logs in SQLValidator	Evaluation of submitted code and quizzes in LiaScript
Student exam performance	Exam results (CSV/Excel)	Exam results (CSV/Excel)

Digitalization increased the use of learning management systems and promoted usage of learning analytics. As a result, data from learners are generated every day, which enables learning and teaching to become more personalized.

Collaborative Programming Use Case. In this paper, we rely on a specific use case where we apply learning analytics. The use case is teaching collaborative programming at a university, with the goal to understand and optimize how students learn to program collaboratively.

Abstractly, for each student, researchers gather data, such as: How many points did they reach in Assignment a, how often did they commit source code, etc. From the perspective of machine learning, this is a feature vector – the basis for automatic analyses. In addition, a quantification of the learning outcome is stored, such as the final grade or points per assignment. Then, researchers aim at identifying a relationship between the feature vector and the learning outcome. Often they are interested in whether a certain sub-set of the feature vector, like usage of a specific tool, suggests a particularly good (or bad) learning outcome.

Data Collection in Our Use Case. In our research, we use two different frameworks to monitor collaborative learning of programming languages at University of Magdeburg (OVGU) and TU Bergakademie Freiberg (TU BAF).

Data Collection at OVGU. Moodle and SQLValidator [19] deliver different data in different formats (cf. Table 1). Moodle records student's accesses of course material, which gives an interaction profile for each user, and stores the score for each exercise task.

Data Collection at TU BAF. Students visit weekly theoretical exercises and submit solutions to different C programming tasks via the lecture project on GitHub (cf. Table 1). Hence, we monitor student activity by commits on the platform, including timestamps. In addition, students submit quizzes, surveys, and theoretical exercises via LiaScript [6] as an integrated learning environment, which stores the results in a database.

2.2 Data Sharing: Challenge and Reuse Scenarios

The objective within our use case is that the generated data can be shared with other learning analytics scientists.

Challenge. Learning analytics research includes in most cases the use of information about real persons, human behavior, or attitude as well as current context. Consequently, research data management in learning analytics is strongly related to complex matters in data ownership and ethics [21, 27]. When collecting personal data, researchers have to consider regional regulations regarding privacy, data ownership, anonymity, and data security. For instance, since 2018, the General Data Protection Regulation (GDPR) applies in the European Union.[1] When collected data are completely anonymized, these regulations do not apply. However, depending on the aim of the project, current and future research can be hindered if too much data is anonymized or obscured (e.g., hiding the gender of the students). This means in some application differentiation is useful, but anonymization boycotts the use of such attributes. Therefore, different use cases require a specific handling of the participant data along the data lifecycle.

Reuse Scenarios. Possible data reuse scenarios are manifold and, especially in learning analytics, the potential of data reuse is high. A particularly important reuse of data is reproduction of research results. Therefore, already existing data from a prior study is reanalyzed by asking the same research questions and using the same data and analysis method. Another option is aiming at reproducing core results of prior studies with newly acquired data using the same data acquisition and analysis method. However, reproduction needs associated documentation of software, code, and scientific models. More complex is a data integration scenario, when already existing datasets are reused and combined at once with other data for comparison, building new models, or research questions [22].

A serious issue of sensitive research data are protection regulations. Here, we apply a three-domain model along Treloars data curation continuum (see Fig. 1), which makes data sharing possible between a scientific research group and the public [31]. As seen in Table 1, we collect different data from different tools. Nonetheless, we tend to share our data among our research team and to analyze them across different courses. To make the collected data reusable, the research designs and aims must be picked up by the informed consent given from the study participants. According to the privacy and ethical issues, the DELICATE checklist can be applied for creating an informed consent. The checklist makes the research more transparent for the participants [7]. Furthermore, a data management plan is required that gives information about kind of produced data and data sharing and archiving concept [17]. When these points are considered, a research scenario along the three domains of data sharing would be possible like described in the following.

---

[1] https://dsgvo-gesetz.de/.

Private Domain. The private domain is the environment of the initial data collection at the project partners. For instance, a researcher from OVGU executes an initial skill assessment. This may include a student characterization by questionnaires or measures the students' learning behavior with error data. After data collection, data are stored in their finest granularity in the private data storage. This storage is secured, such that only the researchers who collected the data can assess it. Hence, analyzing the data with respect to gender, field of study, and programming success is possible by involving the aforementioned personal information that is else hidden.

Collaboration Domain. In the collaboration domain, the collected data leaves the protected area of a single researcher and is to be shared with researchers from the whole project group. Therefore, all data must be properly pseudonymized. This means, e.g., study participant's names must be modified but individuals (without their personal information) are still trackable from the researcher involved in the data generation. Nonetheless, a comparison for example between the data about people's success of programming with less or more skill or depending on the field of study can be run as well. Finding a balance between privacy and data quality is a general issue named privacy-utility challenge.

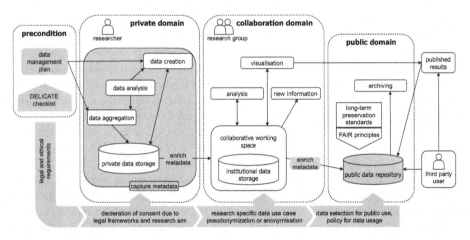

Fig. 1. Collaborative research data sharing in a learning analytics scenario

Public Domain. For public data sharing, all data must be fully anonymized. This means that all personal data collected must be deleted or aggregated accordingly. Therefore, one may rely on notions like k-anonymity [30], which conceptually aggregates individual information into groups. This means, for instance, that students of underrepresented study plans may be deleted, or several study plans could be summarized into "other study plans" in order to not reveal their identity. In addition, in case data are vulnerable to the differential snapshot problem allowing to re-identify data of an individual despite proper aggregation, noise is injected into the aggregated data to reach differential privacy [8].

Despite the anonymization, with properly described metadata captured during the research process, the research scenario could be reproduced and pretests for a further study of a third-party scientist could be run.

2.3   Requirements

A data sharing system based on the concept in Fig. 1 makes it easy for the researcher to share the data produced. In each domain, different information, including metadata, are important for researchers. In this setting, there is the possibility to fine-tune what data are shared with what group of people. However, we also identified additional requirements on the research data management solutions in this scenario, as we detail in the following.

R1 – Reusability [33]: To enable third-party researchers to use the data for the reuse scenarios above, complete structured information about the whole life-cycle of the data is needed. This includes information about the stakeholder that produced the data and his institution where the data was collected. Both person and institutions need an identifier, like an ORCID, for traceability. The data creation process can only be reproduced with a detailed description of the research design. This refers to the type of instrument (e.g., questionnaires, software) with detailed description. Information about measured activity and attributes used as variables for computations and calculations to make the learning process visible, as well as information about learner and learning environment (e.g., learning concept) are essential for reusability of datasets. On the level of a data package, details of data modification regarding data protection must be shown.

R2 – Findability [33]: Librarians ensure findability by giving a persistent identifier to the dataset and embed it into existing classification systems like the Dewey decimal classification for searching engines: for learning analytics, we can apply the class 300 for social science and the division 370 for education [5]. Existing repositories should be indexed in the re3data[2], the Registry of Research Data Repositories [20].

R3 – Privacy: Whenever a project works with sensitive data (i.e., user-related, personal data), it needs to be assured that the user agrees with the processing of this data. Usually, participants agree on an informed consent, which contains information about the whole research data life cycle [23]. It details who works with the data, how the data are processed, as well as how are the data shared (usually in an anonymized form), and the duration of storage [12]. As a result, what data have to be stored for each domain is also regulated by the informed consent and builds the basis for data storage.

R4 – Provenance of Data Curation: In order to implement the privacy concerns as well as different information requirements from the domains of the research data management, data have to be curated and transformed from its initial state to the desired state of each domain. Since each domain bases their

---

[2] https://www.re3data.org/.

decisions and research results on this curated data, data provenance is an important property that needs to be guaranteed. That means that not only the data's origin due to metadata, but also applied curation methods need to be transparently described for all researchers.

R5 – Systematic Data Duplication: One of our requirements is to propose a methodology that integrates data curation to systematically duplicate the data in a (semi-)automated fashion without human intervention. As a result, when data are changed, the curation pipeline should be executed with the updated version of the data, which systematically produces the data for each domain.

R6 – Universality: Since our collaborative use case is just one example among numerous applications using different repositories, the proposed solution needs to be universally applicable. This means, it should base on standard technologies and has to be easily implemented in state-of-the-art research data repositories.

R7 – Usability: Collaborative research data management involves scientists from different domains as well as data librarians. Each of them has different expectations, knowledge, and responsibilities, which means that the workflow and tooling should hide the complexity of the research data management that the data librarian architects [13,14]. An improved usability will, thus, assure a general acceptance of the approach in the team as well as with other scientists.

3   Preliminaries on Relational Databases

Before explaining how we solve the aforementioned requirements with our proposed workflow, we introduce preliminary background of (semi-)structured data management, whose functionality can be used to adapt the data for different stakeholders. To this end, we first introduce the data model of relational database systems and their operations and functions that can be used in the concept of views as a use-case-specific data management. Furthermore, we review functionalities of current research data repositories.

3.1   Structured Data Management – Relational Database Systems

For a formal definition of structured (i.e., relational or tabular) data, we refer to the definition of Codd [3]. He defines a relation as an array of values $(v_1, v_2, ..., v_n)$ forming a tuple over a specific array of attributes $(A_1, A_2, ..., A_n)$, called a schema S. Each attribute has a specific domain (i.e., value type as $D_1, D_2, ..., D_n$). The most common domains are integers or floating points numbers, characters, or strings.

View Definition. Views are an essential benefit of database management systems. They are virtual relations that allow for a better structuring and use-case-specific data preparation [10]. A view is represented by an SQL query built from the aforementioned operations and functions, and only shows the excerpt of the database that is visible through the SQL query. Hence, it can be used to limit the accessible content for specific users. For example, a view for the public domain could limit the view on the results of the questionnaires by aggregating data of underrepresented groups (e.g., study courses with too little students are added up to "others") to keep anonymity. Notably, views are only virtual relations, in the sense that there is no physical relation stored that holds the data of the view. When accessing the view, the corresponding data is fetched from the base relations of the view by applying the SQL query.

3.2 State-of-the-Art Research Data Management Repositories

Data management repositories in a library context have to fit different purposes, like storing digitized content collections, rare book collections, electronic dissertation collections, media art collections, and for us important, scientific data collections [24]. A broad scope of different software frameworks has been developed over the last decades, but regarding scientific research data management, repositories should match the requirements of librarians and researchers. Librarians are mostly concerned with provenance aspects and maintenance of the collections over time, which includes the use of persistent IDs, a moderation stage for data ingestion with an option to embargo the publication of datasets, as well as the support of restricted access to datasets. Furthermore, options for metadata export and migration as well as the easy extraction of metadata should be included. In contrast, researchers require aspects in depositing, managing, discovery, and reuse of data. Therefore, a repository needs proper search options, standardized citation formats, use of correct licenses, no restriction to size, upload, and editing functions of metadata, and features, such as controlled vocabularies. Furthermore, it is important to share data across different domains (cf. Fig. 1) and to provide an optimized discovery, download, and reuse of data.

Not all repository software fit these requirements. The OpenDOAR[3] (Directory of Open Access Repositories) has listed about 5,800 repositories (state, January 2022), while DSpace is used for 39% of these repositories, which can be explained with its closeness to the OAIS framework [28,29]. Just 418 repositories are used exclusively for datasets. 108 repositories use DSpace, which sets apart other appropriate frameworks like EPrints with 61 and Fedora with 16 instances. Regarding technical features, all frameworks are open source, support the configuration of user roles, customizing their metadata, and adapt to existing standards [1,24]. Thereby, metadata configuration meets the requirement of reusability and provenance of data curation. Content and control of datasets by licensing, e.g., Creative Commons[4] license, is possible and meets the privacy requirement by giving reuse restrictions. Findability requirements are served by content discovery within the frameworks with integrated search engines and a metadata harvesting with an OAI-PMH gateway for the dataset metadata is configurable. Just for Fedora, Google Scholar indexing is not possible [4]. Persistent identifiers, like handles or DOIs, are supported in all frameworks. All three

---

[3] https://v2.sherpa.ac.uk/opendoar/.
[4] https://creativecommons.org/.

frameworks support reporting of downloads and accesses. EPrints offers a format migration risk tool for preservation and migration of metadata, while the other both give the option to implement one by the managed institution. None of the frameworks offer a publication tool to supervise or administer the publication process for data, which is already possible in the area of open access publication of journal articles.[5] Therefore, our approach takes the already existing database frameworks used in the context of libraries to address privacy issues in research data management of sensitive personal data.

4   A Framework for Sharing of Research Data in Collaborative Usage Scenarios

To achieve a collaborative research data management, we propose to implement the view concept in research data repositories. Views are a powerful feature of relational database systems, which are already the standard backbone of most research data repositories [9]. Hence, exploiting this feature solves our requirements for free. In the following, we describe a generalized workflow of how to apply views on the data management for arbitrary (semi-)structured data of research projects. As a proof of concept, we exemplarily describe how we implemented the workflow in our project.

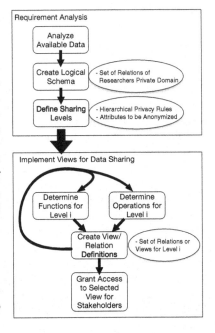

Fig. 2. Workflow of view definitions for collaborative data sharing

4.1   Workflow

Based on the definition of views and available functions, we define a workflow how to apply views on a given scenario in Fig. 2.

The workflow is split into two phases. The first phase represents the requirement analysis, where a scientist communicates details about gathered data with the responsible person for research data management (i.e., a data librarian). In the second phase, the data librarian implements the requirements by implementing different views for stakeholders and grants access rights. We, now, briefly describe the necessary steps of each phase.

Requirement Analysis. The requirement analysis starts by gathering data about the study or experiment whose data is to be stored. To this end, the data librarian interviews scientists, analyzes their data (e.g., often in (semi-)

---

[5] https://pkp.sfu.ca/ojs/.

structured form as a csv or JSON file), and gathers metadata as well as regulatory rules (e.g., informed consents). Based on this information, a logical schema is built, which is the second step during requirement analysis. In this step, the data librarian creates a schema as a set of relations storing the (semi-)structured data. Usually, one file is mapped to a relation whose attributes represent columns or properties of the data from the files. While this will probably not create minimal and redundancy-free relations, the focus is here on the easy mapping between research data and database schema. The resulting logical schema is the first level of data storage and represents the fine-grained original data of the study or experiment. Thus, the exchange of information between data librarian and scientist should be as detailed as possible to allow for a holistic data management, which reuses the data for the other publishing levels. The last step in the requirement analysis is to define the sharing levels and determine their requirements. Notably, although we define only three levels for our scenario in Fig. 1, it is also possible to create more levels in case of more stakeholders involved. Each of the defined sharing levels consists of a set of privacy rules (i.e., attributes to be anonymized or pseudonymized) based on the informed consent of study participants, copyright, and licensing regulations. These rules are usually represented as a set of written documents (e.g., mails, word, or PDF files). After this step, a logical schema of the whole data storage and post-processing actions is passed to the second phase, implementing these models and actions.

Implement Views for Data Sharing. In the second phase of our proposed workflow, the data librarian uses the gathered information to create physical data management for the stakeholders. That means, the goal is to create one stakeholder-specific schema such that requirements are reflected in the schema of that level. This process follows a recursive flow because, usually, views on level $i + 1$ are based on the more fine-grained level i. Furthermore, it is possible that some views or tables can be used for several levels if there is nothing to be changed (e.g., one of the relations is already fully anonymized in level i).

To create views, we use the gathered information from the requirement analysis (i.e., base relations and privacy rules) to derive a set of functions and operators that transfers a single or several relations to a set of target views for the current level i. For these generated views, it is important to decide whether these are simple views or materialized views. The last step in this phase is to assign each stakeholder their views by granting specific access rights. For further information on access rights within databases and views see [18,25].

Notably, this workflow is flexible and can be redone once certain requirements change. While the view definitions can simply be adapted to suit the new requirements, one should be cautiously when updating dependent views. Since the definition of the views is done hierarchically, changing the views of level i may change the view definitions of level $i + 1$. Hence, these changes propagate to views in a higher hierarchy level. As a result, the deeper the change in these levels, the more effort is caused for updating dependent views.

4.2   Exemplary Application on Our Research Data Management

After defining the workflow for a collaborative research data management, we now present a proof-of-concept by applying this workflow to our own research data management in the learning analytics context described in Sect. 2.1. We chose this use case because (apart from our availability of the data) it allows for a suitable hierarchy of sharing levels, as well as the usage of different operators and functions due to different anonymization requirements per level. Furthermore, we limit our example to the data gathered at OVGU focusing on the Moodle log, questionnaire data, and error logs from SQLValidator.

In the following, we first present the logical schema representing the base relations from the use case. Second, we derive sharing levels from the description in Sect. 2.2 and then define suitable views.

Logical Schema. After the initial requirements analysis and analysis of the data sources, we create a set of relations that represents the logical schema of the research data to be stored. This logical schema is shown in Fig. 3. We define three relations – one for each dataset – which are **Student_Moodle_Action**, **Student_Questionnaire_Answers**, and **Student_Error_Logs**.

Student_Moodle_Action contains all interactions of users with the course site and material in moodle. Apart from the actions on specific material (components), the data also comprise several confidential attributes, such as name of the student and their IP.

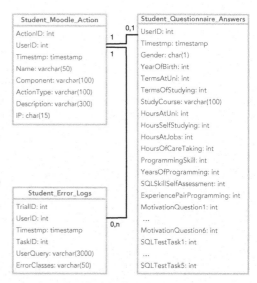

Fig. 3. Basic relations of the repository

Student_Questionnaire_Answers contains answers of the questionnaire that students fill when starting to use SQLValidator. We record personal information, which also includes the summed up semesters at any university (**TermsAtUni**) and the semesters in the current study course (**TermsOfStudying**) as well as an average number of hours per week for different activities (course work, self studying, jobbing, taking care of children or relatives). As skill assessment, we ask participants for their self assessment of their programming skills, their SQL skills, and whether they have got experience in pair programming due to the focus on collaborative task solutions in the course. Their motivation is analyzed through six questions rated on a Likert scale, and their actual SQL skill is assessed through five small single-choice questions about SQL.

Finally, in the **Student_Questionnaire_Answers** relation, we store user trials for solving an SQL task in SQLValidator. For each query that the user tests, we store encountered errors as a set of error classes. From this relation, learning analytics can infer usage patterns (trial-&-error vs. thoughtful improvements) when solving exercise tasks.

Sharing Levels and Requirements. For defining the sharing levels, we use the defined relations from the previous step and all gathered information that define attributes to be pseudonymized or anonymized. In our use case, the necessary information is the *informed consent* of the questionnaires and *terms of use* of the tools and our hierarchy of users of the data. From this information, we define the three levels from Fig. 1.

View Definitions

Simple Views in Public and Collaborative Domain. In the private domain, having no (additional) privacy requirements, the view definitions are equivalent to the ones shown in Fig. 3. The only difference to the raw data is that we correct certain obvious data errors, such as null-value entries. Technically, the creation of this level means copying the entire dataset and perform a sequence of **Update** statements on the data. For reproducibility reasons (i.e., to ensure provenance), the whole procedure is encapsulated into a single user-defined function [16], permanently stored in the database system.

In the level implementing the collaboration domain, we need to ensure additional privacy requirements. To this end, we exclude certain attributes from the view schema, such as the **Name** attribute. Moreover, we pseudonymize various attributes, our compliance department deems privacy relevant. This applies, for instance, to the **IP** attribute, where we mask the final block. Technically, we create a view for each of the three tables requiring only projections, that the standard SQL offers. This includes string manipulation (e.g., to mask the IP addresses). We depict the corresponding view definition of the table Student_Moodle_Action in Listing 1.1. This view now hides the name of the student and masks the IP by extracting the first parts of the IP-address (due to the usage of the substr function) and concatenates three #'s for the masked part.

Listing 1.1. Exemplary Collaborative View Definition for Student_Moodle_Action

```
1  Create View Collab_Student_Moodle_Action As
2  Select ActionID, UserID, Timestmp, Component, ActionType, Description,
3    Concat(Substr(IP, 0, Len(IP)-3),'###')
4  From Student_Moodle_Action
```

Complex Data Access in Public Domain. When sharing data publicly, privacy is a major concern. While some attributes of the public domain can be directly provided in the form of views on the collaborative domain, various attributes may reveal private data when seen individually, or in combination. In this case, we cannot give access to the underlying data itself, but a user may issue a well-defined set of queries on the database to compute *statistics*. The statistics are a histogram containing the frequency of attribute values. There is a white list of attributes one may compute the statistics on. The statistics additionally ensure *k*-anonymity and differential privacy. We explain the details of this concept and its technical realization with the help of an example next. In the example, we rely on the `Gender` attribute. Note, in the project there was a vivid discussion whether one should include such attributes at all, finally motivating this solution.

For an explanation of our concept, we refer to Fig. 4. Part (a) of the figure illustrates the first layer of our concept: we give access only to aggregated statistics. This way, one knows that there are 68 male, 37 female and one diverse students questioned. At implementation level, one specifies the attribute where one wants to compute the statistics on. Then the system generates the corresponding query. For the `Gender` attribute, the query is as follows: `select count(*), gender from t group by gender order by count(*)`.

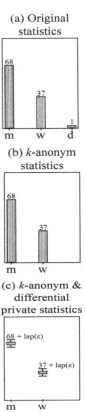

(a) Original statistics

(b) *k*-anonym statistics

(c) *k*-anonym & differential private statistics

Obviously, this aggregation does not protect the privacy of the diverse student. Therefore (cf. Fig. 4(b)), we introduce a second layer to protect e.g., privacy of the diverse student using the *k*-anonymity notion [30]. That is, we do not output a group having less than *k* tuples, where *k* is a parameter one can configure. Setting $k = 20$ results in the statistics shown in part (b) of Fig. 4. Technically, we introduce a having clause in the above SQL statement: `having count(*)>k`. Note, altering the attribute values, e.g., changing 'm' to -1, using 0 for 'w', and 1 for 'd', does not improve privacy, as simple frequency attacks break this encoding [26]. Besides computing statistics on a single attribute, we also allow attribute combination (e.g., `Gender` and `YearOfBirth`). Moreover, the user may specify arbitrary `where` conditions for filtering the data.

Despite, giving access only to aggregated statistics satisfying k-anonymity, we may still compromise the privacy of individuals [8]. As compensation, one sanitizes the statistics with a well-defined amount of noise to achieve ϵ-differential privacy. To achieve differential privacy, we rely on the Laplace mechanism, adding noise following a zero-mean Laplace distribution. Parameter ϵ is the privacy budget. Lower values of ϵ indicate better privacy, but implicate higher noise. Common values for ϵ are 0.1 to 10. We use $\epsilon = 1.0$. This means that the expected difference per group between the original statistics and the sanitized statistics is 1. That is,

Fig. 4. Illustration of privacy concept for the public domain

sanitation only marginally affects data quality. Technically, we modify the projection clause of the above SQL as follows: `select round(count(*) + lap(ε))`.

Here, lap(ϵ) generates a random Laplace number (i.e., the noise) with zero mean and shape parameter $\lambda = \frac{1}{\epsilon}$. The additional round() maps the real-valued statistics back to integers to represent a proper count value.

5   Conclusion and Discussion on Open Challenges

In this paper, we propose a research data management framework that uses database views to share structured data among different stakeholders and collaborators. This framework fulfills our requirements of (R1) reusability that is given through the integration into a research data repository, (R2) findability through common metadata among all derived views, (R3) fine-tuned privacy due to flexible view definitions, (R4) provenance, since the view definitions resemble the data curation steps, (R5) systematic data duplication where the system handles all sharing levels semi-automatically, (R6) can be universally applied in all research data repositories using relational databases as backend, and (R7) can be used easily used when implementing a respective frontend. Still, there are further open challenges to be addressed, which we detail in the following.

Systematic Versioning. Versioning of changes of datasets is a powerful possibility that comes almost automatically with a database. It requires to model data in such a way that time information is added to each data entry – a common concept from domain of data warehousing [15]. These historization concepts are well known and could be applied for our data model according their requirements.

Complex Structure of Sharing Domains. In our solution, we address a three-level model with private, collaborative, and public domain. However, the view concept also enables other hierarchy scenarios, for instance, more fine-granular levels where different groups collaborate, or even a group-in-group approach (i.e., each scientist inside a group has her own domain).

Advanced Data Curation. Besides the above challenges there has to be a definition, which data processing and curation is done within the database and in what cases further interfaces (e.g., for advanced data processing algorithms such as statistical and data mining techniques or domain-specific data preprocessing) are necessary. With the computation outside the database environment and usage of interfaces, a loss of data process description and data provenance is possible. Therefore, these challenges must be addressed at the development of interfaces. In such a case, a metadata description comparable to our model is necessary for each interface.

Privacy Utility Challenge. In this work, we face the privacy utility challenge, i.e., as a learning analytics researcher (or, generally, data analyst), we want to share as much data as possible. However, following a privacy perspective, one is highly reluctant about sharing data that may potentially reveal private information. Investigating how to find a meaningful and legal trade off between privacy and utility is not the main intention of our paper. This is additional work, we negotiated with various stakeholders in the course of our project. Instead, the presented solution is an exemplary, project-specific solution illustrating how one can use views in a relational database system to implement collaborative data sharing. The implementation thereby reveals that, using standard SQL features, a) one can easily implement well-known privacy notions and b) the view definitions – by design – serve as proof how data is anonymized.

Data Model Selection. In our paper, we only address a very structural data model. With the emergence of unstructured data (e.g., in big data scenarios), techniques for NoSQL data models [11] are applied inside database systems. This enables a more flexible way in the metadata definition phase, but requires more knowledge of such data processing. Additionally, the use of free text fields enables a flexibility that creates ambiguities at the same time.

Funding Information. German Federal Ministry of Education and Research [16DHB 3008].

References

1. Amorim, R.C., Castro, J.A., Rocha da Silva, J., Ribeiro, C.: A comparison of research data management platforms: architecture, flexible metadata and interoperability. Univ. Access Inf. Soc. **16**(4), 851–862 (2016). https://doi.org/10.1007/s10209-016-0475-y
2. Bloemers, M., Montesanti, A.: The FAIR funding model: providing a framework for research funders to drive the transition toward FAIR data management and stewardship practices. Data Intell. **2**(1–2), 171–180 (2020). https://doi.org/10.1162/dint_a_00039
3. Codd, E.F.: A relational model of data for large shared data banks. Commun. ACM **26**(1), 64–69 (1983). https://doi.org/10.1145/357980.358007
4. Devarakonda, R., Palanisamy, G., Green, J., Wilson, B.: Data sharing and retrieval using OAI-PMH. Earth Sci. Inf. **4**(1), 1–5 (2011). https://doi.org/10.1007/s12145-010-0073-0
5. Dewey, M.: Dewey decimal classification and relative index. 2, Schedules 000-599. OCLC Library (1989)
6. Dietrich, A.: Liascript: a domain-specific-language for interactive online courses. In: Multi Conference on Computer Science and Information Systems, p. 186 (2019)
7. Drachsler, H., Greller, W.: Privacy and analytics: it's a delicate issue a checklist for trusted learning analytics. In: Gašević, D., Lynch, G., Dawson, S., Drachsler, H., Penstein Rosé, C. (eds.) Proceedings of the Sixth International Conference on Learning Analytics and Knowledge, LAK 2016, pp. 89–98. Association for Computing Machinery, New York (2016). https://doi.org/10.1145/2883851.2883893
8. Dwork, C.: Differential privacy. In: Bugliesi, M., Preneel, B., Sassone, V., Wegener, I. (eds.) ICALP 2006. LNCS, vol. 4052, pp. 1–12. Springer, Heidelberg (2006). https://doi.org/10.1007/11787006_1
9. Garcia-Molina, H., Ullman, J.D., Widom, J.: Database Systems: The Complete Book, 2nd edn. Pearson International Edition, London (2008)

10. Gray, J., Reuter, A.: Transaction Processing: Concepts and Techniques. Elsevier, Amsterdam (1992)
11. Grolinger, K., Higashino, W.A., Tiwari, A., Capretz, M.A.M.: Data management in cloud environments: NoSQL and NewSQL data stores. J. Cloud Comput. Adv. Syst. Appl. **2**(1), 1–24 (2013). https://doi.org/10.1186/2192-113X-2-22
12. Hildt, E., Laas, K.: Informed consent in digital data management. In: Laas, K., Davis, M., Hildt, E. (eds.) Codes of Ethics and Ethical Guidelines. TILELT, vol. 23, pp. 55–81. Springer, Cham (2022). https://doi.org/10.1007/978-3-030-86201-5_4
13. Jørn Nielsen, H., Hjørland, B.: Curating research data: the potential roles of libraries and information professionals. J. Doc. **70**(2), 221–240 (2014). https://doi.org/10.1108/JD-03-2013-0034
14. Kim, Y., Zhang, P.: Understanding data sharing behaviors of stem researchers: the roles of attitudes, norms, and data repositories. Libr. Inf. Sci. Res. **37**(3), 189–200 (2015). https://doi.org/10.1016/j.lisr.2015.04.006
15. Kimball, R.: Slowly Changing Dimensions. Unlike OLTP Systems, Data Warehouse Systems Cab Track Historical Data. DBMS Online, vol. 9, no. 4 (1996)
16. Linnemann, V., et al.: Design and implementation of an extensible database management system supporting user defined data types and functions. In: VLDB, pp. 294–305 (1988)
17. Michener, W.K.: Ten simple rules for creating a good data management plan. PLoS Comput. Biol. **11**(10), 1–9 (2015). https://doi.org/10.1371/journal.pcbi.1004525
18. Motro, A.: An access authorization model for relational databases based on algebraic manipulation of view definitions. In: ICDE Fifth International Conference on Data Engineering, pp. 339–347 (1989). https://doi.org/10.1109/ICDE.1989.47234
19. Obionwu, V., Broneske, D., Hawlitschek, A., Köppen, V., Saake, G.: SQLValidator - an online student playground to learn SQL. Datenbank-Spektrum (2021)
20. Pampel, H., et al.: Making research data repositories visible: the re3data.org registry. PLoS ONE **8**(11), 1–10 (2013). https://doi.org/10.1371/journal.pone.0078080
21. Pardo, A., Siemens, G.: Ethical and privacy principles for learning analytics. Br. J. Edu. Technol. **45**(3), 438–450 (2014). https://doi.org/10.1111/bjet.12152
22. Pasquetto, I.V., Randles, B.M., Borgman, C.L.: On the reuse of scientific data. Data Sci. J. (2017)
23. Pouchard, L.: Revisiting the data lifecycle with big data curation. Int. J. Digit. Curation (2015)
24. Pyrounakis, G., Nikolaidou, M., Hatzopoulos, M.: Building digital collections using open source digital repository software: a comparative study. Int. J. Digital Libr. Syst. (IJDLS) **4**(1), 10–25 (2014). https://doi.org/10.4018/ijdls.2014010102
25. Rizvi, S., Mendelzon, A., Sudarshan, S., Roy, P.: Extending query rewriting techniques for fine-grained access control. In: Proceedings of the 2004 ACM SIGMOD International Conference on Management of Data, SIGMOD 2004, pp. 551–562. Association for Computing Machinery, New York (2004). https://doi.org/10.1145/1007568.1007631
26. Sanamrad, T., Kossmann, D.: Query log attack on encrypted databases. In: Jonker, W., Petković, M. (eds.) SDM 2013. LNCS, vol. 8425, pp. 95–107. Springer, Cham (2014). https://doi.org/10.1007/978-3-319-06811-4_14
27. Scheffel, M., Drachsler, H., Slavi, S., Specht, M.: Quality indicators for learning analytics. Educ. Technol. Soc. **17**(4), 117–132 (2014)
28. Smith, M., et al.: DSpace: an open source dynamic digital repository. D-Lib Mag. **9**(1) (2003). https://www.dlib.org/dlib/january03/smith/01smith.html

29. International Organization for Standardization: Space data and information transfer systems - Open archival information system (OAIS) - Reference model. International Organization for Standardization, Vernier, Geneva, Switzerland, ISO 14721:2012-09 edn. (2012). https://www.iso.org/standard/57284.html
30. Sweeney, L.: K-anonymity: a model for protecting privacy. Int. J. Uncertain. Fuzziness Knowledge-Based Syst. **10**(5), 557–570 (2002)
31. Treloar, A., Klump, J.: Updating the data curation continuum. IJDC **14**(1), 87–101 (2019). https://doi.org/10.2218/ijdc.v14i1.643
32. Viberg, O., Hatakka, M., Bälter, O., Mavroudi, A.: The current landscape of learning analytics in higher education. Comput. Hum. Behav. **89**, 98–110 (2018). https://doi.org/10.1016/j.chb.2018.07.027
33. Wilkinson, M.D., et al.: The fair guiding principles for scientific data management and stewardship. Sci. Data **3**, 160018 (2016). https://doi.org/10.1038/sdata.2016.18

Towards Efficient Data Access Through Multiple Relationship in Graph-Structured Digital Archives

Kazuma Kusu[1]([envelope]) [iD], Takahiro Komamizu[2] [iD], and Kenji Hatano[1] [iD]

[1] Doshisha University, Kyotanabe, Kyoto, Japan
{kkusu,hatano}@acm.org
[2] Nagoya University, Nagoya, Aichi, Japan
taka-coma@acm.org

Abstract. The research field of digital libraries mainly deals with data with graph structure. Graph database management systems (GDBMSs) are suitable for managing data in the digital library because the data size is large and its structure is complex. However, when performing a non-simple search or analysis on a graph, GDBMSs cannot avoid reaching already-scanned nodes from different starting nodes by repeatedly traversing edges such as property paths pattern in SPARQL. Therefore, when a GDBMS reaches high degree nodes, the number of graph traversals increases in proportion to the number of its adjacent nodes. Consequently, the cost of traversing multiple paths extremely increases affected by nodes connected enormous the number of edges in conventional GDBMSs. In this paper, we propose a data access approach by repeatedly traversing edges belonging to a specific relationship or anything one while distinguishing between high degree nodes and low degree ones. Finally, a result of our experiment indicated our approach can increase the speed of repeat traversals by a factor of a maximum of ten.

Keywords: Graph-structured digital archives · Property paths · Repeat traversal · Digital archive management

1 Introduction

A transition from digitally archiving various information individually to connecting related information in archives has got attention from digital library researchers [4,8,9]. Subsequently, researchers in that field have proposed convenient applications for accessing and analyzing digital archives by combining several kinds of data. The connectivity among several types of digital libraries is available because the entity in the data has a relationship with other entities.

In practice, needless to note about social networks and knowledge bases, scholarly data have linked components in many pieces of data [8]. Hence, it should be conscious to frequently focus on links or the relationships between the entities in data for manners of data access and analysis. The size of data in the

Y.-H. Tseng et al. (Eds.): ICADL 2022, LNCS 13636, pp. 377–391, 2022.
https://doi.org/10.1007/978-3-031-21756-2_29

digital library increases year after year. Therefore, it is required to employ an efficient way of accessing and analyzing the data.

Researchers and companies have studied graph database management systems (GDBMSs) [5,22] to manage a huge graph-structured data and process traversals on the data efficiently. Moreover, each GDBMS has a data structure for rapidly obtaining edges or nodes called a graph index or an adjacent list. A GDBMS-based *relation* structure, which is also known as table structure, is good performance at global search of sub-graphs with indexes, but the size of index tends to become huge. Such GDBMS is called non-native one because the data store do not shape up graph-like. In contrast, a native GDBMS employs a storage that manages nodes with pointers referencing their adjacent-nodes; this data store keeps a shape of a graph on storage. Therefore, native GDBMSs have an impactive characteristic for efficient traversal, called *index-free adjacency*, in a local search because the cost for searching sub-graphs depends only on an adjacent list of each node. This characteristic is suitable for digital archives that more complex and bigger the graph tend to be year by year, because the older entries are increasing links and relationships to other data. In this paper, we presupposes employing a native GDBMS because our study considers that it requires to ensure the efficiency of graph traversal.

However, GDBMSs execute a graph traversal indiscriminately without considering the degrees of nodes which are the numbers of nodes connected from them. Hence, this traversal approach can be inefficient, because the number of graph traversal increases enormously due to the presence of high-degree nodes. To realize efficient graph traversal, graph traversal beginning from a node connected an enormous number of edges should be avoided.

In the research field of network science, real-world networks have graph-topological properties named *scale-free* or *small-world networks*. Scale-free property is a characteristic of a graph that the small number of nodes have significantly higher degree than other nodes. Small-world property (a.k.a. six degrees of separation in social networks) is another property that the average shortest path lengths between every pairs of nodes is small because nodes having huge degrees are easily reachable from other nodes. Moreover, scholarly data, knowledge graphs, and Web archives has the properties as we described above without exception [2]. Therefore, when traversing a graph in a repeated manner, high-degree nodes are easily reachable.

On the contrary, GDBMSs often call an operation performing repeated traversal when users want to obtain paths consisting of edges labeled a few types of specific relationship like "a friend-of-a-friend" relationship. In the above case, a chance to reach high-degree nodes is raised due to the small-world property. Therefore, it is easily surmised that the number of candidate nodes for next traversals significantly is increased so that the performance of repeated traversals can be largely degraded.

In this study, our goal is to solve the bottleneck of a GDBMS, which causes when it repeatedly traverses edges in the graph due to the existing networks' properties. Our previous study [10] defined a repetition path as long paths obtained by repeatedly traversing edges labeled a specified relationship or any ones, and moreover, the process querying the paths was called repeated traversal. Furthermore, our previous study proposed a structure of a graph index for scanning paths specified length from a high-degree node to avoid the bottleneck process [10]. However, the proposed index had two shortcomings when the graph size becomes large. One is that the performance of scanning repetition paths is unstable, and the other is that the construction time of the index becomes unacceptably large. Therefore, in this paper, we propose a method for compressing the size of our graph index for scanning destination nodes of repetition paths, then it simultaneously enables us to construct our index faster.

Our contributions in this study is to:

- develop efficient construction approach for our index [10] by a compression approach; and
- enable GDBMSs to traverse long paths consist of a specified type or any ones of edges by a low cost.

As we described above, our index enables GDBs to improve the performance for a repeat graph traversal operation, which tends to be a high cost in real-world graphs.

The rest of this paper is structured as follows. In Sect. 2, we describe an index-free adjacency of native GDBMs and studies aimed to improve the performance of sub-graph extraction. In Sect. 3, we propose an approach for reducing redundant of our previous index [10]. In Sect. 4, to confirm the effectiveness of our compression approach, we conduct an experiment to evaluate the performance of our index construction compared with a previous our approach for constructing our index.

2   Related Works

A considerable number of studies have been conducted on graph management methods and indexes for improving traversing performances [20]. This section discusses studies focusing on native GDBMSs employing *index-free adjacency* and those concerning indexes for searching paths in a query.

Section 2.1 describes management approach for a huge graph on native GDBMSs that employ index-free adjacency. Section 2.2 introduces indexing approaches for inquiring paths fast. Finally, in Sect. 2.3, we advocate the differences of our approach compared with conventional approaches in the light of conventional ones.

2.1   The Index-Free Adjacency of Native GDBMSs

Native GDBMSs with index-free adjacency [19] can efficiently retrieve adjacent nodes by using a small adjacent list of each node. This adjacent list of each node has pointers referring to the address of its adjacent nodes in database storage. Moreover, there is the case that the nodes' edges consist of a large variety of labeled edges, but native GDBMSs do not affect the performance of a graph traversal in such a case. This is because native GDBMSs have a hash map of edges grouped by their relationship so these can get edges having the relationship specified in a query from the hash map. To retrieve matching sub-graphs, furthermore, a native GDBMS first scans origin nodes as sub-graphs from a database; subsequently, it consecutively expands them by traversing edges based on adjacent lists of the target nodes.

In contrast, conventional native GDBMSs are not efficient for queries requiring larger hops of traversals. They only grasp adjacent connectivity of nodes, in other words, they cannot grasp connectivity of nodes which are more than one-hop away from each other. When the conventional GDBMSs process the queries requiring larger hops of traversals, they are affected by high-degree nodes because such nodes explosively increase the number of paths being traversed.

However, conventional native GDBMSs cannot grasp the all connectivities between nodes in a graph, which cannot be revealed using anything but the adjacency list of each node.

Consequently, it occasionally happens to traverse the edges even if the target node for traversing is a high-degree node. Hence, it traverses edges if the target node is that node nevertheless. As mentioned above, index-free adjacency is the most powerful characteristic for traversing the graph regionally. However, in the case of traversing the graph globally, this is not an efficient approach.

2.2   Path Index

Path index-based approaches are roughly classified into two categories of approaches. Those in the first category are that DB administrators construct indices by their estimation of graph pattern queries in the future. Those in the other category assume to use query logs to extract frequent graph patterns for indexing [21].

There are two ways for managing the graph: one is to handle a huge graph, the other is to perform numerous small graphs [21]. Example graphs of the former methods are social graphs, the Web graph, coauthor graphs, citation graphs, etc. By contrast, the latter is applicable in the case of chemical structures and protein-protein interaction networks.

Most conventional graph indexes have been focused on GDBMSs for numerous small graphs. However, in the case of managing a large single graph, graph index with same way as numerous small graphs is inefficient due to its size. In a large single graph, the number of nodes and edges is larger, therefore, the number of paths in the graph is also larger than that in the numerous small graphs. As a result, the index size of the graph becomes considerably large due to the large number of path candidates, and, hence, the index scan becomes inefficient.

2.3   Our Goal

Conventional approaches for extracting sub-graphs have been realized by graph traversals and the graph index described in Sect. 2.1 and 2.2. In the case of management for the graph, it is efficient to extract sub-graphs with index-free adjacency regionally, but native GDBMSs have not considered an inefficiency affected by nodes having too many node degrees. Hence, in this study, we should deal with nodes having a large number of edges labeled one type of relationship. In the case of using a graph index, on the other hand, indexing a specified pattern of a path and extracting sub-graphs with the index becomes inefficient caused by the graph size. Thus, these approaches suffer from extracting sub-graphs from a large single graph in an efficient way.

In the research field of network science, researchers have reported that real-world networks have properties named scale-free and small world [16]. The scale-free property implies that the degree distribution of such a network follows a power-law distribution. The small world property indicates that arbitrary two nodes in a networks can be reached within a small number of hops. Conventional native GDBMSs traverse edges with regardless of node's degree because these do not take into account the aforementioned properties of real-world networks. Moreover, it gradually becomes easy to reach high-degree nodes by repeatedly traversing edges because of the small world property.

In this study, therefore, we aim to enable native GDBMSs to efficiently traverse a long path extracted by traversing edges labeled one type of relationship repeatedly from a huge real-world graph. We pay attention to the fact that traversing repetition paths makes the opportunity to reach the nodes from other nodes increase because of the properties of real-world graphs such as scale-free and small-world. Therefore, we propose an approach for managing the graph that enables native GDBMSs to make it efficient to traverse repetition paths by considering the nodes.

3   Proposed Method

Our study aims to improve the efficiency when GDBMSs repeatedly traverse long paths extracted by the traversing edges labeled by one type of relationship from a prominent actual graph such as social networks that grows larger with time. In this paper, we name a high-degree node *HDN* which overlaps with another concept called *hub* in network science [2]. In contrast, we define the exclusive nodes of HDNs, low-degree nodes called LDNs. We focus on the fact that traversing *repetition paths* from other nodes increases the probability of reaching to HDNs because of the properties such as scale-free and small-world of the real-world graphs. Therefore, native GDBMSs aiming to be versatile at managing a variety of graphs should be able to grasp whether a node is an HDN or not because lacking this ability would render them inefficient at dealing with HDNs.

Our previous study proposed a graph index (PR-index) for repeatedly traversing edges by collecting repetition paths, consisting of edges labeled the

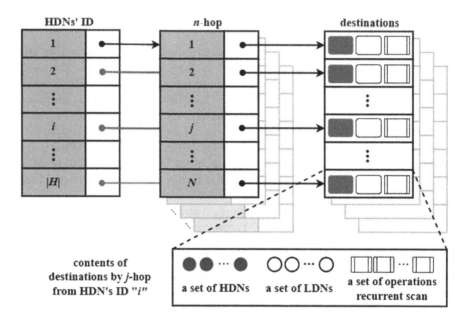

Fig. 1. This figure is a schema of RPD-index.

same relationship, from HDNs. RP-index enabled a GDBMS to traverse repetition paths faster than one without our index. However, RP-index included redundancy in its structure that repetition paths beginning from a specified HDN are also contained other HDNs. Moreover, expected results of queries with repetition paths generally are destination nodes of these paths.

In this paper, to rid redundancy of RP-index, we propose an algorithm for indexing compressed RP-index by judging whether reached node is HDN or LDN. Subsequently, our approach memories an operation of scanning RP-index for the ID of HDN and the length of hops into RP-index to enable GDBMSs to obtain destinations required a query later.

3.1 A Schema of Compressed RPD-Index

RP-index can become fast to query repetition paths, such as "-[Relation* 2..4]->" in a graph query language like Cypher [7], PGQL [18], G-core [1], and GQL [24], but indexing these paths generate a huge index. The pattern in Fig. 2 means to traverse a relationship named Relation from two to four times recursively. This pattern is also called property path pattern [23] in SPARQL 1.1, and queries including the patterns will be issued against data in digital libraries [9]. Our approach is compatible with index-free adjacency in order to minimize the cost of graph traversal, even if the data volume is massive. Hence, we redefine repetition path's destinations index (RPD-index) to reduce the redundancy of RP-index [10] in this section.

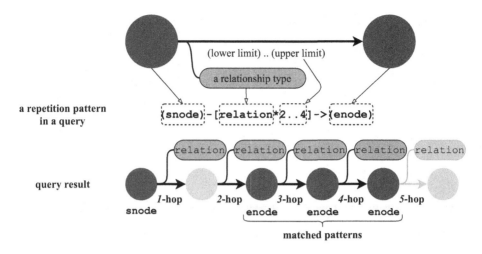

Fig. 2. A description of repetition paths

To construct the index scalably, we reform the structure of our index by changing the unit of indexing graph elements and compressing repetition paths being indexed. This study aims to enable GDBMSs to traverse repetition paths efficiently while judging whether or not a node is an HDN, as well as our previous study. Therefore, it is necessary to consider the labels of the edges that are often traversed repeatedly in an application to differentiate HDNs from all other nodes. Note that our approach requires one type of label for edges to collect while traversing repetition paths. Accordingly, this study set the repetition paths consisting of edges with just the selected label to make it easy enabling us to understand the meaning of traversing the paths.

Figure 1 shows a schema of RPD-index structured with a hash map, whose keys are a pair of an HDN's ID and a length of repetition paths, and values are destinations of the paths. Differences in our approach compared with our previous study are as follows:

– A unit of RPD-index is changed to destination nodes (hereinafter we shortly called destinations) from repetition paths to be manageable in size, so our index is renamed to RPD-index. This is because almost all queries with repetition paths use destinations but paths.
– RPD-index's values store destinations, which contain three sets of categorized nodes by HDNs, LDNs, and operations performing recurrent index-scan.
– We innovate an operation enabling us to decompress omitted destinations by recurrently scanning RPD-index.

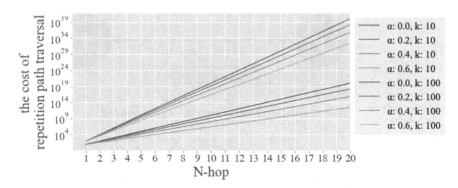

Fig. 3. The cost of repetition path traversal depends on nodes' degree (α: $\frac{\text{\# of HDNs}}{\text{\# of LDNs}}$, k: average degree of nodes).

3.2 The Cost of Constructing RPD-Index

In this section, we deal with the problem that an RP-index contains redundancy caused by duplicates of a part of the repetition path. The reason why the duplicates are included is that our indexing algorithm of RP-index likewise performs a traversal for other HDNs in the middle of repetition paths from an HDN of the index target. Moreover, this redundant process makes the consumed time for indexing repetition paths long; the time would be endless for a huge graph.

Traversing long repetition paths has a significant cost that depends on the degrees of the nodes in the paths. We can roughly estimate the cost of naïve repetition path traversal $E_{\text{cost}}^{\text{RP}}$ at n-hop with Formula (1):

$$E_{\text{cost}}^{\text{RP}} = k^n. \tag{1}$$

Thus, $E_{\text{cost}}^{\text{RP}}$ exponentially increases depending on the average degree k of nodes and the number n of hops.

Our approach for compressing an RPD-index introduces an operation of the recurrent scan, and it eliminates the cost of constructing redundant nodes being indexed. Given the average ratio α of the number of HDNs over that of LDNs in the neighbor nodes of each node, the cost of constructing RPD-index can be estimated as Formula (2):

$$\begin{aligned} E_{\text{cost}}^{\text{RPD}} &= k \times (1 - \alpha)k \times \cdots \times (1 - \alpha)k \\ &= (1 - \alpha)^{n-1} k^n, \end{aligned} \tag{2}$$

where the first cost is just k exceptionally because the initial hop requires scanning all neighbor nodes.

Figure 3 shows that the estimated cost of repetition path traversal of constructing RPD-index for different α and k, in which the x-axis denotes the number n of hops of a repetition path, and the y-axis represents the estimated costs by Formula (2) in logarithmic scale. In typical real-world networks following the power-law degree distribution, α ranges $[0.0, 0.6]$ and k ranges $[10, 100]$ depend on the size of the graph [2]. The figure indicates that omitting redundant traversals when reaching to HDNs in repetition paths can reduce the costs in a number of magnitudes, which can be seen from the comparison between $\alpha = 0.0$ (equivalent to $E_{\text{cost}}^{\text{RP}}$) to the other values of α.

3.3   HDN Selection

To construct RPD-index, a target edge label and a criterion of HDN need to be decided. After the choice of a target edge label, HDNs can be determined by the following steps:

1. Extracting sub-graphs by scanning edges with the chosen label, then getting nodes connected with these edges,
2. Calculating degree of each node,
3. Creating degree distribution of whole extracted sub-graph described above,
4. Determining threshold θ_{HDN} of node degrees for distinguishing between HDNs and LDNs.

From Step (1) to Step (3) are to draw degree distribution of each sub-graph constructed by target labeled edges. At the final step, though the threshold θ_{HDN} must be given, in practice, a heuristic approach called the Pareto law (a.k.a. 80:20 principle) [17] can be used, that is, nodes with the highest 20% degrees are determined as HDNs. This can be supported by the report by Barabási [3]. As a result, the time complexity of the above steps is $\mathcal{O}(n)$, which major cost is node degree calculation that depends on n.

3.4   An Algorithm for Constructing RPD-Index

We describe an algorithm for constructing compressed RPD-index as shown in Algorithm 1 and 2. Algorithm 1 assumes that an input is a set of HDNs decided in Sect. 3.3. Algorithm 1 collects destinations of repetition paths from each HDN by invoking a function named CREATECOMPRESSEDRPDINDEX in Line 3.

Algorithm 2 defines CREATECOMPRESSEDRPDINDEX constructing RPD-index of a specified HDN. Indexing destinations of repetition paths begins from an inputted HDN, and a function TRAVERSE1HOPFROM performs to collect destinations of the first hop from the HDN. Indexing destinations of repetition paths continue until candidate nodes of the next traversal are nothing as written in Line 5 of Algorithm 2. As described in Sect. 3.1, destinations contain of HDNs, LDNs, and recurrent scan operations. Hence, Algorithm 2 indexes destinations while judging a type of a destination in "next" between Line 10 and 16. If a type of destination is an LDN, RPD-index appends the node as is, but in the case of otherwise our index generates or updates an operation performing recurrent index-scan, the operations are CREATERECURRENTSCAN and UPDATERECURRENTSCAN, respectively. Here, our algorithm does not perform

---

Algorithm 1. Collecting destinations from each HDN

Input H: a set of HDNs.
Output RPDi: RPD-index
1: RPDi ← {}
2: **for each** hdn ∈ H **do**
3:     RPDi[hdn] ← CREATECOMPRESSEDRPDINDEX(hdn)
4: **end for**
5: **return** RPDi

Table 1. Our experimental environment

Property	Description
OS	CentOS 7.6.1801 (×86_64)
CPU	Intel Xeon Silver 4114 (2.20 GHz, 10 core) × 2
RAM	256 GB
Neo4j	ver. 4.0.0

TRAVERSE1HOPFROM for HDNs, then it realizes compression against the redundancy of RPD-index such as described in Sect. 3.2. When Algorithm 2 finishes traversing for the candidates, it returns an RPD-index for a specified HDN.

Finally, Algorithm 1 creates RPD-index for each HDN, which segregates the collected destinations of repetition paths by their lengths.

4   Experimental Evaluation

To evaluate whether our approach can construct RPD-index faster, we conducted an experiment to compare our method for constructing a compressed RPD-index with a non-compressed one. We employed Neo4j version 4.0.0 [15] as a target for comparison because it exhibits the ability of high-speed graph traversing [14]. Our computational environment in our experiment is shown in Table 1.

4.1   Benchmark

For this experiment, we required vast and complex real graph data and its queries to evaluate the performance of traversing repetition paths and its scalability. Therefore, we utilize the social network benchmark (SNB) developed by Linked Data Benchmark Council (LDBC) [12] because it enables us to adjust the dataset volume.

The LDBC SNB can generate a dataset modeled as a social network and adjust data volume with a scale factor (SF). Hence, this benchmark enables us to evaluate the scalability of GDBMSs.

We performed the following tasks to prepare for this experiment.

– We prepared three sizes of LDBC SNB dataset by setting the SF values of 1, 10, and 100 to the program [11] as shown in Table 2,

---

Algorithm 2. Constructing compressed RPD index

Input hdn: an HDN
Output hop2nodes: a hash map (hop $n \rightarrow$ destinations)
 1: **function** INDEXCOMPRESSEDRPD(next)
 2:     hop $\leftarrow$ 1
 3:     next $\leftarrow$ TRAVERSE1HOPFROM(hdn)
 4:     hop2nodes[hop] $\leftarrow$ next
 5:     **while** next.**size**() != 0 **do**
 6:         current $\leftarrow$ next
 7:         next $\leftarrow$ {}
 8:         hop $\leftarrow$ hop + 1
 9:         **for each** c $\in$ current **do**
10:             **if** c $\in$ LDN **then**
11:                 next.**add**(TRAVERSE1HOPFROM(c))
12:             **else if** c $\in$ HDN **then**
13:                 next.**add**(CREATERECURRENTSCAN(c))
14:             **else if** c $\in$ RSO **then**
15:                 next.**add**(UPDATERECURRENTSCAN(c))
16:             **end if**
17:         **end for**
18:         hop2nodes[hop] $\leftarrow$ next
19:     **end while**
20:     **return** hop2nodes
21: **end function**

Table 2. Datasets of LDBC SNB

SF	# of nodes	# of edges	# of properties
1	3,181,724	17,256,038	22,981,116
10	29,987,835	176,623,445	228,484,141
100	337,403,991	2,286,478,782	2,037,611,697

- stored the datasets into Neo4j by using the program [13], and
- finally decided whether each node is an HDN or an LDN according to degree distribution as described in Sect. 3.3. In this experiment, we prepared three types of threshold θ_{HDN} at $\theta_{1\%}$, $\theta_{10\%}$, and $\theta_{20\%}$ to permit us to observe the trends of a consumed time.

The queries in the IC [6] include two kinds of repetition paths. The first kind consists of edges labeled relationship knows, representing an acquainted relationship between two users. In contrast, the second kind consists of edges labeled replyOf, which indicates a reply message to a post or a comment. In this experiment, we employ knows relationships for an indexing target because the pattern is a many-to-many connection, and a repeated traversal becomes easily heavy cost. This is because replyOf relationships tend to have a small node degree owing to the non-complexity derived from LDBC SNB data schema, according

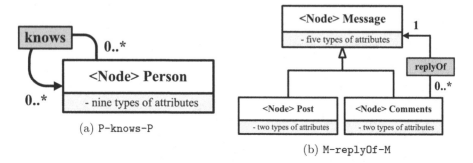

Fig. 4. Two types of patterns: "knows" and "replyOf" of the repetition paths in the LDBC SNB dataset.

to which only `Comment` nodes in `Message` nodes can have `replyOf` relationships. Hence, sub-graphs constructed only using relationships labeled `replyOf` become tree-structure like an e-mail thread that does not have complexity required for this experiment (Fig. 4).

4.2   The Performance for Constructing RPD-index

We assessed the effectiveness of our approach by constructing a compressed RPD-index in various data volumes, as shown in Table 2. In particular, we evaluate the consumed time for constructing a compressed RPD-index compared with a non-compressed one.

As described in Sect. 4.1, we conducted RPD-index construction for the `Person-knows-Person` pattern in this experiment. We measured a consumed time for constructing RPD-index and compressed one five times under each SF and threshold θ_{HDN}, and calculated each average of the times.

Figure 5 shows the results comparing the consumed times for constructing RPD-index and compressed one. To visualize how many times faster constructing a compressed RPD-index compares with a non-compressed one, Fig. 5 draws the ratio of the consumed time by the compressed approach compared with the naïve approach, on each length of a repetition path. Note that the naïve approach is a baseline in this experiment so its ratio of the consumed time is one in any length of a repetition path. Moreover, each x-axis in Fig. 5 denotes the length of repetition paths, and the value means the number n of n-hop from each HDN by indexing approaches. Furthermore, our compressed approach's processes absolutely finish indexing by shorter compared by naïve approaches. Hence, Fig. draws naïve approaches' results in accordance with the maximum length of compressed ones. In invisible results of the naïve approaches, the processes for indexing do not terminate for one day under SF is 100. Finally, the lines show the average value of consumed time for indexing five times, and the bands aligned with the lines do the error range. The upper limit e_{upper} and lower

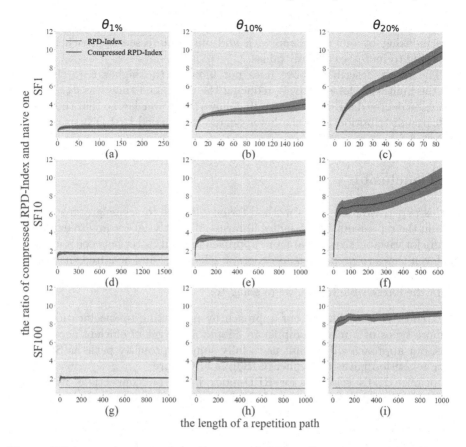

Fig. 5. Efficiency of compression. Compressed RPD-index can construct efficiently compared with the case of non-compressed one (i.e., our previous RP-index).

one e_{lower} of the error range were calculated by our formula (3) and (4):

$$e_{\text{upper}} = \frac{\mu_r + \sigma_r}{\mu_c - \sigma_r}, \tag{3}$$

$$e_{\text{lower}} = \frac{\mu_r - \sigma_r}{\mu_c + \sigma_c}, \tag{4}$$

where μ_r and μ_c denote the average of consumed times by our naïve approach and the compressed approach, respectively, σ_r and σ_c do the standard deviation of the times. Therefore, the range of bands is $[r_\mu - e_{\text{lower}}, e_{\text{upper}} - r_\mu]$, where r_μ is the ratio of the average consumed time for indexing between two approaches.

According to Fig. 5, in the aspect of scale factors, our compressed approach was able to finish indexing destinations, but the speeds did not depend on SFs but were constant. On the contrary, with regard to the thresholds θ_{HDN}, it indicated the values influence the consumed time for indexing RPD-index as compared among Fig. 5(a), (b), and (c) or (d), Fig. 5(d), (e), and (f) for instance.

As observed θ_{HDN} and scale factor simultaneously, the ratio of the consumed time indexing by our naïve approach and our compressed approach increased according to increases of both values.

The result described above does not indicate the higher θ_{HDN} is better, but the limitation for effectively reducing the consumed time was $\theta_{20\%}$. This is because a degree distribution generally follows the power-law so that the top 80% of degree distribution from the lower degree is occupied by LDNs as described in Sect. 3.3.

5   Conclusion

In this paper, we proposed a method for enabling us to access graph-structured data in the representative of digital libraries efficiently. According to experiment results for variable sizes of data, our approach made it faster between a maximum of eleven times to prepare to access graph effectively and acquired the property of scalability.

In the foreseeable future, we're going to:

- extend the versatility of our approach by permitting to specification two or more types of a relationship as an adoptable target of efficient access. That is, our approach will permit us to fully support property paths in SPARQL, or repetition paths in Cypher, GHQL, and G-Core,
- optimize HDN selection for RPD-index based on connections with other nodes. Our current selection of HDN is simply applying a threshold regardless of the connection information of other nodes,
- assess the performance of repeated traversal to prove our approach enables conventional GDBMSs to traverse repetition paths fast.

Acknowledgment. This research was partially supported by the Grants-in-Aid for Academic Promotion, Graduate School of Culture and Information Science, Doshisha University, and JSPS KAKENHI Grant Number JP21H03555 and JP22H03594.

References

1. Angles, R., et al.: G-CORE: a core for future graph query languages. In: Proceedings of the 2018 International Conference on Management of Data, SIGMOD 2018, pp. 1421–1432. ACM (2018). https://doi.org/10.1145/3183713.3190654
2. Barabási, A.L., Pósfai, M.: Network Science. University Press, Cambridge (2016)
3. Barabási, A.L., Frangos, J.: Linked: The New Science of Networks Science of Networks. Perseus Books Group, New York (2002)
4. Candela, G., Escobar, P., Carrasco, R.C., Marco-Such, M.: Evaluating the quality of linked open data in digital libraries. J. Inf. Sci. **48**(1), 21–43 (2022). https://doi.org/10.1177/0165551520930951
5. DB-Engines: Ranking of Graph DBMS. https://db-engines.com/en/ranking/graph+dbms. Accessed 8 Aug 2022

6. Erling, O., et al.: The LDBC social network benchmark: interactive workload. In: Proceedings of the 2015 ACM SIGMOD International Conference on Management of Data, SIGMOD 2015, pp. 619–630. ACM (2015). https://doi.org/10.1145/2723372.2742786

7. Francis, N., et al.: Cypher: an evolving query language for property graphs. In: Proceedings of the 2018 International Conference on Management of Data, SIGMOD 2018, pp. 1433–1445. ACM (2018). https://doi.org/10.1145/3183713.3190657

8. Haris, M., Farfar, K.E., Stocker, M., Auer, S.: Federating scholarly infrastructures with GraphQL. In: Ke, H.-R., Lee, C.S., Sugiyama, K. (eds.) ICADL 2021. LNCS, vol. 13133, pp. 308–324. Springer, Cham (2021). https://doi.org/10.1007/978-3-030-91669-5_24

9. Hogan, A., et al.: Knowledge graphs. ACM Comput. Surv. **54**(4), 1–37 (2021). https://doi.org/10.1145/3447772

10. Kusu, K., Hatano, K.: A hub-based graph management for efficient repetition path traversing. In: 2021 IEEE International Conference on Big Data and Smart Computing (BigComp), pp. 188–191. IEEE (2021). https://doi.org/10.1109/BigComp51126.2021.00043

11. LDBC: ldbc/ldbc_snb_datagen.git. https://github.com/ldbc/ldbc_snb_datagen. Accessed 8 Aug 2022

12. LDBC: LDBC's HP. http://ldbcouncil.org/. Accessed 8 Aug 2022

13. LDBC: ldbc_snb_implementations.git. https://github.com/ldbc/ldbc_snb_implementations. Accessed 8 Aug 2022

14. Lissandrini, M., Brugnara, M., Velegrakis, Y.: Beyond macrobenchmarks: microbenchmark-based graph database evaluation. Proc. VLDB Endow. **12**(4), 390–403 (2018). https://doi.org/10.14778/3297753.3297759

15. Neo4j Inc: Neo4j's HP. https://neo4j.com/. Accessed 8 Aug 2022

16. Newman, M.: Networks: An Introduction. Oxford University Press, Oxford (2010)

17. Pareto, V.F.D.: La courbe des revenus. In: Cours d'Èconomie Politique, vol. (II), chap. (I), pp. 299–345. Librairie Droz (1964)

18. van Rest, O., Hong, S., Kim, J., Meng, X., Chafi, H.: PGQL: a property graph query language. In: Proceedings of the Fourth International Workshop on Graph Data Management Experiences and Systems, GRADES 2016, pp. 1–6. ACM (2016). https://doi.org/10.1145/2960414.2960421

19. Robinson, I., Webber, J., Eifrem, E.: Graph Databases. O'Reilly Media, Inc., Sebastopol (2015)

20. Rodriguez, M.A., Neubauer, P.: The graph traversal pattern. In: Sakr, S., Pardede, E. (eds.) Graph Data Management: Techniques and Applications, chap. 2, pp. 29–46. IGI Global (2012). https://doi.org/10.4018/978-1-61350-053-8.ch002

21. Sakr, S., Al-Naymat, G.: The overview of graph indexing and querying techniques. In: Sakr, S., Pardede, E. (eds.) Graph Data Management: Techniques and Applications, chap. 4, pp. 71–88. IGI Global (2012). https://doi.org/10.4018/978-1-61350-053-8.ch004

22. Sakr, S., Pardede, E.: Graph Data Management: Techniques and Applications. IGI Global, Hershey (2011)

23. Seaborne, A.: SPARQL 1.1 Property Paths. World Wide Web Consortium (W3C). https://www.w3.org/TR/sparql11-property-paths/

24. THE GQL MANIFESTO: GQL Is Now a Global Standards Project alongside SQL. https://gql.today/. Accessed 8 Aug 2022

Adopting the Europeana Data Model (EDM) for Describing Resources in Cultural Heritage Systems: A Case Study of Taiwan Memory

Wei-Hsiang Hung and Hao-Ren Ke[✉]

Graduate Institute of Library and Information Studies, National Taiwan Normal University,
Taipei, Taiwan
{weldon,clavenke}@ntnu.edu.tw

Abstract. Taiwan Memory (TM) is a digital library that stores digital cultural heritage (CH) resources from the National Central Library and other CH institutions in Taiwan and provides public access. In this paper, we adopt the Europeana Data Model (EDM) as the foundation and map the metadata elements of TM to EDM classes in order to improve the current metadata landscape for the system and to make the digital objects more discoverable and accessible on the Internet. Four postcards of Taiwanese aboriginal Amis are selected to demonstrate the feasibility of the proposed Taiwan Memory Conceptual Data Model in describing the TM resources. This study provides experiences of adopting EDM for an existing CH system. The processes of EDM mapping, entity enrichment, institution identification, and resource description are elaborated. It is hoped that the implication and the adoption of EDM in this study might provide invaluable information for the future development of TM or be beneficial to other CH systems that are planning to adopt EDM or other semantic data models.

Keywords: Cultural heritage system · Europeana Data Model (EDM) ·
Metadata · Metadata aggregation

1 Introduction

Taiwan Memory (TM)[1] is a digital library that holding a rich collection of Taiwanese historical documents, including postcards, old photos, old books, local historical records, ancient contracts, stone tablets, and rubbings. The system was established around 2003, was structurally modified in 2016, and is maintained by National Central Library in Taiwan (NCL). NCL has not only digitized its own collection, but also been helping other cultural heritage (CH) institutions convert their materials into digital forms; in this manner, Taiwanese historical documents and materials can be preserved collaboratively. The metadata schemas of the resources in TM do not strictly follow widely known metadata standards and the metadata schemas of the different types of resources are developed separately, without holistic consideration. In addition, the system does

---

[1] https://tm.ncl.edu.tw/index?lang=eng.

Y.-H. Tseng et al. (Eds.): ICADL 2022, LNCS 13636, pp. 392–400, 2022.
https://doi.org/10.1007/978-3-031-21756-2_30

not use any conceptual entity-relationship models like Functional Requirements for Bibliographic Records (FRBR) or BIBFRAME to organize the resources.

Europeana[2] is a system that provides access to millions of materials from libraries, archives, and museums in Europe, and is supported by the Europeana Data Model (EDM). EDM is an open, cross-domain, Semantic Web-based framework which offers great potential for supporting Linked Data. EDM works as a basis for enriching various descriptions of CH materials which may overlap across institutions. Unlike Europeana, TM lacks the support of a data model like EDM, which is crucial to the provision of a metadata framework to link resources semantically. This paper proposes a data model for TM which is based on EDM definitions to enhance discoverability and accessibility to the digital resources of TM. The development process of the Taiwan Memory Data Model from the practical viewpoints involved in adopting EDM for a CH system is elaborated in the paper.

2 Research Goals

The current metadata schemas of TM are designed separately and in accordance with their different material types. These schemas, moreover, do not strictly follow any widely-accepted metadata standards and are not designed with the consideration of Linked Data in mind. The discoverability and accessibility of the TM resources on the Internet is therefore limited. In order to provide better knowledge organization, and to improve the current metadata landscape for TM, we choose EDM from Europeana as the data model owing to the similarities between TM and Europeana. Both of the systems are preserving CHOs such as digitized books and images, and they all cooperate with CH institutions to provide more discoverable information on CHOs. This study proposes a metadata data model for TM using EDM as its basis which aims to aggregate identical resources which were digitized by NCL or collected from other cooperative institutions as a unified collection. The data model will not only provide more descriptive and linkable metadata records within TM but also encourage the exchange and reuse of the metadata on the Semantic Web.

3 Related Works

EDM changes the way that Europeana deals with the metadata harvested from the data providers. It allows different data providers to model their data in a manner that suits their original data and desired functions. There are three core classes in EDM: "edm:ProvidedCHO", "edm:WebResource" and "ore:Aggregation". The "edm:ProvidedCHO" class is the "provided cultural heritage object" itself. The "edm:WebResource" class is one or many accessible digital representations of this cultural heritage object, and the "ore:Aggregation" class is an aggregation to represent the result of the provider's activity which uses the edm:aggregatedCHO and edm:hasView sub-properties to represent the "real" object and its digital view or views [2, 4]. In addition to the core classes, there are five contextual classes (edm:Agent, edm:Event,

---

[2] https://www.europeana.eu/en.

edm:Place, edm:TimeSpan, skos:Concept) that may be used to carry information about the resources. Details of which property should be used in relation to which class is defined in the EDM Mapping Guideline [5], and the dc (with namespace)[3] and dcterms (with namespace)[4] properties from Dublin Core are used to describe an object and its features. Controlled vocabularies such as VIAF and SKOS are also encouraged. The above essential features of EDM improve access to original objects and facilitate the navigation of users through a semantic space of contextual entities before reaching the actual object [2, 4].

There are various studies on integrating EDM into a CH system. The Rijksmuseum provided and published CH collections as Linked Data which were modelled according to EDM. The ore:Aggregation class was used to connect the metadata of a CH object to Web resources. Every item in the system got an aggregation object with its persistent identifier as URI. Plenty of properties were used to describe objects in the system, including dc:creator. dc:title, dc:format, dc:subject. The Rijksmuseum also added a direct conversation layer to the collection management system that allowed other institutions to benefit from the progress made, through easy reuse and the possibility to add new perspectives to the data [1].

Zapounidou, Sfakakis and Papatheodorou attempted to map core semantic paths between BIBFRAME to EDM. They used the concept "edition" to represent the entirety of all identical copies of an item. The EDM-FRBRoo Application Profile Task Force was used to map the library metadata. The basic BIBFRAME path was defined and its "Work-hasInstance-Instance-hasAnnotation-heldMaterial-electronicLocator-URI" paths of the "Don Quixote" test case were successfully mapped to EDM [7].

Kiryakos and Sugimoto built a Linked Data model to aggregate manga from data providers. The core classes of EDM were used and the ore:Proxy property was added to identify different institutions. The FRBR Work level was described using edm:ProvidedCHO which could together represent various media formats, such as a Japanese edition, an English translation and an animate adaptation. The results indicated that transforming data into a BIBFRAME-based RDF schema facilitates the establishment of the relationship between manga resources and the building of connections from related volumes to the associated Work entity; in this manner, it may provide a more complete bibliographic landscape for manga resources [6].

4   The Selected Case and the EDM Mapping

TM preserves Taiwan's historical memory and provides easy accessibility for researchers and public audiences. In order to use EDM to describe resources in TM, following the EDM Mapping Guideline, this paper mapped the metadata elements in TM to the most suitable classes and properties in EDM. The result of the mapping is summarized in Table 1. A test case of Taiwanese aboriginal Amis called "Carrying water by Ami women" from the "Taiwan Postcards (Japanese Colonial Period)" was selected from the dataset in TM. The selected case contains four digitized postcards. Three (postcards

---

[3] http://purl.org/dc/elements/1.1.

[4] http://purl.org/dc/terms.

1,3,4) were provided by NCL and the other (postcard 2) was provided by National Taiwan University Library. Postcards 1 and 2 were printed in color and postcards 3 and 4 in black and white. The selected case is listed in Table 2. These postcards are identical in their content, which means that all of them represent the same Work (same idea) in FRBR, and their Expressions are all displayed in photographs. The Manifestation of the selected case is printed postcard, and it has four Items preserved in two libraries in Taiwan.

Table 1. The mapping of TM metadata elements to EDM classes and properties

Metadata elements	Class	Property	Examples
Main title	edm:ProvidedCHO	dc:title	阿美族的婦女搬運用水
Alternative title	edm:ProvidedCHO	dcterms:alternative	アミ族婦女の用水搬運 Carrying water by Ami women, Formosa
Works type	edm:ProvidedCHO	edm:type	攝影作品[Image]
Medium	edm:ProvidedCHO	dcterms:medium	paper
Place of publication	edm:ProvidedCHO	dcterms:spatial	臺北[Taipei]
Publisher	edm:ProvidedCHO	dc:publisher	生蕃屋本店
Topic	edm:ProvidedCHO skos:Concept	dc:subject skos:prefLabel	原住民—日常生活[Aboriginal-Daily routine]
Keyword	edm:ProvidedCHO	dc:subject	阿美族、服飾、汲水 [Amis, Apparel, Draw Water]
Cameraman	edm:ProvidedCHO	dc:contributor	森丑之助所
Photo location	edm:Place	skos:prefLabel	花蓮縣瑞穗鄉奇美村 [Ruisui Township, Hual-ien County]
Date	edm:ProvidedCHO	dcterms:issued	約1920年代 [c.1920]
Period	edm:ProvidedCHO	dcterms:period	日治時期(1895–1945) [Japanese colonial period (1895–1945)]
Original surrogate	edm:ProvidedCHO	dc:format	原件[original item]
Original format	edm:ProvidedCHO	dc:format	影像-靜畫資料[graphic materials]
Dimension	edm:ProvidedCHO	dcterms:extent	138.5x89(mm)
NCL ID (NCLACN)	edm:ProvidedCHO	dc:identifier	002414057
Series title	edm:ProvidedCHO	dcterms:isPartOf	日治時期臺灣地區明信片[Postcards(Japanese Colonial Period)]

(continued)

Table 1. (*continued*)

Metadata elements	Class	Property	Examples
Place, City, Country, Area[5]	edm:Place	skos:prefLabel	瑞穗鄉奇美村[Qimei Valley], 花蓮縣[Hualien County], 臺灣[Taipei], 亞洲[Asia]
Language	edm:ProvidedCHO	dc:language	Chinese
Owner name	ore:Aggregation	edm:dataProvider	國家圖書館特藏組[Special Collection Division, National Central Library]
Owner country	edm:ProvidedCHO	edm:curremtLocation	臺灣[Taiwan]
TM system ID	ore:Aggregation	edm:aggregatedCHO	001_001_0000360526
Created by	ore:Aggregation	edm:provider	國家圖書館[National Central Library]

Table 2. The selected case

No.	Title	Web Resource	URL
1	Carrying water by Ami women, Formosa.		https://tm.ncl.edu.tw/article?u=001_001_0000360526&lang=chn
2	Carrying water by Ami-women, Formosa		https://tm.ncl.edu.tw/article?u=001_103_NTUv03137&lang=chn
3	Setting to Work Woman Amizoku.		https://tm.ncl.edu.tw/article?u=001_001_0000360530&lang=chn
4	Setting to work Woman Amizoku.		https://tm.ncl.edu.tw/article?u=001_001_0000360525&lang=chn

5 Taiwan Memory Conceptual Data Model

The metadata of the selected case is described using the EDM's classes and properties and the Taiwan Memory Conceptual Data Model is presented in Fig. 1. The "edm:ProvidedCHO" represents a CH object by its identifier (tm:NCLACN), and one digital view (tm:imgURI) is stated by the class "edm:WebResource" to make the digital resource available on the Web. The "ore:Aggregation" (tm:sysID) provides connections

---

[5] Place, City, Country, and Area are four separate metadata elements in TM denoting the location or address of a place from most specific to general; therefore, in the mapping, they are concatenated into edm:Place.

to WebResource and ProvidedCHO using edm:hasView and edm:aggregatedCHO properties. For the purpose of presenting rich contextual relationships, the use of controlled vocabularies is the key point of the model. The "Virtual International Authority File (VIAF)" and "SKOS UNESCO Thesaurus" are used to describe the edm:Agent class and dcterms:subject class instead of one single string value. In Fig. 2, the "tm:cameraman" is identified by https://viaf.org/viaf/114470467, a VIAF authority record for the Chinese "森, 丑之助"and "tm:topic/aboriginal" is labeled by https://skos.um.es/unescothes/ C01939, a SKOS UNESCO thesaurus entry for indigenous peoples, which can be linked for more information about the photographer and related items.

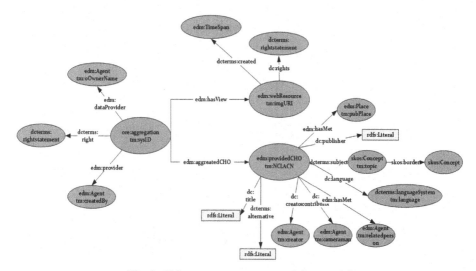

Fig. 1. Taiwan memory conceptual data model

TM not only provides the access to the resources in NCL but also assists and collaborates with other CH institutions to digitize and present their collections. In order to manage system resources originating from different institutions but describing the same ProvidedCHO, the class ore:Proxy is used to distinguish different institutions. In the case of "Carrying water by Ami women", for example, the use of ore:Proxy to distinguish four postcards from NCL and National Taiwan University Library is presented in Fig. 3. While the purpose of this study is to describe the resources in TM using EDM, it should also consider the need to integrate the FRBR entities in EDM. The EDM-FRBRoo application profile Task Force (Europeana Foundation, 2014) translated classes of FRBR model to EDM using skos:Concept, edm:InformationResource and edm:hasType properties with the FRBR vocabularies. The example of the translation of FRBR Work and Expression concept followed by the EDM-FRBRoo application profile Task Force is shown in Fig. 4.

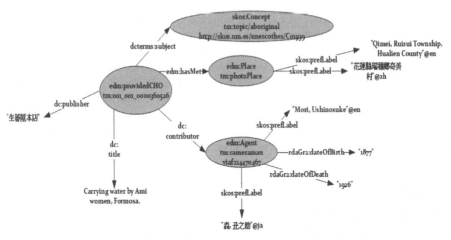

Fig. 2. Enrichment using contextual entities

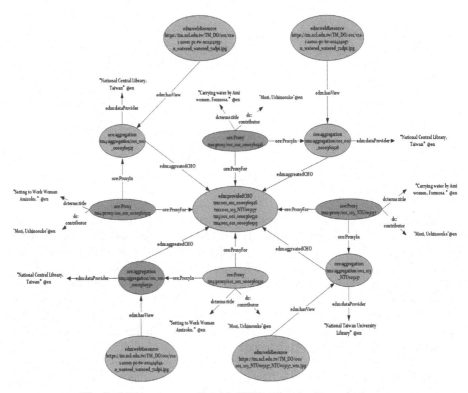

Fig. 3. Linking to same ProvidedCHO using ore:Proxy instances

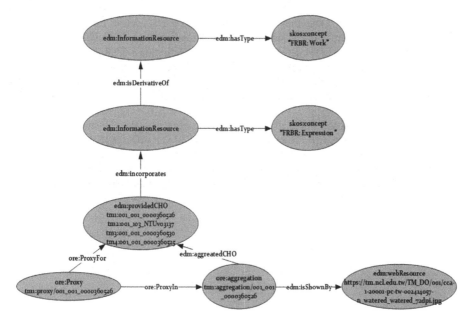

Fig. 4. Integration of EDM with FRBR work and expression entities

6   Conclusion

In this paper, the metadata used to describe resources in TM was mapped to EDM. Also, in Figs. 1, 2, 3 and 4, the Taiwan Memory Conceptual Data Model was designed and proposed. This paper shows an adoption of EDM within a CH system designed for TM. In the adoption process, all elements of TM were mapped to the EDM elements to represent the resource properly in the data model. The enrichment using contextual entities, the usage of the ore:Proxy class in distinguishing content providers and the application of EDM-FRBRoo application profile Task Force were used to enhance the completeness of the metadata and aggregate identical resources. It also enabled the ability to share, interact and reuse the resources in Semantic Web. It is hoped that this study will prove to be a record of practical experiences conducive to the future development of TM or serve as an invaluable reference for other CH systems that are planning to adopt EDM or other semantic data models.

References

1. Dijkshoorn, C., et al.: The Rijksmuseum collection as linked data. Seman. Web **9**(2), 221–230 (2018)
2. Europeana Foundation. Europeana Data Model Primer. Europeana Pro (2013, July 14). https://pro.europeana.eu/files/Europeana_Professional/Share_your_data/Technical_requirements/EDM_Documentation/EDM_Primer_130714.pdf
3. Europeana Foundation. EDM – FRBRoo Application Profile. Europeana Pro (2014, December 12). https://pro.europeana.eu/project/edm-frbroo-application-profile

4. Europeana Foundation: Definition of the Europeana Data Model v5.2.8. Europeana Pro. (2017a, October 6). https://pro.europeana.eu/files/Europeana_Professional/Share_your_data/Technical_requirements/EDM_Documentation//EDM_Definition_v5.2.8_102017.pdf

5. Europeana Foundation: Europeana Data Model – Mapping Guidelines v2.4. Europeana Pro (2017b, October 6). https://pro.europeana.eu/files/Europeana_Professional/Share_your_data/Technical_requirements/EDM_Documentation/EDM_Mapping_Guidelines_v2.4_102017.pdf

6. Kiryakos, S., Sugimoto, S.: A linked data model to aggregate serialized manga from multiple data providers. In: Allen, R.B., Hunter, J., Zeng, M.L. (eds.) ICADL 2015. LNCS, vol. 9469, pp. 120–131. Springer, Cham (2015). https://doi.org/10.1007/978-3-319-27974-9_12

7. Zapounidou, S., Sfakakis, M., Papatheodorou, C.: Library data integration: towards BIBFRAME mapping to EDM. In: Closs, S., Studer, R., Garoufallou, E., Sicilia, M.A. (eds.) MTSR 2014. CCIS, vol. 478, pp. 262–273. Springer, Cham (2014). https://doi.org/10.1007/978-3-319-13674-5_25

Web Archiving as Entertainment

Travis Reid$^{(\boxtimes)}$ ⓘ, Michael L. Nelson ⓘ, and Michele C. Weigle ⓘ

Old Dominion University, Norfolk, VA 23529, USA
treid003@odu.edu, {mln,mweigle}@cs.odu.edu

Abstract. We want to make web archiving entertaining so that it can be enjoyed like a spectator sport. To this end, we have been working on a proof of concept that involves gamification of the web archiving process and integrating video games and web archiving. Our vision for this proof of concept involves a web archiving live stream and a gaming live stream. We are creating web archiving live streams that make the web archiving process more transparent to viewers by live streaming the web archiving and replay sessions to video game live streaming platforms like Twitch, Facebook Gaming, and YouTube. We also want to live stream gameplay from games where the gameplay is influenced by web archiving and replay performance. So far we have created web archiving live streams that show the web archiving and replay sessions for two web archive crawlers and gaming live streams that show gameplay influenced by the web archiving performance from the web archiving live stream. We have also applied the gaming concept of speedruns, where a player attempts to complete a game as quickly as possible. This could make a web archiving live stream more entertaining, because we can have a competition between two crawlers to see which crawler is faster at archiving a set of URIs.

Keywords: Web archiving · Gaming · Live streaming

1 Introduction

Game walkthroughs are guides that show viewers the steps a player would take while playing a video game. Recording and streaming a user's interactive web browsing session is similar to a game walkthrough, because it shows the steps the user would take while browsing different websites. The idea of having game walkthroughs for web archiving was first explored in 2013 [30], but the web archive crawlers at that time were not ideal for this purpose because they did not allow the user to view the web page as it was being archived. Recent advancements in web archive crawlers have made it possible to preserve the experience of dynamic web pages by recording a user's interactive web browsing session, which makes it possible to create a walkthrough of a web archiving session.

Figure 1 applies the analogy of different types of video games and basketball scenarios to types of web archiving sessions. Practicing playing a sport like basketball by yourself, playing an offline single-player game like Pac-Man, and archiving a web page with a browser extension like WARCreate [23] have similar

ⓒ The Author(s), under exclusive license to Springer Nature Switzerland AG 2022
Y.-H. Tseng et al. (Eds.): ICADL 2022, LNCS 13636, pp. 401–411, 2022.
https://doi.org/10.1007/978-3-031-21756-2_31

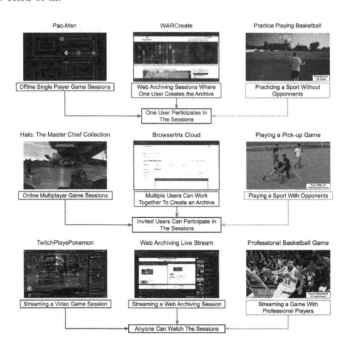

Fig. 1. Different ways to participate in gaming (left), web archiving (center), and sport sessions (right)

qualities, because only one user or player is participating in the session (Fig. 1, top row). Playing team sports with a group of people, playing an online multi-player game like Halo, and collaboratively archiving web pages with Browsertrix Cloud [47] are similar since multiple invited users or players can participate in the sessions (Fig. 1, center row). Watching a professional sport on ESPN+, stream-ing a video game on Twitch, and streaming a web archiving session on YouTube can be similar because anyone can be a spectator and watch the sporting event, gameplay, or web archiving session (Fig. 1, bottom row).

One of our goals in the Game Walkthroughs and Web Archiving project [31] is to create a web archiving live stream like that shown in Fig. 1. We want to create a web archiving live stream that is entertaining so that it can be enjoyed like a spectator sport. To this end, we have been working on a proof of concept that involves integrating video games with web archiving and the gamification of the web archiving process. A part of the vision for this proof of concept is to create web archiving live streams that make the web archiving process more transparent to viewers by live streaming the web archiving and replay sessions. Another part of the vision is to create gaming live streams that show viewers gameplay that is influenced by web archiving and replay performance. We have completed some of the goals for this vision. We have created automated web archiving live streams [38] where the web archiving process has been made transparent by live streaming the crawling of web pages and the playback of the archived web pages. The web archiving process is also gamified during our web archiving live streams by applying the gaming concept of a speedrun to the web archiving process. For video games, a speedrun is a playthrough of a game where the player attempts to complete a section of the game or the entire game as quickly as possible [49]. Applying this concept to web archiving could make the web archiving live stream more entertaining, because we can have a competition between two crawlers to see which crawler is faster at archiving a set of URIs. We have also created automated gaming live streams [33] where the capabilities for the in-game characters were determined by the web archiving performance from a web archiving live stream.

2 Background

Gaming is popular, and over the past twenty years esports (gaming competitions) have become a popular spectator sport that has tens of millions of viewers each year [18], with growth that has also been reflected in the number of esports tournaments [11]. Our goal is to integrate gaming with web archiving so that web archiving can become more entertaining to watch. Recent advancements in web archive crawlers make it possible for us to work on this proof of concept (integrating gaming, web archiving, and live streaming). Traditional archival crawlers like Heritrix [19] do not use a web browser when archiving a web page and cannot perform interactions with a web browser by itself. Some browser-based crawlers like Squidwarc [7], Brozzler [20], Browsertrix Crawler [45], and ArchiveWeb.page [44] allow users to see the interactions being performed on the web page while it is being archived. We also use ReplayWeb.page [46] which is a web archive replay system that is used to view archived content.

We use Selenium [40] and Appium [2] to customize gameplay based on web archiving performance. Selenium is an example of a browser automation tool that can perform automated interactions with a web browser so that a developer can test their web apps. Appium is a tool that can be used to automate tests for desktop, mobile, and web applications.

3 Related Work

One way to measure the performance of a crawler is to use the speed of the crawler, which can be measured by the number of web pages downloaded per second [29,41]. Heydon and Najork [17] used the crawlers' speed, the number of kilobytes per second, and the number of HTTP requests per day. Mohr et al. [28] used the time it took for a crawl to finish and the number of URIs discovered per second to determine the performance of their crawler. The performance of a web archive crawler can also be measured by how well the crawler archived a web page based on the quality of the replayed web page. Gray and Martin [12] determined the quality of an archived webpage, or memento, based on the number of missing embedded resources. Brunelle et al. [8,9] created an algorithm for measuring memento damage, which determines the quality of a memento by calculating the importance of each embedded resource instead of just counting the missing resources. Kiesel et al. [24] used machine learning to predict the quality of a memento from the differences between the screenshots of the original web page and the archived web page. Banos and Manolopoulos [3,4] created the CLEAR and CLEAR+ methods for determining the archivability of a website based on four facets: accessibility, standards compliance, cohesion, and use of metadata. Reyes Ayala [39] used a grounded theory approach to assess how humans evaluate the quality of a web archive capture.

Browsertrix Cloud [47] is a crawling system that allows collaborative archiving where multiple users can work together to create a collection [42]. This crawling system is similar to our work, because it allows multiple users to view the web archiving sessions for the web pages that are currently being archived.

Two related cases for automating a game are for testing a game's features and automating the interactions in a game based on the choices made by a chat during a live stream. Some game developers like Rare [25] have used automated game testing to automate certain gameplay scenarios so that they can detect issues in a video game before the players test the game. TwitchPlaysPokemon [48] is a Twitch streamer bot that reads its live stream chat and then performs those interactions in the game.

Gamification is "the use of game design elements in non-gaming contexts" [10] and has been used in different areas like education [5], commerce [14], data gathering [13], e-health [1], and exercise [15]. Hamari et al. [16] found that studies that used gamification for education/learning contexts had positive outcomes like increased motivation and engagement in the learning tasks. Using gamification to improve the experience of a non-gaming activity is related to our work, because we are going to gamify our web archiving live streams by applying gaming concepts to the web archiving process.

4 Integrating Web Archiving, Gaming, and Live Streaming

We currently have two kinds of live streams: a web archiving live stream and a gaming live stream. For the web archiving live streams, we want to make the web archiving process more transparent to viewers by streaming the archiving and replay sessions. For the gaming live streams, we want to show viewers gameplay from their favorite game where the gameplay is influenced by archiving and replay performance. Figure 2 shows the current process that we are using for the live streams.

For the web archiving live streams (Fig. 2, left side), the viewers watch browser-based web crawlers archive web pages and the replay of the archived web pages. To make the live streams more entertaining, we made each web archiving live stream into a competition between crawlers to see which crawler performs better at archiving the set of seed URIs. The first step for the web archiving live stream is to use Selenium to setup the browsers that will be used during the live stream. The automated browsers are used to show information

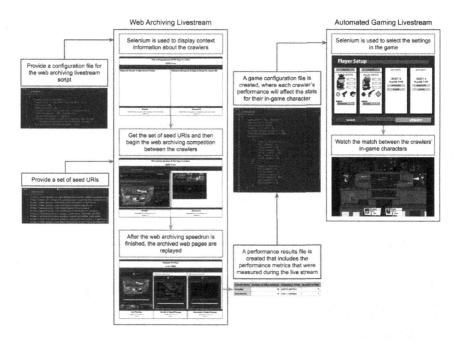

Fig. 2. The current process for running our web archiving live stream and gaming live stream

needed for the live stream, like the name and current progress for each crawler. The information currently displayed for a crawler's progress is the current URI being archived and the number of web pages archived so far. The next step is to get a set of seed URIs that will be used for the competition and then let each crawler start archiving the URIs. During this step, the crawling of the web pages is shown to the viewers, which allows the viewers to observe the web archiving process in action. Since browser-based crawlers used during the live stream, the viewers can observe the interactions that the crawlers perform while archiving a web page like scrolling down the web page and switching between different URI fragments. The next step in the web archiving live stream is to replay the archived web pages after the crawlers are finished archiving the set of URIs. When replaying the archived web pages the live web page is shown beside the replayed web page so the viewers can see how well the crawler archived the web page. Showing the replay sessions allows the viewer to see which web pages are difficult to archive and if any resources are missing on the archived web page. ReplayWeb.page is the replay system that we are currently using for replay sessions. In future live streams we will explore other replay systems, like pywb [43]. At the end of the web archiving live stream a performance results file is created that includes the web archiving and replay performance metrics that were measured during the live stream. Currently this performance result file [37] includes the number of web pages archived by the crawler during the competition, the speedrun completion time for the crawler, the number of resources in the WARC file with an HTTP response status code of 404, the number of resources with a different 400 or 500 level HTTP response status code, and the number of missing resources categorized by the file type (JavaScript, CSS, image, video, audio, and text/HTML). During future web archiving live streams, it will be possible for viewers to observe the results from the crawling session, because we will show a summary of what is included in the performance results file. Usually, third parties cannot observe the results from a crawl when viewing a collection created by Archive-It users or a collection from the Internet Archive's web collections unless the web collection has a CDX summary (example collection with a CDX summary [6]) or a CDX file associated with the collection can be downloaded and used with a CDX summary tool like CDX Summary [21] or cdx-summarize [26,27].

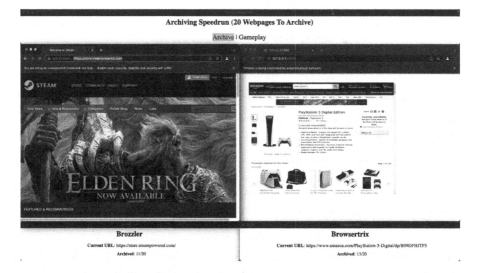

Fig. 3. A screenshot that was taken during a web archiving speedrun (video: https://youtu.be/s2IQERR5V4k) between Brozzler (crawler on the left) and Browsertrix (crawler on the right)

We have also gamified the web archiving process by applying the gaming concept of speedruns to the web archiving process during our web archiving live streams. We created live streams [32] that showed a competition between Brozzler and Browsertrix Crawler where the winner of the competition was determined by which crawler first finished archiving the given set of seed URIs. During the web archiving speedrun shown in Fig. 3, we used a set of 20 URIs [36] and the winner of the match was Brozzler.

The automated gaming live stream (Fig. 2, right side) was created so that viewers can watch a game that has gameplay influenced by the web archiving and replay performance results from a web archiving live stream or any crawling

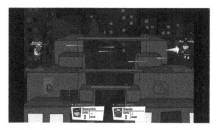

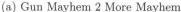

(a) Gun Mayhem 2 More Mayhem   (b) NFL Challenge

Fig. 4. Automated gameplay where the in-game stats for the players were determined based on each crawler's performance.

session. Watching the gameplay is another way to view how well the crawlers and replay system performed during the archiving and replay sessions. This should be more entertaining to watch than viewing a summary of the performance results, especially when applied to long-running crawls, such as the British Library's domain crawl which can take up to three months [22]. Before an in-game match starts, a game configuration file is needed since it contains information about the selections that will be made in the game for the settings. The game configuration file is modified based on how well the crawlers performed during the web archiving live stream. If a crawler had good performance during the web archiving live stream, then the in-game character associated with the crawler will have better items, perks, and other traits. If a crawler performs poorly, then their in-game character will have the worst character traits. At the beginning of the gaming live stream, an app automation tool like Selenium (for browser games) or Appium (for locally installed PC games) is used to select the settings for the in-game characters based on the performance of the web crawlers. After the settings are selected by the app automation tool, the match is started and the viewers of the live stream can watch the match between the crawlers' in-game characters. We have initially implemented this process for two video games, Gun Mayhem 2 More Mayhem and NFL Challenge, however any game with a mode that does not require a human player and that allows character traits or items for each player to be assigned to different values could be used for an automated gaming live stream.

The first game we used for a gaming live stream was Gun Mayhem 2 More Mayhem (Fig. 4a), which is a platform fighting game that is played in a web browser and was automated by using Selenium to simulate mouse clicks on the game's HTML canvas to make the in-game selections. In the Gun Mayhem 2 More Mayhem demo [34], the crawler's speed was used to determine which perk to use and the gun to use. The fastest crawler used the fastest gun and was given an infinite ammo perk. The slowest crawler used the slowest gun and did not get a perk. The second game that was used during our gaming live streams is NFL Challenge (Fig. 4b), which is an NFL football simulator that was popular during the 1980s NFL Challenge is an MS-DOS game that can be played with an emulator named DOSBox and we used Appium to automate the game since NFL Challenge is a locally installed game. Only key presses were simulated by Appium when making selections for NFL Challenge, because this game is executed in a command-line interface. The performance of a team is based on the player attributes that are stored in editable text files. In this demo [35], the fastest crawler gets the team with the fastest players and the other crawler gets the team with the slowest players.

5   Future Work

We plan on making several improvements to the live streams. We will add a mode to the web archiving live stream that shows a summary of the web archiving and replay performance results. We will apply more gaming concepts to the web archiving live streams, like having tournament play. We will evaluate and compare the capture and playback of web pages archived by different web archives and archiving tools like the Wayback Machine, archive.today, and Arquivo.pt. We will also use metrics in addition to the speed of a crawler when determining the crawler's performance, such as the replay quality of mementos. For the web archiving live stream, we need to evaluate if the live streams are entertaining and to determine the benefits of using live streams to add transparency to the web archiving process. The gaming and web archiving live streams will be updated so that both live streams will run at the same time. We will also automate more example games that are from different gaming platforms and game genres.

6   Conclusions

We are developing a proof of concept that involves gamification of the web archiving process and integrating video games with web archiving. We have integrated gaming and web archiving so that web archiving can be more entertaining to watch and enjoyed like a spectator sport. We have applied the gaming concept of a speedrun to the web archiving process by having a competition between two crawlers where the crawler that finished archiving the set of seed URIs first would be the winner. We have also created automated web archiving and gaming live streams where the web archiving performance of web crawlers from the web archiving live streams were used to determine the capabilities of the characters inside of the Gun Mayhem 2 More Mayhem and NFL Challenge video games that were played during the gaming live streams. Our contribution is making the web archiving process more transparent to third parties by live streaming the crawling of web pages during the web archiving session and the playback of the archived web pages during the replay session.

Acknowledgments. We thank the International Internet Preservation Consortium for their support of the Game Walkthroughs and Web Archiving project through a seed grant.

References

1. Allam, A., Kostova, Z., Nakamoto, K., Schulz, P.J.: The effect of social support features and gamification on a web-based intervention for rheumatoid arthritis patients: randomized controlled trial. J. Med. Internet Res. **17**(1), e14 (2015). https://doi.org/10.2196/jmir.3510
2. Appium: Automation for Apps. https://appium.io/
3. Banos, V., Manolopoulos, Y.: A quantitative approach to evaluate Website Archivability using the CLEAR+ method. Int. J. Digit. Libr. **17**(2), 119–141 (2015). https://doi.org/10.1007/s00799-015-0144-4
4. Banos, V., Kim, Y., Ross, S., Manolopoulos, Y.: Clear: a credible method to evaluate website archivability. In: Proceedings of the 10th International Conference on Preservation of Digital Objects (IPRES), Lisbon, Portugal (2013)
5. Barata, G., Gama, S., Fonseca, M.J., Gonçalves, D.: Improving student creativity with gamification and virtual worlds. In: Proceedings of the International Conference on Gameful Design, Research, and Applications, pp. 95–98. Gamification 2013, New York, NY, USA (2013). https://doi.org/10.1145/2583008.2583023
6. Barreau, C.: Ukrainian Web (2022). https://archive.org/details/ukrainian-web?tab=about
7. Berlin, J.: Squidwarc (2017). https://github.com/N0taN3rd/Squidwarc
8. Brunelle, J.F.: Scripts in a Frame: A Framework for Archiving Deferred Representations. Ph.D. thesis, Computer Science, Old Dominion University (2016)
9. Brunelle, J.F., Kelly, M., SalahEldeen, H., Weigle, M.C., Nelson, M.L.: Not all mementos are created equal: measuring the impact of missing resources. Int. J. Digital Librar. (2), 283–301 (2015). https://doi.org/10.1007/s00799-015-0150-6
10. Deterding, S., Dixon, D., Khaled, R., Nacke, L.: From game design elements to gamefulness: defining "gamification". In: Proceedings of the International Academic MindTrek Conference, pp. 9–15. MindTrek 2011, New York, NY, USA (2011). https://doi.org/10.1145/2181037.2181040
11. Esports Earnings: History. https://www.esportsearnings.com/history. Accessed 26 May 2022
12. Gray, G., Martin, S.: Choosing a sustainable web archiving method: a comparison of capture quality. D-Lib Mag. **19**(5/6) (2013)
13. Guin, T.D.L., Baker, R., Mechling, J., Ruyle, E.: Myths and realities of respondent engagement in online surveys. Int. J. Mark. Res. **54**(5), 613–633 (2012). https://doi.org/10.2501/IJMR-54-5-613-633
14. Hamari, J.: Transforming homo economicus into homo ludens: a field experiment on gamification in a utilitarian peer-to-peer trading service. Electron. Commer. Res. Appl. **12**(4), 236–245 (2013). https://doi.org/10.1016/j.elerap.2013.01.004
15. Hamari, J., Koivisto, J.: Social motivations to use gamification: an empirical study of gamifying exercise. In: Proceedings of the European Conference on Information Systems (2013)
16. Hamari, J., Koivisto, J., Sarsa, H.: Does gamification work? - A literature review of empirical studies on gamification. In: Proceedings of the Forty-Seventh Annual Hawaii International Conference on System Sciences, pp. 3025–3034 (2014). https://doi.org/10.1109/HICSS.2014.377
17. Heydon, A., Najork, M.: Mercator: A scalable, extensible Web crawler. World Wide Web, pp. 219–229 (1999)
18. Hollist, K.E.: Time to be grown-ups about video gaming: the rising esports industry and the need for regulation. Ariz. Law Rev. **57**, 823–848 (2015)

19. Internet Archive: Heritrix3 (2011). https://github.com/internetarchive/heritrix3
20. Internet Archive: Brozzler (2014). https://github.com/internetarchive/brozzler
21. Internet Archive: CDX Summary (2021). https://github.com/internetarchive/cdx-summary
22. Jackson, A.: 2020 domain crawl update (2020). https://blogs.bl.uk/webarchive/2020/11/2020-domain-crawl-update.html
23. Kelly, M., Weigle, M.C.: WARCreate - create wayback-consumable warc files from any webpage. In: Proceedings of the ACM/IEEE Joint Conference on Digital Libraries (JCDL), pp. 437–438, Washington, DC (2012). https://doi.org/10.1145/2232817.2232930
24. Kiesel, J., Kneist, F., Alshomary, M., Stein, B., Hagen, M., Potthast, M.: Reproducible web corpora: Interactive archiving with automatic quality assessment. J. Data Inf. Qual. **10**(4) (2018). https://doi.org/10.1145/3239574
25. Masella, R.: Automated Testing of Gameplay Features in 'Sea of Thieves' – GDC (2021). https://youtu.be/X673tOi8pU8
26. Maurer, Y.: cdx-summarize (2021). https://github.com/ymaurer/cdx-summarize
27. Maurer, Y.: Investigate holdings of web archives through summaries: cdx-summarize (2022). https://netpreserveblog.wordpress.com/2022/08/10/investigate-holdings-of-web-archives-through-summaries-cdx-summarize/
28. Mohr, G., Stack, M., Ranitovic, I., Avery, D., Kimpton, M.: An introduction to Heritrix an open source archival quality web crawler. In: Proceedings of the 4th International Web Archiving Workshop (2004). https://citeseerx.ist.psu.edu/viewdoc/summary?doi=10.1.1.676.6877
29. Najork, M., Heydon, A.: High-performance web crawling. In: Handbook of Massive Data Sets, pp. 25–45. Springer (2002). https://doi.org/10.1007/978-1-4615-0005-6_2
30. Nelson, M.L.: Game walkthroughs as a metaphor for web preservation (2013). https://ws-dl.blogspot.com/2013/05/2013-05-25-game-walkthroughs-as.html
31. Nelson, M.L.: Game Walkthroughs and Web Archiving (2022). https://netpreserve.org/projects/game-walkthroughs/
32. Reid, T.: Archiving Speedrun Brozzler vs Browsertrix Part 1 (2022). https://youtube.com/playlist?list=PLDOM9JERow3toWNxaNgwum_198tIfOqso
33. Reid, T.: Automated Gameplay Demos (2022). https://www.youtube.com/playlist?list=PLDOM9JERow3sqYA6TB5-yFhUXWiqo_8db
34. Reid, T.: Gun Mayhem 2 More Mayhem Gameplay Influenced By Web Archiving Performance | Brozzler vs Browsertrix (2022). https://www.youtube.com/watch?v=XK6FdcO5Vko
35. Reid, T.: NFL Challenge Gameplay Influenced By Web Archiving Performance — Brozzler vs Browsertrix Crawler (2022). https://youtu.be/BSm1iQA5Rwg
36. Reid, T.: URI sets for web archiving livestreams (2022). https://github.com/treid003/URI-Sets-For-Web-Archiving-Livestream/blob/main/speedrun_set_20_URLs.txt
37. Reid, T.: Web Archiving Live Stream Results (2022). https://github.com/treid003/Example-Files/blob/4940ed04b121390ceb434f0a8117fa2c44b7a0df/Web-Archiving_Livestream_Results/2022-07-28/web_archiving_livestream_results.csv
38. Reid, T.: Web Archiving Speedrun With Replay Mode (2022–07-28) (2022). https://youtu.be/M5jL7uHQCfw
39. Reyes Ayala, B.: Correspondence as the primary measure of information quality for web archives: a human-centered grounded theory study. Int. J. Digit. Libr. **23**(1), 19–31 (2021). https://doi.org/10.1007/s00799-021-00314-x

40. Selenium: Selenium automates browsers. That's it! What you do with that power is entirely up to you., https://www.selenium.dev/

41. Shkapenyuk, V., Suel, T.: Design and implementation of a high-performance distributed web crawler. In: Proceedings of the 18th International Conference on Data Engineering, pp. 357–368 (2002). https://doi.org/10.1109/ICDE.2002.994750

42. Webrecorder: Features. https://browsertrix.cloud/features/

43. Webrecorder: pywb (2013). https://github.com/webrecorder/pywb

44. Webrecorder: ArchiveWeb.page Interactive Archiving Extension and Desktop App (2020). https://github.com/webrecorder/archiveweb.page

45. Webrecorder: Browsertrix Crawler (2020). https://github.com/webrecorder/browsertrix-crawler

46. Webrecorder: ReplayWeb.page (2020). https://github.com/webrecorder/replayweb.page

47. Webrecorder: Browsertrix Cloud (2021). https://github.com/webrecorder/browsertrix-cloud

48. Wikipedia contributors: Twitch Plays Pokémon. https://en.wikipedia.org/wiki/Twitch_Plays_Pok%C3%A9mon#Legacy

49. Wikipedia contributors: Speedrun – Wikipedia, the free encyclopedia (2022). https://en.wikipedia.org/w/index.php?title=Speedrun&oldid=1101005320. Accessed 1 Aug 2022

YAMAML: An Application Profile Based Lightweight RDF Mapping Language

Nishad Thalhath[1]([envelope]) [ORCID], Mitsuharu Nagamori[2] [ORCID], and Tetsuo Sakaguchi[2] [ORCID]

[1] Graduate School of Library, Information and Media Studies, Tsukuba, Japan
nishad@slis.tsukuba.ac.jp
[2] Faculty of Library, Information and Media Studies, University of Tsukuba,
Tsukuba, Japan
{nagamori,saka}@slis.tsukuba.ac.jp
https://www.slis.tsukuba.ac.jp

Abstract. YAMA Mapping Language (YAMAML) is a lightweight mapping language for generating RDF. YAMAML is based on Yet Another Metadata Application Profiles (YAMA). YAMA is an extensible intermediary application profile authoring format for generating application profile expressions. Application profiles are a combination of vocabularies, which are mixed and matched from different namespaces and optimized for a particular local application. YAMA is based on Description Set Profiles (DSP), a Dublin Core Application Profiles constraint language. YAMA is implemented on YAML, one of the most human-readable data serialization formats. As a superset of JSON, YAML is highly interoperable and has parsers and emitters in all major programming languages. It adapts the basic application profile elements from YAMA and is designed as a simplified markup language to map non-RDF data structures to RDF and generate corresponding RDF based on the application profile. It is proposed as an intermediary format for generating RDF, but not as an RDF representation syntax. The authors demonstrate the capability of YAMAML by developing a basic specification and proof of concept implementations.

Keywords: Metadata · Application profiles · YAMA · RDF · Mapping language · Semantic web · Linked data

1 Introduction

The Resource Description Framework (RDF) is a standard directed labeled graph data format for representing information on the Semantic Web, an extension of the web. RDF is expressed in triples, consisting of a subject, a predicate, and an object [9]. RDF concept and related specifications were introduced by the World Wide Web Consortium (W3C) and are maintained by the W3C. The important formats of RDF include RDF/XML, RDFa, JSON-LD, and Turtle. The main difference between RDF and other data formats is that RDF uses a directed graph model, allowing for more flexible and powerful data representations. The advantages of RDF include its flexibility, extensibility, and interoperability. RDF has importance in the modern web because it provides a standard

Y.-H. Tseng et al. (Eds.): ICADL 2022, LNCS 13636, pp. 412–420, 2022.
https://doi.org/10.1007/978-3-031-21756-2_32

way to represent data that can be shared across different applications and platforms.

The difference between RDF and other data formats like csv and json is that RDF is a graph based data format. This means that data is represented as a set of interconnected nodes in a graph, as opposed to being represented as a table or set of key-value pairs. RDF is also a standard format, which means that there are well-defined rules for how data should be represented in RDF. This makes it easier to exchange data between different systems, and to query data using standard tools.

YAMA Mapping Language (YAMAML) is proposed to improve 5-star level[1] data publication with the notion that a profile-driven RDF generation can streamline the process by mapping multiple non-RDF sources to an RDF application profile of varying complexities.

1.1   Application Profiles, DCAP and DSP

Application profiles, often called Metadata Application Profiles, are a combination of vocabularies, which are mixed and matched from different namespaces and optimized for a particular local application [3]. Application profiles express the terms taken from other namespaces and the structural use of those terms in the local instance data. Application profiles also express constraints on those terms so that the data can be validated as well.

A Dublin Core Application Profile (DCAP) specifies how some metadata description sets are constructed. It includes information on the terms used in the description sets, how they are deployed, and constraints on the values and datatypes of the properties used. A DCAP is a declaration specifying which metadata terms an organization, information provider, or user community uses in its metadata. DCAPs can be used to document the semantics and constraints used for a set of metadata records or instance data. A DCAP can promote interoperability between different metadata models and harmonize metadata practices among different communities. A DCAP can also help communities of implementers harmonize metadata practice among themselves.

The Singapore Framework for Dublin Core Application Profiles [7] is a set of standards for designing metadata applications that are interoperable and reusable. The standards form a basis for reviewing Application Profiles for documentary completeness and conformance with Web-architectural principles. The standards define a set of descriptive components that are necessary or useful for documenting an Application Profile. The standards also describe how these documentary standards relate to standard domain models and Semantic Web foundation standards.

Description Set Profiles (DSP) is a constraint language for Dublin Core Application Profiles [6]. DSP is based on the DCMI Abstract Model (DCAM), which defines Description Set, Description, and Statement [8]. A DSP defines constraints on Description Sets, Descriptions, and Statements. Description Set

---

[1]   https://www.w3.org/DesignIssues/LinkedData.

Templates hold one or more Description Templates composed of Statement Constraints. DSP supports the RDF-oriented data design with properties and datatypes.

1.2 Yet Another Metadata Application Profile (YAMA)

Yet Another Metadata Application Profile (YAMA) is a user-friendly interoperable preprocessor for creating, maintaining, and publishing Metadata Application Profiles [12], developed to be a direct adaption of DublinCore DSP. It is heavily inspired by the Simple-DSP (SDSP) format [5] for the MetaBridge project.[2]. Even though it helps to produce various formats and standards to express the application profiles, YAMA is not defined as a new standard for application profiles but as an easy-to-use preprocessor to create standard application profile formats; extensible [11] with custom elements and structure with a syntax based on YAML 1.2 specification[3]. However, it is parsable with any YAML 1.2 parser; the processing capabilities of the profile depend on implementations.

YAMAML is built with a minimal YAMA application profile concept, that a standard RDF can be expressed in an application profile with `descriptions` and `statements`.

1.3 Related Works

There are different attempts for Application Profiles and RDF mapping languages. A brief overview of the state-of-the-art is provided below.

DC Tabular Application Profiles (DC TAP) is a way to create application profiles in the form of tables. These tables can be read by humans and saved in a CSV format, which can be read by a computer program.[4]

Tarql: SPARQL for Tables is a command-line tool that uses SPARQL 1.1 syntax to convert CSV files to RDF.[5]

LinkML is a flexible modeling language that allows authors to create schemas in YAML that describe the structure of data. LinkML is also a framework for working with and validating data in a variety of formats (JSON, RDF, TSV) and can be used to compile LinkML schemas to other frameworks.[6]

R2RML is a language expressing customized mappings from relational databases to RDF datasets. [1] This language allows different mapping implementations, such as creating a virtual SPARQL endpoint over the mapped relational data, generating RDF dumps, or offering a Linked Data interface.

RDF Mapping Language (RML) is a mapping language that can express customized mapping rules from heterogeneous data structures and serializations to the RDF data model. RML is defined as a superset of the W3C-standardized mapping language R2RML [2].

---

[2] https://metabridge.jp/.
[3] https://yaml.org/spec/1.2.2/.
[4] https://github.com/dcmi/dctap.
[5] http://tarql.github.io.
[6] https://linkml.io.

YARRRML is a human-readable text-based representation for declarative Linked Data generation rules. It is a subset of YAML that can be used to represent R2RML and RML rules.[7]

CSV2RDF defines the procedures and rules for converting tabular data into RDF, including how metadata annotations can describe the structure, meaning, and interrelation of tabular data. [10]

RDF Transform is an extension for OpenRefine[8] that allows users to transform data into RDF formats. The RDF Transform extension provides a graphical user interface (GUI) for transforming OpenRefine project data to RDF-based formats. The transform maps the data with a template graph designed using the GUI.[9]

Among these attempts, DC TAP is to devise a method of creating application profiles in tabular format. Other mapping language attempts are for generating RDF data from different types of input sources, but they are not oriented to application profiles. Considering these facts, YAMAML is a novel approach in devising an RDF mapping language based on application profiles.

2 Methods

The major goals of this attempt are :

1. Derive a subset of YAMA to express minimal RDF as an application profile.
2. Use the derived subset as a general purpose RDF data mapping language, suitable for both RDF generation and minimal profiling.
3. Use data mapping in a descriptive and opinionated format to make RDF mapping easier.
4. Develop a set of ready-to-use and simplified tooling for basic RDF generation.

2.1 Modeling Application Profile of RDF with Data Mapping

Application profiles are constrainers as well as explainers of the data. A typical YAMA application profile also includes constraining options to help generate data validation formats and ensure data quality. These constraining elements, such as cardinality and value constraints, are not part of the modeling or generating RDF, but they help generate RDF validation formats such as Shape Expressions (ShEx)[10] and Shapes Constraint Language (SHACL) [4]. For modeling a minimal application profile for RDF, YAMA constraining elements were avoided for the YAMAML subset. Also, an application profile is intended to generate human-readable documentation of the profile. Explainer elements such as labels and notes were removed from the YAMA profile to create the subset.

---

[7] https://rml.io/yarrrml/.
[8] https://github.com/AtesComp/rdf-transform.
[9] https://openrefine.org.
[10] https://shex.io.

So the subset required to explain minimal RDF application profile structure is limited to 'descriptions' and 'statements' with essential parameters.

Minimal YAMA application profile, which is based on DSP is adapted for YAMAL as well. A basic overview of YAMAML mapping of the application profile to data is explained in Figure 1.

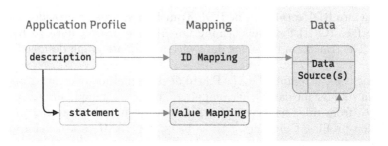

Fig. 1. YAMAML mapping overview - basic application profile and data mapping.

2.2 Data Mapping

YAMAML's data mapping is designed as multi-source capable, so users can use many data sources to generate a single RDF. The sources can be heterogeneous and require only a proper mapping to ID, so various data sources can be mixed and matched to create RDF of any level of complexity. A detailed description of all mapping elements is provided in Table 1.

YAMAML adapts all basic YAML collections from YAMA. Other than the YAMA collections base, namespaces, descriptions, and defaults, a special data collection is defined as a data holder. This optional collection container can store structured data as YAML or JSON. Since YAML is a superset of JSON, valid JSON is treated as valid YAML. All basic collection containers are explained in Table 2.

3   Results

YAMAML basic tooling and documentation are published at https://yamaml. org. The command line (CLI) toolkit can be used to generate relatively big and complex RDF. The playground web app is an in-browser environment, so it may not be sufficient for generating massive RDFs, but it will help to understand the basic implementation. A simple example of converting a basic CSV dataset is illustrated in Fig. 2. The command line tools for YAMAML are written in Javascript for Deno runtime.

Table 1. Elements in YAMAML data mapping

Element	Description	Type	Required	Examples
source	Path of the data source	string	yes	/path/to/example.csv http://ex. tld/ex.csv
type	Type of the data source	string	yes	Csv,xlsx,yaml,json
path	Path to the data element	string	yes	CSV column name, JSON/YAML key path
strip	Strip one or a group of characters, given as a list of strings	list	no	[_," "]
replace	Replace one or a group of characters with the given value. This should be a list of replace pair as a list	list	no	[[0,1],[" ", -]]
separator	A separator character to split the given values into a group of values	string	no	, or |
prepend	Prepend a text string to the value	string	no	
append	Append a text string to the value	string	no	

YAMA is an extensible application profile authoring environment. It was extended to cover many use-cases like versioning, application profile change log management, and provenance [13]. YAMA can be used to generate application profile expressions, documentation, and validation schemas, and now with the data mapping, it can also be an RDF generator. This attempt to subset YAMA as an RDF mapping language is aiding YAMA to be an application profile ecosystem for Semantic Web and Linked Data.

3.1   Comparison with State of the Art

DC TAP is focused more on authoring application profiles in a tabular way and is not extensible as YAMA. So it may not cover the use-case of RDF generation. Though DCTAP and YAMA are primarily based on Dublincore application profiles, YAMA follows the DC-DSP approach in modeling profiles. Thus YAMAML is modeled with a basic DC-DSP structure. Tarql requires a practical knowledge of SPARQL to map CSV to RDF. This is the potential limitation, where YAMAML is relatively simple to author a mapping. Though LinkML uses YAML as the serialization format, it has a steep learning curve. The same challenge is with YARRRML, which demands proper knowledge of R2ML and RML concepts. CSV2RDF requires CSVW to map the data, and it would be challenging to model complex RDF structures with CSVW. OpenRefine is the easiest option for RDF conversion with powerful data transformation capabilities. It has a user-friendly GUI and a sound reconciliation system with Wikidata support. OpenRefine RDF addon requires modeling the data in a certain way, which is not correctly equivalent to the application profile. In short, with all limitations, YAMAML tries to be a minimal, easy-to-use application profile-based RDF mapping language.

Table 2. YAMAML Containers

Component	Description
base	Same as RDF base, preferred a URI as value and will be treated as the base of the generated RDF
namespaces	A discriminatory of key-value pairs indicating prefix and URI of the namespace
descriptions	Same as YAMA descriptions, which holds the basic application profile in YAMA format
defaults	An optional container for declaring default values for the descriptions and data mapping
data	An optional YAMAML-specific structured data holder. Data can be serialized in JSON or YAML format. If the data can be included within the YAMAML file instead of external sources, this data holder can be used for that

4   Discussion

YAMA is proposed as an extensible format [11] so that it can be extended to cover more use-cases and specific needs. With YAML's flexibility, it can be a handy format for various RDF and linked data-related projects. Most of these requirements need custom tooling, which can help grow YAMA as an application profile ecosystem. So the authors believe that an RDF generation mapping language will be an added advantage in adapting YAMA for many real-world scenarios.

4.1   Limitations of This Approach

YAMAML mapping depends on declaring IDs for the descriptions; at least the main or initial description requires an ID mapping. ID can be any common data element similar to the primary key and foreign key concept of traditional relational database systems. This approach is a significant limitation and forces the users to pre-process their data with proper relationships. Another issue is that modeling complex RDF will require essential skills and time. Since YAMAML tries to be simple enough for basic uses, many advanced use-cases and edge cases were not considered in the design decisions. Though YAMAML can be used to map linked data using IRI stems, it is not intended to do a reconciliation of entities to any linked dataset. Tools like OpenRefine can do reconciliation and RDF generation from a GUI environment.

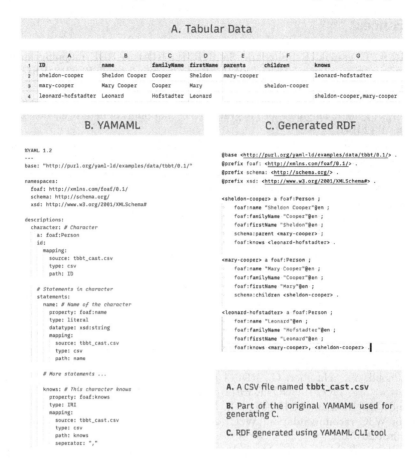

Fig. 2. YAMAML mapping example - a simplified example to demonstrate application profile mapping to a single CSV file with minimal data.

5 Conclusion

There are various tools and mapping languages for RDF, though some have high learning curves, and some are complex for basic use-cases. GUI-oriented tools like OpenRefine helps novice users to convert their data to RDF. The adaption of RDF will be less painstaking and popular if there are many tools from which the users can freely choose something that suits their needs. Many of these attempts have overlapping feature sets but still provide many unique features and options. The authors are optimistic that more accessible tools will eventually help to grow semantic web-oriented data sharing and expand the linked data cloud with more 5-star open data.

Acknowledgements. This work was supported by JSPS KAKENHI Grant Number 21K12579.

References

1. Das, S., Cyganiak, R., Sundara, S.: R2RML: RDB to RDF mapping language. W3C recommendation, W3C (2012). https://www.w3.org/TR/2012/REC-r2rml-20120927/
2. Dimou, A., Sande, M.V., Colpaert, P., Verborgh, R., Mannens, E., de Walle, R.V.: RML: A generic language for integrated RDF mappings of heterogeneous data. In: LDOW (2014)
3. Heery, R., Patel, M.: Application profiles: mixing and matching metadata schemas. Ariadne 25 (2000). http://www.ariadne.ac.uk/issue/25/app-profiles/
4. Kontokostas, D., Knublauch, H.: Shapes constraint language (SHACL). W3C recommendation, W3C (2017). https://www.w3.org/TR/2017/REC-shacl-20170720/
5. Nagamori, M., Kanzaki, M., Torigoshi, N., Sugimoto, S.: Meta-bridge: a development of metadata information infrastructure in Japan. In: Proceedings International Conference on Dublin Core and Metadata Applications 2011, p. 6 (2011)
6. Nilsson, M.: DCMI: description set profiles: a constraint language for dublin core application profiles (2008). http://www.dublincore.org/specifications/dublin-core/dc-dsp/
7. Nilsson, M., Baker, T., Johnston, P.: DCMI: the Singapore framework for Dublin core application profiles (2008). http://dublincore.org/specifications/dublin-core/singapore-framework/
8. Powell, A., Nilsson, M., Naeve, A., Johnston, P., Baker, T.: DCMI: DCMI abstract model (2007). http://www.dublincore.org/specifications/dublin-core/abstract-model/
9. Raimond, Y., Schreiber, G.: RDF 1.1 primer. W3C note, W3C (2014). https://www.w3.org/TR/2014/NOTE-rdf11-primer-20140624/
10. Tandy, J., Herman, I., Kellogg, G.: Generating RDF from tabular data on the web. W3C recommendation, W3C (2015). https://www.w3.org/TR/2015/REC-csv2rdf-20151217/
11. Thalhath, N., Nagamori, M., Sakaguchi, T., Sugimoto, S.: Authoring formats and their extensibility for application profiles. In: Jatowt, A., Maeda, A., Syn, S.Y. (eds.) ICADL 2019. LNCS, vol. 11853, pp. 116–122. Springer, Cham (2019). https://doi.org/10.1007/978-3-030-34058-2_12
12. Thalhath, N., Nagamori, M., Sakaguchi, T., Sugimoto, S.: Yet another metadata application profile (YAMA): authoring, versioning and publishing of application profiles. In: International Conference on Dublin Core and Metadata Applications, pp. 114–125 (2019). https://dcpapers.dublincore.org/pubs/article/view/4055
13. Thalhath, N., Nagamori, M., Sakaguchi, T., Sugimoto, S.: Metadata application profile provenance with extensible authoring format and PAV ontology. In: Wang, X., Lisi, F.A., Xiao, G., Botoeva, E. (eds.) JIST 2019. LNCS, vol. 12032, pp. 353–368. Springer, Cham (2020). https://doi.org/10.1007/978-3-030-41407-8_23

Research Activities & Digital Library

Digital Preservation at GLAMs in Japan

Takafumi Kinoshita$^{(\boxtimes)}$ (iD) and Tahee Onuma (iD)

National Diet Library, Tokyo, Japan
lab@ndl.go.jp

Abstract. In recent years, many GLAMs have come to hold more digital materials than ever before, and the long-term digital preservation of these materials has become an issue. The National Diet Library of Japan (NDL) has actively conducted research into and shared information about digital preservation with other domestic institutions. The implementation of effective preservation measures requires an appropriate understanding of the present state of digital preservation, yet a comprehensive survey targeting the GLAM sector in Japan has never been attempted thus far.

Given this background, we conducted a questionnaire survey on digital preservation activities that targeted nearly all GLAMs in Japan. A total of 5,409 institutions were surveyed, and 2,921 responses were received. The results show that while the majority of GLAMs in Japan hold digital materials intended for long-term preservation, few have established relevant policies or implemented plans to put effective digital preservation measures in practice.

Keywords: Digital preservation · Digital curation · Digital materials · Long-term preservation · GLAMs · Questionnaire survey

1 Introduction

In recent years, many galleries, libraries, archives, museums, and similar institutions (GLAMs) have come to hold digital materials[1] in their collections, and the long-term digital preservation of these materials has become an increasingly complex issue to address. Although it is possible to make identical bit-stream copies of original digital material, the preservation of digital materials presents many challenges that differ from those of analogue or physical materials, including issues such as file format obsolescence and the need to maintain playback environments. And research in this area has been conducted by a variety of institutions and international organizations.[2]

The National Diet Library of Japan (NDL) has been actively conducting research related to digital preservation. Currently, under the *Basic Plan for Digital Preservation*

---

[1] In this paper, the term "digital materials" is used to refer to all types of materials in digital form, including packaged electronic publications (e.g., optical discs, magnetic disks), born-digital materials (e.g., ebooks, web archives, research data), and other digitized materials.

[2] The Open Preservation Foundation (OPF) and the Digital Preservation Coalition (DPC) are well-known international organizations in this field.

© The Author(s), under exclusive license to Springer Nature Switzerland AG 2022
Y.-H. Tseng et al. (Eds.): ICADL 2022, LNCS 13636, pp. 423–429, 2022.
https://doi.org/10.1007/978-3-031-21756-2_33

of National Diet Library's Collections 2021–2025, which was formulated in 2021, the NDL undertakes a variety of measures for the long-term preservation of its vast digital collections. [1, 2].

Since the NDL is Japan's only national library, it is expected to play a principal role in raising awareness and educating other GLAMs about the need for and the importance of digital preservation. In particular, we speculate that digital preservation is still largely unaddressed in Japan, and our primary objective was to test that hypothesis. To this end, we conducted in FY2021 a large-scale survey on digital preservation activities at virtually every GLAM in Japan. This paper analyzes data from what was the first comprehensive nationwide survey of its kind in Japan with the intention of clarifying the present state of digital preservation at GLAMs in Japan[3].

2 Related Work

Although many reports and white papers on digital preservation have been published, there have been few examples of large-scale surveys of digital preservation at GLAMs.

Recent efforts to conduct questionnaire surveys include the Open Preservation Foundation (OPF)'s 2015 and 2020 surveys. [4, 5] They targeted GLAMs that were already involved in digital preservation, and responses were collected from 132 institutions in 31 countries in 2015 and again from 98 institutions in 31 countries in 2020.

In 2005, the Digital Preservation Coalition (DPC) conducted a survey of over 900 professionals at wide range of organizations in different sectors in the UK to identify their needs for digital preservation [6].

In 2016, the National Library of New Zealand conducted a large-scale survey on the state of digital preservation in that country, and attempted to account for all cultural heritage institutions in New Zealand that could hold archival or special collections materials. Although the scope of the survey was limited to born-digital materials, a total of 371 institutions were surveyed, and 107 valid and complete responses were received.

In 2017–2018, a survey on digital preservation for memory institutions that mainly targeted members of the Canadian Association of Research Libraries (CARL) was conducted in, and 52 responses were received [7, 8].

In FY 2019, the NDL conducted a survey of 138 organizations, primarily national GLAM institutions outside Japan, regarding their digital preservation practices, but received only 11 responses due to the Covid-19 pandemic [9].

3 Method

We conducted a questionnaire survey of virtually every GLAM[4] and major local government in Japan. Questionnaires were sent by postal mail, and the targeted institutions

---

[3] A comprehensive report of this survey, including the actual questionnaire used, is already available [3], but only in Japanese.

[4] The International Standard Identifier for Libraries and Related Organizations (ISIL) management ledger was used as a basis, to which was added information made public by the Agency for Cultural Affairs, the National Archives of Japan, the Japanese Association of Museums, and others.

responded via postal mail or web-based survey forms. The survey period was from November to December 2021, and responses were collected from 2,921 of the 5,409 institutions surveyed for a response rate of 54%.

The questionnaire was designed with nine main questions, created with reference to the previous similar surveys mentioned above in Sect. 2. Related Work. Each main question also had several sub-questions that were intended to obtain detailed information. All questions and answers were in the Japanese language.

Main Questions: 1) Basic information about the institution, 2) Characteristics of collections, 3) Practices for digital preservation, 4) Policies and Plans, 5) Technical matters, 6) Metadata for digital preservation, 7) Cooperation with other institutions, 8) Characteristic efforts and Plans (free-text comments), and 9) Details of digital archives or institutional repositories.

4   Results[5]

4.1   Overview of the Respondent Institutions

Table 1 shows the ratio of institutional types[6]. Libraries account for 55% of the total and are the largest for the all respondent institutions (2,921). The mean number of employees was 91 and the median was 12.

Table 1. Types of respondent institutions (n = 2,921).

Institutional type	Number (percentage)
Library	1,593 (55%)
Museum	805 (28%)
Archives	124 (4%)
Other institutions of national or local governments	180 (6%)
Other/No answer	219 (7%)

4.2   State of Digital Material Holdings, Metadata, and Availability

Regarding the state of digital materials holdings, 70% (2,046 institutions) of all respondent institutions hold some form of digital materials.

Institutions that hold digital materials were also asked about the state of metadata preparation and the availability of digital materials. The percentage of institutions that make digital materials available on the web was 50% of those holding digital materials.

---

[5] Due to space limitations, only the most important results will be noted with specific figures or tables from the survey. For details, please refer to the poster.

[6] Each type includes academic affiliated institutions.

4.3 Types of Digital Materials and Ways to Implement Digitization

In libraries, the most frequent mode of acquisition of digital materials is that of networked electronic resources such as electronic journals. On the other hand, in museums and archives, digitization of materials or creation of born-digital materials showed the highest percentage (65%).

As for digitization of materials, 32% of respondent institutions carry out in-house digitization, even if only partially.

4.4 Practices for Digital Preservation

Table 2 shows the results of multiple-answer questions to the 2,046 institutions that hold digital materials on how they position their digital materials in terms of preservation.

The questionnaire also asks the allocation of budget for preservation and management of digital materials and the number of employees in charge of preservation duties. Only 26% of all the institutions with digital material holdings have dedicated budget and only 22% have employees in charge of preservation-related duties.

Table 2. Position of digital materials for preservation (n = 2,046; institutions holding digital materials).

Options	Percentage of responses
Plan to preserve all of their digital materials for at least 30 years or longer	36%
Plan to preserve part of their digital materials for a long term (limit the subject or period of time)	12%
Preserve digital materials, but considering while proceeding with digital material collection and creation	30%
Are not considering long-term preservation	22%

4.5 Policies and Plans

Regarding the state of formulation of policy or plan for digital preservation, only about 13% of the institutions that hold digital materials (2,046 institutions) have some kind of policy or plan for digital preservation. Even if adding institutions planning to formulate such a policy in the future, the total of institutions working on digital preservation policies and plans is still less than 30%.

4.6 Technical Matters

We also inquired about data backup, which is one of the most basic measures for data preservation, particularly with regard to the current state of practice and the number of copies created. The result shows that 41% of the institutions holding digital materials (2,046 institutions) have at least some kind of partial backup. Many institutions, however, did not respond to the question about the number of copies.

The state of implementation of preservation measures for digital materials other than backup (condition check, migration, maintenance of playback environment, etc.) is asked. The largest number of respondents (45%, 924 institutions) answered "none in particular" for those holding digital materials. Only 14% of the institutions holding digital materials have implemented preservation measures beyond backup and simple condition check.

4.7 Cooperation with Other Institutions

In response to the question inquiring cooperation and information sharing with external organizations for preservation and provision of digital materials, some organizations mentioned cooperation with Japan Search[7], the National Archives of Japan, or some national research institutions, while others mentioned participation in an international digital-resource-sharing network, such as the Internet Archive. There are also cases of cross-institutional collaboration in the same region.

5 Discussion

5.1 Current State of Digital Preservation Revealed by Survey Results

The results of the survey indicate that as many as 70% of the respondent institutions have digital materials in their collections, while only 22% of them have no specific intent to undertake digital preservation. On the other hand, only 13% of the institutions holding digital materials have any policy or plan for digital preservation, and only 14% have actually implemented some kind of preservation measures other than backup for their digital materials. Many institutions have inadequate staffing and budget, and this lack of resources may be one of the reasons for this stagnation.

These results indicate that there is little work being done on digital preservation at GLAM institutions in Japan. Therefore, Japanese-language teaching materials is needed. At present, we are planning to release videos and translate foreign handbooks.

5.2 Limitations

The nature of the survey itself means that the latent bias against the population, such higher response rates from institutions with greater awareness of preservation practices or those that hold digital materials, cannot be ruled out. The number of responses was, however, sufficient (2,921 institutions, response rate: 54%) to constitute a representative sample, and the ratio of respondent institutions by type was approximately equal to that in the lists of all GLAMs in Japan prepared for this survey.

---

[7] Japan Search, operated by the NDL, is a Japanese national platform for aggregating metadata of digital resources of various fields. https://jpsearch.go.jp/.

Although not introduced in this paper, the survey also included multiple free-text comments fields (e.g., categories of materials collected, storage media, etc.), and a thorough analysis of those responses should be a future task. In addition, it would be preferable to conduct a statistical analysis of the survey data.

6 Conclusion

In this research, we surveyed the current state of digital preservation practices in virtually every GLAM in Japan and successfully obtained an unprecedentedly large number of responses. The results showed that, while many institutions hold digital materials and intend to preserve them over the long term, few have established policies or plans for long-term preservation, nor have they put effective preservation measures in practice.

Digital preservation is an activity that requires continuing management activities, including checking for obsolete equipment and formats or timely migration, and securing suitable budget is essential for its steady implementation. It is also necessary to assign personnel with relevant expertise in this field. The NDL will continue efforts to raise awareness of the need for and the importance of digital preservation as well as conduct surveys to help GLAMs guarantee access to digital materials.

Acknowledgement. We thank to The Libraries of the Future Research, Inc. (https://www.mirait osyokan.jp/), the contractor of the survey.

References

1. National Diet Library: Basic Plan for Digital Preservation of National Diet Library's Collections 2021–2025 (in Japanese). (2021). https://www.ndl.go.jp/jp/preservation/dlib/pdf/NDLdigita lpreseravation_basicplan2021-2025.pdf. Accessed 25 July 2022
2. Takafumi, K.: NDL Develops Basic Plan for Long-Term Preservation of Digital Materials 2021–2025. Current Awareness-E 416 (2021). https://current.ndl.go.jp/node/45908, Accessed 25 July 2022
3. National Diet Library.: Survey of GLAMs in Japan on Digital Preservation 2021 (2022) (in Japanese). https://doi.org/10.11501/12300247
4. Open Preservation Foundation: 2014–2015 Digital Preservation Community Survey (2015). https://doi.org/10.5281/zenodo.4073070
5. Open Preservation Foundation.: 2019–2020 Digital Preservation Community Survey. (2020). https://doi.org/10.5281/zenodo.4066912
6. Waller, M., Robert, S.: Mind the gap: assessing digital preservation needs in the UK; Prepared for Digital Preservation Coalition. Digital Preservation Coalition (2006). https://www.dpconline.org/docs/miscellaneous/advocacy/340-mind-the-gap-assessing-digital-preservation-needs-in-the-uk/file. Accessed 25 July 2022
7. Jessica, M.: Born Digital in New Zealand: report of survey results. National Library of New Zealand. (2017). https://natlib.govt.nz/files/reports/research-borndigital2017-report.pdf. Accessed 25 July 2022

8. Hurley, G., Kathleen, S.: Final report of the survey on digital preservation capacity and needs at Canadian Memory Institutions, 2017–18. Canadian Association of Research Libraries (2019). http://www.carl-abrc.ca/wp-content/uploads/2019/11/Digital_preservation_capacity_finalreport_EN-1.pdf. Accessed 25 July 2022
9. National Diet Library: Survey Report on the Long-term Preservation of Electronic Information 2019 (in Japanese). (2020). https://doi.org/10.11501/11529765

Evaluating Machine Translation of Latin Interjections in the *Digital Library of Polish and Poland-related News Pamphlets*

Maciej Ogrodniczuk[1]([⊠]) [ID] and Katarzyna Kryńska[2] [ID]

[1] Institute of Computer Science, Polish Academy of Sciences, Jana Kazimierza 5,
01-248 Warszawa, Poland
maciej.ogrodniczuk@ipipan.waw.pl
[2] Institute of Polish Language, Polish Academy of Sciences, al. Mickiewicza 31,
31-120 Kraków, Poland
katarzyna.krynska@ijp.pan.pl

Abstract. In *The Digital Library of Polish and Poland-related Ephemeral Prints from the 16th, 17th and 18th Centuries* a small fraction of items contains manually created Latin–Polish dictionaries explaining Latin fragments injected into Polish content. At the same time, rapid development of machine translation creates new opportunities for creating such dictionaries automatically. In this paper, we verify whether existing translation solutions are already capable of generating useful results in this Latin-Polish setting. We investigate two systems available for this language pair: the familiar Google neural engine and the GPT-3 model, then we test the translation of isolated and context-embedded phrases and evaluate its results with both automatic and human metrics: BLEU and White's 5-point scale of adequacy and fluency.

Keywords: Digital library · Machine translation · Evaluation · Middle Polish

1 Introduction

The process of injecting Latin fragments into Polish texts was a frequent practice in the 16th to 18th centuries. In *The Digital Library of Polish and Poland-related Ephemeral Prints from the 16th, 17th and 18th Centuries* (Pol. *Cyfrowa Biblioteka Druków Ulotnych polskich i Polski dotyczących z XVI, XVII i XVIII wieku*, hereafter abbreviated CBDU[1] [5,9,10], containing pre-press documents from this period such Latin interjections constitute 7–8% of the textual content of

---

[1] See https://cbdu.ijp.pan.pl/.

The work was financed by a research grant from the Polish Ministry of Science and Higher Education under the National Programme for the Development of Humanities for the years 2019–2023 (grant 11H 18 0413 86, grant funds received: 1,797,741 PLN).

Y.-H. Tseng et al. (Eds.): ICADL 2022, LNCS 13636, pp. 430–439, 2022.
https://doi.org/10.1007/978-3-031-21756-2_34

the print[2]. While still understandable for people familiar with Latin and experts, such passages may be difficult to decipher by a non-specialist reader. For this reason, manually created dictionaries of Latin terms and phrases were added to prints. Unfortunately, due to financial constraints of the original project, only 23 prints were annotated in this way with a total of 600 entries.

Today, with new machine translation developments doing reasonably well for modern languages and available also for Latin, we might try to use them in supplementing the previous work. Not only new prints containing Latin can be translated but also existing dictionaries can be extended with missing words and phrases, previously regarded as easy to understand (which is not always the case). But a prerequisite for starting this process should be verification of the quality of existing Latin-to-Polish machine translation solutions. To our best knowledge, no figures have been so far reported for this language pair.

What is important to note is that we do not intend to create a new state-of-the-art Latin-to-Polish translation engine but evaluate existing out-of-the-box solutions on the available manually created dictionaries and to suggest customizations which could improve their usage.

2   Data Preparation

Our translation dataset was based on the manually created Latin-Polish dictionaries attached as metadata to some prints which can already serve as ready-to-use evaluation data. Out of 23 prints with such dictionaries only 21 prints contained Polish equivalents of Latin phrases (with two dictionaries preserving only Latin and no Polish, presumably marked for translation but never completed[3]) and one duplicate, i.e. the same four entries, both Latin originals and translations, in the same context[4]). This filtering step resulted in 566 entries from 20 prints.

The entries were pre-processed to remove line breaks, editorial comments (such as uncertainty signalled with a question mark in brackets or a reference to a particular book in the bible which was the source of the citation). This process also resulted in several corrections in the library, e.g. for one print the dictionary of difficult old Polish words (with explanations in Polish) was found to be swapped with the Latin-Polish dictionary and one Latin entry contained an excessive fragment in Polish. Additionally, seven obvious typos in the Polish texts were corrected.

The dictionary-based dataset could be successfully used for the translation of isolated Latin fragments but we already planned to carry out a context-wise experiment, i.e. test whether the availability of a larger context could improve

---

[2] Calculated based on a sample of 18 transcribed prints containing Latin-Polish dictionaries; 1895 words out of 24506.

[3] See https://cbdu.ijp.pan.pl/id/eprint/700/ and https://cbdu.ijp.pan.pl/id/eprint/2250/.

[4] See https://cbdu.ijp.pan.pl/id/eprint/4210/ and https://cbdu.ijp.pan.pl/id/eprint/4220/.

translation quality. To be able to do that, we needed larger contextual fragments of dictionary phrases which were not available in the CBDU digital library. At the same time, some full texts from the library were transcribed in another project, intended to create *The Electronic Corpus of the 17th and 18th Century Polish Texts (until 1772)* (Pol. *Elektroniczny Korpus Tekstów Polskich z XVII i XVIII w. (do roku 1772)*) [4], also referred to as the *Baroque Corpus* (Pol. *Korpus Barokowy* – hence its acronym KORBA[5], Out of 20 prints with Latin dictionaries available in the digital library, only 18 have been transcribed for the corpus so we limited our further experiments to these prints to be able to perform the evaluation on a fixed dataset. As a result, the final number of samples in the set dropped to 553. For completeness, it is worth noting that for some prints their content was retrieved from duplicates, i.e. different editions of the same content, registered in CBDU as separate prints[6].

The texts were available in TEI P5 XML, following the format of the National Corpus of Polish [13], with Latin parts marked with `<foreign>` tags which were removed before running the translation. Similarly, when two variants of the same fragment have been available (in `<choice>` elements), their regularized versions have been used (cf. `<orig>corporisþ</orig>` vs. `<reg>corporisque</reg>`).

After stripping XML tags from the corpus files, the Latin dictionary fragments were located using fuzzy matching[7] which was very effective in neglecting minor variations between the transcribed content of the print and the dictionary entry, cf. *O Passi graviora* vs. *O Passi grauiora* or parts of content removed from the Latin entry, usually with a Polish interjection, marked with an ellipsis character, cf. *prosequi ... Hostem* corresponding to *prosequi nie mogli Hostem*. The method, apart from producing offsets of the closest match found, also returns Levenshtein edit distance between both matching parts so errors could be easily tracked. In some cases, however, the difference between the dictionary entry and the corpus text made even the fuzzy match impossible, e.g. when acronyms were used in the text but were already expanded in the dictionary (e.g. *jurium coaequationis M. D. L. cum Regno* shown as *jurium coaequationis Magni Ducatus Lituaniae cum Regno*). During the pre-processing step, such abbreviations were inserted into corpus texts in their expanded form.

Another set of decisions had to be made on the size of the context. The most straightforward scope would be a complete syntactically valid unit containing the phrase being translated. This is not easy to obtain for an old Polish text so initially we decided to extract the left and right context surrounding the phrase or sentence of arbitrary 50-character length and then cut it at potentially syntactically valid places, such as commas, widening the window appropriately. Since

---

[5] See also https://korba.edu.pl/overview?lang=en.

[6] See e.g. https://cbdu.ijp.pan.pl/id/eprint/3760/, https://cbdu.ijp.pan.pl/id/eprint/3770/ and https://cbdu.ijp.pan.pl/id/eprint/3780/ with the content available for the first one and the dictionary present only for the last one or a similar case with https://cbdu.ijp.pan.pl/id/eprint/13880/ and https://cbdu.ijp.pan.pl/id/eprint/13890/.

[7] With the `fuzzy_index` function from the `Text::Fuzzy` Perl module.

this procedure became overly complicated, we got back to a simpler solution of passing full paragraphs to the translation module. A positive side-effect of this step was that paragraphs containing many interjections could only be translated once.

Still, extracting full paragraphs resulted in lengthy passages, sometimes exceeding 5 000 characters (while e.g. the GPT-3 Davinci model is capable of processing up to 4 000 tokens per request) which introduced more complications without any observable gains (the translation did not look better as compared to shorter passages). So we reverted to the idea of extracting full sentences containing Latin phrases being translated and one sentence before and after the full translated sentences. In some cases, the contexts were manually fine-tuned (when e.g. a full stop did not finish a sentence but an abbreviation). The length of the largest context extracted using this method was 700 characters.

3   Translation Setting

Our translation experiments have been concentrated along two axes: the approach used to machine translation and the size of context needed for using the model successfully. The most popular engine offering Latin to Polish translation is Google Translate, also powering numerous "independent" interfaces available on the Web. The Google API[8] is used e.g. by TranslateKing[9], TranslateHub[10] or Translatiz[11]. A similar model is used e.g. by Yandex API[12], adapted by e.g. ContDict[13], Latin Online[14] or Lingvanex[15] but after preliminary tests we decided to use only Google because of its much better quality than the competitive systems. The experiment used standard Google Translate API calls.

A competitive approach is offered by a recently popular paradigm of prompting large general-purpose generative language models for various tasks, including translation, so we also decided to test the OpenAI's Davinci GPT-3 large-scale language-generation approach with its default settings[16]. GPT-3 prompts were constructed in the form of the static request: *Przetłumacz łacinę na polski:* (*Translate Latin to Polish:*) "*entry*":.

The scope-based analysis is exploiting the expectation that taking into account contextual information from the text in which the phrase or sentence is embedded might bring more successful results than isolated translation (i.e. just a given phrase or sentence). This might be particularly true for the multilingual generative models which are known for the ability to reuse foreign-language

---

[8] https://translate.google.pl/?sl=la&tl=pl.
[9] https://translateking.com/.
[10] https://livetranslatehub.com/.
[11] https://translatiz.com/.
[12] https://translate.yandex.com/?lang=la-pl.
[13] https://www.contdict.com.
[14] https://www.latin-online-translation.com/.
[15] https://lingvanex.com/demo/.
[16] See e.g. its openly accessible "playground" https://beta.openai.com/playground.

hints, well represented in the main text of our prints. In our experiments, we will try to validate this anticipation by comparing the results of isolated and contextual translation.

In the context-less setting the entries have been fed one by one to the translation engine and results collected.

4   Evaluation

Two basic types of evaluation of machine translation results are usually being carried out: automatic and human evaluation. Below we present both, realizing that each of them has its advantages and flaws: automatic evaluation being low-cost and consistent but not necessarily reliable while human evaluation being more meaningful but also time-consuming and subjective.

For evaluation, we randomly selected 100 entries, following the proportion of phrases to full sentences from the complete dataset (95 entries being phrases). When several translation variants were given, they were treated equally during evaluation.

4.1   Automatic Evaluation

A commonly used method to evaluate machine translation automatically is BLEU (BiLingual Evaluation Understudy) [11], an n-gram precision-based metric. Even though numerous other metrics (cf. NIST [2], METEOR [7], TER [14] or chrF [12]) are also used, many new ones are proposed almost every year[17] and despite the well-known problems with BLEU, the machine translation community still uses it as the primary measure of translation quality so we decided to adopt it for our evaluation.

Table 1 presents the results of the automatic evaluation.

Table 1. Automatic evaluation results

Setting	Engine	Cumulative BLEU score			
		1-gram	2-gram	3-gram	4-gram
Isolated	Google	26.22	18.77	**14.74**	**12.58**
	GPT-3	26.27	16.45	11.35	8.33
Context-wise	Google	23.95	15.46	11.63	8.85
	GPT-3	**31.83**	**20.18**	13.45	9.54

Even though the higher presence of unigrams and bigrams in the translation puts the context-wise GPT-based solution in the best position, the most

---

[17] See e.g. chapter 6 of [8] for more examples and [6] for evaluation of the correlation of various metrics with human judgements.

frequently used 4-gram BLEU score is the highest for isolated Google solution. Still, what is slightly discouraging, it does not reach 20 points regarded as the minimum value required for getting the gist of the text.

However, it is worth noting that BLEU only measures direct word-to-word similarity and good translations using e.g. synonyms get poor scores because they cannot be matched in the reference text. This is where human evaluation can show its usefulness.

4.2 Human Evaluation

Apart from automatic evaluation, we decided to carry out the human evaluation of translation results to compensate for BLEU deficiencies (e.g. in dealing with synonyms), compare how both sets of results correlate and to better assess various properties of the translation. Again, numerous methods of human evaluation have been proposed[18], with the most straightforward one using a 5-point scale of adequacy and fluency [16] (see Table 2). Adequacy is related to the adherence of the translation to the source text while fluency grades the quality of the target text only. Contrary to more detailed evaluation schemes, such as iSTS (Interpretable Semantic Textual Similarity, see [1]) or detailed error typologies (see. e.g. [15]) it requires a moderate evaluation effort while still measuring the two most important properties of the translation.

Table 2. 5-point scale of adequacy and fluency, based on [16] (Table 3)

Value	Adequacy	Fluency
5	All meaning	Flawless Polish
4	Most meaning	Good Polish
3	Much meaning	Non-native Polish
2	Little meaning	Disfluent Polish
1	None	Incomprehensible

The evaluation has been carried out by a single translator proficient in Latin and Polish. Table 3 presents its overall results for both translation engines and translation scopes which show relatively high fluency (good to flawless) while retaining much meaning. What is surprising, adding context does not always help with achieving better translation adequacy and always impairs fluency. The adequacy values seem to correlate with automatic results.

---

[18] See their review e.g. in the Related Work section of [3].

Table 3. Human evaluation results

Setting	Engine	Adequacy	Fluency
Isolated	Google	3.11	4.63
	GPT-3	2.87	4.52
Context-wise	Google	2.61	4.02
	GPT-3	3.00	4.32

5 Qualitative Error Analysis and Translators' Notes

5.1 Analysing Adequacy and Fluency

Passages not translated by the machine translator, whether left in Latin or omitted, were rated lowest on the evaluation scale (1) as *none* or *incomprehensible* in both adequacy and fluency categories.

In many cases, a high degree of fluency can be observed, which we judge following [8]: *"When judging fluency, the source text is not relevant. The evaluators have access to only the translation being judged and not the source data"* while the quality of adequacy in these cases is low. This means that automatic translators mostly do well in generating grammatically and logically correct translations, but often meaningfully distant from the desired version.

The high frequency of adequate translation fluency is influenced by the occurrence of single-word macaronisms in sentences. In the case of a single word translations (e.g. *Februarii, discernere, protrahere*) or short popular phrases (e.g. *prima die, in absentia*), the highest (5) degree of fluency in all four categories is usually recorded, unless the translator leaves a word untranslated in some cases (e.g. *periculum, Julii*). However, cases can be noted where the MT solutions translated a stand-alone Latin word correctly, but failed to translate it in context, e.g. *decernemus (we decide)* was translated as *współbędźie będźie (will co-be*, Google with context) and *dla potrzeb Stanu (for the State*, GPT-3 with context).

In some cases, both adequacy and fluency were rated highest in all four categories of translation (e.g. for isolated words *confirmatio* or *notandum*). However, there were also instances of context-less translations which (according to the principle: how well the target text represents the informational content of the source text [8]) were rated highest on the scale and, although correctly translated, they were semantically distant from respective entries in the manually created dictionary. This fact should be noted when analysing the reported percentages. In reality, their actual usefulness will therefore be lower than the statistics show.

5.2 The Role of Context

In some cases, a correct automatic translation is not possible in the given limited context, while the glossary takes into account a man-made translation adapted to the wider context. E.g. the examined phrase *ultima praeterlapsi* (literally: *last of the past*) requires an addendum specifying the time when the action described in the sentence took place. The time is indicated in a broader, omitted context, and thus in the given limited context, the translator failed to cope with a translation whose meaning (the last day of the past month) should have been guessed from the broader context.

Sometimes the Polish translation present in the dictionary contained excessive explanations, not covered by the original, e.g. *cum omnium applausu & satisfactione* was translated as *zyskując uznanie i zadowolenie wszystkich stanów Królestwa* (En: *gaining recognition and satisfaction from all states of the Kingdom*) which obviously contains more information than the Latin text.

5.3   Transcription Errors

Sometimes the process has been influenced by transcription errors, as in *ludicre* (clearly visible in the original) wrongly transliterated as *ludiere*. At the same time, the neural models are known to deal with such issues successfully.

5.4   Language Model-Induced Consequences

The multilinguality of the GPT model frequently showed when English output was partially produced for translated Latin phrases (e.g. *Salve* rendered as *hello* or *Nobilitatis* as *Nobility*. At the same time, multilinguality is believed to help translate content without the additional step of language identification for individual fragments, previously a necessary step for every mixed-content solution.

The expectation that translation models could make use of syntactic properties of the context to produce properly declined forms was confirmed, cf. *powstały rożne sensus* (*various meanings have emerged*) was translated as *powstały$_{PL}$ rożne$_{PL}$ znaczenie$_{SING}$* by Google and *powstały$_{PL}$ różne$_{PL}$ znaczenia$_{PL}$* by GPT-3 (also note the correction of diacritics, also interpreted properly for misspelt words).

In general, Polish translations retain the proper grammatical form of the tokens, valid in the given context (i.e. making a valid larger whole, e.g. a sentence, when inserted instead of its corresponding Latin interjection). Still, in some cases the translation lacks some essential part, e.g. a preposition, as in *prosił znowu assensum* (*he asked for reconciliation*), when *assensum* was translated as *zgodę* (*reconciliation$_{ACC}$*) while in this context a preposition should be added *o zgodę*. The generative model added this preposition so we corrected such cases in the original translation before running the evaluation.

6   Conclusions

The presented experiment showed that it is still too early to use Latin-to-Polish machine translation in a completely automatic process. None of the four given categories yielded satisfactory results concerning the adequacy, and the chosen

MT solutions should not constitute a reliable end-to-end tool for translating Latin in Polish texts. Moreover, the high percentage of incorrect translations in the Latin survey, both in the wider context (e.g. 45% in Google translator) and stand-alone clearly shows that there is a high risk that automatic translation will generate erroneous results. Still, the evaluator's experiences show that it can prove useful as a translator's aid under human supervision.

The results can be further analysed, taking into account various types of errors produced (wrong syntax, lack of prepositions, inflexion problems, spelling errors etc.)

The fact that the context contained intertwined Latin and Polish text we could also confirm that contemporary translation models can successfully cope with such a multilingual blend. Unfortunately, even though CBDU prints contain interjections in other languages than Latin, no evaluation data is available so no truly multilingual tests could be carried out.

References

1. Agirre, E., Gonzalez-Agirre, A., Lopez-Gazpio, I., Maritxalar, M., Rigau, G., Uria, L.: SemEval-2016 Task 2: interpretable semantic textual similarity. In: Proceedings of the 10th International Workshop on Semantic Evaluation (SemEval-2016), pp. 512–524. Association for Computational Linguistics, San Diego, California (2016). https://aclanthology.org/S16-1082
2. Doddington, G.: Automatic evaluation of machine translation quality using n-gram co-occurrence statistics. In: Proceedings of the Second International Conference on Human Language Technology Research, pp. 138–145. Morgan Kaufmann Publishers Inc., San Francisco, CA, USA (2002). https://aclanthology.org/www.mt-archive.info/HLT-2002-Doddington.pdf
3. Freitag, M., Foster, G., Grangier, D., Ratnakar, V., Tan, Q., Macherey, W.: Experts, errors, and context: a large-scale study of human evaluation for machine translation. Trans. Assoc. Comput. Linguist. **9**, 1460–1474 (2021). https://doi.org/10.1162/tacl_a_00437
4. Gruszczyński, W., Adamiec, D., Bronikowska, R., Wieczorek, A.: Elektroniczny Korpus Tekstów Polskich z XVII i XVIII w. - problemy teoretyczne i warsztatowe. Poradnik Językowy **777**(8), 32–51 (2020). https://doi.org/10.33896/porj.2020.8.3
5. Gruszczyński, W., Ogrodniczuk, M.: Cyfrowa Biblioteka Druków Ulotnych Polskich i Polski dotyczących z XVI, XVII i XVIII w. w nauce i dydaktyce (Digital Library of Poland-related Old Ephemeral Prints in research and teaching. In: Polish). In: Materiały konferencji Polskie Biblioteki Cyfrowe 2010 (Proceedings of the Polish Digital Libraries 2010 conference), pp. 23–27. Poznań, Poland (2010)
6. Kocmi, T., Federmann, C., Grundkiewicz, R., Junczys-Dowmunt, M., Matsushita, H., Menezes, A.: To ship or not to ship: an extensive evaluation of automatic metrics for machine translation. In: Proceedings of the Sixth Conference on Machine Translation, pp. 478–494. Association for Computational Linguistics (2021). https://aclanthology.org/2021.wmt-1.57
7. Lavie, A., Agarwal, A.: METEOR: an automatic metric for mt evaluation with high levels of correlation with human judgments. In: Proceedings of the Second Workshop on Statistical Machine Translation, pp. 228–231. Association for Computational Linguistics, Prague, Czech Republic (2007). https://aclanthology.org/W07-0734

8. Maučec, M.S., Donaj, G.: Machine translation and the evaluation of its quality. In: Sadollah, A., Sinha, T.S. (eds.) Recent Trends in Computational Intelligence, chap. 8. IntechOpen, Rijeka (2019). https://doi.org/10.5772/intechopen.89063

9. Ogrodniczuk, M., Gruszczyński, W.: Digital library of poland-related old ephemeral prints: preserving multilingual cultural heritage. In: Proceedings of the Workshop on Language Technologies for Digital Humanities and Cultural Heritage, pp. 27–33. Hissar, Bulgaria (2011). http://www.aclweb.org/anthology/W11-4105

10. Ogrodniczuk, M., Gruszczyński, W.: Digital library 2.0 – source of knowledge and research collaboration platform. In: Calzolari, N., et al.(eds.) Proceedings of the Ninth International Conference on Language Resources and Evaluation (LREC 2014), pp. 1649–1653. European Language Resources Association, Reykjavík, Iceland (2014). http://www.lrec-conf.org/proceedings/lrec2014/pdf/14_Paper.pdf

11. Papineni, K., Roukos, S., Ward, T., Zhu, W.J.: BLEU: a method for automatic evaluation of machine translation. In: Proceedings of the 40th Annual Meeting of the Association for Computational Linguistics, pp. 311–318. Association for Computational Linguistics, Philadelphia, Pennsylvania, USA (2002). https://aclanthology.org/P02-1040

12. Popović, M.: CHRF: character n-gram F-score for automatic MT evaluation. In: Proceedings of the Tenth Workshop on Statistical Machine Translation, pp. 392–395. Association for Computational Linguistics, Lisbon, Portugal (2015). https://aclanthology.org/W15-3049

13. Przepiórkowski, A., Bańko, M., Górski, R.L., Lewandowska-Tomaszczyk, B. (eds.): Narodowy Korpus Języka Polskiego. Wydawnictwo Naukowe PWN, Warsaw (2012)

14. Snover, M., Dorr, B., Schwartz, R., Micciulla, L., Makhoul, J.: A study of translation edit rate with targeted human annotation. In: Proceedings of the 7th Conference of the Association for Machine Translation in the Americas: Technical Papers, pp. 223–231. Association for Machine Translation in the Americas, Cambridge, Massachusetts, USA (2006). https://aclanthology.org/2006.amta-papers.25

15. Vilar, D., Xu, J., D'Haro, L.F., Ney, H.: Error analysis of statistical machine translation output. In: Proceedings of the Fifth International Conference on Language Resources and Evaluation (LREC 2006), pp. 697–702. European Language Resources Association (ELRA), Genoa, Italy (2006). http://www.lrec-conf.org/proceedings/lrec2006/pdf/413_pdf.pdf

16. White, J.S., O'Connell, T.A., O'Mara, F.E.: The ARPA MT evaluation methodologies: evolution, lessons, and future approaches. In: Proceedings of the First Conference of the Association for Machine Translation in the Americas, pp. 193–205. Columbia, Maryland, USA (1994). https://aclanthology.org/1994.amta-1.25

Extracting Information about Research Resources from Scholarly Papers

Ayahito Saji[1]([✉]) [iD] and Shigeki Matsubara[1,2] [iD]

[1] Graduate School of Informatics, Nagoya University, Nagoya, Japan
saji.ayahito.y7@s.mail.nagoya-u.ac.jp
[2] Information and Communications, Nagoya University, Nagoya, Japan

Abstract. This paper presents a method to extract information about research resource metadata from scholarly papers to expand research resource repositories using an academic knowledge graph. Here, we considered the hypothesis that information extracted from scholarly papers is beneficial to expand research resource repositories from two perspectives: (1) the amount of information in existing metadata, and (2) the number of entries in existing repositories. We constructed an academic knowledge graph, where the nodes and directed edges in the graph correspond to the entities and their relations in scholarly papers, respectively. To verify our hypothesis, we constructed a knowledge graph using 15,721 papers published in international conferences. We then investigated the expandability of a language resource metadata repository using the constructed knowledge graph. The experimental results demonstrated that the constructed knowledge graph could be used to enrich the descriptions of metadata and increase the number of entries in the repository.

Keywords: Information extraction · Data repository · Knowledge graph

1 Introduction

The open science concept promotes the sharing and utilization of papers and research data. One way to realize this is to register the metadata of such resources in repositories. Paper search services are currently available, e.g., CiteSeerX[1], Google Scholar[2], and Semantic Scholar[3], and research data search platforms, e.g., Google Dataset Search [19] and CiNii Research[4], are in development.

Generally, metadata for research resources are created manually and registered in repositories. For example, Google Dataset Search allows dataset registration using metadata according to the schema provided by Schema.org[5]. In the

---

[1] https://citeseerx.ist.psu.edu.
[2] https://scholar.google.com.
[3] https://www.semanticscholar.org.
[4] https://cir.nii.ac.jp.
[5] https://schema.org.

Y.-H. Tseng et al. (Eds.): ICADL 2022, LNCS 13636, pp. 440–448, 2022.
https://doi.org/10.1007/978-3-031-21756-2_35

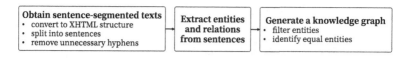

Fig. 1. Flow of knowledge graph construction

CiNii Research platform, metadata must be registered manually in the JAIRO Cloud[6]. However, generating metadata incurs significant costs [4].

In this study, we set and verify the following hypothesis: information extracted from scholarly papers is useful for expanding research resource repositories. Scholarly papers frequently mention research resources, and it is likely that such resources can be used to generate metadata.

Thus, this paper describes a method to acquire an academic knowledge graph from scholarly papers. The nodes and directed edges in the graph correspond to the entities and their relations in scholarly papers, respectively. To verify the above hypothesis experimentally, we constructed a knowledge graph using 15,721 papers published in international conferences on natural language processing (NLP). We also investigated the expandability of the SHACHI [26] language resource metadata repository [25] using the constructed knowledge graph.

2   Related Work

Several studies have been conducted to extract and use statements about research resources that appear in scholarly papers, such as the name of datasets [11,12,20,24] or the names of different software packages [6,7,17]. Kozawa et al. [15,16] proposed a method to automatically extract information about the "usages" of research resources from scholarly papers.

In addition, previous studies have attempted to expand research resource repositories by classifying citing information in scholarly papers. For example, Ikoma et al. [13] proposed a method to identify bibliographic information indicating research resources from reference lists, and Tsunokake et al. [27] proposed a method to classify URLs referring to research resources in scholarly papers.

3   Information Extraction from Scholarly Papers

Here, we describe the proposed method to construct a knowledge graph by extracting information about the metadata of research resources from papers. The flow of the knowledge graph construction process is illustrated in Fig. 1.

First, scholarly papers in PDF format are converted to semi-structured texts using PDFNLT-1.0 [1]. That is, XHTML files retaining the components of papers (e.g., title, paragraph, caption, footnotes, and bibliography) are generated. Each

---

[6] https://jpcoar.repo.nii.ac.jp.

Table 1. List of entity types [18].

Category	Description
Task	Applications, problems to solve, systems to construct
Method	Methods, models, systems to use, or tools, frameworks
Evaluation Metric	Metrics, measures, or entities that can express the quality
Material	Data, datasets, resources, corpus, knowledge base
Other Scientific Terms	Scientific terms that do not fall into any of the above classes
Generic	General terms or pronouns

Table 2. List of relation types [18].

Category	Description
Used-for	B is used for A, B models A, A is trained on B, A is based on B
Feature-of	B belongs to A, B is a feature of A, B is under A domain
Hyponym-of	B is a hyponym of A, B is a type of A
Part-of	B is a part of A
Compare	Opposite of conjunction, compare two models/methods
Conjunction	Function as similar role or use/incorporate
Evaluate-for	B is evaluated with A

paragraph is split into sentences using PySBD [22], a sentence boundary detection module. Dehyphen[7] is employed to remove unnecessary hyphens.

A model to extract entities from scholarly papers is then trained using the SciERC [18] dataset for Information Extraction tasks in academic papers. The SciERC schema extends the definitions of the SemEval-2017 Task 10 [2] and SemEval-2018 Task 7 [9]. Note that SciERC is annotated with the positions and types of entities (six types) and relations between two entities and their types (seven types). Tables 1 and 2 show the types of entities and relations between them, respectively. SpERT [8], which we use for entity extraction, is an attention-based model [28] that employs BERT [5] and SciBERT [3] embeddings. The model achieves high performance on the CoNLL04 [21], ADE [10], and SciERC datasets. SpERT is applied to each preprocessed sentence.

Then, a knowledge graph in which entities and their relations are represented as nodes and directed edges, respectively, is generated. Filtering and identification of equal entities are then performed. Here, the filtering process is performed to remove entities that include tokens of single letters, Greek letters, and alphanumeric mathematical symbols (Unicode U+1D400 to U+1D7FF). Figure 2 shows a part of the knowledge graph constructed in this study.

4   Investigation of Metadata Expansion

To investigate the expansion of metadata, we constructed a knowledge graph using scholarly papers from the NLP field. Here, we used 15,721 ACL, NAACL,

---

[7] https://github.com/pd3f/dehyphen.

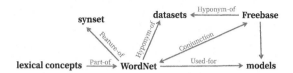

Fig. 2. Part of the constructed knowledge graph

Table 3. Correspondence between the relations and SHACHI database schema

Relation category	SHACHI metadata property
Used-For	`relation.utilization`
Feature-of	`description`
Hyponym-of	`relation.hypernym`
Part-of	`relation.part-of`
Compare	`relation.similar`
Conjunction	`relation.similar`

and EMNLP conference papers from 2000 to 2022 in the ACL Anthology. After preprocessing was applied, the total number of sentences was 1,228,368. For each sentence, the SpERT whose parameters were trained using the SciERC dataset was used to extract entities and their relations. The constructed knowledge graph included 763,305 entities and 1,302,589 relations.

In this study, we used the SHACHI language resources metadata database as an existing repository. SHACHI is described in a metadata vocabulary according to DublinCore [26]. As statements about the entry name from SHACHI, we collected `title`, `title.abbreviation` and `title.alternative`. The number of collected entries was 3,319, and that of different ones was 4,168.

We experimentally verified how much of the existing metadata information stored in SHACHI can be expanded. The existing metadata can be expanded if it is possible to add the relations as information about the corresponding properties of metadata in SHACHI. Table 3 shows the correspondence between the relations and the properties of the SHACHI metadata. A string comparison was conducted between the 4,168 entry names of SHACHI and the 763,305 entities extracted from the papers. We found that 208 entries (6.3% of the total entries) held one or more relations, and a total of 5,845 relations were added to those entries. Figure 3 shows the top 50 entries in terms of the number of added relations. These results confirm that the metadata in SHACHI can be expanded using the constructed knowledge graph.

5   Investigation of Entry Expansion

5.1   Dataset Construction and Classification Model Training

To construct the dataset, we used entities that had a "Material" type ratio of at least 0.5. Here, entities not holding any relations or appearing in only a single

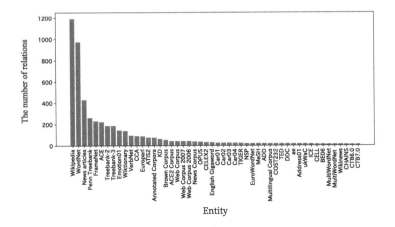

Fig. 3. Top 50 entries in terms of the number of added relations

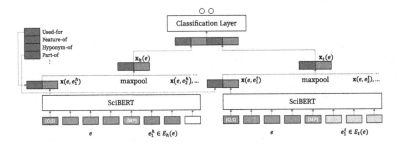

Fig. 4. Structure of the constructed entity classification model

paper were excluded[8]. In the following, E denotes the set of entities obtained by these processes. Note that the size of E was 16,869 entities.

Next, we sampled 1,000 entries from E and manually labeled those indicating language resources (LRs). In the following, we refer to these as *LR entities*. For example, `B-CLS`, `SMS message`, and `reduced document` are not LR entries because they do not indicate the LRs. However, `LCMC Corpus`, `WordNet` and `wikipedia` are LR entries because they indicate the LRs or are data collection targets. As can be seen, 237 (23.7%) entities were determined to be LR entities[9].

An entity classification model was constructed using SciBERT [3] and perceptrons. Figure 4 shows the structure of the model. For entities $e_1, e_2 \in E$ that hold the relationship, the BPE [23] token sequences comprising e_1 and e_2 are $(t_1^1, \ldots, t_{n_1}^1)$ and $(t_1^2, \ldots, t_{n_2}^2)$, respectively. Here, het $\mathbf{c}(e_1, e_2)$ be an embedding vector for `[CLS]` obtained by inputting $(\texttt{[CLS]}, t_1^1, \ldots, t_{n_1}^1, \texttt{[SEP]}, t_1^2, \ldots, t_{n_2}^2)$ to SciBERT. In addition, let $\mathbf{t}(e_1, e_2)$ be an embedding vector of the categories of

---

[8] In addition, if the entity matched a language name included in the ISO 639–3 language code (https://iso639-3.sil.org), it was excluded.

[9] This means that there may be approximately 4,000 LR entities in E.

relations for e_1 and e_2 and let $\mathbf{x}(e_1, e_2) = [\mathbf{t}(e_1, e_2); \mathbf{c}(e_1, e_2)]$ be an embedding vector representing the relation between e_1 and e_2.

For an entity $e \in E$, let $E_h(e)$ and $E_t(e)$ be the set of entities holding relations that start and end with e, respectively. For e, $\{e_1^h, \ldots, e_{m_h}^h\} \subseteq E_h(e)$ $(m_h \leq \psi)$,

$$\mathbf{x}_h(e) = \begin{cases} f\left(\mathbf{x}(e, e_1^h), \ldots, \mathbf{x}(e, e_{m_h}^h)\right) & E_h(e) \neq \emptyset \\ 0 & E_h(e) = \emptyset \end{cases},$$

$\mathbf{x}_t(e)$ is also defined in the same way. Note that f is the max-pooling operation. Finally, the input to the classification layer is $\mathbf{x}(e) = [\mathbf{x}_h(e); \mathbf{x}_t(e)]$. The classification layer is $\hat{y}(e) = \mathrm{softmax}(W \cdot \mathbf{x}(e) + \mathbf{b})$ and outputs probabilities.

5.2   Experiment

First, parameters W and $\mathbf{b}$ were trained, and SciBERT was fine-tuned to classify whether an input entity is an LR entity. Here, used 1,000 labeled entries, which were split into training, validation, and testing sets with 700 entries, 150 entries, and 150 entries, respectively. We used weighted cross-entropy loss as the loss function during training and we employed the reciprocal of the ratio of the number of datasets in each class $(1000/237, 1000/763)$ as weights. Adam [14] was employed as the optimization algorithm with a learning rate of 1e-5 as the base and a decay rate of 0.9 per epoch. In addition, the batch size was set to 16, the number of epochs was set to 64, the embedding vector dimension of the categories of relations was set to 25, and ψ was set to 8. A dropout layer with a dropout rate of 0.1 was also used before the classification layer.

As evaluation metrics, we used precision, recall, their weighted harmonic mean $F_{0.5}$ value and precision for a sampling of 100 entities from all entity sets E classified as LR entities. Among the epochs, the model that obtained the highest $F_{0.5}$ value on the validation set was used for evaluation.

The precision, recall, and $F_{0.5}$ values for the test data were 83.3% (25/30), 61.0% (25/41), and 0.78, respectively. In the annotation of 100 entries sampled from the 3,514 (20.8%) entries classified as LR entities in E, we found that 80 (80.0%) entries were in fact LR entities. Thus, we confirmed that constructed knowledge graph can be used to expand the number of entries in SHACHI.

6   Conclusion

In this paper, we have presented a method to extract knowledge about research resources from paper texts to expand research resource repositories. We constructed an academic knowledge graph from international conference papers and experimentally verified whether the existing LR repositories could be expanded. We found that the constructed knowledge graph can be used to enrich the metadata and increase the number of entries of LRs in the repository.

Acknowledgments. This research was supported in part by the Grant-in-Aid for Scientific Research (B) (No. 21H03773) of the JSPS.

References

1. Abekawa, T., Aizawa, A.: SideNoter: scholarly paper browsing system based on PDF restructuring and text annotation. In: Proceedings of COLING 2016, the 26th International Conference on Computational Linguistics: System Demonstrations, pp. 136–140. The COLING 2016 Organizing Committee, Osaka, Japan (2016). https://aclanthology.org/C16-2029
2. Augenstein, I., Das, M., Riedel, S., Vikraman, L., McCallum, A.: SemEval 2017 task 10: scienceie - extracting keyphrases and relations from scientific publications. In: Proceedings of the 11th International Workshop on Semantic Evaluation (SemEval-2017), pp. 546–555. Association for Computational Linguistics, Vancouver, Canada (2017). https://doi.org/10.18653/v1/S17-2091
3. Beltagy, I., Lo, K., Cohan, A.: SciBERT: a pretrained language model for scientific text. In: Proceedings of the 2019 Conference on Empirical Methods in Natural Language Processing and the 9th International Joint Conference on Natural Language Processing (EMNLP-IJCNLP), pp. 3615–3620. Association for Computational Linguistics, Hong Kong, China (2019). https://doi.org/10.18653/v1/D19-1371
4. Chapman, A., et al.: Dataset search: a survey. VLDB J. **29**(1), 251–272 (2019). https://doi.org/10.1007/s00778-019-00564-x
5. Devlin, J., Chang, M.W., Lee, K., Toutanova, K.: BERT: pre-training of deep bidirectional transformers for language understanding. In: Proceedings of the 2019 Conference of the North American Chapter of the Association for Computational Linguistics: Human Language Technologies, Volume 1 (Long and Short Papers), pp. 4171–4186. Association for Computational Linguistics, Minneapolis, Minnesota (2019). https://doi.org/10.18653/v1/N19-1423
6. Du, C., Cohoon, J., Lopez, P., Howison, J.: Softcite dataset: a dataset of software mentions in biomedical and economic research publications. J. Assoc. Inf. Sci. Technol. **72**(7), 870–884 (2021). https://doi.org/10.1002/asi.24454. https://ideas.repec.org/a/bla/jinfst/v72y2021i7p870-884.html
7. Du, C., Howison, J., Lopez, P.: Softcite: automatic extraction of software mentions in research literature (2020). https://scinlp.org/history/2020/pdfs/softcite-automatic-extraction-of-software-mentions-in-researchliterature.pdf
8. Eberts, M., Ulges, A.: Span-based joint entity and relation extraction with transformer pre-training (2020)
9. Gábor, K., Buscaldi, D., Schumann, A.K., QasemiZadeh, B., Zargayouna, H., Charnois, T.: SemEval-2018 task 7: semantic relation extraction and classification in scientific papers. In: Proceedings of The 12th International Workshop on Semantic Evaluation, pp. 679–688. Association for Computational Linguistics, New Orleans, Louisiana (2018). https://doi.org/10.18653/v1/S18-1111
10. Gurulingappa, H., Rajput, A.M., Roberts, A., Fluck, J., Hofmann-Apitius, M., Toldo, L.: Development of a benchmark corpus to support the automatic extraction of drug-related adverse effects from medical case reports. J. Biomed. Inf. **45**(5), 885–892 (2012)
11. Heddes, J., Meerdink, P., Pieters, M., Marx, M.: The automatic detection of dataset names in scientific articles. Data **6**(8), 84 (2021). https://doi.org/10.3390/data6080084. https://www.mdpi.com/2306-5729/6/8/84
12. Ikeda, D., Nagamizo, K., Taniguchi, Y.: Automatic identification of dataset names in scholarly articles of various disciplines. Int. J. Inst. Res. Manage. **4**(1), 17–30 (2020)

13. Ikoma, T., Matsubara, S.: Identification of research data references based on citation contexts. In: Ishita, E., Pang, N.L.S., Zhou, L. (eds.) ICADL 2020. LNCS, vol. 12504, pp. 149–156. Springer, Cham (2020). https://doi.org/10.1007/978-3-030-64452-9_13

14. Kingma, D.P., Ba, J.: Adam: A method for stochastic optimization. In: International Conference on Learning Representations (ICLR) (2015)

15. Kozawa, S., Tohyama, H., Uchimoto, K., Matsubara, S.: Automatic acquisition of usage information for language resources. In: Proceedings of the Sixth International Conference on Language Resources and Evaluation (LREC'08). European Language Resources Association (ELRA), Marrakech, Morocco (2008). http://www.lrec-conf.org/proceedings/lrec2008/pdf/169_paper.pdf

16. Kozawa, S., Tohyama, H., Uchimoto, K., Matsubara, S.: Collection of usage information for language resources from academic articles. In: Proceedings of the Seventh International Conference on Language Resources and Evaluation (LREC2010). European Language Resources Association (ELRA), Valletta, Malta (2010). http://www.lrec-conf.org/proceedings/lrec2010/pdf/746_Paper.pdf

17. Li, K., Yan, E.: Co-mention network of R packages: scientific impact and clustering structure. J. Informetrics **12**(1), 87–100 (2018). https://doi.org/10.1016/j.joi.2017.12.001. https://www.sciencedirect.com/science/article/pii/S1751157717304108

18. Luan, Y., He, L., Ostendorf, M., Hajishirzi, H.: Multi-task identification of entities, relations, and coreference for scientific knowledge graph construction. In: Proceedings of the 2018 Conference on Empirical Methods in Natural Language Processing, pp. 3219–3232. Association for Computational Linguistics, Brussels, Belgium (2018). https://doi.org/10.18653/v1/D18-1360

19. Noy, N., Burgess, M., Brickley, D.: Google dataset search: building a search engine for datasets in an open web ecosystem. In: 28th Web Conference (WebConf 2019) (2019). https://datasetsearch.research.google.com

20. Prasad, A., Si, C., Kan, M.Y.: Dataset mention extraction and classification. In: Proceedings of the Workshop on Extracting Structured Knowledge from Scientific Publications, pp. 31–36. Association for Computational Linguistics, Minneapolis, Minnesota (2019). https://doi.org/10.18653/v1/W19-2604

21. Roth, D., Yih, W.T.: A linear programming formulation for global inference in natural language tasks. In: Proceedings of the Eighth Conference on Computational Natural Language Learning (CoNLL-2004) at HLT-NAACL 2004, pp. 1–8. Association for Computational Linguistics, Boston, Massachusetts, USA (2004). https://aclanthology.org/W04-2401

22. Sadvilkar, N., Neumann, M.: PySBD: pragmatic sentence boundary disambiguation. In: Proceedings of Second Workshop for NLP Open Source Software (NLP-OSS), pp. 110–114. Association for Computational Linguistics, Online (2020). https://doi.org/10.18653/v1/2020.nlposs-1.15

23. Sennrich, R., Haddow, B., Birch, A.: Neural machine translation of rare words with subword units. In: Proceedings of the 54th Annual Meeting of the Association for Computational Linguistics (vol. 1: Long Papers), pp. 1715–1725. Association for Computational Linguistics, Berlin, Germany (2016). https://doi.org/10.18653/v1/P16-1162

24. Singhal, A., Srivastava, J.: Data extract: mining context from the web for dataset extraction. Int. J. Mach. Learn. Comput. **3**(2) 219–223 (2013)

25. Tohyama, H., Kozawa, S., Uchimoto, K., Matsubara, S., Isahara, H.: Construction of an infrastructure for providing users with suitable language resources. In: Coling 2008: Companion volume: Posters, pp. 119–122. Coling 2008 Organizing Committee, Manchester, UK (2008). https://aclanthology.org/C08-2030

26. Tohyama, H., Kozawa, S., Uchimoto, K., Shigeki, M., Hitoshi, I.: Shachi: a large scale metadata database of language resources. In: Proceedings of the First International Conference on Global Interoperabikity for Language resources (ICGL-2008), pp. 205–212 (2008). http://shachi.org

27. Tsunokake, M., Matsubara, S.: Classification of URLs citing research artifacts in scholarly documents based on distributed representations. In: Proceedings of 2nd Workshop on Extraction and Evaluation of Knowledge Entities from Scientific Documents (EEKE2021) collocated with ACM/IEEE Joint Conference on Digital Libraries (JCDL2021), vol. 3004, pp. 20–25 (2021)

28. Vaswani, A., et al.: Attention is all you need. 6000–6010. NIPS2017, Curran Associates Inc., Red Hook, NY, USA (2017)

Investigating Evolving Collection Support with Simple Tools

Hussein Suleman(✉)(iD)

University of Cape Town, Cape Town, South Africa
hussein@cs.uct.ac.za
http://dl.cs.uct.ac.za/

Abstract. Most digital archive/repository toolkits are designed for the long-term preservation of digital objects and metadata but are not as well suited for evolving collections where the content, structure and presentation are not settled. This is crucial for contested knowledge systems or where knowledge systems change because of changes in society. This paper discusses simple approaches to address the evolution problem in the context of the EMANDULO archive and the Simple DL toolkit. Our initial and ongoing work shows promise to leverage existing practices and underlying tools for a potentially more effective solution for rapidly evolving archives.

Keywords: Simple · Archive · Change

1 Introduction

While archives are traditionally thought of as institutions for the storage and preservation of immutable assets, this conceptualisation has been challenged by the uncertainties and evolution in human knowledge [3].

As an example, Mapungubwe was an ancient African city that existed in pre-colonial Southern Africa and its discovery was obfuscated during the Apartheid era to maintain the fallacy that no such civilizations existed [6]; post-Apartheid, the presentation of history has been updated to highlight such knowledge. The Five Hundred Year Archive project emerged as an attempt to reconceptualise and reframe Southern African history in the pre-colonial era through the collection, organisation and presentation of documentary evidence collected from all over the world [5].

In such environments where knowledge is subject to change over time, the role of the archive is complex. Traditional archives ingest items that seldom change in form or organisation, as a major goal is preservation. Software systems therefore provide matching facilities for this form of archiving. However, evolving forms of knowledge require archiving systems that not only store and disseminate digital objects, but enable the constant evolution of content, organisation and presentation. Presentation in this context refers to where digital objects in an archive are incorporated into exhibitions, productions and presentations, either within the archive or external to it.

© The Author(s), under exclusive license to Springer Nature Switzerland AG 2022
Y.-H. Tseng et al. (Eds.): ICADL 2022, LNCS 13636, pp. 449–455, 2022.
https://doi.org/10.1007/978-3-031-21756-2_36

This paper addresses these questions of change management in evolving archives and presents how these are being addressed in the ongoing development of the EMANDULO archive, designed for the Five Hundred Year Archive project.

2   Related Work

Early digital library research addressed questions of definition, where it was clear what the major problems were but it was not clear precisely what a digital library was, or how this related to repositories and archives. The Reference Model for an Open Archival Information System [2] presented a vocabulary and model by which to understand the notion of a digital archive and its processes, with an underlying premise of the archival objects as mostly immutable. Guédon [4] argues that a range of functions need to be provided by repositories or archives, and the terminology is fluid.

Arguably, the content is fluid as well. Some digital repository/library/archive toolkits have incorporated support for content evolution in their design. Greenstone's librarian interface [11] provided end users (librarians) with a GUI within which to organise digital objects and edit metadata; after changes are made, the collection can be rebuilt. DSpace, EPrints and similar toolkits offer batch import facilities but these are not always easy to use [1]. In addition, revocation and re-importing of items is then necessary to effect changes in the structure of the imported batch.

The Open Archives Initiative defined its Protocol for Metadata Harvesting [7] as a means to maintain data consistency with changing content. Therefore, any changes to individual items can be tracked and shared with downstream harvesters. However, this assumes a relatively flat structure in the repository and changes to set structure and other archive attributes must be communicated out of band.

3   Designing for Change in Simple DL

3.1   Overview

The EMANDULO archive was built on the foundation provided by the Simple DL toolkit[1] [10]. Simple DL is a new experimental software toolkit for the creation of digital archives containing digital objects and metadata. The toolkit has a primary goal to enable preservation of information by creating a foundation of simple data storage and simple data processing. Thus, failure in systems will not result in inaccessible data and data rescue is made easier for the future. The secondary goal of this toolkit is to support users in low-resource environments, by eliminating the need for complex software system and even allowing offline access to collections, thus facilitating large-scale copying of data in the spirit of LOCKSS [8].

---

[1] https://github.com/slumou/simpledl.

A design goal of the toolkit is to avoid or minimise dependencies on abstracted data stores (like DBMSes) and identifier resolution systems (like DOI). The toolkit is designed for small collections but in prior work it was shown that this scales adequately to collections where a search query can result in 100000 results [9]. Simple DL is meant to provide a space for creation and intermediate management of an archive.

Changes in the content, structure and presentation need to be supported in archive software system design and processes. These changes can affect an individual item, multiple items or reflect a reorganization of content. While the archive may change in its fundamental structure, internal and external links need to remain intact and accurate. In addition, if the archive's contents are migrated to a different platform in future, it must be possible for all links to remain functional and accurate.

3.2   Architecture

Digital archives are created as static websites. At any time, the entire digital archive is made of static files served by a simple Web server or served locally to a user's browser - this reduces the risk of software failure and increases the speed of access with minimal server resources. Some dynamic functions are provided when collections are online, such as annotation and archive management.

Simple DL assumes that archivists store digital objects in a directory and metadata (by default in ICA-AtoM or Dublin Core format) in comma–separated–value (CSV) spreadsheets. The toolkit then processes the spreadsheets to create XML files for each metadata record, validating the data during this step. These XML files are converted to static XHTML pages using XSLT stylesheet transformations. The XML files are also indexed for use by a search engine that is wholly based within the browser environment, using Javascript to respond to queries.

Simple DL has 3 core processing operations:

- **Import** spreadsheets and other documents into the archive. This is the step where spreadsheets are converted into XML files and entities are extracted and linked.
- **Index** all metadata in XML files into inverted files for eventual use by the information retrieval system. This includes indexing for search operations, browse operations and faceted search.
- **Generate** all HTML pages. This includes the metadata pages for digital objects and the website containing the archive, and is based on templates and transformations written in XSLT. Annotations and entities are incorporated into this generation of pages.

3.3   Supporting Evolving Collections

Spreadsheets as the Norm. Simple DL uses spreadsheets for all source metadata. Spreadsheets are widely used by metadata creators and are usually translated into other data formats in archives. Simple DL assumes the normative data source is the spreadsheets, thus an archivist can easily change the metadata in a spreadsheet and have this carried through into the archive when it is re-imported and re-generated. This supports both updates in individual items and sets of items, using tools and ways of working that are familiar to archivists.

Incremental and Clean Builds. Spreadsheets are linked to one another to create hierarchies using either hierarchical directories or parent-child links between rows in spreadsheets. Reorganizing, splitting and merging collections is then accomplished by editing spreadsheets and reorganizing files - both processes that are familiar to archivists. When a collection is re-imported by Simple DL, it is then possible to either do a *clean* import or an *incremental* import, with the latter being the default. Simple DL normally scans all files to determine which ones are new and need to be re-processed (analogous to GNU make), leaving previously processed files in place. A clean import, in contrast, will re-process everything and is needed when structural changes are made such that previously-processed places should not be retained.

Local and Global Identifier Resolution. Given the fluid nature of items in the archive, Simple DL uses a 2-tiered system of resolvable identifiers for the EMANDULO archive.

At a global level, a single partial Persistent URL (PURL)[2] has been registered for the archive with the Internet Archive (the current maintainers of the PURL registry). This allows redirection of URLs that start with a common prefix by rewriting the common prefix to point to a local URL. For example, /net/emandulo/object/ does a partial redirect to http://emandulo.apc.uct.ac.za/simpleresolver/.

At a local level, the URLs are then redirected a second time to the actual location of the items in the archive. *simpleresolver* is a directory within the EMANDULO site with small HTML redirect files to redirect to actual locations. An entry is automatically created for every unique identifier whenever metadata is imported. To create an entry, a uniqueIdentifier column is added to the spreadsheet and the archivist can assign identifiers as needed. Thus, when a user visits http://purl.org/net/emandulo/object/7549, they are first redirected to http://emandulo.apc.uct.ac.za/simpleresolver/7549 and finally to the actual location of http://emandulo.apc.uct.ac.za/metadata/Presentations/7549/index.html.

Figure 1 shows the final item page in the archive, with a globally-resolvable link icon in the top right corner for linking purposes.

The advantage of this 2-step link resolution is there is no need to register all digital objects with an external organization while the archive is in a state of rapid evolution. When the archive shifts from one location to another, or the structure of items within the archive changes, the local resolver will maintain link validity within the archive and from external presentations/exhibitions. If the

---

[2] https://purl.archive.org/.

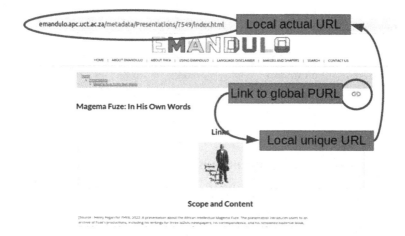

Fig. 1. Example of EMANDULO page, incorporating global and local resolution

entire archive's contents are moved to a different archiving platform altogether, the global resolver can then be updated with individual links.

A second important advantage is that the local resolution only uses static files at resolution-time. Therefore, the entire archive can be accessed offline with local resolution and local links operational without even a Web server being necessary.

4   Evaluating Performance

Emandulo currently has 8046 metadata records, generated from 111 spreadsheets with an average of 72 records per spreadsheet. The spreadsheets are arranged hierarchically such that there are 13 high level collections.

First, the entire collection of metadata was re-imported and re-generated. Then, changes were made to one collection (with 613 entries) and those files were re-imported and re-generated as an incremental update. Finally, the import and generate operations were executed on a data collection with no changes.

The results from executing these tests on a Xeon E5-2407 CPU with the Ubuntu Linux 14.04 operating system, and a 3GB Hard Disk Drive (not an SSD) are listed in Table 1.

With metadata ingest and processing taking 4–5s for a collection being curated, this is arguably a negligible amount of time to update the archive as each change is made.

Table 1. Results from timing of SimpleDL update operations. All times are in seconds and averages over 3 runs.

Operation	Import	Generate
Full update	6.2 s	15.3 s
Single collection update	3.4 s	0.83 s
Check with no update	3.2 s	0.54 s

5   Discussion and Conclusions

Digital archive/repository toolkits are often designed for digital objects as finished products but this is not always the case. In many instances, archival content can change in terms of the digital objects, metadata or even the structural representation of the items. Supporting such operations can require complex systems, but the approach presented in this paper argues for allowing the archivists to instead use common software tools they are already familiar with, and supporting that use in the repository framework.

Toolkits should also plan for change. Simple DL is designed to be replaced. Eventually, all collections will be migrated to a different toolkit as technology evolves. It should therefore be as simple as possible for a software developer to migrate the content, while maintaining critical information, such as resolvable links. There are many systems to do this; this paper presents one case study to enable global resolution and local resolution, thus allowing local changes in the medium term without any impact on the global resolver, but without losing the advantages offered by global resolution services in the long term.

Ongoing experimental work includes investigations into version control, at the level of entire archives and individual items where possible. Whole archive versioning will maintain a history of the archive as it evolves, but without impinging on the freedom of the archivist to freely modify content and structure as needed.

Ultimately, archivists need to straddle the traditional world of the archive with its notions of largely immutable content and the emerging world of constantly reimagined and reconceptualised content. Toolkits for the creation of such archives need to be designed explicitly for change. The ongoing work reported on in this paper illustrates some of the issues and approaches that are being explored.

Acknowledgements. This research was partially funded by the National Research Foundation of South Africa (Grant numbers: 105862, 119121 and 129253) and University of Cape Town. The authors acknowledge that opinions, findings and conclusions or recommendations expressed in this publication are that of the authors, and that the NRF accepts no liability whatsoever in this regard.

We would like to acknowledge the Archive & Public Culture research initiative at the University of Cape Town for allowing this research to use the Five Hundred Year Archive data collection for the purposes of this study.

References

1. Castagné, M.: Institutional repository software comparison: dspace, eprints, digital commons, islandora and hydra (2013)
2. Consultative Committee for Space Data Systems: reference model for an open archival information system (OAIS). CCSDS Secretariat (2002)
3. Featherstone, M.: Archive. Theory, Culture & Society **23**(2–3), 591–596 (2006)
4. Guédon, J.C.: It's a repository, it's a depository, it's an archive...: open access, digital collections and value. Ciencia, Pensamiento y Cultura (2009)
5. Hamilton, C., McNulty, G.: Refiguring the archive for eras before writing: digital interventions, affordances and research futures. History in Africa pp. 1–27 (2022)
6. Kashe-Katya, X.: Carefully hidden away: excavating the archive of the Mapungubwe dead and their possessions. Master's thesis, University of Cape Town (2013)
7. Lagoze, C., Van de Sompel, H., Nelson, M., Warner, S.: Open archives initiative-protocol for metadata harvesting v2.0 (2002)
8. Reich, V., Rosenthal, D.S.: Lockss (lots of copies keep stuff safe). New Rev. Acad. Librariansh. **6**(1), 155–161 (2000)
9. Suleman, H.: Investigating the effectiveness of client-side search/browse without a network connection. In: Jatowt, A., Maeda, A., Syn, S.Y. (eds.) ICADL 2019. LNCS, vol. 11853, pp. 227–238. Springer, Cham (2019). https://doi.org/10.1007/978-3-030-34058-2_21
10. Suleman, H.: Simple DL: a toolkit to create simple digital libraries. In: Ke, H.-R., Lee, C.S., Sugiyama, K. (eds.) ICADL 2021. LNCS, vol. 13133, pp. 325–333. Springer, Cham (2021). https://doi.org/10.1007/978-3-030-91669-5_25
11. Witten, I.H., Bainbridge, D.: Creating digital library collections with greenstone. Library hi tech (2005)

Investigating User Control to Mitigate Bias When Searching African Historical Data

Soham Singh and Hussein Suleman$^{(\boxtimes)}$ ⓘ

University of Cape Town, Cape Town, South Africa
sngsoh004@myuct.ac.za, hussein@cs.uct.ac.za
http://dl.cs.uct.ac.za/

Abstract. Historians have argued that common information retrieval algorithms may bias results presented to users searching through precolonial historical collections. This study therefore investigates how users experience and control bias in the context of commonly used information retrieval pre-processing algorithms for both the textual and image data that are available in typical historical archives. Users were presented with the results generated by multiple algorithmic variations, and the ability to select algorithms. The results show that users have justifiable preferences for multimodal result modes to improve user experience, and, that users believe they can control bias using algorithmic variation.

Keywords: Bias · User control · Heritage data

1 Introduction

Student-led protests at the University of Cape Town in South Africa led to the resurfacing of the discussion of decolonisation [10,13]. Decolonisation is the process of unlearning unjust practices and ideals and dismantling institutions with the intention of facilitating other perspectives of knowledge [13]. In the case of precolonial heritage data, the data contains the bias of the curators of the artefacts in the data and is further processed by potentially biased retrieval algorithms and interfaces. Curators of the artefacts may misattribute the data through their descriptions of the data and negatively impact the retrievability of that data - this occurs in both metadata and digital objects. In addition, the vocabulary used by the curator may not match that of the researchers, and specificities known to the original creators of the artefacts are lost in translation when an archivist thousands of kilometres away curates the object without full knowledge of its context. As such, alternative strategies need to be considered to retrieve such data in the case where textual metadata is inaccurate or incomplete, such as image-based retrieval rather than text-based retrieval, using different pre-processing algorithms that determine relevance by analysing different features within the data, or the presentation of results in different modes that do not rely on the textual metadata alone.

User-control was added to a multimodal information retrieval system containing African heritage data by allowing users to change the query mode, pre-processing algorithms, and the mode of results. The query and results were

© The Author(s), under exclusive license to Springer Nature Switzerland AG 2022
Y.-H. Tseng et al. (Eds.): ICADL 2022, LNCS 13636, pp. 456–463, 2022.
https://doi.org/10.1007/978-3-031-21756-2_37

either in text mode or image mode or both. The text pre-processing algorithms explored were stemming (finding common roots), stopping (removal of common words) and incorporation of a thesaurus to expand coverage of words. These are all classical approaches in information retrieval but may or may not be suitable for a corpus where English is interspersed with some names and concepts in African languages. The image pre-processing algorithms explored were shape-based, colour-based and a hybrid of these. These approaches were motivated by the inherent colour/shape similarity in many historical artefacts e.g., pottery that may confound image matching algorithms.

Our research aimed to answer the following research question: Can users detect bias and control bias using algorithmic variation?

2   Related Work

Bias in retrieval systems has been the recent subject of many research initiatives, with there being a main concern of algorithmic fairness in systems [7] and the following being identified as areas that need to be addressed in computer systems by the ACM: awareness, access, accountability, explanation, data provenance and auditability (among others) [1,4,20]. A potential solution to this problem of bias that has been identified is the notion of control to assist users with overcoming algorithmic errors and biases [7].

Much early research regarding user-control of retrieval systems was conducted to improve retrieval effectiveness mainly in the form of Interactive Query Expansion (IQE) [8,9,14,17]. In fact, when dealing with bias and algorithmic fairness, research tends to go in the opposite direction of user-control by opting to develop and automate the process based on "expert" qualifications and technical validation [7]. For the early research about IQE, much of the justification for it was the control that it gives to the user, as the user has their criteria for relevance and thus is more capable of making decisions about what will be useful to their search [17] and that their interaction with the system is important if performance is to be improved [2,9]. Other possibilities for user-control in search engines are Advanced Search Features, however research has also shown this has a low amount of usage from users [14,19].

Applications of user-control are also demonstrated in other research areas such as user interface design [16], educational systems [15], adaptive systems [21] and recommender systems [19]. Research comparing system-controlled and user-controlled personalization revealed the need for users to control personalization to ensure the feeling of freedom, especially in the instances where there is a lack of trust in the personalization system [15]. Jones [12] went as far as to say that the lack of capacity for human intervention in algorithmic decision making is a "threat to human dignity".

3   Experiment and System Design

3.1   The Five Hundred Year Archive Dataset (FHYA)

The Five Hundred Year Archive is a collection of historical documents and images from the pre-colonial and colonial era [3]. Digital objects are either textual documents or photographs of physical artefacts; in both cases there is associated metadata in the ICA-AtoM format (title, events, scope and content, etc.). 1345 text documents and 5708 images from the FHYA collection were used for this study - this is the entire collection that was available at the time of the study.

3.2   System Design and Implementation

For this experiment, we developed a user interface for an underlying multimodal information retrieval system (using Apache SOLR and LIRE for text and image indexing) and asked users to perform multiple tasks using the user interface, while regularly providing feedback via a survey. The user interface developed for this experiment needed to facilitate algorithmic variation, the submission of text and image queries, and the presentation of results in different modes to determine whether these have any effect on the user experience or the mitigation of bias of heritage data retrieval.

3 text retrieval pre-processing algorithms and 3 image retrieval pre-processing algorithms were included in this experiment. Stemming, Stopping and Synonyms were the three chosen text retrieval pre-processing algorithms [5], while the chosen image retrieval pre-processing algorithms were Edge Histogram (EH) [22], Autocolour Correlogram (AC) [11] and Pyramid Histogram of Oriented Gradients (PH) [6]. The image processing algorithms were chosen as representatives of the different kinds of algorithms in literature.

3.3   Experimental Design

The repeated measures blocked design experiment entailed asking users to perform tasks and then provide feedback via a survey. For each task, participants were to submit a predefined query of a specific mode and then vary algorithms and result modes. 2 images and 2 text queries were used as tasks by participants during the experimental process. This limited number of queries was used because the goal of the experiment was to investigate user experience and control of algorithms, rather than generalise over queries (within the constraint of a reasonable time to perform the experiment).

The two image tasks consist of an image of beadwork and an image of a wooden object. Going forward, this paper will refer to these two tasks as the "bead image task" and the "wooden image task".

The convenience and the snowball sampling methods were used to obtain participants for this experiment. An email invitation was sent to university e-mail lists inviting participants over the age of 18 with Internet-access. The researcher also sent invitations out through a variety of social media platforms. A total of 54 participant responses were recorded for this experiment.

4 Results

4.1 Algorithmic Preferences

If we combine the preferences of image pre-processing algorithms across both image tasks, we observe that PH was preferred over AC and EH, and, that AC was preferred over EH; shape-based pre-processing algorithms perform better for heritage image data retrieval than colour-based pre-processing algorithms. If preferences are combined across both text tasks, Stemming was unanimously preferred over Synonyms and Stopping.

4.2 Result Mode Preferences

Figure 1 shows participant preferences for result modes. Viewing results "As Both Images and Text" was strongly favoured over the other two result modes. This is consistent with research that highlights the importance of interface design integration and diverse results with user-control [17,18].

Some justifications for preferring the image mode over the text result mode included that "bias is more easily conveyed using words" and that "imagery helps to understand the text"

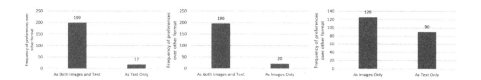

Fig. 1. Pairwise comparisons of preferences for result views

4.3 Perceived Bias Detection

Participants were also asked to identify whether query modes, pre-processing algorithms or result modes can be potential contributors of bias in the system. Figure 2 shows that no single image retrieval pre-processing algorithm was unanimously identified for containing the most bias across the pre-processing algorithms. PH, however, was recorded the least for containing the most bias and this correlates with the overall preference for that pre-processing algorithm. Figures 2, 3 and 4 suggest a potential relationship between user preference of pre-processing algorithms and views and user perception of algorithmic bias.

Both unimodal result modes were identified 52% - 57% more frequently than the multimodal result view for containing the most bias. Similarly, participants were also unable to unanimously identify a query mode for containing more bias than the other. Lastly, it was found that the number of participants who believed algorithmic variation can mitigate bias in retrieval grew from 65% before the experiment to 81% after the experiment (see Fig. 5).

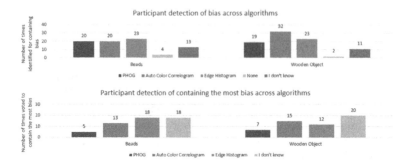

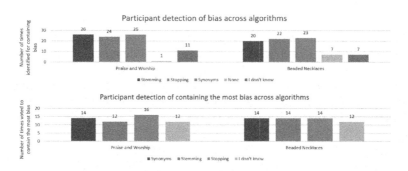

Fig. 2. Participant identification of bias in image algorithms

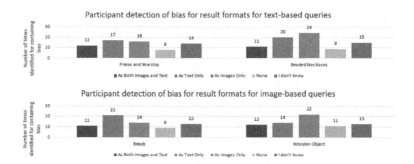

Fig. 3. Participant identification of bias in text algorithms

Fig. 4. Participant identification of bias in result views

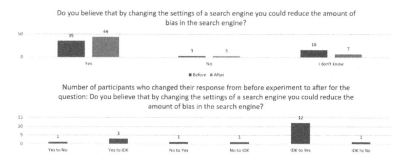

Fig. 5. Participant change in response for whether algorithmic variation can mitigate bias in retrieval for before and after experiment

5 Conclusions

We attempted to adopt decolonisation principles in the digital retrieval of pre-colonial African heritage data through the addition of algorithmic variation and user-control of retrieval. Participants expressed a belief that algorithmic variation can assist with the mitigation of bias in retrieval systems, and they expressed a preference for multimodal information presentation.

While participants were unable to unanimously identify contributors of bias, the results of our research suggest that participants are aware of the presence of bias in query modes, algorithmic processes and result views, and that systems need to be designed in a manner that acknowledges and is transparent to their users about the presence of bias in these components and in their interaction with data.

Acknowledgements. This research was partially funded by the National Research Foundation of South Africa (Grant numbers: 105862, 119121 and 129253) and University of Cape Town. The authors acknowledge that opinions, findings and conclusions or recommendations expressed in this publication are that of the authors, and that the NRF accepts no liability whatsoever in this regard.

We would like to acknowledge the Archive & Public Culture research initiative at the University of Cape Town for allowing this research to use the Five Hundred Year Archive data collection for the purposes of this study.

References

1. ACM U.S. Public Policy Council: statement on algorithmic transparency and accountability (2017). https://www.acm.org/binaries/content/assets/public-policy/2017_usacm_statement_algorithms.pdf
2. Anick, P.: Using terminological feedback for web search refinement: a log-based study. In: Proceedings of the 26th Annual International ACM SIGIR Conference on Research and Development in Informaion Retrieval, pp. 88–95. SIGIR 2003, Association for Computing Machinery, New York, NY, USA (2003). https://doi.org/10.1145/860435.860453

3. Archive public culture research initiative: the five hundred year archive. http://www.apc.uct.ac.za/apc/research/projects/fivehundredyeararchive

4. Baeza-Yates, R.: Bias on the web. Commun. ACM **61**(6), 54–61 (2018). https://doi.org/10.1145/3209581

5. Beaulieu, M.: Experiments on interfaces to support query expansion. J. Documentation **53**(1), 8–19 (1997). https://doi.org/10.1108/eum0000000007187

6. Bosch, A., Zisserman, A., Munoz, X.: Representing shape with a spatial pyramid kernel. In: Proceedings of the 6th ACM International Conference on Image and Video Retrieval, pp. 401–408 CIVR 07, Association for Computing Machinery, New York, NY, USA (2007). https://doi.org/10.1145/1282280.1282340

7. Burrell, J., Kahn, Z., Jonas, A., Griffin, D.: When users control the algorithms: values expressed in practices on twitter. In: Proceedings of the ACM on Human-Computer Interaction. vol. 3, pp. 1–20 (2019). https://doi.org/10.1145/3359240

8. Efthimiadis, E.N.: A user-centred evaluation of ranking algorithms for interactive query expansion. In: Proceedings of the 16th Annual International ACM SIGIR Conference on Research and Development in Information Retrieval, pp. 146–159. SIGIR 1993, Association for Computing Machinery, New York, NY, USA (1993). https://doi.org/10.1145/160688.160710

9. Fonseca, B.M., Golgher, P., Pôssas, B., Ribeiro-Neto, B., Ziviani, N.: Concept-based interactive query expansion. In: Proceedings of the 14th ACM International Conference on Information and Knowledge Management, pp. 696–703. CIKM 2005, Association for Computing Machinery, New York, NY, USA (2005). https://doi.org/10.1145/1099554.1099726

10. Gill, J.: Decolonizing literature and science. Configurations **26**(3), 283–288 (2018). https://doi.org/10.1353/con.2018.0023

11. Huang, J., Kumar, S., Mitra, M., Zhu, W.J., Zabih, R.: Image indexing using color correlograms. In: Proceedings of IEEE Computer Society Conference on Computer Vision and Pattern Recognition, pp. 762–768 (1997). https://doi.org/10.1109/CVPR.1997.609412

12. Jones, M.L.: The right to a human in the loop: political constructions of computer automation and personhood. Soc. Stud. Sci. **47**(2), 216–239 (2017). https://doi.org/10.1177/0306312717699716

13. Kessi, S., Marks, Z., Ramugondo, E.: Decolonizing African studies (2020)

14. Nemeth, Y., Shapira, B., Taeib-Maimon, M.: Evaluation of the real and perceived value of automatic and interactive query expansion. In: Proceedings of the 27th Annual International ACM SIGIR Conference on Research and Development in Information Retrieval, pp. 526–527. SIGIR 2004, Association for Computing Machinery, New York, NY, USA (2004). https://doi.org/10.1145/1008992.1009103

15. Orji, R., Oyibo, K., Tondello, G.F.: A comparison of system-controlled and user-controlled personalization approaches. In: Adjunct Publication of the 25th Conference on User Modeling, Adaptation and Personalization, pp. 413–418. UMAP 17, Association for Computing Machinery, New York, NY, USA (2017). https://doi.org/10.1145/3099023.3099116

16. Rahdari, B., Brusilovsky, P.: User-controlled hybrid recommendation for academic papers. In: Proceedings of the 24th International Conference on Intelligent User Interfaces: Companion, pp. 99–100. IUI 2019, Association for Computing Machinery, New York, NY, USA (2019). https://doi.org/10.1145/3308557.3308717

17. Ruthven, I.: Re-examining the potential effectiveness of interactive query expansion. In: Proceedings of the 26th Annual International ACM SIGIR Conference on Research and Development in Informaion Retrieval, pp. 213–220. SIGIR 2003, Association for Computing Machinery, New York, NY, USA (2003). https://doi.org/10.1145/860435.860475

18. Simpson, T.W.: Evaluating google as an epistemic tool. In: Philosophical Engineering: Toward a Philosophy of the Web, pp. 97–115 (2013)

19. Spink, A., Wolfram, D., Jansen, M.B., Saracevic, T.: Searching the web: the public and their queries. J. Am. Soc. Inform. Sci. Technol. 52(3), 226–234 (2001)

20. Thomas, P., Billerbeck, B., Craswell, N., White, R.W.: Investigating searchers' mental models to inform search explanations. ACM Trans. Inf. Syst. 38(1), 1–25 (2019). https://doi.org/10.1145/3371390

21. Tsandilas, T., schraefel, M.C.: User-controlled link adaptation. In: Proceedings of the Fourteenth ACM Conference on Hypertext and Hypermedia, pp. 152–160. HYPERTEXT 2003, Association for Computing Machinery, New York, NY, USA (2003). https://doi.org/10.1145/900051.900086

22. Won, C.S., Park, D.K., Park, S.J.: Efficient use of mpeg-7 edge histogram descriptor. ETRI J. 24(1), 23–30 (2002). https://doi.org/10.4218/etrij.02.0102.0103

Research Outputs of Vietnam National University, Hanoi: A Bibliometric Analysis on Scopus and Web of Science During 2018–2021

Son Nguyen Hoang[1]([✉]) [ID], Lam Le Ba[1]([✉]) [ID], Phuong Vu Thi Mai[2] [ID],
Tra Nguyen Thanh[3] [ID], Duong Hoang Van[1] [ID], Bac Hoang Minh[1] [ID], Anh Do Diep[1] [ID],
and Tan Nguyen Duy[1] [ID]

[1] Library and Digital Knowledge Center, Vietnam National University, Hanoi, Vietnam
{son.nh,lamlb,duonghv,bachm,anhdd,tannd88}@vnu.edu.vn
[2] Science and Technology Department, Vietnam National University, Hanoi, Vietnam
phuongvtm@vnu.edu.vn
[3] Central Library, Banking Academy of Vietnam, Hanoi, Vietnam
trant@hvnh.edu.vn

Abstract. The present study is a bibliometric assessment of scientific research output of Vietnam National University, Hanoi (VNU) during the 2018 to 2021 on the Scopus and Web of Science database. Research output on Scopus 2018 to 2021 ~3,500 document records and Web of Science ~3,400 document records. The authors have made statistical reports, analyzed and assessed the quantity (use Mendeley check and removal duplicate records) and quality (Q1234 by SJR-Scimago Journal & Country Rank), type of publication, keywords/subjects, collaborations in research, citation numbers and the authors with many published publications, most source title, etc. The result reveals the leaders, managers and scientists VNU's would have the general outline of their institutions' scientific research situation in the previous periods to make the proper decisions for future.

Keywords: Bibliometrics study · Research outputs · Publication trends · Author productivity · Citation · Research collaboration · Higher Education · Vietnam National University · Hanoi

1 Introduction

Research output demonstrates the scientific capacity as well as research productivity of individuals, research organizations, and even countries [1]. Scientific publication data are always used in evaluating the research achievements of scientists, in university rankings, in evaluating the performance of funding and scientific support agencies, as well as state management agencies on science. Current scientific publication data are often extracted from international research output databases, including Web of Science [2] and Scopus [3] which are popular around the world. The quantity and quality evaluation of research output of each country or organization have many different approaches, from which research output database to use, to how to classify and rank the published quality [4]. Research and scientific management activities at VNU in recent years have received strong attention and investment from leaders, reflected in policies to support lecturers, researchers, and the establishment of strong research groups for the scientific fields of member and affiliated units. Therefore, the research outputs have continuously increased in both quantity and quality, which is evidenced by the international ranking indexes of several scientific fields and university rankings in particular. VNU's overall ranking in QS, THE, WEBOMETRICS, etc. have continuously increased and developed sustainably. In the QS World Ranking by Subject 2022 (QS WUR by subject 2022), VNU'sposition in key fields keeps increasing when its 6 out of 51 fields are ranked [5]. In addition to the 5 fields that continue to be ranked (four of which increase in ranking position), VNU has 1 more new field ranked for the first time, which is Electrical and Electronics Engineering (Engineering - Electrical & Electronic). Among the six VNU fields ranked by QS in the QS WUR by subject 2022 including Computer Science and Information Systems, Mechanical Engineering, Aeronautics and Manufacturing, Mathematics, Physics and Astronomy, Business and Science studying management, and Electrical and Electronic Engineering, 5 fields are in the top 500 group in the world. Among these, the three fields of Mathematics, Physics & Astronomy, Business & Management Studies are all ranked No. 1 in Vietnam. The QS ranking criteria emphasize the contribution and impact of an industry/field training quality to society (through the scholars and employers assessment); contributions to research activities (through citation levels and H-index) and internationalization of scientific research (through international research networks).

In the above context, this study focuses on assessing the status of the international research output of VNU in the period 2018–2021 based on Scopus and Web of Science (WoS) databases. VNU's international scientific publications by industry/field of study, by organization leading the research, and by scientific programs/funding sources (research funding) were surveyed, respectively. The main objective of this paper is to identify solutions to promote and improve the quantity and quality of international research output and to support VNU leaders in decision-making in the next period.

Table 1 shows members VNU's are 8 Universities, 4 Schools, 7 Institutes, Centrals and Service Units with 2,500 lectures/researchers, 34 research groups, 210 laboratories and 50,000 students (VNU Annual Report 2021).

Table 1. Members VNU's

Members	Name of English
HUS	VNU - University of Science
USSH	VNU - University of Social Sciences and Humanities
ULIS	VNU - University of Languages and International Studies
UET	VNU - University of Engineering and Technology
UEB	VNU - University of Economics and Business

(continued)

Table 1. (*continued*)

Members	Name of English
UEd	VNU - University of Education
VJU	VNU - Vietnam Japan University
UMP	VNU - University of Medicine and Pharmacy
LS	VNU - School of Law
SHB	VNU - School of Business and Management
SIS	VNU - School of Interdisciplinary Studies
IS	VNU - International School
ITI	VNU - Information Technology Institute
IVIDES	VNU - Institute of Vietnamese Studies and Development Sciences
IMBT	VNU - Institute of Microbiology and Biotechnology
INFEQA	VNU - Institute for Education Quality Assurance
IFI	VNU - International Francophone Institute
CRES	Institute of Natural Resources and Environmental Studies
TNTI	Tran Nhan Tong Institute
SERVICE	Service Units

2 Literature Review

Bibliometric methods have been used to measure scientific progress in many disciplines of science and engineering and are a common research instrument for systematic analysis [6]. Since Narin et al. [7] first proposed the concept of "evaluative bibliometrics", many scientists have tried to evaluate the research trends in the publication outputs of countries, research institutes, journals and subject categories [8, 9], the citation analysis [10] and the peak year citation per publication [11, 12].

In Vietnam, there are also many articles on these issues, which are published online with topics such as "Vietnam's research output in the past 5 years", "Taking attendance at 30 Vietnamese universities with the most research output" or "Vietnam has more than 17,000 international articles published in 2020"[13–15] but none of them are included in the analysis in the possible units. Show this, VNU use the VCGATE software (Vietnam Citation) at the address https://vcgate.vnu.edu.vn/ to save the archive, management, and activities of research output of the Scopus and WoS.

Through the results of this study, it is possible to make a preliminary assessment of the quantity and quality of research output of VNU, which has increased gradually over time. The field research levels are expanded by default. Although there is still an intermediate element of natural science and technology, the field of social sciences has recently received more attention.VNU most fruitful domestic research cooperation is still VAST (Vietnam Academy of Science & Technology) and universities HUST (Hanoi University of Science & Technology), TonDucThang University and DuyTan University.

3   Objectives

- To analyze the quantity, quality, growth, and type of publications
- To know the keywords / subjects of publications
- To explore the top prolific authors and citation impact
- To identify the most preferred journals and collaborating
- To examine the citation distribution of publications
- To identify frequently cited papers

4   Methodology

The research group used Scopus and Web of Sciences databases as sources of data to study the research output of Vietnam National University, Hanoi. The affiliation search was carried out on July 18, 2022, by entering the name of the institution with affiliation Id as 60071364 (Scopus) and OG = Vietnam National University Hanoi (WoS). Records were retrieved covering a period of 2018 to 2021 (4 years).

Advanced search query was initiated:

On Scopus: AF-ID(60071364) AND (PUBYEAR > 2017 AND PUBYEAR < 2022).

On WoS: (OG = Vietnam National University Hanoi) AND (PY = 2018–2021).

Aspects referring to quantity, quality, type of publications, keywords / subjects, journals, affiliations, collaborations, authors, etc. were analyzed by Excel, VOSViewer soft, Mendeley, InCites (Clarivate) and Scival (Elsevier).

5   Data Analysis

5.1   Year-Wise Distribution of Publications

Figure 1 shows VNU's research outputs from 2018–2021 on Scopus & Web of Science databases and mixes 2 databases. Out of the total publications of VNU 3,477 papers were indexed in the Scopus database and 3,393 papers were indexed in the WoS database. After remove papers duplicates on Scopus & Web of Science: 2018 = 876, 2019 = 1040, 2020 = 1097 and 2021 = 1116 papers. Total VNU's research outputs from 2018–2021 were 4,129 papers. Altogether there was increasing in quantity by year and per year ~150 papers.

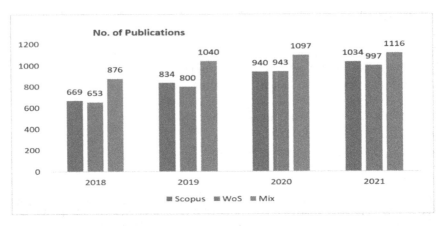

Fig. 1. Year-wise distribution of publications

5.2 Type of Publications

Table 2 depicts the different types of publications of VNU during 2018–2021. The majority of contributions were published in the form of articles (79%), followed by conference proceedings (9%), conference papers (8%), serial (3%), book, chapters (~1%).

Table 2. Type of publications

Publications type	Publications (%)
Journal Article	3267 (79%)
Conference Proceedings	355 (9%)
Conference Paper	312 (8%)
Serial	133 (3%)
Book/Book chapter	62 (1%)
Total	**4,129**

5.3 Keywords of Publications

From keywords have the top 10 most keywords of publications. Shows keywords "Vietnam" and "performance" with the most frequency (> 100), there out keywords "stability", "impact", "adsorption" and "water",… too on the top (Table 3).

Table 3. Top 10 most keywords of publications

No	Keyword	Occurrences	Total link strength
	Vietnam	286	61.00
	Performance	136	84.00
	Stability	77	29.00
	Impact	74	39.00
	Adsorption	69	44.00
	Water	68	46.00
	Hadron-hadron scattering	65	52.00
	Behavior	63	36.00
	Nanoparticles	61	32.00
	Algorithm	59	23.00

5.4 Subjects of Publications

The subject of publication is displayed in Fig. 2, which shows Engineering (12.4%) was the most favored subject category among the faculty followed by Computer Science (12.2%), Physics and Astronomy (8.1%), Mathematics (7.9%), Material Science (7.5%), Environmental Science (7.4%) and so on. The total number of scientific publications listed under different subject categories was found more than the total number of actual publications (4,129) because of overlapping papers.

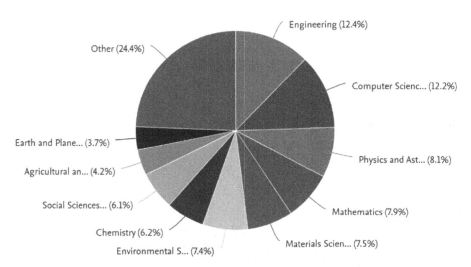

Fig. 2. Subject of publications

Through data on the subjects VNU's research outputs in Fig. 3 shows Engineering, Computer Science is the strength of the University of Engineering and Technology

(UET) and other subjects like Physics and Astronomy, Mathematics, Materials Science Environmental Science,… are the strength of University of Science (HUS). In addition, interdisciplinary science is currently very developed in VNU, so it is not surprising that other subjects account for a large proportion of publications 24.4% .

5.5 Top 10 Authors

A total of 4,129 research outputs were contributed by 23,164 authors. The top 10 authors are given in Table 4. The research output appears to be extremely skewed; the top 10 authors for 606 (14.7%) of the total (4,129) publications.

Statistics by affiliation show authors have most publications are researchers about natural science and technology, by ¾ on the top 10 (7 authors from the University of Science, 2 authors from the University of Engineering and Technology, and 1 author from the Information Technology Institute).

Table 4. Top 10 authors

No	Author	University	Research output	Citations	h-index
1	Duc, N.D	UET	135	1630	44
2	Son, L.H	ITI	131	3047	46
3	Duc, L.M	HUS	51	324	19
4	Tung, B.T	UET	46	142	15
5	Minh, T.B	HUS	44	464	34
6	Minh, N.N	HUS	41	272	14
7	Anh, H.Q	HUS	41	490	15
8	Duc, P.T	HUS	40	670	22
9	Viet, P.H	HUS	39	391	45
10	Dong, P.T	HUS	38	691	24
Total			**606**	-	-
Total Research Output			**4,129**	-	-

Update to 8/6/2022 from https://scival.com/.

5.6 Top 10 Source Title

Table 5 represents the top 10 most source titles (preferred journals) in which the faculty prefer to publish their research paper during 2018–2021. The most source title for publication was Journal Of High Energy Physics 121 papers, Physical Review Letters 68, LNCS (Lecture Notes In Computer Science) 65, IEEE Access 44, AISC (Advances In Intelligent Systems & Computing) 25, JAMC (Journal of Analytical Methods In Chemistry) 22, Materials Transactions 21, etc. These top ten productive journals account for 10.2% of the total publications.

Table 5. Top 10 source title

No	Source title	Publications
	Journal Of High Energy Physics	121
	Physical Review Letters	68
	LNCS	65
	IEEE Access	44
	AISC	25
	JAMC	22
	Materials Transactions	21
	IOP Conference Series Earth And Environmental Science	20
	Journal Of Physics Conference Series	20
	ACM International Conference Proceeding Series	19

5.7 Publications by Journal Quartile

The quartile of publications of VNU during 2018–2021 were increase by years. Publications by Journal quartile Q1 + Q2 ~ 75% (Q1 = 46.5%, Q2 = 29.2%) and Q3 + Q4 ~ 25% (Q3 = 15.3%, Q4 = 9.1%), the data shows publication outputs VNU's were high quality.

5.8 Top 10 Collaborating Institutions

Table 6 shows VNU's research outputs from 2018–2021 have 2.154 collaborating institutions and 3.142 co-authored publications with VNU. Top 10 collaborating have 6 Universities / Institutes in Vietnam and 4 in area and the world.

Table 6. Top 10 most collaborating institutions

No	Institution	Co-authored publications	Field-weighted citation impact
	Vietnam Academy of Science and Technology	575	1.27
	Hanoi University of Science and Technology	266	1.05
	Duy Tan University	230	3.11
	CNRS	200	1.93

(*continued*)

Table 6. (*continued*)

No	Institution	Co-authored publications	Field-weighted citation impact
	Ton Duc Thang University	191	2.45
	Nguyen Tat Thanh University	128	4.07
	Russian Academy of Sciences	125	2.18
	Université Paris-Saclay	121	3.62
	VNU Hochiminh City	113	3.51
	Sorbonne Université	111	2.45

5.9   Top 5 Cited Publications

The complete bibliographic information of the top 5 frequently cited along with the total number of citations received are presented in Table 7. The article contributed by Hoang, D.T. et al. (2018), ranked top as it received the highest citations (2471), Field-Weighted Citation Impact (161.49). Another most cited publications were LHCb (Large Hadron Collider beauty) collaboration program, the University of Science is a member.

Table 7. Top 5 cited publications

No	Publication	Citations	Field-weighted Cit. Imp.
	Hoang, D. T., Chernomor, O., Von Haeseler, A., Minh, B. Q., & Vinh, L. S. (2018). UFBoot2: Improving the ultrafast bootstrap approximation. *Molecular Biology and Evolution, 35*(2), 518–522. https://doi.org/10.1093/molbev/msx281	2471	161.49
	Aaij, R., Abellán Beteta, C., Adeva, B., Adinolfi, M., Aidala, C. A., Ajaltouni, Z.,... Zucchelli, S. (2019). Observation of a narrow pentaquark state, pc (4312) +, and of the two-peak structure of the pc (4450) +. *Physical Review Letters, 122*(22) https://doi.org/10.1103/PhysRevLett.122.222001	302	26.27
	Aaij, R., Abellán Beteta, C., Adeva, B., Adinolfi, M., Aidala, C. A., Ajaltouni, Z.,... Zucchelli, S. (2019). Search for lepton-universality violation in B + → K + l + l- decays. *Physical Review Letters, 122*(19) https://doi.org/10.1103/PhysRevLett.122.191801	301	26.1
	Akhtaruzzaman, M., Boubaker, S., & Sensoy, A. (2021). Financial contagion during COVID–19 crisis. *Finance Research Letters, 38* https://doi.org/10.1016/j.frl.2020.101604	242	96.9
	Aaij, R., Adeva, B., Adinolfi, M., Ajaltouni, Z., Akar, S., Albrecht, J.,... Zucchelli, S. (2018). Measurement of the ratio of the B0 → d ∗ -τ + ντ and B0 → d ∗ -μ + νμ branching fractions using three-prong τ -lepton decays. *Physical Review Letters, 120*(17) https://doi.org/10.1103/PhysRevLett.120.171802	239	16.57

5.10 Research Outputs of VNU-Hanoi and VNU-HCM

Table 8 shows VNU-Hanoi's (Lectures/Researches ~2500) and VNU-HCM's (Lectures/Researches ~3500) and research outputs from 2018–2021. In 2 years 2018–2019 the number of research outputs is the same, but in 2 years 2020–2021 VNU-HCM is more than VNU-Hanoi ~600 documents (2020) and ~800 documents (2021). The above result is because the number of lectures/research VNU-HCM is more than VNU-Hanoi is 1000.

Table 8. Lectures/Researchers and research outputs of VNU-Hanoi and VNU-HCM

	Lectures/Researchers	2018	2019	2020	2021	Notes
VNU-Hanoi	2500	876	1040	1097	1116	Annual report VNU-Hanoi 2021
VNU-HCM	3500	843	1096	1641	1925	Annual report VNU-HCM 2021

6 Summary and Conclusions

The trends of publications under Scopus and WoS of VNU are increasing year by year throughout the period of 2018–2021. The number of study fields has continuously grown, now encompassing 27 scientific topics while remaining primarily focused on engineering, science, and technology.

This outcome appropriately represents the University of Science (HUS) and the University of Engineering and Technology (UET) established strengths. In International School (IS), there has been a lot of investment in research. In terms of both quantity and quality, studies in economics, law, and social sciences have seen considerable improvements. Researchs in health, medicine, and pharmacy will require more attention, promotion, and investment in the future. Two-thirds of VNU publication items were in groups Q1 and Q2. Open access journal publications also account for a bigger percentage than in the past. Research collaboration with Vietnam National University Hochiminh and other universities in Hanoi and Ho Chi Minh City has not been expanded. Collaboration with Southeast Asian countries is limited. Top Collaborations by Country are USA, France, United Kingdom, China, Japan, Russia,…

With 34 members (8 Universities, 4 Affiliated Schools, 7 Research Institutes, and 2 Training & Research Centers, …), 34 research groups (28 strong research groups, 6 promising research groups), 210 laboratories, 2,500 lectures/researchers, and 50,000 students (VNU Annual Report 2021), VNU can affirm that VNU has succeeded in taking national responsibility, has enough potential and internal resources to take the lead in scientific research in Vietnam and stewardship. To do so, it is necessary to strengthen and expand cooperation in all fields of research, particularly scientific and technological research, with the Vietnam Academy of Science and Technology and the Vietnam Academy of Social Sciences, as well as local universities such as Thai Nguyen, Hue, Da Nang, Can Tho, and others. Other topics include ASEAN, Asia, and the world. Promoting research groups and laboratories, and frequently updating information resources such as ScienceDirect, Springer, Jstor, Emerald, Taylor & Francis, Mc-Graw hill, IEEE, CNKI, and databases regarding health science are needed. Databases such as Scopus, Web of Science, and SciVal are required for frequent study, evaluation, and bibliometrics on scientific research.

Acknowledgments. This research was funded by the research project QG 2022 of Vietnam National University, Hanoi: "Statistic, analysis and assessed research outputs of Vietnam National University, Hanoi" on Scopus and Web of Science databases.

References

1. Hiển Phạm Duy: So sánh năng lực nghiên cứu khoa học của 11 nước Đông Á dựa trên các công bố quốc tế và bài học rút ra cho Việt Nam. High. Educ. **60**(4), 122–132 (2010)
2. Clarivate: Web of Sciences. https://webofknowledge.com/
3. Elsevier: Scopus, Elsevier. https://scopus.com/
4. Hirsch, J.E.: An index to quantify an individual's scientific research output. Proc. Natl. Acad. Sci. **102**(46), 16569–16572 (2005)
5. INFEQA: "Bảng xếp hạng QS 2022: ĐHQGHN có thêm lĩnh vực mới được xếp hạng và gia tăng vị trí trên 4 lĩnh vực," *VNU* (2022). Accessed 7 Apr 2022. 1BC. https://vnu.edu.vn/ttsk/?C1654/N30658/Bang-xep-hang-QS-2022:-dHQGHN-co-them-linh-vuc-moi-duoc-xep-hang-va-gia-tang-vi-tri-tren-4-linh-vuc.htm
6. Van Raan, A.F.J.: For your citations only? Hot topics in bibliometric analysis. Meas. Interdiscip. Res. Perspect. **3**(1), 50–62 (2005)
7. Narin, H.H., Pinski, F., Gee, G.: Structure of biomedical literature. J. Am. Soc. Inf. Sci. **27**(1), 24–25 (1976)
8. Garcia-Rio, J., et al.: A bibliometric evaluation of European Union research of the respiratory system from 1987 to 1998. Eur. Respir. J. **17**(6), 1175–1180 (2001)
9. Zhou, F., Guo, H.C., Ho, Y.S., Wu, C.Z.: Scientometric analysis of geostatistics using multivariate methods. Scientometrics **73**(3), 265–279 (2007)
10. Cole, S.: Citation and the evaluation of individual scientist. Trends Biochem. Sci. **14**(1), 9–13 (1989)
11. Chuang, Y.S., Huang, K.Y., Ho, Y.L.: A bibliometric and citation analysis of stroke-related research in Taiwan. Scientometrics **72**(2), 201–212 (2007)
12. Li, Y.S., Ho, Z.: Use of citation per publication as an indicator to evaluate contingent valuation research. Scientometrics **75**(1), 97–110 (2008)
13. Tuấn, N.V.: Năng suất khoa học Việt Nam qua công bố quốc tế 2001–2015, *Tạp chí Khoa học và Công nghệ Việt Nam* **10**(A), 49–54 (2016)
14. Hạnh, H.: Điểm danh 30 trường đại học Việt Nam có công bố quốc tế NGHIÊN CỨU - TRAO ĐỔI THÔNG TIN VÀ TƯ LIỆU - 3/2021 29 nhiều nhất. (2019)
15. Hùng, T.: Việt Nam có hơn 17.000 bài báo quốc tế được công bố năm 2020 (2020). Accessed 02 Feb 2021. https://baoquocte.vn/viet-nam%7B%5C%25%7D02-17000-bai-bao-quoc-te-duoc-cong-bo%7B%5C%25%7D022020.html

Trends in Digital Library

Clustering Semantic Predicates
in the Open Research Knowledge Graph

Omar Arab Oghli[(✉)] [iD], Jennifer D'Souza[iD], and Sören Auer[iD]

TIB Leibniz Information Centre for Science and Technology, Hannover, Germany
{omar.araboghli,jennifer.dsouza,auer}@tib.eu

Abstract. When semantically describing knowledge graphs (KGs), users have to make a critical choice of a vocabulary (i.e. predicates and resources). The success of KG building is determined by the convergence of shared vocabularies so that meaning can be established. The typical lifecycle for a new KG construction can be defined as follows: nascent phases of graph construction experience terminology divergence, while later phases of graph construction experience terminology convergence and reuse. In this paper, we describe our approach tailoring two AI-based clustering algorithms for recommending predicates (in RDF statements) about resources in the Open Research Knowledge Graph (ORKG) https://orkg.org/. Such a service to recommend existing predicates to semantify new incoming data of scholarly publications is of paramount importance for fostering terminology convergence in the ORKG.

Our experiments show very promising results: a high precision with relatively high recall in linear runtime performance. Furthermore, this work offers novel insights into the predicate groups that automatically accrue loosely as generic semantification patterns for semantification of scholarly knowledge spanning 44 research fields.

Keywords: Content-based recommender systems · Open research knowledge graph · Artificial intelligence · Clustering algorithms

1 Introduction

Traditional, discourse-based scholarly communication in "pseudo-digitized" PDF format is being now increasingly transformed to a completely new representation leveraging semantified digital-born formats e.g. within the Open Research Knowledge Graph (ORKG) [3] among other initiatives [2,4,6,9,10,13,18]. This "digital-first" scholarly information representation is based on a fundamentally new information organization paradigm that creates and uses *structured, fine-grained scholarly content*. Such an information organization paradigm facilitates the evolution of scholarly communication from documents for humans to read towards human *and* machine-readable knowledge with the aim of alleviating

Supported by TIB Leibniz Information Centre for Science and Technology, the EU H2020 ERC project ScienceGRaph (GA ID: 819536).

Y.-H. Tseng et al. (Eds.): ICADL 2022, LNCS 13636, pp. 477–484, 2022.
https://doi.org/10.1007/978-3-031-21756-2_39

human reading cognitive tie-ups. To this end, the ORKG-based scholarly communication comprises a crucial machine-actionable unit of scholarly content in the form of *human and machine-readable comparisons* of semantified *scholarly contributions* [15]. These comparisons are meant to be used by researchers to quickly get familiar with existing work in a specific research domain. For example, determining the reproduction number estimate R0 of the Sars-Cov-2 virus from a number of studies in various regions across the world https://orkg.org/comparison/R44930. The respective papers' scholarly contributions are described with an equivalent set of RDF statements. A core semantic construct of these contribution-centric statements are the *predicates* or *properties* used to describe the contribution of an article, i.e. contribution predicate sets (CPS). While the *subject* and *object* are content-based, *predicates* can generically span contributions across articles. E.g., *task name, dataset name, metric*, and *score* are a group of four predicates used to semantically describe the leaderboard contribution across AI articles [12] in the Computer Science domain; the predicates *basic reproduction number, confidence interval (95%), location*, and *time period* are used to describe Covid-19 reproductive number estimates in epidemiology articles [14]. Each such group then becomes a *contribution-centric* predicate group (CPG).

The ORKG follows an agile, iterative Wiki-style editing approach which gives curators the autonomy to coin new predicates easily, however aims in the long-term to discover a coherent contributions vocabulary as an ontology. Generally, the typical lifecycle of a wiki-based editable KG construction starts in nascent phases experiencing terminology divergence or growth, while later phases experience terminology convergence and reuse. In this background setting of building the ORKG, the overarching research question investigated in this paper is: *How to ensure that individuals, free to use arbitrary terminology, converge towards shared vocabularies for contribution-centric semantic predicates?* To this end, this work describes our implementation of an unsupervised AI service based on clustering similar papers and recommending contribution-centric predicate groups (CPG) from the existing ORKG contributions. *Similar scholarly contributions should be semantified with a homogeneous contribution-centric semantic predicate groups.* This is our intuition behind adopting clustering since the method aims to group the data points having similar features, where data points in different groups should have highly offbeat features. We chose hierarchical (Agglomerative) and non-hierarchical (K-means) clustering strategies. We avoid computationally intensive methods (e.g., Affinity) or methods that can handle only small cluster sizes (e.g., Spectral clustering).

2   Our Task

Definition. As mentioned above, the task addressed in this paper deals with discovering CPGs from CPSs in the ORKG knowledge base (KB) to describe a new article's contribution. At a high-level, given an article and the ORKG KB of crowdsourced, structured contributions w.r.t. their CPSs, the most relevant CPG, if found, should be recommended for describing the new article contribution.

Our task formalism is as follows. The ORKG KB comprising structured contributions defined only w.r.t. predicates is $CPS = \{CPS_1, ..., CPS_N\}$ which were used to structure contributions in the set $C = \{c_1, ..., c_N\}$, respectively. Here, the base N represents the total number of contributions in the ORKG, CPS is the knowledge base of predicates sets, and CPS_i is the predicates set used to structure contribution c_i. Furthermore, the set of predicates in each CPS formally is, $CPS_i = \{p_{1i}, p_{2i}, ..., p_{xi}\}$. Finally, $P = \{p_1, p_2, ..., p_y\}$ represents the set of unique predicates aggregated from all CPSs and y is the total number of unique predicates used to structure the knowledge about contributions in ORKG. The recommendation task attempted in this work can then be defined as, given a new paper P as its title T and abstract A, to semantify or describe its contribution C with an automatically discovered CPG from the ORKG KB of CPSs such that the predicates in $CPG \in P$.

Dataset. For our novel task, a novel dataset (https://doi.org/10.5281/zenodo. 6513499) needed to be created. Our objective with creating the dataset is to capture instances of the constructs of CPGs and CPSs with their respective scholarly articles' title T and abstract A. While obtaining CPSs and their corresponding articles may be a relatively straightforward process – for CPSs, we query the ORKG RDF data dump[1] dated 2021-11-10 of contributions and for articles' T and A, we query external services like Crossref – the process of obtaining CPGs is not.

Note ORKG *Comparisons* are a downstream application enabling computing surveys over collections structured contributions with roughly similar CPSs. Given this and our need to obtain CPGs heuristically, we ask ourselves: could the CPSs aggregated in *Comparisons* be considered a CPG? The answer is "yes," but with a caveat. We cannot consider the aggregated CPSs as CPGs from just about any *Comparison*. *We want to generate CPGs that are strong candidates for templates.* For this, we deem that the candidate CPSs need to demonstrate a strong repetition pattern of structuring several contributions as a determiner that they would apply to new contributions that have not yet been structured as well. This was implemented using the following heuristic. The aggregated CPSs in *Comparisons* containing at least 10 contributions were considered as CPGs in turn satisfying our criteria that they represent a strong repetition pattern.

Our final task dataset statistics are shown in Table 1 in terms of total unique papers, contributions, predicates and their research fields' coverages.

3   Our Approach

3.1   Clustering of Contribution Predicates' Groups

When describing our task dataset, we described our heuristic (https://doi.org/ 10.5281/zenodo.6514139) reliance on ORKG *Comparisons* to obtain CPGs. The next question is: how can we develop a recommender of CPGs given a corpus

---

[1] https://orkg.org/orkg/api/rdf/dump.

Table 1. Our final task dataset statistics w.r.t. the ORKG *Comparisons*.

-	Papers	Contributions	Predicates	Research fields
Minimum per comparison	2	10	2	1
Maximum per comparison	202	250	112	5
Average per comparison	23.25	35.47	12.86	1.19
Total	3941	5123	1681	44

of papers as their titles T and abstracts A structured for their contributions with CPSs? We propose an AI-based unsupervised clustering strategy of papers as the solution. With this approach, we aim to automatically obtain CPGs by aggregating all CPSs in a particular cluster of similar papers. Our hypothesis is that papers describing similar contributions are also similar to each other in terms of their unstructured text descriptions as T and A. Thus, the role played by the construct of *Comparisons* in generating CPGs are now replaced, in the context of an automated recommender, by a clustering algorithm.

3.2 Grouped Predicates Recommender System Workflow

Our automated predicates recommender system workflow (see Fig. 1) is as follows: **1.** A user provides the paper's title and/or DOI they wish to add. **2.** We fetch the paper's abstract from external service APIs as discussed in the dataset section. **3.** The paper's title and abstract are concatenated and vectorized. **4.** The vector representation will be fed to a pre-trained clustering model for most relevant cluster prediction. Note, each candidate cluster was constructed based on prior semantified papers already in the ORKG KB. **5.** We fetch the predicates, i.e. CPSs, of all the structured paper contributions in the predicted cluster. **6.** All CPSs are combined to a set to produce a CPG which is then recommended to the user for their query paper.

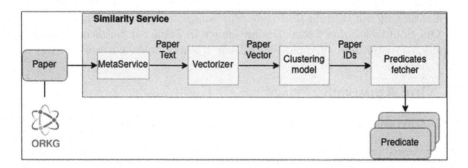

Fig. 1. Our grouped predicates recommender workflow. Arrows indicate the data flow.

For the vectorizer module, we experimented with two different vectorization functions. *1.* TF-IDF *embeddings* computed using scikit-learn [8,16] library on our task corpus of paper T and A into TF-IDF [17] vectors. $260,016$ unique terms were found in our corpus. *2. Pretrained* SCIBERT *embeddings* [5] uncased model fed forward with our text corpus of paper T and A to output its final hidden state and averaged via sentence transformers (https://huggingface.co/sentence-transformers) resulting in a vectorized text of dimension 768. The embeddings are obtained using a max sequence length of 512.

And, for the clustering model, we tried two different clustering algorithms. *1.* K-MEANS. Following [1], we apply the centroid-based clustering algorithm K-means [11] to group similar scholarly contributions represented by their paper T and A. The models were trained on the *Google Colab Pro+* platform due to the complex time and space requirements of K-means. *2.* AGGLOMERATIVE. This bottom-up hierarchical-based clustering algorithm [19] with *ward* linkage was applied. This method, like the K-means objective function, minimizes the variance within a cluster. The scikit-learn (https://scikit-learn.org/stable/modules/generated/sklearn.cluster.AgglomerativeClustering.html) implementation was used and the models were trained on *Google Colab*.

4 Results and Discussion

In this section, we discuss our experimental results for selecting the optimal vectorization and clustering model pair.

Baselines. We implemented two baselines each driven by a research question (RQ). ***Baseline 1 RQ***: what happens if the problem were reduced to a trivial solution where clusters of contributions are created simply based on the research field? For this baseline, the contribution CPSs in our training data were grouped to form a CPG per research field of the training data contributions. The 44 different research fields in our dataset thus resulted in 44 CPGs. Thus a new incoming paper from the test dataset would be assigned the CPG of its research field created from the training dataset contributions. Row 1 in Table 3 shows the results from this baseline. We find that while a perfect recall can be obtained, such an approach is not precise. This reveals an important characteristic of our dataset: i.e., *the structure of contributions within each research field can differ significantly across papers in the same field*. ***Baseline 2 RQ***: what happens when 192 topics are generated from our dataset by topic modeling [7] analogous to the 192 comparisons? To implement this baseline, topic distributions were obtained for all papers in the training dataset and each paper was assigned to the best topic. Thus CPSs were obtained per topic from which CPGs were generated. A new incoming test paper was then classified to best topic and assigned its CPG. Row 2 in Table 3 shows the results from a topic modeling based approach. The results prove to not be promising in terms of both precision and recall. This is contrary to our initial assumption that topic groups could be a correlated semantic construct of comparisons. We find no correlation can be established.

Table 2. Micro-averaged results of automatically generating CPGs.

Agglomerative							K-Means						
-	TF-IDF			SciBERT			-	TF-IDF			SciBERT		
Clusters K	P	R	$F1$	P	R	$F1$	Clusters K	P	R	$F1$	P	R	$F1$
350	0.239	0.964	0.383	0.312	0.032	**0.058**	1850	0.593	0.732	**0.655**	0.603	0.834	0.700
1300	0.760	0.853	**0.804**	0.761	0.023	0.044	2050	0.486	0.696	0.572	0.659	0.808	**0.726**

Table 3. Overall results - Comparison between $Base_{RF}$ (Baseline Research Fields), $Base_{LDA}$ (Baseline Latent Dirichlet Allocation), K-Means and Agglomerative.

-	Macro-average			Micro-average		
Approach	P	R	$F1$	P	R	$F1$
$Base_{RF}$	0.186	1.0	0.250	0.028	1.0	0.055
$Base_{LDA}$	0.040	0.662	0.090	0.023	0.615	0.046
K-Means	0.728	0.844	0.781	0.659	0.808	0.726
Agglomerative	0.823	0.845	0.834	0.760	0.853	0.804

Clustering Results. Table 2 shows the results from applying K-means and Agglomerative clustering with both vectorization methods. The best results are highlighted as bold and underlined.

Each clustering method preferred a different vectorization strategy. The K-means clustering algorithm shows that SciBERT embeddings are the preferred vectorization method obtaining 0.726 micro $F1$ (k = 2050). The Agglomerative clustering algorithm shows that TF-IDF embeddings is the preferred vectorization method obtaining 0.804 micro $F1$ (k = 1300). Thus, Agglomerative clustering surpasses K-means by nearly 10 points. Thus, our optimal model is at $k = 1300$ with the highest micro $F1$ using TF-IDF vectorization and Agglomerative clustering.

5   Conclusion

Our experiments on the hierarchical Agglomerative algorithm have shown a quantitative result of 80.4% F1 and a qualitative result of similar recommendations of comparison predicates to those predefined in ORKG templates. Thus, the content-based recommender system based on clustered predicate units satisfies the templating concept of the ORKG. Overall, we offer among our methodology a semantification system for research contributions in the Semantic Web that does not limit the user autonomy, but instead directs the user to choose from an existing vocabulary, and hence prevent terminology divergence during later phases of graph construction.

References

1. Anteghini, M., D'Souza, J., dos Santos, V.A.P.M., Auer, S.: Easy semantification of bioassays (2021). https://arxiv.org/abs/2111.15182
2. Aryani, A., et al.: A research graph dataset for connecting research data repositories using RD-switchboard. Sci. Data **5**, 180099 (2018)
3. Auer, S., et al.: Improving access to scientific literature with knowledge graphs. Bibliothek Forschung und Praxis **44**(3), 516–529 (2020)
4. Baas, J., Schotten, M., Plume, A., Côté, G., Karimi, R.: Scopus as a curated, high-quality bibliometric data source for academic research in quantitative science studies. Quant. Sci. Stud. **1**(1), 377–386 (2020)
5. Beltagy, I., Lo, K., Cohan, A.: SciBERT: a pretrained language model for scientific text. In: Proceedings of the 2019 Conference on Empirical Methods in Natural Language Processing and the 9th International Joint Conference on Natural Language Processing (EMNLP-IJCNLP), pp. 3606–3611 (2019)
6. Birkle, C., Pendlebury, D.A., Schnell, J., Adams, J.: Web of science as a data source for research on scientific and scholarly activity. Quant. Sci. Stud. **1**(1), 363–376 (2020)
7. Blei, D.M., Ng, A.Y., Jordan, M.I.: Latent Dirichlet allocation. J. Mach. Learn. Res. **3**, 993–1022 (2003)
8. Buitinck, L., et al.: API design for machine learning software: experiences from the scikit-learn project. In: ECML PKDD Workshop: Languages for Data Mining and Machine Learning, pp. 108–122 (2013)
9. Dessì, D., Osborne, F., Reforgiato Recupero, D., Buscaldi, D., Motta, E., Sack, H.: AI-KG: an automatically generated knowledge graph of artificial intelligence. In: Pan, J.Z., et al. (eds.) ISWC 2020. LNCS, vol. 12507, pp. 127–143. Springer, Cham (2020). https://doi.org/10.1007/978-3-030-62466-8_9
10. Fricke, S.: Semantic scholar. J. Med. Libr. Assoc. JMLA **106**(1), 145 (2018)
11. Jin, X., Han, J.: K-means clustering. In: Sammut, C., Webb, G.I. (eds.) Encyclopedia of Machine Learning and Data Mining, pp. 695–697. Springer, Boston (2017). https://doi.org/10.1007/978-1-4899-7687-1_431
12. Kabongo, S., D'Souza, J., Auer, S.: Automated mining of leaderboards for empirical AI research. In: Ke, H.-R., Lee, C.S., Sugiyama, K. (eds.) ICADL 2021. LNCS, vol. 13133, pp. 453–470. Springer, Cham (2021). https://doi.org/10.1007/978-3-030-91669-5_35
13. Manghi, P., et al.: OpenAIRE research graph dump, December 2019. https://doi.org/10.5281/zenodo.3516918
14. Oelen, A., et al.: Covid-19 reproductive number estimates (2020). https://doi.org/10.48366/R44930. https://www.orkg.org/orkg/comparison/R44930
15. Oelen, A., Jaradeh, M.Y., Stocker, M., Auer, S.: Generate FAIR literature surveys with scholarly knowledge graphs, pp. 97–106. Association for Computing Machinery, New York (2020). https://doi.org/10.1145/3383583.3398520
16. Pedregosa, F., et al.: Scikit-learn: machine learning in Python. J. Mach. Learn. Res. **12**, 2825–2830 (2011)
17. Sammut, C., Webb, G.I. (eds.): TF-IDF. In: Sammut, C., Webb, G.I. (eds.) Encyclopedia of Machine Learning, pp. 986–987. Springer, Boston (2010). https://doi.org/10.1007/978-0-387-30164-8_832

18. Wang, K., Shen, Z., Huang, C., Wu, C.H., Dong, Y., Kanakia, A.: Microsoft academic graph: when experts are not enough. Quant. Sci. Stud. **1**(1), 396–413 (2020)
19. Zepeda-Mendoza, M.L., Resendis-Antonio, O.: Hierarchical agglomerative clustering. In: Dubitzky, W., Wolkenhauer, O., Cho, KH., Yokota, H. (eds.) Encyclopedia of Systems Biology, pp. 886–887. Springer, New York (2013). https://doi.org/10.1007/978-1-4419-9863-7_1371

Data Librarians: Changes in Role and Job Duties Over 25 Years

Tokinori Suzuki ⓘ, Emi Ishita⁽✉⁾ ⓘ, Xinyu Ma ⓘ, Widiatmoko Adi Putranto ⓘ,
and Yukiko Watanabe ⓘ

Kyushu University, Fukuoka 819-0395, Japan
`tokinori@inf.kyushu-u.ac.jp`, `ishita.emi.982@m.kyushu-u.ac.jp`

Abstract. The role and the job duties of librarians may evolve owing to social changes and users' needs. It is important to know academic libraries have adapted to their needs. Data librarians have held a key position in academic libraries. In this study, we investigated the adaptation in their job duties over 25 years. We conducted content analyses using descriptions of job advertisements to examine changes in the role and job duties of data librarians to clarify libraries' adaptation. All job advertisements for data librarians posted in the IFLA - Library and Information Science Jobs Mailing List from 1995 to 2022 were collected, and 36 job advertisements were obtained after the preprocessing procedures. Based on job titles, data librarians for specific subjects were needed in the early days, and research data librarians appeared in recent years. Job descriptions indicate that data librarians were required to have knowledge of data about various subjects and use statistical analysis software to process data from 2000–2004; however, knowledge of research data was required from 2015–2022. There have been many other changes in work performed by data librarians over the past 25 years, and libraries have regularly adapted their job descriptions.

Keywords: Content analysis · Data librarian · Job advertisement · Job description · Job titles

1 Introduction

Liscouski [1] first proposed the term "data librarian" in an article published in 1997 and predicted the transformation of librarian responsibilities in the era of Big Data. In 2008, Swan and Brown [2] used the title "data librarian" for professionals in the role of collecting, storing, analyzing, and managing data in the library. In 2020, Ming and Ren [3] proposed that data librarians are data professionals with specialized talents in data literacy education and data management, and libraries should provide additional training to ensure the libraries and the data librarians conform to the development of the times and meet users' new and changing data needs.

For academic libraries, not only digitized information but also digital data itself has become a major resource. The data librarian, who first appeared around the 1990s, symbolizes this change. However, about 30 years have since passed and, in the meantime,

Y.-H. Tseng et al. (Eds.): ICADL 2022, LNCS 13636, pp. 485–491, 2022.
https://doi.org/10.1007/978-3-031-21756-2_40

the environment of "Big Data" and data-driven research have become popular. It is expected that the role and duty of data librarians will be affected by these changes in the scholarly world. By analyzing the changes in the roles and job duties of the "Data Librarian," we can understand whether academic libraries were well adapted to the needs of society and users in scholarly communication. In addition, analysis of changes in their jobs according to the job titles and the required skills may reflect changes necessary in higher education for new information specialists and recurrent (continuing) education programs for current librarians.

Job analysis is conducted by analyzing the job descriptions in advertisements for specific job titles. For example, Khan and Du [4] examined the job title, required skills, and preferred skills of 50 randomly selected data librarian job advertisements from multiple job notice websites. There have also been some studies focusing on digital librarians [5], system librarians [6], and copyright librarians [7]; however, many of those researchers used job advertisements posted currently.

In this study, we sought to understand the changes in data librarians' roles and job duties over 25 years using content analysis of job advertisements, a commonly used method in library and information science research.

2 Methods

2.1 Data Collection

We referred the framework of the Cross's study [8], who explored the similarities and differences between the skills and requirements of academic communication librarians by analyzing job descriptions. We examined the job advertisements for data librarian positions from 1995 to 2022 in the IFLA LIBJOBS. In this paper, we reported the preliminary analysis of the job titles and changes in job descriptions. Job advertisements for librarians are available online, such as at ALA JobLIST[1], Indeed[2] and HigherEd-Jobs[3]. Most of them, however, only display current advertisements, and past postings are not available. In this study, we needed to obtain past advertisements to investigate the changes in data librarians' job duties over the years. There are some websites that, to the best of our knowledge, do archive past job advertisements, for example, IASSIST Jobs Repository[4] and IFLA LIBJOBS[5]. The IASSIST Jobs Repository, which archived records of job descriptions for data librarians posted to the members' email list from 2005 to the present, might be a useful resource for our study. However, it also included "Research data system archivist," "Information management specialist," and so on. The criteria of this job repository were unclear, so we excluded it from our study. Although the number of job advertisements is small, we used the archive of the IFLA LIBJOBS mailing list, which archives job advertisements from 1995 until now.

---

[1] https://joblist.ala.org/

[2] https://indeed.com/

[3] https://www.higheredjobs.com/

[4] https://iassistdata.org/jobs-repository/

[5] https://mail.iflalists.org/wws/info/libjobs/

We searched advertisements for "data librarian" from IFLA LIBJOBS (total of 25,482 postings) from August 1995 to April 2022 by querying the phrase "data librarian," ignoring the case of characters. We obtained 240 advertisements. Job advertisements including the phrase "data librarian" were searched. In our searching method, "metadata librarians" were also searched because the phrase "data librarian" was included. One of the authors manually categorized 240 advertisements into three categories: "data librarian," "others," and "for consideration." The basic criterion for data librarian is that job title included "data librarian." If they are not related to data librarians obviously, they were categorized to "others." If it is difficult to make a decision, they were categorized as "consideration." Advertisements classified as "Consideration" were discussed with other authors, and final decisions were made. For example, an advertisement recruited multiple kinds of librarians, and each librarian's job description was short. After the discussion, we determined that this was advertisement for a data librarian because it existed as a job offer. In addition, some same advertisements were posted multiple times on the mailing list. Advertisements posted within a month which had the same content as in the prior month were deleted. There were also cases where the same content was posted one year later, but this was included in the analysis. Because it was difficult to know whether they were new advertisements or the same opening posted more than once until the job was not filled.

After the above process, 36 job advertisements were finally analyzed. Although the number of advertisements is small, they include that from 1995 to 2022. It enables us to analyze the general changes over 25 years. Among those classified as "Other," advertisements for cataloging librarians and metadata librarians dominated. In some cases, detailed information was not posted on the mailing list, and many of them displayed the URL of each institution's website; however, it was difficult to check the content now. The description of advertisements posted to the mailing list was analyzed.

2.2 Data Analysis

The typical job advertisements comprise a job title, the job responsibilities or duties, required qualifications, preferred qualifications and salary, a description of the institution, and so on. As the first step, we created a spreadsheet including job title, institution's names, countries, posted date, job description, qualifications, and job type (full-time or part-time).

To investigate changes in job descriptions over the years, we made scatter plot diagrams of job advertisements by characterizing their descriptions using a word embedding [9] as a first step. Other analysis techniques, e.g., a co-occurrence network analysis of words can provide additional information, which is our future study. We selected a word embedding to characterize the descriptions. Given the limited number of available advertisements, traditional word-count-based approaches may not work well due to the sparsity of the words. However, with word embedding, it is possible to learn the characteristics of words in a large text corpus in advance and apply it to the smaller descriptions. Word embedding is a technique for converting words into vectors of real numbers that capture contextual meanings; the vectors of similar words are close to each other based on the distributional hypothesis that words in a similar context tend to have similar meanings.

We used the skip-gram model [9] to learn the word embeddings and denoted a context as $w(t - n), \ldots, w(t - i), w(t), w(t + 1), \ldots, w(t + n)$. In this context, $w(t)$ and $w(t \pm i)$, $(i = 1, \ldots, n)$ are the current word and the surrounding words of $w(t)$, respectively. The model learns the word embedding to predict the surrounding words $w(t \pm i)$ given the current word $w(t)$ using a neural network. Since there are no corpora of job advertisements with a sufficient volume for the training with the best of our knowledge, we trained a word embedding model with the English version of Wikipedia articles provided as a data dump on October 1st, 2020, by the Wikimedia Foundation with the word2vec model of Python's genism library[6]. The learning parameters were as follows: the vector size of 300, 5 surrounding words, and 10 for the minimum occurrence of words. Using the trained word embeddings model, we converted the texts in the job description part of the advertisements into the corresponding vectors. The average number of words in a single description is 250. After completing word removal, we calculated a mean vector of all the words in a job description, representing the whole description for each posting. To visualize the descriptions, we reduced the dimensions of the descriptions' vectors with a dimension reduction technique, Uniform Manifold Approximation [10]. Then, we plotted the scatter diagrams of the descriptions and made groups of advertisements to analyze the changes.

3   Results

3.1   Outline of Job Advertisements

Among 36 job advertisements, 27 were from university libraries and nine were from companies. Although the IFLA is the world library association, there were 33 advertisements were from the USA, two from Canada, and one from England. As for job types, seven institutions advertised full-time positions, and only one was hiring for a part-time job. The other 27 cases did not specify the type; however, the terms "annual salary" and "annual leave" indicated they were for full-time jobs. We also examined the actual job titles displayed in the postings.

Table 1 demonstrates the job titles from five periods. Though the number of job advertisements fluctuates over the periods, advertisements were found in every period. Many data librarians were also required to have knowledge of or a background in specific subjects, such as social science, business, GIS/spatial, and sciences. Most were posted in the earlier years, around 1995 to 2004. In recent years, research data librarian, as an emerging profession, has also appeared in advertisements. The results indicate that, even in recent years, if the word "data librarian" is included, such as in "research data librarian," the job duties differ slightly from the traditional descriptions in recent years.

---

[6] https://github.com/RaRe-Technologies/gensim.

Table 1. The number of job advertisements for data librarians and system librarians.

	'95–'99	'00–'04	'05–'09	'10–'14	'15–'19	'20–'22	Total
Data librarian (L)	3	4	3	2	1		13
Social science data L	1	2	3	2	2		9
Business/market data L		1		3			4
GIS/Spatial data L		3					3
Science data L				2	1		3
Research data L				1	1	1	3

3.2 Changes in Job Description and Skills

Figure 1 shows the scatter plot of the job description consisting of job duties and responsibilities. They were divided into five groups, and we labeled them Groups A to E. In the figure, the color of the dots indicates the year the advertisements were posted. Most of the jobs within a job description group had been advertised within the same period, indicating that the job descriptions changed over time.

To understand changes in job descriptions in each group, we examined the required qualifications. Job descriptions were also examined, but it was difficult to identify their characteristics because some job duties were described in broader contexts, such as "serving researchers and students" and "developing effective collections and services." Thus, we examined the required skills. To identify the changes within the periods, we selected Group E, which included advertisements from 2000 to 2004, and Group C, which included those from 2015 to 2022.

Group E included many postings for data librarians for specific subjects, and knowledge of data in specific subjects was required. The following characteristics were also requisite: knowledge of quantitative methods of data extraction, analysis, and use; experience with the development of digital online resources; familiarity with statistical software, familiarity with metadata schema, familiarity with management of and access to numeric databases in various disciplines; experience using office software; and knowledge of mark-up languages. These skills and knowledge were necessary to manage and analyze data and develop an environment wherein they can provide data to users. Therefore, it can be said that such duties were expected of data librarians at that time.

Group C included data librarians, data librarians for specific subjects, and research data librarians. They were required to have knowledge of issues and experience with technical challenges related to data management and curation; understand the research process and impact in some disciplines; understand scientific work and the scientific process; have knowledge of research data management and common challenges regarding data sharing and curation; have knowledge of data issues in research; understand the data creation life cycle. Compared to Group E, they were expected to have a higher-level concept of research data management, such as managing research data in research activities, rather than only handling data.

As mentioned above, we found that the job duties changed depending on the years' group; however, some of the same skills were required in more than one group. For example, skills such as oral and written communication skills, interpersonal skills, and an ability to work collaboratively and effectively with others in many places were required for both Group E and Group C. These skills are fundamental for all librarians and are not limited to data librarians.

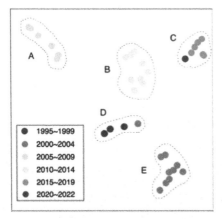

Fig. 1. Scatter diagram of job descriptions for data librarians. Advertisements close to each other in the content of job descriptions are grouped within dotted lines.

4   Conclusion

We analyzed the description of job advertisements and found the changes in over 25 years. Job advertisements are grouped based on that in posted years. Data librarians were expected to manage data or use data 20 years ago. In recent years, the handling of "research data" has been more focused. On the other hand, there are common skills that have been required over the years.

In this report, we have only revealed the preliminary results of our investigation, but we will also analyze all of the findings in greater detail using the qualitative methods to identify required knowledge, experience, and skills. For example, we plan to examine changes in the required and preferred skills and degree requirements.

Acknowledgments. This work is supported by the Japan Society for the Promotion of Science (JSPS) KAKENHI Grant Number JP18K18508.

References

1. Liscouski, J.: The data librarian: introducing the data librarian. J. Autom. Chem. **19**(6), 199–204 (1997). https://doi.org/10.1155/S1463924697000242

2. Swan, A., Brown, S.: The skills, role and career structure of data scientists and curators: an assessment of current practice and future needs. Key Perspectives Ltd., Truro, UK (2008). http://www.jisc.ac.uk/media/documents/programmes/digitalrepositories/dataskillsca reersfinalreport.pdf
3. Ming, X., Ren, S.: Study on the construction of data librarian team in libraries of medical colleges and universities in the new era [in Chinese]. Yixue Xinxi Xue Zazhi **41**(8), 85–88 (2020)
4. Khan, H.R., Du, Y.: What is a data librarian?: a content analysis of job advertisements for data librarians in the United States academic libraries. IFLA WLIC 2018, (2018). https://lib rary.ifla.org/id/eprint/2255/1/139-khan-en.pdf
5. Shahbazi, R., Hedayati, A.: Identifying digital librarian competencies according to the analysis of newly emerging IT-based LIS jobs in 2013. J. Acad. Librariansh. **42**(5), 542–550 (2016). https://doi.org/10.1016/j.acalib.2016.06.014
6. Ratledge, D., Sproles, C.: An analysis of the changing role of systems librarians. Library Hi Tech **35**(2), 303–311 (2017). https://doi.org/10.1108/LHT-08-2016-0092
7. Kawooya, D., Veverka, A., Lipinski, T.: The copyright librarian: a study of advertising trends for the period 2006–2013. J. Acad. Librariansh. **41**(3), 341–349 (2015). https://doi.org/10.1016/j.acalib.2015.02.011
8. Cross, W.M.: The State of the Scholarly Communication Librarian: a Content Analysis of Position Descriptions from Association of Research Libraries Member Institutions. Masters Paper, University of North Carolina at Chapel Hill (2011). https://doi.org/10.17615/j2ka-m178
9. Mikolov, T., Sutskever, I., Chen, K., Corrado, G., Dean, J.: Distributed representations of words and phrases and their compositionality. In: Proceedings of the 26th International Conference on Neural Information Processing Systems, vol. 2, pp. 3111–3119. Curran Associates Inc., Red Hook (2013)
10. McInnes, L., Healy, J., Melville, J.: UMAP: uniform manifold approximation and projection for dimension reduction. ArXiv (2018). https://doi.org/10.48550/arXiv.1802.03426

Data Spaces for Cultural Heritage: Insights from GLAM Innovation Labs

Milena Dobreva[1,2]([✉]) [iD], Krassen Stefanov[2] [iD], and Krassimira Ivanova[3] [iD]

[1] GATE Institute, Sofia University "St. Kliment Ohridski", 125 Tsarigradsko Shose, Sofia, Bulgaria
milena.dobreva@gate-ai.eu
[2] Faculty of Mathematics and Informatics, Sofia University "St. Kliment Ohridski", 5, J. Bourchier Blvd., Sofia, Bulgaria
[3] Institute of Mathematics and Informatics, Bulgarian Academy of Sciences, Bl. 8, Acad. G. Bontchev St., 1113 Sofia, Bulgaria

Abstract. The accumulation of digital cultural heritage collections for decades was shaped by centralised approaches based on the aggregation, harmonisation and enrichment of digital assets from a variety of sources. Currently, there is an ongoing transition towards decentralised infrastructures employing intelligent tools for answering more diversified user demands: the data spaces. This paper looks at the current understanding of what a European data space for cultural heritage should provide and takes as an inspirational example the work of innovation labs in galleries, libraries, archives and museums (GLAM labs). It focuses on the data users within data spaces. This paper is a first attempt to explore user requirements within the context of data spaces and the transition from aggregated to decentralised e-infrastructures for digital heritage.

Keywords: Data spaces · Digital heritage · GLAM labs · Europeana

1 Introduction

Digitisation of cultural heritage has been an integral part of the work of most cultural and scientific heritage institutions now for decades. The initial motivation for introducing digitisation was two-prong, improving *access* to collections and contributing to their *preservation* [1]. With the accumulation of digitised objects, the understanding of what digitisation was about from the 20th century was outgrown by a new understanding that heritage objects are digitised in order to be *analysed*, benefitting from the accumulation of digitised objects and the big data methods being applied to digitised heritage. In the early 21st century, this shift was embodied in the question, what do you do with a million books [2]? Several aspects of large digital collections, including scale, heterogeneity of content, the granularity of the objects, noise, audience needs, as well as issues around collection development and distribution were first summarised in [2].

The number of large-scale collections quickly expanded as a result of the efforts of large-scale digitisation projects and initiatives. For example, Europeana was conceived in

2005, launched digitally in 2008 and currently offers metadata on over 58 mln cultural and scientific heritage objects from over 4000 institutions [3]. A contemporary distributed digital library aggregating contents from the Middle East is [4]; links to growing digital heritage collections from China, Taiwan and Korea are provided in [5]. The COVID-19 pandemic acted as an additional factor to strengthen the services around digital heritage. For example, a study by UNESCO [6] showed significant discrepancies in the provision of digital services across the globe.

The build-up of issues around collecting digital content and providing adequate services to the users calls for a new infrastructural approach. At this time, there is a high hope that the emerging *data spaces* will provide solutions to the accumulated problems. A recent example of the potential usefulness of data spaces was provided by the archival sector. Gaël Chenard argued that some 200 digital archive collections in France do not have a federated search facility (or guaranteed interoperability) [7].

Digital heritage is not a unique domain exploring how it can employ intelligent decentralised solutions. For example, the need for decentralised data spaces in mobility and industry was analysed in [8]. The aggregated infrastructures were beneficial in accumulating digital content, but they have their limitations in the increasing data storage costs; the difficulties in providing seamless resource discovery; as well as the constraints in the search options provided to the users, which mostly follow the search engines' keyword search style. The transition from centralised to decentralised environments also provides a more robust opportunity to integrate big-scale analytical methods into the services provided to users [9]. It appeals to using more tools for large-scale analysis. This paper is an early attempt to explore what this infrastructural shift means with a focus on users.

2 Literature Survey

2.1 Data Space Definitions

The European data space for cultural heritage [10] is still in the process of conceptualisation and will start taking practical shape later this year. While there are a number of documents which discuss what this space should provide, possibly the most detailed technical guidance was summarised in [11].

One of the difficulties in discussing the data space for cultural heritage is the lack of a common understanding of what it means in practical terms. According to IDSA (International Data Spaces Association), data space is "a domain-specific or cross-domain ecosystem of trusted partners that share data" in a sovereign way "to benefit from the added-value potential in many different use cases" [12].

A high-level view of data space architecture includes a data space which can communicate with data owners and data users. The data owners can have intermediaries serving as data providers while the data users could go via data consumers as intermediaries. There are also technological components – connectors, which support the communications and are facilitated by brokers, app stores, identity providers, clearing houses and vocabularies. Data spaces follow life cycles similarly to other infrastructures. The scale on which IDSA measures the maturity of data spaces includes four categories:

lead-in, committed case, pilot, and *live.* Data spaces in other domains such as mobility, manufacturing, smart cities, reached the *pilot* or *live* stages.

Cultural heritage data spaces are still not mapped on the IDSA radar [13], but Europeana [3] can be considered either as a large-scale data provider in the terminology used within data spaces, or as a rudimentary data space.

2.2 Capturing User Requirements in the Digital Heritage Domain

Decades of digitisation contributed to the accumulation of digital collections, their aggregation, and the advancement of digital humanities. European-wide infrastructures like DARIAH [14] and CLARIN [15] are streamlining the use of scholarly content and tools, supported by a network of national infrastructures. However, one question which looks deceitfully simple remains vastly unanswered – what are the needs of the users making use of these resources? A substantial number of studies addressed the scholarly use of digital heritage, and we will focus on this type of users in this literature survey to illustrate several remaining substantial gaps.

In a systematic review of scholarly publications on users of digital cultural heritage resources, [16] summarised 86 publications. Over 50 categories related to users had been identified in these publications; their suggested grouping into four categories is presented in Fig. 1. A report from 2019 [17] summarises the outcomes of a survey consisting of 83 questions, and the focus is on the perceptions of research libraries on the scholarly use of digital resources. This report follows a data lifecycle structure in analysing the scholarly use of digital resources (see Figs. 2 and 3).

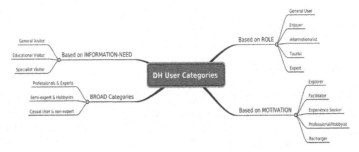

Fig. 1. User categories according to [16].

A further relevant publication [18] emphasises the communication between scholars and digital heritage institutions and access to digital content. An example of an extensive institutional report on the scholarly use and planning for innovative services is [19] from the National Library of France. This is an interesting analysis from the point of view of opening an innovation lab in the spirit of the disruptive innovation units in GLAM institutions discussed in [20]. This model has the advantage of incorporating several relevant axes which allow to construct more comprehensive multi-dimensional user spaces (see the four dimensions of aims, skills, engagement type and institutional affiliation on Fig. 4). Additional insights on the scholarly use of digital heritage can be gathered from the work on the European flagship digital library Europeana [21, 22].

Fig. 2. Scholarly activities in libraries according to [17]

Fig. 3. Research and innovation in digital cultural heritage according to [18].

Fig. 4. User categories in innovation labs in GLAM institutions [20]

The overview of studies summarising users and their engagement with digital heritage shows that there are multiple not well-aligned models of users and their needs.

3 Methodology

What a data space for cultural heritage is, requires further discussion. Hence we focused our effort on collecting examples of work which can be inspirational to understand in particular the user demands within data spaces. The user needs in the cultural heritage domain as illustrated in our literature survey are a particular challenge. We explored the approaches applied within GLAM Labs because they can serve as glimpses into potential user journeys and areas where personalisation is essential. This study combines desk research and proposes an initial framework for potential use cases within data spaces for cultural heritage. It is exploratory in nature, and we hope it will be a basis for opening a wider professional discussion which will help to arrive at a shared understanding of the actual building blocks of the data spaces for cultural heritage.

4   Data Spaces vs GLAM Labs

The European data space for cultural heritage has the ambitious task to transform the delivery and use of digital cultural heritage collections. The recent Recommendation of the EC states: *"Cultural heritage is not only a key element in building a European identity... but also an important contributor to the European economy"* [10]. The introduction of the European data space for cultural heritage places the cultural and scientific heritage sectors at the doorstep of a catalytic change. It will be a significant evolutionary stage in the technological infrastructure, data sharing and use regulations. It will impact the day-to-day work practices in the cultural heritage sector. This process will also require the **reshaping of research in the domain of digital cultural heritage infrastructure**. For example, E. Curry proposed the following research areas essential to enabling the next generation of dataspaces: decentralised support services, support for multimedia data, trusted data sharing, governance and economic models, incremental systems engineering, and human-centricity [25]. The cultural heritage domain will have to coin its own priorities within the data space research domain.

4.1   The Nature of Transition to Data Spaces

The documents specifying the European data space for cultural heritage identify a number of indicators which need to be delivered but the actual blueprint of the data space, which will provide the transition into new ways of serving the users, still needs to be refined and implemented. However, the most challenging work remains to identify how data spaces can serve the users better. Table 1 summarises some key aspects of the use of the data spaces for cultural heritage.

Table 1. Key aspects within data spaces for cultural heritage in relation to actors

Actor	Intermediary	Key aspects
Data owner	Data provider	• Availability and quality of datasets • Trustworthiness in providing content • Rights regime for using the data owners' content • Calculating rights for compound objects
Data user	Data Consumer	• Going beyond the keyword search: answering more complex demands • Clarity on the provenance and the coverage of the data used in the responses to user's requests • Reproducibility of query results • Explainability when AI is applied

4.2   Useful Lessons from GLAM Labs

While large cultural heritage institutions accumulated vast digital collections, they also encountered some of the questions currently at stake with the transition to data spaces from having aggregated collections. The British Library, the Library of Congress among others [20], established innovation labs which worked closely with users to understand how to answer their needs better within the context of accumulated vast digital resources. This experience brings components which can facilitate the data spaces:

Collections as data: A major shift in the cultural institutions is the targeted effort to create new datasets based on digital collections and the interpretation of collections as data [26, 27]. The GLAM lab community also has started developing practical tools for collections which provide guidance on datafication of collections (e.g. [28]).

Open innovation: In the last years, there has been growing interest in combining the efforts of smaller institutions in particular. eCHOing, an ongoing Erasmus + project, is exploring the various shapes such collaborations can efficiently take [29].

Use cases: The work of GLAM labs [20] is a treasure trove for unconventional user scenarios illustrating innovative uses of digital collections. It would be extremely useful to summarise experiences from different institutions and arrive at a repertory of scenarios that can be recreated on a large scale. Some examples of recent work are [30–33].

Towards formalising use cases for the DCH domain: More advanced data spaces are arriving at formalised use cases. For example, [8] lists seven use cases from industry which cover the use of own institutional data across (1. Dashboard 2. Transparency 3. Monitoring), and of shared data (4. Comparable monitoring 5. Anomaly detection 6. Predictive maintenance 7. New business models). For example, all three related to intra-institutional use can be applied in the cultural heritage domain.

Closing the skills gap: The transition into data spaces will require extensive work with multiple institutions. Europeana currently works with some 4,000 institutions, and only the museums in Europe are around 15,000. A massive upskilling of heritage professionals is needed. As an initial training, we delivered training for small museums' professionals [34].

5   Conclusions and Future Work

The need to support the digital transformation of Europe's cultural heritage sector is currently clearly set on the EC agenda. [10] sets up an agenda for substantially increased reuse and adding 40 mln additional digitised items to the European data space. In addition, [35] sees a CH sector transformed radically and [36] explores the interconnection between tangible, intangible, and digital dimensions of CH that are core for the understanding and appreciation of heritage. The essential role of digitisation is also emphasised in [37–39]. All these developments shape the stage for supporting work on the cultural heritage data space.

Our paper illustrated some areas which can provide useful examples for the deployment of the data space. A priority for the future is to develop a robust research agenda for this domain so that previous useful knowledge is properly expanded and supports a smooth transition into the new technological realm.

Acknowledgements. The contribution of M. Dobreva is supported by GATE project, funded by OP Science and Education for Smart Growth under Grant Agreement No. BG05M2OP001-1.003-0002-C01. The contribution of K. Stefanov is partially supported by the project KP-06-DB/6 DISTILL funded by the NSF of Bulgaria Project and by UNITe BG05M2OP001-1.001-0004 funded by the OP "Science and Education for Smart Growth" and co-funded by the EU through the ESI Funds.

References

1. Smith, A.: Why Digitise? CLIR, 13 pp., ISBN 1-887334-65-3 (1999)
2. Crane, G.: What Do You Do with a Million Books? D-Lib Magazine, vol. 12, no. 7 (2006). http://www.dlib.org/dlib/march06/crane/03crane.html
3. Europeana About Us. https://www.europeana.eu/en/about-us
4. The Digital Library of the Middle East (DLME). https://dlmenetwork.org/library
5. Digital Archives of Cultural Institutions in Asia (2020). https://rnavi.ndl.go.jp/en/post-440747.html
6. UNESCO: Museums around the world in the face of COVID-19. 31p. (2020). https://unesdoc.unesco.org/ark:/48223/pf0000373530
7. Building the Common European Data Space for Cultural Heritage. The Role of Europeana, Content Aggregation and Strategic Frameworks (2022). https://pro.europeana.eu/event/building-the-common-european-data-space-for-cultural-heritage-together
8. Schlueter Langdon, C., Schweichhart, K.: Data spaces: first applications in mobility and industry. In: Otto, B., ten Hompel, M., Wrobel, S. (eds) Designing Data Spaces. Springer, Cham (2022). https://doi.org/10.1007/978-3-030-93975-5_30
9. Unsworth, J., Clement, T., Steger, S., Uszkalo, K.: How Not To Read a Million Books, Cambridge, MA (2008). https://johnunsworth.name/hownot2read.html
10. EC. Commission Recommendation of 10.11.2021 on a common European data space for cultural heritage. C 7953. Brussels (2021). https://www.europeansources.info/record/commission-recommendation-eu-2021-1970-on-a-common-european-data-space-for-cultural-heritage/
11. Deployment of a common European data space for cultural heritage - CNECT/LUX/2021/OP/0070 (2022). https://digital-strategy.ec.europa.eu/en/funding/deployment-common-european-data-space-cultural-heritage-cnectlux2021op0070
12. IDSA: International Data Space Association. https://internationaldataspaces.org/
13. IDSA Radar. https://internationaldataspaces.org/adopt/data-space-radar/
14. DARIAH-EU. The Digital Research Infrastructure for the Arts and Humanities (DARIAH). https://www.dariah.eu/
15. CLARIN - European Research Infrastructure for Language Resources and Technology. https://www.clarin.eu/
16. Walsh, D., Clough, P., Foster, J.: User categories for digital cultural heritage. In: Proceedings of the International Workshop Accessing Cultural Heritage Scale, pp. 3–9 (2016)
17. Wilms, L., Derven, C., O'Dwyer, L., Lingstadt, K., Verbeke, D.: Europe's Digital Humanities Landscape: A Study From LIBER's Digital Humanities & Digital Cultural Heritage Working Group. Zenodo (2019). https://doi.org/10.5281/zenodo.3247286
18. Angelaki, G., et al.: How to Facilitate Cooperation between Humanities Researchers and Cultural Heritage Institutions. Guidelines. Warsaw, Poland: Digital Humanities Centre at the Institute of Literary Research of the Polish Academy of Sciences (2019). https://doi.org/10.5281/zenodo.2587481

19. Moiraghi, E.: Le projet Corpus et ses publics potentiels: Une étude prospective sur les besoins et les attentes des futurs usagers. [Rapport de recherche] Bibliothèque nationale de France. (hal-01739730) (2019). https://hal-bnf.archives-ouvertes.fr/hal-01739730

20. Mahey, M., Al-Abdulla, A., Ames, S., Bray, P., Candela, G., Chambers, S., et al.: Open a GLAM Lab, 164p. International GLAM Labs Community, Doha (2019)

21. Europeana Innovation Agenda. (2018). https://pro.europeana.eu/page/europeana-innovation-agenda

22. Final Recommendations from the Audiovisual Media in Europeana Task Force (2017). https://pro.europeana.eu/files/Europeana_Professional/Europeana_Network/Europeana_Network_Task_Forces/Final_reports/FinalRecommendationsTaskForceAudiovisualMediainEuropeana_20170711.pdf

23. Birrell, D., Dobreva, M., Dunsire, G., Griffiths, J., Hartley, R., Menzies, K.: The DiSCmap project. New Library World **112**(1/2), 19–44 (2011). https://doi.org/10.1108/03074801111100436

24. Task Force on Research Requirements. Europeana (2019). https://pro.europeana.eu/project/research-requirements

25. Curry, E.: The DCH domain-specific needs which are tackled in Section 1.2. In: Real-time Linked Dataspaces. Springer (2020). https://doi.org/10.1007/978-3-030-29665-0

26. Padilla, T., Allen, L., Frost, H., et al.: Final report – always already computational: Collections as data, Zenodo (2019). https://doi.org/10.5281/zenodo.3152935

27. Padilla, T., Kettler, H., Varner, S., et al.: Collections as data: part to whole (2019). https://collectionsasdata.github.io/part2whole/

28. Things You Can Do. (2020). https://collectionsasdata.github.io/fiftythings/

29. eCHOing website. Recovery of cultural heritage through higher education-driven open innovation. https://echoing.eu/

30. Beshirov, A., Hadzhieva, S., Koychev, I., Dobreva, M.: DuoSearch: a novel search engine for Bulgarian historical documents. In: Hagen, M., et al. (eds.) ECIR 2022. LNCS, vol. 13186, pp. 265–269. Springer, Cham (2022). https://doi.org/10.1007/978-3-030-99739-7_31

31. Birkholz, J.M., Chambers, S.: Data-level access to born-digital and digitised collections at KBR, Royal Library of Belgium : a "Labs" approach. In: IIPC General Assembly & Web Archiving Conference 2021, Abstracts (2021)

32. Williams, O., Farquhar, A.: Enabling complex analysis of large-scale digital collections: humanities research, high performance computing, and transforming access to British library digital collections. In: Digital Humanities 2016: Conference Abstracts, pp. 376–379. Jagiellonian University & Pedagogical University, Kraków (2016). http://dh2016.adho.org/abstracts/230

33. Doucet, A., et al.: NewsEye: a digital investigator for historical newspapers. In: Digital Humanities 2020, DH 2020, Conference Abstracts, Ottawa, Canada, 22–24 July 2020. Alliance of Digital Humanities Organizations (ADHO) (2020). https://zenodo.org/record/3895269

34. Dobreva, M.: Masterclass on practical datafication (2022). https://distill.page/category/datafication/

35. Europeana Strategy 2020–2025. (2020). https://pro.europeana.eu/post/europeana-strategy-2020-2025-empowering-digital-change

36. European Framework for Action on Cultural Heritage. (2018). https://ec.europa.eu/culture/document/european-framework-action-cultural-heritage

37. New European Agenda for Culture. (2018). https://www.cultureinexternalrelations.eu/2018/06/01/new-european-agenda-for-culture/

38. European Digital Action Plan 2021–2027. (2021). https://education.ec.europa.eu/document/digital-education-action-plan
39. Digital Agenda for Europe. (2010). https://eur-lex.europa.eu/LexUriServ/LexUriServ.do?uri=COM%3A2010%3A0245%3AFIN%3AEN%3APDF

EduArc: Federated Infrastructures for Digital Educational Resources

Ahmed Saleh$^{(\boxtimes)}$ ⓘ, Mohammad Abdel-Qader ⓘ, and Klaus Tochtermann ⓘ

ZBW – Leibniz Information Centre for Economics, Kiel/Hamburg, Germany
{a.saleh,m.abdel-qader,k.tochtermann}@zbw.eu

Abstract. The goals of the EduArc project are to explore the conditions for successful dissemination of open educational resources (OER) at universities and the provision of a federated infrastructure for digital educational resources. The project aims to develop a design concept (EduArc platform) for distributed learning infrastructures that provide federated access to digital educational resources. The EduArc platform connects decentralized systems via open standards and interfaces and is open for the integration of content from future providers and users.

Keywords: Digital libraries · Search engine · Learning management system

1 Introduction

The project addresses the question of what infrastructural requirements are necessary to build a sustainable platform for digital educational resources for universities. Marine et al. published a study on the state of digital educational resources (OER) in the context of digital transformation of various higher education systems [1]. The results of the study were taken into consideration while developing EduArc infrastructure. In order to successfully build such a platform, the functional requirements and design concepts were defined through use case studies. Afterwards, a common data model (CDM) for learning resources was developed based on the Learning Object Metadata standard (LOM) [2]. The common data model enables the metadata of open educational resources from different repositories to be mapped to the EduArc standard and stored in a central search index (EduArc index). Based on this common data model, a concept for an overall system architecture of the EduArc platform for connecting distributed learning resources was designed. A search engine, that searches for OERs based on the stored metadata, was developed. In addition, we developed various subject indexing models to analyze the indexed documents and generate new metadata. The generated metadata contains additional information about the content of a document (e.g., business, computer science, etc.). Finally, the repositories used in the EduArc project were documented in the common project wiki. A guide for linking repositories to EduArc has been made publicly available. This guide allows universities to link their repositories to the EduArc infrastructure. More information can be found in the reproducibility section.

Y.-H. Tseng et al. (Eds.): ICADL 2022, LNCS 13636, pp. 501–508, 2022.
https://doi.org/10.1007/978-3-031-21756-2_42

2   Case Studies and Requirements Specification

A user-centered approach was used. The approach focuses on the needs of the users and includes evaluations at different stages of the development process with appropriate feedback in the design or development process. The following research questions were defined:

RQ1: How do educators currently work with resources?
RQ2: How can EduArc be integrated into teachers' workflows?
RQ3: What are the functional requirements of EduArc from the teachers' perspective?

Case studies were developed to answer these three sequential research questions.

2.1   Interviews: Data Collection

Data collection and data analysis were conducted in an iterative process, resulting in a robust requirements specification. One iteration consisted of multiple data collections. Data collection was based on interviews. This technique had the advantage of focusing directly on the case study objectives and allowing for perceived causal relationships [3]. An interview guide was created to ensure a logical structure to the research questions. The interview questions were open-ended in order to elicit teachers' ways of working and motivations during the interviews without prescribing answers. Since the learning resource is the central element and starting point for the technical implementation of EduArc, the functionalities of the learning resource were considered as use cases for the creation of the guide. Specifically, three use cases were considered: Creating a resource, Searching a resource, and Viewing a resource.

2.2   Data Analysis

Qualitative data analysis is based on Lamnek's approach [4], which includes four phases: (1) transcription, (2) individual analysis, (3) generalizing analysis, (4) control phase. The first phase involved transcription of the interviews using the audio recording. In the second phase, irrelevant passages were deleted and relevant passages were highlighted to reduce the density of details in a single transcript. The analysis of each interview was done by highlighting all passages that are answers to the interview questions, grouping the highlighted passages into categories, reviewing the relationships between the highlighted passages, and finally comparing the results with the transcript. In EduArc, the user stories represented the categories. In the third phase, all similarities and differences between each analysis were noted. The final phase ensured that all relevant information was included. To this end, the results of the third phase were verified to be consistent with the transcripts, and errors were corrected as necessary. In addition, unclear passages were removed. Prior to conducting the interviews, a set of initial wireframes was developed to give the interviewees the idea of two alternative implementation approaches. The wireframes were used to design an initial graphical user interface. The approach was based on the user interface of the Hamburg Open Online University (HOOU) repository[1]. During the interview, both approaches were demonstrated to the participants along the use cases.

2.3   Usage Scenarios, Personas and Requirements Specification

Based on the interview responses, user requirements were defined in terms of user stories. As explained earlier, three use cases were considered: creating, searching, and viewing resources. However, when answering RQ1 and RQ2, it became clear that resource reuse was a critical issue for teachers. For this reason, another use case was added: reusing a resource. Below is a summary of the main scenarios along the use cases, along with some of the wireframes.

Create a Resource. As shown in Fig. 1, the teacher clicks browse and has the option to select files in different formats (1). The teacher clicks on a file, which is added to the list of selected resources (2). The file type is displayed (mp4) and the resource type (video) is determined automatically. If the resource type is not supported, the user has the option to change it before uploading by clicking the Change Document Type link [3]. If the teacher selects a folder that contains, for example, a video and a slide set, both files will be included in the list. Alternatively, the teacher can simply drag and drop files or folders. Then the teacher clicks Next and a window opens asking the teacher to enter more information (3). The teacher assigns his or her resource to a topic and determines the target audience and access. Before specifying access, the teacher reads an explanation of the relevant CC licenses. For references, the teacher searches EduArc and adds two resources as references (Fig. 1 and Slides 4). Additionally, the teacher can upload a bibliography, e.g. a BibTex file. Finally, the teacher briefly describes the content of the resource and clicks Add (4). The files are saved in the EduArc hub and their metadata is added to the index.

Search a Resource. The teacher has entered the search term "bitcoin" and the search view opens with two search results. The teacher tries to assess which resources are relevant and considers the given information: one resource about Block Chain from 2018 with the resource type slides and a short description; another resource about crypto currency from 2010 with the resource type video and a short description. By default, the results are sorted by relevance, but the teacher can also sort them in reverse chronological order (date). Then the teacher can narrow the search results by setting the creation date to 2015. The teacher sets the access to the license type to CCv4.

View a Resource. The teacher clicks on the resource Block Chain after searching with the keyword bitcoin. The teacher can view various information such as the title, creator, topic, scope, summary, and some references and keywords.

---

[1] https://www.hoou.de/.

Fig. 1. Create a resource

Reusing a resource. The teacher wants to save the Block Chain resource locally to use it again later.

3 Metadata for Learning Resources

A common data model for learning resources was developed based on the LOM standard. LOM was chosen because it clearly focuses on learning resources. In addition, LOM forms the basis for metadata representation in several German OER repositories for higher education, such as the Central Repository for Open Educational Resources in Baden-Württemberg (ZOERR)[2]. The common data model (CDM) made it possible to map the metadata of OERs from different repositories to this project standard and to store them in a central search index (EduArc index).

EduArc's CDM consists of 20 fields. It distinguishes between two levels of commitment:

- Mandatory properties that must be present, and
- recommended properties that can be optionally present.

The EduArc CDM incorporates the FAIR principles [5], which originated with Wilkinson [6]. The four FAIR principles describe guiding principles for discoverability, accessibility, interoperability, and reuse of digital resources.

4 System Architecture

The development of the software and system architecture includes the central services located at EduArc and the existing systems and infrastructures for storing learning resources. Based on EduArc's CDM, a concept for an overall system architecture of the EduArc platform was designed to connect distributed learning resources. The overall EduArc infrastructure pipeline is shown in Fig. 2.

---

[2] https://www.oerbw.de/.

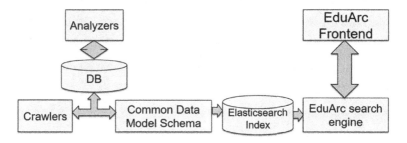

Fig. 2. The infrastructure of the EduArc project

The main components of the pipeline are:

1. Crawler: a computer program that automatically searches documents on the web [7]. Their job is to collect web content. Crawlers can search for any information, and are also called web spiders or web robots.
2. Common data model: the EduArc CDM is described in Sect. 3.
3. Subject Indexing Model for Metadata Generation: The subjects of the documents in the index are automatically generated using Learning-To-Rank models. Learning-To-Rank consists of a set of supervised ranking models that are trained with a numerical set of vectors to find the top-k relevant documents for a user query. The numerical set of vectors, called feature vectors, is computed based on the content of the documents and/or queries.
4. Search engine frontend: To help users of the EduArc platform find the most relevant results for their search query, a user-friendly frontend was developed, consisting of four main components: search bar, advanced search form, faceted search widgets, and search results form. The faceted search widgets allow users to filter search results based on some common data model fields such as language, author, or date ranges. In addition, users of the platform can download the metadata of the results. Figure 3 shows the search results form of the EduArc platform.

The process of collecting metadata, mapping it and storing it in the index is shown in Fig. 4. The figure shows three scenarios. The first scenario is when the OER repositories use the LOM standard to model their metadata. As a result, no mapper is needed for those types of repositories. The second scenario is when the repository uses another known standard rather than LOM. Then, a mapper is required for those repositories based on their standard. The last scenario is when a repository does not use any standard. Therefore, a mapper is needed for each repository of that type.

4.1   Subject Indexing

Various subject indexing models were developed to parse the indexed documents and generate new metadata. The generated metadata contains supplementary information about the content of a document (e.g., business, computer science,

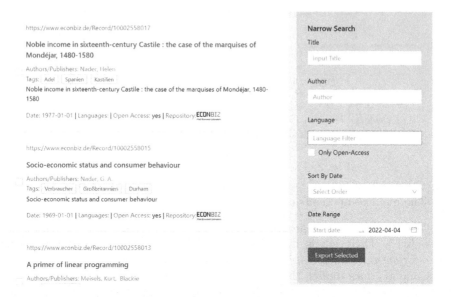

Fig. 3. The frontend of EduArc search.

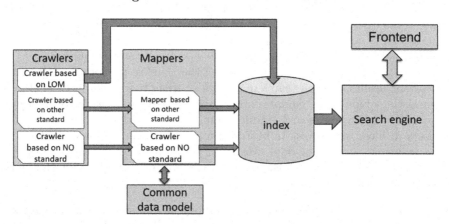

Fig. 4. The scenarios of capturing and mapping OER metadata modeled using the LOM standard, as well as other standards from capturing the metadata to storing the results and presenting them on the front end.

etc.). The Standard Thesaurus for Economics (STW) was used to generate the new metadata. The STW consists of nearly 6,200 keywords. In addition, the following subjects were used:

- Education Server Annotations: 53,580 German subjects.
- Confederation of Open Access Repositories (COAR): 234 German subjects and 274 English subjects.
- Skohub: 730 English and German subjects.

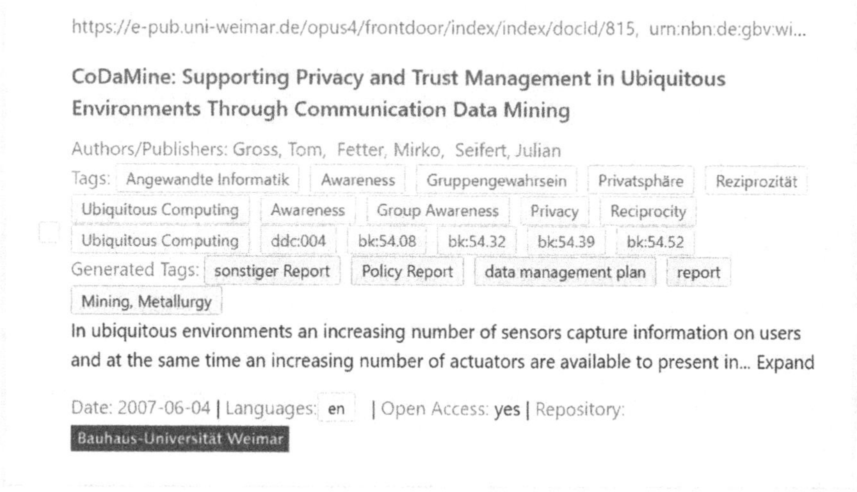

Fig. 5. Appearance of generated metadata (generated tags) on the search frontend of the EduArc platform

These thesauri were used to annotate the documents using various subject indexing models. The generated annotations for each document are added to the "generatedmetadata" field. The generated metadata is made available to data providers and other interested parties through the search frontend (Generated Tags) (Fig. 5).

5   Conclusion

A federated infrastructure was developed for connecting various Open Educational Resources (OER) repositories. Six data providers were connected to the EduArc platform. The connection was made through EduArc's Common Data Model (CDM). Five of these repositories are related to educational and research institutions, and one is a source of figures. In addition, the platform automatically generates the topics of the documents in the index using learning-to-rank models. EduArc's platform includes four main services: search and advanced search with the ability to filter results, adding OER metadata to the index, storing resource metadata, and collecting OER repositories and adding the collected records to the index.

Reproducibility. The EduArc platform was developed on top of Moodle. The platform's code repository has been published online[3]. A limited demo is accessable[4]. Interested universities and institutes are invited to use the platform.

---

[3] https://git.informatik.uni-kiel.de/asal/eduarcbox.
[4] http://eduarc.zbw.uni-kiel.de.

Acknowledgement. This article is part of the project "Digital educational architectures: Open learning resources in distributed learning infrastructures - EduArc" funded by the German Federal Ministry of Education and Research (grant #16DHB2129).

References

1. Marín, V.I., et al.: A comparative study of national infrastructures for digital (open) educational resources in higher education. Open Praxis **12**(2), 241–256 (2020)
2. Menzel, M.: "Lom for higher education oer repositories: Ein metadatenprofil für open educational resources im hochschulbereich zur förderung der interoperabilität von oer-länderrepositorien," o-bib. Das offene Bibliotheksjournal/Herausgeber VDB, vol. 7, no. 1, pp. 1–10 (2020)
3. Perry, D.E., Sim, S.E., Easterbrook, S.M.: "Case studies for software engineers. In: Proceedings of the 26th International Conference on Software Engineering, pp. 736–738. IEEE (2004)
4. Lamnek, S., Krell, C.: Qualitative sozialforschung. Psychologie Verlags Union München (2005)
5. Saleh, A., Vagliano, I., Heck, T., Kullmann, S.: "Eduarc. a fair and user-centred infrastructure for learning resources" (2020)
6. Wilkinson, M.D., et al.: "Andra waagmeester," Peter Wittenburg, Katherine Wolstencroft, Jun Zhao, and Barend Mons (2016)
7. Olston, C., Najork, M.: Web crawling. Now Publishers Inc (2010)

Question Support Method to Promote Critical Thinking Using Lecture Slide Structure in On-Demand Courses

Saki Inoue[1]([✉]) [iD], Yuanyuan Wang[2] [iD], Yukiko Kawai[3,4] [iD],
and Kazutoshi Sumiya[1] [iD]

[1] Kwansei Gakuin University, 1 Gakuen Uegahara, Sanda, Hyogo 669-1330, Japan
{hms54907,sumiya}@kwansei.ac.jp
[2] Yamaguchi University, 2-16-1 Tokiwadai, Ube, Yamaguchi 755-8611, Japan
y.wang@yamaguchi-u.ac.jp
[3] Kyoto Sangyo University, Motoyama, Kamigamo, Kita-ku, Kyoto 603-8555, Japan
kawai@cc.kyoto-su.ac.jp
[4] Osaka University, 5-1 Mihogaoka, Ibaraki, Osaka 567-0047, Japan

Abstract. Online learning has been widely conducted in educational institutions. Students typically take some time to formulate and reflect on questions on learning material. Therefore, in this study, we consider on-demand classes that students can take at their own pace. In particular, we investigate critical thinking, which is defined as a way of critically questioning the rationale for an idea or belief. We aim to provide on-demand classes that support and improve the critical thinking skills of students. To this end, in this study, we propose a method to support question generation and a method to present related slides in the question assistance task, and evaluated related slides by the proposed method based on the results of a questionnaire. The results of an evaluation experiment showed that the lecture slides that should be recommended for each question may vary considerably depending on the subject of the lecture.

Keywords: e-Learning · On-demand lectures · Question generation · Slide recommendation · Critical thinking

1 Introduction

Critical thinking is a type of introspective thinking in which one consciously considers one's reasoning processes [1]. Gray stated that questions are an essential part of critical thinking [2]. However, Japanese students tend to be too shy to ask questions about the content of lectures. For example, Ikuta et al. found that 47.7% of children did not generate or ask questions [3]. Therefore, in this study, we aimed to promote critical thinking by encouraging students to generate questions and supporting the process of careful thinking. To this end, we propose a learning support system. The UI of the implemented system is shown in Fig. 1. Our proposed UI transitions from "question generation support" to the

© The Author(s), under exclusive license to Springer Nature Switzerland AG 2022
Y.-H. Tseng et al. (Eds.): ICADL 2022, LNCS 13636, pp. 509–515, 2022.
https://doi.org/10.1007/978-3-031-21756-2_43

Important Question Keywords   Generated Questions

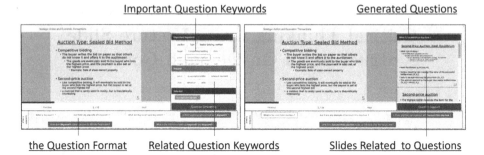

the Question Format   Related Question Keywords   Slides Related to Questions

Fig. 1. Question generation support (left) and presentation of slides related to question (right) for critical thinking

"presentation of related slides" according to the student's behavior[1]. First, we define a question suggestion support task, in which the "target slide" at which the student is currently looking is displayed on the upper-left corner of the UI. In addition, the keywords of the target slide are displayed on the upper-right corner according to the proposed method. Furthermore, when a student selects the "Important Keyword Suggestion" option, the keywords in the target slide are colored according to their importance, and the student can visually grasp the important keywords. The calculation of the importance of each keyword is described in Sect. 2.1. In addition, when a student selects a "Related Keyword Suggestion," the system recommends keywords related to the selected keyword through the proposed method. The suggestion of related keywords is described in Sect. 2.2. At the bottom of the screen, the "Question Formats," are then shown, as described in detail in Sect. 2.3. Furthermore, the lower part shows the slides related to the question obtained by the proposed method. The method for presenting slides related to the question is described in Sect. 3.

1.1 Related Research

King [4] [5] and Ikuta et al. [6] proposed teaching students how to generate questions by using a list of question stems to promote critical thinking. Incidentally, this list was translated into Japanese by Ikuta et al. The results of this approach show that encouraging students to generate questions for study materials facilitates their learning.

Shinogaya et al. [7] categorized students' questions into low- and high-level versions. In this study, we revised these definitions of low- and high-level questions for use as a keyword-based question classification frame.

2   Question Generation Support

Slides used in lectures (e.g., PowerPoint and keynote) have a hierarchical structure with indentation.

---

[1] Demo:https://www.youtube.com/watch?v=tYl_2KHBYfY.

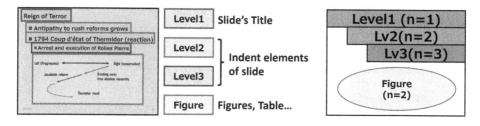

Fig. 2. Indentation and hierarchy level examples

2.1 Extraction of Important Question Keywords

We propose ranking question keywords by their importance using the hierarchical structure of the slides. The hierarchical structure of the slide is reprocessed by assigning the indentation the hierarchical levels we defined. As shown in Fig. 2, the highest hierarchy level is $n = 1$ for the title, and the hierarchy level then increases by one level in descending order.

First, we conduct a morphological analysis and extract nouns as question keywords from the target slide. The importance of keyword k in target slide x is calculated using the following equations.

$$I(x, k) = \sum_{n=1}^{N} \frac{1}{l_n(x, k)} \times \frac{1}{L(x, k)} \times \sum_{m=1}^{M} |l_m(x, k)| \times \frac{1}{M} \qquad (1)$$

Here, $I(x, k)$ is the importance of keyword k in slide x. N is a different type of indentation hierarchy, $l_n(x, k)$ is the hierarchy n in which the keyword k appears in slide x, and $L(x, k)$ is the total number of hierarchies in which the keyword k appears in slide x. M is the total number of indentations in slide x, and $|l_m(x, k)|$ is the total number of indentations m in which keyword k appears in slide x. In this way, students can select important keywords from a target slide as question keywords. We assume that the more the keyword k appears at a higher hierarchical level and the more indentations it appears in slide x, the more important (topical) the keyword is. In this study, the texts that appear in figures, tables, independence texts are calculated as follows.

- Define all text outside the hierarchy as a figure
- Figures appearing on one slide are all calculated as a single indent
- All hierarchy levels of text appearing in a figure are assigned level 2.

2.2 Extraction of Related Question Keywords

Next, when students select keywords, they may want to select related keywords that do not appear on the target slide. In this case, we respond to this request by calculating the relationship between the keywords in the content and extracting the upper-lower relationship between the selected and other keywords. In this

Table 1. Question format

Low	Q_{L_1}: What is k_1?
	Q_{L_2}: Are there any examples of k_1?
	Q_{L_3}: What are k_1 and k_2?
High	Q_{H_1}: Is anything synonymous with k_1?
	Q_{H_2}: How does k_1 relate to before and after the target slide?
	Q_{H_3}: What is the difference between k_1 and k_2?

study, we extract a thesaurus in the lecture slides using the hierarchical structure of the slides. We calculate the value of the upper-lower relationship between keywords k_1 and k_2 of slide x using the following equation.

$$R(x,\ k_1,\ k_2) = \sum_{m=1}^{M}\left(\frac{1}{l(m,\ x,\ k_1)}\right) - \sum_{m=1}^{M}\left(\frac{1}{l(m,\ x,\ k_2)}\right) \qquad (2)$$

In Eq. (2), $l(m,x,k)$ is the hierarchical level of indentation m where keyword k appears in slide x.

2.3 Presenting the Question Format

We propose a question format that generates questions by simply combining keywords. The question format shown in Table 1 was created by referring to the question stem list created by Ikuta et al. [6] and the question classification method proposed by Shinogaya. [7]. In this study, we redefine low-level questions as those that confirm the facts of the keywords themselves, and high-level questions as those that encourage associations between keywords and prior knowledge. In addition, we consider the case in which students select one keyword as a single keyword question, and multiple keywords as a multiple keyword question. In the question format, Q_{L_3} and Q_{H_3} support multiple keywords. In this study, the question format is used in the sliding rank calculation related to the question.

3 Recommendation of Slides Related to Questions

We propose a ranking method to recommend candidate slides that are relevant to the question by using the hierarchical structure of the slides and the occurrence rate of the keywords.

Q_{L_1}: *What is* k_1?

$$Q_{L_1}(x,k) = \sum_{n=1}^{N}\frac{1}{l_n(x,k)} \times \frac{1}{L(x,k)} \times (D(x,k)+1) \qquad (3)$$

Table 2. Rank correlation between the proposed method and the evaluation experiments

Number of Selected Keywords	Single						Multi		Master
Question Format	Q_{L_1}	Q_{L_2}	**Ave**	Q_{H_1}	Q_{H_2}	**Ave**	Q_{L_3}	Q_{H_3}	Subjects
Lecture "Data Structures and Algorithms"	0.51	0.96	**0.74**	0.81	0.62	**0.72**	0.86	0.77	2%
Lecture "the French Revolution" (1) Jacobins	0.54	0.39	**0.47**	0.54	0.59	**0.57**	0.97	0.97	14%
Lecture "the French Revolution" (2) Directoire	0.56	0.50	**0.53**	0.46	0.47	**0.47**	0.85	0.50	17%

In Eq. (3), $D(x, k)$ is the number of indentations at the lower hierarchical level where keyword k appears in slide x, $l_n(x, k)$ is the hierarchy level n at which keyword k appears in slide x, and $L(x, k)$ denotes the number of levels at which keyword k appears in slide x. Here, the hierarchy level of the indents in the lower hierarchy is counted, and a new value is added when the hierarchy changes from the lower hierarchy to the upper hierarchy. With this formula, the question keyword appears in the upper hierarchy of the slide, and slides in which the lower hierarchy is present in the indent in which a question keyword appears are highly evaluated. Here, we hypothesized that the more indents there are in the lower hierarchy of the appearance indent of the question keyword, the greater is the explanatory power of the question keyword is.

4   Evaluation Experiment

To evaluate the effectiveness of our proposed method, we conducted evaluation experiments three times using lecture slides from different fields. The lecture used included "Data Structures and Algorithms" once and "the French Revolution" twice. There were a total of 326 participants in the evaluation experiment. The subjects answered the following questions.

- Preliminary Survey : Do you have any previous experience learning about the content of "Data Structures and Algorithms"?
- Ranking evaluation of the candidate slides : How appropriate are the candidate slides for recommendation a material to support critical thinking on a scale of 1 to 5?

4.1   Preliminary Survey

The subjects answered the first question to determine how much knowledge they already had of the subject matter of that lecture. We set the percentage of subjects who answered that they had learned and understood the title of the lecture as "master" and are shown in Table 2.

4.2   Ranking Evaluation

The questions are assumed to be created by the proposed method, and the experiment was conducted with the question keywords applied to the six question formats. We formulated the questions used in the survey based on important and relevant keywords selected by 12 college students. The question format used all six suggested question formats. However, the user-selected question keyword appears in both slides. We compared the ranking of slide candidates calculated by the proposed method and the ranking by questionnaire using normalized discounted cumulative gain (nDCG). The results are shown in Table 2. This shows that the nDCG value differs depending on the type of question format and our proposed method of presenting related slides was evaluated slightly higher.

4.3   Discussion

In this evaluation experiment, we conducted an experiment on one lecture instead of multiple lectures. Therefore, this experiment involved some computational problems such as the limit on the number of times the question keyword appeared and the lack of movement in the appearance hierarchy. We consider that this problem may be solved by performing calculations for multiple lectures, but it is necessary to reconsider the formula that allows calculations for fewer lectures. Table 2 shows the ranking evaluation of the slides recommended to the user calculated by nDCG and the degree of understanding of the lecture theme of the subjects who evaluated the slides. From this data, it may be observed that the more the subject understood the lecture theme, the lower the evaluation value of the slide recommendation. We consider the lecture themes that are difficult for subjects to understand tend to refer to the structure of the slides, and lecture themes that are easy to understand tend to refer to the meaning of the text. This indicates that this method may be similar to learners' thinking processes in trying to understand a lecture theme that is difficult to understand semantically.

5   Conclusion

In this study, we have proposed an online learning support system to promote critical thinking in students, and performed an experiment to evaluate the proposed approach. The results showed that the evaluation of the ranking of the proposed recommendation candidate slides varied greatly depending on the lectures targeted. In addition, the visual information obtained from the lecture slides may be important for learners with little or no learning experience studying difficult themes. In future research, we would like to improve the proposed formula and consider compound words and multiple groups of slide pages.

References

1. Ennis, R.H.: A taxonomy of critical thinking dispositions and abilities. In: Baron, J.B., Sternberg, R.J. (Eds.), Teaching Thinking Skills: Theory and Practice, pp. 9–26. W H Freeman/Times Books/ Henry Holt Co. (1987)
2. Gray, P.: Engaging students' intellects: The immersion approach to critical thinking in psychology instruction. Teach. Psychol. 20(2), 68–74 (1993)
3. Junichi IKUTA and Shunichi MARUNO: Does the child generate a question in elementary school class? : Relation between interrogative feeling and the question generation, and expression. Psycholl. Res. Kyushu Univ. 5, 9–18 (2004)
4. Alison, K.I.N.G.: Effects of training in strategic questioning on children's problem-solving performance. J. Educ. Psychol. 83, 307–317 (1991)
5. Alison, K.I.N.G.: Facilitating elaborative learning through guided student-generated questioning. Educ. Psychol. 27(1), 111–126 (1992)
6. Junichi IKUTA and Shunichi MARUNO: Student question generation in the classroom?: a review. Psychol. Res. Kyushu Univ. 6, 37–48 (2005)
7. Keita SHINOGAYA. An examination of the impact of interventions in question generation and answer generation during preparatory activities on class comprehension and its process Educ. Psychol. Res. 61(4), 351–361 (2013). [in japanese]

VNU-LIC Digital Knowledge Center Model: Transforming Big Data into Knowledge

Nguyen Hoang Son[1](✉) ⓘ, Le Ba Lam[1] ⓘ, Hoang Van Duong[1] ⓘ,
Hoang Minh Bac[1] ⓘ, Do Diep Anh[1] ⓘ, Vu Thi Thanh Thuy[1] ⓘ, Ngo Thuy Quynh[1] ⓘ,
Nguyen Duy Tan[1] ⓘ, Le Huong Giang[1] ⓘ, Vu Son Hai[1] ⓘ, Trinh Van Khanh[2] ⓘ,
Tran van Thi Thanh[2] ⓘ, and Nguyen Thi Kim Lan[2] ⓘ

[1] Library and Digital Knowledge Center, National University, Hanoi, Vietnam
son.nh@vnu.edu.vn
[2] University of Social Sciences and Humanities, National University, Hanoi, Vietnam

Abstract. Digital knowledge centers transforming big data into knowledge is the future of VNU-LIC development. The paper presents the context of big data booming, a comparison between Data Center - Information Center - Knowledge Center, brief overview of models of digital knowledge hubs/centers around the world and the reason for building and developing digital knowledge center. Particularly, a VNU-LIC digital knowledge center model is set up to deal with the chaos of big data issues.

Keywords: Digital knowledge center · Digital knowledge hub · Knowledge management · Big data management

1 Introduction

Everyday, people need data, information and knowledge for decision making. In the time of big data booming, the most important thing is not only how to collect and archive as much as possible data/information but also to select, process, analyse, synthesize the data and information into knowledge assisting and supporting an individual or an organization to make decision quickly, smartly and efficiently. In the time of Vietnam digital transformation, data (Input) is as fuel/ energy to run digital knowledge centers (DKCs) that process, filter, analyse, synthesize and change all the big data to valued and smart knowledge (Output) for the usage of individuals, organizations, cities and a nation.

In the context of a university, a library is needed to update new mission dealing with big data booming issues such as: 1. How to capture, select, organize, store, create and use learning resources from big data; how to transform big data to valued knowledge findings for research and science process; 2. How to upgrade and change a digital academic library to a DKC that not only works with traditional digital learning resources (ebooks, digital thesis…) but also deals with big learning and researching data from various formats (social media data, artificial machined - created data, human – computer interaction data…); 3. How to plan and make data – information – knowledge management strategies to run the DKC model…

As a leading digital academic library in Vietnam (Top 50 among over 3903 Institutional Repositories globally and No1 in Vietnam) [1], the Library and Information Center of Vietnam National University, Hanoi (VNU-LIC) plays a very important role in the university digital transformation. However, the VNU-LIC library has been challenged by those 1, 2, 3 issues and a new DKC model transforming big data to smart knowledge is needed to solve the problems.

2   Model of VNU-LIC Digital Knowledge Center

On June 11, 2020, the Party Committee of the VNU-LIC successfully organized the 6th Congress, term 2020 - 2030. Congress determined that the goal for the period 2020 - 2030 is the digital transition period developing the VNU-LIC to become a **"Digital Knowledge Center"**. The DKC was formed and developed to meet the development needs of VNU in the new period of digital transformation, digitized learning materials, technology development 4.0, digital data – digital information - digital knowledge management, creating a smart - creative digital ecosystem and especially making an important contribution to making VNU become one of the top 100 universities in Asia and the top 500 universities in world academic leader (2020–2025). The resolution of the VNU-LIC Party Committee on the development of the DKC (2020–2030) showed that this is the right time condition for VNU-LIC on the basis of the development of former different stages (Fig. 1):

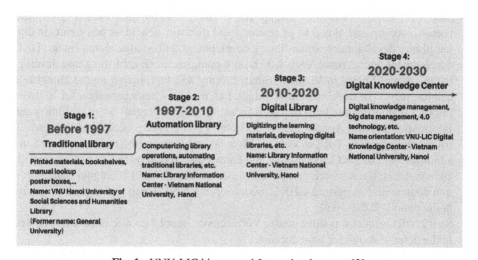

Fig. 1. VNU-LIC history and future development [2].

- Phase 1. Traditional Library before 1997: Emphasis mostly on organizing and archiving traditional documents (printed books, periodicals, newspapers, etc.), preserving bookcases, and manually searching for documents in bookcase boxes.

- Phase 2: Automation library (1997–2010): Concentrating mostly on the computerization and automation of the traditional library's business processes: supplemental, cataloging, archiving, searching, and reader service. This stage corresponds to the automation and computerization of the conventional library starting to concentrate on science and technology-related information activities for VNU research and training: scientific bibliographic information, thematic information service, etc.
- Phase 3: Digital Library (2010–2020): Concentrating particularly on digital libraries, digital learning management, textbooks, reference books, theses, and dissertations. This is the stage where traditional libraries are changed over to digital libraries. Focusing on activities related to science and technology information for VNU research and training, themed information service, scientific bibliographic information…
- Phase 4 (2020–2030): This phase will concentrate on developing DKC, Digital knowledge management, Technology 4.0, Big data management and the creation of an innovation ecosystem. The transition from the Library - Information Center model to the Library - Knowledge Center model is currently in its fourth stage. In essence, the development of the Digital University - Smart University, VNU (2020–2030) model involves the transition from the Digital Library model to the DKC model.

3   Methodology: Steps Building up VNU-LIC Digital Knowledge Center (2020–2030)

To develop the DKC, VNU-LIC has spent 5 years to work with 5 steps as follows:

– Step 1: Team up a Research Group: Since 2017, a VNU-LIC research group has been teamed up and aimed to do research and discover new ideas and trends in digital library development; smart library development; knowledge management; DKC development, etc… Also, VNU-LIC hold 4 conferences (Establishing and developing the digital library in Vietnam; Smart Library 4.0; Optimizing digital knowledge management; The development of a digital knowledge center paradigm for Vietnam libraries) gathering hundreds of papers focusing on the emergent issues on library and information science. Among 229 papers in the 4 conference proceedings, there are 10 papers on suggesting DKC models for Vietnam and 30 papers on the management and administration of DKC, technology and knowledge. Based on the 40 papers analysis and synthesis, the research group has investigated the VNU-LIC digital transformation context and suggested a DKC model serving VNU smart and digital university in the period (2020–2030)
– Step 2: DKC model was submitted to VNU science board then discussed and reviewed in the defense round for final decision
– Step 3: The DKC model with new functions and missions was approved and applied to VNU-LIC
– Step 4: New services has been developed for the DKC mission "Transforming Data into Knowledge and Digital Knowledge Management (Fig. 2)"

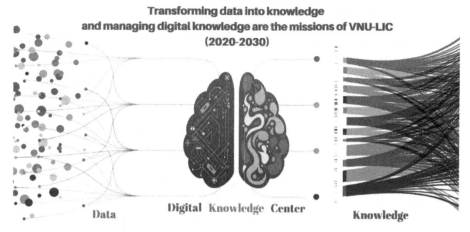

Fig. 2. VNU-LIC missions (2020–2030); The brain shape shows the human and artificial intelligence collecting, storing, organizing, disseminating, and managing digital knowledge [3]

4   VNU-LIC Digital Knowledge CENTer's Specific Tasks (2020–2030)

The VNU-LIC DKC model (2020–2030) has the following basic points:

- Completely digitize educational content for use in digital learning, training, and research

    VNU-LIC must accelerate digitization, continue to work and cooperate closely with training institutions, lecturers and researchers, and with many other sources inside and outside VNU to borrow, receive, and digitize with the fastest speed, highest quality, digital cataloging, and organization into a system of scientifically categorized learning materials on the basis of collected, supplemented, and digitized learning resources from training institutions in previous years. This is a prerequisite for developing VNU's elearning, digital teaching, and digital learning system [4].

- Collect, store, organize, and develop the VNU Big Data system

    The DKC is built on the foundation of a big data system, using artificial intelligence to analyze and process data, convert raw data into scientific knowledge, and respond quickly to the researcher, lecturer, and learner demand for academic knowledge. As a result, VNU-LIC not only constructs a system of learning materials based on Bookworm but also integrates and connects with the endogenous data system: digital dissertations, digital dissertations, scientific research results, inventions - inventions of VNU based on Dspace, as well as many other scientific database sources such as ScienceDirect, Springer, Bookboon, MathSciNet.In addition to these three large data sources, VNU-LIC must develop cutting-edge technology and a software platform to store and manage the Vietnam Hoc Documentation Center's data system as well as data warehouses for other databases. VNU's training units, Institutes, and Centers to create a unified, interconnected, and user-friendly VNU Big Data system across VNU, managed and administered by the Digital Knowledge Center VNU-LIC [4].

- Creating and developing a cutting-edge 4.0 technology platform

  With a massive and diverse big data system and distributed data warehouses on a variety of software platforms, along with Bookworm, Dspace, Virtua, Academic Databases: ScienceDirect, Springer… Through the intelligent centralized search system URD2, The DKC has succeeded in connecting search and access to unified data, attempting to make the data search process fast and unified on a specific search interface. The DKC has made a breakthrough in big data governance. However, technological advancements are continuous in order to meet the needs of increasingly intelligent and convenient software and data, as well as rapid digital knowledge transfer and effective knowledge use in the context of Artificial Intelligence, the Internet of Things, Big Data, Interactive Social networks…VNU, in particular, requires a unified technology platform that is compatible with VNU's entire digital ecosystem (technology, data, users, administrators, etc.). As a result, The DKC must quickly build and develop a unified data management platform with several features such as reading e-books, reading VNU news, interacting and socializing in VNU, tools supporting research - teaching – learning, creating a unified digital ecosystem, easy to administer, comprehension of user needs and marketing, statistics - analysis-synthesis of behavioral data users' behavior in real-time… so that both VNU and VNU-LIC can effectively manage data [4].

- Augment as well as develop digital data, information, and knowledge management services

  In the future, VNU Digital University will be built on large data warehouses that are unified and synchronized in real-time. When VNU's big data is constantly expanding over time, it is critical to manage, organize, and use data effectively, quickly, conveniently, and selectively based on needs. What researchers, lecturers, and learners require is more advanced data which is knowledge, and this is the mission of the DKC, which will have to assist VNU in collecting, selecting and filtering, classifying, organizing, storing, using, and managing this big data system in order to turn it into valuable knowledge and meet VNU's needs for effective use.

  The DKC must focus on ensuring not only the basic tasks of the library, such as providing learning materials for lecturers and learners, but also expanding the tasks, such as knowledge management and converting data into academic knowledge for research, training, and learning at VNU. These are critical tasks that must be completed immediately in order to meet the digital transformation and development of VNU digital university.

  The specific tasks of digital data - digital information - digital knowledge management are as follows: effectively organizing and managing the VNU system of digital learning materials; deploying ISI/Scopus bibliometrics to analyze, evaluate, report, and forecast research trends at VNU; deploying DoiT anti-plagiarism service to ensure the quality of theses - theses; creating a digital author profile of the entire VNU to store and manage the scientists' gray matter; developing a shared university digital library system connecting many endogenous data repositories of Vietnamese universities to contribute to the creation of the Government's Digital Vietnamese Knowledge System; providing service packages for researchers searching and serving scientific data, etc. [4].

- Create and develop a future generation of creative, self-learning, and self-researching users

More than 52,000 VNU users, including students (mostly from Generation Z), graduate students, lecturers, researchers, leaders/managers/experts, etc., are served directly by VNU-LIC, demonstrates the importance of the purpose it is carrying out to provide and disseminate knowledge input for users to receive, use, study, teach, research, and generate knowledge output. The DKC is in direct rivalry with technological platforms like Facebook, Youtube, Instagram, Zalo, Google Books, Kindle, Apple Books, and Netflix, etc. in the context of booming big data, ubiquitous data, and mobile devices connecting constantly on the Internet and social networking platforms in order to involve VNU users, encourage them to care about and put effort into reading books, and help them build their spirit and self-study and self-study abilities helping them become scientists and researchers capable of self-exploration, self-discovery, self-discovery, and skill growth by actively and actively encouraging rich imagination to consistently produce knowledge products of high scientific value and practical applicability, one must engage in lifelong self-study and research. To accomplish such amazing things, the DKC not only pays attention to technology and data but also pays particular attention to users, listening to and understanding their requirements, approaches, training generate and equip skills and knowledge to use data, information, and knowledge for information users, such as services as follows: *the introduction of VNU-LIC resource warehouse, goods, and services; skills in utilizing search engines, such as URD2, Google, etc.; analyze, synthesize, evaluate and process data into knowledge; methods of reading and self-study; applications for processing and creating reference documents such as Endnote, Zotezo, Mendeley; ISI/Scopus bibliometrics; Anti-plagiarism and research ethics, etc.* [4].

5   Conclusion

The DKC transforming big data into knowledge is the future of VNU-LIC development (2020–2030). This is also the first advanded DKC model in Vietnam strongly influencing and shaping the trend of the Vietnam library development. Coping with the big data booming, the DKC is not suitable to the library sectors but also to goverment, business, office sectors dealing with the chaos of big data issues.

References

1. https://repositories.webometrics.info/en/node/32
2. Son, N.H., et al.: Knowledge-Library Center: Transforming Digital Libraries into Digital Knowledge Centers to Cope with the Big Data Explosion, The Development of a Digital Knowledge Center Paradigm for Vietnamese Libraries, pp. 14–28. Vietnam National University Publishing House, Hanoi (2020)
3. Son, N.H.: VNU-LIC Digital Transformation (2021–2025): Developing a Digital Knowledge Center on the Basis of a Digital Library, Digital Transformation Based on The Paradigm of a Digital Knowledge Hub, pp. 26–32. Vietnam National University Publishing House, Hanoi (2021)

4. Son, N.H.: Developing digital universities – smart universities on the basis of 4.0 VNU-LIC digital knowledge center- digital learning- digital research. In: Developing Digital Universities – Smart Universities on the Basis of VNU-LIC Digital Learning Resources, pp. 17–34. Vietnam National University Publishing House, Hanoi (2019)

Author Index

Printed in the United States
by Baker & Taylor Publisher Services